ADOPTION – THE
PROCEDURE

ADOPTION – THE MODERN PROCEDURE

HHJ Heather Swindells QC

Clive Heaton
Barrister, Zenith Chambers, Leeds

 **Family Law**

2006

Published by Family Law
a publishing imprint of
Jordan Publishing Limited
21 St Thomas Street
Bristol BS1 6JS

Whilst the publishers and the author have taken every care in preparing the material included in this work, any statements made as to the legal or other implications of particular transactions are made in good faith purely for general guidance and cannot be regarded as a substitute for professional advice. Consequently, no liability can be accepted for loss or expense incurred as a result of relying in particular circumstances on statements made in this work.

©Jordan Publishing Limited 2006

Crown copyright material is reproduced under Class Licence Number C01W0000451 with the permission of the Controller of HMSO and the Queen's Printer for Scotland.

All rights reserved. No part of this publication may be reproduced, stored in a retrieval system, or transmitted in any way or by any means, including photocopying or recording, without the written permission of the copyright holder, application for which should be addressed to the publisher.

British Library Cataloguing-in-Publication Data
A catalogue record for this book is available from the British Library.

ISBN 0 85308 969 8

Typeset by Columns Design Ltd, Reading, Berkshire
Printed in Great Britain by Antony Rowe Ltd, Chippenham, Wilts

Preface

On 30 December 2005 the Adoption and Children Act 2002 came into force and heralds a new approach to adoption law. This book provides a detailed guide through the new procedure relating to domestic adoption against the backdrop of the Act and is intended as a practice companion to *Adoption – The Modern Law* (Family Law, 2003). It includes the full text not only of the Adoption and Children Act 2002 but also of the Family Procedure (Adoption) Rules 2005 (together with the Practice Directions and Forms) and the principal Regulations.

We are grateful to Caroline Bridge for her encouragement during the planning stages of the book and to the Honourable Mr Justice McFarlane for his invaluable contribution, which we have gratefully included in the text. Our thanks also go to Tom Inglis for his computer re-mastering of a lekythos by the Achilles Painter for the front cover.

We dedicate the book to our respective families for their patience and support.

HH Judge Heather Swindells QC

Clive Heaton

January 2006

Contents

Preface		v
Table of Cases		xiii
Table of Statutes		xv
Table of Statutory Instruments		xix
Table of Abbreviations		xxv

Chapter 1	WELFARE		1
	Paramount consideration		1
	Delay		1
		Wishes and feelings	2
		Needs	2
		Having ceased to be a member of the original family and become an adopted person	2
		Age, sex, background and characteristics	3
		Harm	3
		Relationship which the child has with relatives	3
	Religion, racial origin, cultural background: section 1(5)		4
	Range of powers: section 1(6)		4
		The whole range of powers	4
		'No order principle': section 1(6)	9
Chapter 2	PARENTAL CONSENT		11
	Parental consent and placement		11
	Parental consent and adoption		11
	Meaning of consent		12
	Advance consent		13
	Withdrawal of consent		13
	Procedure for consent		14
		Role of the reporting officers	15
	Dispensing with consent		16
		Paramountcy principle	16
		Welfare checklist	16
		The grounds for dispensation	16
		Procedure for dispensing with consent: FP(A)R 2005, rule 27	18
Chapter 3	PLACEMENT FOR ADOPTION		19
	The new system		19
	Placing a child for adoption		19
		Local authority foster parents	20
		The demise of 'freeing orders'	20
	The two routes		21

	The consensual route	21
	The placement order route	23
	Reviews/independent reviewing officers	29
	Revocation: section 24	30
	Variation: section 23	32
	Consequences of placement	32
	Parental responsibility: section 25	32
	Contact: section 26	33
	Procedure	35
	Surname and removal from the UK: section 28(2)	37
	Removal	38
	Agency cases	38
	Consensual placements: sections 30–33	38
	Placement orders: section 34	38
	Return of the child: section 35	39
	Non-agency cases: sections 36–40	39
	Recovery orders: section 41	39
	Procedure: FP(A)R 2005, rule 107	40
	Interaction between care proceedings and placement order proceedings	41
Chapter 4	THE MAKING OF ADOPTION ORDERS	45
	Adoption order	45
	Status of the adopted child: section 67	45
	Requirements for obtaining an adoption order	46
	Who may apply	46
	Eligibility	47
	Preliminaries to making an adoption order	48
	Suitability of any person or couple to adopt	49
	Suitability of the child to be adopted	50
	Probationary periods	50
	Reports	52
	Notice	53
	Other considerations before making an adoption order	53
	Has a previous application for a British adoption order been made by the same applicants and been refused?	53
	Has there been any contravention by the applicant of any restriction on arranging an adoption?	53
	Duty to consider post-adoption contact arrangements	54
	Alternative conditions for making an adoption order	54
	First condition – consent: section 47(2)	54
	Second condition – placement: section 47(4)	54
	The third condition – section 47(6)	56
	Summary of the procedural steps	57
	Post-adoption contact: section 46(6)	59
	Family relationships	60
	Step-parents and partners	60
	Unmarried fathers	62
	Baby adoptions	63
	Orphans	64

Contents

Chapter 5	ILLEGAL PLACEMENTS AND TRANSACTIONS	65
	Prohibition upon making arrangements: section 92	65
	Prohibitions on reports: section 94	66
	Prohibitions on payments: section 95	67
	Prohibition on advertisements: section 123	68
Chapter 6	ACCESS TO INFORMATION	71
	The registers	71
	Adopted Children Register	71
	Person adopted before commencement	72
	A person adopted after commencement	73
	The Adoption Contact Register: section 80	74
	Disclosure of information about a person's adoption	75
	The system for disclosure: in brief	76
	The system under sections 61–62	78
	Confidentiality	80
	Privacy	80
Chapter 7	THE FAMILY PROCEDURE (ADOPTION) RULES 2005	83
	The overriding objective: FP(A)R 2005, rule 1	83
	Case management: FP(A)R 2005, rule 4	85
	How to start proceedings: FP(A)R 2005, Part 4	86
	Procedure for applications in adoption and placement proceedings: Part 5	88
	Application of the Part 5 procedure	88
	Who are the parties: FP(A)R 2005, rule 23	89
	What the court will do on the issue of the application: FP(A)R 2005, rule 24	89
	The first directions hearing: FP(A)R 2005, rule 26	91
	The final hearing: FP(A)R 2005, rule 32	93
	The role of children's guardian	94
	Appointment: FP(A)R 2005, rules 59–61	94
	Powers and duties: FP(A)R 2005, rules 62–64	95
	Exercise of the duties: FP(A)R 2005, rules 65–67	96
	Solicitor for the child: FP(A)R 2005, rule 68	97
	Role of the reporting officer: FP(A)R 2005, rules 69–72	98
	Role of the children and family reporter: FP(A)R 2005, rules 73–74	98
	Role of the litigation friend: FP(A)R 2005, rules 49–58	99
	Who can act as a children's guardian, reporting officer, or children and family reporter: FP(A)R 2005, rules 75–76	101
	Part 9 procedure: FP(A)R 2005, rules 86–96	101
	Part 10 procedure: FP(A)R 2005, rules 97–105	106
	Experts	108
	Appeals	112
	Grounds	112
	Permission	112
	Procedure after permission is obtained	114
	The appeal	115
	Costs	118
	Some signposts to other rules	118

Chapter 8	ADOPTION AGENCIES	119
	The Adoption Agencies Regulations 2005	119
	Duties of an adoption agency where the agency is considering adoption: regulations 11 to 17	120
	Function of the adoption panel: regulation 18	121
	Adoption agency decision and notification: regulation 19	121
	CAFCASS/Welsh family proceedings officer: regulation 20	122
	Duties of an adoption agency in respect of a prospective adopter: regulations 21 to 30	122
	Duties of an adoption agency in respect of a proposed placement of a child with a prospective adopter: regulations 31 to 34	123
	Requirements imposed on the adoption agency before the child may be placed for adoption: regulation 35	125
	Reviews: regulations 36 and 37	125
	Withdrawal of consent	127
	Contact	127
	The Suitability of Adopters Regulations 2005	127
	Assessment	128
	Determinations and decisions	129
	Regulation 4(2)	129
	Adoption support services	129
	Meaning of adoption support services	130
	Assessments and plans	130
	Financial support	132
	Procedure	133
	Reviews	134
	Urgent cases	134
	Independent review of determinations	134
Appendix A	TRANSITIONAL ARRANGEMENTS	137
Appendix B	ADOPTION AND CHILDREN ACT 2002	145
Appendix C	THE FAMILY PROCEDURE (ADOPTION) RULES 2005, SI 2005/2795	231
Appendix D	PRACTICE DIRECTIONS	303
Appendix E	FORMS	421
Appendix F	ADOPTION SUPPORT SERVICES REGULATIONS 2005, SI 2005/691	601
Appendix G	THE INDEPENDENT REVIEW OF DETERMINATIONS (ADOPTION) REGULATIONS 2005, SI 2005/3332	615
Appendix H	THE DISCLOSURE OF ADOPTION INFORMATION (POST-COMMENCEMENT ADOPTIONS) REGULATIONS 2005, SI 2005/888	621

Appendix I	THE ADOPTION INFORMATION AND INTERMEDIARY SERVICES (PRE-COMMENCEMENT ADOPTIONS) REGULATIONS 2005, SI 2005/890	629
Appendix J	THE ADOPTION AGENCIES REGULATIONS 2005, SI 2005/389	637
Appendix K	THE SUITABILITY OF ADOPTERS REGULATIONS 2005, SI 2005/1712	675
Appendix L	THE SPECIAL GUARDIANSHIP REGULATIONS 2005, SI 2005/1109	677
Appendix M	THE ADOPTIONS WITH A FOREIGN ELEMENT REGULATIONS 2005, SI 2005/392	691
Appendix N	THE ADOPTION AND CHILDREN ACT 2002 (COMMENCEMENT NO 10 TRANSITIONAL AND SAVINGS PROVISIONS) ORDER 2005, SI 2005/2897	715
Appendix O	THE LOCAL AUTHORITY (ADOPTION) (MISCELLANEOUS PROVISIONS) REGULATIONS 2005, SI 2005/3390	731
Appendix P	NATIONAL ADOPTION STANDARDS FOR ENGLAND	735
Appendix Q	ADOPTION AND CHILDREN ACT 2002 GUIDANCE – ANNEX I: TRANSITIONAL ARRANGEMENTS	743
Index		759

Table of Cases

A (A Child) (Adoption of a Russian Child), Re [2000] 1 FLR 539, [2000] 1 FCR 673, [2000] Fam Law 596	2.37
Arbuthnot Latham Bank Ltd v Trafalgar Holdings Ltd; Chishty Coveney & Co v Raja [1998] 1 WLR 1426, [1998] 2 All ER 181, [1998] CLC 615	7.8
Ashingdane v United Kingdom (A/93), *sub nom* Ashingdane v United Kingdom (8225/78) (1985) 7 EHRR 528	4.47
B (A Child) (Adoption Order), Re [2001] EWCA Civ 347, [2001] 2 FLR 26, [2001] 2 FCR 89	1.20
B (A Minor), Re [2001] UKHL 70, [2002] 1 WLR 258, [2002] 1 All ER 641	4.19
B (Disclosure to Other Parties), Re [2001] 2 FLR 1017, [2002] 2 FCR 32, [2001] Fam Law 798	6.47
B v B (A Minor) (Residence Order) [1992] 2 FLR 327, [1993] 1 FCR 211, [1992] Fam Law 490	1.38
Berry Trade Ltd v Moussavi (No 1) [2002] EWCA Civ 477, [2002] 1 WLR 1910, [2002] CPLR 427	7.8
Buchholz v Federal Republic of Germany (A/42) (1981) 3 EHRR 597	7.8
C (A Minor) (Adopted Child: Contact), Re, *sub nom* Re A (A Minor) (1993), Re S (Adopted Child: Contact) [1993] Fam 210, [1993] 3 WLR 85, [1993] 3 All ER 259, [1993] 2 FLR 431	4.67
C (A Minor) (Adoption: Freeing Order), Re, *sub nom* Re SC (A Minor) [1999] Fam 240, [1999] 1 WLR 1079, [1999] 1 FLR 348	3.7
C (A Minor) (Adoption Order: Conditions), Re, *sub nom* Re C (A Minor) (Adoption: Contract with Sibling) [1989] AC 1, [1988] 2 WLR 474, [1988] 1 All ER 705	4.64
C and B (Children) (Care Order: Future Harm), Re, *sub nom* Re C and J (Children) [2001] 1 FLR 611, [2000] 2 FCR 614, [2001] Fam Law 253	1.38
CSC (An Infant), Re [1960] 1 WLR 304, [1960] 1 All ER 711, 124 JP 260	4.29
D (A Minor) (Adoption Order: Conditions), Re [1992] 1 FCR 461	4.64
D (An Infant) (Adoption: Parent's Consent), Re [1977] AC 602, [1977] 2 WLR 79, [1977] 1 All ER 145	1.2
D (Minors) (Adoption Reports: Confidentiality), Re [1996] AC 593, [1995] 3 WLR 483, [1995] 4 All ER 385	6.47
D and K (Children) (Care Plan: Twin Track Planning), Re, *sub nom* Re D and K (Children) (Care Plan: Concurrent Planning) [2000] 1 WLR 642, [1999] 4 All ER 893, [1999] 2 FLR 872	1.20
Flintshire CC v K [2001] 2 FLR 476, [2001] 2 FCR 724, [2001] Fam Law 578	5.2

G (A Minor) (Adoption: Illegal Placement), Re [1995] 1 FLR 403, [1995] 3 FCR 26, [1995] Fam Law 230	5.3
Golder v United Kingdom (A/18) (1979–80) 1 EHRR 524	4.47
Goode v Martin [2001] EWCA Civ 1899, [2002] 1 WLR 1828, [2002] 1 All ER 620	7.5
H (A Child) (Adoption: Consultation of Unmarried Fathers), Re; Re G (A Child) (Adoption: Disclosure), sub nom Re H (A Child) (Adoption: Disclosure) [2001] 1 FLR 646, [2001] 1 FCR 726, [2001] Fam Law 175	4.83
J (Specific Issue Orders: Child's Religious Upbringing and Circumcision), Re [2000] 1 FLR 571, [2000] 1 FCR 307, [2000] Fam Law 246	1.26
K v Finland (25702/94) (No 2), sub nom T v Finland (25702/94) (No 2) [2001] 2 FLR 707, [2001] 2 FCR 673, (2003) 36 EHRR 18	3.24
KT (A Minor) (Adoption), Re [1993] Fam Law 567	4.29
M (A Minor) (Adoption or Residence Order), Re [1998] 1 FLR 570, [1998] 1 FCR 165, [1998] Fam Law 188	1.19
McMichael v United Kingdom (A/308), sub nom McMichael v United Kingdom (16424/90) [1995] 2 FCR 718, (1995) 20 EHRR 205, [1995] Fam Law 478	4.47
O (A Child) (Supervision Order: Future Harm), Re [2001] EWCA Civ 16, [2001] 1 FLR 923, [2001] 1 FCR 289, (2001) 165 JPN 606	1.38
O (A Minor) (Adoption: Withholding Agreement), Re, sub nom Re O (A Minor) (Adoption: Withholding Consent) [1999] 1 FLR 451, [1999] 2 FCR 262, [1999] Fam Law 76	1.9
O (Minors) (Care or Supervision Order), Re [1996] 2 FLR 755, [1997] 2 FCR 17, [1997] Fam Law 87	1.38, 1.40
Olsson v Sweden (A/130), sub nom Olsson v Sweden (10465/83) (1989) 11 EHRR 259, (1988) The Times, March 28	3.24
Oxfordshire CC v L (Care or Supervision Order), sub nom Oxfordshire CC v B (Care or Supervision Order) [1998] 1 FLR 70, [1998] 3 FCR 521, [1998] Fam Law 22	1.38
R (Adoption), Re [1967] 1 WLR 34, [1966] 3 All ER 613, (1967) 131 JP 1	2.37
R (Adoption: Father's Involvement), Re [2001] 1 FLR 745	4.83
S (Contact: Application by Sibling), Re [1999] Fam 283, [1999] 3 WLR 504, [1999] 1 All ER 648	4.67
S v M (Consent: Missing Parent), sub nom Re S, Petitioners, ES, Petitioner (Adoption), S (Adoption), M v S (Consent: Missing Parent) 1999 SC 388, 1999 SLT 571, 1999 SCLR 738	2.37
SL (Adoption: Home in Jurisdiction), Re [2004] EWHC 1283, [2005] 1 FLR 118, [2004] Fam Law 860	4.31
TP and KM v United Kingdom (28945/95) [2001] 2 FLR 549, [2001] 2 FCR 289, (2002) 34 EHRR 2	4.47
V (A Minor) (Adoption: Consent), Re [1987] Fam 57, [1986] 3 WLR 927, [1986] 1 All ER 752	4.64
X (Children) (Adoption: Confidential Procedure), Re, sub nom Re X (Children) (Adoption by Foster Parents: Disclosure), Re X (Children) (Adoption: Confidentiality) [2002] EWCA Civ 828, [2002] 2 FLR 476, [2002] 3 FCR 648	6.47

Table of Statutes

Paragraph references printed in **bold** type indicate where the Act is set out in part or in full.

Access to Justice Act 1999	
s 57	7.170
Administration of Justice Act 1960	6.50
s 12	6.50
Adoption Act 1976	2.37, 4.28, 5.1, 5.2, 6.47, 8.1
s 15(3)	4.19
s 16(2)(a)	2.34
(b)	2.36
s 18	3.7, 4.49
ss 19–21	4.49
s 21	4.49
Adoption and Children Act 2002	1.12, 1.15, 1.17, 1.22, 1.23, 1.24, 2.2, 2.36, 3.1, 3.7, 3.22, 3.30, 3.111, 4.9, 4.28, 4.29, 4.50, 4.62, 4.68, 4.69, 4.75, 4.76, 5.1, 5.2, 5.14, 6.1, 6.23, 7.3, 7.24, 8.1, 8.4, 8.49
Pt 1	6.18, 6.19, 6.22
Ch 4	1.9
Pt 2	6.20, 6.22
s 1	1.1, 2.32, 2.33, 3.33, 3.44, 3.95, 4.6, 4.47, 4.90
(2)	1.2, 1.16, 3.87, 8.12, 8.28
(3)	1.4
(4)	1.4, 2.33, 3.87, 8.12, 8.28
(a)	1.5
(c)	1.7, 1.14, 2.41
(e)	1.12
(f)	1.13, 2.41, 4.78
(i)–(iii)	8.51
(5)	1.15, 8.12, 8.28
(6)	1.16, 1.17, 1.38, 2.42, 3.131, 4.62, 8.12
(7)	1.1, 4.47
(8)	4.78
s 2(1)	5.3, 8.3
s 3	8.2
(2)(b)	8.1

Adoption and Children Act 2002 – *contd*	
s 4	8.1, 8.52
(2)	8.51
s 12	6.46, 8.1
s 18	3.2
(1)	4.85
(5)	3.3
s 19	2.2, 2.18, 2.19, 2.22, 2.23, 2.24, 2.25, 2.26, 3.2, 3.10, 3.16, 3.19, 3.36, 4.50, 4.77, 4.85, 4.86, 4.87, 4.88, 8.5, 8.6
(1)	3.11
(2)	3.12
(3)(a)	3.17
(b)	3.17
(4)	3.15
s 20	2.4, 2.14, 2.15, 2.16, 2.18, 2.19, 2.22, 2.24, 2.25, 2.26, 4.50, 4.59, 7.33, 7.43, 8.5, 8.6
(2)	2.15
(4)(a)	2.15, 2.26, 4.56, 4.59, 7.30, 7.33, 7.43, 8.5
(b)	2.26, 4.56, 7.33, 8.5
s 21	2.2, 3.9, 3.26, 3.36
(2)(a)	3.27
(b)	3.27
(c)	4.89
(3)(a)	3.27, 3.35, 3.75
(b)	3.27, 3.35, 3.75
s 22	2.25, 3.36, 3.131
(1)	3.36
(2)	3.17, 3.36
(3)	3.37
(4)	3.4
s 23	3.76, 7.24
s 24	3.28, 3.69
(2)	3.28, 3.69
(3)	3.28, 3.69
(4)	3.71
(5)	3.70

Adoption and Children Act 2002 – contd

s 25	3.5, 3.29, 3.81
(4)	3.83
s 26	3.8, 3.21, 3.85, 3.90, 3.92, 3.94, 3.95, 3.96, 3.97, 3.98, 3.99, 3.100, 3.101, 3.103, 4.88, 5.14, 7.26
(1)	3.85, 3.88, 3.100
(2)(a)	3.20, 3.85
(b)	3.92
(3)(f)	7.88, 7.89
(4)	3.90
s 27	3.103, 4.88, 7.26
(1)(a)	3.96
(b)	3.96
(2)	3.93, 3.94
(4)	3.91
(5)	3.97
s 28(1)	3.18
(a)	3.18
(b)	3.19
(2)	3.107, 7.20, 7.26
(3)	3.107, 7.26
s 29(1)	3.39
(2)	3.40
(a)	3.41
(3)	3.41
(5)	1.37, 3.43
(b)	1.37
(6)	1.32
s 30(2)	3.13
ss 30–33	3.113
ss 30–35	3.2, 3.112, 3.121
s 31	3.13
(4)	3.121
s 32(2)	3.121
s 33(3)	3.121
s 34	3.114
s 35	3.116, 3.118
s 36	3.119
ss 36–40	3.112, 3.119
ss 37–40	3.119
s 39(1)	4.74
(2)	4.74
(3)	4.74
s 41	3.121
(2)	3.122, 3.125
(4)	3.123
(5)	3.123
(6)–(8)	3.123
s 42	4.8, 4.21
(2)	2.19, 4.28
(3)	4.28, 4.73
(4)	4.28
(5)	4.28
(6)	3.119, 4.28, 7.88, 7.89, 7.90

Adoption and Children Act 2002 – contd

s 42(7)	4.8, 4.30
s 43	4.8, 4.21, 4.32, 4.65, 4.81, 5.11
s 44	3.128, 4.8, 4.21, 4.54, 7.30, 7.89
(2)	4.35, 4.73
(3)	4.35, 4.73
(5)	4.36, 5.11
s 45	4.8
s 46(1)	4.1
(2)	4.2
(3)	4.3
(6)	4.8, 4.40, 4.62
s 47	4.7, 4.8, 4.50, 4.77, 4.90
(2)	2.4, 4.42, 4.44, 4.73
(a)	4.59, 7.43
(c)	2.5, 2.9, 4.59
(3)	2.7, 2.10, 2.20, 4.43, 7.44, 7.88
(4)	4.45, 4.50, 4.86
(5)	2.7, 2.10, 2.20, 3.14, 4.46, 4.59, 7.43, 7.44, 7.88
(6)	4.48, 4.49
(7)	2.7, 2.10, 2.21, 3.14, 4.43, 4.46, 4.47, 7.88
(8)	4.24
(9)	4.24
s 48	4.8, 4.37, 4.38
(1)	7.29
s 49	4.11
(1)	4.13
(4)	4.8, 4.24
(5)	4.8
ss 49–51	4.8
s 50	4.10, 7.46
s 51	4.10
(2)	4.4, 4.15, 4.71, 4.72
(3)	4.17
(4)	4.18
s 52	2.1, 2.34, 3.10, 3.27, 4.41
(1)	**2.31**, 2.43, 4.44
(a)	**2.31**, 2.36
(b)	**2.31**, 2.33, 2.37
(3)	4.86
(4)	2.19, 3.13, 4.86
(5)	2.11, 2.16
(6)	2.12
(8)	2.24, 2.25
(9)	2.12, 4.77
(10)	2.12, 4.77
s 54	6.24, 6.29, 6.30
s 55(2)	3.121
s 56	6.24, 6.26
ss 56–65	6.8, 6.24
s 57	6.28
ss 57–65	6.28
s 58	6.24
(2)	6.29

Table of Statutes

Adoption and Children Act 2002 – *contd*	
s 58(3)	6.29
s 59	6.28
s 60	6.7, 6.30, 6.36
(2)(a)	6.14, 6.35
(3)	6.16, 6.30, 7.87, 7.112
s 61	6.36, 6.37, 6.43, 6.46
(3)	6.26, 6.37, 6.45
ss 61–62	6.37
s 62	6.36, 6.38, 6.43
(3)	6.26, 6.40, 6.45
(4)	6.26, 6.45
s 67	4.4, 4.72
s 77	6.1, 6.4
s 78	6.5
s 79	6.7
(3)	6.24, 7.87
(4)	6.11, 7.87, 7.112
(5)	6.9, 6.15, 6.24, 6.26
s 80	6.17
s 84	5.14, 7.26
s 85	5.18
s 88	7.26
s 89	7.26
s 92	5.3, 5.6, 5.7
(2)	5.4, 5.13
(a)–(e)	5.17
(f)	5.7
(g)–(i)	5.17
(3)	5.5
(4)	5.5
(7)(a)	5.4
ss 92–96	5.3
ss 92–97	4.8
s 93	5.18
(2)	5.7
(3)	5.7
s 94	5.8
(1)	5.9, 5.12, 5.13
(2)(a)	5.9
(5)	5.9
s 95	5.13, 5.16
s 96	5.14
s 101	6.49
(2)	6.50
s 103	6.48, 7.62
s 109	7.10
(1)	1.4
s 110	4.35
s 112	1.23, 4.69
s 113	1.24, 1.30
s 114	1.22, 4.69
s 115	1.20, 1.24
s 118	3.58, 3.65
s 120	1.12
s 123	5.17, 5.20, 5.22

Adoption and Children Act 2002 – *contd*	
s 123(1)	5.20, 5.21
s 124	5.21
s 138	5.6, 5.9, 5.16
s 141(1)(a)	3.35
(3)	3.35, 3.80, 7.43, 7.45
(4)	3.75, 7.43, 7.45
(a)	3.35
(b)	3.80
(c)	4.59, 7.43
s 144(1)	3.35, 4.35, 8.51
(4)	4.14
(5)	4.14
(6)	4.14
Sch 1	6.2, 6.3
Sch 2	6.7, 6.12
Sch 4, para 7(3)	4.49
Adoption (Scotland) Act 1978	
s 18	4.48
Births and Deaths Registration Act 1953	2.13, 6.3
s 10(1)(a)	4.76
(b)	4.76
(c)	4.76
s 10A(1)(a)	4.76
(b)	4.76
(c)	4.76
Children Act 1989	1.2, 1.4, 1.12, 1.15, 1.17, 1.23, 1.25, 3.4, 3.20, 3.23, 3.27, 3.30, 3.41, 3.46, 3.85, 3.88, 3.100, 3.101, 4.2, 4.62, 4.69, 4.76
s 1	1.25
(3)(b)	1.6
(f)	1.13
(5)	1.38
s 4	4.79, 4.80
(4)	8.64
s 4A	4.69
s 8	1.28, 3.20, 3.40, 3.41, 3.85, 3.97, 4.63, 4.79, 7.45, 7.48
s 9	1.24
(3)	1.30
s 10	4.67
(5)(b)	1.30
(c)	1.30
(7A)	1.36
(8)	1.31
(9)	1.31
s 12	1.22, 4.69, 8.70
s 14(11)	1.32
s 14A(3)	1.30
(5)	1.30
(d)	1.30

Children Act 1989 – *contd*		Children Act 1989 – *contd*	
s 14A(6)	1.30	s 34(4)	3.41
(7)	1.32, 1.37	s 41(3)	7.63
(8)	1.32	(4)(b)	7.64
(9)	1.32	s 42	7.62
(12)	1.31	s 47(3)	3.42
(13)	1.37	(5)	1.37, 3.42, 3.43
ss 14A–14G	1.20, 1.24	s 59	8.53
s 14B(1)(a)	1.28	s 91(14)	1.20
s 14C(1)(a)	1.26	s 97	6.52
(b)	1.26	Sch 2, para 15	3.85
(2)	1.26	Children Act 2004	
(b)	1.28	s 37(1)	7.59
(3)(a)	1.33	Civil Partnership Act 2004	4.14
s 14D(1)	1.34	Criminal Justice and Court Services Act 2000	
(2)	1.34		
(3)(a)–(d)	1.35	s 15(1)	7.59
(5)	1.35	Human Fertilisation and Embryology Act 1990	
s 14F	1.25		
s 14G	1.25	s 28	4.18
s 20	3.59	Human Rights Act 1998	3.66, 7.5, 7.181
s 23	8.53	s 3	7.5
s 26	3.58, 3.65	Sch 1	7.5
(2A)	3.64	Magistrates' Courts Act 1980	
s 26A	8.38	Sch 6, Pt I	4.49
s 31	1.12, 3.30	Marriage Act 1949	6.10
(2)	3.22, 3.23, 3.30, 3.36, 3.131	Mental Health Act 1983	7.73, 7.78
(9)	1.12	Supreme Court Act 1981	
s 31A	3.59	s 9	7.174
s 34	1.36, 3.85, 4.79		

Table of Statutory Instruments

Adopted Children and Adoption Contact Registers Regulations 2005 (SI 2005/924)		Adoption Agencies Regulations 2005 (SI 2005/889) – *contd*	
reg 2	6.2	reg 25(3)(a)	4.23
reg 6	6.18	(b)	4.23
reg 7	6.20	(4)	4.23
reg 8	7.22	(5)	4.23
reg 11	6.9	reg 26	4.23, 8.21
reg 12	6.12	(2)(b)	4.23
reg 13	6.10	reg 27	8.22
reg 18	6.6	(4)	8.71
Sch 3	6.18	(4)–(10)	8.22
Sch 4	6.20	reg 28	8.22
Adoption Agencies Regulations 1983 (SI 1983/1964)	6.26	reg 29	8.23
		(4)	4.23
Adoption Agencies Regulations 2005 (SI 2005/889)	2.23, 3.9, 3.86, 3.131, 4.65, 4.79, 6.26, 8.4, 8.43	reg 31	8.24, 8.25
		(1)(b)	4.65
		(c)(ii)	4.65
		(2)(c)	4.65
Pt 4	4.22, 4.23	(d)(iv)	4.65
regs 3–10	8.11	regs 31–34	8.23
regs 11–17	8.5	reg 32	8.27
reg 12	2.26, 8.5	reg 33	8.29, 8.31
reg 13	8.6	reg 35	8.31
reg 14	4.79, 8.6	reg 36	3.60, 8.34, 8.38
(3)	8.6, 8.14	(3)	3.61
(4)	8.6	(5)	3.62
reg 15	8.7	(6)	3.62
reg 16	8.8	reg 37	3.64, 8.34, 8.38
reg 17	8.9	(7)	3.66
reg 18	8.5, 8.10	(8)	3.67
reg 19	8.5, 8.14	reg 38	2.25, 8.41
reg 20	8.15	regs 39–44	8.5
reg 21	4.23, 8.17	reg 46	8.42
regs 21–30	8.17	(1)	3.86
reg 22	4.23, 8.18	(2)	3.86
reg 23	4.23, 8.18, 8.20	(4)	3.88
(1)(a)	4.23	(5)	3.89
(b)	4.23	(6)	3.89
reg 24	4.23, 8.19, 8.20	reg 47	8.42
reg 25	4.23, 8.20	(1)	3.94
(2)	4.23	(2)	3.98
		(3)	3.94, 3.98

Adoption Agencies Regulations 2005 (SI
    2005/889) – contd
  Sch 2   2.23
  Sch 4, Pt 1   4.23
  Sch 5, Pt 1   8.46
Adoption Information and Intermediary
    Services (Pre-Commencement
    Adoptions) Regulations 2005
    (SI 2005/890)   6.13
Adoption (Northern Ireland) Order 1987
    (SI 1987/2203)
  Art 17(1)   4.48
  Art 18(1)   4.48
Adoption Support Services
    Regulations 2005 (SI 2005/691)   8.25
  Pt 3   8.53, 8.59, 8.61
  Pt 5   8.66
  reg 3   8.53
  reg 6   8.58
  reg 8   8.60
  reg 9   8.61
  reg 10   8.62
  reg 11   8.62
  reg 12   8.63, 8.66, 8.68
    (2)   8.64
  reg 13   8.51
  reg 14   8.54
    (2)   8.54
    (3)   8.55
  reg 15(4)   8.56
    (5)   8.56
  reg 16   8.57
    (4)   8.66
  reg 17   8.64
    (5)   8.65
  reg 18   8.66
  reg 19   8.67
  reg 20   8.68
  reg 21   8.69
  reg 22   8.64
Adoption Support Services (Local
    Authorities) (England)
    Regulations 2003 (SI 2003/1348)   8.25
Adoptions with a Foreign Element
    Regulations 2005 (SI 2005/392)   8.43
  Pt 3, Ch 1   8.48
  reg 12   8.46, 8.48
  reg 15(4)   8.46

Children (Allocation of Proceedings)
    Order 1991 (SI 1991/1677)   7.24
Children (Allocation of Proceedings)
    (Amendment) Order 2005
    (SI 2005/520)   3.76, 7.24
  Sch 3   7.24
  Sch 4   7.24

Civil Procedure Rules 1998
    (SI 1998/3132)   7.1, 7.5
  Pt 43   7.180
  Pt 44   7.180
  Pt 47   7.1
  Pt 50   7.1
  Pt 52   7.147
  Pts 70–74   7.1
  r 1.1   7.3
  r 1.2   7.3
  r 35.15   7.1
    (3)   7.1
  r 44.3(2)   7.180
    (3)   7.180
  rr 44.9–44.12A   7.180
  r 44.13(i)   7.105
  r 45.6   7.180
  r 47   7.180
  rr 47.20–47.23   7.146
  r 48   7.180
  Sch 1   7.1
  Sch 2   7.1
Disclosure of Adoption Information
    (Post-Commencement Adoptions)
    Regulations 2005 (SI 2005/888)   6.25,
                                               8.71
  reg 4   6.26
  reg 10   6.26
  reg 11   6.26
  reg 12   6.43
  reg 13   6.44
  reg 14   6.26, 6.45
  reg 15   6.46
    (1)   8.71
  reg 18   6.26
  reg 19   6.35
  reg 20   6.36
  reg 21   6.28
Family Procedure (Adoption) Rules 2005
    (SI 2005/2795)   7.1, 7.2
  Pt 2   7.181
  Pt 3   7.14
  Pt 4   7.15
  Pt 5   2.28, 3.106, 3.126, 7.26, 7.52, 7.58,
                                    7.69, 7.71, 7.88
  Pt 6   7.181
  Pt 9   4.47, 7.15, 7.86, 7.87, 7.88, 7.111
  Pt 10   7.15, 7.25, 7.111, 7.112, 7.113, 7.114,
                                 7.115, 7.116, 7.123,
                                               7.126
  Pt 12   7.181
  Pt 13   7.181
  Pt 14   7.181
  Pt 15   7.181
  Pt 16   7.181

Family Procedure (Adoption) Rules 2005 (SI 2005/2795) – contd		Family Procedure (Adoption) Rules 2005 (SI 2005/2795) – contd	
Pt 17	7.127, 7.128	r 25	7.29, 7.36
Pt 18	7.181	r 26	3.53, 4.57, 7.6, 7.35, 7.36
Pt 19	8.146	(1)(c)	4.84
r 1	7.2	(f)(i)	4.84
(2)(e)	7.8	(g)	7.37
r 2	7.5	(3)	7.36
r 3	7.6	(4)	7.40
r 4	7.10, 7.12	(6)	7.41
(1)	7.10	r 27	2.44, 3.51, 4.55, 7.30, 7.87, 7.114
(2)	7.11	(1)	2.44
r 5(1)	7.1	(2)	2.44
(2)–(5)	7.1	(3)	2.44
(3)	7.180	(4)(a)	2.45
r 6	2.27, 2.45, 7.12, 7.73	(b)	2.46
r 7	7.12, 7.29	r 28	2.22
(1)(c)(ii)(bb)	7.14	(1)(a)	2.22
r 8	7.14, 7.23	(b)	2.22
r 9	7.14	(2)	2.27
(4)	7.14, 7.181	r 29	4.33, 4.65, 4.81
r 10	7.14	(1)	7.34
r 11	7.14	(2)	3.54, 7.31
r 12	7.14	r 30	4.34, 4.52
rr 12–16	7.14	r 31	3.35, 3.56, 4.59, 7.42
r 13	7.14	r 32	7.42
r 14	7.14	(1)	7.44
r 15	7.14	(3)	7.44
r 16	7.14, 7.168	(6)	4.60, 7.46
r 17	2.22, 2.24, 3.48, 7.17	(7)	7.46, 7.47
r 18	7.17	(8)	7.46
r 19	7.16	(9)	3.56, 7.51
r 20	2.44, 7.18, 7.49	r 33	7.17
(2)	7.38	r 37(1)	7.62, 7.66
r 21	7.20	(2)(a)	7.66
(1)	7.38	(b)	7.62
(2)	7.38	r 49	7.73
r 22	7.26	rr 49–58	7.73
r 23	3.45, 3.46, 3.72, 3.73, 3.77, 3.78, 3.101, 3.103, 3.104, 3.108, 3.109, 7.27, 7.62, 7.89	r 50	7.74
		r 51	7.74, 7.75
		(1)(a)	7.75
		(b)(i)	7.75
(1)	3.100	(ii)	7.75
(2)	3.47, 7.37	r 52(2)	7.74
(a)	7.28	(3)	7.74
(b)	7.28	r 53(2)	7.78
(3)	3.47, 7.37	(3)	7.78
(a)	4.84, 7.28	(a)–(c)	7.77
(b)	7.28	r 54	7.80
(4)	7.28	(6)	7.80
r 24	7.28	r 55	7.74, 7.76
(1)	3.49, 4.53	(1)	2.46
(b)	3.50, 4.54	(3)	2.46
(2)	4.56	r 58(1)	7.81
(3)	3.52	(2)	7.82
(4)	7.35	r 59	7.29

Family Procedure (Adoption) Rules 2005 (SI 2005/2795) – contd

r 59(1)	7.52
(2)	7.87, 7.114
(a)	7.53
(3)	7.53
(4)	7.52
rr 59–61	7.52
r 60(1)	7.54
(2)	7.55
(3)	7.56
r 61	7.57
r 62	7.58
rr 62–64	7.58
rr 62–67	7.60
r 63	7.59
(2)(a)	7.60, 7.63
(c)	7.60
(3)	7.59
(a)	7.59
r 64	7.60
(2)	7.60, 7.63
r 65(1)	7.61
(2)–(5)	7.62
rr 65–67	7.61
r 66	7.62
(1)	7.62
(2)	7.62
r 67	7.62
r 68	7.63
(1)(a)	7.63
(2)	7.66
(3)–(5)	7.67
(6)	7.68
r 69	7.29, 7.69
(a)	2.28
(b)	2.28
rr 69–72	7.69
r 70	2.28, 7.69
r 71	2.29, 7.70
r 72	2.30
(2)	2.30
(3)	2.30
r 73	7.29, 7.71
rr 73–74	7.71
r 74	7.72
rr 75–76	7.84
r 76	7.85
r 77	7.37
(2)	7.38
(3)	7.39
r 78	6.51
r 84	6.30, 6.33, 7.87, 7.114
r 86(3)	7.87
(4)	7.89
rr 86–96	7.86

Family Procedure (Adoption) Rules 2005 (SI 2005/2795) – contd

r 87	7.90
r 88	7.90
(2)	7.90
r 90	7.90
(2)	7.90
r 91	7.91
(2)	7.90
(3)	7.91
r 92	7.94
r 93(1)	7.93
(2)	7.93
(3)	7.93
r 94	7.93
r 95	7.103
r 96	7.107
r 97(3)	7.115
(4)	7.114
rr 97–105	7.111
r 98	7.116
(3)	7.117
r 100	7.119
(4)	7.120
r 101	7.121
r 102	7.118, 7.125
(2)	7.118
(3)	7.122
(5)	7.124
(6)	7.124
(7)	7.118
r 103	7.125
r 104	7.123
r 105	7.112
r 106	7.21, 7.87, 7.114
r 107	3.124, 7.87, 7.114
(1)	3.125
(2)	3.126
(3)	3.128
r 108	4.82, 7.25, 7.112
r 110	7.179
r 122	7.22, 7.181
r 123	7.181
r 124	7.181
r 125	7.181
r 128	7.181
r 129	7.181
r 130	7.181
r 131	7.181
r 132	7.181
r 133	7.181
r 134	7.181
r 138	7.181
r 154	7.127
r 156	7.129
r 157	7.130

Family Procedure (Adoption) Rules 2005 (SI 2005/2795) – contd		Independent Review of Determinations (Adoption) Regulations 2005 (SI 2005/3332) – contd	
r 158	7.131	reg 12	8.75
r 159	7.136	reg 13	8.76
(2)	7.136	The Local Authority (Adoption) (Miscellaneous Provisions) Regulations 2005 (SI 2005/3390)	4.36
(4)	7.137		
r 160	7.138		
r 161	7.139	Restriction on the Preparation of Adoption Reports Regulations 2005 (SI 2005/1711)	5.10, 5.11
r 162	7.134		
r 163	7.132		
(4)	7.135	reg 3	5.10
r 164	7.142	reg 4	5.11
r 165	7.143	Review of Children's Cases Regulations 1991 (SI 1991/895)	
r 166	7.144		
r 167	7.145	reg 2	3.65
r 171	7.146	reg 3	3.65
r 172	7.148	reg 8	3.65
r 173	7.150	Review of Children's Cases (Amendment) (England) Regulations 2004 (SI 2004/1419)	3.65, 3.66
(6)	7.151		
(7)	7.156		
r 174	7.159	Special Guardianship Regulations 2005 (SI 2005/1109)	1.25
(1)	7.155		
r 175	7.159	reg 21	1.32
(3)	7.155	Sch	1.32
r 177	7.165	Suitability of Adopters Regulations 2005 (SI 2005/1712)	4.22, 8.43, 8.44, 8.49
r 178	7.159		
r 179	7.166	reg 3	4.23, 8.45
r 180	7.167	(a)	8.46
(4)	7.168	(b)	8.46
(5)	7.168	(c)	8.46
r 181	7.169	(d)	8.46
(3)	7.149	(e)	8.46
r 182	7.170	(f)(i)	8.46
r 183	7.171	(ii)	8.46
Family Proceedings Rules 1991 (SI 1991/1247)		(iii)	8.46
		reg 4(1)	4.23, 8.48
r 4.11B	1.32	(a)	8.48
Independent Review of Determinations (Adoption) Regulations 2005 (SI 2005/3332)	8.71	(b)	8.48
		(c)	8.48
		(d)	8.48
Pt 2	8.72	(e)	8.48
Pt 3	8.73	(f)	8.48
reg 3	8.71	(2)	4.14, 4.23, 8.49, 8.50
regs 10–11	8.74	reg 5	4.23, 8.47

Table of Abbreviations

AA 1976	Adoption Act 1976
AAR 1983	Adoption Agencies Regulations 1983
AAR 2005	Adoption Agencies Regulations 2005
ACA 2002	Adoption and Children Act 2002
ACACRR 2005	Adopted Children and Adoption Contact Registers Regulations 2005
AFER 2005	Adoption with a Foreign Element Regulations 2005
ASSR 2005	Adoption Support Services Regulations 2005
CA 1989	Children Act 1989
CAFCASS	Children and Family Court Advisory and Support Service
CPR 1998	Civil Procedure Rules 1998
DAI(PCA)R 2005	Disclosure of Adoption Information (Post-Commencement Adoptions) Regulations 2005
FP(A)R 2005	Family Procedure (Adoption) Rules 2005
IRD(A)R 2005	Independent Review of Determinations (Adoption) Regulations 2005
IRO	Independent reviewing officer
SAR 2005	Suitability of Adopters Regulations
SGO	Special guardianship order

Chapter 1

WELFARE

1.1 Section 1 of the Adoption and Children Act 2002 (ACA 2002) is the overarching provision of the Act. 'Coming to a decision relating to the adoption of a child' triggers the obligation on the court and adoption agency to apply the s 1 principles: s 1(7).

PARAMOUNT CONSIDERATION

1.2 ACA 2002, s 1(2) provides that 'the paramount consideration of the court or adoption agency must be the child's welfare throughout his life'. The paramountcy principle makes welfare the pre-eminent consideration outweighing all others.[1] This aligns adoption with the Children Act 1989 (CA 1989).

1.3 It is the welfare of the child 'throughout his life' which must be considered.

DELAY

1.4 Section 1(3) applies the general principle that delay is prejudicial to the child's welfare and places delay amongst the foremost mandatory considerations, although still subject to the welfare principle. The words 'any delay' constitute the widest concept of delay. Section 1(3) complies with Art 6(1) of the European Convention on Human Rights, which requires that cases be heard within a reasonable time:

– There is a statutory obligation on the court to draw up a timetable.[2]

– A key player in the battle against delay will be the National Adoption Standards, which include the production of a plan for permanence for all looked after children at the 4-monthly review and a decision on prospective adopters within 6 months of application.

– A further key part of the drive to reduce delay has been the establishment of an Adoption and Children Act Register, which holds information on children waiting to be adopted and on approved adoptive families waiting to adopt.

---

1 *Re D (An Infant) (Adoption: Parent's Consent)* [1977] AC 602.
2 ACA 2002, s 109(1).

Welfare checklist

> Section 1(4) of ACA 2002 provides that 'the court or adoption agency must have regard to the following matters (among others):
> (a) the child's ascertainable wishes and feelings regarding the decision (considered in the light of the child's age and understanding);
> (b) the child's particular needs;
> (c) the likely effect on the child (throughout his life) of having ceased to be a member of the original family and become an adopted person;
> (d) the child's age, sex, background and any of the child's characteristics which the court or agency considers relevant;
> (e) any harm (within the meaning of the Children Act 1989) which the child has suffered or is at risk of suffering;
> (f) the relationship which the child has with relatives and with any other person in relation to whom the court or agency considers the question to be relevant, including:
>   (i) the likelihood of any such relationship continuing and the value to the child of its doing so;
>   (ii) the ability and willingness of any of the child's relatives, or of any such person, to provide the child with a secure environment in which the child can develop and otherwise meet the child's needs;
>   (iii) the wishes and feelings of any of the child's relatives, or of any such person, regarding the child.'

Wishes and feelings

1.5 As the trend is towards the adoption of older children, s 1(4)(a) is of key importance, particularly in those cases where the child has a strong sense of identity with his natural family.

Needs

1.6 It is implicit that the 'physical, emotional and educational' needs in s 1(3)(b) of CA 1989 will be included. 'Needs' will also embrace social, moral, psychological and health needs.

Having ceased to be a member of the original family and become an adopted person

1.7 Section 1(4)(c) looks at the 'life long' prospects. In addition to the clear need to consider the emotional and psychological impact of adoption, it also brings into consideration such issues as succession, contingent interests under inheritance and trust law, nationality and the right of abode. It has a twofold focus.

Having ceased to be a member of the original family

1.8 This raises important issues such as:

- The extinction of the parents' parental responsibility and the complete severing of all legal ties with the family of birth.
- The loss of the child's sense of identity with the birth family and the risk of damage to the child's self esteem and psychological well-being.
- The damaging sense of loss to such a child in seeing himself as abandoned or unloved by his parents or extended birth family.
- The Art 8 'family life' provisions are relevant in this context.

Becoming an adopted person

1.9 'Becoming an adopted person' confers upon the child the legal status set out in Part 1, Chapter 4 of ACA 2002 and provides for the child a permanent substitute family, where the adopters are legally responsible and, therefore, fully committed to fulfilling their parental responsibilities.[1]

Age, sex, background and characteristics

1.10 Where the adoption of an older child with strong links with the birth family is being considered, the factors of 'age' and 'background' may carry particular weight.

1.11 Considerations such as special educational needs or physical disability may also be included.

Harm

1.12 Section 1(4)(e) employs the same definition as in s 31(9) of CA 1989. The s 31 definition is amended by ACA 2002,[2] which adds 'including, for example, impairment suffered from seeing or hearing the ill-treatment of another'. Domestic violence including the impact on children of witnessing abuse is, therefore, to be considered in all CA 1989 and adoption proceedings.

Relationship which the child has with relatives

1.13 Section 1(4)(f) casts a wider shadow than that under s 1(3)(f) of CA 1989. It has widened the focus of capability. It embraces consideration of (i) *the value* to the child of a continuing relationship with his relatives and (ii) the wishes and feelings of those relatives. This includes the important sibling relationship. These subsections give significant emphasis to those issues which are especially critical for the older child with identity links with his birth family.

---

1 *Re O (A Minor) (Adoption: Withholding Agreement)* [1999] 1 FLR 451.
2 ACA 2002, s 120.

1.14 Whether this factor, taken with the s 1(4)(c) factor, is sufficient to redress the inherent imbalance against the birth family – stemming from the paramountcy principle and the removal of the 'unreasonableness' ground from dispensing with consent – is a matter for debate.

RELIGION, RACIAL ORIGIN, CULTURAL BACKGROUND: SECTION 1(5)

1.15 ACA 2002 gives statutory force to the guidance given in the CA 1989 Guidance and Regulations[1] and the Local Authority Circular 'Adoption – Achieving the Right Balance'.[2] The factors in s 1(5) must be considered by adoption agencies, but not at the expense of harmful delay to the child. 'Due consideration' is a subjective test and will depend on the circumstances.

RANGE OF POWERS: SECTION 1(6)

1.16 ACA 2002, s 1(6) sets out two key principles, both of which provide the context within which the welfare principle in s 1(2) itself must operate:

– the whole range of powers;
– the 'no order' principle.

The whole range of powers

1.17 Section 1(6) places the obligation on the court or adoption agency 'always' to consider the whole range of powers available under (i) ACA 2002 (including placement and adoption orders), and (ii) CA 1989 (including residence orders, care orders, supervision orders and special guardianship orders).

Alternative options for permanence

1.18 Chapter 5 of the White Paper highlighted the need to establish a full range of options for permanent families where the child can no longer live with the birth parents. One of the key objectives of the White Paper was to 'set adoption within a context of permanence, with a spectrum of options for finding families for looked after children who need them[3] ... securing it as a mainstream service'.[4] The intention is to encourage the wider use of adoption, particularly of children looked after by a local authority.

---

1   Volume 3, paras 2.40 and 2.41.
2   LAC (98) 20 (28 August 1998).
3   White Paper *Adoption: A New Approach*, para 3.8.
4   *Adoption: A New Approach*, para 3.5.

1.19 The weighing up of the nature and effect of each order and the advantages and disadvantages which each brings to the child's welfare remains a crucial exercise under the new legislation: see Ward LJ in *Re M (A Minor) (Adoption or Residence Order)*.[1]

Range of options

1.20 The range of options includes:

(1) Rehabilitation with birth parents.
(2) Home with extended family members or friends.
(3) Residence orders/residence orders coupled with a s 91(14) restriction.[2]
(4) Fostering.
(5) Special guardianship orders (SGOs): the new ss 14A to 14G of CA 1989.[3]
(6) Adoption.

Both 'twin track planning' and 'concurrent planning' remain important players in the range of options: see *Re D and K (Care Plan)*,[4] per Bracewell J.

RESIDENCE ORDERS

1.21 Residence orders provide an important option for permanence, particularly for relatives and friends, step-parents and local authority foster parents. One of the main objections to adoption by relatives is the potential for distorting family relationships.

1.22 ACA 2002[5] amends s 12 of CA 1989 to empower the court to direct an *extension of a residence order to age 18*.

1.23 ACA 2002 also amends CA 1989 in the case of step-parents with the intention of boosting alternatives to adoption by enabling a *step-parent to acquire parental responsibility for the child of his spouse*: either (i) by agreement between the step-parent and the parents who have parental responsibility, or (ii) by order of the court.[6]

1.24 The position of local authority foster parents, who wish to apply for a residence order, has also been ameliorated by ACA 2002 which has reduced the residence requirement to one year.[7]

SPECIAL GUARDIANSHIP ORDERS[8]

1.25 SGOs are intended to meet the needs of those children who cannot live with their birth parents, for whom adoption is not appropriate, but who could still benefit

---

1 [1998] 1 FLR 570 at 588D–F and 589A–D.
2 See *Re B (A Child) (Adoption Order)* [2001] 2 FLR 26 at [24]–[27].
3 Amended by ACA 2002, s 115.
4 [1999] 2 FLR 872.
5 ACA 2002, s 114.
6 ACA 2002, s 112.
7 ACA 2002, s 113 amends s 9 of CA 1989 by substituting one year for 3 years.
8 ACA 2002, s 115 amends CA 1989 by inserting new provisions in ss 14A–14G, which deal with SGOs.

from a legally secure placement. The aim is to offer more than a residence order in terms of the security it brings and the support services to be made available, including financial support,[1] which are set out in the Special Guardianship Regulations 2005. It is important to remember:

– that the child's welfare is the paramount consideration; and
– that the welfare checklist in CA 1989, s 1 applies to SGOs.

1.26 The special guardian appointed by the order has parental responsibility for the child and (subject to any other order in force with respect to the child[2]) is *entitled to exercise that parental responsibility to the exclusion of any other person with parental responsibility*[3] with two exceptions. The special guardian's responsibility does not:

(1) affect the operation of any rule of law which requires the consent of all those with parental responsibility (for example, the sterilisation or circumcision of the child[4]), nor
(2) any rights which a natural parent has in relation to the child's adoption or placement for adoption.[5]

1.27 The special guardian, therefore, has the responsibility for the day-to-day decisions about caring for the child and for taking decisions about his upbringing.

1.28 The parents, however, retain some limited rights:

– They have the right to consent or not to the child's placement for adoption or adoption.[6]
– Before making a special guardianship order, an express duty is imposed upon the court to consider whether a contact order should be made, which would enable continued contact with the birth family.[7]
– The special guardian must also take reasonable steps to inform the parents if the child dies.

1.29 The aim, therefore, is to provide legal security, whilst preserving the 'basic' link between the child and his birth family. Unlike adoption, the child's relationship with his birth parents is not severed, but preserved. Although their ability to exercise their parental responsibility is circumscribed, they nevertheless remain legally the child's parents.

---

[1] CA 1989, ss 14F and 14G deal with special guardian support services.
[2] See the position in relation to placement orders.
[3] CA 1989, s 14C(1)(a) and (b).
[4] *Re J (Specific Issue Orders: Child's Religious Upbringing and Circumcision)* [2000] 1 FLR 571 at 577D, per Dame Elizabeth Butler-Sloss P.
[5] CA 1989, s 14C(2).
[6] CA 1989, s 14C(2)(b).
[7] CA 1989, s 14B(1)(a). Before considering whether an SGO should be made, the court must consider whether a contact order should be made and whether any s 8 order in force should be varied or discharged.

Procedure in relation to SGOs

1.30 A court may make an SGO on the application of:[1]

(1) any guardian of the child;
(2) any individual in whose favour a residence order is in force in respect of the child or who has the consent of all those in whose favour a residence order is in force;
(3) anyone with whom the child has lived for at least 3 years out of the last 5 years;
(4) where the child is in the care of the local authority, anyone with the local authority's consent;
(5) in any other case, anyone who has the consent of all those with parental responsibility;
(6) a local authority foster parent with whom the child has lived for a period of at least one year immediately preceding the application – they may apply as of right;[2]
(7) anyone else, including the child, who has the leave of the court.[3]

1.31 Where a person is applying for leave to make an application for a special guardianship order, the court is under a duty to have particular regard to:[4]

– the nature of the proposed application for the special guardianship order;
– the applicant's connection with the child;
– any risk there might be of that proposed application disrupting the child's life to such an extent that he would be harmed by it; and
– where the child is being looked after by the local authority:
  (a) the authority's plans for the future, and
  (b) the wishes and feelings of the child's parents.

In the case of a child seeking leave, the court may grant leave only if it is satisfied that he or she has sufficient understanding to make the proposed application.[5]

1.32 Applicants have to give 3 months' written notice to the local authority of their intention to apply for an order.[6] The application may be a joint application and the persons concerned need not be married, but they must be aged 18 or over and must not be the natural parents. Furthermore:

---

1 CA 1989, s 14A(3), (5) and (6); see also s 10(5)(b) and (c). The court may also make an SGO with respect to any child in family proceedings in which a question arises with respect to the welfare of the child (a) if an application for an SGO has been made by an individual entitled to make the application or has obtained leave to do so, or (b) the court considers that an SGO should be made even though no such application was made: s 14A(6).
2 CA 1989, s 14A(5)(d).
3 CA 1989, s 9((3) as amended by ACA 2002, s 113 applies in relation to an application for leave to apply for a special guardianship order (ie a person who has been within the last 6 months a local authority foster parent may not apply unless he has the consent of the authority, or he is a relative of the child, or the child has lived with him for at least one year preceding the application).
4 CA 1989, s 14A(12) and s 10(9).
5 CA 1989, s 14A(12) and s 10(8).
6 The only exception to this is where a person has the leave of the court to make a competing application for a special guardianship order at a final hearing, in which case the 3-month period does not apply: ACA 2002, s 29 (6) and CA 1989, s 14A(7).

- the local authority is under a duty to investigate and prepare a report to the court as to the suitability of the applicants;[1] the matters to be dealt with in the report are set out in the Schedule to the Special Guardianship Regulations 2005;[2]
- the court may not make a special guardianship order unless it has received such a report;[3]
- an officer of the Children and Family Court Advisory and Support Service (CAFCASS) will be appointed in most cases.[4]

1.33 On making a special guardianship order, the court may give leave for the child to be known by a new surname and give permission for the child to be taken out of its jurisdiction for any period longer than 3 months.[5] Otherwise, whilst the SGO is in force, no one may cause the child to be known by a new surname or remove him from the UK without the written notice of every person with parental responsibility or the leave of the court.

1.34 A further distinction from an adoption order is that SGOs can be varied or discharged by the court of its own motion[6] or on the application of:[7]

- the special guardian;
- the child's parents or guardian (but only with leave of the court);
- the child (with leave of the court, and provided the court is satisfied that he has sufficient understanding to make the application);
- any individual in whose favour a residence order is in force in respect of the child;
- if a care order is made in respect of the child, the local authority.

1.35 The following must obtain leave:[8]

- the child;
- any parent or guardian;
- any step-parent who has acquired and has not lost parental responsibility;
- any individual who immediately before the making of the SGO had, but no longer has, parental responsibility.

Save for the case of the child, the court may grant leave only if it is satisfied that there has been a significant change in circumstances since the making of the SGO.[9]

1.36 Schedule 3 of ACA 2002 provides that an SGO discharges any existing care order or related contact order under CA 1989, s 34.[10] If, however, the need arises, a

---

1   CA 1989, s 14A(8) and (9).
2   The Special Guardianship Regulations 2005, reg 21.
3   CA 1989, s 14(11).
4   See Family Proceedings Rules 1991, r 4.11B.
5   CA 1989, s 14C(3)(a).
6   CA 1989, s 14D(2).
7   CA 1989, s 14D(1).
8   CA 1989, s 14D(3)(a)–(d).
9   CA 1989, s 14D(5).
10 ACA 2002, Sch 3, para 68.

care order or a residence order may be made while an SGO is in force.[1] In these circumstances, the SGO is not automatically discharged, but the local authority or person with the residence order has a right to apply for discharge or variation of the SGO.

1.37 Where a placement order is in force, no SGO may be made in respect of the child unless:[2]

- an application has been made for a final order;
- the person applying for the special guardianship order has obtained leave under ACA 2002, s 29(5)(b) or if he is the guardian under s 47(5).[3]

'No order principle': section 1(6)

1.38 The 'no order' principle in ACA 2002, s 1(6) is in line with s 1(5) of CA 1989. It encapsulates the 'least interventionist' approach[4] and the principle of proportionality under the European Convention.[5]

1.39 It is suggested that the court or adoption agency, in working their way through the range of options, should always ask themselves whether the option under consideration is a proportionate response to the current needs of the child.

1.40 It is further suggested that the court or adoption agency ought to consider the whole range of options, with the least interventionist first.[6]

---

1 Schedule 3 inserts a new subsection (7A) into s 10 of CA 1989.
2 CA 1989, s 14A(13) and ACA 2002, s 29(5).
3 Written notice of the intention to make the application must be given to the local authority looking after the child or in whose area the individual is ordinarily resident, but 3 months' notice is not required: CA 1989, s 14A(7) and ACA 2002, s 29(5).
4 See *B v B (A Minor) (Residence Order)* [1992] 2 FLR 327 at 328B; *Re O (Minors) (Care or Supervision Order)* [1996] 2 FLR 755 at 760A; *Oxfordshire County Council v L (Care or Supervision Order)* [1998] 1 FLR 70 at 74E.
5 See *Re C and B (Care Order: Future Harm)* [2001] 1 FLR 611 at [34]; *Re O (A Child) (Supervision Order)* [2001] 1 FLR 923 at [28].
6 *Re O (Care or Supervision)* [1996] 2 FLR 755 at 759H–760B.

Chapter 2

PARENTAL CONSENT

2.1 Section 52 of ACA 2002 is of general application to both placement and adoption and is central to the whole adoption process.

PARENTAL CONSENT AND PLACEMENT

2.2 ACA 2002 establishes two routes for placing a child for adoption.

(1) Each parent may consent to the child being placed for adoption (in which case no placement order is required): s 19.
(2) A local authority may secure a placement order from the court authorising it to place a child with adopters: s 21. The preconditions for making a placement order include the parents' consenting to placement and not withdrawing their consent or their consent being dispensed with. The local authority must apply for a placement order where it is satisfied that a child should be adopted but the parents do not consent to placement or have withdrawn such consent.

PARENTAL CONSENT AND ADOPTION

2.3 The court can now establish jurisdiction to make an adoption order by a variety of routes (see Chapter 4). The provisions relating to the role and timing of parental consent are now more complex and may encompass consent to placement and/or adoption, depending on the facts of the case.

2.4 Section 47(2) makes the making of an adoption order conditional upon consent. It provides that the court must be satisfied that:

(a) each parent consents to the making of the adoption order; or
(b) each parent has given advance consent under s 20 (see below) and does not oppose the making of an adoption order; or
(c) the parents' consent should be dispensed with.

2.5 In a non-agency placement case, the traditional model of prospective adopters applying within the adoption application to dispense with parental consent will still occur: ACA 2002, s 47(2)(c).

2.6 In agency cases, at an earlier stage prior to placement, one or more of the following events will have taken place:

- The parent consents to placement.
- The parent may also give advance consent to adoption (see below).
- The parent's consent to placement is dispensed with.
- A placement order is made.

2.7 Where the adoption application arises from an agency placement with prospective adopters (which must be the result of one or more of the above consents or a placement order) the only potential for a parent to oppose the adoption application arises if the court gives the parent leave to so oppose (being satisfied that there is a change of circumstance): ACA 2002, s 47(3), (5) and (7).

2.8 In an agency placement case, if the leave to oppose the making of an adoption order is not granted, the court will not have to consider dispensing with parental consent to adoption and the parent is prevented from opposing the making of the adoption order.

2.9 If a parent is given leave to oppose an agency placement application, then the application can only be granted if the court is satisfied that the parent's consent to adoption should be dispensed with: ACA 2002, s 47(2)(c).

2.10 Thus, consent plays a crucial role in the making of an adoption order, in particular in non-agency cases, such as relative adoptions, and in cases where the parents obtain leave to oppose the making of an adoption order under s 47(3), (5) and (7).

MEANING OF CONSENT

2.11 'Consent' to the placement of a child for adoption or the making of an adoption order means 'consent given unconditionally and with full understanding of what is involved, but a person may consent to adoption without knowing the identity of the persons in whose favour the order will be made'.[1] 'Freely' has been omitted in recognition that many parents struggle against their own feelings in giving consent in the children's best interests.

2.12 The persons who have the right to consent are the parent 'having parental responsibility'[2] or the guardian of the child (which includes a special guardian).

2.13 Those 'parents' who qualify are:
(1) the birth mother;
(2) the birth father, where he is married to the child's mother at the time of the child's birth or if he subsequently marries the mother;
(3) an unmarried father if:

---

1 ACA 2002, s 52(5).
2 ACA 2002, s 52(6). See also s 52(9) and (10).

    (a) he becomes registered as the child's father under the Births and Deaths Registration Act 1953, or
    (b) he makes a parental responsibility agreement with the child's mother, or
    (c) he is granted a parental responsibility order by the court;
(4) the child's adoptive parent, where the child has been the subject of a previous adoption.

ADVANCE CONSENT

2.14 Section 20 of ACA 2002 introduces a new concept of 'advance consent', which enables a parent (who consents to placement by an adoption agency) at the same time or a subsequent time to give consent to the making of a future adoption order ('advance consent').

2.15 'Advance consent' may be to adoption (i) by the prospective adopters identified in the consent and/or (ii) by *any* prospective adopters who may be chosen by the agency.[1] Under s 20(4)(a) and (b), a person giving consent under s 20 may at the same time or any subsequent time, by notice to the adoption agency:

(a) state that he does not wish to be informed of any application for an adoption order; or
(b) withdraw such a statement.

2.16 If a parent only gives advance consent under s 20 to the making of a future adoption order to prospective adopters identified in the consent and the 'identified' adoption breaks down, there is no valid consent under s 52(5) to adoption by other prospective adopters chosen by the agency. The parent has in these circumstances only given unconditional consent to the prospective adopters identified in the consent. Thus, if the specified adoption breaks down, the adoption agency will have to return to the court for a further order.

2.17 The consent to a future adoption with identified prospective adopters may be combined with consent to a future adoption with any prospective adopters chosen by the agency. This combination is likely to be encouraged by the agency because, if the child is removed from or returned by the identified prospective adopters, it will not have to return to court for a further order.

WITHDRAWAL OF CONSENT

2.18 Where consent has been given under s 19 (placement with consent) or s 20 (advance consent), the consent can be withdrawn.

---

1 ACA 2002, s 20(2).

2.19 Once, however, an application for an adoption order has been made, any consent that has been given under s 19 or s 20 cannot be withdrawn.[1] In an agency placement case, the prospective adopters only have to satisfy a 10-week residence qualification under s 42(2) before they can apply for an adoption order. Thus, the window of opportunity for a parent to withdraw consent may be very narrow.

2.20 There is, therefore, a 'cut-off point' by which consent must be withdrawn. Once the point is passed, if the parents wish to oppose the adoption order, they have to seek the court's leave where they have given advance consent[2] or where the child has been placed for adoption.[3]

2.21 Leave cannot be given unless the court is satisfied that there has been *a change of circumstances* since either the consent was given or the placement order made.[4]

PROCEDURE FOR CONSENT

2.22 Consent under ss 19 and 20 to the child being placed for adoption and under s 20 to the making of a future adoption order must be given in the form prescribed by the *Practice Direction 'Forms'* (which supplements the Family Procedure (Adoption) Rules 2005, r 28 and r 17) or a form to the like effect.[5] Table 2 lists the forms required or permitted by FP(A)R 2005, r 28, which include:

(1) consent to placement for adoption:
   - with any prospective adopters [A100],
   - with identified prospective adopters [A101],
   - with identified adopters and, if the placement breaks down, with any prospective adopters [A102];
(2) advance consent to adoption [A103].

2.23 Where the parent is prepared to consent to the placement of the child for adoption under s 19 or consent to the making of a future adoption order under s 20, the adoption agency must under reg 20 of the Adoption Agencies Regulations 2005 (AAR 2005) request CAFCASS to appoint an officer of the Service or the National Assembly of Wales to appoint a Welsh family proceedings officer for the purposes of signification by that officer of the consent to placement or to adoption by that parent, and send with that request the information which is specified in Sch 2 to the Regulations: (see Chapter 8).

2.24 Withdrawal of consent under s 19 or s 20 (other than by notice given to the adoption agency) must be in the Form A106 or a form to the like effect.[6]

---

1 ACA 2002, s 52(4).
2 ACA 2002, s 47(3).
3 ACA 2002, s 47(5).
4 ACA 2002, s 47(7).
5 FP(A)R 2005, r 28(1)(a) and (b).
6 ACA 2002, s 52(8); FP(A)R 2005, r 17; *Practice Direction – Forms*, Table 2.

2.25 Where the consent given under ACA 2002, s 19 or s 20 is withdrawn in accordance with s 52(8) of the Act, under reg 38 of the AAR 2005:

(1) Where the agency is the local authority, on receipt of the form or notice the authority must immediately review its decision to place the child for adoption and, where it decides to apply for a placement order under s 22, it must notify as soon as possible:
   (a) the parent;
   (b) the child's father (where he does not have parental responsibility, but his identity is known); and
   (c) the prospective adopter with whom the child is placed.
(2) Where the agency is a registered adoption society, it must immediately consider whether it is appropriate to inform the local authority in whose area the child is living.

2.26 The s 19 and s 20 consents, any form or notice withdrawing consent and any notices under s 20(4)(a) or (b) must be placed on the child's case record by the adoption agency: reg 12 of the AAR 2005 (see Chapter 8).

2.27 Consent to the making of an adoption order may be given in Form 104 or a form to like effect.[1]

Role of the reporting officers[2]

2.28 In proceedings to which Part 5 of FP(A)R 2005 applies (which include placement proceedings and adoption proceedings), the court will appoint a reporting officer where it appears that a parent is willing to consent to the placing of a child for adoption or to the making of an adoption order, and the parent is within the jurisdiction.[3] The same person may be appointed as the reporting officer for two or more parents or guardians of the child.[4]

2.29 The reporting officer's duty is to witness the signature by the parent on the document in which consent is given to (i) placing the child for adoption and (ii) the making of the adoption order.[5]

2.30 The officer is under a duty:[6]

(a) to ensure so far as reasonably practicable that the parent is giving consent unconditionally and with full understanding of what is involved;
(b) to investigate all the circumstances relevant to a parent's consent;

---

1 FP(A)R 2005, r 28(2); *Practice Direction – Forms*, Table 2.
2 FP(A)R 2005, r 6, Interpretation: 'Reporting Officer' means an officer of the Service or a Welsh proceedings officer appointed to witness the documents which signify a parent or guardian's consent to the placing of the child for adoption or the making of an adoption order.
3 FP(A)R 2005, r 69 (a) and (b).
4 FP(A)R 2005, r 70.
5 FP(A)R 2005, r 71.
6 FP(A)R 2005, r 72.

(c) on completing his investigation:
- to make a confidential report in writing to the court in accordance with a timetable set by the court, drawing attention to any matters which in his opinion may be of assistance to the court, and
- to make an interim report[1] to the court if a parent is *unwilling to consent* to the placing of the child for adoption or to the making of an adoption order. Upon receipt of this report, the court officer *must* inform the applicant that the parent is unwilling;[2]
- to attend all the directions hearings unless the court otherwise directs.

DISPENSING WITH CONSENT

2.31 Section 52(1), which sees ACA 2002 in its most radical clothing, reads:

'The court cannot dispense with the consent of any parent or guardian of a child to the child being placed for adoption or the making of an adoption order in respect of the child unless the court is satisfied that –

(a) the parent or guardian cannot be found or is incapable of giving consent, or
(b) the welfare of the child requires the consent to be dispensed with.'

Paramountcy principle

2.32 Section 1 of ACA 2002 applies. The child's welfare throughout his life is, therefore, the paramount consideration in dispensing with parental consent.

Welfare checklist

2.33 The welfare checklist under s 1(4) applies to dispensing with parental consent. This is crucial, as the welfare checklist recognises the importance of the child's relationship with his birth parents and, therefore, goes some way to redressing the imbalance against the family of birth, which s 1, taken together with s 52(1)(b), has created.

The grounds for dispensation

2.34 There are now only two grounds for dispensation. The first limb of s 52, 'the parent cannot be found or is incapable of giving consent', which derives from s 16(2)(a) of the Adoption Act 1976 (AA 1976), remains. However, the second limb, 'the welfare of the child requires the consent to be dispensed with', breaks new ground in adoption law.

---

1 FP(A)R 2005, r 72(3): the reporting officer may at any time before the final hearing make an interim report to the court, if he considers it necessary, and ask the court for directions.
2 FP(A)R 2005, r 72(2).

2.35 The second limb is intended to be a key component of the drive towards the child-centred approach, where children are 'the paramount priority of the adoption process'[1] and where the aim of the new system is to ensure that decisions are made earlier in the adoption process.

2.36 As part of this drive, ACA 2002 has deleted the unreasonableness ground under AA 1976, s 16(2)(b)[2] and, thus, at a stroke, removed the legal hurdle under the old law whereby an adoption considered to be in the child's best interests could nevertheless be prevented by the parent 'reasonably' withholding his consent ('the parent's veto').

First ground for dispensation: cannot be found or incapable of giving consent: section 52(1)(a)

2.37 For the authorities under AA 1976 (which are likely still to apply) see *Re R (Adoption)*;[3] *Re S (Adoption)*;[4] and *Re A (A Child) (Adoption of Russian Child)*.[5]

Second ground for dispensing with consent: the welfare requirement: section 52(1)(b)

2.38 The overwhelming probability is that this will be the ground used for dispensing with consent in the majority of cases.

2.39 Parental consent is the cornerstone of adoption law, not only historically in our domestic law, but also internationally. The objective underlying the requirement for parental consent is to safeguard the rights of the parents.

2.40 This new ground for dispensation lies at the central core of the reforms driving the new legislation. However, by placing reliance upon the paramountcy principle for dispensing with consent, it fundamentally alters the balance between the child's welfare and birth parents' rights. The welfare of the child must always outweigh parental rights.

2.41 Section 1(4)(c) and 1(4)(f) in the welfare checklist are intended to 'make up' for the loss of the parental right of 'reasonably withholding consent'.

2.42 Further, arguably the word 'requires' imports an imperative into the subsection as an additional safeguard, ie a further obligation upon the court to be satisfied that the child's welfare interests 'compel' or make necessary dispensing with consent. The 'least interventionist' approach in s 1(6), together with Art 8 of the European Convention on Human Rights and the principle of proportionality, also have a key part to play in dispensing with parental consent.

1　Paragraph 1.21 of the White Paper, *Adoption: A New Approach*.
2　No one is likely to miss that imaginary legal paragon, 'the hypothetical reasonable parent'.
3　[1967] 1 WLR 34, per Buckley J.
4　[1999] 2 FLR 374 at 379A–D, per Lord Prosser.
5　[2000] 1 FLR 539.

2.43 Despite the fact that welfare has been brought expressly into the test for dispensing with consent, the consent issue remains separate from the welfare issue. Thus, the question under s 52(1) is *not*: 'Does the child's welfare require a placement/adoption order?' It is: 'Does the child's welfare require parental consent to be dispensed with?'

Procedure for dispensing with consent: FP(A)R 2005, rule 27

2.44 Where an applicant requests the court to dispense with the consent of any parent to the child being placed for adoption or the making of an adoption order:[1]

- he must give notice of the request in the application form or at any later stage by filing a written request setting out the reasons for the request; and
- he must file a statement of facts setting out a summary of the history of the case and any other facts to satisfy the court that –
    (i) the parent cannot be found or is incapable of giving consent, or
    (ii) the welfare of the child requires the consent to be dispensed with;
- if a serial number has been assigned to the applicant under FP(A)R 2005, r 20, the statement of facts must be framed so that it does not disclose the identity of the applicant.[2]

2.45 The court officer,[3] upon receipt of the notice of the request, will:

- inform the parent of the request; and
- send a copy of the statement of facts to –
    (i) the parent,
    (ii) any children's guardian, reporting officer, and children and family reporter,
    (iii) any local authority to whom notice under s 44 (notice of intention to adopt) has been given, and
    (iv) any adoption agency which has placed the child for adoption.[4]

2.46 If the applicant considers that the parent is incapable of giving consent, the court will consider whether to appoint a litigation friend for the parent under FP(A)R 2005, r 55(1), or give directions for an application to be made under r 55(3) (unless a litigation friend has already been appointed).[5]

---

1 FP(A)R 2005, r 27(1) and (2).
2 FP(A)R 2005, r 27(3).
3 FP(A)R 2005, r 6: 'Court Officer' means in the High Court and county court a member of the court staff and in the magistrates' court a designated officer.
4 FP(A)R 2005, r 27(4)(a).
5 FP(A)R 2005, r 27(4)(b).

Chapter 3

PLACEMENT FOR ADOPTION

THE NEW SYSTEM

3.1 ACA 2002 introduces a new legal process for placing children for adoption.

'The new system is intended to provide greater certainty and stability for children by dealing as far as possible with parental consent *before* they have been placed with the prospective new family, so as (a) to reduce the uncertainty for the prospective adopters, who possibly face a contested hearing at the adoption order stage (b) to reduce the extent to which birth families are faced with a fait accompli at the final adoption hearing, if the child has been placed with prospective adopters for some time.'[1]

PLACING A CHILD FOR ADOPTION

3.2 Section 18[2] sets the new process in motion by specifying that an adoption agency may place a child for adoption 'only under s 19 or a placement order'.[3] A child may, therefore, only be placed for adoption:

— where there is the consent of the parent; or
— where there is no parental consent, under a placement order of the court.

3.3 *Placing a child for adoption* by an adoption agency is defined as 'placing a child for adoption with prospective adopters' and includes 'where it has placed a child with any persons (whether under this Act or not), leaving the child with them as prospective adopters.[4]

---

[1] *Hansard*, vol 365, no 59, col 708, Mr John Hutton in respect of Bill 69 (26 March 2001), the first in a long line of Bills.
[2] ACA 2002, s 18 is expressly made subject to ss 30–35 which deal with the removal of children placed by adoption agencies.
[3] An adoption agency may place a child who is less than 6 weeks old for adoption (*a baby placement*) with the voluntary agreement of the parents. The baby is not placed under s 19 or under a placement order during those first 6 weeks. The placement regime does not apply. The child is, however, a 'looked after' child of the local authority. When the child attains the age of 6 weeks, if adoption continues to be the plan, the agency must obtain the consent of the parents or, if a local authority, a placement order.
[4] ACA 2002, s 18(5).

3.4 If a child is placed for adoption or authorised to be placed for adoption by a local authority as adoption agency, the child is a 'looked after' child under the auspices of CA 1989.[1]

3.5 The intention is to ensure that the local authority has the continuing responsibility for managing and overseeing the child's progress until a future adoption order is made and regularly reviewing his progress. The prospective adopters obtain parental responsibility, whilst the parents retain it with the local authority holding the ring under ACA 2002, s 25.

Local authority foster parents

3.6 The position as to local authority foster parents is as follows:

(1) Local authority foster parents will be able to seek formal approval from the local authority as prospective adopters of children being fostered by them. If they are approved and the agency leaves the child with them as prospective adopters, the placement will be *an agency placement* and there will be no need for them to give formal notice.

(2) If the agency does not approve of them as prospective adopters, they can give notice of intention to apply to adopt *as a non-agency case*, subject to them satisfying the residence requirement (ie the child must have had his home with the applicants at all times during the period of one year preceding the application).

The demise of 'freeing orders'

3.7 ACA 2002 has sounded the death knell for the widely criticised freeing for adoption orders.[2] All too often a freeing order consigned the child to an indefinite legal limbo.[3]

3.8 The placement provisions, therefore, replace freeing orders. They differ from freeing orders in the following respects:

(1) The birth parents remain the child's parents until the final adoption order, irrespective of whether the consensual route or placement order route is taken. Although a parent will not lose parental responsibility, he will be required to share parental responsibility with the prospective adopters and the adoption agency.

---

1 ACA 2002, s 22(4): If a local authority is under a duty to apply for a placement order or has applied for a placement order which is still pending, the child is 'looked after' by the authority. The 'looked after' provisions in CA 1989 are amended to make clear that local authorities have power to provide assistance in kind, accommodation or, in exceptional circumstances, cash.
2 Under the former s 18 of the Adoption Act 1976.
3 An example of the traumas of 'adoptive limbo' is to be found in *Re C (A Minor) (Adoption: Freeing Order)* [1999] 1 FLR 348. See also *Re G (Adoption: Freeing Order)* [1997] 2 FLR 202 at 206C–F, per Lord Browne-Wilkinson.

(2) There is a wider (albeit still limited) ability to reverse a placement order or withdraw consent, whereas a freeing order could only be reversed on appeal or revoked in very circumscribed circumstances.

(3) The court has jurisdiction to make a contact order during the currency of a placement for adoption under ACA 2002, s 26.

THE TWO ROUTES[1]

3.9 There are two routes for placement:

(1) The first route is where the placement is consensual.

(2) The second route is where a placement order under ACA 2002, s 21 is required.

The consensual route

Placement and consent

3.10 Section 19 of ACA 2002 authorises an adoption agency to place children for adoption where it is satisfied each parent has consented to placement and that consent has not been withdrawn. The section is subject to s 52 as to the meaning of 'parental consent'.[2]

3.11 The placement with consent may be with:[3]

– the prospective adopters identified in the consent; or
– any prospective adopters who may be chosen by the agency.

3.12 The consent to placement with identified prospective adopters may be combined with consent to a subsequent placement with any prospective adopters chosen by the agency.[4]

3.13 Where a child is placed with consent, the birth parents can at any time, until an application for an adoption order is made, withdraw their consent.[5] However:

– Under the removal provisions (see **3.111 ff** below), where the child is placed for adoption and the consent is withdrawn, the child must be returned within 14 days.

---

1 The Adoption Agencies Regulations 2005 set out the provisions dealing with: (i) the establishment of an adoption panel; (ii) the duties of the adoption agency where the agency is considering adoption; (iii) the agency's duties in respect of prospective adopters; (iv) the agency's duties in respect of a proposed placement with prospective adopters; (v) placements and reviews; (vi) records (see Chapter 8).
2 See **2.11** above.
3 ACA 2002, s 19(1).
4 ACA 2002, s 19(2).
5 ACA 2002, s 52(4).

- If the consent is withdrawn before the child has been placed, the child must be returned within one week.[1]
- Where the child is being accommodated by the local authority and the authority has applied for a placement order, the child may not be removed from the accommodation without the court's leave.[2]

3.14 Where consent has not been withdrawn before an adoption application is made, he or she may oppose the final adoption order only with leave of the court and the court may give leave only if there has been a change of circumstances.[3]

3.15 Where a child is placed with prospective adopters and consent is then withdrawn, the child continues to be treated as placed for adoption until the child is returned to the parents or any placement order application is determined.[4]

Effect on other orders/applications

3.16 Placement of a child for adoption under ACA 2002, s 19 fits in with other proceedings and orders as follows.

PENDING APPLICATION FOR CARE ORDER

3.17 The consensual route does not apply where there is a pending application as a result of which a care order may be made,[5] or a care order or placement order has been made after the consent was given.[6] In these circumstances, if the local authority is satisfied that the child should be adopted, they must take the placement order route under s 22(2).

RESIDENCE ORDER

3.18 A parent may not apply for a residence order once a child is placed for adoption or the agency is authorised to place under the consensual route.[7] There is an exception where an application for adoption has been made and the parent has obtained the court's leave to oppose the adoption order. This is to allow competing applications for residence orders from parents at contested final adoption order hearings.[8]

SPECIAL GUARDIANSHIP ORDER

3.19 Where a child is placed for adoption with consent and an SGO is subsequently made, the authority to place the child no longer applies unless the special guardian

---

1 ACA 2002, s 31.
2 ACA 2002, s 30(2).
3 ACA 2002, s 47(5) and (7). The imposition of a 'leave fetter' upon the parents' ability to contest a final hearing is intended to fulfil the Government's objective in shifting the issue of consent to a point earlier in the process so as to reduce the opportunity to contest.
4 ACA 2002, s 19(4).
5 ACA 2002, s 19(3)(a).
6 ACA 2002, s 19(3)(b).
7 ACA 2002, s 28(1).
8 ACA 2002, s 28(1)(a).

consents under s 19. Where the child is placed for adoption or the agency is authorised to place the child and an application is made for an adoption order, a special guardian may not apply for an SGO without obtaining leave to oppose the adoption.[1]

Existing contact order

3.20 On an agency being authorised to place a child, contact orders under CA 1989 cease to have effect and no application may be made for a contact order under CA 1989, s 8 (save where the contact application is to be heard together with the application to adopt).[2]

3.21 During the period, in which an adoption agency is authorised to place a child for adoption, contact may be regulated by orders under ACA 2002, s 26.

The placement order route

3.22 The making of a placement order by the court is a new concept in adoption law, in that it brings together under one banner at an early stage in the adoption process the threshold criteria from CA 1989, s 31(2) and the provisions for dispensing with parental consent in ACA 2002.

3.23 The link to CA 1989, s 31(2) is intended as a part of the general design to align adoption law with the Children Act. The threshold test is intended to safeguard the rights of birth families so as to achieve a consistent threshold for compulsory state intervention in family life across adoption legislation and the 1989 Act.

3.24 It further brings home the necessity for there to be relevant and sufficient reasons to justify such state intervention for the purposes of Art 8 of the European Convention on Human Rights.[3]

3.25 Only local authorities are able to apply for placement orders.

Placement order

3.26 Under s 21 of ACA 2002 a 'placement order' is 'an order made by the court authorising a local authority to place a child for adoption with any prospective adopters who may be chosen by the authority'.

3.27 The court may not make a placement order unless:[4]

(a) the child is subject to a care order, or the court is satisfied that the conditions in CA 1989, s 31(2) are met (or the child has no parent or guardian); and

---

1 ACA 2002, s 28(1)(b).
2 ACA 2002, s 26(2)(a).
3 *Olsson v Sweden (No 1)* (1989) 11 EHRR 259, para 68; *K and T v Finland* [2001] 2 FLR 707 at 733.
4 ACA 2002, s 21(2)(a) and (b) and s 21(3)(a) and (b).

(b) each parent has consented to the child being placed for adoption and has not withdrawn consent, or the parent's consent should be dispensed with under ACA 2002, s 52.

3.28 A placement order remains in force until it is revoked,[1] or an adoption order is made, or the child marries or attains the age of 18. The parents may not apply to revoke the order unless:

(1) the court gives leave; and
(2) the child is not placed for adoption by the authority.

The court may only give leave if the parents' circumstances have changed since the order was made.[2]

3.29 Once a placement order has been made, only the local authority may remove the child. A placement order gives the local authority considerable protective powers. Under the order it has parental responsibility and the power to restrict the parents' and the prospective adopters' ability to exercise their parental responsibility.[3]

Threshold criteria

3.30 The court may only make a placement order where the child is already subject to a care order under CA 1989 or the threshold criteria under s 31(2) of CA 1989 are met, or the child is an orphan. Furthermore:

– Except in the case of an orphan, the court has to be satisfied of the existence or likelihood of significant harm attributable either to the care the child is receiving or is likely to receive, or whether the child is beyond parental control.
– The principles established under s 31 are likely to be directly translated into ACA 2002.
– Whether the child being 'subject to a care order' includes an interim care order (with the lower threshold) may need judicial clarification.

Consent

3.31 Two of the key components to the making of a placement order are (i) consent to the child being placed for adoption or, alternatively, (ii) dispensing with consent.

3.32 Thus, the statutory scheme for dispensing with parental consent under the new legislation is brought forward in time to the earlier placement decision.

3.33 This enables the court to be brought in at this early stage with a critical part of its role being to consider the essential elements of s 1. This judicial exercise reinforces the duty imposed on the authority to be 'satisfied that the child ought to be placed for adoption', which necessarily involves a consideration of all the alternative options.

---

1 ACA 2002, s 24 (see below).
2 ACA 2002, s 24(2) and (3). See **3.69** below.
3 ACA 2002, s 25.

3.34 These are not only crucial safeguards for the interests of the birth family but also essential if the making of a placement order is to be Convention compliant.

3.35 The court cannot make a placement order unless an effort has been made to notify the parents or guardians with parental responsibility (amongst others) (i) of the date and place where the application will be heard and (ii) of the fact that (unless the person wishes or the court requires) the person need not attend.[1] Section 141(4)(a) and FP(A)R 2005, r 31 set out who is to receive notice of the final hearing:

– Every person who can be found whose consent to the making of a placement order is required under s 21(3)(a) (ie the parent or guardian with parental responsibility) or would be required but for s 21(3)(b) (ie their consent should be dispensed with).
– If no such person can be found, s 141(4)(a) provides that any relative 'prescribed by rules' who can be found should be notified.
– FP(A)R 2005, r 31 provides that the court officer will give notice to 'any other person that may be referred to in a practice direction'.
– Currently there is no practice direction which prescribes 'any relative' for the purposes of s 141(4)(a).[2]

Relevant circumstances for applying for a placement order: section 22

3.36 There is a *mandatory* requirement placed upon a local authority to apply for a placement order in the following circumstances:

(1) Where a child is placed[3] for adoption by them or is being provided with accommodation by them, and:
 – no adoption agency is authorised to place the child for adoption;
 – they consider that the conditions in s 31(2) of CA 1989 are met (or that the child has no parent or guardian);
 – they are satisfied that the child ought to be placed for adoption.[4]
(2) Where:
 – there is a pending application for a care order (which has not been disposed of); or
 – the child is the subject of a care order and the appropriate local authority is not authorised to place; and
 – they are satisfied that the child ought to be placed for adoption.[5]

---

1 ACA 2002, s 141(3).
2 In the absence of 'prescription', it does not appear to be legitimate simply to rely upon the wide definition of 'relative' in ACA 2002, s 144(1) for the purposes of s 141(1)(a).
3 'Placed' here presumably refers to 'voluntarily' placed for adoption rather than 'formally' placed with prospective adopters under ACA 2002, s 19 or under an existing s 21 order.
4 ACA 2002, s 22(1). This does not apply where a notice of intention to adopt is given unless 4 months has expired without them applying for an adoption order, or such application is withdrawn or refused, or an application for an adoption order is pending.
5 ACA 2002, s 22(2).

3.37 The authority has a *discretion* whether to apply for a placement order where a child is subject to a care order and they are the appropriate authority authorised to place under the consensual route. Alternatively, they could simply decide to place the child with parental consent under the consensual route.[1]

Effect on other orders

3.38 A placement order has the following effects upon other orders.

CARE ORDERS

3.39 Where a child is subject to a care order or a care order is made at the same time as the placement order, the care order does not have any effect whilst the placement order is in force.[2] The care order is, therefore, suspended for the duration of the placement order, but it will automatically revive if the placement order is revoked.

SECTION 8 ORDERS AND SUPERVISION ORDERS

3.40 On the making of a placement order, any CA 1989, s 8 order or any supervision order ceases to have effect.[3]

3.41 Whilst it is in force, the court may not make a s 8 order, supervision order or child assessment order[4] or a s 34(4) contact order[5] under CA 1989.

3.42 Where a placement order is in force and an application for a final adoption order has been made, a parent may make a competing application for a residence order where they have leave to oppose the making of an adoption order under s 47(3) or (5).

SPECIAL GUARDIANSHIP ORDERS

3.43 Where a placement order is in force, no SGO may be made in respect of the child until an application for a final adoption order is made, when a person entitled to do so may make a competing application for an SGO with the leave of the court under s 29(5) or, if he is the guardian of the child, with leave under s 47(5).[6]

3.44 The making of an SGO does not automatically discharge the placement order. The court will have to make a positive decision to revoke the order, governed by s 1 of ACA 2002 and the adoption welfare checklist.

---

1   ACA 2002, s 22(3).
2   ACA 2002, s 29(1).
3   ACA 2002, s 29(2).
4   ACA 2002, s 29(3).
5   ACA 2002, s 29(2)(a).
6   ACA 2002, s 29(5).

Procedure

PARTIES

3.45 The local authority is the applicant in an application for a placement order.[1]

3.46 The respondents to an application for a placement order[2] are:

- each parent who has parental responsibility for the child;
- any person in whose favour an order under the CA 1989 is in force;
- any adoption agency or voluntary organisation which has parental responsibility for, is looking after, or is caring for the child;
- the child;
- the parties or any persons who are or have been parties to the proceedings for a care order where those proceeding have led to the application for the placement order.

3.47 The court may at any time direct that any other person or body be made a respondent or a respondent be removed.[3] It may also direct that a child who is not already a respondent be made a respondent in the circumstances set out in FP(A)R 2005, r 23(2).

3.48 The *Practice Direction – Forms* specifies that the relevant form for a placement order application is Form A50.[4] The following persons receive a copy of the application form:[5]

- each parent with parental responsibility for the child or the guardian of the child;
- any appointed children's guardian, children and family reporter, and reporting officer;
- any other person directed by the court.

SUMMARY OF THE PROCEDURAL STEPS.

3.49 As soon as practicable after the application has been issued, the court will, under FP(A)R 2005, r 24(1):

(1) set a date for the first directions hearing (which must be within 4 weeks, beginning with the date on which the application is issued);
(2) appoint a children's guardian and/or a reporting officer;
(3) request a report on welfare (if required); and
(4) set a date for the hearing of the application.

Instead of setting a date for the first directions, the court may give the first directions.

---

1 FP(A)R 2005, r 23, Table 1.
2 FP(A)R 2005, r 23, Table 2.
3 FP(A)R 2005, r 23(3).
4 FP(A)R 2005, r 17.
5 *Practice Direction – Who Receives a Copy of the Application Form for Orders in Proceedings.*

3.50 The court officer will carry out the tasks set out in FP(A)R 2005, r 24(1)(b), including serving copies of the application form to the persons referred to at **3.48** (above).

3.51 If a notice has been given under FP(A)R 2005, r 27 requesting that the parent's consent be dispensed with, the court officer must inform the parent of the request and send a copy of the statement of facts to:

(1) the parent;
(2) the children's guardian, reporting officer, or children and family reporter;
(3) the local authority to whom a notice under s 44 has been given; and
(4) any adoption agency which has placed the child for adoption.

3.52 Additionally under FP(A)R 2005, r 24(3), in the case of a placement order application, as soon as practicable after issue:

– the court will consider whether a report giving the local authority's reasons for placing the child for adoption is required and, if so, direct the local authority to prepare such a report; and
– the court or court officer will ask either the Service or the Assembly to file any form of consent to the child being placed for adoption.

3.53 FP(A)R 2005, r 26 sets out the steps to be taken at the first directions hearing which include:

(1) fixing a timetable for the filing of the local authority report on placement and any report from the children's guardian, reporting officer, or children and family reporter;
(2) considering the joining of other parties;
(3) transfer;
(4) directions about the final hearing.

The parties or their legal representatives must attend the first directions hearing, unless the court otherwise directs.

3.54 Where a local authority is directed to prepare a report on the placement of the child for adoption, under FP(A)R 2005, r 29(2) it must file the report within the timetable fixed by the court. The report must cover the matters specified in the *Practice Direction – Reports by the Adoption Agency or Local Authority*, Annex B.

3.55 As to the final hearing, notice is given as set out at **3.35** above.

3.56 Under FP(A)R 2005, r 31 any person who has been given notice may attend the final hearing and be heard on the question of whether an order should be made. The court cannot make a placement order unless a legal representative of the applicant (ie the local authority) attends the final hearing (r 32(9)).

3.57 See Chapter 7 for the details on:

– how to start proceedings (**7.15 ff**);
– steps when the application has been issued (**7.29 ff**);

- the first directions hearing (**7.36 ff**);
- the final hearing (**7.42 ff**).

REVIEWS/INDEPENDENT REVIEWING OFFICERS

3.58 All children looked after by a local authority are under an independent reviewing system.[1] This system includes all children accommodated, whether they are voluntarily placed or actually placed with prospective adopters or simply accommodated pending placement. Each child will have a care plan, which will be reviewed regularly by the local authority.

3.59 Care plans have been placed on a statutory basis requiring local authorities to keep under review CA 1989, s 31A care plans and care plans for children voluntarily looked after under CA 1989, s 20.

3.60 Under AAR 2005, reg 36, where an adoption agency is authorised to place a child for adoption but the child is not for the time being placed for adoption, the agency must carry out a review of the child's case not more than 3 months after the date on which the agency first has authority to place; and thereafter not more than 6 months after the date of the previous review ('the six months review') until the child is placed. (see Chapter 8).

3.61 Where the child is placed for adoption, the adoption agency must carry out a review of the child's case (i) not more than 4 weeks after the date on which the child is placed for adoption ('the first review'); (ii) not more than 3 months after the first review; and (iii) thereafter not more than 6 months after the date of the previous review, unless the child is returned to the agency by the prospective adopter or an adoption order is made[2].

3.62 When carrying out the review the adoption agency must consider (amongst other things): (i) whether the adoption agency remains satisfied that the child should be placed for adoption; and (ii) the existing arrangements for contact and whether they should be continued or altered.[3]

3.63 Where a child is subject to a placement order and has not been placed for adoption at the time of the first six months review, the local authority must at that review: (i) establish why the child has not been placed for adoption and consider what further steps it should take in relation to the placement of the child; and (ii) consider whether it remains satisfied that the child should be placed for adoption.[4]

---

1 CA 1989, s 26 as amended by ACA, s 118.
2 AAR 2005, reg 36(3).
3 AAR 2005, reg 36(5) and (6).
4 AAR 2005, reg 36(7).

3.64 An adoption agency must also appoint an independent reviewing officer (IRO) in respect of each child authorised to be placed for adoption by the agency to carry out the functions set out in CA 1989, s 26(2A).[1]

3.65 The Review of Children's Cases (Amendment) (England) Regulations 2004[2] require the appointment of an IRO independent of the case and its management, who has the following functions:

– to participate in the review of the case;
– to monitor the performance of the authority's functions;
– to refer the case to the CAFCASS officer, if he considers it appropriate to do so.

3.66 Under AAR 2005, reg 37(7), if a child whose case is reviewed wishes to take proceedings on his own account (eg to apply for a revocation of a placement order), it is the function of the IRO to assist the child to obtain legal advice or to establish whether an appropriate adult is able and willing to provide such assistance or bring the proceedings on the child's behalf. Under the 2004 Regulations, as a remedy where there has been a failure, the reviewing officer is empowered to refer the case to CAFCASS, who will be able to bring proceedings on behalf of the child under the Human Rights Act 1998.

3.67 The local authority is required under AAR 2005, reg 37(8) to inform the IRO about any significant failure to make the arrangements agreed at a review and any significant change in the child's circumstances.

3.68 The review system and the role of the IRO provide important safeguards to avoid local authority drift and limbo for the child.

REVOCATION: SECTION 24

3.69 The placement order remains in force until it is revoked under s 24 or an adoption order is made or the child marries or attains the age of 18. Although the child or local authority may apply to revoke a placement order at any time, other persons, including the parents, may not apply to revoke the order unless they meet each of the following pre-conditions:[3]

– the court gives leave, which it cannot do unless satisfied that there has been a change of circumstances since the order was made;[4] and
– the child is not yet placed for adoption by the authority.

---

1 AAR 2005, reg 37.
2 Implemented 27 September 2004. The 2004 Regulations amend the Review of Children's Cases Regulations 1991 ('the Principal Regulations'), regs 2, 3 and 8. The power to require local authorities to appoint IROs was inserted in s 26 of CA 1989 by ACA 2002, s 118.
3 ACA 2002, s 24(2).
4 ACA 2002, s 24(3).

3.70 Where, however, an application for revocation has been made and not disposed of and the child is not placed for adoption, the child may not be placed for adoption by the authority without the court's leave.[1]

3.71 At the final adoption hearing, if the court decides not to make an adoption order and further considers that the child should not even be placed for adoption, it has the discretion to revoke the placement order.[2] If, however, the court decides that the child should still be placed for a future adoption, then it may order the placement order to continue.

3.72 The application form for revocation of a placement order is Form A52 in the *Practice Direction – Forms*[3] and the applicants are:[4]

– the child;
– the local authority authorised to place the child for adoption; or
– where the child has not been placed by the authority, any other person with permission of the court to apply.

3.73 The respondents are:[5]

– the parties to the proceedings leading to the placement order sought to be revoked;
– any person in whose favour there is provision for contact;

3.74 The persons who are to receive a copy of the application are:[6]

– each parent with parental responsibility for the child, or the guardian of the child;
– any appointed children's guardian, and children and family reporter;
– the local authority authorised by the placement order to place the child for adoption;
– any other person directed by the court to receive a copy.

3.75 In the case of a revocation of a placement order, under ACA 2002, s 141(4) the persons to be notified:

(i) of the date and place where the application will be heard; and
(ii) of the fact that (unless the person wishes or the court requires) the person need not attend hearing,

are all persons who can be found whose consent to the making of the placement order was required under s 21(3)(a) of the Act (or would have been required except for s 21(3)(b)).

---

1 ACA 2002, s 24(5).
2 ACA 2002, s 24(4).
3 Table 1.
4 FP(A)R 2005, r 23, Table 1.
5 FP(A)R 2005, r 23, Table 2.
6 *Practice Direction – Who Receives a Copy of the Application Form for Orders in Proceedings.*

VARIATION: SECTION 23

3.76 On a joint application by both authorities, the court (which must be the magistrates' court[1]) may vary a placement order so as to substitute another local authority for the authorised authority.

3.77 The joint applicants are (i) the local authority authorised by the placement order to place the child; and (ii) the local authority which is substituted for that authority.[2] The application form is Form A51 in the *Practice Direction – Forms*.

3.78 The respondents are:[3]

– the parties to the proceedings leading to the placement order which it is sought to have varied, except for the child who is the subject of those proceedings;
– any person in whose favour there is provision for contact.

3.79 The persons who receive a copy of the application form are:[4]

– each parent with parental responsibility for the child or the guardian of the child;
– any appointed children's guardian, child and family reporter, and reporting officer;
– any other person directed by the court to receive a copy.

3.80 The same requirements as to notification of the date and place of the hearing apply in relation to variation of a placement order as in relation to a revocation order.[5]

CONSEQUENCES OF PLACEMENT

Parental responsibility: section 25

3.81 Parental responsibility for the child is given to (i) the agency and (ii) to the prospective adopters while:

(1) the child is placed for adoption under the consensual route; or
(2) the adoption agency is authorised to place the child for adoption under the consensual route; or
(3) a placement order is in force.

3.82 The parents' parental responsibility is not extinguished upon placement for adoption or on the making of a placement order. It is shared with the prospective adopters and the agency, with the agency holding the ring.

---

1   Children (Allocation of Proceedings) (Amendment) Order 2005, SI 2005/520.
2   FP(A)R 2005, r 23, Table 1.
3   FP(A)R 2005, r 23, Table 2.
4   *Practice Direction – Who Receives a Copy of the Application Form for Orders in Proceedings.*
5   ACA 2002, s 141(3) and (4)(b).

3.83 It is left to the agency to determine to what extent the parental responsibility of any parent or of the prospective adopters is to be restricted.[1] It is important to stress that the discipline of s 1 applies just as much to this agency determination as to others under the Act. The agency also has to have regard to Art 8 and the principle of proportionality in setting the parameters of parental responsibility.

3.84 If the birth parents are dissatisfied with the way in which the agency restricts their ability to exercise responsibility, the expectation is that this will be discussed with the agency in the first instance and, if they remain dissatisfied, the relevant complaints procedure will be utilised. If this is exhausted, the remedy will be judicial review. However, in the case of placement with consent, it is open to the parents to withdraw consent and to request the child be returned to their sole responsibility.

CONTACT: SECTION 26

3.85 One of the consequences of an agency being authorised to place a child for adoption is that any contact order under s 8 or s 34 of CA 1989 ceases to have effect.[2] Nor can any application for a contact order under CA 1989 thereafter be made,[3] except where the contact application is heard together with an application for an adoption order. This means that at the final adoption hearing the court may make a contact order under s 8. Otherwise, the objective is to agree whatever new arrangements for contact are appropriate, given the adoptive placement (the assumption being that the arrangements set out in previous contact orders may no longer be appropriate). Unlike under the CA 1989,[4] the local authority is not under a statutory duty to promote contact between the child and his parents.

3.86 Under the AAR 2005, where an adoption agency decides that a child should be placed for adoption, it must consider what arrangements it should make for allowing any person contact with the child once the agency is authorised to place the child for adoption ('the contact arrangements').[5]

3.87 In coming to a decision in relation to contact arrangements, the agency must take into account:

– the wishes and feelings of the parent or guardian (and the child's father where he does not have parental responsibility but his identity is known and where the agency considers it appropriate);
– any advice given by the adoption panel;
– the considerations set out in ACA 2002, s 1(2) and (4).

3.88 The agency must give notification of the contact arrangements to:

---

1 ACA 2002, s 25(4).
2 ACA 2002, s 26(1).
3 ACA 2002, s 26(2)(a).
4 CA 1989, Sch 2, para 15.
5 Regulation 46(1) and (2).

(1) the child (of sufficient age and understanding);
(2) the parents, if their whereabouts are known;
(3) the father of the child without parental responsibility whose identity is known and if the agency considers it appropriate;
(4) any person in whose favour there was a provision for contact under CA 1989 which ceased to have effect by virtue of s 26(1);
(5) any other person considered relevant by the agency.[1]

3.89 Where the agency decides that a child should be placed for adoption with a particular prospective adopter, the agency is under a duty to review the contact arrangements in the light of the views of the prospective adopter and any advice given by the adoption panel.[2] If the agency proposes to make any change to the contact arrangements which affects any of the five categories of persons (above), it must seek the views of that person and take those views into account in deciding what arrangements it should make for allowing any person contact with the child, while he is placed for adoption with the prospective adopter.[3] It must also set out the contact arrangements in the placement plan and keep the arrangements under review.

3.90 Where agreement is not possible, there is provision for a freestanding application for contact to be made under ACA 2002, s 26. The court may also make an order of its own motion.[4]

3.91 Before making a placement order, the court is *under a duty* to consider the arrangements made or proposed by the agency for allowing contact with the child and to invite the parties to the proceedings to comment on those arrangements.[5]

3.92 The court may make a 's 26 contact order' requiring the person with whom the child lives or is to live to allow the child to visit or stay with the person named in the order, or for the person named in the order and the child otherwise to have contact with each other.[6]

3.93 Provision is also made under s 27(2) for an agency to refuse to allow contact without a court order if:

– it is satisfied that it is necessary to do so in order to safeguard or promote the child's welfare; and
– the refusal is decided upon as a matter of urgency and does not last for more than 7 days.

3.94 Where an adoption agency has decided under s 27(2) to refuse the contact, the agency must as soon as the decision is made:

---

1 AAR 2005, reg 46(4).
2 AAR 2005, reg 46(5).
3 AAR 2005, reg 46(6).
4 ACA 2002, s 26(4).
5 ACA 2002, s 27(4).
6 ACA 2002, s 26(2)(b).

(a) inform:
    (i) the child, if of sufficient age and understanding;
    (ii) the person in whose favour the order under s 26 was made; and
    (iii) the prospective adopter, if the child is placed; and
(b) notify them of the decision, the reasons for the decision and the duration of the period.[1]

3.95 In making any s 26 order the court will have to have regard to s 1.

3.96 A contact order under s 26 has effect while the adoption agency is authorised to place the child for adoption or is placed for adoption, but may be varied or revoked by the court on an application by the child, the agency or the person named in the order.[2]

3.97 Unlike a contact order under s 8 of CA 1989, an order under ACA 2002, s 26 can include an order for 'no contact'. An order under s 26 may also provide for contact on any conditions the court considers appropriate.[3]

3.98 The terms of an order under s 26 may be departed from by agreement between the agency and any person for whose contact with the child the order provides subject to the following conditions:[4]

– where the child is of sufficient age and understanding, subject to his agreement;
– where the child is placed for adoption, subject to consultation before the agreement is reached with the prospective adopter; and
– written confirmation of the terms of the agreement must be given by the agency to:
    (i) the child (if of sufficient age and understanding),
    (ii) the person in whose favour the s 26 order is made, and
    (iii) the prospective adopter, if the child is placed.

Procedure

3.99 The form to be used for an application for a s 26 contact order is Form A53.[5]

3.100 The potential applicants for a s 26 order are:[6]

(1) the child ;
(2) the adoption agency;
(3) any parent or guardian or relative;
(4) any person in whose favour there was a CA 1989 contact order (which ceased to have effect on an adoption agency being authorised to place a child for adoption or placing a child for adoption who is less than six weeks old under s 26(1));

---

1 AAR 2005, reg 47(1) and (3).
2 ACA 2002, s 27(1)(a) and (b).
3 ACA 2002, s 27(5).
4 AAR 2005, reg 47(2) and (3).
5 *Practice Direction – Forms*, Table 1.
6 FP(A)R 2005, r 23(1), Table 1.

(5) the person with a residence order in force immediately before the adoption agency was authorised to place or placed the child for adoption at a time when he was less than six weeks old;[1]
(6) the person who had care of the child by an order under the High Court's inherent jurisdiction immediately before the agency was authorised to place;
(7) any person with the court's permission.

3.101 The respondents are:[2]

(1) the adoption agency authorised to place the child for adoption or which has placed the child for adoption;
(2) the person with whom the child lives or is to live;
(3) each parent with parental responsibility for the child;
(4) the child where:
- the adoption agency authorised to place the child for adoption or which has placed the child for adoption or a parent with parental responsibility for the child opposes the making of a contact order under s 26,
- the child opposes the making of the contact order under s 26,
- existing provision for contact is to be revoked,
- relatives of the child do not agree to (i) the arrangements for allowing any person contact with the child, or (ii) a person not being allowed contact with the child,
- the child is suffering or is at risk of suffering harm within the meaning of CA 1989.

3.102 The following persons are to receive a copy of the application:[3]

(1) all the parties;
(2) any appointed children's guardian, and children and family reporter;
(3) any other person directed by the court to receive a copy.

3.103 In respect of an order under s 27 varying or revoking a s 26 contact order, the appropriate form is Form A54[4] and the applicants are:[5]

(1) the child;
(2) the adoption agency;
(3) any person named in the contact order.

3.104 The respondents are:[6]

(1) the parties to the proceedings leading to the contact order sought to be varied or revoked;
(2) any person named in the contact order.

---

1   Or placed the child for adoption at a time he was less than 6 weeks old.
2   FP(A)R 2005, r 23, Table 2.
3   *Practice Direction – Who Receives a Copy of the Application Form for Orders in Proceedings.*
4   *Practice Direction – Who Receives a Copy of the Application Form for Orders in Proceedings.*
5   FP(A)R 2005, r 23, Table 1.
6   FP(A)R 2005, r 23, Table 2.

3.105 The following persons are to receive a copy of the application form:[1]

(1) all parties;
(2) any appointed children's guardian, and children and family reporter;
(3) any other person directed by the court to receive a copy.

3.106 Part 5 of the FP(A)R 2005 sets out the procedural steps in relation to an application for a contact order or variation/revocation of an order. See Chapter 7 for the details on:

– how to start proceedings (**7.15 ff**);
– steps when the application has been issued (**7.29 ff**);
– the first directions hearing (**7.36 ff**);
– the final hearing (**7.42 ff**).

SURNAME AND REMOVAL FROM THE UK: SECTION 28(2)

3.107 Where a child is placed for adoption, either under the consensual route or the placement order route, whilst in force no one may:

(1) cause a child to be known by a new surname, or
(2) remove the child from the UK (save for a period of less than one month),

without the court's leave or each parent's written consent.[2]

3.108 The applicants to an application for an order permitting the child's name to be changed or the removal of the child from the UK are any person, including the adoption agency or the local authority, authorised to place the child for adoption or who has placed the child.[3] The relevant application form for permission to change a child's surname is Form A55. The relevant form for permission to take a child out of the jurisdiction is Form A56.

3.109 The respondents to the application are:[4]

(1) the parties to the proceedings leading to any placement order;
(2) the adoption agency authorised to place the child for adoption or which has placed the child for adoption;
(3) any prospective adopters with whom the child is living;
(4) each parent with parental responsibility for the child.

3.110 The following persons are to receive a copy of the application:[5]

(1) all the parties;
(2) any appointed children's guardian, and children and family reporter; and

---

1 *Practice Direction – Who Receives a Copy of the Application Form for Orders in Proceedings.*
2 ACA 2002, s 28(2) and (3).
3 FP(A)R 2005, r 23, Table 1.
4 FP(A)R 2005, r 23, Table 2.
5 *Practice Direction – Who Receives a Copy of the Application Form for Orders in Proceedings.*

(3) any other person directed by the court to receive a copy.

REMOVAL

3.111 ACA 2002 has not reinstated the status of 'protected child', but has substituted detailed removal measures which ensure that children placed for adoption are not peremptorily removed and the adoption process disrupted. Removal or failure to return in contravention of the Act constitutes an offence.

3.112 The Act draws a distinction between agency cases (ss 30–35) and non-agency cases (ss 36–40).

AGENCY CASES

Consensual placements: sections 30–33

3.113 In respect of consensual placements, there are three basic rules:

(1) Only an adoption agency may remove a child from placement.
(2) Where parents withdraw consent to placement and request their child to be returned, the agency must return the child within 7 days if the child has not been placed and 14 days where the child has been placed.
(3) The only exception is where the agency is the local authority and it considers that the child should still be adopted. In that case, application for a placement order must be made within 7 or 14 days.

Placement orders: section 34

3.114 Where the placement order:

(a) is in force, or
(b) has been revoked (but the child has not been returned by the prospective adopters),

only the local authority may remove the child from the prospective adopters.

3.115 Where the placement order is revoked, it will be for the court to determine whether the child remains with the prospective adopters or is to be returned to the parent:

– If the court determines that the child should not remain with the prospective adopters, then they must return the child to the local authority within the period set by the court.
– If the court determines that the child is to be returned to the parent, the authority must return the child to the parent:
  (i) as soon as the child is returned to the authority by the prospective adopters,
  (ii) at once, where the child is in accommodation provided by the authority.

Return of the child: section 35

3.116 Where the child is placed for adoption and the prospective adopters give notice that they wish to return the child, the agency must:

(a) receive the child before the end of 7 days; and
(b) give notice to any parent of the prospective adopters' wish.

3.117 Where the agency is of the opinion that the child should not remain with the prospective adopters, and gives them notice to that effect:

(a) the prospective adopters must return the child not later than the end of 7 days;
(b) the agency must also give notice to any parent of the obligation to return the child to the agency.

3.118 If, before notice under s 35 is given, an application for an adoption order, or SGO, or residence order, or leave to apply for an SGO or residence order was made and has not been disposed of, then the prospective adopters are not required to return the child to the agency unless the court makes an order to that effect.

NON-AGENCY CASES: SECTIONS 36–40

3.119 Section 36 provides that a person may only remove children in non-agency cases in accordance with ss 37–40. A 'child' means a child whose home is with persons ('the people concerned') with whom the child is not placed by an adoption agency and they have:

– applied for an adoption order and the application has not been disposed of;
– given notice of an intention to adopt;
– applied for leave for an adoption order under s 42(6) and the application has not been disposed of.

3.120 To remove the child is an offence. Where a parent is able to remove his child, the people concerned must (at the request of the parent) return the child to the parent at once; failure to do so is an offence.

RECOVERY ORDERS: SECTION 41

3.121 Section 41 applies where it appears to the court that:

– a child has been removed or withheld and not returned in contravention of ss 30–35; or
– there are reasonable grounds for believing that a person intends to remove a child in contravention of those provisions; or
– there is a failure to comply with ss 31(4), 32(2), 33(3) or 55(2).

3.122 In those circumstances, the court may, under s 41(2), on application of any person, by order:

- direct any person who is in a position to do so to produce him on request to an authorised person;
- authorise the removal of the child by an authorised person;
- require anyone who has information as to the child's whereabouts to disclose that information to a constable or officer of the court;
- authorise a constable to enter any premises specified in the order (if there are reasonable grounds for believing that the child is there) and search for the child, using reasonable force if necessary.

3.123 'Authorised persons' are (a) any person named by the court, (b) any constable, or (c) any person who is authorised to exercise any power under the order by the authorised adoption agency (s 41(4)). A person who intentionally obstructs an authorised person exercising the power of removal is guilty of an offence (s 41(5)).

3.124 A person must comply with a request for disclosure, even if it might constitute evidence that he or she has committed an offence (s 41(6)–(8)).

Procedure: FP(A)R 2005, rule 107

3.125 An application for any of the orders referred to in s 41(2) may be made:[1]
- in the High Court or county court without notice, in which case the applicant must file the application –
  - (i) where the application is made by telephone, the next business day after the making of the application, or
  - (ii) in any other case, at the time when the application is made;
- in the magistrates' court, without notice with the permission of the court, in which case the applicant must file the application at the time when the application is made or as directed by the court.

3.126 Where the court refuses to make an order on an application without notice, it may direct that the application is made on notice, in which case the application will proceed in accordance with Part 5 of FP(A)R 2005.[2]

3.127 The relevant form for a recovery order is Form A57.[3]

3.128 The respondents are:[4]

(1) all the parties to any pending placement or adoption proceedings;
(2) any adoption agency authorised to place the child for adoption, or which has placed the child for adoption;
(3) any local authority to whom notice under s 44 has been given;
(4) any person having parental responsibility;

---

[1] FP(A)R 2005, r 107(1).
[2] FP(A)R 2005, r 107(2).
[3] *Practice Direction – Forms.*
[4] FP(A)R 2005, r 107(3).

(5) any person in whose favour there is provision for contact;
(6) any person who was caring for the child immediately prior to the making of the application; and
(7) any person whom the applicant alleges to have effected or to have been or to be responsible for taking or keeping the child.

3.129 The following persons are to receive a copy of the application:[1]

(1) all the parties;
(2) any appointed children's guardian;
(3) any other person directed by the court to receive a copy.

INTERACTION BETWEEN CARE PROCEEDINGS AND PLACEMENT ORDER PROCEEDINGS

3.130 A frequently asked question is whether public law proceedings are typically going to start with an application for a care order or a placement order or both.

3.131 There are a variety of permutations and only time will tell as to which (if any) becomes the norm. What follows are some suggestions:

(1) There will be cases where a local authority removes the child under an Emergency Protection Order, issues care proceedings and applies for an interim care order.
  – Once, after considering the whole range of powers under s 1(6), the local authority considers that the child should be placed for adoption and the child's care plan becomes adoption, then, where parental consent is not forthcoming or is withdrawn, the authority must apply for a placement order under ACA 2002, s 22.
  – If the care proceedings are well advanced, then the likelihood is that the placement order application will be dealt with sequentially to the care proceedings and reliance placed by the local authority on the care order as satisfying one of the preconditions for a placement order.
  – If the care proceedings are still in their early stages, then the court may direct that the two applications be heard together; the threshold criteria under CA 1989, s 31(2) being common ground to both applications (which the court may decide to split off as a preliminary 'finding of fact' hearing).
(2) There will be cases, for example, where there have been previous care proceedings with serious findings made in respect of older children, all of whom have been adopted, and consequently the local authority's plan is to remove the child at birth and place for adoption.
  – In these circumstances, the local authority may simply apply for a placement order or make a twin 'belt and braces' application for both a care

---

1 *Practice Direction – Who Receives a Copy of the Application Form for Orders in Proceedings.*

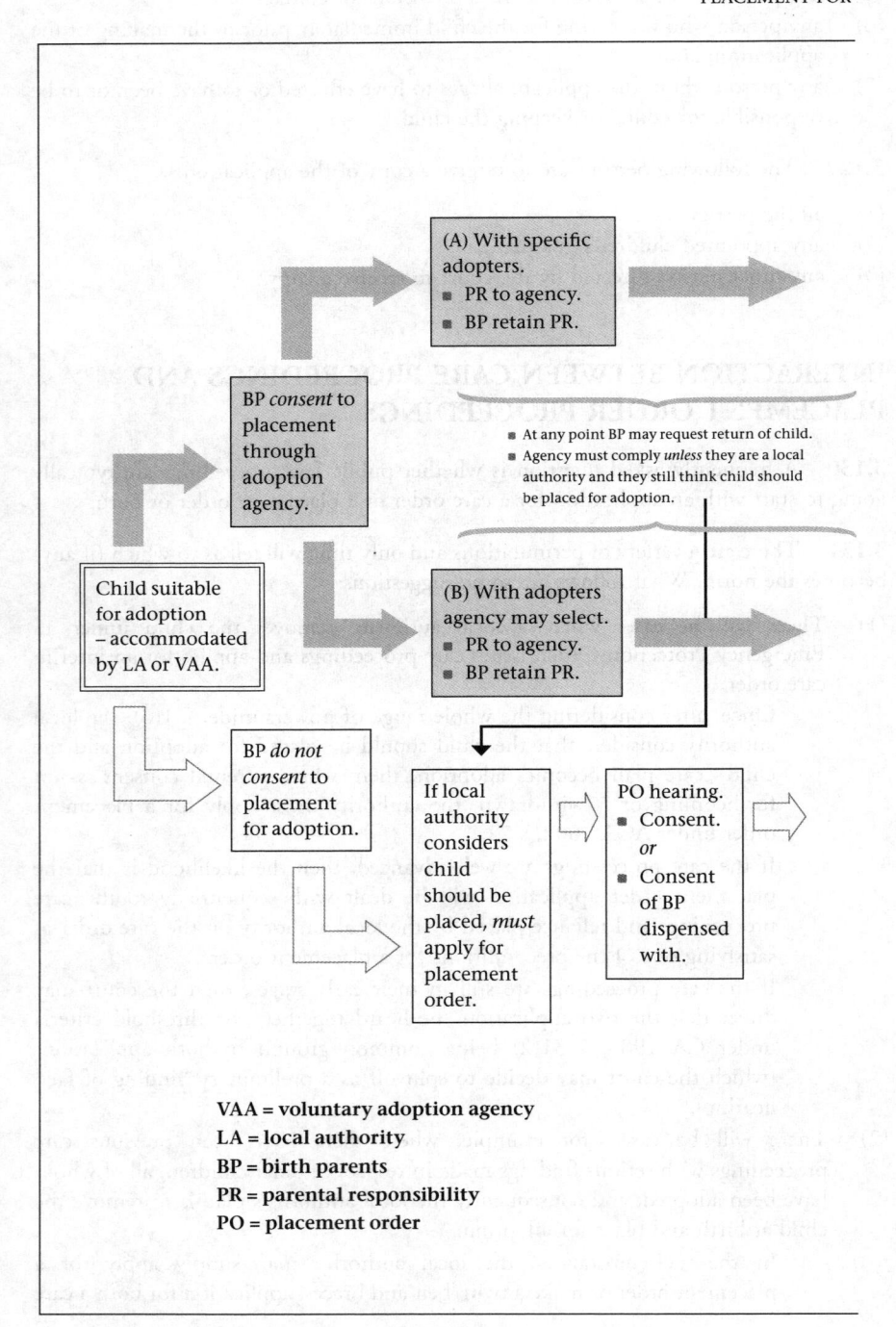

PLACEMENT FOR

```
                          ┌──────────────────────────┐
                          │ (A) With specific        │
                          │ adopters.                │
                     ──▶  │ ■ PR to agency.          │ ──▶
                          │ ■ BP retain PR.          │
                          └──────────────────────────┘

    ┌──────────────┐
    │ BP consent to│
    │ placement    │       ■ At any point BP may request return of child.
    │ through      │       ■ Agency must comply *unless* they are a local
    │ adoption     │         authority and they still think child should
    │ agency.      │         be placed for adoption.
    └──────────────┘

                          ┌──────────────────────────┐
    ┌──────────────┐      │ (B) With adopters        │
    │ Child suitable│     │ agency may select.       │
    │ for adoption  │ ──▶ │ ■ PR to agency.          │ ──▶
    │ - accommodated│     │ ■ BP retain PR.          │
    │ by LA or VAA. │     └──────────────────────────┘
    └──────────────┘
```

- **VAA** = voluntary adoption agency
- **LA** = local authority
- **BP** = birth parents
- **PR** = parental responsibility
- **PO** = placement order

BP *do not* consent to placement for adoption.

If local authority considers child should be placed, *must* apply for placement order.

PO hearing.
- Consent.
or
- Consent of BP dispensed with.

Placement for adoption 43

ADOPTION CHART

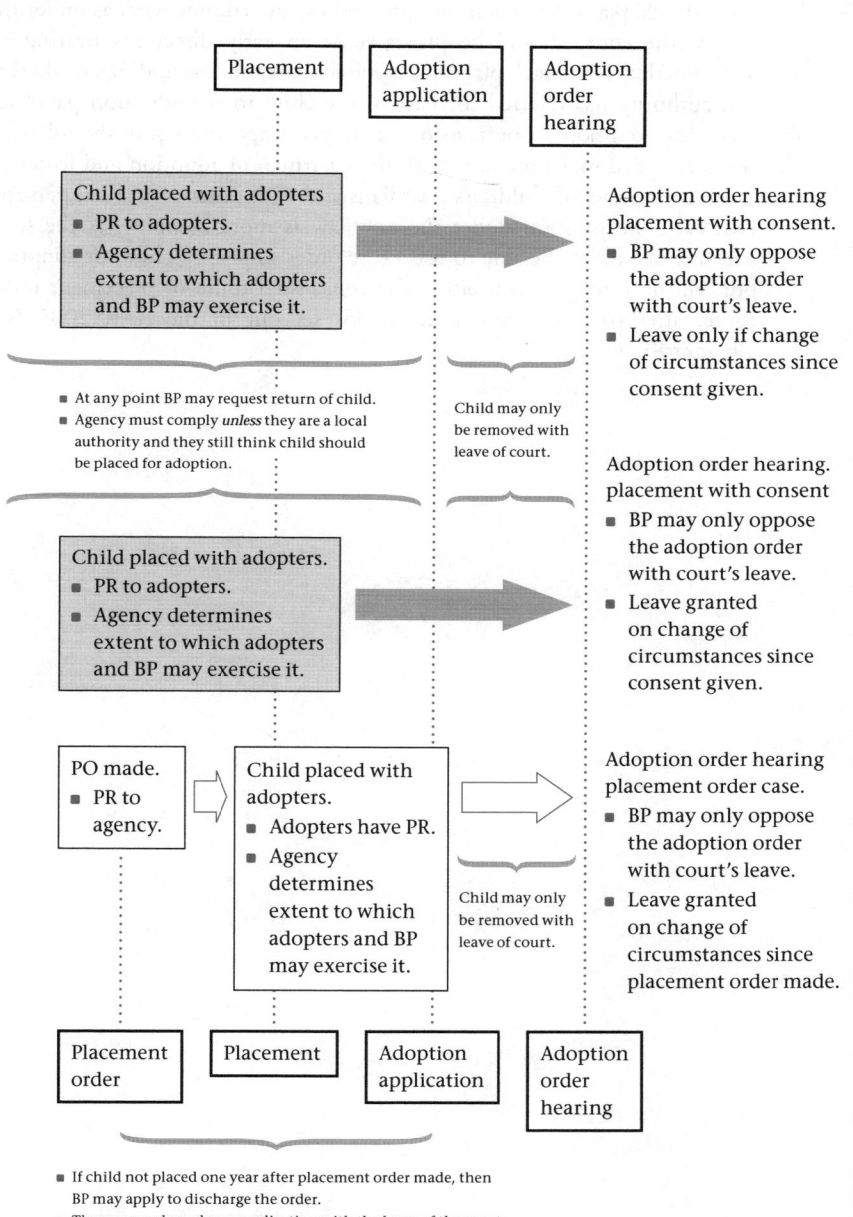

Top row headings
Placement | Adoption application | Adoption order hearing

Row 1
Child placed with adopters
- PR to adopters.
- Agency determines extent to which adopters and BP may exercise it.

→ (Adoption application)

Adoption order hearing placement with consent.
- BP may only oppose the adoption order with court's leave.
- Leave only if change of circumstances since consent given.

- At any point BP may request return of child.
- Agency must comply *unless* they are a local authority and they still think child should be placed for adoption.

Child may only be removed with leave of court.

Row 2
Child placed with adopters.
- PR to adopters.
- Agency determines extent to which adopters and BP may exercise it.

→

Adoption order hearing. placement with consent
- BP may only oppose the adoption order with court's leave.
- Leave granted on change of circumstances since consent given.

Row 3
PO made.
- PR to agency.

⇨ **Child placed with adopters.**
- Adopters have PR.
- Agency determines extent to which adopters and BP may exercise it.

⇨

Child may only be removed with leave of court.

Adoption order hearing placement order case.
- BP may only oppose the adoption order with court's leave.
- Leave granted on change of circumstances since placement order made.

Bottom row headings
Placement order | Placement | Adoption application | Adoption order hearing

- If child not placed one year after placement order made, then BP may apply to discharge the order.
- They may only make an application with the leave of the court.
- Court will only grant leave if there has been a change of circumstances since order was made.

order and a placement order (in case the placement order should be revoked, in which case they can still rely upon the 'revived' care order).

(3) As to 'twin-track' planning, when care proceedings are commenced, as under the former law, the court should be proactive at an early directions hearing by enquiring whether twin-track planning is suitable for the case and, if so, whether the local authority has referred the case of the child to the adoption panel for placement for adoption to be considered. If necessary, the court should liaise with the director of social services, with the chairman of adoption and fostering panels, with the panel of children's guardians and with other concerned persons.

– However, the position under the new law is more complex, as the local authorities will not be able to use a care order to place a child for adoption but will have to go down either the consensual route or placement order route, after passing through the hoops set out in the AAR 2005 (see Chapter 8).

Chapter 4

THE MAKING OF ADOPTION ORDERS

ADOPTION ORDER

4.1 An adoption order is defined as an order which gives parental responsibility for a child to the adopters[1] and extinguishes the parental responsibility which any person, including the mother and father, has for the child immediately before making the order. The legal effect is absolute and irrevocable. Unlike other orders relating to children, it is for life.

4.2 The adoption order also extinguishes any orders under CA 1989 and any duty arising by virtue of an agreement or court order to make payments for the adopted person's maintenance (unless governed by a trust or expressly stated to survive post-adoption).[2]

4.3 Parental responsibility relating to any period before the making of the order is unaffected and an adoption order in favour solely of the partner of the child's parent does not alter that parent's parental responsibility.[3]

STATUS OF THE ADOPTED CHILD: SECTION 67

4.4 An adopted person is to be treated in law:

- as if born as a child of the adopter(s);
- as the child of the relationship of the couple, where adopted by a couple or one of a couple under s 51(2);
- as not being the child of any person other than the adopter and the other one of the couple, where adopted by one of a couple under s 51(2), and in any other case, as not being the child of any person other than the adopter(s).

4.5 This marks a new departure from the old law in specifically recognising the status of the child in a step-parent/partner adoption.

---

1 ACA 2002, s 46(1).
2 ACA 2002, s 46(2).
3 ACA 2002, s 46(3).

REQUIREMENTS FOR OBTAINING AN ADOPTION ORDER

4.6 The primary ground for the making of an adoption order is that such an order is justified in all the circumstances, the paramount consideration being given to the child's welfare throughout his life under ACA 2002, s 1.

4.7 An adoption order can only be made if the conditions relating to parental consent are satisfied under s 47.

4.8 When an adoption application has been made the court may only make an adoption order if each of the following requirements is satisfied.

Each applicant is qualified to apply in terms of (i) age, (ii) domicile or residence, (iii) status as a couple or single applicant	ss 49–51
Where an application relates to a child placed for adoption by an adoption agency, the agency must submit a report on the suitability of the applicants	ss 43, 45
The child's age and status	s 49(4)–(5)
The child has lived with the applicant for the relevant period of time prior to making the order ('the probationary periods')	s 42
The adoption agency has had sufficient opportunity to see the child with the applicants	s 42(7)
In the case of an non-agency placement, the provisions regarding notice have been satisfied	s 44
No previous application for a British adoption order has been made by the same applicant(s) in relation to the same child, unless it appears to the court that either because of a change of circumstances or for any other reason it is proper to hear the application	s 48
There has been no contravention by the applicant of the provisions relating to illegal transactions	ss 92–97
The requirements regarding parental consent are satisfied	s 47
The court must consider any arrangement for post-adoption contact	s 46(6)

WHO MAY APPLY

4.9 ACA 2002 continues the policy of imposing certain restrictions on the eligibility of those persons who may adopt. The qualifications for eligibility relate to (i) age and (ii) domicile and residence. These conditions must be satisfied before an adoption order can be made.

Eligibility

Age

4.10 Each applicant must have attained the age of 21 years, unless one of a couple is either the mother or father of the child, in which case that person needs only to have attained the age of 18 years.[1]

Domicile and residence

4.11 One of the following conditions must be met under ACA 2002, s 49:

(1) at least one of the couple or the single applicant is domiciled in part of the British Isles; or
(2) both of the couple or the single applicant have been habitually resident in part of the British Isles for a period of not less than one year preceding the date of the application.

Couples and single persons

4.12 A new change of direction is the deletion of the marital status qualification for joint applications. The objective is to widen the pool of prospective adopters.

4.13 An application for adoption may be made by a 'couple' or one person.[2]

4.14 A couple is defined as 'a married couple or two people (whether of different sexes or the same sex) living as partners in an enduring family relationship'.[3] Regulation 4(2) of the Suitability of Adopters Regulations 2005 makes it a requirement, when an agency is determining the suitability of a couple, that it should have proper regard to the need for stability and permanence in their relationship. The definition of 'couple' was further amended by the Civil Partnership Act 2004 to include two people who are civil partners of each other. The definition of a couple does not include close relatives.[4]

STEP-PARENT OR PARTNER

4.15 The eligibility of a step-parent or partner to adopt as a single applicant under s 51(2) is a further new departure.

4.16 An adoption order may be made on the application of one person if the court is satisfied that the person is a partner of a parent of the person to be adopted. The effect is that the step-parent becomes an adoptive parent, whilst the birth parent retains his

---

1　ACA 2002, ss 50 and 51.
2　ACA 2002, s 49(1).
3　ACA 2002, s 144(4).
4　ACA 2002, s 144(5) and (6).

or her status. This removes the previous anomaly of the birth parent being required to make a joint application with the step-parent to adopt his own child.

A SINGLE MARRIED PERSON

4.17 One person who is married may successfully apply for an adoption order if the court is satisfied[1] that:

– the other spouse cannot be found; or
– the spouses have separated and are living apart and the separation is likely to be permanent; or
– the person's spouse is by reason of ill health, whether physical or mental, incapable of making an application for an adoption order.

SOLE APPLICATION BY MOTHER OR FATHER

4.18 An adoption order may not be made on the application by the mother or father of the child as a single applicant unless the court is satisfied[2] that:

– the other natural parent is dead or cannot be found; or
– by virtue of the Human Fertilisation and Embryology Act 1990, s 28 there is no other parent; or
– there is some other reason justifying the child being adopted by the applicant alone.

4.19 This last ground is a more open-ended interpretation than its predecessor, AA 1976, s 15(3) (*Re B (A Minor)*[3]), in that it deletes the notion of 'exclusion'.

4.20 Where the court makes an adoption order on such an application, the court must record that it is satisfied as to one of the reasons referred to above.

PRELIMINARIES TO MAKING AN ADOPTION ORDER

4.21 There are five preliminary requirements which have to be satisfied before an adoption order can be made. They relate to:

(1) the suitability of any person or couple to adopt;
(2) the suitability of the child to be adopted;
(3) the probationary periods which are prescribed in both agency adoptions and non-agency adoptions;[4]
(4) Reports required by the court;[5]

---

1   ACA 2002, s 51(3).
2   ACA 2002, s 51(4).
3   [2001] UKHL 70.
4   ACA 2002, s 42.
5   ACA 2002, s 43.

(5) in the case of non-agency adoptions, notice provisions.[1]

Suitability of any person or couple to adopt

4.22 The suitability of the applicants must be assessed in accordance with the Suitability of Adopters Regulations 2005[2] (which have to be read with Part 4 of AAR 2005) (see Chapter 8).

4.23 Part 4 of AAR 2005 makes provision for the assessment of prospective adopters. The agency is required to do the following:

(1) Provide counselling and information for a prospective adopter (reg 21).
(2) Consider an application by a prospective adopter for an assessment of his suitability to adopt a child (reg 22).
(3) Carry out police checks (reg 23). An agency may not consider a person suitable to adopt if he or any member of his household aged 18 or over has been convicted of, or cautioned for, certain specified offences.
(4) Arrange for the prospective adopter to receive preparation for adoption, including the provision of information about the child and his family (reg 24).
(5) Obtain the information about the prospective adopter set out in Part 1 of Sch 4 (reg 25(2)) and prepare a written report ('the prospective adopter's report') (reg 25(5)) which includes the information specified in Part 1 of Sch 4 and the agency's assessment of the prospective adopter's suitability to adopt.
(6) In making the prospective adopter's report (and the prospective adopter's review report under reg 29(4), the agency must take into account, under reg 3 of the Suitability of Adopters Regulations 2005, any information obtained as a consequence of:
 – providing the counselling service under AAR 2005, reg 21;
 – the preparation for adoption under AAR 2005, reg 24;
 – obtaining an enhanced criminal record certificate under AAR 2005, reg 23(1)(a) and (b);
 – obtaining information about the prospective adopters under AAR 2005, reg 25(2);
 – the written report obtained from the registered medical practitioner (under AAR 2005, reg 25(3)(a)) of each of the interviews of the personal referees (under AAR 2005, reg 25(3)(b)) from the local authority in whose area the prospective adopter has his home (under AAR 2005, reg 25(4)).
(7) Under reg 4(1) of the Suitability of Adopters Regulations 2005, in determining the suitability of any person to adopt a child, the matters to be taken into account by the adoption agency are:
 – the prospective adopter's report;
 – the medical report;
 – the personal references;
 – the recommendation of the adoption panel under AAR 2005, reg 26;

---

1 ACA 2002, s 44.
2 Note: these Regulations only apply in England.

– any other relevant information as a consequence of AAR 2005 reg 26(2)(b).

(8) Under reg 4(2) of the Suitability of Adopters Regulations 2005, in determining the suitability of a couple to adopt, the agency is under a duty to have proper regard to the need for stability and permanence in their relationship.

(9) Regulation 5 of the Suitability of Adopters Regulations 2005 provides for the matters to be taken into account by the agency where it is of the opinion that the prospective adopter is unlikely to be considered suitable, notwithstanding that it may not have obtained all the information required under AAR 2005, reg 25.

Suitability of the child to be adopted

4.24 An application for an adoption order may only be made if the child to be adopted has not attained the age of 18 on the date of the application, but an adoption order may be made at any time before the child reaches the age of 19 years.[1] An order can be made with respect to an adopted child, but not a child who is or who has been married.[2]

Probationary periods

4.25 In the case of an agency adoption where the child was placed with the applicants by an adoption agency, a child must have *had his home* with the applicants at all times *in the 10 weeks before* the application for an adoption order is made.

4.26 In a non-agency case involving:

– *a partner of a parent*, the time required is a continuous preceding period of 6 *months*;

– *local authority foster parents*, they may not apply to adopt, unless the child's home has been with them for a continuous period of not less than *one year*, or if the court gives *leave*.

4.27 In any other non-agency case (for example, involving relatives), the prospective adopters may not apply unless the child's home has been with them for a period of not less than 3 years (whether continuous or not) during the period of 5 years ending with the application, or unless the court gives leave to make the application.

4.28 The cumulative probationary period of 3 years for non-agency adoptions, where relatives are concerned, has been extended from the 13 weeks under AA 1976. This reflects the thinking that a residence order is generally more appropriate in these types of cases.

---

1 ACA 2002, ss 47(9) and 49(4).
2 ACA 2002, s 47(8).

Type of placement	Child to live with adopters before application	ACA 2002
If the child was *placed* for adoption with the applicant(s) either: (a) by an *adoption agency*, or (b) in pursuance of a *High Court order* or the applicant is a *parent* of the child	The child must have had his home with the applicant (or with one or both of a couple) at all times during the period of *10 weeks* preceding the application	s 42(2)
If the above is not applicable, then ...		
If the applicant, or one of the applicants, is the *partner of a parent* of the child	The child must have had his home with the applicant(s) at all times during the period of *6 months* preceding the application	s 42(3)
If the applicants are *local authority foster parents*	The child must have had his home with the applicant(s) at all times during the period of *one year* preceding the application (unless the court gives leave for earlier application)	s 42(4) s 42(6)
In any other case	The child must have had his home with the applicant, or one or both of a couple, for not less than a total of *3 years out of the 5 years* preceding the application (unless the court gives leave for earlier application)	s 42(5) s 42(6)

4.29 The question of where a child has his home is one of fact. It has been established that if the child is physically absent, he may still be held to have his home with the applicants if they remain in effective parental control of the child's life.[1] (The statutory disregard of periods in hospital, boarding school or other temporary absence, which applied under the former law, is not replicated in ACA 2002.)

4.30 Additionally, the adoption cannot be made unless the court is satisfied that 'sufficient opportunities to see the child' with the applicant or both of joint applicants

---

1   *Re CSC (An Infant)* [1960] 1 WLR 304; *Re KT (A Minor) (Adoption Application)* [1993] Fam Law 567.

together in the home environment have been given either to the adoption agency who placed the child for adoption or, if there was no agency placement, to the local authority within whose area the home is.[1]

4.31 The requirement that the local authority has sufficient opportunity to see the child in the home environment means that the applicant must actually have a home within the local authority's area.[2]

Reports

4.32 Under ACA 2002, s 43, where a placement has been made by an adoption agency, the agency must provide the court with a report dealing with the suitability of the applicants and any other matters relevant to the child's welfare and must assist the court as the court may direct.

4.33 FP(A)R 2005, r 29 provides that the agency or local authority must provide 'the suitability report' within the timetable fixed by the court and it must cover the matters set out in the *Practice Direction – Reports by the Adoption Agency or Local Authority*, Annex A:

– This includes information about the child, each parent of the child, the contact arrangements and views of the child, parents and relatives, together with information about the prospective adopter of the child, including their suitability to adopt and their wishes and feelings in relation to contact.
– The information as to parents includes unmarried fathers without parental responsibility. If the identity or whereabouts of the father is not known, the report must set out the information about him that has been ascertained and from whom and the steps that have been taken to establish paternity.
– It further contains recommendations as to:
  (i) the relative merits of adoption and other orders with an assessment of whether the child's long-term interests would be best met by an adoption order or other orders;
  (ii) whether the order sought should be made; and
  (iii) as to whether there should be future contact arrangements.

4.34 FP(A)R 2005, r 30 provides that health reports by a registered medical practitioner are to be made not more than 3 months earlier (than the application for adoption) on the health of the child and each applicant and must be attached to an application for adoption except:

– where the child was placed for adoption with the applicant by an adoption agency; or
– the applicant (or one of the applicants) is a parent of the child or the applicant is a partner of a parent of the child.

---

1 ACA 2002, s 42(7).
2 *Re SL (Adoption: Home in Jurisdiction)* [2004] EWHC 1283 (Fam).

These reports are confidential and must contain the information set out in the *Practice Direction – Reports by a Registered Medical Practitioner ('Health Reports')*.

Notice

4.35 In a non-agency placement, no adoption order can be made unless the proposed adopters have given notice to the appropriate local authority of their intention to apply for an adoption order.[1] The notice must be given not more than 2 years before and not less than 3 months before the date on which the application is made.[2] It must be in writing[3] and may be given by post.[4]

4.36 On receipt of the notice, the local authority must investigate the matter, in particular the applicant's suitability and relevant welfare issues, and submit a report to the court.[5] The Local Authority (Adoption) (Miscellaneous Provisions) Regulations 2005 prescribe the local authority responsible for assessing the suitability of prospective adopters and providing a report to the court, and require the local authority to carry out Criminal Records Bureau checks in respect of the applicants.

OTHER CONSIDERATIONS BEFORE MAKING AN ADOPTION ORDER

Has a previous application for a British adoption order been made by the same applicants and been refused?

4.37 The court may not hear an application for an adoption order in relation to a child where a previous application for an adoption order made in relation to the same child by the same person(s) was refused by any court, unless it appears to the court that either (i) because of a change of circumstances or (ii) for any other reason it is proper to hear the application.[6]

4.38 An 'adoption order' in the context of ACA 2002, s 48 means not only an England and Wales adoption order, but also a Scottish, Northern Irish, Manx or Channel Island adoption order.

Has there been any contravention by the applicant of any restriction on arranging an adoption?

4.39 See Chapter 5 on illegal placements and transactions.

---

1   ACA 2002, s 44(2).
2   ACA 2002, s 44(3).
3   ACA 2002, s 144(1).
4   ACA 2002, s 110.
5   ACA 2002, s 44(5).
6   ACA 2002, s 48.

Duty to consider post-adoption contact arrangements

4.40 Before making an adoption order, the court must consider whether there should be arrangements for allowing any person to have contact with the child. For that purpose the court must consider any existing or proposed arrangements and obtain any views of the parties to the proceedings: ACA 2002, s 46(6) (see **4.62 ff**).

ALTERNATIVE CONDITIONS FOR MAKING AN ADOPTION ORDER

4.41 Subject to ACA 2002, s 52, one of three conditions must be met before an adoption order can be made.

First condition – consent: section 47(2)

4.42 The court must be satisfied that:

- each parent consents to the making of the adoption order; or
- each parent has given advance consent and does not oppose the making of the adoption order; or
- each parent's consent should be dispensed with.

4.43 Where a parent has given advance consent to the making of an adoption order, he may not oppose the making of the order without the court's leave, which cannot be given unless the court is satisfied that there has been a change of circumstances since the consent was given.[1]

4.44 The court cannot dispense with the consent of any parent to the making of an adoption order under s 47(2) unless either of the two grounds under s 52(1) is satisfied.

Second condition – placement: section 47(4)

4.45 The second condition is that:

(1) the child must have been placed for adoption by the agency with the prospective adopters in whose favour the order is proposed to be made; *and*
(2) either:
   (a) the child was placed with the consent of each parent and the consent of the mother was given when the child was at least 6 weeks old; or
   (b) the child was placed for adoption under a placement order; *and*
(3) no parent opposes the making of the adoption order.

4.46 'Parental opposition' for the purposes of the second condition is controlled by the requirement for leave:

---

1   ACA 2002, s 47(3) and (7).

- A parent may not oppose the making of an adoption order under the second condition without the leave of the court.[1]
- Leave, however, cannot be given by the court unless it is satisfied that there has been 'a change of circumstances', since the consent was given or the placement order was made.[2]
- To gain access to the court, therefore, parents must establish 'a change of circumstances'.

4.47 Some suggestions as to the procedure to be adopted are as follows:

(1) The 'leave to oppose' issue should be determined as a preliminary issue prior to the main hearing.
(2) The applicant should use the Part 9 procedure (see Chapter 7).
(3) The parents should be directed to provide written statements setting out the circumstances upon which they rely as showing a change of circumstances.
(4) There should be full reports (including from the children's guardian) before the court dealing with (i) the issue of change of circumstances and (ii) the welfare of the child.
(5) An oral hearing should be directed to give the parents effective access to the court for the purposes of Arts 6 and 8 of the European Convention on Human Rights.[3]
(6) In deciding whether there is 'a change in circumstances', the s 1 principles apply. Under s 1(7), 'coming to a decision relating to the adoption of a child in relation to a court' triggers the s 1 principles. Coming to such a decision is defined as including 'coming to a decision about granting leave in respect of any action (other than the initiation of proceedings in any court) which may be taken by ... an individual under the Act'.
(7) What does a change of circumstances in s 47(7) mean and how high should the threshold be set?
   - Examples of a relevant change of circumstances are: successful and proven rehabilitation where a placement order was made because of parental drug or alcohol abuse, or recovery from mental illness to allow the parent to care for the child, or the identification of a previously unknown father willing and able to provide a home.
   - The court is, therefore, likely to interpret the 'change' of circumstances as requiring a 'significant' rather than 'de minimis' change.
   - Setting a higher jurisdictional hurdle for parents to cross, such as a 'fundamental' or 'exceptional' change of circumstances would run the risk of becoming a legal and evidential bar and consequently an infringement under Arts 6 and 8 of the European Convention on Human Rights.[4]
   - Where consent of the parent was given or a placement order has been

---

1 ACA 2002, s 47(5).
2 ACA 2002, s 47(7).
3 *Golder v UK* (1979–80) 1 EHRR 524 at paras 35 and 36; *Ashingdane v UK* (1985) 7 EHRR 528 at 546–547; and *TP and KM v UK* [2001] 2 FLR 549 at [72] and [98]; *McMichael v UK* (1995) 20 EHRR 205 at 241.
4 Ibid.

made, the change of circumstances will be confined to considering what has changed since the consent was given or the order was made.
- It is unlikely that the fact that any original consent was only given for placement and the issue now is full adoption will be a sufficient 'change of circumstances' by itself.

The third condition – section 47(6)

4.48 The third condition is that the child is free for adoption by virtue of an order made in Scotland under s 18 of the Adoption (Scotland) Act 1978 or in Northern Ireland, under Art 17(1) or 18(1) of the Adoption (Northern Ireland) Order 1987. Given the movement of families these days, this may not be so rare in the England and Wales courts.

4.49 It should be noted that in ACA 2002, Sch 4, para 7 it is provided that nothing in the Act affects any freeing order made under s 18 of AA 1976 and that ss 19–21 of the 1976 Act are to continue to have effect in relation to such an order.[1] Where a child is free for adoption under s 18 of the 1976 Act, the third condition in s 47(6) is to be treated as satisfied.[2]

Some pointers

4.50 Section 47 is a key provision within ACA 2002. The following pointers are offered to assist those who will have to interpret its impact on particular cases:

(1) Depending on the facts, an 'agency placement' may fall to be considered under either the first or second conditions.
(2) Where a parent has given consent to placement (which has not been withdrawn prior to the adoption application being made), he/she may only oppose the adoption application with the leave of the court (which may only be given if there is a change of circumstances).
(3) Consent to placement therefore places a parent in the same position as a parent who has either consented to adoption or whose consent to adoption has been dispensed with, *unless* the court gives leave to oppose the adoption application.
(4) Advance consent to adoption (s 20) also prevents a parent opposing the adoption application, unless the court gives leave to do so.
(5) Both s 19 (consent to placement) and s 20 (advance consent) provide for the option of consenting either to a specific placement with identified individuals or generally to a placement chosen by the agency, yet neither of the two conditions under s 47 makes any distinction between these two options and their relationship to the actual placement made.
(6) Where, under the second condition (placement with consent or placement order), leave is given for a parent to oppose the adoption, that condition can no

---

1   Part 1 of Sch 6 to the Magistrates' Courts Act 1980 is also to continue to have effect for the purposes of an application under s 21 of AA 1976 in relation to a freeing order.
2   ACA 2002, Sch 4, para 7(3).

longer be met (as each of the three elements in s 47(4) must be in place). Such a case will then have to proceed under the first condition, with an application to dispense with the parent's consent.

(7) It will be seen that the application for 'leave to oppose', if refused, will effectively determine the adoption application so far as the parent's involvement is concerned (save for issues of contact).

SUMMARY OF THE PROCEDURAL STEPS

4.51 Part 5 procedure applies to applications for adoption orders.

4.52 The *Practice Direction – Forms* specifies that the relevant form for an adoption order application is Form A58. A health report must be attached to the application for an adoption order under FP(A)R 2005, r 30, which covers the matters set out in the *Practice Direction – Reports by a Registered Medical Practitioner* ('Health Reports'). Any consent to the making of an adoption order may be given in Form 104 or a form to the like effect.

4.53 As soon as practicable after the application has been issued, the court will, under FP(A)R 2005, r 24(1):

– set a date for the first directions hearing (which must be within 4 weeks beginning with the date on which the application is issued);
– appoint a children's guardian and/or reporting officer;
– request a report on welfare (if required); and
– set a date for the hearing of the application.

Instead of setting a date for the first directions, the court may give the first directions.

4.54 The court officer will carry out the tasks set out in FP(A)R 2005, r 24(1)(b), including serving copies of the application form on:[1]

– any appointed children's guardian, children and family reporter, and reporting officer;
– the local authority to whom a notice under s 44 has been given;
– the adoption agency which placed the child for adoption with the applicants;
– any person directed by the court to receive a copy.

4.55 If a notice has been given under FP(A)R 2005, r 27 requesting the parent's consent be dispensed with, the court officer must inform the parent of the request and send a copy of the statement of facts to (i) the parent; (ii) the children's guardian, reporting officer, or children and family reporter; (iii) the local authority to whom a notice under s 44 has been given; and (iv) any adoption agency which has placed the child for adoption.

---

1 *Practice Direction – Who Receives a Copy of the Application Form for Orders in Proceedings.*

4.56 Additionally, under FP(A)R 2005, r 24(2), in the case of an adoption order, as soon as practicable after issue, the court or the court officer will:

(a) where the child is not placed for adoption by an adoption agency:
  – ask either the Service or the Assembly to file any relevant form of consent to an adoption order; and
  – ask the local authority to prepare a report on the suitability of the prospective adopters; and
(b) where the child is placed for adoption by an adoption agency, ask the agency to:
  – file any relevant form of consent to (i) the child being placed for adoption (Forms A100–A102), (ii) an adoption order (Form 104), (iii) a future adoption order (Form 103) (or forms to like effect);
  – confirm whether a statement has been made under s 20(4)(a) and, if so, file that statement;
  – file any statement made under s 20(4)(b) as soon as it is received by the agency;
  – prepare a report on the suitability of the prospective adopters.

4.57 FP(A)R 2005, r 26 sets out the steps to be taken at the first directions hearing, which include:

(1) fixing a timetable for the filing of any report relating to the suitability of the applicants to adopt, any report from the local authority, any report from the children's guardian, reporting officer, or children and family reporter and giving directions relating to the reports and other evidence;
(2) considering the joining of other parties;
(3) transfer;
(4) directions about the final hearing.

4.58 The report as to suitability must cover the matters specified in the *Practice Direction – Reports by the Adoption Agency or Local Authority*, Annex A.

4.59 As to the final hearing, notice of the date and place where the application will be heard, and of the fact that (unless the person wishes or the court requires) the person need not attend, is given pursuant to ACA 2002, s 141(4)(c) to the following persons:

– every person who can be found whose consent to the making of an adoption order is required under ACA 2002, s 47(2)(a) (ie the parents with parental responsibility), or would be required but for s 47(2)(c) (or if no such person can be found, any relative prescribed by the rules who can be found);[1]
– every person who has consented to the making of the order under s 20 (and has not withdrawn the consent), unless he has given notice under s 20(4)(a) which has effect;

---

1 Note: the Rules do not currently prescribe any relative. FP(A)R 2005, r 31 provides that a court officer will give notice to '… any other person that may be referred to in a Practice Direction'. There is currently no Practice Direction which prescribes 'any relative'.

– every person who, if leave were given under s 47(5) would be entitled to oppose the making of the order.

4.60 Under FP(A)R 2005, r 32(6) the court cannot make an adoption order unless the applicant and child attend the final hearing.

4.61 See: Chapter 7 for the details as to:

– how to start proceedings (**7.15 ff**);
– steps when the application has been issued (**7.29 ff**);
– first directions hearing (**7.36 ff**);
– final hearing (**7.42 ff**).

POST-ADOPTION CONTACT: SECTION 46(6)

4.62 ACA 2002, s 46(6) imposes the duty upon the court to consider whether there should be arrangements for allowing any person contact with the child; and for that purpose the court must consider any existing or proposed arrangements and obtain any views of the parties. This must be read alongside the duty to consider the whole range of powers available under ACA 2002 and CA 1989 (ACA 2002, s 1(6)). Neither provision creates any presumption one way or the other on the question of post-adoption contact.

4.63 At the final adoption hearing, therefore, the court may make a s 8 contact order. The intention is to replicate the position under the current legislative framework.

4.64 It is unlikely that there will be any significant change in approach to making contact orders post-adoption.[1]

4.65 There are, however, some important pointers which at least keep the issue of post-adoption contact on the radar screen:

(1) The National Adoption Standards published in 2001 provide for links or contact with birth parents, wider birth family members and other people who are significant to them:
A10 The child's needs, wishes and feelings and their welfare and safety are the most important concerns when considering links or contact.
A11 Adoption plans will include details of arrangements for maintaining links (including contact).
C4 Adoptive parents will be involved in discussions as to how they can best maintain any links, including contact.
D7 Where it is in the child's best interest for there to be ongoing links, including contact (and including in relation to siblings separated by

---

1 *Re V (A Minor) (Adoption: Consent)* [1987] Fam 57, [1987] 2 FLR 89 at 107; *Re C (A Minor) (Adoption Order: Conditions)* [1989] AC 1 at 17, [1988] 2 FLR 159 at 168; *Re D (A Minor) (Adoption Order: Conditions)* [1992] 1 FCR 461.

adoption), birth family members will be involved in discussions about how best to achieve this and help to fulfil agreed plans, eg through practical or financial help.

(2) Under the AA 2005 (see Chapter 8):
- Where the adoption agency is considering placing a child for adoption with a particular prospective adopter, it must meet the prospective adopter to discuss the proposed placement and ascertain the views of the prospective adopter about the arrangements the agency proposes to make for allowing any person contact with the child.[1]
- Where the agency decides that the proposed placement should proceed, it must consider the arrangements for allowing any person contact with the child and prepare the adoption placement report, which shall include any proposed contact arrangements,[2] and which must be considered by the adoption panel.

(3) The report on suitability required under ACA 2002, s 43 and FP(A)R 2005, r 29 covers in relation to contact: (i) the child's wishes and feelings; (ii) each parent's wishes and feelings; (iii) the prospective adopter's wishes and feelings; (iv) the arrangements concerning siblings; (v) the extent of contact with the child's mother and father and, in each case, the nature of the relationship enjoyed; (vi) the child's relationship with relatives or other relevant person and their wishes and feelings: *Practice Direction – Reports by the Adoption Agency or Local Authority.*

4.66 Further, under Art 8, the court must be satisfied that the cutting off of all contact between the child and his natural family is a proportionate response and justified by the overriding necessity of the interests of the child. If it is not, then irrespective of the prospective adopters' unwillingness, the court, under its duty to act compatibly with Art 8, ought to override any discretion given to the adopters under the adoption order.

4.67 Given the value of post-adoption contact, particularly in cases involving older children, it is important that the court should explore and deal fully with the issue in every case. This is particularly so, as once an adoption order is made, the jurisdictional hurdle for a member of the natural family in seeking leave for contact under CA 1989, s 10 is set exceptionally high.[3]

FAMILY RELATIONSHIPS

Step-parents and partners

4.68 Although ACA 2002 has made some important amendments to the position of step-parents, the direction of the reforms has been towards alternatives to adoption.

---

1 AAR 2005, reg 31(1)(b) and (c)(ii).
2 AAR 2005, reg 31(2)(c) and (d)(iv).
3 *Re C (A Minor) (Adopted Child: Contact)* [1993] Fam 210 at 216A, [1993] 2 FLR 431 at 436B; *Re S (Contact: Application by Sibling)* [1998] 2 FLR 897 at 912C–D.

4.69 This is illustrated by the amendments which ACA 2002 has made to CA 1989:

– Under the new s 4A of CA 1989,[1] a married step-parent may acquire parental responsibility for the child of his spouse by an agreement between the step-parent and the parents, who have parental responsibility, or by a court order.
– However, parental responsibility, whether under a parental responsibility agreement or court order, is not indefeasible. It may be brought to an end by an order of the court.
– Section 12 of CA 1989 has also been amended[2] so as to enable the court to direct that a residence order in favour of a step-parent or partner may continue in force until the child reaches the age of 18, as a further means of delivering enhanced security where the step-parent or partner is caring for the child on a long-term basis.

4.70 There may, however, be circumstances where a step-parent or partner adoption may be in the child's best interests: for example, where one of the natural parents is a stranger to the child and the child has no knowledge of this parent's extended family.

4.71 Under s 51(2) an adoption order may now be made on the single application of a step-parent or partner.

4.72 Under s 67 the status of a child adopted by a couple or one of a couple under s 51(2) is expressly recognised. A child so adopted is to be treated as a child of the relationship of a couple.

4.73 As a preliminary requirement for a step-parent or partner to obtain an adoption order, the child must have had his home with the step-parent at all times during the period of 6 months preceding the application.[3] The step-parent or partner must also give notice in writing to the appropriate local authority of his intention to apply for an adoption order not more than 2 years or less than 3 months before applying for an order.[4] The step-parent or partner must then satisfy the consent condition under s 47(2).

4.74 Where a step-parent or partner has given notice of intention to apply to adopt:

(1) If the child has had his home with the step-parent/partner for not less than 3 years out of the last 5, the child may be removed only:[5]
   – with the court's leave;
   – by a local authority or other person in exercise of statutory powers.
(2) If the child's home has been with the step-parent/partner for less than 3 years, then the child may be removed:[6]
   – by the child's parents;

---

1 Inserted by ACA 2002, s 112.
2 By ACA 2002, s 114.
3 ACA 2002, s 42(3).
4 ACA 2002, s 44(2) and (3).
5 ACA 2002, s 39(1) and (2).
6 ACA 2002, s 39(3).

– with the court's leave;
– by a local authority or other person in exercise of statutory powers.

Unmarried fathers

4.75 Under ACA 2002 the key to the parental right to give or withdraw consent to placement for adoption and adoption remains 'parental responsibility'.

4.76 CA 1989, as amended by ACA 2002, now extends the means whereby an unmarried father may acquire parental responsibility to include where he becomes registered as the child's father under paragraphs (a), (b) and (c) of s 10(1) and of s 10A(1) of the Births and Deaths Registration Act 1953.

4.77 Where the agency has placed the child for adoption under s 19 pursuant to a consent given by the mother, and the father subsequently acquires parental responsibility, he is deemed to have consented in the same terms as the mother under s 52(9) and (10). He is, however, entitled to withdraw his 'deemed' consent, provided he does so before an application for adoption has been made. Once an adoption application has been made, if he wishes to oppose the making of the adoption order, then he must obtain leave on the basis that there has been a change of circumstances under s 47.

Role of unmarried father without parental responsibility

4.78 The unmarried father without parental responsibility has a voice under ACA 2002, s 1(4)(f), which requires the adoption agency to consider the wishes and feelings of any of the child's relatives. 'Relative' is defined in s 1(8) as including 'the child's mother and father', ie *both* parents.

4.79 Under the AAR 2005 (see Chapter 8) there is a requirement upon the agency, where the father does not have parental responsibility, but his identity is known:[1]

– to provide a counselling service;
– to explain to him the procedure in relation to placement for adoption, and adoption, and the legal implications of adoption;
– to ascertain his wishes and feelings regarding:
  (a) the child;
  (b) the placement of the child for adoption, including any wishes and feelings about the child's religious and cultural upbringing;
  (c) contact with the child if the child is authorised to be placed for adoption or the child is adopted;
– to ascertain so far as is possible whether the father wishes
  (a) to acquire parental responsibility for the child under s 4 of CA 1989;
  (b) intends to apply for a residence or contact order under s 8 of CA 1989 or, where the child is subject to a care order, an order under s 34 of CA 1989.

---

1 AAR 2005, reg 14.

4.80 Where the child has been placed with prospective adopters by the agency, there will be a minimum period of only 10 weeks within which it is possible for an unmarried father to apply for a parental responsibility order under CA 1989, s 4. When an application for parental responsibility is pending and an application for a placement order or an adoption order is made at the same time, then the expectation is that the court will ensure that the matter of parental responsibility is dealt with first.

4.81 In the report on suitability, required under ACA 2002, s 43 and FP(A)R 2005, r 29, the information covered includes whether the unmarried father has parental responsibility and, if so, how it was acquired and if the identity and whereabouts of the father are not known, the information about him that has been ascertained and from whom and the steps that have been taken to establish paternity. The report also includes a summary of the adoption agency's actions, which includes details of the steps taken to inform an unmarried father without parental responsibility of the application for an adoption order.

4.82 Where no proceedings have started and an adoption agency or local authority is in any doubt as to whether to consult an unmarried father without parental responsibility, under FP(A)R 2005, r 108 the agency or authority may ask the High Court for directions on the need to give a father without parental responsibility notice of the intention to place for adoption. The procedure which applies in this case is the Part 10 procedure (see Chapter 7). It is unlikely that these applications will be routine.

4.83 Under the former law, with an eye towards Art 8 of the European Convention on Human Rights, the court had increased the involvement of unmarried fathers in the adoption process: *Re R (Adoption: Father's Involvement* [2001] 1 FLR 745 and *Re H; Re G (Adoption: Consultation of Unmarried Fathers)* [2001] 1 FLR 646. In *Re H; Re G,* Dame Elizabeth Butler-Sloss P established that, as a matter of general practice, judges giving directions in adoption applications would be expected to inform natural fathers of the proceedings, unless for good reason it was inappropriate to do so. This expectation will continue under the new adoption law.

4.84 Under FP(A)R 2005, r 23(3)(a) the court has a discretion at any time to direct that any person may be made a respondent to proceedings. Further, under r 26(1)(c), at the first directions hearing the court has to consider the joining of parties and, under r 26(1)(f)(i), the tracing of parents.

Baby adoptions

4.85 Under s 18(1) an adoption agency may place for adoption a child under 6 weeks old without either formal consent under s 19 or a placement order.

4.86 Sections 52(3) and (4) provide that any consent given by the mother to placement under s 19 or to the making of an adoption order is ineffective for an adoption order if given less than 6 weeks after the child's birth. She must formally re-affirm her consent after 6 weeks for there to be a valid basis for the making of an adoption order under s 47(4).

4.87 Where a child under 6 weeks old has been placed for adoption but after 6 weeks the agency does not have authorisation under s 19, the rules for removal still apply. Only the adoption agency may remove the child from the placement.

4.88 The provisions for placement contact orders in ss 26 and 27 cover baby placements which begin when the child is under 6 weeks old but continue after that point without a s 19 consent being obtained.

Orphans

4.89 Section 21(2)(c) ensures that the court may make a placement order in respect of a child of any age, where the child has no parent.

4.90 The conditions for making an adoption order under s 47 do not apply where the child has no parent. The court may make an order on application, provided that it is satisfied that it is in the child's best interests and consistent with the obligations placed on the court by s 1.

Chapter 5

ILLEGAL PLACEMENTS AND TRANSACTIONS

5.1 ACA 2002 reaffirms and strengthens the safeguards existing under AA 1976 which permitted only adoption agencies to make arrangements for adoption and to advertise for adoption.

5.2 In the wake of the 'internet twins' case,[1] ACA 2002 has:

– extended and reinforced the former prohibitions on illegal placements under AA 1976, including tougher penalties;
– extended and reinforced the restrictions on advertising to include both traditional media and electronic means, including the internet;
– imposed for the first time express restrictions on the preparation and submission of reports.

PROHIBITION UPON MAKING ARRANGEMENTS: SECTION 92[2]

5.3 Section 92 of ACA 2002 sets out the restrictions in relation to arranging an adoption imposed on persons who are neither an adoption agency nor acting in pursuance of an order of the High Court.[3]

5.4 The nine steps a person must not take are:[4]

(1) asking a person other than an adoption agency to provide a child for adoption;
(2) asking a person other than an adoption agency to provide prospective adopters for a child;
(3) offering to find a child for adoption;

---

1 *Flintshire County Council v K* [2001] 2 FLR 476.
2 In ACA 2002, ss 92–96, references to 'adoption' are to the adoption of a person wherever they may be habitually resident, effected under the law of any country or territory, whether within or outside the British Isles. Under s 2(1), a local authority or registered adoption society is an adoption agency. The definition of 'adoption agency' does not include adoption agencies abroad.
3 Under the former law in *Re G (A Minor) (Adoption: Illegal Placement)* [1995] 1 FLR 403 at 409H–410A the Court of Appeal held that where there had been an illegal placement, the adoption application is 'appropriate for determination in the High Court' and should be commenced or transferred to that court. There is unlikely to be any change in this practice.
4 ACA 2002, s 92(2). They are designed to cover (i) making contact with birth parents on behalf of prospective adopters; (ii) obtaining the birth parents' consent to adoption; and (iii) taking forward agreed matches between children and adoptive families by placing a child for adoption.

(4) offering a child for adoption to a person other than an adoption agency;
(5) handing over a child for adoption to any person other than an adoption agency;
(6) receiving a child handed over to him in contravention of (5);
(7) entering into an agreement[1] with any person for the adoption of a child, or for the purpose of facilitating the adoption of a child, where no adoption agency is acting on behalf of the child in the adoption;
(8) initiating or taking part in negotiations of which the purpose is the conclusion of an agreement within (7);
(9) causing any other person to take any of the steps mentioned in (1) to (8).

5.5 Where the prospective adopters are parents, relatives, guardians, or one of them is a partner of a parent of the child, steps (4), (5), (7), (8) and (9) do not apply.[2]

5.6 A contravention of s 92 is a summary offence punishable with imprisonment for a term not exceeding 6 months or a fine not exceeding £10,000 or both. Under s 138 of ACA 2002, the prosecution may be brought within 6 months from the date on which the prosecutor has sufficient evidence to do so and must not be brought more than 6 years after the commission of the offence.

5.7 There are certain defences available. Where a person is charged with receiving a child handed over to him under s 92(2)(f) (step (6)), that person is not guilty unless it is proved that he knew or had reason to suspect that the child was handed over to him in contravention of step (5).[3] A similar defence is available to someone in contravention of s 92 by causing a person to take any of the steps (1) to (8).[4] In each case the defence only applies if he adduces sufficient evidence to raise the issue as to whether he had the specified knowledge or reason.

PROHIBITIONS ON REPORTS: SECTION 94

5.8 Section 94 is a new provision which imposes restrictions on the preparation of certain reports in connection with adoption. It is intended to ensure that only professionally qualified staff carry out the necessary assessments and the preparation of reports, and thus aims at eradicating the difficulty which arose from privately commissioned home study reports.

5.9 Under s 94(1) of ACA 2002, a person (who does not fall within a prescribed description and certain prescribed circumstances) may not prepare a report about the suitability of a child for adoption or of a person to adopt or about the adoption or placement for adoption of a child. To do so constitutes a summary offence punishable with imprisonment for a term not exceeding 6 months or a fine not exceeding level 5

---

1 'Agreement' includes an arrangement (whether enforceable or not): ACA 2002, s 92(7)(a).
2 ACA 2002, s 92(3) and (4).
3 ACA 2002, s 93(2).
4 ACA 2002, s 93(3).

(£5,000), or both.[1] Additional offenders include someone who causes a person to prepare a report or submits a report prepared in contravention of s 94(1) and, if the person concerned works for an adoption society, the manager of the society.

5.10 The Restriction on the Preparation of Adoption Reports Regulations 2005 identify the persons who fall within 'the prescribed description'. They include a social worker employed by a local authority or registered adoption society.[2]

5.11 The circumstances prescribed under the Restriction on the Preparation of Adoption Reports Regulations 2005[3] include:

– preparing a report about whether the child should be placed for adoption;
– preparing a report about the suitability of the prospective adopter to adopt a child;
– preparing a report about whether a child should be placed for adoption with a particular prospective adopter;
– preparing a report of a visit;
– preparing a pre-adoption report;
– preparing a post-adoption report;
– preparing a report in accordance with ACA 2002, s 43 (reports in agency cases) or s 44(5) (reports in non-agency cases).

5.12 A person is not guilty of an offence of causing someone to prepare a report in contravention of s 94(1) unless it is proved that he knew or had reasonable cause to suspect that the report had been so prepared. This applies only if sufficient evidence is adduced by him to raise an issue as to whether he had the requisite knowledge or reason.

PROHIBITIONS ON PAYMENTS: SECTION 95

5.13 Section 95 prohibits certain payments or rewards in connection with the adoption of a child. It is an offence for a person;

(a) to make any such payment or reward;
(b) to agree or offer to make such payment;
(c) to receive or agree to receive or to attempt to obtain such payment for:
 – the adoption of a child;
 – the giving of any consent required in connection with the adoption of a child;
 – the taking of any of the nine steps prohibited in s 92(2);
 – the preparing or submitting of a report in contravention of s 94(1).

---

1 ACA 2002, s 94(2)(a) and (5). The proceedings may be brought more than 6 years after the commission of the offence but subject to that may be brought within a period of 6 months from the date on which evidence, sufficient in the opinion of the prosecutor to warrant the proceedings, came to his knowledge: s 138.
2 Restriction on the Preparation of Adoption Reports 2005, SI 2005/1711, reg 3.
3 Restriction on the Preparation of Adoption Reports 2005, reg 4.

5.14 The prohibition does not apply to certain 'excepted payments' which are defined in s 96 as those made:[1]

- by virtue of or in accordance with the provision made by or under ACA 2002;
- to a registered adoption society by a parent or an adopter or proposed adopter in respect of expenses reasonably incurred by the society in connection with the adoption;
- in respect of any legal or medical expenses incurred in connection with a court application for an adoption order, placement order or a contact order under s 26.

5.15 The intention is to prohibit money changing hands in relation to the adoption of a child, while still permitting the payment of legitimate expenses of adoption agencies and persons applying or proposing to apply for adoption.

5.16 A contravention of s 95 is a summary offence punishable with imprisonment for a term not exceeding 6 months, or a fine not exceeding £10,000, or both, with an extended time limit for prosecution under s 138.

PROHIBITION ON ADVERTISEMENTS: SECTION 123

5.17 Section 123 of ACA 2002 imposes restrictions carrying criminal sanctions on publishing or distributing an advertisement or information indicating that:

- the parent wants his child to be adopted; or
- a person wants to adopt a child; or
- a person (other than an adoption agency) is willing to take any step in arranging for the adoption of a child as specified in s 92(2)(a)–(e), (g)–(i) (ie steps 1–5, 7–9); or
- a person (other than an adoption agency) is willing to receive a child handed over to him with a view to the child's adoption by him or another;
- a person is willing to remove a child from the UK for the purposes of adoption.

5.18 'Information' includes (i) information about how to do anything, which, if done, would constitute an offence under s 93 (or under s 85), whether or not the information contains a warning that it may constitute an offence; and (ii) information about a particular child as a child available for adoption.

5.19 'Publishing or distributing' means doing so 'to the public' and covers all forms of publication and distribution, including electronic means (for example, by means of the internet).

---

1   They also include payments in respect of expenses reasonably incurred in connection with an application for an order under s 84 and payments made in respect of the removal of the child from the UK for the purpose of adoption where the proposed adopters are the parent, relatives or guardian, or one of them is a step-parent and the payment is in respect of travel and accommodation expenses.

5.20   Section 123(1) does not apply to publication or distribution by or on behalf of an adoption agency.[1]

5.21   Section 124 makes contravention of s 123(1) a summary criminal offence for anyone who publishes or distributes an advertisement or information in breach of the section. The penalty is imprisonment not exceeding 3 months, or a fine not exceeding level 5 on the standard scale, or both.

5.22   The following defence is available. A person is not guilty of an offence under s 123 unless it is proved that he knew or had reason to suspect that the section applied to the advertisement or information. The defence applies only if sufficient evidence is adduced to raise the issue of knowledge or reason.

---

1   This may include a person outside the UK exercising functions corresponding to those of an adoption agency. The Secretary of State will prescribe which bodies are to be treated as a UK adoption agency for the purposes of s 123.

Chapter 6

ACCESS TO INFORMATION

THE REGISTERS

Adopted Children Register

6.1 ACA 2002 continues to place a duty upon the Registrar General to continue to maintain the Adopted Children Register: s 77. The Register itself is not open to public inspection or search.

6.2 Every adoption order must contain a direction to make an entry in the Register in the form prescribed by reg 2 of the Adopted Children and Adoption Contact Registers Regulations 2005. No entries may be made in the Register other than entries directed by adoption orders or required to be made under ACA 2002, Sch 1.

6.3 Records include certified copies kept by the Registrar General of entries in any register of births and 'registers of live-births' mean the registers of live-births under the Births and Deaths Registration Act 1953.

The entry system: section 77 and Schedule 1

6.4 The entry system works as follows:

(1) Provision is made for the marking of the register of live-births with the word 'Adopted'.
(2) The officer of the court, which made the order, must communicate the order to the Registrar General, who must then comply with the directions as to marking.
(3) Errors in the particulars contained in the adoption order can be corrected by amending the order, either on the application of the adopter or the adopted person, including the substitution or addition of a name, within 12 months from the beginning of the order.
(4) Provision is also made for rectification and re-registration of the birth, and cancellation in registers on legitimisation.

Index: section 78

6.5 The Registrar General is under a duty to maintain an index of the Adopted Children Register and any person may search the index and have a certified copy of any entry.

6.6 A person is not, however, entitled to a certified copy of an entry in the Adopted Children Register relating to an adopted person who has not attained the age of 18 years, unless the applicant has provided the Registrar General with the following prescribed particulars:[1]

– the full name of the adopted person;
– the date of birth of the adopted person; and
– the full name of the adoptive parent(s).

Connecting information/birth record information: sections 79, 60 and Schedule 2

6.7 The Registrar General must make traceable the connection between any entry in the registers of live-births or other records which have been marked 'Adopted' and any corresponding entry in the Adopted Children Register, but only in accordance with s 79. The information kept by the Registrar General is not to be open to public inspection or search.

6.8 Where the adoptee was adopted before 'the appointed day' (ie the day appointed for the commencement of ss 56–65), the court may, in exceptional circumstances, order the Registrar General to give the connecting information or birth record information to the adoptee.

6.9 Under ACA 2002, s 79(5), on an application by the appropriate[2] adoption agency, a duty is imposed on the Registrar General to give to that agency the 'connecting/birth record' information. The application must be made in writing.[3]

6.10 On an application by an adopted person, a record of whose birth is kept by the Registrar General, and who is under the age of 18 and intends to marry or form a civil partnership, the Registrar General is under an obligation to inform the applicant whether or not it appears from the information contained in the register of live-births or other records that the applicant and the person whom the applicant intends to marry may be within the prohibited degrees of relationship for the purposes of the Marriage Act 1949. The application by the adoptee must be in writing and signed by him.[4]

Person adopted before commencement

6.11 In order to obtain the 'connecting/birth record information', the adopted adult has to apply to the court and satisfy the 'exceptional circumstances' test under s 79(4).

1　Adopted Children and Adoption Contact Registers Regulations 2005, reg 18.
2　'Appropriate adoption agency' means (i) the placing adoption agency; or (ii) (if different) the agency keeping the information in relation to the adoption; or (iii) (in any other case) the local authority to which notice of intention to adopt was given.
3　ACACRR 2005, reg 11.
4　ACACRR 2005, reg 13.

6.12 The Registrar General remains under a statutory duty to disclose the information to the adult adoptee, provided he applies in accordance with Sch 2, and subject to certain conditions such as the payment of a fee:

- The application by the adopted person must be in writing and signed by him.[1]
- Before the Registrar General gives any information to an applicant, he must inform the applicant that counselling services are available and where they may be obtained.
- If the applicant chooses to receive counselling, the Registrar General must send to the person or body providing the counselling the information to which the applicant is entitled.
- Where a person applies for information under Sch 2 and was adopted before 12 November 1975, the Registrar General must not give the information to the applicant unless the applicant has attended an interview with a counsellor arranged by a person or body from whom counselling services are available.
- Where the Registrar General is prevented in cases where the person was adopted before 12 November 1975 from giving information to a person who is not living in the United Kingdom, he may give the information to any body which he is satisfied is suitable to provide counselling for that person and which has notified the Registrar General that it is prepared to provide such counselling.

6.13 The Adoption Information and Intermediary Services (Pre-Commencement Adoptions) Regulations 2005 provide a scheme for registered adoption support agencies or an adoption agency to operate an intermediary service for the purposes of:

(1) assisting adopted persons aged 18 or over, who were adopted before 30 December 2005, to obtain information in relation to their adoption; and
(2) facilitating contact between such persons and their relatives.

A person adopted after commencement

6.14 Under ACA 2002, s 60(2)(a), the adopted adult retains a right, at his request, to receive information which would enable him to obtain a certified copy of his birth certificate, but he may only do so through the intermediary of the appropriate adoption agency.

6.15 On an application by the appropriate adoption agency, the Registrar General must under s 79(5) give the agency the 'connecting/birth record' information for the adopted adult. The adoption agency must then pass on the information to the adopted adult.

6.16 If the adoption agency wishes to withhold the information, it must apply to the High Court for an order denying the adopted adult access to the information under s 60(3). Such order will only be granted where the court is satisfied that the circumstances are exceptional.

---

1   ACACRR 2005, reg 12.

The Adoption Contact Register: section 80

6.17 The Registrar General remains under a duty to continue to maintain the Adoption Contact Register, which is not open to public inspection or search. The Adoption Contact Register is in two parts, designed to facilitate contact between adopted persons and their birth relatives where both parties have expressed a wish for such contact.

6.18 Part 1 contains the following information relating to the adopted person who has given requisite notice[1] expressing their wish to make contact with their relatives:[2]

- the full name address and date of birth of the adopted person;
- any relative with whom they wish to have contact, together with the name of the relative, if known;
- any relative with whom they do not wish to have contact, together with the name of that relative, if known.

6.19 There are *three pre-requisites* for an entry in Part 1:

(1) A record of the adoptee's birth must be kept by the Registrar General.

(2) The adopted person must have attained 18.

(3) The Registrar General has to be satisfied that the adoptee has the necessary information to enable him to obtain a certified copy of his birth.

6.20 Part 2 contains the following information relating to the persons who have given the requisite notice[3] expressing their wishes, as relatives of the adopted persons, to make contact with them:[4]

- the full name and address and date of birth of the relative of an adopted person;
- the name of the adopted person with whom they wish to have contact; or
- the fact that they do not wish to have contact.

6.21 There are *two pre-requisites* to an entry:

(1) The person has to have attained 18.

(2) The Registrar General has to be satisfied that the person is a relative[5] of the adopted person and has the necessary information to enable him to obtain a certified copy of the record of the adopted person's birth.

---

1 The notice prescribed under ACACRR 2005, reg 6 is set out in Sch 3.
2 ACACRR 2005, reg 6.
3 The notice prescribed under ACACRR 2005, reg 7 is set out in Sch 4.
4 ACACRR 2005, reg 7.
5 'Relative' means 'any person who (but for his adoption) would be related to him by blood (including half blood) or marriage ie parents, siblings, grandparents, great grandparents, uncles, aunts, cousins, nephews, nieces and relatives by marriage.

6.22 The Registrar General must give an adopted person whose name is in Part 1 the name in writing of any relative whose name is in Part 2 and who has asked for contact with that adopted person, together with the address at or through which the relative may be contacted.[1]

DISCLOSURE OF INFORMATION ABOUT A PERSON'S ADOPTION

6.23 Under ACA 2002 access to information is filtered through adoption agencies so as to provide an intermediary safeguard before disclosure is made.

6.24 Sections 54 and 56–65 ('the disclosure group of sections') deal with different types of information:

- *Section 54 information,* which an adoption agency is required to disclose to prospective adopters.
- *Section 56 information* or 'protected' information, which an adoption agency must keep in relation to a person's adoption:
  (a) information about the adopted person, including his birth parents and siblings, his adoptive parents and siblings, and other relatives;
  (b) any information kept by the adoption agency (i) which is necessary to enable the adopted person to obtain a certified copy of the record of his birth,[2] or (ii) which is information about an entry relating to an adopted person in the Adoption Contact Register;
  (c) 'identifying' information, which means information which identifies the person or enables the person to be identified: this includes residence, educational and employment addresses, photographic or audiovisual material, case records and legal and medical information held by adoption agencies.
- *Section 58 information* or 'background' information (which does not fall into either category).[3]

6.25 The Disclosure of Adoption Information (Post-Commencement Adoptions) Regulations 2005 provide for the keeping of information in relation to persons adopted on or after 30 December 2005.

6.26 The s 56 information which the agency must keep under DAI(PCA)R 2005, reg 4 (for at least 100 years from the date of the adoption order) includes the case record set up in respect of the adopted person under the AAR 2005,[4] together with:

---

1   ACACRR 2005, reg 8.
2   See ACA 2002, s 79(3) and (5).
3   Information such as the child's birth details, medical history, interests, any special needs and progress, which (i) will help adopters and (ii) can be disclosed to the birth family without compromising the adoptee's new identity or whereabouts.
4   Or the AAR 1983.

- any information supplied by a natural parent or relative or other significant person in the adopted person's life with the intention that the adopted person may be given that information;
- any information supplied by the adoptive parents or other persons which is relevant to matters arising after the making of the adoption order;
- any information that the adopted person has requested should be kept;
- any information given to the adoption agency by the Registrar General under s 79(5);
- any information disclosed to the adoption agency about an entry relating to the adopted person on the Adoption Contact Register;
- any information required by reg 10 (a record of disclosure for research or inquiries), reg 14 (the written views obtained under ACA 2002, s 61(3) or s 62(3) or (4)) or reg 18 (disclosure for counselling);
- the record of any agreement under reg 11 (the prescribed agreement for the disclosure of protected information).

In the first three cases, the adoption agency is not required to keep any such information where it would be prejudicial to the adopted person's welfare to keep it or it would not be reasonably practicable to keep it.

The system for disclosure: in brief

6.27 The adoption agency is the single point of access for 'identifying information', including the information necessary to access a birth record.

6.28 Protected information may only be disclosed by the agency pursuant to ss 57–65. The system for disclosure of protected information is subject to criminal sanctions imposed on adoption agencies who contravene the disclosure provisions.[1]

6.29 Certain background information must be disclosed to adopters[2] and may be disclosed to certain persons for the purposes of the agency's functions.[3]

6.30 The adopted adult has the right, at his request, under s 60:

- To receive from the agency the information disclosed to the adopters by the agency under s 54.
- To receive from the adoption agency the information necessary to obtain his birth record ('the birth record information'), unless the High Court orders otherwise. For the High Court to do so, there must be an application by the agency for permission not to disclose, and the High Court must be satisfied that the circumstances are exceptional.[4]

---

1 ACA 2002, s 57 and s 59. A registered adoption society which discloses any information in contravention of s 57 is guilty of an offence and is liable on summary conviction to a fine not exceeding level 5 on the standard scale: DAI(PCA)R 2005, reg 21.
2 ACA 2002, s 54 and s 58(3).
3 ACA 2002, s 58(2).
4 ACA 2002, s 60(3).

– Under FP(A)R 2005, r 84, to receive from the court, which made the adoption order, a copy of:

(a) the application form for an adoption order (but not the documents attached);

(b) the adoption order and any other orders relating to the adoption proceedings;

(c) orders allowing a person contact with the child after the adoption order was made;

(d) any document or order referred to in any relevant practice direction.

6.31 The *Practice Direction – Disclosing Information to an Adopted Adult* supplements FP(A)R 2005, r 84 and provides that the adopted adult is also entitled to receive (i) any transcript or written reasons of the court's decision, and (ii) a report made to the court by a children's guardian, reporting officer, or children and family reporter, a local authority or an adoption agency.

6.32 The court will remove any protected information from any such copy document or order before it is given to the adopted person.[1]

6.33 An application under FP(A)R 2005, r 84 must be made in Form A64 and must have attached to it a full certified copy of the entry in the Adopted Children Register relating to the applicant.[2]

6.34 The completed application form must be taken to the court which made the adoption order, together with evidence of the applicant's identity showing a photograph and signature (such as a passport or driving licence).

6.35 Where an adult adoptee requests information from the agency under s 60(2)(a) that would enable him to obtain a certified copy of the record of his birth and the agency does not have that information, the agency must seek the information from the Registrar General.[3]

6.36 The Registrar General must disclose:

– to any person (including an adopted person) at his request any information that the person requires to assist him to make contact with the adoption agency which is the appropriate adoption agency in the case of the person specified in the request; and

– to the appropriate adoption agency any information that the agency requires, in relation to an application under ss 60, 61 or 62 about any entry relating to a person on the Adoption Contact Register.[4]

---

1 *Practice Direction – Disclosing Information to an Adopted Adult*, para 3.
2 *Practice Direction – Disclosing Information to an Adopted Adult*, para 1.2 and 1.3.
3 DAI(PCA)R 2005, reg 19.
4 DAI(PCA)R 2005, reg 20.

The system under sections 61–62

Disclosure not involving a child

6.37   Where a person applies to the agency for the disclosure of protected information, *none of which involves a child*, the agency has a discretion under s 61 whether or not to proceed with the application:

– It is not required to do so unless it considers it appropriate.
– If it does proceed, it must take all reasonable steps under s 61(3) to obtain the views of persons to whom the information relates, including whether they consent to the release of the information.
– It may then disclose the information if it considers it appropriate.
– In determining whether it is appropriate to proceed to disclose, it must consider all the circumstances including:
   (a) the welfare of the adopted person;
   (b) the views of the persons to whom the information refers obtained by the agency under s 61(3);
   (c) prescribed matters.[1]

Disclosure involving a child

6.38   Where a person applies to the agency for the disclosure of protected information, *any of which involves a child*, the agency has a discretion under s 62 whether or not to proceed with the application, and is not required to do so unless it considers it appropriate:

6.39   If it decides to proceed, then it must, in relation to any information about the child, take all reasonable steps to obtain the views of:

– any parent or guardian or adoptive parent of the child; and
– the child (if the agency considers it appropriate to do so, having regard to his age and understanding).

6.40   In deciding whether to proceed with the application or disclose the information, the agency must:

– have regard to the paramountcy principle in respect of the adopted child and, in the case of any other child, have particular regard to the child's welfare; and
– consider all the circumstances of the case including –
   (i) the welfare of the adoptee (where the adoptee is not an adopted person whose welfare is not the paramount consideration);
   (ii) the views obtained under s 62(3) from the parents or guardian and the child;
   (iii) prescribed matters.

---

1   Currently there are no regulations or proposals for regulations which prescribe any such matters.

Disclosure where person aged 18

6.41 Where the information is about a person *who has attained the age of 18*, the agency must:

(1) take all reasonable steps to obtain his views as to disclosure; and
(2) consider all the circumstances of the case including:
- his views;
- the welfare of the adoptee (where the adoptee is not an adopted child to whom the paramountcy principle applies);
- prescribed matters.[1]

6.42 The agency must then disclose, if it considers it appropriate:

- If there is consent, the expectation is that the information would normally be disclosed.
- The agency can still withhold disclosure, if it considers it inappropriate.
- If consent is refused or cannot be obtained, the agency can still disclose, if it considers it appropriate.

Further requirements

6.43 An application to an adoption agency for the disclosure of protected information under s 61 or s 62 must be in writing and state the reasons for the application.[2]

6.44 On receipt of the application, the agency must take reasonable steps to confirm (i) the identity of the applicant or any person acting on his behalf; and (ii) that person is authorised to act on the applicant's behalf.[3]

6.45 The agency must ensure that any views obtained under s 61(3) or s 62(3) or (4) are recorded in writing.[4]

Qualifying determinations

6.46 The following determinations by the agency in relation to an application under s 61 are 'qualifying determinations' and subject to review by an independent panel under s 12:[5]

- not to proceed with an application from any person for disclosure of protected information;
- to disclose information against the express views of the person the information is about;

---

1 Currently there are no regulations or proposals for regulations which prescribe such matters.
2 DAI(PCA)R 2005, reg 12.
3 DAI(PCA)R 2005, reg 13.
4 DAI(PCA)R 2005, reg 14.
5 DAI(PCA)R 2005, reg 15.

– not to disclose information about a person to the applicant where that person has expressed the view that that information should be disclosed.

CONFIDENTIALITY

6.47 The law and procedure established under AA 1976 continues to provide a guide to the disclosure of confidential material to natural parents: see *Re D (Minors) (Adoption Reports: Confidentiality)* [1996] AC 593; *Re X (Children) (Adoption: Confidential Procedure)* [2002] 2 FLR 476; *Re B (Disclosure to Other Parties)* [2001] 2 FLR 1017.

6.48 CAFCASS officers have the right under ACA 2002, s 103 to examine and to take copies of an adoption agency's records relating to a proposed or actual application in respect of the child concerned. Any copy of such a document (or any part of it) will be admissible as evidence of any matter referred to in any report he may produce to the court in the proceedings or in any evidence which he gives in the proceedings.

PRIVACY

6.49 Adoption proceedings in the High Court or county court may be heard and determined in private: ACA 2002, s 101. This is to ensure that only those concerned in the case are present and the public are not admitted. It gives the High Court and county court judges the discretion to hear adoption proceedings in public when they consider it appropriate (eg where it is in the child's best interests, such as a judgment given in public).

6.50 Section 12 of the Administration of Justice Act 1960 sets out the circumstances in which it would be contempt of court to publish information given in private proceedings, which includes adoption proceedings.[1]

6.51 For the purposes of the law relating to contempt of court, under FP(A)R 2005, r 78 information relating to proceedings held in private may be communicated:

– where the court gives permission;
– in accordance with a relevant practice direction (unless the court directs otherwise); or
– where the communication is to:
    (i) a party,
    (ii) a legal representative of a party,
    (iii) a professional legal adviser,
    (iv) an officer of the Service or a Welsh family proceedings officer,
    (v) a welfare officer,
    (vi) the Legal Services Commission,

---

1   ACA 2002, s 101(2) amends the Administration of Justice Act 1960 to include adoption proceedings.

(vii) an expert whose instruction by a party has been authorised by the court, or

(viii) a professional acting in furtherance of the protection of children (eg a local authority officer or police officer exercising child protection functions, or an officer of NSPCC).

6.52 Section 97 of CA 1989 applies to adopted children so as to bar their identification in the High Court and county court.

Chapter 7

THE FAMILY PROCEDURE (ADOPTION) RULES 2005

7.1 The Family Procedure (Adoption) Rules 2005 are the first rules to be made by the Family Procedure Rules Committee. The rules provide a procedural code which is new in two principal respects:

(1) The rules apply to proceedings in all three court tiers: High Court, county court and the magistrates' court.[1]
(2) Mirroring the Civil Procedure Rules 1998, many of the practical details are contained in Practice Directions, which have mandatory force.

Certain provisions of CPR 1998 are to be applied with modifications.[2]

THE OVERRIDING OBJECTIVE: FP(A)R 2005, RULE 1

7.2 The overriding objective of the FP(A)R 2005 contained in r 1 is to enable the court to deal with cases justly, having regard to the welfare issues involved.

7.3 It is an overarching statement of purpose intended to provide a compass to guide the courts, legal advisers and litigants as to their general course through proceedings under ACA 2002. It tailors the overriding objective in CPR, r 1.1 and r 1.2 to the special circumstances of family cases, where the welfare principle is paramount. It also gives voice to the rights guaranteed under Art 6 of the European Convention on Human Rights, for example the right to equality of arms.

7.4 Dealing with a case justly includes, so far as is practicable:

– ensuring that it is dealt with expeditiously and fairly;
– dealing with the case in ways which are proportionate to the nature, importance and complexity of the issues;
– ensuring that the parties are on an equal footing;
– saving expense; and

---

1 FP(A)R 2005, r 5(1).
2 FP(A)R 2005, r 5(2)–(5): (i) CPR, r 35.15 applies in detailed assessment proceedings in the High Court and county court; (ii) CPR, r 35.15(3) deals with the modifications to the rules on costs; (iii) CPR, Part 47 does not apply to magistrates' court proceedings; (iv) CPR Parts 50 and 70–74, Schs 1 and 2 apply to the enforcement of orders.

– allotting to it an appropriate share of the court's resources, while taking into account the need to allot resources to other cases.

7.5 The duty imposed upon the court in FP(A)R 2005, r 2 is to give effect to the overriding objective when it (a) exercises any power given to it by the rules, or (b) interprets any rule. The achievement of the overriding objective is, therefore, the duty of the court.[1]

7.6 Although no such duty is directly imposed upon the parties, they are required to help the court to further the overriding objective.[2] This help will include:

(1) complying with the rules, practice directions and court orders;

(2) co-operating with each other and the court in the fixing of hearing dates (such as providing accurate and timely information as to the availability of expert witnesses);

(3) ensuring that all relevant material is available to the court.

Parties must be prepared to deal with all matters which may be raised at any allocation hearing, the first directions hearing under FP(A)R 2005, r 26, and any subsequent hearings.

7.7 Although proportionality is not a new concept to family law, by making the principle an integral part of the overriding objective, the rules clearly bring into focus its importance in the procedural context. It is relevant to the allocation of cases to one of the three court levels.

7.8 Dealing with a case justly includes 'allotting to it an appropriate share of the court's resources, while taking into account the need to allot resources to other cases': FP(A)R 2005, r 1(2)(e). This recognises that any delay which occurs will be assessed not only from the viewpoint of the prejudice caused in the particular case, but also in relation to other litigants and the prejudice caused to the administration of justice.[3] It gives emphasis to the duty of the parties and their professional advisers to keep the court informed immediately of case developments which may impact upon the

---

1 The effect of the overriding objective and the Human Rights Act 1998 was set out in *Goode v Martin* [2002] 1 All ER 620 where Brooke LJ said: 'We now possess more tools for enabling us to do justice than were available before April 1999. Since then, the CPR and the provisions of the 1998 Act have come into force. By the former we must seek to give effect to the overriding objective of dealing with cases justly when we interpret any rule. By the latter we must read and give effect to subordinate legislation, so far as it is possible to do so, in a way which is compatible with the convention rights set out in Sch 1 to the Act (s 3 of the 1998 Act).'
2 FP(A)R 2005, r 3.
3 *Arbuthnot Latham Bank Limited v Trafalgar Holdings Ltd* (1997) *The Times*, December 27, per Lord Woolf MR (as he then was).

administration of the court's business. However, organisational deficiencies arising from a shortage of resources cannot be a reason for denying the right to a fair hearing under Art 6.[1]

7.9 Examples of the circumstances in which the court will have the overriding objective in mind are applications for any extensions of time for taking procedural steps, for parties to be added to proceedings, for adjournments, for expert evidence and for permission to appeal.

CASE MANAGEMENT: FP(A)R 2005, RULE 4

7.10 Under FP(A)R 2005, r 4(1) the court must further the overriding objective by actively managing cases (as required by ACA 2002, s 109).

7.11 *Active case management* includes the exercise of various judicial powers, as listed in FP(A)R 2005, r 4(2):

(a) encouraging the parties to co-operate with each other in the conduct of the proceedings;
(b) identifying at an early stage –
    (i) the issues; and
    (ii) who should be a party to the proceedings;
(c) deciding promptly –
    (i) which issues need full investigation and hearing and which do not; and
    (ii) the procedure to be followed in each case;
(d) deciding the order in which issues are to be resolved;
(e) encouraging the parties to use an alternative dispute resolution procedure, if the court considers that appropriate, and facilitating the use of such procedure;
(f) helping the parties to settle the whole or part of the case;
(g) fixing timetables or otherwise controlling the progress of the case;
(h) considering whether the likely benefits of taking a particular step justify the cost of taking it;
(i) dealing with as many aspects of the case as it can on the same occasion;
(j) dealing with the case without the parties needing to attend at court;
(k) making use of technology; and
(l) giving directions to ensure that the hearing of the case proceeds quickly and efficiently.

---

[1] *Buchholz v FRG* (1981) 3 EHRR 597 at 608, para 51; *Berry Trade Ltd v Moussavi* [2002] 1 WLR 1910 where the Court of Appeal held that, in the circumstances of the case, the judge's refusal to grant the defendant's application for an adjournment of a committal hearing breached Art 6. The court held that affording the defendant a proper opportunity to exercise those rights should outweigh other considerations, such as the use of court resources and the convenience of other parties.

7.12 The list in FP(A)R 2005, r 4 is not exhaustive or prescriptive. The power to control case progress by 'fixing timetables or otherwise' complements and supplements the time limits in the rules and practice directions.[1]

7.13 The case management powers include encouraging the parties to use alternative dispute resolution procedures, where appropriate. The circumstances in which this is likely to arise include contact disputes or non-agency adoption applications by relatives, where alternative options for permanence such as a residence order or SGO ought properly to be canvassed first.

7.14 FP(A)R 2005, Part 3, rr 12–16 amplify the court's management powers to cover:

– the court's general powers of management (r 12), which include:
 (a) extending or shortening time for compliance;
 (b) adjourning or bringing forward a hearing;
 (c) requiring a party or his legal representative to attend court;
 (d) holding a hearing and receiving evidence by telephone or other methods;
 (e) directing that part of the proceedings be dealt with as separate proceedings;
 (f) staying the whole or part of any proceedings or judgment, either generally or until a specified date;
 (g) consolidating proceedings;
 (h) hearing two applications on the same occasion;
 (i) directing a separate hearing of any issue;
 (j) deciding the order in which issues are to be heard;
 (k) excluding an issue from consideration;
 (l) dismissing or giving judgment on an application after a decision on a preliminary issue;
 (m) directing any party to file and serve an estimate of costs;
 (n) taking any further step or giving any other direction for the purpose of managing the case and furthering the overriding objective;
– the exercise of powers of the court's own initiative (r 13);
– the court officer's power to refer to the court (r 14);
– general power to rectify matters where there has been an error of procedure (r 15);
– the power of the court to make civil restraint orders (r 16): see **7.107–7.109**.

HOW TO START PROCEEDINGS: FP(A)R 2005, PART 4

7.15 Part 4 applies to all proceedings, including those for which the Part 9 or Part 10 procedure is used.

---

[1] *NB*: FP(A)R 2005, r 6 is the interpretation rule; rule 7 deals with the power to perform the functions of the court; rule 8 gives the court discretion as to where it hears cases; rule 9 deals with court documents; rule 10 deals with computation of time; rule 11 provides for the dates for compliance to be calendar dates and to include time of day. The *Practice Direction – Hearings by a Single Justice of the Peace* supplements r 7(1)(c)(ii)(bb). The *Practice Direction – Court Documents* supplements r 9(4).

7.16 Under FP(A)R 2005, r 19, proceedings are started when the court officer issues an application at the request of the applicant. The date entered on the form by the court officer is the issue date.

7.17 The forms are set out in the *Practice Direction – Forms* and these, or forms to the like effect, must be used.[1] FP(A)R 2005, r 18 provides that the application form must have attached to it any documents referred to in the application form.

7.18 If the proposed applicant for an adoption order wishes his identity to be kept confidential in the proceedings, he may, before the commencement of proceedings, request the court officer to assign a serial number to him under FP(A)R 2005, r 20.

7.19 If a serial number has been assigned:

– the court officer will ensure that any application form or notice sent out does not contain information which discloses or is likely to disclose the identity of that person to any other party who is not already aware of his identity; and
– the proceedings will be conducted with a view to securing that the applicant is not seen by or made known to any party who is not already aware of his identity except with his consent.

The court may at any time direct that a serial number identifying the applicant in the adoption proceedings must be removed.

7.20 Under FP(A)R 2005, r 21, unless the court directs otherwise, a party is not required to reveal:

(a) the address or telephone number of their private residence;
(b) the address of the child;
(c) the name of the person with whom the child is living (if not the applicant); or
(d) the proposed new surname of the child (where the application is for permission to change the child's surname under s 28(2)).

Where a party does not wish to reveal these personal details, he must give notice of those particulars to the court and the particulars will not be revealed (unless the court directs otherwise); the confidential information form is A65 in the *Practice Direction – Forms*. If a party changes his address during the course of the proceedings, he must give notice of the change to the court.

7.21 An application may be withdrawn with the permission of the court under FP(A)R 2005, r 106. A written request for permission must be filed setting out the reasons for the request. The other parties and any children's guardian, reporting officer,

---

1 FP(A)R 2005, r 17. Under r 33, unless the contrary is shown, the child referred to in the application will be deemed to be the child referred to in the form of consent to the child being placed for adoption or to the making of an adoption order where (i) the application identifies the child by reference to a full certified copy of an entry in the registers of live-births; (ii) the form of consent identified the child by reference to a full certified copy of the entry in the registers of live-births attached to the form; and (iii) the copy of the entry in the registers of live-births is the same or relates to the same entry in the registers of live-births as the copy of the entry in the registers of live-births attached to the form of consent.

or children and family reporter will be notified of the request by the court officer. The request can be dealt with by the court without a hearing if the other parties and any of the CAFCASS officers have had an opportunity to make written representations.

7.22 By a notice in writing a party may admit the truth of the whole or any part of another party's case: FP(A)R 2005, r 122. The court has a discretion as to whether to allow a party to amend or withdraw an admission.

7.23 The court has a discretion as to where it deals with cases, under FP(A)R 2005, r 8.

7.24 Restrictions on where proceedings may be started are set out in the Children (Allocation of Proceedings) Order 1991 (as amended).[1] Two new classes of county court have been inserted: adoption centres and intercountry adoption centres:

– An application under ACA 2002 to be made to a county court must be commenced in an adoption centre.
– Where ACA 2002 proceedings[2] are to be transferred to a county court from the High Court or magistrates' court, they must be transferred to an adoption centre.
– An application under s 23 of ACA 2002 (varying placement orders) must be made to the magistrates' court.

7.25 It should be noted that under FP(A)R 2005, r 108, where no proceedings have started, an adoption agency or local authority may ask the High Court for directions on the need to give a father without parental responsibility notice of the intention to place a child for adoption The appropriate procedure to be used is the Part 10 procedure (see below).

PROCEDURE FOR APPLICATIONS IN ADOPTION AND PLACEMENT PROCEEDINGS: PART 5

Application of the Part 5 procedure

7.26 The FP(A)R 2005, Part 5 procedure applies to:[3]

(a) adoption proceedings;
(b) placement proceedings;
(c) proceedings for:
 – the making of a s 26 contact order;

---

1 Amended by the Children (Allocation of Proceedings) (Amendment) Order 2005, which in Sch 3 sets out the adoption centres and in Sch 4 the intercountry adoption centres. The Principal Registry of the Family Division of the High Court is to be treated as an adoption centre and an intercountry adoption centre.
2 Save for s 23, which must be made in the magistrates' court. Otherwise proceedings to vary or revoke an order must be made to the court which made the order.
3 FP(A)R 2005, r 22.

- variation or revocation of a contact order under s 27;
- an order giving permission to change a child's surname or remove the child from the UK under s 28(2) and (3);
- s 84 orders, s 88 directions and s 89 orders;
- any other order that may be referred to in a practice direction.

Who are the parties: FP(A)R 2005, rule 23

7.27 This is governed by FP(A)R 2005, r 23, which sets out in Table 1 which persons are to be applicants and in Table 2 which persons are to be respondents. (The relevant parties are set out here separately under the specific proceedings).

7.28 The court retains a general discretion at any time to direct that:

- a child, who is not already a respondent, should be made a respondent where –
  (a) the child wishes to make an application or has evidence to give or a legal submission to make which has not been made by any other party; or
  (b) there are other special circumstances;[1]
- a person or body should be made a respondent or that a respondent should be removed;[2]
- where the court makes a direction for the addition or removal of a party, it may give consequential directions about –
  (a) serving a copy of the application form on any new respondent;
  (b) serving relevant documents on the new party; and
  (c) the management of the proceedings.[3]

What the court will do on the issue of the application: FP(A)R 2005, rule 24

As soon as practicable after the application has been issued

7.29 The court[4] will:

- if ACA 2002, s 48(1) (restrictions on making an adoption order) applies, consider whether it is proper to hear the application;
- set a date for the first directions hearing, which must be within 4 weeks beginning with the date on which the application is issued;[5]
- appoint a children's guardian (r 59);
- appoint a reporting officer (r 69);
- consider whether a report relating to the welfare of the child is required and, if so, request such a report (r 73);

---

1 FP(A)R 2005, r 23(2)(a) and (b).
2 FP(A)R 2005, r 23(3)(a) and (b).
3 FP(A)R 2005, r 23(4).
4 FP(A)R 2005, r 7 sets out the power to perform the functions of the court.
5 FP(A)R 2005, r 25.

- set a date for the hearing of the application; and
- do anything else set out in a practice direction.

7.30 The court officer will:

- give notice of any directions hearing set by the court to the parties and to any children's guardian, reporting officer, or children and family reporter, subject to receiving confirmation whether a statement has been made under s 20(4)(a) (statement of wish not to be informed of any application for an adoption order);
- serve a copy of the application form (but not the documents attached, save for below) on the persons referred to in the *Practice Direction – Who Receives a Copy of the Application Form for Orders in Proceedings*;
- send a copy of the certified copy of the entry in the register of live-births or Adopted Children Register and any health report attached to an application for an adoption order to –
  (a) any children's guardian, reporting officer, or children and family reporter; and
  (b) the local authority to whom notice has been given under s 44;
- if a notice under r 27 has been given (request to dispense with consent of parent), inform the parent of the request and send a copy of the statement of facts to –
  (i) the parent;
  (ii) any CAFCASS officer;
  (iii) the local authority to whom a notice under s 44 has been given; and
  (iv) any adoption agency which has placed the child for adoption;
- do anything else that may be set out in a practice direction.

As soon as practicable after an application for a placement order has been issued, additionally

7.31 The court will consider whether a report giving the local authority's reasons for placing the child for adoption is required and, if so, will direct the local authority to prepare such a report:

- Under r 29(2) a local authority that is directed to prepare a report on the placement of a child for adoption must file a report within a timetable fixed by the court. The report must cover the matters specified in the *Practice Direction – Reports by the Adoption Agency or Local Authority*, Annex B.
- The court may at any stage request a further report, or ask the local authority to assist the court in any other manner.
- The court officer will send a copy of the report to any children's guardian, reporting officer, or children and family reporter.
- The report will be confidential.

7.32 The court or court officer will ask the Service or the Assembly to file any form of consent to the child being placed for adoption.

As soon as practicable after an application for an adoption order has been issued, additionally

7.33 The court officer will:

(1) where the child is not placed for adoption by an adoption agency:
- ask the Service or the Assembly to file any relevant form of consent to an adoption order;
- ask the local authority to prepare a report on the suitability of the prospective adopters (if not already done); and

(2) where the child is placed for adoption by an adoption agency, ask the adoption agency to:
- file any relevant form of consent to (a) the child being placed for adoption, (b) an adoption order, (c) a future adoption order under s 20;
- confirm whether a statement has been made under s 20(4)(a) and, if so, file that statement;
- file any statement made under s 20(4)(b) (withdrawal of wish not to be informed of any application for an adoption order);
- prepare a report on the suitability of the prospective adopters (if not already done).

7.34 Under r 29(1), the adoption agency or local authority must file the report on the suitability of the applicant to adopt the child within the timetable fixed by the court:

- The report must cover the matters specified in the *Practice Direction – Reports by the Adoption Agency or Local Authority*, Annex A.
- The court may request a further report or ask for further assistance.
- The court officer will send a copy of the report to any children's guardian, reporting officer, or children and family reporter.
- The report will be confidential.

7.35 It should be noted that, where it considers it appropriate, the court may, instead of setting a date for a first directions hearing, give the first directions under r 26.[1]

The first directions hearing: FP(A)R 2005, rule 26

7.36 The date for the first directions hearing must within 4 weeks beginning with the date on which the application form is issued.[2] The parties or their legal representatives must attend the first directions hearing (unless the court orders otherwise).[3]

7.37 At the first direction hearing the court will:

1　FP(A)R 2005, r 24(4).
2　FP(A)R 2005, r 25.
3　FP(A)R 2005, r 26(3).

(1) fix a timetable for the filing of the following reports and give directions relating to the reports and other evidence:
- any report relating to the suitability of the applicant to adopt;
- any report from the local authority;
- any report from the children's guardian, reporting officer, and children and family reporter;
- if a statement of facts has been filed, any amended statement of facts;
- any other evidence;

(2) consider whether alternative dispute resolution is appropriate and, if so, give directions;

(3) consider whether the child or any other person should be a party to the proceedings and give directions relating to the joining as a party (r 23(2) and (3));

(4) give directions for the appointment of a litigation friend for any patient or non-subject child (ie a person under the age of 18 who is a party to the proceedings but is not the subject of the proceedings);

(5) consider whether the case needs to be transferred to another court and, if so, give directions relating to the transfer;

(6) give directions about:
- tracing parents or any other person the court considers to be relevant to the proceedings;
- service of the documents;
- disclosure as soon as possible of information and evidence to the parties subject to r 77 (which deals with the disclosure of confidential reports[1]);
- the final hearing.

7.38 Rule 77(2) applies to any direction given in relation to disclosure of information and evidence to the parties. Before the court gives a direction that a confidential report be disclosed to each party, it has to consider whether any information should be deleted, including information which:

- discloses or is likely to disclose the identity of a person who has been assigned a serial number under r 20(2); or
- discloses the personal details referred to in r 21(1) where a party has given notice under r 21(2).

7.39 The court has a discretion not to disclose the report to a party.[2]

7.40 Directions may be given at any stage of the proceedings, either of the court's own initiative or on the application of a party or any children's guardian (or where the report concerns a report by a reporting officer, or children and family reporter, that officer).[3] For the purpose of giving directions:

- the court may set a date for a further directions hearing or other hearing; and

---

1 FP(A)R 2005, r 26(1)(g).
2 FP(A)R 2005, r 77(3).
3 FP(A)R 2005, r 26(4).

— the court officer will give notice of any date so fixed to the parties and to any child's guardian, reporting officer or children and family reporter.

7.41 After the first directions hearing, it is the court's duty to monitor compliance with the court's fixed timetable and directions by the parties.[1]

The final hearing: FP(A)R 2005, rule 32

7.42 Under r 31 the court officer gives notice to the parties, any children's guardian, reporting officer, or children and family reporter and to any other person who may be referred to in a practice direction:[2]

(a) of the date and place where the application will be heard; and
(b) of the fact that the person need not attend (unless he wishes or the court requires).

7.43 ACA 2002, s 141(3) expressly provided that in the case of an application for an adoption order, the rules must require any person mentioned in s 141(4) to be so notified. The persons to be notified under s 141(4)(c) in the case of an adoption order are:

— every person who can be found whose consent to the making of the order is required under s 47(2)(a) or would be required but for their consent being dispensed with (ie the parents having parental responsibility) or, if no such person can be found, any relative prescribed by the rules who can be found;[3]
— every person who has consented under s 20 (and has not withdrawn consent) unless he gave notice of his wish not to be informed of any application for an adoption order under s 20(4)(a);
— every person who if leave were given under s 47(5) would be entitled to oppose the making of the order.

7.44 A person who has been given notice may attend the hearing[4] and be heard on the question of whether an order should be made (save where the court has refused permission to oppose the making of an adoption order under s 47(3) or (5)). A member or employee of a party which is a local authority or adoption agency may address the court if authorised to do so.[5]

7.45 It follows that the door is left open to parents in the circumstances set out in s 141(3) and (4) to be notified of the date and place where a final adoption hearing will be heard and to be heard on the question whether an order should be made (though in fact the person who has given advance consent and not withdrawn that consent is unable to oppose the order without leave). The 'open door' reflects no doubt a wish to

---

1 FP(A)R 2005, r 26(6).
2 Currently there is no practice direction.
3 No relative is currently prescribed by the rules.
4 FP(A)R 2005, r 32(1).
5 FP(A)R 2005, r 32(3).

comply with the parties' right to access to the court under Art 6 and to enable applications for contact under CA 1989, s 8 to be made at the time of the final adoption hearing.

7.46 In relation to an adoption order, r 32(6) provides that the court cannot make an order unless the applicant and the child personally attend the final hearing. This subrule is, however, subject to two qualifications. Under r 32(7) the court may direct that the applicant or the child need not attend the final hearing. Under r 32(8), in the case of an adoption by a couple under s 50, the court may make an adoption order after personal attendance of only one of the applicants, if there are special circumstances.

7.47 Serious concern has been raised concerning the potential for confrontation between (i) the parents who, on receipt of the notice of date and place, decide to attend the final adoption hearing and (ii) the applicant and the child, whose personal attendance is required before the court can make the order. Although r 32(7) enables the court to exercise its discretion to dispense with the personal attendance of the applicant and the child at the final hearing, this fails to address the serious issue that the final hearing is regarded as an important event for the adopters and the child, and generally their personal attendance would be required and welcomed.

7.48 One possible solution is that the court should direct a substantive 'final' hearing where the decision is made as to the making of the adoption order (and the making of any CA 1989, s 8 contact order) with the child's attendance dispensed with, followed by an informal occasion where the adopters and child do personally attend, at which the adoption order is pronounced.

7.49 It is important to recall that where a serial number has been assigned to the applicant,[1] the proceedings are to be conducted so as to secure that the applicant is not seen or made known to the respondent, who is not aware of his identity, except with his consent.

7.50 The court may direct that any person must attend a final hearing.

7.51 A legal representative of the applicant must attend the final hearing of the application for a placement order; otherwise the court cannot make the order.[2]

THE ROLE OF CHILDREN'S GUARDIAN

Appointment: FP(A)R 2005, rules 59–61

7.52 In proceedings to which Part 5 applies, a children's guardian is appointed where the child is a party (unless the court is satisfied that it is not necessary to do so to

---

1 Under FP(A)R 2005, r 20.
2 FP(A)R 2005, r 32(9).

safeguard the interests of the child).[1] When appointing, the court will consider the appointment of anyone who has previously acted as a children's guardian to the same child.[2]

7.53 At any stage in the proceedings where the child is a party, the court may appoint a children's guardian of its own initiative. A party may also apply for the appointment of a children's guardian, without notice to the other parties (unless the court otherwise directs), and the court will grant such an application (unless it considers such an appointment unnecessary to safeguard the child).[3]

7.54 In the event that the court refuses to appoint a children's guardian, it will give reasons for the refusal and the court or the court officer will record the refusal and the reasons for it. As soon as practicable, the decision will be notified to the parties and the Service or the Assembly.[4]

7.55 Where a children's guardian is appointed, the court officer will record the appointment and as soon as practicable:[5]

- inform the parties and the Service or the Assembly; and
- send copies of the application and any documents filed with the court in the proceedings to the children's guardian.

7.56 The court officer has a continuing duty to send the children's guardian a copy of any document filed with the court during the course of the proceedings.[6]

7.57 The appointment continues for the time specified in the appointment or until terminated by the court. When terminating the appointment, the court must give reasons for doing so, a note of which will be taken by the court or a court officer.[7]

Powers and duties: FP(A)R 2005, rules 62–64

7.58 Under FP(A)R 2005, r 62 the children's guardian's role is to act on behalf of the child upon the hearing of any application. In proceedings to which Part 5 applies, his duty is to safeguard the interests of the child. Additionally, he is obliged to provide the court with such assistance as it may require.

7.59 His duties under FP(A)R 2005, r 63 include:

- making such investigations as may be necessary to carry out his duties; in particular he must:
    (a) contact or seek to interview such persons as he thinks appropriate or as the court directs;

---

1 FP(A)R 2005, r 59(1).
2 FP(A)R 2005, r 59(4).
3 FP(A)R 2005, r 59(2)(a) and (3).
4 FP(A)R 2005, r 60(1).
5 FP(A)R 2005, r 60(2).
6 FP(A)R 2005, r 60(3).
7 FP(A)R 2005, r 61.

(b) obtain such professional assistance as is available to him which he thinks is appropriate or which the court directs him to obtain;
- appointing a solicitor for the child;[1]
- giving such advice to the child as is appropriate, having regard to his understanding;
- instructing the solicitor representing the child on all matters relevant to his interest, including the possibility of appeal.

7.60 If it appears to the children's guardian that the child (a) is instructing his solicitor direct, or (b) intends to conduct and is capable of conducting the proceedings on his own behalf, under FP(A)R 2005, r 64 the court must be informed of that fact. The children's guardian's role in those circumstances is to:[2]

- perform the duties under rr 62–67 (save for the duties in r 63(2)(a) and (c), ie appointing a solicitor and instructing the solicitor on all matters relevant to the child) or such other duties as the court may direct;
- take part in the proceedings as the court may direct;
- have legal representation in the conduct of those duties with the permission of the court.

Exercise of the duties: FP(A)R 2005, rules 65–67

7.61 Under FP(A)R 2005, r 65(1), the children's guardian or the child's solicitor is under a duty to attend all directions hearings (unless the court directs otherwise).

7.62 Under FP(A)R 2005, r 65(2)–(5) and r 66 the children's guardian must:

(1) advise the court orally or in writing:
- whether the child is of sufficient understanding for any purpose (including the child's refusal to submit to medical or psychiatric examination or other assessment),
- the wishes of the child in respect of any matter relevant to the proceedings (including his attendance at court),
- the appropriate forum,
- the appropriate timing,
- the options available and the suitability of each option,
- any other matter on which the court seeks his advice or he considers that the court should be informed;

(2) file a written report (which will be confidential) advising on the interests of the child in accordance with the timetable set by the court;

---

1 The exceptions to the duty to appoint are (i) where a solicitor has already been appointed, or (ii) he is authorised under s 15(1) of the Criminal Justice and Court Services Act 2000, or s 37(1) of the Children Act 2004 (ie he has a right to conduct litigation and has a right of audience). In the latter case the duty to appoint a solicitor does not apply, unless the child wishes to instruct the solicitor direct and the children's guardian or the court considers that he is of sufficient understanding to do so: FP(A)R 2005, r 63(3)(a) and (3).
2 FP(A)R 2005, r 64(2).

(3) where practicable, notify any person, the joining of whom as a party would be likely to safeguard the interests of the child, of the court's power to join that party as a party under r 23 and inform the court:
- of any notification,
- of anyone whom he attempted to notify but was unable to contact,
- of anyone whom he believes may wish to be joined to the proceedings;

(4) serve and accept documents on behalf of the child in accordance with r 37(2)(b) and the table set out in r 37(1), and advise the child of the contents where the child has not been served himself and has sufficient understanding[1] – where the children's guardian inspects records of the kind specified in CA 1989, s 42 (right to have access to local authority records) or ACA 2002, s 103 (right to have access to adoption agency records), he must bring all records and documents which, in his opinion, may assist in the proper determination of the proceedings to the attention of the court and to the other parties (unless the court directs otherwise);[2]

(5) ensure that the child (if considered appropriate to his age and understanding) is notified of the court's decision and has it explained to him in a manner appropriate to his age and understanding.[3]

Solicitor for the child: FP(A)R 2005, rule 68

7.63 A solicitor[4] must represent the child in accordance with the instructions received from the children's guardian.[5] If the solicitor considers (having taken into account the views of the children's guardian and any court direction under r 64(2)) that the child wishes to give instructions which conflict with those of the children's guardian, and he is able, having regard to his understanding, to give instructions, the solicitor must conduct the proceedings in accordance with the child's instructions.[6]

7.64 Where no children's guardian has been appointed and the condition in CA 1989, s 41(4)(b) is satisfied, the solicitor must act in accordance with the child's instructions.

7.65 In default of instructions (as above), the solicitor must act in furtherance of the best interests of the child.

7.66 The solicitor must serve and accept service of documents on behalf of the child in accordance with r 37(2)(a) and the table in r 37(1) and advise the child of the contents where the child has not himself been served and has sufficient understanding.[7]

---

1 FP(A)R 2005, r 66(1).
2 FP(A)R 2005, r 66(2).
3 FP(A)R 2005, r 67.
4 Appointed under s 41 (3) of CA 1989, or under FP(A)R 2005, r 63(2)(a).
5 FP(A)R 2005, r 68(1)(a).
6 FP(A)R 2005, r 68(1)(a).
7 FP(A)R 2005, r 68(2).

7.67 Where the child wishes to terminate an appointment of a solicitor, he may apply to the court for an order terminating the appointment. The solicitor and the children's guardian will have an opportunity to make representations. Where the children's guardian wishes the appointment of a solicitor to be terminated, he may apply to the court for a termination order. The solicitor and the child (if of sufficient understanding) will have an opportunity to make representations. The court will give reasons for terminating an appointment, a note of which will be taken by the court or court officer.[1]

7.68 A record of the appointment of, or refusal to appoint, a solicitor will be recorded by the court or court officer.[2]

ROLE OF THE REPORTING OFFICER: FP(A)R 2005, RULES 69–72

7.69 In proceedings to which Part 5 applies, a reporting officer is appointed by the court where it appears that a parent or guardian is willing to consent to the placing of the child for adoption or to the making of an adoption order, and the parent or guardian is in England or Wales.[3] The same person may be appointed as the reporting officer for two or more parents or guardians of the child.[4]

7.70 His duties under FP(A)R 2005, r 71 are to witness the signature by a parent on the document in which consent is given to (a) placing the child for adoption, or (b) the making of an adoption order. (How the reporting officer exercises his duties is more fully set out at **2.28–2.30**).

ROLE OF THE CHILDREN AND FAMILY REPORTER: FP(A)R 2005, RULES 73–74

7.71 Where the court is considering an application for an order in Part 5 proceedings, the court may, under FP(A)R 2005, r 73, ask a children and family reporter to prepare a confidential report on matters relating to the welfare of the child. The children and family reporter is under a duty to comply with such a request and provide the court with such other assistance as it may require.

7.72 The children and family reporter has the following obligations under FP(A)R 2005, r 74; he must:

(1) make such investigations as may be necessary to perform his powers and duties, and must in particular:

---

1 FP(A)R 2005, r 68(3)–(5).
2 FP(A)R 2005, r 68(6).
3 FP(A)R 2005, r 69.
4 FP(A)R 2005, r 70.

- contact or seek to interview such persons as he thinks appropriate or the court directs,
- obtain such professional assistance as is available to him which he thinks is appropriate or as the court directs;

(2) notify the child of such contents of his report as he considers appropriate to the child's age and understanding, including any reference to the child's own views on the application and his recommendation, and explain them in a manner appropriate to his age and understanding;

(3) attend all directions hearings (unless the court orders otherwise);

(4) advise the court of the child's wishes and feelings;

(5) advise the court if he considers that the joining of a person as a party would be likely to safeguard the child's interests;

(6) consider whether it is in the child's best interests to be made a party and, if so, notify the court of his opinion, together with reasons;

(7) where a written report has been directed, file the report in accordance with the timetable set by the court.

ROLE OF THE LITIGATION FRIEND: FP(A)R 2005, RULES 49–58

7.73 Special provisions relating to the requirement for a litigation friend apply in proceedings involving:

- a 'non-subject' child (ie a person under the age of 18 years who is a party to the proceeding *but not the subject of* the proceedings) who does not have a children's guardian;
- a subject child who does not have a children's guardian;
- a patient within the meaning of the Mental Health Act 1983.[1]

7.74 In each case, he must have a litigation friend to conduct proceedings on his behalf[2] (save in the circumstances set out in r 51). Unless a r 51 order is made, except for filing an application form or applying for the appointment of a litigation friend under r 55, a person may not take any step in proceedings without the permission of the court until there is a litigation friend.[3] If a party becomes a patient during the proceedings, no party may take any step without the permission of the court until the patient has a litigation friend.[4]

7.75 The exceptions to the requirement for a litigation friend under FP(A)R 2005, r 51 are:

---

1 FP(A)R 2005, r 49 and r 6 (interpretation rule).
2 FP(A)R 2005, r 50.
3 FP(A)R 2005, r 52(2).
4 FP(A)R 2005, r 52(3).

(a) where he has obtained the court's permission to conduct proceedings without a litigation friend;[1] or
(b) where a solicitor (i) considers that the non-subject child is able, having regard to his understanding, to give instructions in the proceedings, and (ii) has accepted instructions from the child to act.[2]

7.76 The court may, under FP(A)R 2005, r 55, either (i) on its own initiative. or (ii) on the application of a person who wishes to be the litigation friend or a party, appoint as a litigation friend:

– the Official Solicitor;
– an officer of the Service or a Welsh family proceedings officer (if he consents) in the case of a non-subject child;
– some other person (if he consents);

and a person so appointed shall be treated as a party for the purposes of service of documents or notice.

7.77 The court must be satisfied that the 'some other person' complies with the following conditions[3] ('the three preconditions'), that he:

– can fairly and competently conduct proceedings on behalf of the non-subject child or patient;
– has no interest adverse to that of the non-subject child or patient;
– undertakes to pay the costs which the non-subject child or patient may be ordered to pay (subject to any right he may have to be repaid from the assets of the non-subject child or the patient); this does not apply to the Official Solicitor or an officer of the Service.

7.78 A person authorised under the Mental Health Act 1983 to conduct proceedings on behalf of a patient is entitled to be a litigation friend of the patient in any proceedings to which his authority extends without a court order.[4]

7.79 If nobody has been appointed by the court (or, in the case of a patient, authorised under the 1983 Act), a person may only act as a litigation friend if he can satisfy the three pre-conditions.[5]

7.80 If the court has not appointed a litigation friend, a person wishing to become a litigation friend must follow the procedure under FP(A)R 2005, r 54 (this does not apply to the Official Solicitor or an officer of the Service).[6]

---

1   FP(A)R 2005, r 51(1)(a).
2   FP(A)R 2005, r 51(1)(b)(i) and (ii).
3   FP(A)R 2005, r 53(3)(a)–(c). The application for a certificate of suitability of a litigation friend is in Form FP9 in the *Practice Direction – Forms*.
4   FP(A)R 2005, r 53(2).
5   FP(A)R 2005, r 53(3).
6   FP(A)R 2005, r 54(6).

7.81 When a non-subject child who is not a patient reaches the age of 18, a litigation friend's appointment ceases: FP(A)R 2005, r 58(1).

7.82 When a party ceases to be a patient, the litigation friend's appointment continues until ended by court order: FP(A)R 2005, r 58(2).

7.83 The *Practice Direction – Litigation Friends* supplements the rules dealing with litigation friends.

WHO CAN ACT AS A CHILDREN'S GUARDIAN, REPORTING OFFICER, OR CHILDREN AND FAMILY REPORTER: FP(A)R 2005, RULES 75–76

7.84 In the case of adoption proceedings, the following persons may not be appointed:

- a member, officer or servant of a local authority which is a party;
- a person who is or has been a member, officer or servant of a local authority or voluntary organisation who has been directly concerned in arrangements relating to the care, accommodation or welfare of the child during the 5 years prior to the commencement of the proceedings;
- a serving probation officer who in that capacity has been previously concerned with the child or his family.

In placement proceedings, the latter two categories may not be appointed as a children's guardian, reporting officer or children and family reporter.

7.85 Under FP(A)R 2005, r 76 the same person may be appointed to act as one or more of the following:

- the children's guardian;
- the reporting officer; and
- the children and family reporter.

PART 9 PROCEDURE: FP(A)R 2005, RULES 86–96

7.86 An applicant may use the Part 9 procedure if the application is made:

(1) in the course of existing proceedings;
(2) to commence proceedings other than those to which Part 5 applies; or
(3) in connection with proceedings which have concluded.

7.87 The Part 9 procedure does not apply to applications under:

- ACA 2002, s 60(3) (order to prevent disclosure of information to an adopted person);
- ACA 2002, s 79(4) (order for Registrar General to give any information referred to in s 79(3));

- FP(A)R 2005, r 27 (a request to dispense with consent);
- FP(A)R 2005, r 59(2) (appointment of children's guardian);
- FP(A)R 2005, r 84 (disclosure of information to an adopted child);
- FP(A)R 2005, r 106 (withdrawal of application);
- FP(A)R 2005, r 107 (recovery orders).

It also does not apply if a practice direction provides that the Part 9 procedure may not be used in relation to the type of application in question.[1]

7.88 The *Practice Direction – Other Applications in Proceedings* provides that all applications for the court's permission should be made under Part 9 (save for applications for permission to change a child's surname or remove a child from the jurisdiction, which should be made under Part 5). This will include:

(1) permission to apply for a contact order under s 26(3)(f);
(2) permission to apply for an adoption order under s 42(6); and
(3) leave to oppose the making of an adoption order under s 47(3), (5) and (7).

7.89 The following persons are to be respondents:[2]

- where there are existing proceedings or the proceedings have concluded, the parties to those proceedings;
- where there are no existing proceedings:
  (i) the local authority to whom notice has been given under ACA 2002, s 44 (notice of intention to adopt),
  (ii) if an application is made under s 26(3)(f) (permission to apply for a contact order) or s 42(6) (permission to apply for an adoption order), any person who will be a party under r 23 if permission is granted,
  (iii) any other person the court may direct.

7.90 The applicant must file an application notice (unless permitted by a rule or practice direction not to do so, or the court dispenses with the requirement):[3]

- An application notice (which may be in Form FP2[4]) must be signed and state (i) the order the applicant is seeking, and (ii) briefly, why the applicant is seeking the order,[5] together with the matters set out in the Practice Direction, para 2.1 and, where the notice relates to an application under s 42(6), the matters set out in para 2.2.
- When he files the application notice he must file a copy of any written evidence in support.[6]
- A copy will be served on each respondent, together with any written evidence in support.[7]

---

1 FP(A)R 2005, r 86(3).
2 FP(A)R 2005, r 86(4).
3 FP(A)R 2005, r 87.
4 *Practice Direction – Forms.*
5 FP(A)R 2005, r 90.
6 FP(A)R 2005, r 91(2).
7 FP(A)R 2005, r 88.

- The exception to service on each respondent is where this is permitted by a rule or practice direction or the court[1] (see below).
- The contents of an application notice may be used as evidence, provided the contents have been verified by a statement of truth.[2]

7.91 Under FP(A)R 2005, r 91, the court officer will serve a copy of the application notice as soon as practicable after it is filed, and in any event at least 7 days before the court is to deal with the application. It will be accompanied by:

(a) a notice of the date and place where the application will be heard;
(b) a copy of any witness statement in support; and
(c) a copy of any draft order.[3]

7.92 An application may be made without the court officer serving an application notice only:[4]

- where there is exceptional gravity;
- where the overriding objective is best furthered by doing so;
- by the consent of the parties;
- with the permission of the court;
- where para 2.10 applies (see below);
- where a rule or practice direction permits.

7.93 Where the court permits an application to be made without service of the application notice and makes an order granting or dismissing the application, a copy of the application notice and any evidence in support will be served with the order on all the parties to the proceedings.[5] The order must contain a statement of the right to make an application to set aside or vary the order.[6] An application to set aside or vary under r 94 must be made within 7 days beginning with the date on which the order was served on the person making the application.

7.94 The court may deal with an application without a hearing if:

(1) the parties agree as to the terms of the order;
(2) the parties agree that the court should dispose of the application without a hearing; or
(3) the court does not consider that it would be appropriate.[7]

7.95 The parties to an application for a consent order must ensure that they provide the court with any material it needs to be satisfied that it is appropriate to make the order. A letter will generally be acceptable for this purpose.[8] Where a judgment or

---

1 FP(A)R 2005, r 88(2).
2 FP(A)R 2005, r 90(2); *Practice Direction – Other Applications in Proceedings*, para 8.7.
3 FP(A)R 2005, r 91(3).
4 *Practice Direction – Other Applications in Proceedings*, para 3.
5 FP(A)R 2005, r 93(1) and (2).
6 FP(A)R 2005, r 93(3).
7 FP(A)R 2005, r 92.
8 *Practice Direction – Other Applications in Proceedings*, para 9.1.

order has been agreed in respect of an application where a hearing date has been fixed, the parties must inform the court immediately.[1]

7.96 Where the parties agree that the court should dispose of the application without a hearing, they should inform the court in writing and each should confirm that all evidence and any other material on which he relies has been disclosed to the other parties.[2]

7.97 Where the court does not consider it would be appropriate to deal with an application without a hearing, the court will treat the application as if it were proposing to make an order of its own initiative.[3]

7.98 On receipt of an application notice containing a request for a hearing, unless the court considers that the application is suitable for consideration without a hearing, the court officer will notify the applicant of the time and date fixed for the hearing.[4]

7.99 Where an application notice requests that the application be dealt with without a hearing and the court considers this to be suitable, the court officer will inform the applicant and the respondents of the court's decision and may give directions for the filing of evidence.[5]

7.100 Where the court does not agree that the application is suitable for consideration without a hearing, it may give directions as to the filing of evidence and the court officer will notify the applicant and the respondent of the time, date and place for the hearing of the application.[6]

7.101 The parties must anticipate that at any hearing the court may wish to review the conduct of the case as a whole and give any necessary directions. They must be ready to assist the court in doing so and to answer questions the court may ask for this purpose.[7]

7.102 Under the *Practice Direction – Other Applications in Proceedings*, para 2.10, where the date of a hearing has been fixed and a party wishes to make an application but does not have sufficient time to file an application notice, he should inform the court (if possible in writing) and, if possible, the other parties as soon as he can of the nature of the application and the reason for it. He should then make the application orally at the hearing.[8]

7.103 Where the applicant or any respondent fails to attend the hearing of an application, the court may proceed in his absence and, where the court makes an order,

---

1 *Practice Direction – Other Applications in Proceedings*, para 9.2.
2 *Practice Direction – Other Applications in Proceedings*, para 10.1.
3 *Practice Direction – Other Applications in Proceedings*, para 10.2.
4 *Practice Direction – Other Applications in Proceedings*, para 2.3.
5 *Practice Direction – Other Applications in Proceedings*, paras 2.4 and 2.5.
6 *Practice Direction – Other Applications in Proceedings*, para 2.6.
7 *Practice Direction – Other Applications in Proceedings*, para 2.9.
8 *Practice Direction – Other Applications in Proceedings*, para 2.10.

it may, on application or its own initiative, re-list the application.[1] This is in addition to any other powers of the court with regard to the order (for example, to set aside, vary, discharge or suspend the order).[2]

7.104 Save for the most simple applications the applicant should bring to any hearing a draft of the order sought. If the case is in the High Court and the order is unusually long or complex, it should also be supplied on disk for use by the court office.[3]

7.105 Attention should also be drawn to CPR, r 44.13(i), which provides that if an order makes no mention of costs, none are payable in respect of the proceedings to which it relates.

7.106 The court or court officer should keep, either by way of a note or a tape recording, the brief details of all proceedings before the court, including the dates of the proceedings and a short statement of the decision taken at each hearing.[4]

7.107 If the High Court or a county court dismisses the application (including an application for permission to appeal) and it considers the application totally without merit, the court must record that fact and at the same time consider whether it is appropriate to make a *civil restraint order*.[5]

7.108 'A civil restraint order' means an order restraining a party from:

(1) making any further applications in current proceedings ('a limited restraint order');
(2) making certain applications in specified courts ('an extended civil restraint order'); or
(3) making any application in specified courts ('a general civil restraint order').

7.109 The *Practice Direction – Civil Restraint Orders* sets out:

(1) The circumstances in which the court has the power to make a civil restraint order against a party:
　－　a limited restraint order may be made by a judge or district judge of the High Court or a county court where a party has made two or more applications which are totally without merit;
　－　an extended civil restraint order may be made by a judge of the High Court where a party has persistently made applications which are totally without merit;
　－　a general civil restraint order may be made by a judge of the High Court where the party against whom the order is made persists in making applications which are totally without merit in circumstances where an extended civil restraint order would not be sufficient or appropriate.

1　FP(A)R 2005, r 95.
2　*Practice Direction – Other Applications in Proceedings*, para 11.2.
3　*Practice Direction – Other Applications in Proceedings*, para 11.1.
4　*Practice Direction – Other Applications in Proceedings*, para 7.
5　FP(A)R 2005, r 96.

(2) The procedure where the party applies for a civil restraint order against another party.
(3) The consequences of the court making a civil restraint order.

7.110 The *Practice Direction – Other Applications in Proceedings* also deals with:

– telephone hearings: para 5;
– video conferencing: para 6.

PART 10 PROCEDURE: FP(A)R 2005, RULES 97–105

7.111 The Part 10 procedure may be used where the procedure in Part 9 does not apply and:

– there is no form prescribed by a rule or practice direction, in which to make the application; or
– the applicant seeks the court's decision on a question which is unlikely to involve a substantial dispute of facts; or
– a rule or practice direction may, in relation to a specified type of proceedings:
   (a) require or permit the use of the Part 10 procedure; and
   (b) disapply or modify any rules set out in Part 10 as they apply to those proceedings (where it does modify or disapply the Part 10 procedure, it is the practice directions which must be complied with).

7.112 The *Practice Direction – Alternative Procedure for Applications* specifies that the Part 10 procedure must be used for an order under:

– ACA 2002, s 60(3), to prevent disclosure of information to an adopted person;
– ACA 2002, s 79(4), to require the Registrar General to provide information (where the Registrar is the respondent); or
– FP(A)R 2005, r 108, to request the directions of the High Court regarding fathers without parental responsibility.[1]

Applications under FP(A)R 2005, r 108 and ACA 2002, s 60(3) may be issued without naming a respondent.[2]

7.113 The Practice Direction identifies the type of application for which the Part 10 procedure may be used as including an application for an order or direction which is unopposed by each respondent before the commencement of proceedings where the sole purpose is to obtain the approval of the court to the agreement.[3]

7.114 The Part 10 procedure does not apply to applications under:[4]

– r 27 (request to dispense with consent);

---

1 FP(A)R 2005, r 105.
2 *Practice Direction – Alternative Procedure for Applications*, para 2.2.
3 *Practice Direction – Alternative Procedure for Applications*, para 1.5.
4 FP(A)R 2005, r 97(4).

- r 59(2) (appointment of children's guardian);
- r 84 (disclosure of information to an adopted child);
- r 106 (withdrawal of an application);
- r 107 (recovery orders); or
- if a practice direction provides that the Part 10 procedure may not be used in relation to the type of application in question.

7.115 The court has the discretion at any stage to direct that the application is to continue as if the applicant had not used the Part 10 procedure and, if it does, the court may give any directions it considers appropriate.[1]

7.116 Where an applicant uses the Part 10 procedure, the application form Form FP1 (Form FP1A and FP1B set out the notes for applicants and respondents) should be used and must state the matters set out in r 98, namely:

(a) that Part 10 applies;
(b) the question which the applicant wants the court to decide or the order which the applicant is seeking and the legal basis of the application for that order;
(c) if the application is being made under an enactment, what that is;
(d) if the applicant is applying in a representative capacity, what that capacity is; and
(e) if the respondent appears in a representative capacity, what that is.

7.117 The court officer will serve a copy of the application on the respondent.[2]

7.118 Under FP(A)R 2005, r 102, the applicant must file written evidence on which he intends to rely when he files his application, which the court officer will serve on the respondent with the application.[3] Evidence will normally be in the form of a witness statement or an affidavit, but the applicant may rely on the matters set out in his application as evidence if the application is verified by a statement of truth.[4]

7.119 Each respondent must file an acknowledgement of service within 14 days beginning with the date on which the application is served, which the court officer will then serve on the applicant and any other party.[5] The acknowledgement of service should be in Form FP5, but can alternatively be given in an informal document such as a letter.[6]

7.120 The acknowledgement of service must:

(a) state whether the respondent contests the application;
(b) state if the respondent seeks a different order from that set out in the application, what that order is; and
(c) be signed by the respondent or his legal representative.[7]

---

1 FP(A)R 2005, r 97(3).
2 FP(A)R 2005, r 98(3).
3 FP(A)R 2005, r 102(2).
4 FP(A)R 2005, r 102(7); *Practice Direction – Alternative Procedure for Applications*, para 5.2.
5 FP(A)R 2005, r 100.
6 *Practice Direction – Alternative Procedure for Applications*, para 3.1.
7 FP(A)R 2005, r 100(4).

7.121 If the respondent fails to file an acknowledgement of service and the time period expires for doing so, the respondent must attend the hearing of the application but may not take part without the court's permission.[1]

7.122 If the respondent wishes to rely upon written evidence, he must, under FP(A)R 2005, r 102(3), file it when he files his acknowledgment of service.

7.123 Where a respondent objects to the use of the Part 10 procedure because (i) there is a substantial dispute of fact, and (ii) the use of Part 10 procedure is not required or permitted by a rule or practice direction, then he must state his reasons when he files the acknowledgment of service.[2]

7.124 The applicant may, within 14 days beginning with the date on which a respondent's evidence was served on him, file further written evidence in reply, which the court officer will serve on the other parties.[3]

7.125 No written evidence can be relied upon at the hearing unless it has been served in accordance with FP(A)R 2005, r 102, or the court gives permission. The court has a discretion as to whether to require or permit oral evidence at the hearing. It may also give directions requiring the attendance for cross-examination of a witness who has given written evidence.[4]

7.126 The court may give directions immediately after a Part 10 application is issued, either on the application of a party or on its own initiative. The directions may include fixing a hearing date where there is no dispute, or where there may be a dispute but a hearing date could conveniently be given.[5] Where the court does not fix a hearing date, it will give directions for the disposal of the application as soon as practicable after each respondent has acknowledged service of the application, or after the period for acknowledging service has expired.[6]

EXPERTS

7.127 FP(A)R 2005, Part 17 deals with experts. Rule 154 imposes a duty to restrict expert evidence to that which is reasonably required to resolve the proceedings.

7.128 Part 17 is, therefore, intended to limit the use of oral expert evidence to that which is reasonably required.[7] In addition, where possible, matters requiring expert evidence should be dealt with by a single expert. Permission of the court is always required, either to call an expert or to put an expert's report in evidence.

---

1 FP(A)R 2005, r 101.
2 FP(A)R 2005, r 104.
3 FP(A)R 2005, r 102(5) and (6).
4 FP(A)R 2005, r 103.
5 *Practice Direction – Alternative Procedure for Applications*, para 4.1.
6 *Practice Direction – Alternative Procedure for Applications*, paras 4.1 and 4.2.
7 *Practice Direction – Experts*.

7.129 The expert's overriding duty is to help the court on the matters within his expertise (FP(A)R 2005, r 156). It is a duty which overrides any obligation to the person from whom he has received instructions or by whom he is paid. Thus:

(1) Expert evidence should be the independent product of the expert uninfluenced by the pressures of litigation.[1]
(2) The expert should assist the court by providing objective, unbiased opinion upon matters within his expertise and should not assume the role of advocate.
(3) An expert should make clear (i) when a question or issue falls outside his expertise and (ii) when he is not able to reach a definite opinion (eg because he has insufficient information).
(4) If, after producing the report, the expert changes his mind on any material matter, such a change of view must be communicated to all parties without delay and, when appropriate, to the court.

7.130 No party may call or put in evidence an expert's report without the court's permission.[2] When applying for permission, the party must identify (i) the field in which he wishes to rely on expert evidence and (ii) where practicable, the expert in that field. The permission will only relate to the expert named or the field identified.

7.131 Expert evidence is to be given in a written report[3] (unless the court directs otherwise).

7.132 The expert's report must comply with the requirements set out in the *Practice Direction – Experts*.[4] It must state the substance of all material instructions (whether written or oral) on the basis of which the report was written. The report should be addressed to the court and not to the party from whom he has received his instructions. It must:[5]

– give details of the expert's qualifications;
– give details of any literature or other material which the expert has relied upon in making the report;
– contain a statement setting out the substance of the facts and instructions given to the expert which are material to the opinions expressed in the report or upon which those opinions are based;
– make clear which of the facts stated in the report are within the expert's own knowledge;
– say who carried out any examination, measurement, test or experiment which the expert has used for the report, give the qualifications of that person and say whether or not the test or experiment has been carried out under the expert's supervision;
– where there is a range of opinion, summarise the range and give reasons for his own opinion;

---

1 *Practice Direction – Experts*, paras 1.2–1.6.
2 FP(A)R 2005, r 157.
3 FP(A)R 2005, r 158.
4 FP(A)R 2005, r 163.
5 *Practice Direction – Experts*, para 2.2.

- contain a summary of the conclusions reached;
- if he is not able to give his opinion without qualification, state the qualification; and
- contain a statement that the expert understands his duty to the court and has complied with it and will continue to comply with it;

7.133 The report must be verified by a statement of truth as follows:

'I confirm that insofar as the facts stated in my report are within my own knowledge, I have made clear which they are and I believe them to be true, and that the opinions I have expressed represent my true and complete professional opinion.'

7.134 The court may under r 162 direct a party with access to information, which is not reasonably available to another party, to prepare and file a document which records the information. It must include sufficient details of all the facts, tests and assumptions which underlie the information, so as to enable the other party to make or obtain a proper interpretation of the information and an assessment of its significance. The court officer will send a copy of this document to the other party.

7.135 The instructions given to the expert are not privileged against disclosure.[1] Cross-examination of the expert on the contents of his instructions will not be allowed unless the court permits it (or unless the party who gave the instructions consents to it).[2] Before it gives permission, the court must be satisfied that there are reasonable grounds to consider that the statement in the report of the substance of the instructions is inaccurate or incomplete. If the court is so satisfied, it will allow the cross-examination where it appears in the interest of justice to do so.

7.136 A party may put to an expert instructed by another party or a single joint expert written questions about his report.[3] Written questions:

- may only be put once;
- must be put not later than 5 days after receipt of the report; and
- must be for the purpose only of clarification of the report.[4]

7.137 The expert's answers to written questions shall be treated as part of the expert's report. Where a party puts a question to an expert instructed by another party and does not get an answer, the court may order that the party who instructed the expert may not rely on the evidence of that expert, or that the party may not recover the fees and expenses of that expert from any other party.[5]

7.138 Under FP(A)R 2005, r 160, the court has a power to direct that evidence be given by a single joint expert, where two or more parties ('the instructing parties') wish to submit evidence on a particular issue.

---

1 FP(A)R 2005, r 163(4).
2 *Practice Direction – Experts*, para 4.
3 FP(A)R 2005, r 159.
4 FP(A)R 2005, r 159(2).
5 FP(A)R 2005, r 159(4).

7.139 Where the instructing parties cannot agree who should be the expert, the court may select the expert from a list prepared or identified by the instructing parties, or direct that the expert be selected in such a manner as the court directs. Where a direction for a single joint expert is made, each instructing party may give instructions to the expert and at the same time send a copy of the instructions to the other instructing parties.[1]

7.140 Where the court has directed that the evidence on a particular issue is to be given by one expert only, but there are a number of disciplines relevant to that issue, a leading expert in the dominant discipline should be identified as the single expert. He should prepare the general part of the report and be responsible for annexing or incorporating the contents of any reports from experts in other disciplines.[2]

7.141 The court may give directions about the payment of the expert's fees and expenses and any inspection, examination or experiments which the expert wishes to carry out. The court may limit the amount of fees and expenses before an expert is instructed. The instructing parties are jointly and severally liable for the payment of the expert's fees and expenses.

7.142 Where a party has disclosed an expert's report, any party may use that report as evidence at the final hearing.[3]

7.143 At any stage the court may direct a discussion between experts for the purpose of requiring the experts to identify and discuss the expert issues and, where possible, reach an agreed opinion.[4] It may specify the issues which the experts must discuss, and may direct that, following the discussion, the experts must prepare a statement showing the issues on which they agree and those on which they disagree and a summary of their reasons for disagreeing.

7.144 A party who fails to disclose an expert's report may not use the report at the final hearing or call the expert to give evidence orally (unless the court directs otherwise).[5]

7.145 The expert may file a written request for directions to assist him in carrying out his function as an expert.[6] He must provide a copy of the request to the party instructing him at least 7 days before he files the request, and to all other parties at least 4 days before he files it.

---

1 FP(A)R 2005, r 161.
2 *Practice Direction – Experts*, para 6.
3 FP(A)R 2005, r 164.
4 FP(A)R 2005, r 165.
5 FP(A)R 2005, r 166.
6 FP(A)R 2005, r 167.

APPEALS

7.146 FP(A)R 2005, Part 19 applies to appeals to the High Court and county court, but not to an appeal in detailed assessment proceedings against a decision of an authorised court officer.[1] 'Appeal' includes an appeal by way of case stated.

7.147 Appeals to the Court of Appeal are governed by CPR, Part 52.

7.148 All parties must comply with the *Practice Direction – Appeals*.[2] The following table sets out to which court or judge an appeal is to be made (subject to obtaining any necessary permission):

Decision of …	Appeal made to …
Magistrates' court	High Court
District judge of a county court	Circuit judge
District judge of High Court	High Court judge
District judge of the principal registry of the Family Division	High Court judge
Costs judge	High Court judge
Circuit judge or recorder	Court of Appeal
High Court judge	Court of Appeal

Grounds

7.149 Under FP(A)R 2005, r 181(3) the appeal court will allow an appeal where the decision of the lower court was:

(a) wrong, or
(b) unjust because of a serious procedural or other irregularity in the proceedings in the lower court.

Permission

7.150 Under FP(A)R 2005, r 173 an appellant or respondent requires permission to appeal (a) against a decision in assessment proceedings relating to costs where the decision appealed against was made by a district judge or a costs judge (ie taxing master of the Supreme Court), or (b) as provided by the *Practice Direction – Appeals*.[3]

---

1 FP(A)R 2005, r 171. CPR, rr 47.20 to 47.23 deal with appeals in detailed assessment proceedings.
2 FP(A)R 2005, r 172.
3 FP(A)R 2005, r 173.

7.151 Permission to appeal will only be given where (i) the court considers that the appeal would have a real prospect of success, or (ii) there is some other compelling reason why the appeal should be heard.[1]

7.152 An application for permission to appeal may be made to the lower court (ie the court from whose decision the appeal is sought), if that court is a county court or the High Court, (i) at the hearing at which the decision to be appealed was made, or (ii) to the appeal court in an appeal notice. Where the lower court refuses an application for permission to appeal, a further application for permission to appeal may be made to the appeal court.

7.153 Applications for permission to appeal may be considered by the appeal court without a hearing. Where the appeal court refuses permission to appeal without a hearing, the person seeking permission may request the decision to be reconsidered at the hearing, provided the request is filed within 7 days beginning with the date on which notice that permission has been refused was served.

7.154 Where a represented appellant requests that the decision be reconsidered at an oral hearing, his advocate must, at least 4 days before the hearing, in a brief written statement:

(a) inform the court and the respondent of the points which he proposes to raise at the hearing;
(b) set out his reasons why permission should be granted, notwithstanding the reasons given for the refusal of permission; and
(c) confirm, where applicable, that the appellant is in receipt of services funded by the Legal Services Commission.[2]

7.155 Where the appellant or the respondent seeks permission from the appeal court, the request must be made in the appeal notice (r 174(1) and r 175(3)).

7.156 Any order giving permission may:

(a) limit the issues to be heard; and
(b) be made the subject of conditions.[3]

Appellant's/respondent's notices

7.157 The appellant must file the following documents, together with an appeal bundle with his appellant's notice:[4]

– two additional copies of the appellant's notice;
– one copy of the appellant's notice for each of the respondents;

---

1 FP(A)R 2005, r 173(6).
2 *Practice Direction – Appeals*, paras 4.9 and 4.12.
3 FP(A)R 2005, r 173(7).
4 *Practice Direction – Appeals*, para 5.8.

- one copy of his skeleton argument for each copy of the notice filed (*Practice Direction – Appeals*, paras 5.13–5.22 deal with the contents of skeleton arguments);
- a sealed or stamped copy of the order being appealed;
- a copy of any order giving or refusing permission to appeal, together with a copy of the judge's reasons; and
- any witness statements or affidavits in support.

7.158 In his appeal bundle the appellant must include:[1]

- a sealed or stamped copy of the appellant's notice;
- a sealed or stamped copy of the order being appealed;
- a copy of any order giving or refusing permission to appeal, together with the judge's reasons;
- any affidavit or witness statement filed in support;
- a copy of the skeleton argument;
- a transcript or note of the judgment or, in the magistrates' court, written reasons for the court's decision;
- the application form;
- any relevant application notice (or case management document);
- any other document which the appellant reasonably considers necessary to enable the appeal court to reach its decision, or which the court may direct.

7.159 Rules 174 and 175 set out the time limits for the filing and serving of an appellant's notice and a respondent's notice. The appeal notice may not be amended without the permission of the appeal court.[2]

7.160 A respondent who wishes to ask the appeal court to vary the lower court's order must appeal, and permission will be required on the same basis as for an appellant.

Procedure after permission is obtained

7.161 Where the permission to appeal is given by the appeal court, or the appellant's notice is filed in the appeal court and permission was given by the lower court, or is not required, the appeal bundle must be served on each of the respondents within 7 days beginning with the date that the order giving permission to appeal is made.[3] The court officer will effect service.

7.162 The appeal court will send to the parties:

(1) notification of the date of the hearing or listing window during which the appeal is likely to be heard;

---

1 *Practice Direction – Appeals*, para 5.9.
2 FP(A)R 2005, r 178.
3 *Practice Direction – Appeals*, paras 6.1 and 6.2.

(2) where permission is granted by the appeal court, a copy of the order giving permission; and
(3) any other directions given by the court.[1]

7.163 Where the appeal court grants permission to appeal, the appellant must add the following documents to the appeal bundle:

(a) the respondent's notice and skeleton argument (if any);
(b) those parts of the transcripts of evidence which are directly related to any question at issue on the appeal;
(c) the order granting permission to appeal and, where permission was granted at an oral hearing, the transcript or note of any judgment given; and
(d) any document which the appellant and respondent have agreed to add.[2]

7.164 If the appellant is legally represented, the appeal court must be notified in writing of the advocate's time estimate for the hearing of the appeal (ie the advocate who will argue the appeal). It should exclude the time required by the court to give judgment.[3] The appellant's time estimate will be notified to the respondent and, if he disagrees, he must inform the court within 7 days of the notification.

The appeal

7.165 An appeal does not operate as a stay of any order or decision of the lower court (unless the appeal court or the lower court, other than the magistrates' court, orders otherwise).[4]

7.166 Where there is a compelling reason for doing so, the court may:

(a) strike out the whole or part of an appeal notice;
(b) set aside permission to appeal in whole or in part; or
(c) impose or vary conditions upon which an appeal may be brought.[5]

Where, however, a party was present at the hearing at which permission was given, he may not subsequently apply for an order to set aside the permission, or impose or vary any conditions attached to it.

7.167 The appeal court has all the powers of the lower court in relation to the appeal.[6] It may:

(a) affirm, set aside or vary any order or judgment made or given by the lower court in whole or in part;
(b) refer any application or issue for determination by the lower court;
(c) order a new hearing;

---

1 *Practice Direction – Appeals*, para 6.3.
2 *Practice Direction – Appeals*, para 6.4.
3 *Practice Direction – Appeals*, paras 6.6–6.8.
4 FP(A)R 2005, r 177.
5 FP(A)R 2005, r 179.
6 FP(A)R 2005, r 180.

(d) make orders for the payment of interest; and
(e) make a costs order.

7.168 If the appeal court (i) refuses an application for permission to appeal, or (ii) strikes out the appellant's notice, or (iii) dismisses the appeal, and it considers that the application or the appellant's notice or the appeal were totally without merit, then:[1]

(a) the court's order must record that fact; and
(b) the court must at the same time consider whether it is appropriate to make a civil restraint order (see FP(A)R 2005, r 16 above).

7.169 Under FP(A)R 2005, r 181 every appeal will be limited to a review of the decision of the lower court (unless (i) a practice direction makes different provision, or (ii) the court considers that in the circumstances of an individual appeal it would be in the interests of justice to hold a rehearing). Furthermore:

– The appeal court will not receive oral evidence or evidence which was not before the lower court (unless it orders otherwise).
– It may draw any inference of fact which it considers justified on the evidence.
– A party may not rely on any matter not contained in his appeal notice, unless the appeal court gives permission.

7.170 The court from or to which an appeal is made, or from which permission to appeal is sought ('the relevant court'), may order the appeal to be transferred to the Court of Appeal,[2] where it considers that:

(a) an appeal which is to be heard by a county court or the High Court would raise an important point of principle or practice; or
(b) there is some other compelling reason for the Court of Appeal to hear it.

7.171 The High Court will not reopen a final determination of any appeal (including an application for permission to appeal) unless:

(a) it is necessary to do so in order to avoid real injustice;
(b) the circumstances are exceptional and make it appropriate to reopen the appeal; and
(c) there is no alternative effective remedy.[3]

7.172 Permission is needed to make an application to reopen a final determination (the procedure is set out in *Practice Direction – Appeals*). Moreover:

– There is no right to an oral hearing of an application for permission unless, exceptionally, the judge so directs.
– The judge must direct that the application be served on the other party to the original appeal and give him the opportunity to make representations.

---

1   FP(A)R 2005, r 180(4) and (5).
2   FP(A)R 2005, r 182. Under s 57 of the Access to Justice Act 1999 the Master of the Rolls has the power to direct that an appeal be heard by the Court of Appeal instead of the county court or the High Court.
3   FP(A)R 2005, r 183.

– There is no right of appeal or review from the decision of the judge on the application for permission, which is final.

Rule 183 does not apply to appeals to the county court.

7.173 Where the appeal lies to the High Court from a decision of the magistrates' court, the appellant's notice must be filed in:

(a) the principal registry of the Family Division; or

(b) the district registry, being in the same place as an adoption centre or an intercountry adoption centre, which is nearest to the court from which the appeal lies.[1]

7.174 In appeals from district judges of the High Court, the appeal and application for permission may be given by a High Court judge or any person authorised under s 9 of the Supreme Court Act 1981 to act as a judge of the High Court.[2]

7.175 The Designated Family Judge in consultation with the Family Division Liaison Judges has responsibility for allocating appeals from the decision of district judges to circuit judges.[3]

7.176 Where an appellant does not wish to pursue his appeal, he may request an order that his appeal be dismissed:[4]

(1) The request must state whether the appellant is a child, non-subject child or a patient.

(2) The request must be accompanied by a consent signed by the other parties stating whether the respondent is a child, a non-subject child, or a patient and whether he consents to the dismissal of the application or appeal.

(3) Where the application relates to an appeal from the magistrates' court, it may be heard by a district judge of the appeal court.

7.177 Although the appeal court will not normally make an order allowing an appeal unless satisfied that the decision of the lower court was wrong, it may set aside or vary the order with consent and without determining the merits of the appeal, if it is satisfied that there are good and sufficient reasons for doing so.[5]

7.178 An application to withdraw an appeal from the decision of a magistrates' court may be heard by a district judge of the appeal court.[6]

---

1 *Practice Direction – Appeals*, paras 8.1–8.2.
2 *Practice Direction – Appeals*, para 8.4.
3 *Practice Direction – Appeals*, para 8.5.
4 *Practice Direction – Appeals*, paras 10.1–10.3.
5 *Practice Direction – Appeals*, para 11.
6 *Practice Direction – Appeals*, para 12.

COSTS

7.179 The court may at any time make such order as to costs as it thinks fit, including an order relating to the payment of expenses incurred by any officer of the Service or a Welsh family proceedings officer.[1]

7.180 Parts 43, 44 (except r 44.3(2), (3) and r 44.9–44.12A), 47 and 48 as well as r 45.6 of the CPR apply to costs in proceedings: FP(A)R 2005, r 5(3).

SOME SIGNPOSTS TO OTHER RULES

7.181

(1) Court documents: FP(A)R 2005, Part 2, r 9(4) and *Practice Direction – Court Documents*.
(2) Evidence: see FP(A)R 2005, Part 15 and *Practice Direction – Evidence*, including:
  – Making an admission (r 122).
  – Power of court to control evidence (r 123).
  – Evidence of witnesses (r 124).
  – Evidence by video link (r 125; *Practice Direction – Evidence*, Annex 3).
  – Evidence in proceedings other than the final hearing (r 128).
  – Cross-examination (rr 129 and 132).
  – Form of witness statement (r 130; *Practice Direction – Evidence*, paras 17–23).
  – Witness summaries (r 131).
  – False statements (r 133).
  – Affidavit evidence (r 134; *Practice Direction – Evidence*, paras 2–10).
  – Use of plans and photographs as evidence (r 138).
(3) Witnesses, depositions and evidence for foreign courts: see FP(A)R 2005, Part 16; *Practice Direction – Depositions and Court Attendance*.
(4) Service: see FP(A)R 2005, Part 6 and *Practice Direction – Service*.
(5) Human Rights Act 1998 claims: see FP(A)R 2005, Part 13; *Practice Direction – Human Rights, Joining the Crown*.
(6) Interim injunctions: see FP(A)R 2005, Part 14; *Practice Direction – Interim Injunctions* and *Practice Direction – Forms*, Form FP3.
(7) Disputing the court's jurisdiction: see FP(A)R 2005, Part 12.
(8) Change of solicitor: see FP(A)R 2005, Part 18; *Practice Direction – Change of Solicitor* and Form FP8.

---

1 FP(A)R 2005, r 110.

Chapter 8

ADOPTION AGENCIES

8.1 ACA 2002 provides a structure for an 'adoption service'. Although largely modelled on AA 1976, there are some key new measures which are designed to encourage more people to come forward as adopters. These include:

(1) a duty on a local authority to make arrangements for the provision of adoption support services;[1]

(2) a new right to request and receive an assessment of needs for adoption support services;[2]

(3) the establishment of an independent body to review qualifying adoption agency determinations.[3]

8.2 Under ACA 2002, s 3 each local authority must continue to maintain within its area an adoption service designed to meet the needs of (i) children who may be adopted, their parents and guardians, (ii) persons wishing to adopt a child, and (iii) adopted persons, their parents, natural parents and former guardians. This is a wider group than under the former law, which did not include adopted adults, their birth or adopted parents or former guardians.

8.3 These services are collectively referred to as 'the Adoption Service'.[4] An 'adoption agency' refers either to a local authority or to a registered adoption society.[5]

THE ADOPTION AGENCIES REGULATIONS 2005

8.4 The Adoption Agencies Regulations 2005 (AAR 2005) make provision for the exercise by the adoption agencies of their functions in relation to adoption under ACA 2002. They are an important backdrop to the functioning of the Act in the courts.

---

1 ACA 2002, s 3(2)(b).
2 ACA 2002, s 4.
3 ACA 2002, s 12.
4 ACA 2002, s 2(1).
5 ACA 2002, s 2(1).

Duties of an adoption agency where the agency is considering adoption: regulations 11 to 17

8.5 The adoption agency has to set up a 'child's case record' (reg 12) which includes:[1]

(a) the child's permanence report;
(b) a written record of the proceedings of the adoption panel under reg 18;
(c) a record of the agency's decision under reg 19;
(d) any consent to placement for adoption under ACA 2002, s 19 or any advance consent under s 20;
(e) any form or notice withdrawing consent or any notice under s 20(4)(a) and (b) (a copy of the notice under s 20(4)(a) and (b) must be sent to the court which gave notice of the issue of an application for an adoption order to the agency);
(f) a copy of a placement order.

8.6 The adoption agency is under a duty to provide, so far as is reasonably practicable:

(1) a counselling service for the child (a) explaining the legal implications of adoption and (b) ascertaining his wishes and feelings regarding:
  (i) placement for adoption with a new family,
  (ii) his religious and cultural upbringing, and
  (iii) contact with his parent or relative or other important person (reg 13);
(2) a counselling service for the parent (a) explaining the procedure and legal implications of giving consent under ss 19 and 20, placement orders and adoption, and (b) ascertaining his wishes and feelings regarding the child, placement and contact (reg 14).

The counselling service also applies to a father who does not have parental responsibility but whose identity is known to the adoption agency (reg 14(3) and (4)). In his case, the agency must ascertain whether the father wishes to obtain parental responsibility or to apply for residence or contact.

8.7 The agency is required to obtain the following information in respect of the child (reg 15):

(1) the information set out in AAR 2005, Sch 1, Part 1 (which includes his racial origins, cultural and linguistic background, a chronology of the child's care since birth, his educational history and information about his relationship with his parents, siblings, relatives and other important persons, and the arrangements for contact);
(2) the child's health report dealing with the matters set out in AAR 2005, Sch 1, Part 2.

8.8 The agency is also required to obtain in respect of the child's family (reg 16):

---

1 Regulations 39–44 deal with the preservation of, confidentiality of, access to and transfer of case records.

(1) information set out in AAR 2005, Sch 1, Part 3 about each parent, the child's siblings, relatives and other important persons, and the family history;
(2) in respect of an unmarried father, information as to whether he has acquired parental responsibility and, if his identity or whereabouts are not known, the information that has been ascertained and from whom, and the steps that have been taken to establish paternity (Sch 1, Part 3, paras 16 and 17);
(3) information about the health of each of the child's natural parents and his brothers and sisters, as set out in Sch 1, Part 3.

8.9 The agency must prepare in writing 'the child's permanence report' (reg 17), which must be sent to the adoption panel, and which includes:

(1) the views of the agency about the child's need for contact with his parent or relative or other important person, and the arrangements the agency proposes to make for allowing contact;
(2) an assessment of the child's emotional and behavioural and any related needs;
(3) an analysis of the options for the future care of the child which have been considered by the agency, and why placement for adoption is considered the preferred option.

Function of the adoption panel: regulation 18

8.10 The adoption panel is under a duty to consider the case of every child referred to it by the adoption agency and make a recommendation to the agency as to whether the child should be placed for adoption.

8.11 Regulations 3 to 10 deal with the constitution, tenure and meetings of the panel.[1]

8.12 In considering what recommendation to make, the panel must have regard to the duties imposed on the agency under ACA 2002, s 1(2), (4), (5) and (6) and the permanence report, and obtain legal advice.

8.13 Where the panel makes a recommendation that the child be placed for adoption, it must consider and may at the same time give advice to the agency about:

(1) contact arrangements;
(2) where the agency is a local authority, whether an application should be made by the authority for a placement order.

Adoption agency decision and notification: regulation 19

8.14 The agency must take into account the recommendation of the adoption panel in coming to a decision about whether the child should be placed for adoption. The

---

1 All members of an adoption panel established before 30 December 2005 (the 'old adoption panel') ceased to hold office and, with effect from 30 December 2005, the agency has to establish a new adoption panel.

agency must notify the parents in writing of its decision, if their whereabouts are known. Where the father does not have parental responsibility, but his identity is known (reg 14 (3)) and the agency considers it appropriate, the father must be notified of the decision.

CAFCASS/Welsh family proceedings officer: regulation 20

8.15 Where a parent is prepared to consent to the placement of the child for adoption or to give advance consent, the adoption agency must request CAFCASS to appoint an officer of the Service for the purposes of signifying the consents.

8.16 With the request, the agency must send to CAFCASS the information specified in AAR 2005, Sch 2, which includes:

(1) a certified copy of the child's birth certificate;
(2) the name and address of the child's parent;
(3) a chronology of actions and decisions taken by the adoption agency; and
(4) confirmation that the agency has counselled and explained to the parents the legal implications of consent.

Duties of an adoption agency in respect of a prospective adopter: regulations 21 to 30

8.17 Where an adoption agency is considering a person's suitability to adopt, the agency must provide a counselling service and explain the procedure and legal implications (reg 21).

8.18 Where the adoption agency receives an application in writing from a prospective adopter for an assessment of his suitability to adopt the child, the agency must set up 'the prospective adopter's case record' and consider his suitability to adopt a child (reg 22). The agency is required to carry out police checks (reg 23).

8.19 Where the agency is considering a person's suitability to adopt, the agency must make arrangements for the prospective adopter to receive 'preparation for adoption', which includes (reg 24) the provision of information to the prospective adopter about:

(a) the age range, sex, likely needs and background of the children who may be placed for adoption;
(b) the significance of adoption for a child and his family;
(c) contact between a child and his parent or other relatives where the child is authorised to be placed for adoption or is adopted;
(d) the skills which are necessary for an adoptive parent;
(e) the agency's procedures in relation to the assessment;
(f) the procedure in relation to placement for adoption and to adoption.

8.20 Where, following the procedures in regs 23 and 24, the agency considers the prospective adopter may be suitable to adopt the child, it must (under reg 25):

(1) obtain the information about the prospective adopter as set out in AAR 2005, Sch 4, Part 1, which includes personal details, a family history, the reasons for wishing to adopt, and his views and feelings about contact;
(2) obtain (i) a written report from a registered medical practitioner about the health of the prospective adopter and (ii) a written report of each of the interviews with persons nominated to provide personal references;
(3) ascertain whether the local authority in whose area the prospective adopter has his home has any relevant information about the prospective adopter and, if so, obtain a written report;
(4) prepare the 'prospective adopter's report' which will include the agency's assessment of the prospective adopter's suitability to adopt;
(5) notify the prospective adopter that his application is to be referred to the adoption panel, and give him a copy of the prospective adopter's report, inviting him to make observations within 10 working days, at the end of which the agency must send the reports and observations to the adoption panel.

8.21 It is the function of the adoption panel to consider the case and make a recommendation to the agency as to whether the prospective adopter is suitable to adopt (reg 26). It may also give advice to the agency about the number of children the prospective adopter may be suitable to adopt, their age range, sex, likely needs and background. Before making any recommendation, the panel must invite the prospective adopters to attend a meeting of the panel.

8.22 The adoption agency must make a decision about whether the prospective adopter is suitable to adopt a child (reg 27). If it decides to approve, it must notify the prospective adopter in writing of its decision. If it decides that the prospective adopter is not suitable to adopt a child, it must notify the prospective adopter in writing that it proposes not to approve him as suitable to adopt a child (a 'qualifying determination') and advise the prospective adopter as to his entitlement to apply to the Secretary of State for a review by an independent review panel of the qualifying determination (regs 27(4)–(10) and 28).

8.23 The adoption agency must review the approval of each prospective adopter whenever the agency considers it necessary but otherwise not more than one year after approval and thereafter at intervals of not more than a year (reg 29).

Duties of an adoption agency in respect of a proposed placement of a child with a prospective adopter: regulations 31 to 34

8.24 Where an adoption agency is considering placing a child for adoption with a particular adopter ('the proposed placement'), the agency must (reg 31):

(a) provide the prospective adopter with a copy of the child's permanence report;
(b) meet with the prospective adopter to discuss the proposed placement;
(c) ascertain the views of the prospective adopter about (i) the proposed placement and (ii) the arrangements the agency proposes to make for allowing any person contact with the child;
(d) provide a counselling service for the prospective adopter.

8.25 Where the agency considers that the proposed placement should proceed, the agency must (reg 31):

(a) where the agency is the local authority, carry out an assessment of the needs of the child, prospective adopter and any children of the prospective adopter ('the adoptive family') for adoption support services;[1]

(b) where the agency is a registered adoption society, notify the prospective adopter that he may request the local authority in whose area he has his home to carry out an assessment of his needs for adoption support services and pass to the authority a copy of the child's permanence report and a copy of the prospective adopter's report;

(c) consider the arrangements for allowing any person contact with the child;

(d) prepare an 'adoption placement report' which includes:
   (i) the agency's reasons for proposing placement, and
   (ii) the arrangements the agency proposes to make for allowing any person contact with the child.

8.26 The adoption agency must notify the prospective adopter that the proposed placement is to be referred to the adoption panel and give him a copy of the adoption placement report, inviting him to send any observations in writing to the agency within 10 working days.

8.27 At the end of 10 working days, the adoption agency must send the adoption placement report, the child's permanence report, and the prospective adopter's report and his observations to the adoption panel. The adoption panel must consider the proposed placement and make a recommendation to the agency as to whether the child should be placed for adoption with the particular prospective adopter (reg 32).

8.28 In considering what recommendation to make, the panel has to have regard to the duties imposed on the agency under ACA 2002, s 1(2), (4) and (5) and consider the reports. It must also consider and may give advice to the agency as to:

(1) where the agency is a local authority, the proposals for the provision of adoption support services for the adoptive family;

(2) the arrangements the agency proposes to make for allowing any person contact with the child;

(3) whether the parental responsibility of any parent should be restricted and, if so, the extent of any such restriction.

8.29 The adoption agency must take into account the adoption panel's recommendation and, as soon as possible after making the decision, the agency must notify in writing of its decision (reg 33):

(a) the prospective adopter;

(b) if their whereabouts are known to the agency, the parents.

---

1   See the Adoption Support Services (Local Authorities) (England) Regulations 2003 (and Guidance) and the Adoption Support Services Regulations 2005.

Where the father does not have parental responsibility but his identity is known, the father must be notified of the fact that his child is to be placed for adoption.

8.30 If the agency decides that the proposed placement should proceed, the agency must, in an appropriate manner and having regard to the child's age and understanding, explain its decision to the child and place on the child's case record:

(1) the prospective adopter's report;
(2) the adoption placement report and the prospective adopter's observations;
(3) the written record of the adoption panel proceedings, its recommendation and the reasons;
(4) the record and notification of the agency's decision.

Requirements imposed on the adoption agency before the child may be placed for adoption: regulation 35

8.31 Where the adoption agency has decided to place a child for adoption with a particular adopter (in accordance with reg 33) and has met with the prospective adopter to consider the arrangements it proposes to make for the placement of the child with him, the agency must send to the prospective adopters 'the adoption placement plan', which covers the matters set out in AAR 2005, Sch 5, including:

(1) the date on which it is proposed to place the child;
(2) whether parental responsibility is to be restricted;
(3) whether adoption services are to be provided for the adoptive family;
(4) the arrangements for contact and the dates on which the child's life story book and later life letter are to be passed to the prospective adopter.

8.32 Where the prospective adopter notifies the agency that he wishes to proceed and the agency is authorised to place the child for adoption, or the child is less than 6 weeks old, the agency may then place the child with the prospective adopter. Unless there is a placement order, the agency may not place a child who is less than 6 weeks old unless the parent has agreed in writing with the agency that the child may be placed for adoption. Where the child already has his home with the prospective adopter, the agency must notify the prospective adopter in writing of the date on which the child is 'placed for adoption' with him.

8.33 The agency must notify the prospective adopter of any changes to the adoption placement plan and place a copy of the plan and any changes on the child's case record.

Reviews: regulations 36 and 37

8.34 Where an adoption agency is authorised to place a child for adoption but the child is not for the time being placed for adoption, the agency must carry out a review of the child's case until the child is placed:

(a) not more than 3 months after the date on which the agency first has authority to place; and

(b) thereafter not more than 6 months after the date of the previous review ('6 months review').

8.35 Where the child is placed for adoption, the agency must carry out a review of the child's case, unless the child is returned to the agency by the prospective adopter or an adoption order is made:

(a) not more than 4 weeks after the date on which the child is placed for adoption ('the first review');
(b) not more than 3 months after the first review; and
(c) thereafter not more than 6 months after the date of the previous review.

8.36 When carrying out the review, the agency must ascertain the views of the child (having regard to his age and understanding), the prospective adopter and any other relevant person, and consider:

(1) whether the adoption agency remains satisfied that the child should be placed for adoption;
(2) the child's needs, welfare and development and whether any changes need to be made to meet his needs;
(3) the existing arrangements for contact and whether they should continue or be altered;
(4) where the child is placed for adoption, the arrangements in relation to the exercise of parental responsibility for the child and whether they should continue or be altered;
(5) the arrangements for adoption support services;
(6) in consultation with appropriate agencies, the arrangements for assessing the child's health care and educational needs;
(7) the frequency of reviews.

8.37 Where the child is subject to a placement order and has not been placed for adoption at the time of the first 6 months review, the local authority must at that review:

(a) establish why the child has not been placed for adoption and consider what further steps should be taken; and
(b) consider whether it remains satisfied that the child should be placed for adoption.

It must then notify the child, the prospective adopter and any other relevant person of the outcome of the review and any decision taken by the authority.

8.38 The adoption agency must, under reg 37, appoint an 'independent reviewing officer' (IRO) to carry out the functions set out in s 26A of CA 1989, who must ensure, as far as is reasonably practicable, that the review is conducted in accordance with reg 36 and, in particular, that:

(a) the child's views are understood and taken into account;
(b) the persons responsible for implementing any decision taken in consequence of the review are identified; and

(c) any failure to review the case or to take proper steps to make the arrangements agreed is brought to the attention of persons at an appropriate level of seniority within the adoption agency.

8.39 If the child wishes to take proceedings on his own account (eg apply for the revocation of a placement order), it is the function of the IRO (i) to assist the child to obtain legal advice or (ii) to establish whether an appropriate adult is able and willing to provide such assistance or bring proceedings on the child's behalf;

8.40 The agency must inform the IRO of (i) any significant failure to make the arrangements agreed at a review and (ii) any significant change in the child's circumstances after a review.

Withdrawal of consent

8.41 Regulation 38 is dealt with at **2.24–2.25**.

Contact

8.42 Regulations 46 and 47 are dealt with at **3.86 ff**.

THE SUITABILITY OF ADOPTERS REGULATIONS 2005

8.43 The Suitability of Adopters Regulations 2005 (SAR 2005) set out those matters to be taken into account by an adoption agency when determining or making any report about the suitability of prospective adopters to adopt a child. There are three main stages in the assessment of suitability of adopters:

(1) Obtaining and gathering information about the prospective adopters. This is provided for in the AAR 2005 (above) and the Adoption with a Foreign Element Regulations 2005 (AFER 2005).
(2) The second stage is the preparation of reports about the prospective adopters which will be considered by the adoption panel. SAR 2005 sets out what matters must be taken into account in preparing those reports
(3) The third stage is the making of a decision. SAR 2005 sets out the factors to be taken into account when making any decision about the suitability of prospective adopters

8.44 The intention of the regulations is to set out a framework which will address the changed circumstances of many modern adoptions:

– Most adoptions now are of children from the looked-after system who have been abused or neglected and whose birth parents do not consent.
– A small percentage of children each year have been brought from abroad for adoption and are therefore extremely vulnerable; additionally they often have significant health problems.

- The challenges such children present mean that prospective adopters must have a parenting capacity over and above that generally needed for parenting birth children.
- Even greater care than in the past is therefore needed in assessing prospective adopters.[1]

Assessment

8.45 Regulation 3 sets out the matters to be taken into account when preparing:

(1) the prospective adopters report (the report to the panel making a recommendation about suitability);
(2) a review report (a report to the adoption panel reviewing the suitability of the prospective adopter after a change of circumstances which may indicate the need for de-approval).

8.46 Those matters are:

(1) Information derived from the counselling of prospective adopters. The intention is to seek to ensure that those who make an application after counselling are really motivated and committed to the challenges of adoption.[2]
(2) Information obtained in the 'preparation for adoption' process. The intention is that those who continue after the preparation for adoption process are more likely to continue to the end of the process as a whole and be more able to care for adopted children.[3]
(3) Information from any enhanced criminal record certificate.[4]
(4) All the information in AAR 2005, Sch 5, Part 1.[5]
(5) Information obtained about a prospective adopter pursuant to AFER 2005, reg 15(4) as to the ability of the prospective adopter to care for a child from a foreign country where those regulations apply pursuant to AFER 2005, reg 12.[6]
(6) The written report from the medical practitioner.[7]
(7) The information from interviews with personal referees.[8]
(8) The information obtained from the local authority in whose area the prospective adopter has his home.[9]

8.47 The adoption agency may undertake a brief (ie truncated) assessment if it comes to the view at the time of application that the prospective adopter is unlikely to be suitable.[10]

---

1 The Full Regulatory Impact Assessment (RIA) for the SAR 2005.
2 SAR 2005, reg 3(a).
3 SAR 2005, reg 3(b).
4 SAR 2005, reg 3(c).
5 SAR 2005, reg 3(d).
6 SAR 2005, reg 3(e).
7 SAR 2005, reg 3(f)(i).
8 SAR 2005, reg 3(f)(ii).
9 SAR 2005, reg 3(f)(iii).
10 SAR 2005, reg 5.

Determinations and decisions

8.48 Regulation 4(1) sets out the matters the adoption agency must take into account in determining or making a decision about suitability. Those matters are:

(1) the prospective adopter's report;[1]
(2) the medical report;[2]
(3) the report of the personal interviews;[3]
(4) the recommendation of the adoption panel;[4]
(5) any other relevant information;[5]
(6) any additional information obtained about a prospective adopter as a consequence of AFER 2005, Part 3, Ch 1 where those regulations apply pursuant to AFER 2005, reg 12.[6]

Regulation 4(2)

8.49 ACA 2002 recognises that, although its measures widen the pool of prospective adopters, a clear duty should be placed on adoption agencies to pay particular attention to the stability and permanence of a couple's relationship as part of the assessment process.[7]

8.50 Regulation 4(2) requires the agency, when determining the suitability of a couple to adopt, 'to have proper regard for the stability and permanence of their relationship'. This is intended to highlight for agencies that a couple's relationship is likely to come under intense pressure when an adopted child joins the family and, in consequence, careful assessment of the relationship is required.

ADOPTION SUPPORT SERVICES

8.51 ACA 2002, s 4 (as extended by the Adoption Support Services Regulations 2005, reg 13) imposes upon a local authority a duty to carry out an assessment of the need for adoption support services at the request of:

(a) children who may be adopted, their parents and guardians;
(b) persons wishing to adopt a child;
(c) adopted persons, their parents, natural parents and former guardians;
(d) a child of an adoptive parent (whether or not adopted);
(e) a child who is a natural sibling (whether full or half blood) of an adopted child;

---

1 SAR 2005, reg 4(1)(a).
2 SAR 2005, reg 4(1)(b).
3 SAR 2005, reg 4(1)(c).
4 SAR 2005, reg 4(1)(d).
5 SAR 2005, reg 4(1)(e).
6 SAR 2005, reg 4(1)(f).
7 The Full Regulatory Impact Assessment (RIA) for the SAR 2005.

(f)   a related person[1] in relation to an adoptive child.

The authority also has a discretionary power to carry out an adoption support service assessment at the request of any person.[2]

8.52   ACA 2002, s 4 gives people affected by adoption the right to request and receive *an assessment* of their needs for adoption support services, but does not confer the right to receive the services. Where a person's needs are identified in an assessment, it is for the local authority to decide whether to provide those services to that person.

Meaning of adoption support services

8.53   'Adoption support services' (which may include giving assistance in cash) means:[3]

(a)   counselling, advice and information;
(b)   financial support payable under ASSR 2005, Part 3;
(c)   services to enable groups of adoptive children, adoptive parents and natural parents, or former guardians of an adoptive child, to discuss matters relating to adoption;
(d)   assistance (including mediation services) in relation to contact between an adoptive child and a natural parent, natural sibling, former guardian, or a related person of the adoptive child;
(e)   services in relation to the therapeutic needs of an adoptive child;
(f)   assistance for the purpose of ensuring the continuance of the relationship between an adoptive child and his adoptive parent, including (i) training for the adoptive parents for the purpose of meeting any special needs of the child, and (ii) respite care;[4]
(g)   assistance where disruption of an adoptive placement or an arrangement following the making of an adoption order has occurred or is in danger of occurring, including (i) mediation services, and (ii) meetings to discuss the disruptions.

Assessments and plans

8.54   Where a local authority carries out an assessment of a person's needs for adoption support services, it must have regard to:[5]

(a)   the needs of the person being assessed and how these may be met;

---

1   'A related person' means a relative within the meaning of ACA 2002, s 144(1) and any person with whom the adoptive child has a relationship which appears to the local authority to be beneficial, having regard to ACA 2002, s 1(4)(f)(i)–(iii): ASSR 2005, reg 2(1).
2   ACA 2002, s 4(2).
3   ASSR 2005, reg 3.
4   The accommodation provided for respite care must be accommodation provided by a local authority under CA 1989, s 23 or by a voluntary organisation under CA 1989, s 59.
5   ASSR 2005, reg 14.

(b)   the needs of the adoptive family[1] and how these might be met;
(c)   the needs, including the developmental needs, of the adoptive child and how these should be met;
(d)   the parenting capacity of the adoptive parent;
(e)   wider family and environmental factors;
(f)   in the case of a child who is or was placed for adoption or matched for adoption, the circumstances which led to the child being placed or matched; and
(g)   any previous assessment of needs for adoption support services.

8.55 The local authority must interview the person (where they consider it appropriate to do so) and, where the person is an adoptive child, his adoptive parents, and prepare a written report of the assessment.[2] Where the person may have a need for services from a primary care trust, a local health board, or a local education authority, the local authority shall consult those bodies as part of the assessment.

8.56 Where the local authority carries out an assessment of a person's needs for financial support, it must take into account:

(1)   any other grant, benefit, allowance or resource available to the person in respect of his needs as a result of the adoption of the child;
(2)   (save for certain disregards)[3] the person's financial resources, including any tax credit or benefit;
(3)   the amount required in respect of reasonable outgoings and commitments (excluding outgoings on the child);
(4)   the financial needs and resources of the child.

8.57 The local authority must prepare a plan, if it proposes to provide adoption support services on more than one occasion, and the services are not limited to advice and information.[4] It must also (i) consult a primary care trust, a local health board, or local education authority before preparing the plan, where the need for their services arises, and (ii) nominate a person to monitor the provision of services in accordance with the plan.

8.58 An 'adoption support services' adviser must be appointed to:[5]

–   give advice and information to persons who may be affected by the adoption or proposed adoption;
–   give advice, information and assistance to the local authority which appointed him, including as to the assessment of needs, the availability of services and preparation of plans.

---

1   'Adoptive family' here means the family consisting of the adoptive child, the adoptive parents and any other child of the adoptive parents (whether or not adopted): ASSR 2005, reg 14(2).
2   ASSR 2005, reg 14(3).
3   Set out in ASSR 2005, reg 15(4) and (5).
4   ASSR 2005, reg 16.
5   ASSR 2005, reg 6.

Financial support

8.59 Financial support is payable under ASSR 2005, Part 3 to an adoptive parent for the purpose of supporting the placement of the adoptive child or the continuation of adoption arrangements after an adoption order is made.

8.60 Support is only payable as follows:[1]

(1) where it is necessary to ensure that the adoptive parent can look after the child;
(2) where the child needs special care which requires greater expenditure of resources by reason of illness, disability, emotional or behavioural difficulties, or the continuing consequences of past abuse or neglect;
(3) where it is necessary for the local authority to make special arrangements to facilitate the placement or the adoption by reason of –
   (i) age or ethnic origin of the child, or
   (ii) the desirability of the child being placed with the same adoptive parent as his brother or sister (whether full or half blood) or with a child with whom he has previously shared a home;
(4) where such support is to meet recurring costs in respect of travel for the purpose of visits between the child and a related person;
(5) where the local authority considers it appropriate to make a contribution to meet the following kinds of expenditure –
   (i) legal costs,
   (ii) for the purpose of introducing an adoptive child to his adoptive parent,
   (iii) for the purpose of accommodating and maintaining the child, including the provision of furniture and domestic equipment, alterations and adaptations of the home, provision of transport and provision of clothing toys and other items necessary for looking after the child.

8.61 Financial support under ASSR 2005, Part 3 may include an element of remuneration.[2] This is only where the decision to include it is taken before the adoption order is made and the local authority considers it to be necessary to facilitate the adoption in a case where:

(a) the adoptive parent has been a local authority foster parent in respect of the child;
(b) an element of remuneration was included in the payments made by the local authority to the adoptive parent in relation to his fostering the child.

This element ceases to be payable at the end of two years from the adoption order unless the local authority considers its continuation necessary, having regard to the exceptional needs of the child or any other exceptional circumstances.

8.62 The financial support may be paid periodically, or by a single payment, or by instalments.[3] It ceases to be payable to an adoptive parent if:

---

1 ASSR 2005, reg 8.
2 ASSR 2005, reg 9.
3 ASSR 2005, reg 10.

(1) the child ceases to have his home with him;
(2) the child ceases full-time education or training and commences employment;
(3) the child qualifies for income support or jobseeker's allowance in his own right; or
(4) the child attains the age of 18, unless he continues in full-time education when it may continue until the end of the course or training.[1]

8.63 ASSR 2005, reg 12 provides for conditions to be imposed. For example, where financial support is to be paid periodically, it is not payable until the adoptive parent has agreed to conditions that he will inform the local authority if there is a change in his financial circumstances and that he will supply an annual statement as to his financial circumstances and the financial needs and resources of the child.

Procedure

8.64 Before making any decision under ACA 2002, s 4(4) as to whether to provide adoption support services, the local authority must allow the person an opportunity to make representations:[2]

(1) It must first give the person notice in writing[3] of its proposed decision and the time allowed for making representations.
(2) The notice must contain:
 (i) a statement as to the person's needs for adoption support services;
 (ii) where the assessment relates to his need for financial support, the basis upon which financial support is determined;
 (iii) whether the local authority proposes to provide him with adoption support services;
 (iv) the services proposed to be provided;
 (v) the proposed amount of any financial support;
 (vi) any proposed conditions under ASSR 2005, reg 12(2).
(3) A draft of the plan should accompany the notice where services are proposed and a plan required.

8.65 No decision should be made until:[4]

(a) the person has made the representations to the local authority or notified that he is satisfied with the decision and the draft plan; or
(b) the period of time for making representations has expired.

8.66 After making the decision, the local authority must give the person notice of the decision and the reasons for it.[5] Where the local authority is required to prepare a

---

1 ASSR 2005, reg 11.
2 ASSR 2005, reg 17.
3 ASSR 2005, reg 22.
4 ASSR 2005, reg 17(5).
5 ASSR 2005, reg 18.

plan, the notice must include details of the plan and the person nominated under ASSR 2005, reg 16(4). Where financial support is to be provided, the notice must include:

(a) the method of determination of the amount of financial support;
(b) where the support is to be paid in instalments or periodically, the amount, frequency, period and when the first payment is to be made;
(c) where the support is a single payment, when the payment is to be made;
(d) where any conditions are imposed under reg 12, those conditions, the date by which the conditions are to be met and the consequences of failing to meet the conditions;
(e) the arrangements and procedure for review, variation and termination;
(f) the responsibilities of the local authority under ASSR 2005, Part 5 (reviews) and the adoptive parent pursuant to any reg 12 agreement.

Reviews

8.67 Where the local authority provides adoption support services (other than financial support payable periodically), a review of the provision of such services must be made:[1]

(a) if any change in the person's circumstances which may affect the provision of adoption support services comes to their notice;
(b) at such stage in the implementation of the plan as they consider appropriate;
(c) in any event, at least annually.

8.68 Where the local authority provides financial support periodically, it shall review the financial support:[2]

– annually, on receipt of the statement mentioned in reg 12;
– if any relevant change of circumstances or any breach of a condition under reg 12 comes to their notice;
– at any stage in the implementation of the plan that it considers appropriate.

Urgent cases

8.69 Where any requirement on the local authority in relation to carrying out an assessment, preparing a plan or giving notice would delay the provision of a service in a case of urgency, that requirement does not apply.[3]

INDEPENDENT REVIEW OF DETERMINATIONS

8.70 ACA 2002, s 12 provides for the establishment of a review procedure in respect of certain determinations made by adoption agencies. The purpose of the review mechanism is to make recommendations to the adoption agencies, not to override their decisions.

---

1   ASSR 2005, reg 19.
2   ASSR 2005, reg 20.
3   ASSR 2005, reg 21.

8.71 The Independent Review of Determinations (Adoption) Regulations 2005 (IRD(A)R 2005) make provision for a review by an independent panel in two types of case:

(1) a determination made under AAR 2005, reg 27(4) that the adoption agency does not propose to approve a prospective adopter as suitable to adopt a child;[1]
(2) a determination made by an adoption agency under the Disclosure of Adoption Information (Post-Commencement Adoptions) Regulations 2005.[2]

8.72 IRD(A)R 2005, Part 2 makes provision for the constitution and membership of the panels, their functions and the payment of fees, meetings and record keeping.

8.73 IRD(A)R 2005, Part 3 provides for the procedure to be followed when a review is sought. An application to the Secretary of State for a review of the qualifying determination must be made by the applicant in writing and include the grounds of the application.

8.74 Upon receipt of the application, the Secretary of State shall:[3]

(a) notify the adoption agency who made the qualifying determination that the application has been made by sending to the agency a copy of the application;
(b) send a written acknowledgement of the application to the applicant and notify him of the steps taken above;
(c) constitute a panel;
(d) fix a date, time and venue for the panel to meet for the purposes of a review meeting;
(e) inform in writing the applicant and the adoption agency which made the qualifying determination of the appointment of the panel and the date, time and venue of the review meeting; and
(f) inform the applicant in writing that he may, if he wishes, provide to the panel further details of the grounds of his application in writing in the period up to 2 weeks before the review meeting and orally at the review meeting.

8.75 The panel's recommendation may be that of the majority.[4] The recommendation and the reason for it and whether it was unanimous or that of the majority must be recorded without delay in a document signed and dated by the chair. The panel must without delay send a copy of the recommendation and the reasons for it to the applicant and the adoption agency which made the qualifying determination.

8.76 The panel may make an order for the payment by the adoption agency, by which the qualifying determination review was made, of such costs as the panel considers reasonable.[5]

---

1 IRD(A)R 2005, reg 3.
2 Disclosure of Adoption Information (Post-Commencement Adoptions) Regulations 2005, reg 15(1).
3 IRD(A)R 2005, regs 10–11.
4 IRD(A)R 2005, reg 12.
5 IRD(A)R 2005, reg 13.

Appendix A

TRANSITIONAL ARRANGEMENTS

The Adoption Act 1976 will be repealed with effect from 30 December 2005 by Sch 5 to ACA 2002.

The Adoption Rules 1984 will lapse when the 1976 Act is repealed.

The Magistrates' Courts (Adoption) Rules 1984 will not automatically lapse as they were made under a different enabling power, which is not being repealed. The intention is, however, that these Rules and any rules which amend them will be revoked.

The transitional arrangements are set out in Sch 4 to ACA 2002,[1] which is modified by the Adoption and Children Act 2002 (Commencement No 10 Transitional and Savings Provisions) Order 2005 ('the Transitionals Order'[2]).

General summary

An application for an adoption order or a freeing order made, but not disposed of, before 30 December 2005 will continue and the 1984 Rules will apply.
Applications under AA 1976, s 52 (revocation on legitimation) made, but not disposed of, before 30 December 2005 will convert to become an application under ACA 2002, s 55 and the FP(A)R 2005 will apply.
Applications under AA 1976, ss 20, 21, 27(1) and (2) and 29 may continue to be made after 30 December 2005 under the 1984 Rules, despite those sections being repealed.
The FP(A)R 2005 will apply, as far as practicable, to (i) appeals made, but not disposed of, before 30 December 2005 and (ii) enforcement orders made before that date. Where it is not practicable, the old rules will apply.
Applications under AA 1976, s 53 (annulment of a Convention order) or s 55 (adoption of children abroad) made, but not disposed of, before 30 December 2005 will continue under the 1984 Rules.

---

1   ACA 2002 s 139(2).
2   The Transitionals Order is made under ACA 2002, s 140(7) and (8), s 142(4)–(6) and s 148(1).

Summary relating to freeing orders

Freeing orders made under AA 1976, s 18 will remain in place unless they are revoked.	ACA 2002, Sch 4, para 7
Any application to vary or revoke a freeing order will continue to be dealt with under AA 1976, ss 20 and 21.	ACA 2002, Sch 4, para 7(1)(a)
A freeing order application pending on 30 December 2005 *where the child has been placed for adoption* by the adoption agency and the child is living with the prospective adopters continues under AA 1976.	ACA 2002, Sch 4, para 6
A freeing order application pending on 30 December 2005 *where the child has not been placed* will continue under AA 1976.	Transitionals Order, art 10
New freeing order applications cannot be made on or after 30 December 2005.	ACA 2002, Sch 5; ACA 2002 Statutory Guidance, Annex I, para 10
Where a child is free for adoption by virtue of a freeing order, the third condition for making an adoption order under ACA 2002, s 47(6) is treated as satisfied.	ACA 2002, Sch 4, para 7(3)
Where a child is free for adoption but not yet placed, the local authority may place the child for adoption and ACA 2002, ss 18 and 22 do not apply. The Adoption Agency Regulations 2005, reg 36 (placement and reviews) applies as if the child is subject to a placement order.	Transitionals Order, art 4
Where a child is freed for adoption, the prospective adopters will not exercise any parental responsibility prior to the adoption order being made. The adoption agency will have parental responsibility for the child.	ACA 2002 Statutory Guidance, Annex I, para 10
Where a freeing order application is pending on 30 December 2005 and the child has not been placed for adoption, unless a proposed placement has been considered by the adoption panel prior to 30 December 2005 (in which case the placement goes ahead under Adoption Agencies Regulations 1983) the local authority will not be able to place the child until the freeing order is made or an alternative authority to place is obtained.	ACA 2002 Statutory Guidance, Annex I, para 10

Summary relating to adoption orders

Adoption orders made before 30 December 2005 will not be affected. A child adopted under AA 1976 will derive their adoptive status from AA 1976, Chapter 4 (which has not been repealed).	ACA 2002 Statutory Guidance, Annex I, para 11
All adoption applications under AA 1976, s 12 (non-agency cases) made before 30 December 2005 will be dealt with under AA 1976, and the AR 1984 or MCAR 1984 will apply.	The Transitionals Order, art 11
Applications for adoption orders made on or after 30 December 2005 must be made under ACA 2002. *Where parents have agreed to their child being adopted prior to 30 December 2005, it will be for the court to determine whether or not this meets the requirements of ACA 2002.*	ACA 2002 Statutory Guidance, Annex I, para 11
Where one member of an unmarried couple or civil partnership has applied for an adoption order and that application is pending on 30 December 2005, the agency may wish to discuss with the prospective adopter whether it would be appropriate to withdraw the application and make a new joint application with their partner under ACA 2002.	ACA 2002 Statutory Guidance, Annex I, para 11
The disclosure regime in ACA 2002, ss 56–65 will apply in any case where an adoption is made on or after 30 December 2005, regardless as to whether the adoption order is made under AA 1976 or ACA 2002.	ACA 2002 Statutory Guidance, Annex I, para 11

Summary relating to placement

Where the adoption panel has decided under AAR 1983 that a prospective adopter is suitable to adopt a particular child before, on or after 30 December 2005, any decision that the child should be placed for adoption with the prospective adopters will be made under Adoption Agencies Regulations 1983 (ACA 2002, ss 18 and 22 will not apply), but such placement will be treated as if it were made under AAR 2005.	The Transitionals Order, art 3(6)
Placements that have not been considered by the panel prior to 30 December 2005 will be made under ACA 2002, ie the local authority must secure authority to place the child for adoption before making a placement.	ACA 2002 Statutory Guidance, Annex I, para 27
Where a child is placed for adoption prior to 30 December 2005, or is placed using the AAR 1983 after 30 December 2005, there will be no requirement on the local authority to secure retrospective authority to place. ACA 2002, s 22 does not apply.	The Transitionals Order, art 3(6) and (7).
Where a child is free for adoption but is not placed for adoption prior to 30 December 2005, the agency may place the child for adoption and ACA 2002, ss 18 and 22 do not apply.	The Transitionals Order, art 4
In the above circumstances, the AAR 2005, reg 36 applies as if the adoption agency is authorised to place the child but has not yet placed the child for adoption and the child is subject to a placement order.	The Transitionals Order, art 4
Where a freeing order is pending and the adoption panel has not made a recommendation in respect of the proposed placement with a prospective adopter prior to 30 December 2005, the child may not be placed until either the freeing order is made or an alternative authority to place is secured.	ACA 2002 Statutory Guidance, Annex I, para 31

Schedule 4 to the Adoption and Children Act 2002

Adoption orders and freeing orders

Paragraphs 6 and 8 of Sch 4 provide that the repeal of AA 1976 does not affect applications for freeing order (s 18) and adoption orders (s 12) which have been made and not disposed of before 30 December 2005, where the child in relation to whom the application is made has, on that date, his home with a person with whom he has been placed for adoption by an adoption agency. Those applications will, therefore, continue.

Paragraph 7 of Sch 4 provides that the repeal of AA 1976 does not affect any freeing order made under AA 1976, s 18. It also provides that the following sections will continue to have effect in relation to freeing orders:

– section 19 (progress reports to former parents);
– section 20 (revocation of a freeing order);
– section 21 (variation of a freeing order to substitute one adoption agency for another).

Paragraph 1(1) of Sch 4 to ACA 2002 provides that any reference in any instrument to a provision of ACA 2002, Part 1, or things done or falling to be done under or for the purposes of any provision of Part 1, is to be construed as including a reference to the corresponding provision repealed by ACA 2002, or things to be done or falling to be done under or for the purposes of that corresponding provision, so far as the nature of the reference permits.

Transitional arrangements effected by the Transitionals Order

Adoption orders and freeing orders

The transitional arrangements provide that the 1984 Rules will continue to apply to applications for adoption orders and freeing orders which have been made, but not disposed of, before 30 December 2005, where the child has been placed by an adoption agency. This enables the 1984 Rules to apply to any application under AA 1976, s 20 or s 21 made on or after 30 December 2005.

Although Sch 4 to ACA 2002 does not permit applications to continue for freeing orders and adoption orders which have not been completed by 30 December 2005, where the child has not been placed by an adoption agency, this was modified by the Transitionals Order and these applications are, therefore, permitted to continue. Consequently, the transitional arrangements provide for the 1984 Rules to apply to *all* applications for freeing orders and adoption orders which are pending on 30 December 2005.

Cases in progress under the Adoption Agencies Regulations 1983

Where a case is still in progress on 30 December 2005, the general rule is that any action or decision taken before that day under the AAR 1983 shall be treated, on or after 30 December 2005, as if it were an action or decision under the corresponding provision of AAR 2005: art 3.

This is subject to three exceptions. Where before 30 December 2005 an adoption panel has considered (i) whether adoption is in the child's best interests, (ii) whether a prospective adopter is suitable to adopt a child, or (iii) whether the child should be placed for adoption and no decision has been made, the AAR 1983 continue to apply for the purposes of that decision.

Where an adoption agency has made a decision under AAR 1983 (whether before, on or after 30 December 2005) that a prospective adopter is suitable to adopt a particular child:

- the AAR 1983 continue to apply for the purposes of placing the child with the prospective adopter, and ACA 2002, s 18 (placement for adoption by agencies) does not apply to such placement; and
- any such placement is treated as if it were made under AAR 2005.

Where a child is placed for adoption by an adoption agency before 30 December 2005 or a decision has been made under AAR 1983 that a prospective adopter is suitable, ACA, s 22 (applications for placement orders) does not apply.

Where an adoption agency is minded to make a decision under AAR 1983 (whether before, on or after 30 December 2005) as to whether a prospective adopter is suitable to adopt a child, the AAR 1983 and the Independent Review of Determinations (Adoption) Regulations 2004 continue to apply for the purposes of making representations or reviewing any qualifying determination.

Child ceasing to be a protected child

The Transitionals Order, art 5 sets out the transitional arrangements in the case of a child who, because of the repeal of AA 1976, ss 32–36, ceases to be a protected child and so becomes privately fostered. It looks at the implications for the Children (Private Arrangements for Fostering) Regulations 2005.

Where notice of intention to adopt under AA 1976, s 22 is given prior to 30 December 2005, this will be treated as if notice was given under ACA 2002, s 44 (by virtue of ACA 2002, Sch 4, para 1). ACA 2002 does not, however, replicate protected status, and so AA 1976, s 32 will not apply. It follows that the local authority is no longer obliged to protect the welfare of the child under AA 1976, s 33.

Other safeguards may be invoked by the local authority in a non-agency case. In carrying out the investigation required by ACA 2002, s 44(5), if the local authority becomes concerned for the child's welfare, it may apply for an EPO under CA 1989. The local authority will also remain obliged to provide adoption services and assessments of the need for adoption services under ACA 2002, ss 3 and 4.

Revocation of an adoption order on legitimation (AA 1976, section 52)

AA 1976, s 52 is re-enacted in ACA 2002, which makes identical provision to s 52 (whilst updating its terminology) and enables the court, which made the adoption order, to revoke it on legitimation.

FP(A)R, r 113 makes provision for an application under ACA 2002, s 55. The provision is identical to that made in the 1984 Rules. By virtue of Sch 4, para 1(1), references to s 55 orders must be construed as including s 52 orders. No further transitional provisions are, therefore, required and an application for such an order will be made under FP(A)R, r 113. This should not cause any difficulty in relation to applications that have not been completed by 30 December 2005, since the provisions in the old and new rules are the same.

Restrictions on the removal of children (AA 1976, sections 27 and 29)

ACA 2002 makes a number of provisions on the removal and recovery of children, which mirror the former provisions under AA 1976.

Under the Transitionals Order, art 9, notwithstanding the repeal of ss 27 and 29 of AA 1976 set out in Sch 5 to ACA 2002, these sections continue to have effect where an application for an adoption order has been made under AA 1976, s 12 or s 18 and has not immediately been disposed of before 30 December 2005.

Interim orders (AA 1976, section 25)

AA 1976, s 25 permitted the court to make an interim adoption order giving the applicants parental responsibility for the child for a probationary period, which could be extended.

A party is not entitled to apply for an interim order under s 25, which can only be made on the court's initiative. In consequence, there are no 'pending' proceedings on 30 December 2005. There are no transitional arrangements relating to s 25 and therefore the court will not be able to make or extend an interim order on or after 30 December 2005.

Residence orders

The power of the court to direct (on request) that a residence order continue in force until the child reaches the age of 18 applies to all residence orders made on or after 30 December 2005, irrespective of whether the application was made before or after that date.[1]

Special guardianship orders/step-parent parental responsibility orders

As neither SGOs nor step-parent parental responsibility orders are introduced until 30 December 2005, there are no transitional arrangements.

Appeals

Under AA 1976, an appeal against the making of, or refusal to make, any order under the Act was made by virtue of r 3(2) of the Adoption Rules 1984, in accordance with RSC, Ord 55.

Appeals to the High Court and county court under ACA 2002 are made in accordance with FP(A)R 2005, Pt 19.

By virtue of ACA 2002, Sch 4, para 1(1), the reference in CA 1989, s 94 to appeals made under ACA 2002 must be construed as including reference to appeals made under AA 1976. This means that if an appeal is made on or after 30 December 2005 in relation to an order made before that date under AA 1976, FP(A)R 2005, Pt 19 will apply to such an appeal.

In respect of appeals pending on 30 December 2005, FP(A)R 2005 will apply, so far as is practicable, to such an appeal. Where they do not apply, the rules in force immediately before that day will continue to apply.

Enforcement

The FP(A)R 2005 will apply so far as is practicable to the enforcement of orders made before 30 December 2005. Where they do not apply, the rules previously applied will continue to apply.

---

1   ACA 2002 Statutory Guidance, Annex I, para 15.

How do the adoption agencies manage ongoing adoption cases during the transfer from AA 1976 to ACA 2002?

The ACA 2002 Statutory Guidance, Annex I sets out the details of how the adoption agencies are to manage ongoing cases. The key points appear below as 'signposts' to the significant elements of the guidance:

- Any ongoing case is a 'transitional case'. The 'old system' means the AA 1976 arrangements and regulations. The 'new system' means the ACA 2002 arrangements & regulations.
- The new system will apply to all cases which take place on or after 30 December 2005. To facilitate the transfer, ACA 2002, Sch 4, para 1 permits some actions taken under AA 1976 to be treated as if they were actions under ACA 2002.[1] For example:
  - an agency decision that a person is suitable to adopt under AAR 1983 may be treated as a decision made under AAR 2005;
  - a reference to a child placed for adoption in an agency document dated prior to 30 December 2005 can be construed as a child placed for adoption under ACA 2002.
- During the transition from the old system to the new, the following general principles apply:[2]
  - Cases should continue to be handled in the usual way in the run up to implementation.
  - The transfer should not require previous work to be undone.
  - Adoption agencies should make clear that from 30 December 2005 a new system will apply.
  - Decisions already taken should stand and should generally not be re-opened.
  - Existing adoption and freeing orders are not affected by implementation.
  - Local authorities will continue to be required to supply the courts with reports which meet the requirements under AA 1976 where pending applications for adoption orders and freeing orders continue to be considered.
  - Some cases must continue to be handled using the old system until they reach a particular point in the process, where the case may then be processed under the new system.
  - The details as to how the ongoing adoption cases should be transferred into the new system are set out in the ACA 2002 Statutory Guidance, Annex I, para 48, which provides checklists relating to children in agency cases, parents and prospective adopters in domestic adoptions.
  - Limited additional checks or information may be needed to allow some cases to be processed under the new system. The checklists provide the relevant advice.

---

1 ACA 2002 Statutory Guidance, Annex I, paras 6 and 7.
2 ACA 2002 Statutory Guidance, Annex I, para 9.

Appendix B

ADOPTION AND CHILDREN ACT 2002

PART 1
ADOPTION

Chapter 1
Introductory

1 Considerations applying to the exercise of powers

(1) This section applies whenever a court or adoption agency is coming to a decision relating to the adoption of a child.

(2) The paramount consideration of the court or adoption agency must be the child's welfare, throughout his life.

(3) The court or adoption agency must at all times bear in mind that, in general, any delay in coming to the decision is likely to prejudice the child's welfare.

(4) The court or adoption agency must have regard to the following matters (among others) –

- (a) the child's ascertainable wishes and feelings regarding the decision (considered in the light of the child's age and understanding),
- (b) the child's particular needs,
- (c) the likely effect on the child (throughout his life) of having ceased to be a member of the original family and become an adopted person,
- (d) the child's age, sex, background and any of the child's characteristics which the court or agency considers relevant,
- (e) any harm (within the meaning of the Children Act 1989) which the child has suffered or is at risk of suffering,
- (f) the relationship which the child has with relatives, and with any other person in relation to whom the court or agency considers the relationship to be relevant, including –
    - (i) the likelihood of any such relationship continuing and the value to the child of its doing so,
    - (ii) the ability and willingness of any of the child's relatives, or of any such person, to provide the child with a secure environment in which the child can develop, and otherwise to meet the child's needs,
    - (iii) the wishes and feelings of any of the child's relatives, or of any such person, regarding the child.

(5) In placing the child for adoption, the adoption agency must give due consideration to the child's religious persuasion, racial origin and cultural and linguistic background.

(6) The court or adoption agency must always consider the whole range of powers available to it in the child's case (whether under this Act or the Children Act 1989); and the court must not make any order under this Act unless it considers that making the order would be better for the child than not doing so.

(7) In this section, 'coming to a decision relating to the adoption of a child', in relation to a court, includes –

(a) coming to a decision in any proceedings where the orders that might be made by the court include an adoption order (or the revocation of such an order), a placement order (or the revocation of such an order) or an order under section 26 (or the revocation or variation of such an order),
(b) coming to a decision about granting leave in respect of any action (other than the initiation of proceedings in any court) which may be taken by an adoption agency or individual under this Act,

but does not include coming to a decision about granting leave in any other circumstances.

(8) For the purposes of this section –

(a) references to relationships are not confined to legal relationships,
(b) references to a relative, in relation to a child, include the child's mother and father.

Chapter 2
The Adoption Service

The Adoption Service

2 Basic definitions

(1) The services maintained by local authorities under section 3(1) may be collectively referred to as 'the Adoption Service', and a local authority or registered adoption society may be referred to as an adoption agency.

(2) In this Act, 'registered adoption society' means a voluntary organisation which is an adoption society registered under Part 2 of the Care Standards Act 2000; but in relation to the provision of any facility of the Adoption Service, references to a registered adoption society or to an adoption agency do not include an adoption society which is not registered in respect of that facility.

(3) A registered adoption society is to be treated as registered in respect of any facility of the Adoption Service unless it is a condition of its registration that it does not provide that facility.

(4) No application for registration under Part 2 of the Care Standards Act 2000 may be made in respect of an adoption society which is an unincorporated body.

(5) In this Act –

'the 1989 Act' means the Children Act 1989,
'adoption society' means a body whose functions consist of or include making arrangements for the adoption of children,
'voluntary organisation' means a body other than a public or local authority the activities of which are not carried on for profit.

(6) In this Act, 'adoption support services' means –

(a) counselling, advice and information, and
(b) any other services prescribed by regulations,

in relation to adoption.

(7) The power to make regulations under subsection (6)(b) is to be exercised so as to secure that local authorities provide financial support.

(8) In this Chapter, references to adoption are to the adoption of persons, wherever they may be habitually resident, effected under the law of any country or territory, whether within or outside the British Islands.

3 Maintenance of Adoption Service

(1) Each local authority must continue to maintain within their area a service designed to meet the needs, in relation to adoption, of –

(a) children who may be adopted, their parents and guardians,
(b) persons wishing to adopt a child, and
(c) adopted persons, their parents, natural parents and former guardians;

and for that purpose must provide the requisite facilities.

(2) Those facilities must include making, and participating in, arrangements –

(a) for the adoption of children, and
(b) for the provision of adoption support services.

(3) As part of the service, the arrangements made for the purposes of subsection (2)(b) –

(a) must extend to the provision of adoption support services to persons who are within a description prescribed by regulations,
(b) may extend to the provision of those services to other persons.

(4) A local authority may provide any of the requisite facilities by securing their provision by –

(a) registered adoption societies, or
(b) other persons who are within a description prescribed by regulations of persons who may provide the facilities in question.

(5) The facilities of the service must be provided in conjunction with the local authority's other social services and with registered adoption societies in their area, so that help may be given in a co-ordinated manner without duplication, omission or avoidable delay.

(6) The social services referred to in subsection (5) are the functions of a local authority which are social services functions within the meaning of the Local Authority Social Services Act 1970 (which include, in particular, those functions in so far as they relate to children).

4 Assessments etc for adoption support services

(1) A local authority must at the request of –

(a) any of the persons mentioned in paragraphs (a) to (c) of section 3(1), or
(b) any other person who falls within a description prescribed by regulations (subject to subsection (7)(a)),

carry out an assessment of that person's needs for adoption support services.

(2) A local authority may, at the request of any person, carry out an assessment of that person's needs for adoption support services.

(3) A local authority may request the help of the persons mentioned in paragraph (a) or (b) of section 3(4) in carrying out an assessment.

(4) Where, as a result of an assessment, a local authority decide that a person has needs for adoption support services, they must then decide whether to provide any such services to that person.

(5) If –

 (a) a local authority decide to provide any adoption support services to a person, and
 (b) the circumstances fall within a description prescribed by regulations,

the local authority must prepare a plan in accordance with which adoption support services are to be provided to the person and keep the plan under review.

(6) Regulations may make provision about assessments, preparing and reviewing plans, the provision of adoption support services in accordance with plans and reviewing the provision of adoption support services.

(7) The regulations may in particular make provision –

 (a) as to the circumstances in which a person mentioned in paragraph (b) of subsection (1) is to have a right to request an assessment of his needs in accordance with that subsection,
 (b) about the type of assessment which, or the way in which an assessment, is to be carried out,
 (c) about the way in which a plan is to be prepared,
 (d) about the way in which, and time at which, a plan or the provision of adoption support services is to be reviewed,
 (e) about the considerations to which a local authority are to have regard in carrying out an assessment or review or preparing a plan,
 (f) as to the circumstances in which a local authority may provide adoption support services subject to conditions,
 (g) as to the consequences of conditions imposed by virtue of paragraph (f) not being met (including the recovery of any financial support provided by a local authority),
 (h) as to the circumstances in which this section may apply to a local authority in respect of persons who are outside that local authority's area,
 (i) as to the circumstances in which a local authority may recover from another local authority the expenses of providing adoption support services to any person.

(8) A local authority may carry out an assessment of the needs of any person under this section at the same time as an assessment of his needs is made under any other enactment.

(9) If at any time during the assessment of the needs of any person under this section, it appears to a local authority that –

 (a) there may be a need for the provision of services to that person by a Primary Care Trust (in Wales, a Health Authority or Local Health Board), or
 (b) there may be a need for the provision to him of any services which fall within the functions of a local education authority (within the meaning of the Education Act 1996),

the local authority must notify that Primary Care Trust, Health Authority, Local Health Board or local education authority.

(10) Where it appears to a local authority that another local authority could, by taking any specified action, help in the exercise of any of their functions under this section, they may request the help of that other local authority, specifying the action in question.

(11) A local authority whose help is so requested must comply with the request if it is consistent with the exercise of their functions.

5 Local authority plans for adoption services

(1) Each local authority must prepare a plan for the provision of the services maintained under section 3(1) and secure that it is published.

(2) The plan must contain information of a description prescribed by regulations (subject to subsection (4)(b)).

(3) The regulations may make provision requiring local authorities –

  (a) to review any plan,
  (b) in the circumstances prescribed by the regulations, to modify that plan and secure its publication or to prepare a plan in substitution for that plan and secure its publication.

(4) The appropriate Minister may direct –

  (a) that a plan is to be included in another document specified in the direction,
  (b) that the requirements specified in the direction as to the description of information to be contained in a plan are to have effect in place of the provision made by regulations under subsection (2).

(5) Directions may be given by the appropriate Minister for the purpose of making provision in connection with any duty imposed by virtue of this section including, in particular, provision as to –

  (a) the form and manner in which, and the time at which, any plan is to be published,
  (b) the description of persons who are to be consulted in the preparation of any plan,
  (c) the time at which any plan is to be reviewed.

(6) Subsections (2) to (5) apply in relation to a modified or substituted plan (or further modified or substituted plan) as they apply in relation to a plan prepared under subsection (1).

(7) Directions given under this section may relate –

  (a) to a particular local authority,
  (b) to any class or description of local authorities, or
  (c) except in the case of a direction given under subsection (4)(b), to local authorities generally,

and accordingly different provision may be made in relation to different local authorities or classes or descriptions of local authorities.

6 Arrangements on cancellation of registration

Where, by virtue of the cancellation of its registration under Part 2 of the Care Standards Act 2000, a body has ceased to be a registered adoption society, the appropriate Minister may direct the body to make such arrangements as to the transfer of its functions relating to children and other transitional matters as seem to him expedient.

7 Inactive or defunct adoption societies etc

(1) This section applies where it appears to the appropriate Minister that –

(a) a body which is or has been a registered adoption society is inactive or defunct, or
(b) a body which has ceased to be a registered adoption society by virtue of the cancellation of its registration under Part 2 of the Care Standards Act 2000 has not made such arrangements for the transfer of its functions relating to children as are specified in a direction given by him.

(2) The appropriate Minister may, in relation to such functions of the society as relate to children, direct what appears to him to be the appropriate local authority to take any such action as might have been taken by the society or by the society jointly with the authority.

(3) A local authority are entitled to take any action which –

(a) apart from this subsection the authority would not be entitled to take, or would not be entitled to take without joining the society in the action, but
(b) they are directed to take under subsection (2).

(4) The appropriate Minister may charge the society for expenses necessarily incurred by him or on his behalf in securing the transfer of its functions relating to children.

(5) Before giving a direction under subsection (2) the appropriate Minister must, if practicable, consult both the society and the authority.

8 Adoption support agencies

(1) In this Act, 'adoption support agency' means an undertaking the purpose of which, or one of the purposes of which, is the provision of adoption support services; but an undertaking is not an adoption support agency –

(a) merely because it provides information in connection with adoption other than for the purpose mentioned in section 98(1), or
(b) if it is excepted by virtue of subsection (2).

'Undertaking' has the same meaning as in the Care Standards Act 2000.

(2) The following are excepted –

(a) a registered adoption society, whether or not the society is registered in respect of the provision of adoption support services,
(b) a local authority,
(c) a local education authority (within the meaning of the Education Act 1996),
(d) a Special Health Authority, Primary Care Trust (in Wales, a Health Authority or Local Health Board) or NHS trust,
(e) the Registrar General,
(f) any person, or description of persons, excepted by regulations.

(3) ...

Regulations

9 General power to regulate adoption etc agencies

(1) Regulations may make provision for any purpose relating to –

(a) the exercise by local authorities or voluntary adoption agencies of their functions in relation to adoption, or
(b) the exercise by adoption support agencies of their functions in relation to adoption.

(2) The extent of the power to make regulations under this section is not limited by sections 10 to 12, 45, 54, 56 to 65 and 98 or by any other powers exercisable in respect of local authorities, voluntary adoption agencies or adoption support agencies.

(3) Regulations may provide that a person who contravenes or fails to comply with any provision of regulations under this section is to be guilty of an offence and liable on summary conviction to a fine not exceeding level 5 on the standard scale.

(4) In this section and section 10, 'voluntary adoption agency' means a voluntary organisation which is an adoption society.

10 Management etc of agencies

(1) In relation to local authorities, voluntary adoption agencies and adoption support agencies, regulations under section 9 may make provision as to –

(a) the persons who are fit to work for them for the purposes of the functions mentioned in section 9(1),
(b) the fitness of premises,
(c) the management and control of their operations,
(d) the number of persons, or persons of any particular type, working for the purposes of those functions,
(e) the management and training of persons working for the purposes of those functions,
(f) the keeping of information.

(2) Regulations made by virtue of subsection (1)(a) may, in particular, make provision for prohibiting persons from working in prescribed positions unless they are registered in, or in a particular part of, one of the registers maintained under section 56(1) of the Care Standards Act 2000 (registration of social care workers).

(3) In relation to voluntary adoption agencies and adoption support agencies, regulations under section 9 may –

(a) make provision as to the persons who are fit to manage an agency, including provision prohibiting persons from doing so unless they are registered in, or in a particular part of, one of the registers referred to in subsection (2),
(b) impose requirements as to the financial position of an agency,
(c) make provision requiring the appointment of a manager,
(d) in the case of a voluntary adoption agency, make provision for securing the welfare of children placed by the agency, including provision as to the promotion and protection of their health,
(e) in the case of an adoption support agency, make provision as to the persons who are fit to carry on the agency.

(4) Regulations under section 9 may make provision as to the conduct of voluntary adoption agencies and adoption support agencies, and may in particular make provision –

(a) as to the facilities and services to be provided by an agency,
(b) as to the keeping of accounts,
(c) as to the notification to the registration authority of events occurring in premises used for the purposes of an agency,

(d) as to the giving of notice to the registration authority of periods during which the manager of an agency proposes to be absent, and specifying the information to be given in such a notice,

(e) as to the making of adequate arrangements for the running of an agency during a period when its manager is absent,

(f) as to the giving of notice to the registration authority of any intended change in the identity of the manager,

(g) as to the giving of notice to the registration authority of changes in the ownership of an agency or the identity of its officers,

(h) requiring the payment of a prescribed fee to the registration authority in respect of any notification required to be made by virtue of paragraph (g),

(i) requiring arrangements to be made for dealing with complaints made by or on behalf of those seeking, or receiving, any of the services provided by an agency and requiring the agency or manager to take steps for publicising the arrangements.

11 Fees

(1) Regulations under section 9 may prescribe –

(a) the fees which may be charged by adoption agencies in respect of the provision of services to persons providing facilities as part of the Adoption Service (including the Adoption Services in Scotland and Northern Ireland),

(b) the fees which may be paid by adoption agencies to persons providing or assisting in providing such facilities.

(2) Regulations under section 9 may prescribe the fees which may be charged by local authorities in respect of the provision of prescribed facilities of the Adoption Service where the following conditions are met.

(3) The conditions are that the facilities are provided in connection with –

(a) the adoption of a child brought into the United Kingdom for the purpose of adoption, or
(b) a Convention adoption, an overseas adoption or an adoption effected under the law of a country or territory outside the British Islands.

(4) Regulations under section 9 may prescribe the fees which may be charged by adoption agencies in respect of the provision of counselling, where the counselling is provided in connection with the disclosure of information in relation to a person's adoption.

12 Independent review of determinations

(1) Regulations under section 9 may establish a procedure under which any person in respect of whom a qualifying determination has been made by an adoption agency may apply to a panel constituted by the appropriate Minister for a review of that determination.

(2) The regulations must make provision as to the description of determinations which are qualifying determinations for the purposes of subsection (1).

(3) The regulations may include provision as to –

(a) the duties and powers of a panel (including the power to recover the costs of a review from the adoption agency by which the determination reviewed was made),
(b) the administration and procedures of a panel,
(c) the appointment of members of a panel (including the number, or any limit on the number, of members who may be appointed and any conditions for appointment),

(d) the payment of expenses of members of a panel,
(e) the duties of adoption agencies in connection with reviews conducted under the regulations,
(f) the monitoring of any such reviews.

(4) The appropriate Minister may make an arrangement with an organisation under which functions in relation to the panel are performed by the organisation on his behalf.

(5) If the appropriate Minister makes such an arrangement with an organisation, the organisation is to perform its functions under the arrangement in accordance with any general or special directions given by the appropriate Minister.

(6) The arrangement may include provision for payments to be made to the organisation by the appropriate Minister.

(7) Where the appropriate Minister is the Assembly, subsections (4) and (6) also apply as if references to an organisation included references to the Secretary of State.

(8) In this section, 'organisation' includes a public body and a private or voluntary organisation.

Supplemental

13 Information concerning adoption

(1) Each adoption agency must give to the appropriate Minister any statistical or other general information he requires about –

(a) its performance of all or any of its functions relating to adoption,
(b) the children and other persons in relation to whom it has exercised those functions.

(2) The following persons –

(a) the justices' chief executive for each magistrates' court,
(b) the relevant officer of each county court,
(c) the relevant officer of the High Court,

must give to the appropriate Minister any statistical or other general information he requires about the proceedings under this Act of the court in question.

(3) In subsection (2), 'relevant officer', in relation to a county court or the High Court, means the officer of that court who is designated to act for the purposes of that subsection by a direction given by the Lord Chancellor.

(4) The information required to be given to the appropriate Minister under this section must be given at the times, and in the form, directed by him.

(5) The appropriate Minister may publish from time to time abstracts of the information given to him under this section.

14 Default power of appropriate Minister

(1) If the appropriate Minister is satisfied that any local authority have failed, without reasonable excuse, to comply with any of the duties imposed on them by virtue of this Act or of section 1 or 2(4) of the Adoption (Intercountry Aspects) Act 1999, he may make an order declaring that authority to be in default in respect of that duty.

(2) An order under subsection (1) must give the appropriate Minister's reasons for making it.

(3) An order under subsection (1) may contain such directions as appear to the appropriate Minister to be necessary for the purpose of ensuring that, within the period specified in the order, the duty is complied with.

(4) Any such directions are enforceable, on the appropriate Minister's application, by a mandatory order.

15 Inspection of premises etc

(1) The appropriate Minister may arrange for any premises in which –

   (a) a child is living with a person with whom the child has been placed by an adoption agency, or
   (b) a child in respect of whom a notice of intention to adopt has been given under section 44 is, or will be, living,

to be inspected from time to time.

(2) The appropriate Minister may require an adoption agency –

   (a) to give him any information, or
   (b) to allow him to inspect any records (in whatever form they are held),

relating to the discharge of any of its functions in relation to adoption which the appropriate Minister specifies.

(3) An inspection under this section must be conducted by a person authorised by the appropriate Minister.

(4) An officer of a local authority may only be so authorised with the consent of the authority.

(5) A person inspecting any premises under subsection (1) may –

   (a) visit the child there,
   (b) make any examination into the state of the premises and the treatment of the child there which he thinks fit.

(6) A person authorised to inspect any records under this section may at any reasonable time have access to, and inspect and check the operation of, any computer (and associated apparatus) which is being or has been used in connection with the records in question.

(7) A person authorised to inspect any premises or records under this section may –

   (a) enter the premises for that purpose at any reasonable time,
   (b) require any person to give him any reasonable assistance he may require.

(8) A person exercising a power under this section must, if required to do so, produce a duly authenticated document showing his authority.

(9) Any person who intentionally obstructs another in the exercise of a power under this section is guilty of an offence and liable on summary conviction to a fine not exceeding level 3 on the standard scale.

...

17 Inquiries

(1) The appropriate Minister may cause an inquiry to be held into any matter connected with the functions of an adoption agency.

(2) Before an inquiry is begun, the appropriate Minister may direct that it is to be held in private.

(3) Where no direction has been given, the person holding the inquiry may if he thinks fit hold it, or any part of it, in private.

(4) Subsections (2) to (5) of section 250 of the Local Government Act 1972 (powers in relation to local inquiries) apply in relation to an inquiry under this section as they apply in relation to a local inquiry under that section.

Chapter 3
Placement for Adoption and Adoption Orders

Placement of children by adoption agency for adoption

18 Placement for adoption by agencies

(1) An adoption agency may –

- (a) place a child for adoption with prospective adopters, or
- (b) where it has placed a child with any persons (whether under this Part or not), leave the child with them as prospective adopters,

but, except in the case of a child who is less than six weeks old, may only do so under section 19 or a placement order.

(2) An adoption agency may only place a child for adoption with prospective adopters if the agency is satisfied that the child ought to be placed for adoption.

(3) A child who is placed or authorised to be placed for adoption with prospective adopters by a local authority is looked after by the authority.

(4) If an application for an adoption order has been made by any persons in respect of a child and has not been disposed of –

- (a) an adoption agency which placed the child with those persons may leave the child with them until the application is disposed of, but
- (b) apart from that, the child may not be placed for adoption with any prospective adopters.

'Adoption order' includes a Scottish or Northern Irish adoption order.

(5) References in this Act (apart from this section) to an adoption agency placing a child for adoption –

- (a) are to its placing a child for adoption with prospective adopters, and
- (b) include, where it has placed a child with any persons (whether under this Act or not), leaving the child with them as prospective adopters;

and references in this Act (apart from this section) to a child who is placed for adoption by an adoption agency are to be interpreted accordingly.

(6) References in this Chapter to an adoption agency being, or not being, authorised to place a child for adoption are to the agency being or (as the case may be) not being authorised to do so under section 19 or a placement order.

(7) This section is subject to sections 30 to 35 (removal of children placed by adoption agencies).

19 Placing children with parental consent

(1) Where an adoption agency is satisfied that each parent or guardian of a child has consented to the child –

(a) being placed for adoption with prospective adopters identified in the consent, or
(b) being placed for adoption with any prospective adopters who may be chosen by the agency,

and has not withdrawn the consent, the agency is authorised to place the child for adoption accordingly.

(2) Consent to a child being placed for adoption with prospective adopters identified in the consent may be combined with consent to the child subsequently being placed for adoption with any prospective adopters who may be chosen by the agency in circumstances where the child is removed from or returned by the identified prospective adopters.

(3) Subsection (1) does not apply where –

(a) an application has been made on which a care order might be made and the application has not been disposed of, or
(b) a care order or placement order has been made after the consent was given.

(4) References in this Act to a child placed for adoption under this section include a child who was placed under this section with prospective adopters and continues to be placed with them, whether or not consent to the placement has been withdrawn.

(5) This section is subject to section 52 (parental etc consent).

20 Advance consent to adoption

(1) A parent or guardian of a child who consents to the child being placed for adoption by an adoption agency under section 19 may, at the same or any subsequent time, consent to the making of a future adoption order.

(2) Consent under this section –

(a) where the parent or guardian has consented to the child being placed for adoption with prospective adopters identified in the consent, may be consent to adoption by them, or
(b) may be consent to adoption by any prospective adopters who may be chosen by the agency.

(3) A person may withdraw any consent given under this section.

(4) A person who gives consent under this section may, at the same or any subsequent time, by notice given to the adoption agency –

(a) state that he does not wish to be informed of any application for an adoption order, or
(b) withdraw such a statement.

(5) A notice under subsection (4) has effect from the time when it is received by the adoption agency but has no effect if the person concerned has withdrawn his consent.

(6) This section is subject to section 52 (parental etc consent).

21 Placement orders

(1) A placement order is an order made by the court authorising a local authority to place a child for adoption with any prospective adopters who may be chosen by the authority.

(2) The court may not make a placement order in respect of a child unless –

  (a) the child is subject to a care order,
  (b) the court is satisfied that the conditions in section 31(2) of the 1989 Act (conditions for making a care order) are met, or
  (c) the child has no parent or guardian.

(3) The court may only make a placement order if, in the case of each parent or guardian of the child, the court is satisfied –

  (a) that the parent or guardian has consented to the child being placed for adoption with any prospective adopters who may be chosen by the local authority and has not withdrawn the consent, or
  (b) that the parent's or guardian's consent should be dispensed with.

This subsection is subject to section 52 (parental etc consent).

(4) A placement order continues in force until –

  (a) it is revoked under section 24,
  (b) an adoption order is made in respect of the child, or
  (c) the child marries or attains the age of 18 years.

'Adoption order' includes a Scottish or Northern Irish adoption order.

22 Applications for placement orders

(1) A local authority must apply to the court for a placement order in respect of a child if –

  (a) the child is placed for adoption by them or is being provided with accommodation by them,
  (b) no adoption agency is authorised to place the child for adoption,
  (c) the child has no parent or guardian or the authority consider that the conditions in section 31(2) of the 1989 Act are met, and
  (d) the authority are satisfied that the child ought to be placed for adoption.

(2) If –

  (a) an application has been made (and has not been disposed of) on which a care order might be made in respect of a child, or
  (b) a child is subject to a care order and the appropriate local authority are not authorised to place the child for adoption,

the appropriate local authority must apply to the court for a placement order if they are satisfied that the child ought to be placed for adoption.

(3) If –

  (a) a child is subject to a care order, and
  (b) the appropriate local authority are authorised to place the child for adoption under section 19,

the authority may apply to the court for a placement order.

(4) If a local authority –

  (a) are under a duty to apply to the court for a placement order in respect of a child, or
  (b) have applied for a placement order in respect of a child and the application has not been disposed of,

the child is looked after by the authority.

(5) Subsections (1) to (3) do not apply in respect of a child –

(a) if any persons have given notice of intention to adopt, unless the period of four months beginning with the giving of the notice has expired without them applying for an adoption order or their application for such an order has been withdrawn or refused, or

(b) if an application for an adoption order has been made and has not been disposed of.

'Adoption order' includes a Scottish or Northern Irish adoption order.

(6) Where –

(a) an application for a placement order in respect of a child has been made and has not been disposed of, and

(b) no interim care order is in force,

the court may give any directions it considers appropriate for the medical or psychiatric examination or other assessment of the child; but a child who is of sufficient understanding to make an informed decision may refuse to submit to the examination or other assessment.

(7) The appropriate local authority –

(a) in relation to a care order, is the local authority in whose care the child is placed by the order, and

(b) in relation to an application on which a care order might be made, is the local authority which makes the application.

23 Varying placement orders

(1) The court may vary a placement order so as to substitute another local authority for the local authority authorised by the order to place the child for adoption.

(2) The variation may only be made on the joint application of both authorities.

24 Revoking placement orders

(1) The court may revoke a placement order on the application of any person.

(2) But an application may not be made by a person other than the child or the local authority authorised by the order to place the child for adoption unless –

(a) the court has given leave to apply, and

(b) the child is not placed for adoption by the authority.

(3) The court cannot give leave under subsection (2)(a) unless satisfied that there has been a change in circumstances since the order was made.

(4) If the court determines, on an application for an adoption order, not to make the order, it may revoke any placement order in respect of the child.

(5) Where –

(a) an application for the revocation of a placement order has been made and has not been disposed of, and

(b) the child is not placed for adoption by the authority,

the child may not without the court's leave be placed for adoption under the order.

25 Parental responsibility

(1) This section applies while –

(a) a child is placed for adoption under section 19 or an adoption agency is authorised to place a child for adoption under that section, or
(b) a placement order is in force in respect of a child.

(2) Parental responsibility for the child is given to the agency concerned.

(3) While the child is placed with prospective adopters, parental responsibility is given to them.

(4) The agency may determine that the parental responsibility of any parent or guardian, or of prospective adopters, is to be restricted to the extent specified in the determination.

26 Contact

(1) On an adoption agency being authorised to place a child for adoption, or placing a child for adoption who is less than six weeks old, any provision for contact under the 1989 Act ceases to have effect.

(2) While an adoption agency is so authorised or a child is placed for adoption –

(a) no application may be made for any provision for contact under that Act, but
(b) the court may make an order under this section requiring the person with whom the child lives, or is to live, to allow the child to visit or stay with the person named in the order, or for the person named in the order and the child otherwise to have contact with each other.

(3) An application for an order under this section may be made by –

(a) the child or the agency,
(b) any parent, guardian or relative,
(c) any person in whose favour there was provision for contact under the 1989 Act which ceased to have effect by virtue of subsection (1),
(d) if a residence order was in force immediately before the adoption agency was authorised to place the child for adoption or (as the case may be) placed the child for adoption at a time when he was less than six weeks old, the person in whose favour the order was made,
(e) if a person had care of the child immediately before that time by virtue of an order made in the exercise of the High Court's inherent jurisdiction with respect to children, that person,
(f) any person who has obtained the court's leave to make the application.

(4) When making a placement order, the court may on its own initiative make an order under this section.

(5) This section does not prevent an application for a contact order under section 8 of the 1989 Act being made where the application is to be heard together with an application for an adoption order in respect of the child.

(6) In this section, 'provision for contact under the 1989 Act' means a contact order under section 8 of that Act or an order under section 34 of that Act (parental contact with children in care).

27 Contact: supplementary

(1) An order under section 26 –

(a) has effect while the adoption agency is authorised to place the child for adoption or the child is placed for adoption, but

(b) may be varied or revoked by the court on an application by the child, the agency or a person named in the order.

(2) The agency may refuse to allow the contact that would otherwise be required by virtue of an order under that section if –

(a) it is satisfied that it is necessary to do so in order to safeguard or promote the child's welfare, and

(b) the refusal is decided upon as a matter of urgency and does not last for more than seven days.

(3) Regulations may make provision as to –

(a) the steps to be taken by an agency which has exercised its power under subsection (2),

(b) the circumstances in which, and conditions subject to which, the terms of any order under section 26 may be departed from by agreement between the agency and any person for whose contact with the child the order provides,

(c) notification by an agency of any variation or suspension of arrangements made (otherwise than under an order under that section) with a view to allowing any person contact with the child.

(4) Before making a placement order the court must –

(a) consider the arrangements which the adoption agency has made, or proposes to make, for allowing any person contact with the child, and

(b) invite the parties to the proceedings to comment on those arrangements.

(5) An order under section 26 may provide for contact on any conditions the court considers appropriate.

28 Further consequences of placement

(1) Where a child is placed for adoption under section 19 or an adoption agency is authorised to place a child for adoption under that section –

(a) a parent or guardian of the child may not apply for a residence order unless an application for an adoption order has been made and the parent or guardian has obtained the court's leave under subsection (3) or (5) of section 47,

(b) if an application has been made for an adoption order, a guardian of the child may not apply for a special guardianship order unless he has obtained the court's leave under subsection (3) or (5) of that section.

(2) Where –

(a) a child is placed for adoption under section 19 or an adoption agency is authorised to place a child for adoption under that section, or

(b) a placement order is in force in respect of a child,

then (whether or not the child is in England and Wales) a person may not do either of the following things, unless the court gives leave or each parent or guardian of the child gives written consent.

(3) Those things are –

(a) causing the child to be known by a new surname, or

(b) removing the child from the United Kingdom.

(4) Subsection (3) does not prevent the removal of a child from the United Kingdom for a period of less than one month by a person who provides the child's home.

29 Further consequences of placement orders

(1) Where a placement order is made in respect of a child and either –

(a) the child is subject to a care order, or
(b) the court at the same time makes a care order in respect of the child,

the care order does not have effect at any time when the placement order is in force.

(2) On the making of a placement order in respect of a child, any order mentioned in section 8(1) of the 1989 Act, and any supervision order in respect of the child, ceases to have effect.

(3) Where a placement order is in force –

(a) no prohibited steps order, residence order or specific issue order, and
(b) no supervision order or child assessment order,

may be made in respect of the child.

(4) Subsection (3)(a) does not apply in respect of a residence order if –

(a) an application for an adoption order has been made in respect of the child, and
(b) the residence order is applied for by a parent or guardian who has obtained the court's leave under subsection (3) or (5) of section 47 or by any other person who has obtained the court's leave under this subsection.

(5) Where a placement order is in force, no special guardianship order may be made in respect of the child unless –

(a) an application has been made for an adoption order, and
(b) the person applying for the special guardianship order has obtained the court's leave under this subsection or, if he is a guardian of the child, has obtained the court's leave under section 47(5).

(6) Section 14A(7) of the 1989 Act applies in respect of an application for a special guardianship order for which leave has been given as mentioned in subsection (5)(b) with the omission of the words 'the beginning of the period of three months ending with'.

(7) Where a placement order is in force –

(a) section 14C(1)(b) of the 1989 Act (special guardianship: parental responsibility) has effect subject to any determination under section 25(4) of this Act,
(b) section 14C(3) and (4) of the 1989 Act (special guardianship: removal of child from UK etc) does not apply.

Removal of children who are or may be placed by adoption agencies

30 General prohibitions on removal

(1) Where –

(a) a child is placed for adoption by an adoption agency under section 19, or

(b) a child is placed for adoption by an adoption agency and either the child is less than six weeks old or the agency has at no time been authorised to place the child for adoption,

a person (other than the agency) must not remove the child from the prospective adopters.

(2) Where –

(a) a child who is not for the time being placed for adoption is being provided with accommodation by a local authority, and
(b) the authority have applied to the court for a placement order and the application has not been disposed of,

only a person who has the court's leave (or the authority) may remove the child from the accommodation.

(3) Where subsection (2) does not apply, but –

(a) a child who is not for the time being placed for adoption is being provided with accommodation by an adoption agency, and
(b) the agency is authorised to place the child for adoption under section 19 or would be so authorised if any consent to placement under that section had not been withdrawn,

a person (other than the agency) must not remove the child from the accommodation.

(4) This section is subject to sections 31 to 33 but those sections do not apply if the child is subject to a care order.

(5) This group of sections (that is, this section and those sections) apply whether or not the child in question is in England and Wales.

(6) This group of sections does not affect the exercise by any local authority or other person of any power conferred by any enactment, other than section 20(8) of the 1989 Act (removal of children from local authority accommodation).

(7) This group of sections does not prevent the removal of a child who is arrested.

(8) A person who removes a child in contravention of this section is guilty of an offence and liable on summary conviction to imprisonment for a term not exceeding three months, or a fine not exceeding level 5 on the standard scale, or both.

31 Recovery by parent etc where child not placed or is a baby

(1) Subsection (2) applies where –

(a) a child who is not for the time being placed for adoption is being provided with accommodation by an adoption agency, and
(b) the agency would be authorised to place the child for adoption under section 19 if consent to placement under that section had not been withdrawn.

(2) If any parent or guardian of the child informs the agency that he wishes the child to be returned to him, the agency must return the child to him within the period of seven days beginning with the request unless an application is, or has been, made for a placement order and the application has not been disposed of.

(3) Subsection (4) applies where –

(a) a child is placed for adoption by an adoption agency and either the child is less than six weeks old or the agency has at no time been authorised to place the child for adoption, and

(b) any parent or guardian of the child informs the agency that he wishes the child to be returned to him,

unless an application is, or has been, made for a placement order and the application has not been disposed of.

(4) The agency must give notice of the parent's or guardian's wish to the prospective adopters who must return the child to the agency within the period of seven days beginning with the day on which the notice is given.

(5) A prospective adopter who fails to comply with subsection (4) is guilty of an offence and liable on summary conviction to imprisonment for a term not exceeding three months, or a fine not exceeding level 5 on the standard scale, or both.

(6) As soon as a child is returned to an adoption agency under subsection (4), the agency must return the child to the parent or guardian in question.

32 Recovery by parent etc where child placed and consent withdrawn

(1) This section applies where –

(a) a child is placed for adoption by an adoption agency under section 19, and
(b) consent to placement under that section has been withdrawn,

unless an application is, or has been, made for a placement order and the application has not been disposed of.

(2) If a parent or guardian of the child informs the agency that he wishes the child to be returned to him –

(a) the agency must give notice of the parent's or guardian's wish to the prospective adopters, and
(b) the prospective adopters must return the child to the agency within the period of 14 days beginning with the day on which the notice is given.

(3) A prospective adopter who fails to comply with subsection (2)(b) is guilty of an offence and liable on summary conviction to imprisonment for a term not exceeding three months, or a fine not exceeding level 5 on the standard scale, or both.

(4) As soon as a child is returned to an adoption agency under this section, the agency must return the child to the parent or guardian in question.

(5) Where a notice under subsection (2) is given, but –

(a) before the notice was given, an application for an adoption order (including a Scottish or Northern Irish adoption order), special guardianship order or residence order, or for leave to apply for a special guardianship order or residence order, was made in respect of the child, and
(b) the application (and, in a case where leave is given on an application to apply for a special guardianship order or residence order, the application for the order) has not been disposed of,

the prospective adopters are not required by virtue of the notice to return the child to the agency unless the court so orders.

33 Recovery by parent etc where child placed and placement order refused

(1) This section applies where –

(a) a child is placed for adoption by a local authority under section 19,
(b) the authority have applied for a placement order and the application has been refused, and
(c) any parent or guardian of the child informs the authority that he wishes the child to be returned to him.

(2) The prospective adopters must return the child to the authority on a date determined by the court.

(3) A prospective adopter who fails to comply with subsection (2) is guilty of an offence and liable on summary conviction to imprisonment for a term not exceeding three months, or a fine not exceeding level 5 on the standard scale, or both.

(4) As soon as a child is returned to the authority, they must return the child to the parent or guardian in question.

34 Placement orders: prohibition on removal

(1) Where a placement order in respect of a child –

(a) is in force, or
(b) has been revoked, but the child has not been returned by the prospective adopters or remains in any accommodation provided by the local authority,

a person (other than the local authority) may not remove the child from the prospective adopters or from accommodation provided by the authority.

(2) A person who removes a child in contravention of subsection (1) is guilty of an offence.

(3) Where a court revoking a placement order in respect of a child determines that the child is not to remain with any former prospective adopters with whom the child is placed, they must return the child to the local authority within the period determined by the court for the purpose; and a person who fails to do so is guilty of an offence.

(4) Where a court revoking a placement order in respect of a child determines that the child is to be returned to a parent or guardian, the local authority must return the child to the parent or guardian as soon as the child is returned to the authority or, where the child is in accommodation provided by the authority, at once.

(5) A person guilty of an offence under this section is liable on summary conviction to imprisonment for a term not exceeding three months, or a fine not exceeding level 5 on the standard scale, or both.

(6) This section does not affect the exercise by any local authority or other person of a power conferred by any enactment, other than section 20(8) of the 1989 Act.

(7) This section does not prevent the removal of a child who is arrested.

(8) This section applies whether or not the child in question is in England and Wales.

35 Return of child in other cases

(1) Where a child is placed for adoption by an adoption agency and the prospective adopters give notice to the agency of their wish to return the child, the agency must –

(a) receive the child from the prospective adopters before the end of the period of seven days beginning with the giving of the notice, and

(b) give notice to any parent or guardian of the child of the prospective adopters' wish to return the child.

(2) Where a child is placed for adoption by an adoption agency, and the agency –

(a) is of the opinion that the child should not remain with the prospective adopters, and
(b) gives notice to them of its opinion,

the prospective adopters must, not later than the end of the period of seven days beginning with the giving of the notice, return the child to the agency.

(3) If the agency gives notice under subsection (2)(b), it must give notice to any parent or guardian of the child of the obligation to return the child to the agency.

(4) A prospective adopter who fails to comply with subsection (2) is guilty of an offence and liable on summary conviction to imprisonment for a term not exceeding three months, or a fine not exceeding level 5 on the standard scale, or both.

(5) Where –

(a) an adoption agency gives notice under subsection (2) in respect of a child,
(b) before the notice was given, an application for an adoption order (including a Scottish or Northern Irish adoption order), special guardianship order or residence order, or for leave to apply for a special guardianship order or residence order, was made in respect of the child, and
(c) the application (and, in a case where leave is given on an application to apply for a special guardianship order or residence order, the application for the order) has not been disposed of,

prospective adopters are not required by virtue of the notice to return the child to the agency unless the court so orders.

(6) This section applies whether or not the child in question is in England and Wales.

Removal of children in non-agency cases

36 Restrictions on removal

(1) At any time when a child's home is with any persons ('the people concerned') with whom the child is not placed by an adoption agency, but the people concerned –

(a) have applied for an adoption order in respect of the child and the application has not been disposed of,
(b) have given notice of intention to adopt, or
(c) have applied for leave to apply for an adoption order under section 42(6) and the application has not been disposed of,

a person may remove the child only in accordance with the provisions of this group of sections (that is, this section and sections 37 to 40).

The reference to a child placed by an adoption agency includes a child placed by a Scottish or Northern Irish adoption agency.

(2) For the purposes of this group of sections, a notice of intention to adopt is to be disregarded if –

(a) the period of four months beginning with the giving of the notice has expired without the people concerned applying for an adoption order, or

(b) the notice is a second or subsequent notice of intention to adopt and was given during the period of five months beginning with the giving of the preceding notice.

(3) For the purposes of this group of sections, if the people concerned apply for leave to apply for an adoption order under section 42(6) and the leave is granted, the application for leave is not to be treated as disposed of until the period of three days beginning with the granting of the leave has expired.

(4) This section does not prevent the removal of a child who is arrested.

(5) Where a parent or guardian may remove a child from the people concerned in accordance with the provisions of this group of sections, the people concerned must at the request of the parent or guardian return the child to the parent or guardian at once.

(6) A person who –

(a) fails to comply with subsection (5), or
(b) removes a child in contravention of this section,

is guilty of an offence and liable on summary conviction to imprisonment for a term not exceeding three months, or a fine not exceeding level 5 on the standard scale, or both.

(7) This group of sections applies whether or not the child in question is in England and Wales.

37 Applicants for adoption

If section 36(1)(a) applies, the following persons may remove the child –

(a) a person who has the court's leave,
(b) a local authority or other person in the exercise of a power conferred by any enactment, other than section 20(8) of the 1989 Act.

38 Local authority foster parents

(1) This section applies if the child's home is with local authority foster parents.

(2) If –

(a) the child has had his home with the foster parents at all times during the period of five years ending with the removal and the foster parents have given notice of intention to adopt, or
(b) an application has been made for leave under section 42(6) and has not been disposed of,

the following persons may remove the child.

(3) They are –

(a) a person who has the court's leave,
(b) a local authority or other person in the exercise of a power conferred by any enactment, other than section 20(8) of the 1989 Act.

(4) If subsection (2) does not apply but –

(a) the child has had his home with the foster parents at all times during the period of one year ending with the removal, and
(b) the foster parents have given notice of intention to adopt,

the following persons may remove the child.

(5) They are –

   (a) a person with parental responsibility for the child who is exercising the power in section 20(8) of the 1989 Act,
   (b) a person who has the court's leave,
   (c) a local authority or other person in the exercise of a power conferred by any enactment, other than section 20(8) of the 1989 Act.

39 Partners of parents

(1) This section applies if a child's home is with a partner of a parent and the partner has given notice of intention to adopt.

(2) If the child's home has been with the partner for not less than three years (whether continuous or not) during the period of five years ending with the removal, the following persons may remove the child –

   (a) a person who has the court's leave,
   (b) a local authority or other person in the exercise of a power conferred by any enactment, other than section 20(8) of the 1989 Act.

(3) If subsection (2) does not apply, the following persons may remove the child –

   (a) a parent or guardian,
   (b) a person who has the court's leave,
   (c) a local authority or other person in the exercise of a power conferred by any enactment, other than section 20(8) of the 1989 Act.

40 Other non-agency cases

(1) In any case where sections 37 to 39 do not apply but –

   (a) the people concerned have given notice of intention to adopt, or
   (b) the people concerned have applied for leave under section 42(6) and the application has not been disposed of,

the following persons may remove the child.

(2) They are –

   (a) a person who has the court's leave,
   (b) a local authority or other person in the exercise of a power conferred by any enactment, other than section 20(8) of the 1989 Act.

Breach of restrictions on removal

41 Recovery orders

(1) This section applies where it appears to the court –

   (a) that a child has been removed in contravention of any of the preceding provisions of this Chapter or that there are reasonable grounds for believing that a person intends to remove a child in contravention of those provisions, or
   (b) that a person has failed to comply with section 31(4), 32(2), 33(2), 34(3) or 35(2).

(2) The court may, on the application of any person, by an order –

(a) direct any person who is in a position to do so to produce the child on request to any person mentioned in subsection (4),
(b) authorise the removal of the child by any person mentioned in that subsection,
(c) require any person who has information as to the child's whereabouts to disclose that information on request to any constable or officer of the court,
(d) authorise a constable to enter any premises specified in the order and search for the child, using reasonable force if necessary.

(3) Premises may only be specified under subsection (2)(d) if it appears to the court that there are reasonable grounds for believing the child to be on them.

(4) The persons referred to in subsection (2) are –

(a) any person named by the court,
(b) any constable,
(c) any person who, after the order is made under that subsection, is authorised to exercise any power under the order by an adoption agency which is authorised to place the child for adoption.

(5) A person who intentionally obstructs a person exercising a power of removal conferred by the order is guilty of an offence and liable on summary conviction to a fine not exceeding level 3 on the standard scale.

(6) A person must comply with a request to disclose information as required by the order even if the information sought might constitute evidence that he had committed an offence.

(7) But in criminal proceedings in which the person is charged with an offence (other than one mentioned in subsection (8)) –

(a) no evidence relating to the information provided may be adduced, and
(b) no question relating to the information may be asked,

by or on behalf of the prosecution, unless evidence relating to it is adduced, or a question relating to it is asked, in the proceedings by or on behalf of the person.

(8) The offences excluded from subsection (7) are –

(a) an offence under section 2 or 5 of the Perjury Act 1911 (false statements made on oath otherwise than in judicial proceedings or made otherwise than on oath),
(b) an offence under section 44(1) or (2) of the Criminal Law (Consolidation) (Scotland) Act 1995 (false statements made on oath or otherwise than on oath).

(9) An order under this section has effect in relation to Scotland as if it were an order made by the Court of Session which that court had jurisdiction to make.

Preliminaries to adoption

42 Child to live with adopters before application

(1) An application for an adoption order may not be made unless –

(a) if subsection (2) applies, the condition in that subsection is met,
(b) if that subsection does not apply, the condition in whichever is applicable of subsections (3) to (5) applies.

(2) If –

(a) the child was placed for adoption with the applicant or applicants by an adoption agency or in pursuance of an order of the High Court, or
(b) the applicant is a parent of the child,

the condition is that the child must have had his home with the applicant or, in the case of an application by a couple, with one or both of them at all times during the period of ten weeks preceding the application.

(3) If the applicant or one of the applicants is the partner of a parent of the child, the condition is that the child must have had his home with the applicant or, as the case may be, applicants at all times during the period of six months preceding the application.

(4) If the applicants are local authority foster parents, the condition is that the child must have had his home with the applicants at all times during the period of one year preceding the application.

(5) In any other case, the condition is that the child must have had his home with the applicant or, in the case of an application by a couple, with one or both of them for not less than three years (whether continuous or not) during the period of five years preceding the application.

(6) But subsections (4) and (5) do not prevent an application being made if the court gives leave to make it.

(7) An adoption order may not be made unless the court is satisfied that sufficient opportunities to see the child with the applicant or, in the case of an application by a couple, both of them together in the home environment have been given –

(a) where the child was placed for adoption with the applicant or applicants by an adoption agency, to that agency,
(b) in any other case, to the local authority within whose area the home is.

(8) In this section and sections 43 and 44(1) –

(a) references to an adoption agency include a Scottish or Northern Irish adoption agency,
(b) references to a child placed for adoption by an adoption agency are to be read accordingly.

43 Reports where child placed by agency

Where an application for an adoption order relates to a child placed for adoption by an adoption agency, the agency must –

(a) submit to the court a report on the suitability of the applicants and on any other matters relevant to the operation of section 1, and
(b) assist the court in any manner the court directs.

44 Notice of intention to adopt

(1) This section applies where persons (referred to in this section as 'proposed adopters') wish to adopt a child who is not placed for adoption with them by an adoption agency.

(2) An adoption order may not be made in respect of the child unless the proposed adopters have given notice to the appropriate local authority of their intention to apply for the adoption order (referred to in this Act as a 'notice of intention to adopt').

(3) The notice must be given not more than two years, or less than three months, before the date on which the application for the adoption order is made.

(4) Where –

(a) if a person were seeking to apply for an adoption order, subsection (4) or (5) of section 42 would apply, but
(b) the condition in the subsection in question is not met,

the person may not give notice of intention to adopt unless he has the court's leave to apply for an adoption order.

(5) On receipt of a notice of intention to adopt, the local authority must arrange for the investigation of the matter and submit to the court a report of the investigation.

(6) In particular, the investigation must, so far as practicable, include the suitability of the proposed adopters and any other matters relevant to the operation of section 1 in relation to the application.

(7) If a local authority receive a notice of intention to adopt in respect of a child whom they know was (immediately before the notice was given) looked after by another local authority, they must, not more than seven days after the receipt of the notice, inform the other local authority in writing that they have received the notice.

(8) Where –

(a) a local authority have placed a child with any persons otherwise than as prospective adopters, and
(b) the persons give notice of intention to adopt,

the authority are not to be treated as leaving the child with them as prospective adopters for the purposes of section 18(1)(b).

(9) In this section, references to the appropriate local authority, in relation to any proposed adopters, are –

(a) in prescribed cases, references to the prescribed local authority,
(b) in any other case, references to the local authority for the area in which, at the time of giving the notice of intention to adopt, they have their home,

and 'prescribed' means prescribed by regulations.

45 Suitability of adopters

(1) Regulations under section 9 may make provision as to the matters to be taken into account by an adoption agency in determining, or making any report in respect of, the suitability of any persons to adopt a child.

(2) In particular, the regulations may make provision for the purpose of securing that, in determining the suitability of a couple to adopt a child, proper regard is had to the need for stability and permanence in their relationship.

The making of adoption orders

46 Adoption orders

(1) An adoption order is an order made by the court on an application under section 50 or 51 giving parental responsibility for a child to the adopters or adopter.

(2) The making of an adoption order operates to extinguish –

(a) the parental responsibility which any person other than the adopters or adopter has for the adopted child immediately before the making of the order,
(b) any order under the 1989 Act or the Children (Northern Ireland) Order 1995 (SI 1995/755 (NI 2)),
(c) any order under the Children (Scotland) Act 1995 other than an excepted order, and
(d) any duty arising by virtue of an agreement or an order of a court to make payments, so far as the payments are in respect of the adopted child's maintenance or upbringing for any period after the making of the adoption order.

'Excepted order' means an order under section 9, 11(1)(d) or 13 of the Children (Scotland) Act 1995 or an exclusion order within the meaning of section 76(1) of that Act.

(3) An adoption order –

(a) does not affect parental responsibility so far as it relates to any period before the making of the order, and
(b) in the case of an order made on an application under section 51(2) by the partner of a parent of the adopted child, does not affect the parental responsibility of that parent or any duties of that parent within subsection (2)(d).

(4) Subsection (2)(d) does not apply to a duty arising by virtue of an agreement –

(a) which constitutes a trust, or
(b) which expressly provides that the duty is not to be extinguished by the making of an adoption order.

(5) An adoption order may be made even if the child to be adopted is already an adopted child.

(6) Before making an adoption order, the court must consider whether there should be arrangements for allowing any person contact with the child; and for that purpose the court must consider any existing or proposed arrangements and obtain any views of the parties to the proceedings.

47 Conditions for making adoption orders

(1) An adoption order may not be made if the child has a parent or guardian unless one of the following three conditions is met; but this section is subject to section 52 (parental etc consent).

(2) The first condition is that, in the case of each parent or guardian of the child, the court is satisfied –

(a) that the parent or guardian consents to the making of the adoption order,
(b) that the parent or guardian has consented under section 20 (and has not withdrawn the consent) and does not oppose the making of the adoption order, or
(c) that the parent's or guardian's consent should be dispensed with.

(3) A parent or guardian may not oppose the making of an adoption order under subsection (2)(b) without the court's leave.

(4) The second condition is that –

(a) the child has been placed for adoption by an adoption agency with the prospective adopters in whose favour the order is proposed to be made,
(b) either –
 (i) the child was placed for adoption with the consent of each parent or guardian and the consent of the mother was given when the child was at least six weeks old, or
 (ii) the child was placed for adoption under a placement order, and

(c) no parent or guardian opposes the making of the adoption order.

(5) A parent or guardian may not oppose the making of an adoption order under the second condition without the court's leave.

(6) The third condition is that the child is free for adoption by virtue of an order made –

(a) in Scotland, under section 18 of the Adoption (Scotland) Act 1978, or
(b) in Northern Ireland, under Article 17(1) or 18(1) of the Adoption (Northern Ireland) Order 1987 (SI 1987/2203 (NI 22)).

(7) The court cannot give leave under subsection (3) or (5) unless satisfied that there has been a change in circumstances since the consent of the parent or guardian was given or, as the case may be, the placement order was made.

(8) An adoption order may not be made in relation to a person who is or has been married.

(9) An adoption order may not be made in relation to a person who has attained the age of 19 years.

48 Restrictions on making adoption orders

(1) The court may not hear an application for an adoption order in relation to a child, where a previous application to which subsection (2) applies made in relation to the child by the same persons was refused by any court, unless it appears to the court that, because of a change in circumstances or for any other reason, it is proper to hear the application.

(2) This subsection applies to any application –

(a) for an adoption order or a Scottish or Northern Irish adoption order, or
(b) for an order for adoption made in the Isle of Man or any of the Channel Islands.

49 Applications for adoption

(1) An application for an adoption order may be made by –

(a) a couple, or
(b) one person,

but only if it is made under section 50 or 51 and one of the following conditions is met.

(2) The first condition is that at least one of the couple (in the case of an application under section 50) or the applicant (in the case of an application under section 51) is domiciled in a part of the British Islands.

(3) The second condition is that both of the couple (in the case of an application under section 50) or the applicant (in the case of an application under section 51) have been habitually resident in a part of the British Islands for a period of not less than one year ending with the date of the application.

(4) An application for an adoption order may only be made if the person to be adopted has not attained the age of 18 years on the date of the application.

(5) References in this Act to a child, in connection with any proceedings (whether or not concluded) for adoption, (such as 'child to be adopted' or 'adopted child') include a person who has attained the age of 18 years before the proceedings are concluded.

50 Adoption by couple

(1) An adoption order may be made on the application of a couple where both of them have attained the age of 21 years.

(2) An adoption order may be made on the application of a couple where –

(a) one of the couple is the mother or the father of the person to be adopted and has attained the age of 18 years, and
(b) the other has attained the age of 21 years.

51 Adoption by one person

(1) An adoption order may be made on the application of one person who has attained the age of 21 years and is not married.

(2) An adoption order may be made on the application of one person who has attained the age of 21 years if the court is satisfied that the person is the partner of a parent of the person to be adopted.

(3) An adoption order may be made on the application of one person who has attained the age of 21 years and is married if the court is satisfied that –

(a) the person's spouse cannot be found,
(b) the spouses have separated and are living apart, and the separation is likely to be permanent, or
(c) the person's spouse is by reason of ill-health, whether physical or mental, incapable of making an application for an adoption order.

(4) An adoption order may not be made on an application under this section by the mother or the father of the person to be adopted unless the court is satisfied that –

(a) the other natural parent is dead or cannot be found,
(b) by virtue of section 28 of the Human Fertilisation and Embryology Act 1990, there is no other parent, or
(c) there is some other reason justifying the child's being adopted by the applicant alone,

and, where the court makes an adoption order on such an application, the court must record that it is satisfied as to the fact mentioned in paragraph (a) or (b) or, in the case of paragraph (c), record the reason.

Placement and adoption: general

52 Parental etc consent

(1) The court cannot dispense with the consent of any parent or guardian of a child to the child being placed for adoption or to the making of an adoption order in respect of the child unless the court is satisfied that –

(a) the parent or guardian cannot be found or is incapable of giving consent, or
(b) the welfare of the child requires the consent to be dispensed with.

(2) The following provisions apply to references in this Chapter to any parent or guardian of a child giving or withdrawing –

(a) consent to the placement of a child for adoption, or
(b) consent to the making of an adoption order (including a future adoption order).

(3) Any consent given by the mother to the making of an adoption order is ineffective if it is given less than six weeks after the child's birth.

(4) The withdrawal of any consent to the placement of a child for adoption, or of any consent given under section 20, is ineffective if it is given after an application for an adoption order is made.

(5) 'Consent' means consent given unconditionally and with full understanding of what is involved; but a person may consent to adoption without knowing the identity of the persons in whose favour the order will be made.

(6) 'Parent' (except in subsections (9) and (10) below) means a parent having parental responsibility.

(7) Consent under section 19 or 20 must be given in the form prescribed by rules, and the rules may prescribe forms in which a person giving consent under any other provision of this Part may do so (if he wishes).

(8) Consent given under section 19 or 20 must be withdrawn –

   (a)   in the form prescribed by rules, or
   (b)   by notice given to the agency.

(9) Subsection (10) applies if –

   (a)   an agency has placed a child for adoption under section 19 in pursuance of consent given by a parent of the child, and
   (b)   at a later time, the other parent of the child acquires parental responsibility for the child.

(10) The other parent is to be treated as having at that time given consent in accordance with this section in the same terms as those in which the first parent gave consent.

53 Modification of 1989 Act in relation to adoption

(1) Where –

   (a)   a local authority are authorised to place a child for adoption, or
   (b)   a child who has been placed for adoption by a local authority is less than six weeks old,

regulations may provide for the following provisions of the 1989 Act to apply with modifications, or not to apply, in relation to the child.

(2) The provisions are –

   (a)   section 22(4)(b), (c) and (d) and (5)(b) (duty to ascertain wishes and feelings of certain persons),
   (b)   paragraphs 15 and 21 of Schedule 2 (promoting contact with parents and parents' obligation to contribute towards maintenance).

(3) Where a registered adoption society is authorised to place a child for adoption or a child who has been placed for adoption by a registered adoption society is less than six weeks old, regulations may provide –

   (a)   for section 61 of that Act to have effect in relation to the child whether or not he is accommodated by or on behalf of the society,
   (b)   for subsections (2)(b) to (d) and (3)(b) of that section (duty to ascertain wishes and feelings of certain persons) to apply with modifications, or not to apply, in relation to the child.

(4) Where a child's home is with persons who have given notice of intention to adopt, no contribution is payable (whether under a contribution order or otherwise) under Part 3 of Schedule 2 to that Act (contributions towards maintenance of children looked after by local authorities) in respect of the period referred to in subsection (5).

(5) That period begins when the notice of intention to adopt is given and ends if –

  (a) the period of four months beginning with the giving of the notice expires without the prospective adopters applying for an adoption order, or
  (b) an application for such an order is withdrawn or refused.

(6) In this section, 'notice of intention to adopt' includes notice of intention to apply for a Scottish or Northern Irish adoption order.

54 Disclosing information during adoption process

Regulations under section 9 may require adoption agencies in prescribed circumstances to disclose in accordance with the regulations prescribed information to prospective adopters.

55 Revocation of adoptions on legitimation

(1) Where any child adopted by one natural parent as sole adoptive parent subsequently becomes a legitimated person on the marriage of the natural parents, the court by which the adoption order was made may, on the application of any of the parties concerned, revoke the order.

(2) In relation to an adoption order made by a magistrates' court, the reference in subsection (1) to the court by which the order was made includes a court acting for the same petty sessions area.

Disclosure of information in relation to a person's adoption

56 Information to be kept about a person's adoption

(1) In relation to an adopted person, regulations may prescribe –

  (a) the information which an adoption agency must keep in relation to his adoption,
  (b) the form and manner in which it must keep that information.

(2) Below in this group of sections (that is, this section and sections 57 to 65), any information kept by an adoption agency by virtue of subsection (1)(a) is referred to as section 56 information.

(3) Regulations may provide for the transfer in prescribed circumstances of information held, or previously held, by an adoption agency to another adoption agency.

57 Restrictions on disclosure of protected etc information

(1) Any section 56 information kept by an adoption agency which –

  (a) is about an adopted person or any other person, and
  (b) is or includes identifying information about the person in question,

may only be disclosed by the agency to a person (other than the person the information is about) in pursuance of this group of sections.

(2) Any information kept by an adoption agency –

(a) which the agency has obtained from the Registrar General on an application under section 79(5) and any other information which would enable the adopted person to obtain a certified copy of the record of his birth, or
(b) which is information about an entry relating to the adopted person in the Adoption Contact Register,

may only be disclosed to a person by the agency in pursuance of this group of sections.

(3) In this group of sections, information the disclosure of which to a person is restricted by virtue of subsection (1) or (2) is referred to (in relation to him) as protected information.

(4) Identifying information about a person means information which, whether taken on its own or together with other information disclosed by an adoption agency, identifies the person or enables the person to be identified.

(5) This section does not prevent the disclosure of protected information in pursuance of a prescribed agreement to which the adoption agency is a party.

(6) Regulations may authorise or require an adoption agency to disclose protected information to a person who is not an adopted person.

58 Disclosure of other information

(1) This section applies to any section 56 information other than protected information.

(2) An adoption agency may for the purposes of its functions disclose to any person in accordance with prescribed arrangements any information to which this section applies.

(3) An adoption agency must, in prescribed circumstances, disclose prescribed information to a prescribed person.

59 Offence

Regulations may provide that a registered adoption society which discloses any information in contravention of section 57 is to be guilty of an offence and liable on summary conviction to a fine not exceeding level 5 on the standard scale.

60 Disclosing information to adopted adult

(1) This section applies to an adopted person who has attained the age of 18 years.

(2) The adopted person has the right, at his request, to receive from the appropriate adoption agency –

(a) any information which would enable him to obtain a certified copy of the record of his birth, unless the High Court orders otherwise,
(b) any prescribed information disclosed to the adopters by the agency by virtue of section 54.

(3) The High Court may make an order under subsection (2)(a), on an application by the appropriate adoption agency, if satisfied that the circumstances are exceptional.

(4) The adopted person also has the right, at his request, to receive from the court which made the adoption order a copy of any prescribed document or prescribed order relating to the adoption.

(5) Subsection (4) does not apply to a document or order so far as it contains information which is protected information.

61 Disclosing protected information about adults

(1) This section applies where –

(a) a person applies to the appropriate adoption agency for protected information to be disclosed to him, and
(b) none of the information is about a person who is a child at the time of the application.

(2) The agency is not required to proceed with the application unless it considers it appropriate to do so.

(3) If the agency does proceed with the application it must take all reasonable steps to obtain the views of any person the information is about as to the disclosure of the information about him.

(4) The agency may then disclose the information if it considers it appropriate to do so.

(5) In deciding whether it is appropriate to proceed with the application or disclose the information, the agency must consider –

(a) the welfare of the adopted person,
(b) any views obtained under subsection (3),
(c) any prescribed matters,

and all the other circumstances of the case.

(6) This section does not apply to a request for information under section 60(2) or to a request for information which the agency is authorised or required to disclose in pursuance of regulations made by virtue of section 57(6).

62 Disclosing protected information about children

(1) This section applies where –

(a) a person applies to the appropriate adoption agency for protected information to be disclosed to him, and
(b) any of the information is about a person who is a child at the time of the application.

(2) The agency is not required to proceed with the application unless it considers it appropriate to do so.

(3) If the agency does proceed with the application, then, so far as the information is about a person who is at the time a child, the agency must take all reasonable steps to obtain –

(a) the views of any parent or guardian of the child, and
(b) the views of the child, if the agency considers it appropriate to do so having regard to his age and understanding and to all the other circumstances of the case,

as to the disclosure of the information.

(4) And, so far as the information is about a person who has at the time attained the age of 18 years, the agency must take all reasonable steps to obtain his views as to the disclosure of the information.

(5) The agency may then disclose the information if it considers it appropriate to do so.

(6) In deciding whether it is appropriate to proceed with the application, or disclose the information, where any of the information is about a person who is at the time a child –

(a) if the child is an adopted child, the child's welfare must be the paramount consideration,

(b) in the case of any other child, the agency must have particular regard to the child's welfare.

(7) And, in deciding whether it is appropriate to proceed with the application or disclose the information, the agency must consider –

   (a) the welfare of the adopted person (where subsection (6)(a) does not apply),
   (b) any views obtained under subsection (3) or (4),
   (c) any prescribed matters,

and all the other circumstances of the case.

(8) This section does not apply to a request for information under section 60(2) or to a request for information which the agency is authorised or required to disclose in pursuance of regulations made by virtue of section 57(6).

63 Counselling

(1) Regulations may require adoption agencies to give information about the availability of counselling to persons –

   (a) seeking information from them in pursuance of this group of sections,
   (b) considering objecting or consenting to the disclosure of information by the agency in pursuance of this group of sections, or
   (c) considering entering with the agency into an agreement prescribed for the purposes of section 57(5).

(2) Regulations may require adoption agencies to make arrangements to secure the provision of counselling for persons seeking information from them in prescribed circumstances in pursuance of this group of sections.

(3) The regulations may authorise adoption agencies –

   (a) to disclose information which is required for the purposes of such counselling to the persons providing the counselling,
   (b) where the person providing the counselling is outside the United Kingdom, to require a prescribed fee to be paid.

(4) The regulations may require any of the following persons to provide counselling for the purposes of arrangements under subsection (2) –

   (a) a local authority, a council constituted under section 2 of the Local Government etc (Scotland) Act 1994 or a Health and Social Services Board established under Article 16 of the Health and Personal Social Services (Northern Ireland) Order 1972 (SI 1972/1265 (NI 14)),
   (b) a registered adoption society, an organisation within section 144(3)(b) or an adoption society which is registered under Article 4 of the Adoption (Northern Ireland) Order 1987 (SI 1987/2203 (NI 22)),
   (c) an adoption support agency in respect of which a person is registered under Part 2 of the Care Standards Act 2000.

(5) For the purposes of subsection (4), where the functions of a Health and Social Services Board are exercisable by a Health and Social Services Trust, the reference in sub-paragraph (a) to a Board is to be read as a reference to the Health and Social Services Trust.

64 Other provision to be made by regulations

(1) Regulations may make provision for the purposes of this group of sections, including provision as to –

- (a) the performance by adoption agencies of their functions,
- (b) the manner in which information may be received, and
- (c) the matters mentioned below in this section.

(2) Regulations may prescribe –

- (a) the manner in which agreements made by virtue of section 57(5) are to be recorded,
- (b) the information to be provided by any person on an application for the disclosure of information under this group of sections.

(3) Regulations may require adoption agencies –

- (a) to give to prescribed persons prescribed information about the rights or opportunities to obtain information, or to give their views as to its disclosure, given by this group of sections,
- (b) to seek prescribed information from, or give prescribed information to, the Registrar General in prescribed circumstances.

(4) Regulations may require the Registrar General –

- (a) to disclose to any person (including an adopted person) at his request any information which the person requires to assist him to make contact with the adoption agency which is the appropriate adoption agency in the case of an adopted person specified in the request (or, as the case may be, in the applicant's case),
- (b) to disclose to the appropriate adoption agency any information which the agency requires about any entry relating to the adopted person on the Adoption Contact Register.

(5) Regulations may provide for the payment of a prescribed fee in respect of the disclosure in prescribed circumstances of any information in pursuance of section 60, 61 or 62; but an adopted person may not be required to pay any fee in respect of any information disclosed to him in relation to any person who (but for his adoption) would be related to him by blood (including half-blood) or marriage.

(6) Regulations may provide for the payment of a prescribed fee by an adoption agency obtaining information under subsection (4)(b).

65 Sections 56 to 65: interpretation

(1) In this group of sections –

'appropriate adoption agency', in relation to an adopted person or to information relating to his adoption, means –
- (a) if the person was placed for adoption by an adoption agency, that agency or (if different) the agency which keeps the information in relation to his adoption,
- (b) in any other case, the local authority to which notice of intention to adopt was given,

'prescribed' means prescribed by subordinate legislation,
'regulations' means regulations under section 9,
'subordinate legislation' means regulations or, in relation to information to be given by a court, rules.

(2) But –

(a) regulations under section 63(2) imposing any requirement on a council constituted under section 2 of the Local Government etc (Scotland) Act 1994, or an organisation within section 144(3)(b), are to be made by the Scottish Ministers,

(b) regulations under section 63(2) imposing any requirement on a Health and Social Services Board established under Article 16 of the Health and Personal Social Services (Northern Ireland) Order 1972 (SI 1972/1265 (NI 14)), or an adoption society which is registered under Article 4 of the Adoption (Northern Ireland) Order 1987 (SI 1987/2203 (NI 22)), are to be made by the Department of Health, Social Services and Public Safety.

(3) The power of the Scottish Ministers or of the Department of Health, Social Services and Public Safety to make regulations under section 63(2) includes power to make –

(a) any supplementary, incidental or consequential provision,
(b) any transitory, transitional or saving provision,

which the person making the regulations considers necessary or expedient.

(4) Regulations prescribing any fee by virtue of section 64(6) require the approval of the Chancellor of the Exchequer.

(5) Regulations making any provision as to the manner in which any application is to be made for the disclosure of information by the Registrar General require his approval.

Chapter 4
Status of Adopted Children

66 Meaning of adoption in Chapter 4

(1) In this Chapter 'adoption' means –

(a) adoption by an adoption order or a Scottish or Northern Irish adoption order,
(b) adoption by an order made in the Isle of Man or any of the Channel Islands,
(c) an adoption effected under the law of a Convention country outside the British Islands, and certified in pursuance of Article 23(1) of the Convention (referred to in this Act as a 'Convention adoption'),
(d) an overseas adoption, or
(e) an adoption recognised by the law of England and Wales and effected under the law of any other country;

and related expressions are to be interpreted accordingly.

(2) But references in this Chapter to adoption do not include an adoption effected before the day on which this Chapter comes into force (referred to in this Chapter as 'the appointed day').

(3) Any reference in an enactment to an adopted person within the meaning of this Chapter includes a reference to an adopted child within the meaning of Part 4 of the Adoption Act 1976.

67 Status conferred by adoption

(1) An adopted person is to be treated in law as if born as the child of the adopters or adopter.

(2) An adopted person is the legitimate child of the adopters or adopter and, if adopted by –

(a) a couple, or
(b) one of a couple under section 51(2),

is to be treated as the child of the relationship of the couple in question.

(3) An adopted person –

(a) if adopted by one of a couple under section 51(2), is to be treated in law as not being the child of any person other than the adopter and the other one of the couple, and
(b) in any other case, is to be treated in law, subject to subsection (4), as not being the child of any person other than the adopters or adopter;

but this subsection does not affect any reference in this Act to a person's natural parent or to any other natural relationship.

(4) In the case of a person adopted by one of the person's natural parents as sole adoptive parent, subsection (3)(b) has no effect as respects entitlement to property depending on relationship to that parent, or as respects anything else depending on that relationship.

(5) This section has effect from the date of the adoption.

(6) Subject to the provisions of this Chapter and Schedule 4, this section –

(a) applies for the interpretation of enactments or instruments passed or made before as well as after the adoption, and so applies subject to any contrary indication, and
(b) has effect as respects things done, or events occurring, on or after the adoption.

68 Adoptive relatives

(1) A relationship existing by virtue of section 67 may be referred to as an adoptive relationship, and –

(a) an adopter may be referred to as an adoptive parent or (as the case may be) as an adoptive father or adoptive mother,
(b) any other relative of any degree under an adoptive relationship may be referred to as an adoptive relative of that degree.

(2) Subsection (1) does not affect the interpretation of any reference, not qualified by the word 'adoptive', to a relationship.

(3) A reference (however expressed) to the adoptive mother and father of a child adopted by –

(a) a couple of the same sex, or
(b) a partner of the child's parent, where the couple are of the same sex,

is to be read as a reference to the child's adoptive parents.

69 Rules of interpretation for instruments concerning property

(1) The rules of interpretation contained in this section apply (subject to any contrary indication and to Schedule 4) to any instrument so far as it contains a disposition of property.

(2) In applying section 67(1) and (2) to a disposition which depends on the date of birth of a child or children of the adoptive parent or parents, the disposition is to be interpreted as if –

(a) the adopted person had been born on the date of adoption,
(b) two or more people adopted on the same date had been born on that date in the order of their actual births;

but this does not affect any reference to a person's age.

(3) Examples of phrases in wills on which subsection (2) can operate are –

1. Children of A 'living at my death or born afterwards'.
2. Children of A 'living at my death or born afterwards before any one of such children for the time being in existence attains a vested interest and who attain the age of 21 years'.
3. As in example 1 or 2, but referring to grandchildren of A instead of children of A.
4. A for life 'until he has a child', and then to his child or children.

Note. Subsection (2) will not affect the reference to the age of 21 years in example 2.

(4) Section 67(3) does not prejudice –

(a) any qualifying interest, or
(b) any interest expectant (whether immediately or not) upon a qualifying interest.

'Qualifying interest' means an interest vested in possession in the adopted person before the adoption.

(5) Where it is necessary to determine for the purposes of a disposition of property effected by an instrument whether a woman can have a child –

(a) it must be presumed that once a woman has attained the age of 55 years she will not adopt a person after execution of the instrument, and
(b) if she does so, then (in spite of section 67) that person is not to be treated as her child or (if she does so as one of a couple) as the child of the other one of the couple for the purposes of the instrument.

(6) In this section, 'instrument' includes a private Act settling property, but not any other enactment.

70 Dispositions depending on date of birth

(1) Where a disposition depends on the date of birth of a person who was born illegitimate and who is adopted by one of the natural parents as sole adoptive parent, section 69(2) does not affect entitlement by virtue of Part 3 of the Family Law Reform Act 1987 (dispositions of property).

(2) Subsection (1) applies for example where –

(a) a testator dies in 2001 bequeathing a legacy to his eldest grandchild living at a specified time,
(b) his unmarried daughter has a child in 2002 who is the first grandchild,
(c) his married son has a child in 2003,
(d) subsequently his unmarried daughter adopts her child as sole adoptive parent.

In that example the status of the daughter's child as the eldest grandchild of the testator is not affected by the events described in paragraphs (c) and (d).

71 Property devolving with peerages etc

(1) An adoption does not affect the descent of any peerage or dignity or title of honour.

(2) An adoption does not affect the devolution of any property limited (expressly or not) to devolve (as nearly as the law permits) along with any peerage or dignity or title of honour.

(3) Subsection (2) applies only if and so far as a contrary intention is not expressed in the instrument, and has effect subject to the terms of the instrument.

72 Protection of trustees and personal representatives

(1) A trustee or personal representative is not under a duty, by virtue of the law relating to trusts or the administration of estates, to enquire, before conveying or distributing any property, whether any adoption has been effected or revoked if that fact could affect entitlement to the property.

(2) A trustee or personal representative is not liable to any person by reason of a conveyance or distribution of the property made without regard to any such fact if he has not received notice of the fact before the conveyance or distribution.

(3) This section does not prejudice the right of a person to follow the property, or any property representing it, into the hands of another person, other than a purchaser, who has received it.

73 Meaning of disposition

(1) This section applies for the purposes of this Chapter.

(2) A disposition includes the conferring of a power of appointment and any other disposition of an interest in or right over property; and in this subsection a power of appointment includes any discretionary power to transfer a beneficial interest in property without the furnishing of valuable consideration.

(3) This Chapter applies to an oral disposition as if contained in an instrument made when the disposition was made.

(4) The date of death of a testator is the date at which a will or codicil is to be regarded as made.

(5) The provisions of the law of intestate succession applicable to the estate of a deceased person are to be treated as if contained in an instrument executed by him (while of full capacity) immediately before his death.

74 Miscellaneous enactments

(1) Section 67 does not apply for the purposes of –

   (a) the table of kindred and affinity in Schedule 1 to the Marriage Act 1949,
   (b) sections 10 and 11 of the Sexual Offences Act 1956 (incest), or
   (c) section 54 of the Criminal Law Act 1977 (inciting a girl to commit incest).

(2) Section 67 does not apply for the purposes of any provision of –

   (a) the British Nationality Act 1981,
   (b) the Immigration Act 1971,
   (c) any instrument having effect under an enactment within paragraph (a) or (b), or
   (d) any other provision of the law for the time being in force which determines British citizenship, British overseas territories citizenship, the status of a British National (Overseas) or British Overseas citizenship.

75 Pensions

Section 67(3) does not affect entitlement to a pension which is payable to or for the benefit of a person and is in payment at the time of the person's adoption.

76 Insurance

(1) Where a child is adopted whose natural parent has effected an insurance with a friendly society or a collecting society or an industrial insurance company for the payment on the death of the child of money for funeral expenses, then –

(a) the rights and liabilities under the policy are by virtue of the adoption transferred to the adoptive parents, and
(b) for the purposes of the enactments relating to such societies and companies, the adoptive parents are to be treated as the person who took out the policy.

(2) Where the adoption is effected by an order made by virtue of section 51(2), the references in subsection (1) to the adoptive parents are to be read as references to the adopter and the other one of the couple.

Chapter 5
The Registers

Adopted Children Register etc

77 Adopted Children Register

(1) The Registrar General must continue to maintain in the General Register Office a register, to be called the Adopted Children Register.

(2) The Adopted Children Register is not to be open to public inspection or search.

(3) No entries may be made in the Adopted Children Register other than entries –

(a) directed to be made in it by adoption orders, or
(b) required to be made under Schedule 1.

(4) A certified copy of an entry in the Adopted Children Register, if purporting to be sealed or stamped with the seal of the General Register Office, is to be received as evidence of the adoption to which it relates without further or other proof.

(5) Where an entry in the Adopted Children Register contains a record –

(a) of the date of birth of the adopted person, or
(b) of the country, or the district and sub-district, of the birth of the adopted person,

a certified copy of the entry is also to be received, without further or other proof, as evidence of that date, or country or district and sub-district, (as the case may be) in all respects as if the copy were a certified copy of an entry in the registers of live-births.

(6) Schedule 1 (registration of adoptions and the amendment of adoption orders) is to have effect.

78 Searches and copies

(1) The Registrar General must continue to maintain at the General Register Office an index of the Adopted Children Register.

(2) Any person may –

(a) search the index,

(b) have a certified copy of any entry in the Adopted Children Register.

(3) But a person is not entitled to have a certified copy of an entry in the Adopted Children Register relating to an adopted person who has not attained the age of 18 years unless the applicant has provided the Registrar General with the prescribed particulars.

'Prescribed' means prescribed by regulations made by the Registrar General with the approval of the Chancellor of the Exchequer.

(4) The terms, conditions and regulations as to payment of fees, and otherwise, applicable under the Births and Deaths Registration Act 1953, and the Registration Service Act 1953, in respect of –

(a) searches in the index kept in the General Register Office of certified copies of entries in the registers of live-births,
(b) the supply from that office of certified copies of entries in those certified copies,

also apply in respect of searches, and supplies of certified copies, under subsection (2).

79 Connections between the register and birth records

(1) The Registrar General must make traceable the connection between any entry in the registers of live-births or other records which has been marked 'Adopted' and any corresponding entry in the Adopted Children Register.

(2) Information kept by the Registrar General for the purposes of subsection (1) is not to be open to public inspection or search.

(3) Any such information, and any other information which would enable an adopted person to obtain a certified copy of the record of his birth, may only be disclosed by the Registrar General in accordance with this section.

(4) In relation to a person adopted before the appointed day the court may, in exceptional circumstances, order the Registrar General to give any information mentioned in subsection (3) to a person.

(5) On an application made in the prescribed manner by the appropriate adoption agency in respect of an adopted person a record of whose birth is kept by the Registrar General, the Registrar General must give the agency any information relating to the adopted person which is mentioned in subsection (3).

'Appropriate adoption agency' has the same meaning as in section 65.

(6) In relation to a person adopted before the appointed day, Schedule 2 applies instead of subsection (5).

(7) On an application made in the prescribed manner by an adopted person a record of whose birth is kept by the Registrar General and who –

(a) is under the age of 18 years, and
(b) intends to be married,

the Registrar General must inform the applicant whether or not it appears from information contained in the registers of live-births or other records that the applicant and the person whom the applicant intends to marry may be within the prohibited degrees of relationship for the purposes of the Marriage Act 1949.

(8) Before the Registrar General gives any information by virtue of this section, any prescribed fee which he has demanded must be paid.

(9) In this section –

'appointed day' means the day appointed for the commencement of sections 56 to 65, 'prescribed' means prescribed by regulations made by the Registrar General with the approval of the Chancellor of the Exchequer.

Adoption Contact Register

80 Adoption Contact Register

(1) The Registrar General must continue to maintain at the General Register Office in accordance with regulations a register in two Parts to be called the Adoption Contact Register.

(2) Part 1 of the register is to contain the prescribed information about adopted persons who have given the prescribed notice expressing their wishes as to making contact with their relatives.

(3) The Registrar General may only make an entry in Part 1 of the register for an adopted person –

- (a) a record of whose birth is kept by the Registrar General,
- (b) who has attained the age of 18 years, and
- (c) who the Registrar General is satisfied has such information as is necessary to enable him to obtain a certified copy of the record of his birth.

(4) Part 2 of the register is to contain the prescribed information about persons who have given the prescribed notice expressing their wishes, as relatives of adopted persons, as to making contact with those persons.

(5) The Registrar General may only make an entry in Part 2 of the register for a person –

- (a) who has attained the age of 18 years, and
- (b) who the Registrar General is satisfied is a relative of an adopted person and has such information as is necessary to enable him to obtain a certified copy of the record of the adopted person's birth.

(6) Regulations may provide for –

- (a) the disclosure of information contained in one Part of the register to persons for whom there is an entry in the other Part,
- (b) the payment of prescribed fees in respect of the making or alteration of entries in the register and the disclosure of information contained in the register.

81 Adoption Contact Register: supplementary

(1) The Adoption Contact Register is not to be open to public inspection or search.

(2) In section 80, 'relative', in relation to an adopted person, means any person who (but for his adoption) would be related to him by blood (including half-blood) or marriage.

(3) The Registrar General must not give any information entered in the register to any person except in accordance with subsection (6)(a) of that section or regulations made by virtue of section 64(4)(b).

(4) In section 80, 'regulations' means regulations made by the Registrar General with the approval of the Chancellor of the Exchequer, and 'prescribed' means prescribed by such regulations.

General

82 Interpretation

(1) In this Chapter –

'records' includes certified copies kept by the Registrar General of entries in any register of births,
'registers of live-births' means the registers of live-births made under the Births and Deaths Registration Act 1953.

(2) Any register, record or index maintained under this Chapter may be maintained in any form the Registrar General considers appropriate; and references (however expressed) to entries in such a register, or to their amendment, marking or cancellation, are to be read accordingly.

Chapter 6
Adoptions with a Foreign Element

Bringing children into and out of the United Kingdom

83 Restriction on bringing children in

(1) This section applies where a person who is habitually resident in the British Islands (the 'British resident') –

(a) brings, or causes another to bring, a child who is habitually resident outside the British Islands into the United Kingdom for the purpose of adoption by the British resident, or
(b) at any time brings, or causes another to bring, into the United Kingdom a child adopted by the British resident under an external adoption effected within the period of six months ending with that time.

The references to adoption, or to a child adopted, by the British resident include a reference to adoption, or to a child adopted, by the British resident and another person.

(2) But this section does not apply if the child is intended to be adopted under a Convention adoption order.

(3) An external adoption means an adoption, other than a Convention adoption, of a child effected under the law of any country or territory outside the British Islands, whether or not the adoption is –

(a) an adoption within the meaning of Chapter 4, or
(b) a full adoption (within the meaning of section 88(3)).

(4) Regulations may require a person intending to bring, or to cause another to bring, a child into the United Kingdom in circumstances where this section applies –

(a) to apply to an adoption agency (including a Scottish or Northern Irish adoption agency) in the prescribed manner for an assessment of his suitability to adopt the child, and
(b) to give the agency any information it may require for the purpose of the assessment.

(5) Regulations may require prescribed conditions to be met in respect of a child brought into the United Kingdom in circumstances where this section applies.

(6) In relation to a child brought into the United Kingdom for adoption in circumstances where this section applies, regulations may –

   (a) provide for any provision of Chapter 3 to apply with modifications or not to apply,
   (b) if notice of intention to adopt has been given, impose functions in respect of the child on the local authority to which the notice was given.

(7) If a person brings, or causes another to bring, a child into the United Kingdom at any time in circumstances where this section applies, he is guilty of an offence if –

   (a) he has not complied with any requirement imposed by virtue of subsection (4), or
   (b) any condition required to be met by virtue of subsection (5) is not met,

before that time, or before any later time which may be prescribed.

(8) A person guilty of an offence under this section is liable –

   (a) on summary conviction to imprisonment for a term not exceeding six months, or a fine not exceeding the statutory maximum, or both,
   (b) on conviction on indictment, to imprisonment for a term not exceeding twelve months, or a fine, or both.

(9) In this section, 'prescribed' means prescribed by regulations and 'regulations' means regulations made by the Secretary of State, after consultation with the Assembly.

84 Giving parental responsibility prior to adoption abroad

(1) The High Court may, on an application by persons who the court is satisfied intend to adopt a child under the law of a country or territory outside the British Islands, make an order giving parental responsibility for the child to them.

(2) An order under this section may not give parental responsibility to persons who the court is satisfied meet those requirements as to domicile, or habitual residence, in England and Wales which have to be met if an adoption order is to be made in favour of those persons.

(3) An order under this section may not be made unless any requirements prescribed by regulations are satisfied.

(4) An application for an order under this section may not be made unless at all times during the preceding ten weeks the child's home was with the applicant or, in the case of an application by two people, both of them.

(5) Section 46(2) to (4) has effect in relation to an order under this section as it has effect in relation to adoption orders.

(6) Regulations may provide for any provision of this Act which refers to adoption orders to apply, with or without modifications, to orders under this section.

(7) In this section, 'regulations' means regulations made by the Secretary of State, after consultation with the Assembly.

85 Restriction on taking children out

(1) A child who –

   (a) is a Commonwealth citizen, or

(b) is habitually resident in the United Kingdom,

must not be removed from the United Kingdom to a place outside the British Islands for the purpose of adoption unless the condition in subsection (2) is met.

(2) The condition is that –

(a) the prospective adopters have parental responsibility for the child by virtue of an order under section 84, or
(b) the child is removed under the authority of an order under section 49 of the Adoption (Scotland) Act 1978 or Article 57 of the Adoption (Northern Ireland) Order 1987 (SI 1987/2203 (NI 22)).

(3) Removing a child from the United Kingdom includes arranging to do so; and the circumstances in which a person arranges to remove a child from the United Kingdom include those where he –

(a) enters into an arrangement for the purpose of facilitating such a removal of the child,
(b) initiates or takes part in any negotiations of which the purpose is the conclusion of an arrangement within paragraph (a), or
(c) causes another person to take any step mentioned in paragraph (a) or (b).

An arrangement includes an agreement (whether or not enforceable).

(4) A person who removes a child from the United Kingdom in contravention of subsection (1) is guilty of an offence.

(5) A person is not guilty of an offence under subsection (4) of causing a person to take any step mentioned in paragraph (a) or (b) of subsection (3) unless it is proved that he knew or had reason to suspect that the step taken would contravene subsection (1).

But this subsection only applies if sufficient evidence is adduced to raise an issue as to whether the person had the knowledge or reason mentioned.

(6) A person guilty of an offence under this section is liable –

(a) on summary conviction to imprisonment for a term not exceeding six months, or a fine not exceeding the statutory maximum, or both,
(b) on conviction on indictment, to imprisonment for a term not exceeding twelve months, or a fine, or both.

(7) In any proceedings under this section –

(a) a report by a British consular officer or a deposition made before a British consular officer and authenticated under the signature of that officer is admissible, upon proof that the officer or the deponent cannot be found in the United Kingdom, as evidence of the matters stated in it, and
(b) it is not necessary to prove the signature or official character of the person who appears to have signed any such report or deposition.

86 Power to modify sections 83 and 85

(1) Regulations may provide for section 83 not to apply if –

(a) the adopters or (as the case may be) prospective adopters are natural parents, natural relatives or guardians of the child in question (or one of them is), or
(b) the British resident in question is a partner of a parent of the child,

and any prescribed conditions are met.

(2) Regulations may provide for section 85(1) to apply with modifications, or not to apply, if –
- (a) the prospective adopters are parents, relatives or guardians of the child in question (or one of them is), or
- (b) the prospective adopter is a partner of a parent of the child,

and any prescribed conditions are met.

(3) On the occasion of the first exercise of the power to make regulations under this section –
- (a) the statutory instrument containing the regulations is not to be made unless a draft of the instrument has been laid before, and approved by a resolution of, each House of Parliament, and
- (b) accordingly section 140(2) does not apply to the instrument.

(4) In this section, 'prescribed' means prescribed by regulations and 'regulations' means regulations made by the Secretary of State after consultation with the Assembly.

Overseas adoptions

87 Overseas adoptions

(1) In this Act, 'overseas adoption' –
- (a) means an adoption of a description specified in an order made by the Secretary of State, being a description of adoptions effected under the law of any country or territory outside the British Islands, but
- (b) does not include a Convention adoption.

(2) Regulations may prescribe the requirements that ought to be met by an adoption of any description effected after the commencement of the regulations for it to be an overseas adoption for the purposes of this Act.

(3) At any time when such regulations have effect, the Secretary of State must exercise his powers under this section so as to secure that subsequently effected adoptions of any description are not overseas adoptions for the purposes of this Act if he considers that they are not likely within a reasonable time to meet the prescribed requirements.

(4) In this section references to this Act include the Adoption Act 1976.

(5) An order under this section may contain provision as to the manner in which evidence of any overseas adoption may be given.

(6) In this section –

'adoption' means an adoption of a child or of a person who was a child at the time the adoption was applied for,
'regulations' means regulations made by the Secretary of State after consultation with the Assembly.

Miscellaneous

88 Modification of section 67 for Hague Convention adoptions

(1) If the High Court is satisfied, on an application under this section, that each of the following conditions is met in the case of a Convention adoption, it may direct that section 67(3) does not apply, or does not apply to any extent specified in the direction.

(2) The conditions are –

(a) that under the law of the country in which the adoption was effected, the adoption is not a full adoption,
(b) that the consents referred to in Article 4(c) and (d) of the Convention have not been given for a full adoption or that the United Kingdom is not the receiving State (within the meaning of Article 2 of the Convention),
(c) that it would be more favourable to the adopted child for a direction to be given under subsection (1).

(3) A full adoption is an adoption by virtue of which the child is to be treated in law as not being the child of any person other than the adopters or adopter.

(4) In relation to a direction under this section and an application for it, sections 59 and 60 of the Family Law Act 1986 (declarations under Part 3 of that Act as to marital status) apply as they apply in relation to a direction under that Part and an application for such a direction.

89 Annulment etc of overseas or Hague Convention adoptions

(1) The High Court may, on an application under this subsection, by order annul a Convention adoption or Convention adoption order on the ground that the adoption is contrary to public policy.

(2) The High Court may, on an application under this subsection –

(a) by order provide for an overseas adoption or a determination under section 91 to cease to be valid on the ground that the adoption or determination is contrary to public policy or that the authority which purported to authorise the adoption or make the determination was not competent to entertain the case, or
(b) decide the extent, if any, to which a determination under section 91 has been affected by a subsequent determination under that section.

(3) The High Court may, in any proceedings in that court, decide that an overseas adoption or a determination under section 91 is to be treated, for the purposes of those proceedings, as invalid on either of the grounds mentioned in subsection (2)(a).

(4) Subject to the preceding provisions, the validity of a Convention adoption, Convention adoption order or overseas adoption or a determination under section 91 cannot be called in question in proceedings in any court in England and Wales.

90 Section 89: supplementary

(1) Any application for an order under section 89 or a decision under subsection (2)(b) or (3) of that section must be made in the prescribed manner and within any prescribed period.

'Prescribed' means prescribed by rules.

(2) No application may be made under section 89(1) in respect of an adoption unless immediately before the application is made –

(a) the person adopted, or
(b) the adopters or adopter,

habitually reside in England and Wales.

(3) In deciding in pursuance of section 89 whether such an authority as is mentioned in section 91 was competent to entertain a particular case, a court is bound by any finding of fact

made by the authority and stated by the authority to be so made for the purpose of determining whether the authority was competent to entertain the case.

91 Overseas determinations and orders

(1) Subsection (2) applies where any authority of a Convention country (other than the United Kingdom) or of the Channel Islands, the Isle of Man or any British overseas territory has power under the law of that country or territory –

   (a) to authorise, or review the authorisation of, an adoption order made in that country or territory, or
   (b) to give or review a decision revoking or annulling such an order or a Convention adoption.

(2) If the authority makes a determination in the exercise of that power, the determination is to have effect for the purpose of effecting, confirming or terminating the adoption in question or, as the case may be, confirming its termination.

(3) Subsection (2) is subject to section 89 and to any subsequent determination having effect under that subsection.

Chapter 7
Miscellaneous

Restrictions

92 Restriction on arranging adoptions etc

(1) A person who is neither an adoption agency nor acting in pursuance of an order of the High Court must not take any of the steps mentioned in subsection (2).

(2) The steps are –

   (a) asking a person other than an adoption agency to provide a child for adoption,
   (b) asking a person other than an adoption agency to provide prospective adopters for a child,
   (c) offering to find a child for adoption,
   (d) offering a child for adoption to a person other than an adoption agency,
   (e) handing over a child to any person other than an adoption agency with a view to the child's adoption by that or another person,
   (f) receiving a child handed over to him in contravention of paragraph (e),
   (g) entering into an agreement with any person for the adoption of a child, or for the purpose of facilitating the adoption of a child, where no adoption agency is acting on behalf of the child in the adoption,
   (h) initiating or taking part in negotiations of which the purpose is the conclusion of an agreement within paragraph (g),
   (i) causing another person to take any of the steps mentioned in paragraphs (a) to (h).

(3) Subsection (1) does not apply to a person taking any of the steps mentioned in paragraphs (d), (e), (g), (h) and (i) of subsection (2) if the following condition is met.

(4) The condition is that –

(a) the prospective adopters are parents, relatives or guardians of the child (or one of them is), or
(b) the prospective adopter is the partner of a parent of the child.

(5) References to an adoption agency in subsection (2) include a prescribed person outside the United Kingdom exercising functions corresponding to those of an adoption agency, if the functions are being exercised in prescribed circumstances in respect of the child in question.

(6) The Secretary of State may, after consultation with the Assembly, by order make any amendments of subsections (1) to (4), and any consequential amendments of this Act, which he considers necessary or expedient.

(7) In this section –

(a) 'agreement' includes an arrangement (whether or not enforceable),
(b) 'prescribed' means prescribed by regulations made by the Secretary of State after consultation with the Assembly.

93 Offence of breaching restrictions under section 92

(1) If a person contravenes section 92(1), he is guilty of an offence; and, if that person is an adoption society, the person who manages the society is also guilty of the offence.

(2) A person is not guilty of an offence under subsection (1) of taking the step mentioned in paragraph (f) of section 92(2) unless it is proved that he knew or had reason to suspect that the child was handed over to him in contravention of paragraph (e) of that subsection.

(3) A person is not guilty of an offence under subsection (1) of causing a person to take any of the steps mentioned in paragraphs (a) to (h) of section 92(2) unless it is proved that he knew or had reason to suspect that the step taken would contravene the paragraph in question.

(4) But subsections (2) and (3) only apply if sufficient evidence is adduced to raise an issue as to whether the person had the knowledge or reason mentioned.

(5) A person guilty of an offence under this section is liable on summary conviction to imprisonment for a term not exceeding six months, or a fine not exceeding £10,000, or both.

94 Restriction on reports

(1) A person who is not within a prescribed description may not, in any prescribed circumstances, prepare a report for any person about the suitability of a child for adoption or of a person to adopt a child or about the adoption, or placement for adoption, of a child.

'Prescribed' means prescribed by regulations made by the Secretary of State after consultation with the Assembly.

(2) If a person –

(a) contravenes subsection (1), or
(b) causes a person to prepare a report, or submits to any person a report which has been prepared, in contravention of that subsection,

he is guilty of an offence.

(3) If a person who works for an adoption society –

(a) contravenes subsection (1), or

(b) causes a person to prepare a report, or submits to any person a report which has been prepared, in contravention of that subsection,

the person who manages the society is also guilty of the offence.

(4) A person is not guilty of an offence under subsection (2)(b) unless it is proved that he knew or had reason to suspect that the report would be, or had been, prepared in contravention of subsection (1).

But this subsection only applies if sufficient evidence is adduced to raise an issue as to whether the person had the knowledge or reason mentioned.

(5) A person guilty of an offence under this section is liable on summary conviction to imprisonment for a term not exceeding six months, or a fine not exceeding level 5 on the standard scale, or both.

95 Prohibition of certain payments

(1) This section applies to any payment (other than an excepted payment) which is made for or in consideration of –

- (a) the adoption of a child,
- (b) giving any consent required in connection with the adoption of a child,
- (c) removing from the United Kingdom a child who is a Commonwealth citizen, or is habitually resident in the United Kingdom, to a place outside the British Islands for the purpose of adoption,
- (d) a person (who is neither an adoption agency nor acting in pursuance of an order of the High Court) taking any step mentioned in section 92(2),
- (e) preparing, causing to be prepared or submitting a report the preparation of which contravenes section 94(1).

(2) In this section and section 96, removing a child from the United Kingdom has the same meaning as in section 85.

(3) Any person who –

- (a) makes any payment to which this section applies,
- (b) agrees or offers to make any such payment, or
- (c) receives or agrees to receive or attempts to obtain any such payment,

is guilty of an offence.

(4) A person guilty of an offence under this section is liable on summary conviction to imprisonment for a term not exceeding six months, or a fine not exceeding £10,000, or both.

96 Excepted payments

(1) A payment is an excepted payment if it is made by virtue of, or in accordance with provision made by or under, this Act, the Adoption (Scotland) Act 1978 or the Adoption (Northern Ireland) Order 1987 (SI 1987/2203 (NI 22)).

(2) A payment is an excepted payment if it is made to a registered adoption society by –

- (a) a parent or guardian of a child, or
- (b) a person who adopts or proposes to adopt a child,

in respect of expenses reasonably incurred by the society in connection with the adoption or proposed adoption of the child.

(3) A payment is an excepted payment if it is made in respect of any legal or medical expenses incurred or to be incurred by any person in connection with an application to a court which he has made or proposes to make for an adoption order, a placement order, or an order under section 26 or 84.

(4) A payment made as mentioned in section 95(1)(c) is an excepted payment if –

(a) the condition in section 85(2) is met, and
(b) the payment is made in respect of the travel and accommodation expenses reasonably incurred in removing the child from the United Kingdom for the purpose of adoption.

97 Sections 92 to 96: interpretation

In sections 92 to 96 –

(a) 'adoption agency' includes a Scottish or Northern Irish adoption agency,
(b) 'payment' includes reward,
(c) references to adoption are to the adoption of persons, wherever they may be habitually resident, effected under the law of any country or territory, whether within or outside the British Islands.

Information

98 Pre-commencement adoptions: information

(1) Regulations under section 9 may make provision for the purpose of –

(a) assisting persons adopted before the appointed day who have attained the age of 18 to obtain information in relation to their adoption, and
(b) facilitating contact between such persons and their relatives.

(2) For that purpose the regulations may confer functions on –

(a) registered adoption support agencies,
(b) the Registrar General,
(c) adoption agencies.

(3) For that purpose the regulations may –

(a) authorise or require any person mentioned in subsection (2) to disclose information,
(b) authorise or require the disclosure of information contained in records kept under section 8 of the Public Records Act 1958 (court records),

and may impose conditions on the disclosure of information, including conditions restricting its further disclosure.

(4) The regulations may authorise the charging of prescribed fees by any person mentioned in subsection (2) or in respect of the disclosure of information under subsection (3)(b).

(5) An authorisation or requirement to disclose information by virtue of subsection (3)(a) has effect in spite of any restriction on the disclosure of information in Chapter 5.

(6) The making of regulations by virtue of subsections (2) to (4) which relate to the Registrar General requires the approval of the Chancellor of the Exchequer.

(7) In this section –

'appointed day' means the day appointed for the commencement of sections 56 to 65, 'registered adoption support agency' means an adoption support agency in respect of which a person is registered under Part 2 of the Care Standards Act 2000,

'relative', in relation to an adopted person, means any person who (but for his adoption) would be related to him by blood (including half-blood) or marriage.

Proceedings

99 Proceedings for offences

Proceedings for an offence by virtue of section 9 or 59 may not, without the written consent of the Attorney General, be taken by any person other than the National Care Standards Commission or the Assembly.

...

101 Privacy

(1) Proceedings under this Act in the High Court or a County Court may be heard and determined in private.

(2)–(3) ...

The Children and Family Court Advisory and Support Service

102 Officers of the Service

(1) For the purposes of –

(a) any relevant application,
(b) the signification by any person of any consent to placement or adoption,

rules must provide for the appointment in prescribed cases of an officer of the Children and Family Court Advisory and Support Service ('the Service').

(2) The rules may provide for the appointment of such an officer in other circumstances in which it appears to the Lord Chancellor to be necessary or expedient to do so.

(3) The rules may provide for the officer –

(a) to act on behalf of the child upon the hearing of any relevant application, with the duty of safeguarding the interests of the child in the prescribed manner,
(b) where the court so requests, to prepare a report on matters relating to the welfare of the child in question,
(c) to witness documents which signify consent to placement or adoption,
(d) to perform prescribed functions.

(4) A report prepared in pursuance of the rules on matters relating to the welfare of a child must –

(a) deal with prescribed matters (unless the court orders otherwise), and
(b) be made in the manner required by the court.

(5) A person who –

(a) in the case of an application for the making, varying or revocation of a placement order, is employed by the local authority which made the application,

(b) in the case of an application for an adoption order in respect of a child who was placed for adoption, is employed by the adoption agency which placed him, or
(c) is within a prescribed description,

is not to be appointed under subsection (1) or (2).

(6) In this section, 'relevant application' means an application for –

(a) the making, varying or revocation of a placement order,
(b) the making of an order under section 26, or the varying or revocation of such an order,
(c) the making of an adoption order, or
(d) the making of an order under section 84.

(7) Rules may make provision as to the assistance which the court may require an officer of the Service to give to it.

103 Right of officers of the Service to have access to adoption agency records

(1) Where an officer of the Service has been appointed to act under section 102(1), he has the right at all reasonable times to examine and take copies of any records of, or held by, an adoption agency which were compiled in connection with the making, or proposed making, by any person of any application under this Part in respect of the child concerned.

(2) Where an officer of the Service takes a copy of any record which he is entitled to examine under this section, that copy or any part of it is admissible as evidence of any matter referred to in any –

(a) report which he makes to the court in the proceedings in question, or
(b) evidence which he gives in those proceedings.

(3) Subsection (2) has effect regardless of any enactment or rule of law which would otherwise prevent the record in question being admissible in evidence.

Evidence

104 Evidence of consent

(1) If a document signifying any consent which is required by this Part to be given is witnessed in accordance with rules, it is to be admissible in evidence without further proof of the signature of the person by whom it was executed.

(2) A document signifying any such consent which purports to be witnessed in accordance with rules is to be presumed to be so witnessed, and to have been executed and witnessed on the date and at the place specified in the document, unless the contrary is proved.

...

General

109 Avoiding delay

(1) In proceedings in which a question may arise as to whether an adoption order or placement order should be made, or any other question with respect to such an order, the court must (in the light of any rules made by virtue of subsection (2)) –

(a) draw up a timetable with a view to determining such a question without delay, and

(b) give such directions as it considers appropriate for the purpose of ensuring that the timetable is adhered to.

(2) Rules may –
   (a) prescribe periods within which prescribed steps must be taken in relation to such proceedings, and
   (b) make other provision with respect to such proceedings for the purpose of ensuring that such questions are determined without delay.

110 Service of notices etc

Any notice or information required to be given by virtue of this Act may be given by post.

PART 2
AMENDMENTS OF THE CHILDREN ACT 1989

111 Parental responsibility of unmarried father

(1) Section 4 of the 1989 Act (acquisition of responsibility by the father of a child who is not married to the child's mother) is amended as follows.

(2) In subsection (1) (cases where parental responsibility is acquired), for the words after 'birth' there is substituted ', the father shall acquire parental responsibility for the child if –
   (a) he becomes registered as the child's father under any of the enactments specified in subsection (1A);
   (b) he and the child's mother make an agreement (a "parental responsibility agreement") providing for him to have parental responsibility for the child; or
   (c) the court, on his application, orders that he shall have parental responsibility for the child.'

(3) After that subsection there is inserted –

'(1A) The enactments referred to in subsection (1)(a) are –
   (a) paragraphs (a), (b) and (c) of section 10(1) and of section 10A(1) of the Births and Deaths Registration Act 1953;
   (b) paragraphs (a), (b)(i) and (c) of section 18(1), and sections 18(2)(b) and 20(1)(a) of the Registration of Births, Deaths and Marriages (Scotland) Act 1965; and
   (c) sub-paragraphs (a), (b) and (c) of Article 14(3) of the Births and Deaths Registration (Northern Ireland) Order 1976.

(1B) The Lord Chancellor may by order amend subsection (1A) so as to add further enactments to the list in that subsection.'

(4) For subsection (3) there is substituted –

'(2A) A person who has acquired parental responsibility under subsection (1) shall cease to have that responsibility only if the court so orders.

(3) The court may make an order under subsection (2A) on the application –
   (a) of any person who has parental responsibility for the child; or
   (b) with the leave of the court, of the child himself,

subject, in the case of parental responsibility acquired under subsection (1)(c), to section 12(4).'

(5) Accordingly, in section 2(2) of the 1989 Act (a father of a child who is not married to the child's mother shall not have parental responsibility for the child unless he acquires it in accordance with the provisions of the Act), for the words from 'shall not' to 'acquires it' there is substituted 'shall have parental responsibility for the child if he has acquired it (and has not ceased to have it)'.

(6) In section 104 of the 1989 Act (regulations and orders) –

(a) in subsection (2), after 'section' there is inserted '4(1B),', and
(b) in subsection (3), after 'section' there is inserted '4(1B) or'.

(7) Paragraph (a) of section 4(1) of the 1989 Act, as substituted by subsection (2) of this section, does not confer parental responsibility on a man who was registered under an enactment referred to in paragraph (a), (b) or (c) of section 4(1A) of that Act, as inserted by subsection (3) of this section, before the commencement of subsection (3) in relation to that paragraph.

...

116 Accommodation of children in need etc

(1) In section 17 of the 1989 Act (provision of services for children in need, their families and others), in subsection (6) (services that may be provided in exercise of the functions under that section) after 'include' there is inserted 'providing accommodation and'.

(2) In section 22 of that Act (general duty of local authority in relation to children looked after by them), in subsection (1) (looked after children include those provided with accommodation, with exceptions) before '23B' there is inserted '17'.

(3) In section 24A of that Act (advice and assistance for certain children and young persons aged 16 or over), in subsection (5), for 'or, in exceptional circumstances, cash' there is substituted 'and, in exceptional circumstances, assistance may be given –

(a) by providing accommodation, if in the circumstances assistance may not be given in respect of the accommodation under section 24B, or
(b) in cash'.

...

121 Care plans

(1) In section 31 of the 1989 Act (care and supervision orders), after subsection (3) there is inserted –

'(3A) No care order may be made with respect to a child until the court has considered a section 31A plan.'

(2) After that section there is inserted –

'31A Care orders: care plans

(1) Where an application is made on which a care order might be made with respect to a child, the appropriate local authority must, within such time as the court may direct, prepare a plan ("a care plan") for the future care of the child.

(2) While the application is pending, the authority must keep any care plan prepared by them under review and, if they are of the opinion some change is required, revise the plan, or make a new plan, accordingly.

(3) A care plan must give any prescribed information and do so in the prescribed manner.

(4) For the purposes of this section, the appropriate local authority, in relation to a child in respect of whom a care order might be made, is the local authority proposed to be designated in the order.

(5) In section 31(3A) and this section, references to a care order do not include an interim care order.

(6) A plan prepared, or treated as prepared, under this section is referred to in this Act as a "section 31A plan".'

(3) If –

(a) before subsection (2) comes into force, a care order has been made in respect of a child and a plan for the future care of the child has been prepared in connection with the making of the order by the local authority designated in the order, and

(b) on the day on which that subsection comes into force the order is in force, or would be in force but for section 29(1) of this Act,

the plan is to have effect as if made under section 31A of the 1989 Act.

...

PART 3

MISCELLANEOUS AND FINAL PROVISIONS

Chapter 1
Miscellaneous

Advertisements in the United Kingdom

123 Restriction on advertisements etc

(1) A person must not –

(a) publish or distribute an advertisement or information to which this section applies, or
(b) cause such an advertisement or information to be published or distributed.

(2) This section applies to an advertisement indicating that –

(a) the parent or guardian of a child wants the child to be adopted,
(b) a person wants to adopt a child,
(c) a person other than an adoption agency is willing to take any step mentioned in paragraphs (a) to (e), (g) and (h) and (so far as relating to those paragraphs) (i) of section 92(2),
(d) a person other than an adoption agency is willing to receive a child handed over to him with a view to the child's adoption by him or another, or
(e) a person is willing to remove a child from the United Kingdom for the purposes of adoption.

(3) This section applies to –

(a) information about how to do anything which, if done, would constitute an offence under

section 85 or 93, section 11 or 50 of the Adoption (Scotland) Act 1978 or Article 11 or 58 of the Adoption (Northern Ireland) Order 1987 (SI 1987/2203 (NI 22)) (whether or not the information includes a warning that doing the thing in question may constitute an offence),
  (b) information about a particular child as a child available for adoption.

(4) For the purposes of this section and section 124 –
  (a) publishing or distributing an advertisement or information means publishing it or distributing it to the public and includes doing so by electronic means (for example, by means of the internet),
  (b) the public includes selected members of the public as well as the public generally or any section of the public.

(5) Subsection (1) does not apply to publication or distribution by or on behalf of an adoption agency.

(6) The Secretary of State may by order make any amendments of this section which he considers necessary or expedient in consequence of any developments in technology relating to publishing or distributing advertisements or other information by electronic or electro-magnetic means.

(7) References to an adoption agency in this section include a prescribed person outside the United Kingdom exercising functions corresponding to those of an adoption agency, if the functions are being exercised in prescribed circumstances.

'Prescribed' means prescribed by regulations made by the Secretary of State.

(8) Before exercising the power conferred by subsection (6) or (7), the Secretary of State must consult the Scottish Ministers, the Department of Health, Social Services and Public Safety and the Assembly.

(9) In this section –
  (a) 'adoption agency' includes a Scottish or Northern Irish adoption agency,
  (b) references to adoption are to the adoption of persons, wherever they may be habitually resident, effected under the law of any country or territory, whether within or outside the British Islands.

124 Offence of breaching restriction under section 123

(1) A person who contravenes section 123(1) is guilty of an offence.

(2) A person is not guilty of an offence under this section unless it is proved that he knew or had reason to suspect that section 123 applied to the advertisement or information.

But this subsection only applies if sufficient evidence is adduced to raise an issue as to whether the person had the knowledge or reason mentioned.

(3) A person guilty of an offence under this section is liable on summary conviction to imprisonment for a term not exceeding three months, or a fine not exceeding level 5 on the standard scale, or both.

Adoption and Children Act Register

125 Adoption and Children Act Register

(1) Her Majesty may by Order in Council make provision for the Secretary of State to establish and maintain a register, to be called the Adoption and Children Act Register, containing –

(a) prescribed information about children who are suitable for adoption and prospective adopters who are suitable to adopt a child,

(b) prescribed information about persons included in the register in pursuance of paragraph (a) in respect of things occurring after their inclusion.

(2) For the purpose of giving assistance in finding persons with whom children may be placed for purposes other than adoption, an Order under this section may –

(a) provide for the register to contain information about such persons and the children who may be placed with them, and

(b) apply any of the other provisions of this group of sections (that is, this section and sections 126 to 131), with or without modifications.

(3) The register is not to be open to public inspection or search.

(4) An Order under this section may make provision about the retention of information in the register.

(5) Information is to be kept in the register in any form the Secretary of State considers appropriate.

126 Use of an organisation to establish the register

(1) The Secretary of State may make an arrangement with an organisation under which any function of his under an Order under section 125 of establishing and maintaining the register, and disclosing information entered in, or compiled from information entered in, the register to any person is performed wholly or partly by the organisation on his behalf.

(2) The arrangement may include provision for payments to be made to the organisation by the Secretary of State.

(3) If the Secretary of State makes an arrangement under this section with an organisation, the organisation is to perform the functions exercisable by virtue of this section in accordance with any directions given by the Secretary of State and the directions may be of general application (or general application in any part of Great Britain) or be special directions.

(4) An exercise of the Secretary of State's powers under subsection (1) or (3) requires the agreement of the Scottish Ministers (if the register applies to Scotland) and of the Assembly (if the register applies to Wales).

(5) References in this group of sections to the registration organisation are to any organisation for the time being performing functions in respect of the register by virtue of arrangements under this section.

127 Use of an organisation as agency for payments

(1) An Order under section 125 may authorise an organisation with which an arrangement is made under section 126 to act as agent for the payment or receipt of sums payable by adoption agencies to other adoption agencies and may require adoption agencies to pay or receive such sums through the organisation.

(2) The organisation is to perform the functions exercisable by virtue of this section in accordance with any directions given by the Secretary of State; and the directions may be of general application (or general application in any part of Great Britain) or be special directions.

(3) An exercise of the Secretary of State's power to give directions under subsection (2) requires the agreement of the Scottish Ministers (if any payment agency provision applies to Scotland) and of the Assembly (if any payment agency provision applies to Wales).

128 Supply of information for the register

(1) An Order under section 125 may require adoption agencies to give prescribed information to the Secretary of State or the registration organisation for entry in the register.

(2) Information is to be given to the Secretary of State or the registration organisation when required by the Order and in the prescribed form and manner.

(3) An Order under section 125 may require an agency giving information which is entered on the register to pay a prescribed fee to the Secretary of State or the registration organisation.

(4) But an adoption agency is not to disclose any information to the Secretary of State or the registration organisation –

   (a) about prospective adopters who are suitable to adopt a child, or persons who were included in the register as such prospective adopters, without their consent,
   (b) about children suitable for adoption, or persons who were included in the register as such children, without the consent of the prescribed person.

(5) Consent under subsection (4) is to be given in the prescribed form.

129 Disclosure of information

(1) Information entered in the register, or compiled from information entered in the register, may only be disclosed under subsection (2) or (3).

(2) Prescribed information entered in the register may be disclosed by the Secretary of State or the registration organisation –

   (a) where an adoption agency is acting on behalf of a child who is suitable for adoption, to the agency to assist in finding prospective adopters with whom it would be appropriate for the child to be placed,
   (b) where an adoption agency is acting on behalf of prospective adopters who are suitable to adopt a child, to the agency to assist in finding a child appropriate for adoption by them.

(3) Prescribed information entered in the register, or compiled from information entered in the register, may be disclosed by the Secretary of State or the registration organisation to any prescribed person for use for statistical or research purposes, or for other prescribed purposes.

(4) An Order under section 125 may prescribe the steps to be taken by adoption agencies in respect of information received by them by virtue of subsection (2).

(5) Subsection (1) does not apply –

   (a) to a disclosure of information with the authority of the Secretary of State, or
   (b) to a disclosure by the registration organisation of prescribed information to the Scottish Ministers (if the register applies to Scotland) or the Assembly (if the register applies to Wales).

(6) Information disclosed to any person under subsection (2) or (3) may be given on any prescribed terms or conditions.

(7) An Order under section 125 may, in prescribed circumstances, require a prescribed fee to be paid to the Secretary of State or the registration organisation –

(a) by a prescribed adoption agency in respect of information disclosed under subsection (2), or
(b) by a person to whom information is disclosed under subsection (3).

(8) If any information entered in the register is disclosed to a person in contravention of subsection (1), the person disclosing it is guilty of an offence.

(9) A person guilty of an offence under subsection (8) is liable on summary conviction to imprisonment for a term not exceeding three months, or a fine not exceeding level 5 on the standard scale, or both.

130 Territorial application

(1) In this group of sections, 'adoption agency' means –
  (a) a local authority in England,
  (b) a registered adoption society whose principal office is in England.

(2) An Order under section 125 may provide for any requirements imposed on adoption agencies in respect of the register to apply –
  (a) to Scottish local authorities and to voluntary organisations providing a registered adoption service,
  (b) to local authorities in Wales and to registered adoption societies whose principal offices are in Wales,

and, in relation to the register, references to adoption agencies in this group of sections include any authorities or societies mentioned in paragraphs (a) and (b) to which an Order under that section applies those requirements.

(3) For the purposes of this group of sections, references to the register applying to Scotland or Wales are to those requirements applying as mentioned in paragraph (a) or, as the case may be, (b) of subsection (2).

(4) An Order under section 125 may apply any provision made by virtue of section 127 –
  (a) to Scottish local authorities and to voluntary organisations providing a registered adoption service,
  (b) to local authorities in Wales and to registered adoption societies whose principal offices are in Wales.

(5) For the purposes of this group of sections, references to any payment agency provision applying to Scotland or Wales are to provision made by virtue of section 127 applying as mentioned in paragraph (a) or, as the case may be, (b) of subsection (4).

131 Supplementary

(1) In this group of sections –
  (a) 'organisation' includes a public body and a private or voluntary organisation,
  (b) 'prescribed' means prescribed by an Order under section 125,
  (c) 'the register' means the Adoption and Children Act Register,
  (d) 'Scottish local authority' means a local authority within the meaning of the Regulation of Care (Scotland) Act 2001,
  (e) 'voluntary organisation providing a registered adoption service' has the same meaning as in section 144(3).

(2) For the purposes of this group of sections –

(a) a child is suitable for adoption if an adoption agency is satisfied that the child ought to be placed for adoption,
(b) prospective adopters are suitable to adopt a child if an adoption agency is satisfied that they are suitable to have a child placed with them for adoption.

(3) Nothing authorised or required to be done by virtue of this group of sections constitutes an offence under section 93, 94 or 95.

(4) No recommendation to make an Order under section 125 is to be made to Her Majesty in Council unless a draft has been laid before and approved by resolution of each House of Parliament.

(5) If any provision made by an Order under section 125 would, if it were included in an Act of the Scottish Parliament, be within the legislative competence of that Parliament, no recommendation to make the Order is to be made to Her Majesty in Council unless a draft has been laid before, and approved by resolution of, the Parliament.

(6) No recommendation to make an Order under section 125 containing any provision in respect of the register is to be made to Her Majesty in Council if the register applies to Wales or the Order would provide for the register to apply to Wales, unless a draft has been laid before, and approved by resolution of, the Assembly.

(7) No recommendation to make an Order under section 125 containing any provision by virtue of section 127 is to be made to Her Majesty in Council if any payment agency provision applies to Wales or the Order would provide for any payment agency provision to apply to Wales, unless a draft has been laid before, and approved by resolution of, the Assembly.

…

Chapter 2
Final provisions

140 Orders, rules and regulations

(1) Any power to make subordinate legislation conferred by this Act on the Lord Chancellor, the Secretary of State, the Scottish Ministers, the Assembly or the Registrar General is exercisable by statutory instrument.

(2) A statutory instrument containing subordinate legislation made under any provision of this Act (other than section 14 or 148 or an instrument to which subsection (3) applies) is to be subject to annulment in pursuance of a resolution of either House of Parliament.

(3) A statutory instrument containing subordinate legislation –

(a) under section 9 which includes provision made by virtue of section 45(2),
(b) under section 92(6), 94 or 123(6), or
(c) which adds to, replaces or omits any part of the text of an Act,

is not to be made unless a draft of the instrument has been laid before, and approved by resolution of, each House of Parliament.

(4) Subsections (2) and (3) do not apply to an Order in Council or to subordinate legislation made –

(a) by the Scottish Ministers, or
(b) by the Assembly, unless made jointly by the Secretary of State and the Assembly.

(5) A statutory instrument containing regulations under section 63(2) made by the Scottish Ministers is to be subject to annulment in pursuance of a resolution of the Scottish Parliament.

(6) The power of the Department of Health, Social Services and Public Safety to make regulations under section 63(2) is to be exercisable by statutory rule for the purposes of the Statutory Rules (Northern Ireland) Order 1979 (SI 1979/ 1573 (NI 12)); and any such regulations are to be subject to negative resolution within the meaning of section 41(6) of the Interpretation Act (Northern Ireland) 1954 as if they were statutory instruments within the meaning of that Act.

(7) Subordinate legislation made under this Act may make different provision for different purposes.

(8) A power to make subordinate legislation under this Act (as well as being exercisable in relation to all cases to which it extends) may be exercised in relation to –

(a) those cases subject to specified exceptions, or
(b) a particular case or class of case.

(9) In this section, 'subordinate legislation' does not include a direction.

141 Rules of procedure

(1) The Lord Chancellor may make rules in respect of any matter to be prescribed by rules made by virtue of this Act and dealing generally with all matters of procedure.

(2) Subsection (1) does not apply in relation to proceedings before magistrates' courts, but the power to make rules conferred by section 144 of the Magistrates' Courts Act 1980 includes power to make provision in respect of any of the matters mentioned in that subsection.

(3) In the case of an application for a placement order, for the variation or revocation of such an order, or for an adoption order, the rules must require any person mentioned in subsection (4) to be notified –

(a) of the date and place where the application will be heard, and
(b) of the fact that, unless the person wishes or the court requires, the person need not attend.

(4) The persons referred to in subsection (3) are –

(a) in the case of a placement order, every person who can be found whose consent to the making of the order is required under subsection (3)(a) of section 21 (or would be required but for subsection (3)(b) of that section) or, if no such person can be found, any relative prescribed by rules who can be found,
(b) in the case of a variation or revocation of a placement order, every person who can be found whose consent to the making of the placement order was required under subsection (3)(a) of section 21 (or would have been required but for subsection (3)(b) of that section),
(c) in the case of an adoption order –
  (i) every person who can be found whose consent to the making of the order is required under subsection (2)(a) of section 47 (or would be required but for subsection (2)(c) of that section) or, if no such person can be found, any relative prescribed by rules who can be found,

(ii) every person who has consented to the making of the order under section 20 (and has not withdrawn the consent) unless he has given a notice under subsection (4)(a) of that section which has effect,
(iii) every person who, if leave were given under section 47(5), would be entitled to oppose the making of the order.

(5) Rules made in respect of magistrates' courts may provide –

(a) for enabling any fact tending to establish the identity of a child with a child to whom a document relates to be proved by affidavit, and
(b) for excluding or restricting in relation to any facts that may be so proved the power of a justice of the peace to compel the attendance of witnesses.

(6) Rules may, for the purposes of the law relating to contempt of court, authorise the publication in such circumstances as may be specified of information relating to proceedings held in private involving children.

Amendment—Children Act 2004, s 62(6).

142 Supplementary and consequential provision

(1) The appropriate Minister may by order make –

(a) any supplementary, incidental or consequential provision,
(b) any transitory, transitional or saving provision,

which he considers necessary or expedient for the purposes of, in consequence of or for giving full effect to any provision of this Act.

(2) For the purposes of subsection (1), where any provision of an order extends to England and Wales, and Scotland or Northern Ireland, the appropriate Minister in relation to the order is the Secretary of State.

(3) Before making an order under subsection (1) containing provision which would, if included in an Act of the Scottish Parliament, be within the legislative competence of that Parliament, the appropriate Minister must consult the Scottish Ministers.

(4) Subsection (5) applies to any power of the Lord Chancellor, the Secretary of State or the Assembly to make regulations, rules or an order by virtue of any other provision of this Act or of Her Majesty to make an Order in Council by virtue of section 125.

(5) The power may be exercised so as to make –

(a) any supplementary, incidental or consequential provision,
(b) any transitory, transitional or saving provision,

which the person exercising the power considers necessary or expedient.

(6) The provision which may be made under subsection (1) or (5) includes provision modifying Schedule 4 or amending or repealing any enactment or instrument.

In relation to an Order in Council, 'enactment' in this subsection includes an enactment comprised in, or in an instrument made under, an Act of the Scottish Parliament.

(7) The power of the Registrar General to make regulations under Chapter 5 of Part 1 may, with the approval of the Chancellor of the Exchequer, be exercised so as to make –

(a) any supplementary, incidental or consequential provision,
(b) any transitory, transitional or saving provision,

which the Registrar General considers necessary or expedient.

143 Offences by bodies corporate and unincorporated bodies

(1) Where an offence under this Act committed by a body corporate is proved to have been committed with the consent or connivance of, or to be attributable to any neglect on the part of, any director, manager, secretary or other similar officer of the body, or a person purporting to act in any such capacity, that person as well as the body is guilty of the offence and liable to be proceeded against and punished accordingly.

(2) Where the affairs of a body corporate are managed by its members, subsection (1) applies in relation to the acts and defaults of a member in connection with his functions of management as it applies to a director of a body corporate.

(3) Proceedings for an offence alleged to have been committed under this Act by an unincorporated body are to be brought in the name of that body (and not in that of any of its members) and, for the purposes of any such proceedings in England and Wales or Northern Ireland, any rules of court relating to the service of documents have effect as if that body were a corporation.

(4) A fine imposed on an unincorporated body on its conviction of an offence under this Act is to be paid out of the funds of that body.

(5) If an unincorporated body is charged with an offence under this Act –

(a) in England and Wales, section 33 of the Criminal Justice Act 1925 and Schedule 3 to the Magistrates' Courts Act 1980 (procedure on charge of an offence against a corporation),
(b) in Northern Ireland, section 18 of the Criminal Justice Act (Northern Ireland) 1945 and Schedule 4 to the Magistrates' Courts (Northern Ireland) Order 1981 (SI 1981/1675 (NI 26)) (procedure on charge of an offence against a corporation),

have effect in like manner as in the case of a corporation so charged.

(6) Where an offence under this Act committed by an unincorporated body (other than a partnership) is proved to have been committed with the consent or connivance of, or to be attributable to any neglect on the part of, any officer of the body or any member of its governing body, he as well as the body is guilty of the offence and liable to be proceeded against and punished accordingly.

(7) Where an offence under this Act committed by a partnership is proved to have been committed with the consent or connivance of, or to be attributable to any neglect on the part of, a partner, he as well as the partnership is guilty of the offence and liable to be proceeded against and punished accordingly.

144 General interpretation etc

(1) In this Act –

'appropriate Minister' means –
(a) in relation to England, Scotland or Northern Ireland, the Secretary of State,
(b) in relation to Wales, the Assembly,
and in relation to England and Wales means the Secretary of State and the Assembly acting jointly,
'the Assembly' means the National Assembly for Wales,
'body' includes an unincorporated body,
'by virtue of' includes 'by' and 'under',

'child', except where used to express a relationship, means a person who has not attained the age of 18 years,

'the Convention' means the Convention on Protection of Children and Co-operation in respect of Intercountry Adoption, concluded at the Hague on 29th May 1993,

'Convention adoption order' means an adoption order which, by virtue of regulations under section 1 of the Adoption (Intercountry Aspects) Act 1999 (regulations giving effect to the Convention), is made as a Convention adoption order,

'Convention country' means a country or territory in which the Convention is in force,

'court' means, subject to any provision made by virtue of Part 1 of Schedule 11 to the 1989 Act, the High Court, a county court or a magistrates' court,

'enactment' includes an enactment comprised in subordinate legislation,

'fee' includes expenses,

'guardian' has the same meaning as in the 1989 Act and includes a special guardian within the meaning of that Act,

'information' means information recorded in any form,

'local authority' means any unitary authority, or any county council so far as they are not a unitary authority,

'Northern Irish adoption agency' means an adoption agency within the meaning of Article 3 of the Adoption (Northern Ireland) Order 1987 (SI 1987/2203 (NI 22)),

'Northern Irish adoption order' means an order made, or having effect as if made, under Article 12 of the Adoption (Northern Ireland) Order 1987,

'notice' means a notice in writing,

'registration authority' (in Part 1) has the same meaning as in the Care Standards Act 2000,

'regulations' means regulations made by the appropriate Minister, unless they are required to be made by the Lord Chancellor, the Secretary of State or the Registrar General,

'relative', in relation to a child, means a grandparent, brother, sister, uncle or aunt, whether of the full blood or half-blood or by marriage,

'rules' means rules made under section 141(1) or made by virtue of section 141(2) under section 144 of the Magistrates' Courts Act 1980,

'Scottish adoption order' means an order made, or having effect as if made, under section 12 of the Adoption (Scotland) Act 1978,

'subordinate legislation' has the same meaning as in the Interpretation Act 1978,

'unitary authority' means –

(a) the council of any county so far as they are the council for an area for which there are no district councils,

(b) the council of any district comprised in an area for which there is no county council,

(c) the council of a county borough,

(d) the council of a London borough,

(e) the Common Council of the City of London.

(2) Any power conferred by this Act to prescribe a fee by Order in Council or regulations includes power to prescribe –

(a) a fee not exceeding a prescribed amount,

(b) a fee calculated in accordance with the Order or, as the case may be, regulations,

(c) a fee determined by the person to whom it is payable, being a fee of a reasonable amount.

(3) In this Act, 'Scottish adoption agency' means –

(a) a local authority, or

(b) a voluntary organisation providing a registered adoption service;

but in relation to the provision of any particular service, references to a Scottish adoption agency do not include a voluntary organisation unless it is registered in respect of that service or a service which, in Scotland, corresponds to that service.

Expressions used in this subsection have the same meaning as in the Regulation of Care (Scotland) Act 2001 and 'registered' means registered under Part 1 of that Act.

(4) In this Act, a couple means –

(a) a married couple, or
(b) two people (whether of different sexes or the same sex) living as partners in an enduring family relationship.

(5) Subsection (4)(b) does not include two people one of whom is the other's parent, grandparent, sister, brother, aunt or uncle.

(6) References to relationships in subsection (5) –

(a) are to relationships of the full blood or half blood or, in the case of an adopted person, such of those relationships as would exist but for adoption, and
(b) include the relationship of a child with his adoptive, or former adoptive, parents,

but do not include any other adoptive relationships.

(7) For the purposes of this Act, a person is the partner of a child's parent if the person and the parent are a couple but the person is not the child's parent.

145 Devolution: Wales

(1) The references to the Adoption Act 1976 and to the 1989 Act in Schedule 1 to the National Assembly for Wales (Transfer of Functions) Order 1999 (SI 1999/672) are to be treated as referring to those Acts as amended by virtue of this Act.

(2) This section does not affect the power to make further Orders varying or omitting those references.

(3) In Schedule 1 to that Order, in the entry for the Adoption Act 1976, '9' is omitted.

(4) The functions exercisable by the Assembly under sections 9 and 9A of the Adoption Act 1976 (by virtue of paragraphs 4 and 5 of Schedule 4 to this Act) are to be treated for the purposes of section 44 of the Government of Wales Act 1998 (parliamentary procedures for subordinate legislation) as if made exercisable by the Assembly by an Order in Council under section 22 of that Act.

146 Expenses

There shall be paid out of money provided by Parliament –

(a) any expenditure incurred by a Minister of the Crown by virtue of this Act,
(b) any increase attributable to this Act in the sums payable out of money so provided under any other enactment.

147 Glossary

Schedule 6 (glossary) is to have effect.

148 Commencement

(1) This Act (except sections 116 and 136, this Chapter and the provisions mentioned in subsections (5) and (6)) is to come into force on such day as the Secretary of State may by order appoint.

(2) Before making an order under subsection (1) (other than an order bringing paragraph 53 of Schedule 3 into force) the Secretary of State must consult the Assembly.

(3) Before making an order under subsection (1) bringing sections 123 and 124 into force, the Secretary of State must also consult the Scottish Ministers and the Department of Health, Social Services and Public Safety.

(4) Before making an order under subsection (1) bringing sections 125 to 131 into force, the Secretary of State must also consult the Scottish Ministers.

(5) The following are to come into force on such day as the Scottish Ministers may by order appoint –

- (a) section 41(5) to (9), so far as relating to Scotland,
- (b) sections 132 to 134,
- (c) paragraphs 21 to 35 and 82 to 84 of Schedule 3,
- (d) paragraphs 15 and 23 of Schedule 4,
- (e) the entries in Schedule 5, so far as relating to the provisions mentioned in paragraphs (c) and (d),
- (f) section 139, so far as relating to the provisions mentioned in the preceding paragraphs.

(6) Sections 2(6), 3(3) and (4), 4 to 17, 27(3), 53(1) to (3), 54, 56 to 65 and 98, paragraphs 13, 65, 66 and 111 to 113 of Schedule 3 and paragraphs 3 and 5 of Schedule 4 are to come into force on such day as the appropriate Minister may by order appoint.

149 Extent

(1) The amendment or repeal of an enactment has the same extent as the enactment to which it relates.

(2) Subject to that and to the following provisions, this Act except section 137 extends to England and Wales only.

(3) The following extend also to Scotland and Northern Ireland –

- (a) sections 63(2) to (5), 65(2)(a) and (b) and (3), 123 and 124,
- (b) this Chapter, except sections 141 and 145.

(4) The following extend also to Scotland –

- (a) section 41(5) to (9),
- (b) sections 125 to 131,
- (c) section 138,
- (d) section 139, so far as relating to provisions extending to Scotland.

(5) In Schedule 4, paragraph 23 extends only to Scotland.

150 Short title

This Act may be cited as the Adoption and Children Act 2002.

SCHEDULE 1

REGISTRATION OF ADOPTIONS

Registration of adoption orders

1 (1) Every adoption order must contain a direction to the Registrar General to make in the Adopted Children Register an entry in the form prescribed by regulations made by the Registrar General with the approval of the Chancellor of the Exchequer.

(2) Where, on an application to a court for an adoption order in respect of a child, the identity of the child with a child to whom an entry in the registers of live-births or other records relates is proved to the satisfaction of the court, any adoption order made in pursuance of the application must contain a direction to the Registrar General to secure that the entry in the register or, as the case may be, record in question is marked with the word 'Adopted'.

(3) Where an adoption order is made in respect of a child who has previously been the subject of an adoption order made by a court in England or Wales under Part 1 of this Act or any other enactment –

    (a) sub-paragraph (2) does not apply, and
    (b) the order must contain a direction to the Registrar General to mark the previous entry in the Adopted Children Register with the word 'Re-adopted'.

(4) Where an adoption order is made, the prescribed officer of the court which made the order must communicate the order to the Registrar General in the prescribed manner; and the Registrar General must then comply with the directions contained in the order.

'Prescribed' means prescribed by rules.

Registration of adoptions in Scotland, Northern Ireland, the Isle of Man and the Channel Islands

2 (1) Sub-paragraphs (2) and (3) apply where the Registrar General is notified by the authority maintaining a register of adoptions in a part of the British Islands outside England and Wales that an order has been made in that part authorising the adoption of a child.

(2) If an entry in the registers of live-births or other records (and no entry in the Adopted Children Register) relates to the child, the Registrar General must secure that the entry is marked with –

    (a) the word 'Adopted', followed by
    (b) the name, in brackets, of the part in which the order was made.

(3) If an entry in the Adopted Children Register relates to the child, the Registrar General must mark the entry with –

    (a) the word 'Re-adopted', followed by
    (b) the name, in brackets, of the part in which the order was made.

(4) Where, after an entry in either of the registers or other records mentioned in sub-paragraphs (2) and (3) has been so marked, the Registrar General is notified by the authority concerned that –

    (a) the order has been quashed,
    (b) an appeal against the order has been allowed, or
    (c) the order has been revoked,

the Registrar General must secure that the marking is cancelled.

(5) A copy or extract of an entry in any register or other record, being an entry the marking of which is cancelled under sub-paragraph (4), is not to be treated as an accurate copy unless both the marking and the cancellation are omitted from it.

Registration of other adoptions

3 (1) If the Registrar General is satisfied, on an application under this paragraph, that he has sufficient particulars relating to a child adopted under a registrable foreign adoption to enable an entry to be made in the Adopted Children Register for the child he must make the entry accordingly.

(2) If he is also satisfied that an entry in the registers of live-births or other records relates to the child, he must –

(a) secure that the entry is marked 'Adopted', followed by the name, in brackets, of the country in which the adoption was effected, or
(b) where appropriate, secure that the overseas registers of births are so marked.

(3) An application under this paragraph must be made, in the prescribed manner, by a prescribed person and the applicant must provide the prescribed documents and other information.

(4) An entry made in the Adopted Children Register by virtue of this paragraph must be made in the prescribed form.

(5) In this Schedule 'registrable foreign adoption' means an adoption which satisfies prescribed requirements and is either –

(a) adoption under a Convention adoption, or
(b) adoption under an overseas adoption.

(6) In this paragraph –

(a) 'prescribed' means prescribed by regulations made by the Registrar General with the approval of the Chancellor of the Exchequer,
(b) 'overseas register of births' includes –
  (i) a register made under regulations made by the Secretary of State under section 41(1)(g), (h) or (i) of the British Nationality Act 1981,
  (ii) a record kept under an Order in Council made under section 1 of the Registration of Births, Deaths and Marriages (Special Provisions) Act 1957 (other than a certified copy kept by the Registrar General).

Amendment of orders and rectification of Registers and other records

4 (1) The court by which an adoption order has been made may, on the application of the adopter or the adopted person, amend the order by the correction of any error in the particulars contained in it.

(2) The court by which an adoption order has been made may, if satisfied on the application of the adopter or the adopted person that within the period of one year beginning with the date of the order any new name –

(a) has been given to the adopted person (whether in baptism or otherwise), or
(b) has been taken by the adopted person,

either in place of or in addition to a name specified in the particulars required to be entered in the Adopted Children Register in pursuance of the order, amend the order by substituting or, as the case may be, adding that name in those particulars.

(3) The court by which an adoption order has been made may, if satisfied on the application of any person concerned that a direction for the marking of an entry in the registers of live-births, the Adopted Children Register or other records included in the order in pursuance of paragraph 1(2) or (3) was wrongly so included, revoke that direction.

(4) Where an adoption order is amended or a direction revoked under sub-paragraphs (1) to (3), the prescribed officer of the court must communicate the amendment in the prescribed manner to the Registrar General.

'Prescribed' means prescribed by rules.

(5) The Registrar General must then –

(a) amend the entry in the Adopted Children Register accordingly, or
(b) secure that the marking of the entry in the registers of live-births, the Adopted Children Register or other records is cancelled,

as the case may be.

(6) Where an adoption order is quashed or an appeal against an adoption order allowed by any court, the court must give directions to the Registrar General to secure that –

(a) any entry in the Adopted Children Register, and
(b) any marking of an entry in that Register, the registers of live-births or other records as the case may be, which was effected in pursuance of the order,

is cancelled.

(7) Where an adoption order has been amended, any certified copy of the relevant entry in the Adopted Children Register which may be issued pursuant to section 78(2)(b) must be a copy of the entry as amended, without the reproduction of –

(a) any note or marking relating to the amendment, or
(b) any matter cancelled in pursuance of it.

(8) A copy or extract of an entry in any register or other record, being an entry the marking of which has been cancelled, is not to be treated as an accurate copy unless both the marking and the cancellation are omitted from it.

(9) If the Registrar General is satisfied –

(a) that a registrable foreign adoption has ceased to have effect, whether on annulment or otherwise, or
(b) that any entry or mark was erroneously made in pursuance of paragraph 3 in the Adopted Children Register, the registers of live-births, the overseas registers of births or other records,

he may secure that such alterations are made in those registers or other records as he considers are required in consequence of the adoption ceasing to have effect or to correct the error.

'Overseas register of births' has the same meaning as in paragraph 3.

(10) Where an entry in such a register is amended in pursuance of sub-paragraph (9), any copy or extract of the entry is not to be treated as accurate unless it shows the entry as amended but without indicating that it has been amended.

Marking of entries on re-registration of birth on legitimation

5 (1) Without prejudice to paragraphs 2(4) and 4(5), where, after an entry in the registers of live-births or other records has been marked in accordance with paragraph 1 or 2, the birth is re-registered under section 14 of the Births and Deaths Registration Act 1953 (re-registration of births of legitimated persons), the entry made on the re-registration must be marked in the like manner.

(2) Without prejudice to paragraph 4(9), where an entry in the registers of live-births or other records is marked in pursuance of paragraph 3 and the birth in question is subsequently re-registered under section 14 of that Act, the entry made on re-registration must be marked in the like manner.

Cancellations in registers on legitimation

6 (1) This paragraph applies where an adoption order is revoked under section 55(1).

(2) The prescribed officer of the court must communicate the revocation in the prescribed manner to the Registrar General who must then cancel or secure the cancellation of –

   (a) the entry in the Adopted Children Register relating to the adopted person, and
   (b) the marking with the word 'Adopted' of any entry relating to the adopted person in the registers of live-births or other records.

'Prescribed' means prescribed by rules.

(3) A copy or extract of an entry in any register or other record, being an entry the marking of which is cancelled under this paragraph, is not to be treated as an accurate copy unless both the marking and the cancellation are omitted from it.

SCHEDULE 2

DISCLOSURE OF BIRTH RECORDS BY REGISTRAR GENERAL

1 On an application made in the prescribed manner by an adopted person –

   (a) a record of whose birth is kept by the Registrar General, and
   (b) who has attained the age of 18 years,

the Registrar General must give the applicant any information necessary to enable the applicant to obtain a certified copy of the record of his birth.

'Prescribed' means prescribed by regulations made by the Registrar General with the approval of the Chancellor of the Exchequer.

2 (1) Before giving any information to an applicant under paragraph 1, the Registrar General must inform the applicant that counselling services are available to the applicant –

   (a) from a registered adoption society, an organisation within section 144(3)(b) or an adoption society which is registered under Article 4 of the Adoption (Northern Ireland) Order 1987 (SI 1987/2203 (NI 22)),
   (b) if the applicant is in England and Wales, at the General Register Office or from any local authority or registered adoption support agency,
   (c) if the applicant is in Scotland, from any council constituted under section 2 of the Local Government etc (Scotland) Act 1994,
   (d) if the applicant is in Northern Ireland, from any Board.

(2) In sub-paragraph (1)(b), 'registered adoption support agency' means an adoption support agency in respect of which a person is registered under Part 2 of the Care Standards Act 2000.

(3) In sub-paragraph (1)(d), 'Board' means a Health and Social Services Board established under Article 16 of the Health and Personal Social Services (Northern Ireland) Order 1972 (SI 1972/1265 (NI 14)); but where the functions of a Board are exercisable by a Health and Social Services Trust, references in that sub-paragraph to a Board are to be read as references to the Health and Social Services Trust.

(4) If the applicant chooses to receive counselling from a person or body within sub-paragraph (1), the Registrar General must send to the person or body the information to which the applicant is entitled under paragraph 1.

3 (1) Where an adopted person who is in England and Wales –

(a) applies for information under paragraph 1 or Article 54 of the Adoption (Northern Ireland) Order 1987, or
(b) is supplied with information under section 45 of the Adoption (Scotland) Act 1978,

the persons and bodies mentioned in sub-paragraph (2) must, if asked by the applicant to do so, provide counselling for the applicant.

(2) Those persons and bodies are –

(a) the Registrar General,
(b) any local authority,
(c) a registered adoption society, an organisation within section 144(3)(b) or an adoption society which is registered under Article 4 of the Adoption (Northern Ireland) Order 1987.

4 (1) Where a person –

(a) was adopted before 12th November 1975, and
(b) applies for information under paragraph 1,

the Registrar General must not give the information to the applicant unless the applicant has attended an interview with a counsellor arranged by a person or body from whom counselling services are available as mentioned in paragraph 2.

(2) Where the Registrar General is prevented by sub-paragraph (1) from giving information to a person who is not living in the United Kingdom, the Registrar General may give the information to any body which –

(a) the Registrar General is satisfied is suitable to provide counselling to that person, and
(b) has notified the Registrar General that it is prepared to provide such counselling.

SCHEDULE 3

MINOR AND CONSEQUENTIAL AMENDMENTS

...

The Legitimacy Act 1976

16 The Legitimacy Act 1976 is amended as follows.

17 In section 4 (legitimation of adopted child) –

(a) in subsection (1), after '1976' there is inserted 'or section 67 of the Adoption and Children Act 2002',
(b) in subsection (2) –
  (i) in paragraph (a), after '39' there is inserted 'or subsection (3)(b) of the said section 67',
  (ii) in paragraph (b), after '1976' there is inserted 'or section 67, 68 or 69 of the Adoption and Children Act 2002'.

18 In section 6 (dispositions depending on date of birth), at the end of subsection (2) there is inserted 'or section 69(2) of the Adoption and Children Act 2002'.

...

The Magistrates' Courts Act 1980

36 The Magistrates' Courts Act 1980 is amended as follows.

37 In section 65 (meaning of family proceedings), in subsection (1), for paragraph (h) there is substituted –
   '(h) the Adoption and Children Act 2002;'.

38 In section 69 (sitting of magistrates' courts for family proceedings), in subsections (2) and (3), for 'the Adoption Act 1976' there is substituted 'the Adoption and Children Act 2002'.

39 In section 71 (newspaper reports of family proceedings) –

(a) in subsection (1), '(other than proceedings under the Adoption Act 1976)' is omitted,
(b) in subsection (2) –
  (i) for 'the Adoption Act 1976' there is substituted 'the Adoption and Children Act 2002',
  (ii) the words following '(a) and (b)' are omitted.

40 In Part 1 of Schedule 6 (fees to be taken by justices' chief executives), in the entry relating to family proceedings –

(a) for 'the Adoption Act 1976, except under section 21 of that Act', there is substituted 'the Adoption and Children Act 2002, except under section 23 of that Act',
(b) in paragraph (c), for 'section 21 of the Adoption Act 1976' there is substituted 'section 23 of the Adoption and Children Act 2002'.

...

The Matrimonial and Family Proceedings Act 1984

44 In section 40 of the Matrimonial and Family Proceedings Act 1984 (family proceedings rules), in subsection (2), in paragraph (a), after 'the Adoption Act 1968' the 'or' is omitted and after 'the Adoption Act 1976' there is inserted 'or section 141(1) of the Adoption and Children Act 2002'.

The Child Abduction and Custody Act 1985

45 In Schedule 3 to the Child Abduction and Custody Act 1985 (custody orders), in paragraph 1, the 'and' at the end of paragraph (b) is omitted and after that paragraph there is inserted –
   '(bb) a special guardianship order (within the meaning of the Act of 1989); and',

and paragraph (c)(v) is omitted.

The Family Law Act 1986

46 The Family Law Act 1986 is amended as follows.

47 In section 1 (orders to which Part 1 applies), in subsection (1), after paragraph (a) there is inserted –
'(aa) a special guardianship order made by a court in England and Wales under the Children Act 1989;
(ab) an order made under section 26 of the Adoption and Children Act 2002 (contact), other than an order varying or revoking such an order'.

48 In section 2 (jurisdiction: general), after subsection (2) there is inserted –

'(2A) A court in England and Wales shall not have jurisdiction to make a special guardianship order under the Children Act 1989 unless the condition in section 3 of this Act is satisfied.

(2B) A court in England and Wales shall not have jurisdiction to make an order under section 26 of the Adoption and Children Act 2002 unless the condition in section 3 of this Act is satisfied.'

49 In section 57 (declarations as to adoptions effected overseas) –
(a) for subsection (1)(a) there is substituted –
'(a) a Convention adoption, or an overseas adoption, within the meaning of the Adoption and Children Act 2002, or',
(b) in subsection (2)(a), after '1976' there is inserted 'or section 67 of the Adoption and Children Act 2002'.

The Family Law Reform Act 1987

50 The Family Law Reform Act 1987 is amended as follows.

51 In section 1 (general principle), for paragraph (c) of subsection (3) there is substituted –
'(c) is an adopted person within the meaning of Chapter 4 of Part 1 of the Adoption and Children Act 2002'.

52 In section 19 (dispositions of property), in subsection (5), after '1976' there is inserted 'or section 69 of the Adoption and Children Act 2002'.

...

The Human Fertilisation and Embryology Act 1990

76 The Human Fertilisation and Embryology Act 1990 is amended as follows.

77 In section 27 (meaning of mother), in subsection (2), for 'child of any person other than the adopter or adopters' there is substituted 'woman's child'.

78 In section 28 (meaning of father), in subsection (5)(c), for 'child of any person other than the adopter or adopters' there is substituted 'man's child'.

79 In section 30 (parental orders in favour of gamete donors), in subsection (10) for 'Adoption Act 1976' there is substituted 'Adoption and Children Act 2002'.

...

81 In section 26 of the Child Support Act 1991 (disputes about parentage), in subsection (3), after '1976' there is inserted 'or Chapter 4 of Part 1 of the Adoption and Children Act 2002'.

...

The Family Law Act 1996

85 The Family Law Act 1996 is amended as follows.

86 In section 62 (meaning of 'relevant child' etc) –

(a) in subsection (2), in paragraph (b), after 'the Adoption Act 1976' there is inserted ', the Adoption and Children Act 2002',
(b) in subsection (5), for the words from 'has been freed' to '1976' there is substituted 'falls within subsection (7)'.

87 At the end of that section there is inserted –

'(7) A child falls within this subsection if –
(a) an adoption agency, within the meaning of section 2 of the Adoption and Children Act 2002, has power to place him for adoption under section 19 of that Act (placing children with parental consent) or he has become the subject of an order under section 21 of that Act (placement orders), or
(b) he is freed for adoption by virtue of an order made –
  (i) in England and Wales, under section 18 of the Adoption Act 1976,
  (ii) in Scotland, under section 18 of the Adoption (Scotland) Act 1978, or
  (iii) in Northern Ireland, under Article 17(1) or 18(1) of the Adoption (Northern Ireland) Order 1987.'

88 In section 63 (interpretation of Part 4) –

(a) in subsection (1), for the definition of 'adoption order', there is substituted –
' "adoption order" means an adoption order within the meaning of section 72(1) of the Adoption Act 1976 or section 46(1) of the Adoption and Children Act 2002;',
(b) in subsection (2), after paragraph (h) there is inserted –
'(i) the Adoption and Children Act 2002.'

...

The Criminal Justice and Court Services Act 2000

118 In section 12(5) of the Criminal Justice and Court Services Act 2000 (meaning of 'family proceedings' in relation to CAFCASS), paragraph (b) (supervision orders under the 1989 Act) and the preceding 'and' are omitted.

SCHEDULE 4

TRANSITIONAL AND TRANSITORY PROVISIONS AND SAVINGS

General rules for continuity

1 (1) Any reference (express or implied) in Part 1 or any other enactment, instrument or document to –

(a) any provision of Part 1, or

(b) things done or falling to be done under or for the purposes of any provision of Part 1,

must, so far as the nature of the reference permits, be construed as including, in relation to the times, circumstances or purposes in relation to which the corresponding provision repealed by this Act had effect, a reference to that corresponding provision or (as the case may be) to things done or falling to be done under or for the purposes of that corresponding provision.

(2) Any reference (express or implied) in any enactment, instrument or document to –

(a) a provision repealed by this Act, or
(b) things done or falling to be done under or for the purposes of such a provision,

must, so far as the nature of the reference permits, be construed as including, in relation to the times, circumstances or purposes in relation to which the corresponding provision of Part 1 has effect, a reference to that corresponding provision or (as the case may be) to things done or falling to be done under or for the purposes of that corresponding provision.

General rule for old savings

2 (1) The repeal by this Act of an enactment previously repealed subject to savings does not affect the continued operation of those savings.

(2) The repeal by this Act of a saving made on the previous repeal of an enactment does not affect the operation of the saving in so far as it is not specifically reproduced in this Act but remains capable of having effect.

Adoption support services

3 (1) The facilities to be provided by local authorities as part of the service maintained under section 1(1) of the Adoption Act 1976 include such arrangements as the authorities may be required by regulations to make for the provision of adoption support services to prescribed persons.

(2) Regulations under sub-paragraph (1) may require a local authority –

(a) at the request of a prescribed person, to carry out an assessment of his needs for adoption support services,
(b) if, as a result of the assessment, the authority decide that he has such needs, to decide whether to provide any such services to him,
(c) if the authority decide to provide any such services to a person, and the circumstances fall within a description prescribed by the regulations, to prepare a plan in accordance with which the services are to be provided to him and keep the plan under review.

(3) Subsections (6) and (7) (except paragraph (a)) of section 4 of this Act apply to regulations under sub-paragraph (1) as they apply to regulations made by virtue of that section.

(4) Section 57(1) of the Adoption Act 1976 (prohibited payments) does not apply to any payment made in accordance with regulations under sub-paragraph (1).

Prospective amendment—Paragraph in italics prospectively repealed by Adoption and Children Act 2002, s 139(3), Sch 5, from a date to be appointed.

Regulation of adoption agencies

4 (1) In section 9 of the Adoption Act 1976 –

(a) for 'Secretary of State' in subsections (2) and (3) there is substituted 'appropriate Minister', and
(b) at the end of that section there is inserted –

'(5) In this section and section 9A, "the appropriate Minister" means –
  (a) in relation to England, the Secretary of State,
  (b) in relation to Wales, the National Assembly for Wales,

and in relation to England and Wales, means the Secretary of State and the Assembly acting jointly.'

(2) Until the commencement of the repeal by this Act of section 9(2) of the Adoption Act 1976, section 36A of the Care Standards Act 2000 (inserted by section 16 of this Act) is to have effect as if, after '2002', there were inserted 'or under section 9(2) of the Adoption Act 1976'.

Prospective amendment—Paragraph in italics prospectively repealed by Adoption and Children Act 2002, s 139(3), Sch 5, from a date to be appointed.

Independent review mechanism

5 After section 9 of the Adoption Act 1976 there is inserted –

'9A Independent review of determinations

(1) Regulations under section 9 may establish a procedure under which any person in respect of whom a qualifying determination has been made by an adoption agency may apply to a panel constituted by the appropriate Minister for a review of that determination.

(2) The regulations must make provision as to the description of determinations which are qualifying determinations for the purposes of subsection (1).

(3) The regulations may include provision as to –
  (a) the duties and powers of a panel (including the power to recover the costs of a review from the adoption agency by which the determination reviewed was made),
  (b) the administration and procedures of a panel,
  (c) the appointment of members of a panel (including the number, or any limit on the number, of members who may be appointed and any conditions for appointment),
  (d) the payment of expenses of members of a panel,
  (e) the duties of adoption agencies in connection with reviews conducted under the regulations,
  (f) the monitoring of any such reviews.

(4) The appropriate Minister may make an arrangement with an organisation under which functions in relation to the panel are performed by the organisation on his behalf.

(5) If the appropriate Minister makes such an arrangement with an organisation, the organisation is to perform its functions under the arrangement in accordance with any general or special directions given by the appropriate Minister.

(6) The arrangement may include provision for payments to be made to the organisation by the appropriate Minister.

(7) Where the appropriate Minister is the National Assembly for Wales, subsections (4) and (6) also apply as if references to an organisation included references to the Secretary of State.

(8) In this section, "organisation" includes a public body and a private or voluntary organisation.'

Prospective amendment—Paragraph in italics prospectively repealed by Adoption and Children Act 2002, s 139(3), Sch 5, from a date to be appointed.

Pending applications for freeing orders

6 Nothing in this Act affects any application for an order under section 18 of the Adoption Act 1976 (freeing for adoption) where –

(a) the application has been made and has not been disposed of immediately before the repeal of that section, and
(b) the child in relation to whom the application is made has his home immediately before that repeal with a person with whom he has been placed for adoption by an adoption agency.

Freeing orders

7 (1) Nothing in this Act affects any order made under section 18 of the Adoption Act 1976 and –

(a) sections 19 to 21 of that Act are to continue to have effect in relation to such an order, and
(b) Part 1 of Schedule 6 to the Magistrates' Courts Act 1980 is to continue to have effect for the purposes of an application under section 21 of the Adoption Act 1976 in relation to such an order.

(2) Section 20 of that Act, as it has effect by virtue of this paragraph, is to apply as if, in subsection (3)(c) after '1989' there were inserted –
   '(iia) any care order, within the meaning of that Act'.

(3) Where a child is free for adoption by virtue of an order made under section 18 of that Act, the third condition in section 47(6) is to be treated as satisfied.

Pending applications for adoption orders

8 Nothing in this Act affects any application for an adoption order under section 12 of the Adoption Act 1976 where –

(a) the application has been made and has not been disposed of immediately before the repeal of that section, and
(b) the child in relation to whom the application is made has his home immediately before that repeal with a person with whom he has been placed for adoption by an adoption agency.

Notification of adoption applications

9 Where a notice given in respect of a child by the prospective adopters under section 22(1) of the Adoption Act 1976 is treated by virtue of paragraph 1(1) as having been given for the purposes of section 44(2) in respect of an application to adopt the child, section 42(3) has effect in relation to their application for an adoption order as if for 'six months' there were substituted 'twelve months'.

Adoptions with a foreign element

10 In section 13 of the Adoption Act 1976 (*child to live with adopters before order is made*) –

(a) in subsection (1)(a), at the beginning there is inserted '(subject to subsection (1A))',
(b) after subsection (1) there is inserted –

'(1A) Where an adoption is proposed to be effected by a Convention adoption order, the order shall not be made unless at all times during the preceding six months the child had his home with the applicants or one of them.',
(c) in subsection (2), after 'subsection (1)' there is inserted 'or (1A)',
(d) subsection (4) is omitted.

Prospective amendment—Paragraph in italics prospectively repealed by Adoption and Children Act 2002, s 139(3), Sch 5, from a date to be appointed.

11 In section 56 of the Adoption Act 1976 (restriction on removal of children for adoption outside Great Britain) –

(a) in subsection (1), 'not being a parent or guardian or relative of the child' is omitted,
(b) at the end of that section there is inserted –

'(4) Regulations may provide for subsection (1) to apply with modifications, or not to apply, if –
  (a) the prospective adopters are parents, relatives or guardians of the child in question (or one of them is), or
  (b) the prospective adopter is a step-parent of the child,

and any prescribed conditions are met.

(5) On the occasion of the first exercise of the power to make regulations under subsection (4) –
  (a) the regulations shall not be made unless a draft of the regulations has been approved by a resolution of each House of Parliament, and
  (b) accordingly section 67(2) does not apply to the statutory instrument containing the regulations.

(6) In this section, "prescribed" means prescribed by regulations and "regulations" means regulations made by the Secretary of State, after consultation with the National Assembly for Wales.'

Prospective amendment—Paragraph in italics prospectively repealed by Adoption and Children Act 2002, s 139(3), Sch 5, from a date to be appointed.

12 For section 56A of the Adoption Act 1976 there is substituted –

'56A Restriction on bringing children into the United Kingdom

(1) This section applies where a person who is habitually resident in the British Islands (the 'British resident') –
  (a) brings, or causes another to bring, a child who is habitually resident outside the British Islands into the United Kingdom for the purpose of adoption by the British resident, or
  (b) at any time brings, or causes another to bring, into the United Kingdom a child adopted by the British resident under an external adoption effected within the period of six months ending with that time.

The references to adoption, or to a child adopted, by the British resident include a reference to adoption, or to a child adopted, by the British resident and another person.

(2) But this section does not apply if the child is intended to be adopted under a Convention adoption order.

(3) An external adoption means an adoption, other than a Convention adoption, of a child effected under the law of any country or territory outside the British Islands, whether or not the adoption is –
  (a) an adoption within the meaning of Part IV of this Act, or
  (b) a full adoption (within the meaning of section 39(3A)).

(4) Regulations may require a person intending to bring, or to cause another to bring, a child into the United Kingdom in circumstances where this section applies –
  (a) to apply to an adoption agency (including an adoption agency within the meaning of section 1 of the Adoption (Scotland) Act 1978 or Article 3 of the Adoption (Northern Ireland) Order 1987) in the prescribed manner for an assessment of his suitability to adopt the child, and
  (b) to give the agency any information it may require for the purpose of the assessment.

(5) Regulations may require prescribed conditions to be met in respect of a child brought into the United Kingdom in circumstances where this section applies.

(6) In relation to a child brought into the United Kingdom for adoption in circumstances where this section applies, regulations may provide for any provision of Part II to apply with modifications or not to apply.

(7) If a person brings, or causes another to bring, a child into the United Kingdom at any time in circumstances where this section applies, he is guilty of an offence if –
- *(a) he has not complied with any requirement imposed by virtue of subsection (4), or*
- *(b) any condition required to be met by virtue of subsection (5) is not met,*

before that time, or before any later time which may be prescribed.

(8) A person guilty of an offence under this section is liable –
- *(a) on summary conviction to imprisonment for a term not exceeding six months, or a fine not exceeding the statutory maximum, or both,*
- *(b) on conviction on indictment, to imprisonment for a term not exceeding twelve months, or a fine, or both.*

(9) Regulations may provide for the preceding provisions of this section not to apply if –
- *(a) the adopters or (as the case may be) prospective adopters are natural parents, natural relatives or guardians of the child in question (or one of them is), or*
- *(b) the British resident in question is a step-parent of the child,*

and any prescribed conditions are met.

(10) On the occasion of the first exercise of the power to make regulations under subsection (9) –
- *(a) the regulations shall not be made unless a draft of the regulations has been approved by a resolution of each House of Parliament, and*
- *(b) accordingly section 67(2) does not apply to the statutory instrument containing the regulations.*

(11) In this section, "prescribed" means prescribed by regulations and "regulations" means regulations made by the Secretary of State, after consultation with the National Assembly for Wales.'

Prospective amendment—Paragraph in italics prospectively repealed by Adoption and Children Act 2002, s 139(3), Sch 5, from a date to be appointed.

13 In section 72 of the Adoption Act 1976 (interpretation), subsection (3B) is omitted.

Prospective amendment—Paragraph in italics prospectively repealed by Adoption and Children Act 2002, s 139(3), Sch 5, from a date to be appointed.

Advertising

14 In section 58 of the Adoption Act 1976 (restrictions on advertisements) –

- *(a) after subsection (1) there is inserted –*

'(1A) Publishing an advertisement includes doing so by electronic means (for example, by means of the internet).',

- *(b) in subsection (2), for the words following 'conviction' there is substituted 'to imprisonment for a term not exceeding three months, or a fine not exceeding level 5 on the standard scale, or both'.*

Prospective amendment—Paragraph in italics prospectively repealed by Adoption and Children Act 2002, s 139(3), Sch 5, from a date to be appointed.

15 In section 52 of the Adoption (Scotland) Act 1978 (restriction on advertisements) –

(a) after subsection (1) there is inserted –

'(1A) Publishing an advertisement includes doing so by electronic means (for example, by means of the internet).',

(b) *in subsection (2), for the words following 'conviction' there is substituted 'to imprisonment for a term not exceeding three months, or a fine not exceeding level 5 on the standard scale, or both'.*

Prospective amendment—Paragraph in italics prospectively repealed by Adoption and Children Act 2002, s 139(3), Sch 5, from a date to be appointed.

16 *(1) The Secretary of State may make regulations providing for the references to an adoption agency in –*

(a) *section 58(1)(c) of the Adoption Act 1976, and*
(b) *section 52(1)(c) of the Adoption (Scotland) Act 1978,*

to include a prescribed person outside the United Kingdom exercising functions corresponding to those of an adoption agency, if the functions are being exercised in prescribed circumstances.

'Prescribed' means prescribed by the regulations.

(2) Before exercising the power conferred by sub-paragraph (1) in relation to the Adoption (Scotland) Act 1978, the Secretary of State must consult the Scottish Ministers.

Prospective amendment—Paragraph in italics prospectively repealed by Adoption and Children Act 2002, s 139(3), Sch 5, from a date to be appointed.

Status

17 (1) Section 67 –

(a) does not apply to a pre-1976 instrument or enactment in so far as it contains a disposition of property, and
(b) does not apply to any public general Act in its application to any disposition of property in a pre-1976 instrument or enactment.

(2) Section 73 applies in relation to this paragraph as if this paragraph were contained in Chapter 4 of Part 1; and an instrument or enactment is a pre-1976 instrument or enactment for the purposes of this Schedule if it was passed or made at any time before 1 January 1976.

18 Section 69 does not apply to a pre-1976 instrument.

19 In section 70(1), the reference to Part 3 of the Family Law Reform Act 1987 includes Part 2 of the Family Law Reform Act 1969.

Registration of adoptions

20 (1) The power of the court under paragraph 4(1) of Schedule 1 to amend an order on the application of the adopter or adopted person includes, in relation to an order made before 1 April 1959, power to make any amendment of the particulars contained in the order which appears to be required to bring the order into the form in which it would have been made if paragraph 1 of that Schedule had applied to the order.

(2) In relation to an adoption order made before the commencement of the Adoption Act 1976, the reference in paragraph 4(3) of that Schedule to paragraph 1(2) or (3) is to be read –

(a) in the case of an order under the Adoption of Children Act 1926, as a reference to section 12(3) and (4) of the Adoption of Children Act 1949,

(b) in the case of an order under the Adoption Act 1950, as a reference to section 18(3) and (4) of that Act,

(c) in the case of an order under the Adoption Act 1958, as a reference to section 21(4) and (5) of that Act.

The Child Abduction Act 1984

21 Paragraph 43 of Schedule 3 does not affect the Schedule to the Child Abduction Act 1984 in its application to a child who is the subject of –

(a) an order under section 18 of the Adoption Act 1976 freeing the child for adoption,

(b) a pending application for such an order, or

(c) a pending application for an order under section 12 of that Act.

The Courts and Legal Services Act 1990

22 Paragraph 80 of Schedule 3 does not affect section 58A(2)(b) of the Courts and Legal Services Act 1990 in its application to proceedings under the Adoption Act 1976.

The Children (Scotland) Act 1995

23 *(Applies to Scotland only)*

SCHEDULE 5
REPEALS

Short title and chapter	*Extent of repeal*
Adoption Act 1976 (c 36).	The whole Act, except Part 4 and paragraph 6 of Schedule 2.
Domestic Proceedings and Magistrates' Courts Act 1978 (c 22).	Sections 73(2), 74(2) and 74(4).
Magistrates' Courts Act 1980 (c 43).	In section 71(1) the words '(other than proceedings under the Adoption Act 1976)'. In section 71(2) the words following '(a) and (b)'. In Schedule 7, paragraphs 141 and 142.
Matrimonial and Family Proceedings Act 1984 (c 42).	In section 40(2)(a), after 'the Adoption Act 1968', the word 'or'. In Schedule 1, paragraph 20.
Child Abduction and Custody Act 1985 (c 60).	In Schedule 3, in paragraph 1, the 'and' at the end of paragraph (b). In Schedule 3, in paragraph 1(c), paragraph (v).
Family Law Reform Act 1987 (c 42).	In Schedule 3, paragraphs 2 to 5.

Short title and chapter	Extent of repeal
Children Act 1989 (c 41).	Section 9(4). Section 12(3)(a). In section 20(9), the 'or' at the end of paragraph (a). In section 26(2)(e) and (f), the words 'to consider'. Section 33(6)(b)(i). Section 80(1)(e) and (f). Section 81(1)(b). Section 88(1). Section 102(6)(c). In section 105(1), the definition of 'protected child'. In Schedule 10, Part 1.
Human Fertilisation and Embryology Act 1990 (c 37).	In Schedule 4, paragraph 4.
Adoption (Intercountry Aspects) Act 1999 (c 18).	In section 2(6), the words 'in its application to Scotland'. Section 7(3). Section 14. In section 16(1), the words ', or section 17 or 56A of the 1976 Act,'. In Schedule 2, paragraph 3.
Criminal Justice and Court Services Act 2000 (c 43).	Section 12(5)(b) and the preceding 'and'. In Schedule 7, paragraphs 51 to 53.

SCHEDULE 6

GLOSSARY

In this Act, the expressions listed in the left-hand column below have the meaning given by, or are to be interpreted in accordance with, the provisions of this Act or (where stated) of the 1989 Act listed in the right-hand column.

Expression	Provision
the 1989 Act	section 2(5)
Adopted Children Register	section 77
Adoption and Children Act Register	section 125
adoption (in relation to Chapter 4 of Part 1)	section 66
adoption agency	section 2(1)

Expression	Provision
adoption agency placing a child for adoption	section 18(5)
Adoption Contact Register	section 80
adoption order	section 46(1)
Adoption Service	section 2(1)
adoption society	section 2(5)
adoption support agency	section 8
adoption support services	section 2(6)
appointed day (in relation to Chapter 4 of Part 1)	section 66(2)
appropriate Minister	section 144
Assembly	section 144
body	section 144
by virtue of	section 144
care order	section 105(1) of the 1989 Act
child	sections 49(5) and 144
child assessment order	section 43(2) of the 1989 Act
child in the care of a local authority	section 105(1) of the 1989 Act
child looked after by a local authority	section 22 of the 1989 Act
child placed for adoption by an adoption agency	section 18(5)
child to be adopted, adopted child	section 49(5)
consent (in relation to making adoption orders or placing for adoption)	section 52
the Convention	section 144
Convention adoption	section 66(1)(c)
Convention adoption order	section 144
Convention country	section 144
couple	section 144(4)
court	section 144
disposition (in relation to Chapter 4 of Part 1)	section 73

Expression	Provision
enactment	section 144
fee	section 144
guardian	section 144
information	section 144
interim care order	section 38 of the 1989 Act
local authority	section 144
local authority foster parent	section 23(3) of the 1989 Act
Northern Irish adoption agency	section 144
Northern Irish adoption order	section 144
notice	section 144
notice of intention to adopt	section 44(2)
overseas adoption	section 87
parental responsibility	section 3 of the 1989 Act
partner, in relation to a parent of a child	section 144(7)
placement order	section 21
placing, or placed, for adoption	sections 18(5) and 19(4)
prohibited steps order	section 8(1) of the 1989 Act
records (in relation to Chapter 5 of Part 1)	section 82
registered adoption society	section 2(2)
registers of live-births (in relation to Chapter 5 of Part 1)	section 82
registration authority (in Part 1)	section 144
regulations	section 144
relative	section 144, read with section 1(8)
residence order	section 8(1) of the 1989 Act
rules	section 144
Scottish adoption agency	section 144(3)
Scottish adoption order	section 144

Expression	Provision
specific issue order	section 8(1) of the 1989 Act
subordinate legislation	section 144
supervision order	section 31(11) of the 1989 Act
unitary authority	section 144
voluntary organisation	section 2(5)

Appendix C

THE FAMILY PROCEDURE (ADOPTION) RULES 2005, SI 2005/2795

PART 1
OVERRIDING OBJECTIVE

1 The overriding objective

(1) These Rules are a new procedural code with the overriding objective of enabling the court to deal with cases justly, having regard to the welfare issues involved.

(2) Dealing with a case justly includes, so far as is practicable –

  (a) ensuring that it is dealt with expeditiously and fairly;
  (b) dealing with the case in ways which are proportionate to the nature, importance and complexity of the issues;
  (c) ensuring that the parties are on an equal footing;
  (d) saving expense; and
  (e) allotting to it an appropriate share of the court's resources, while taking into account the need to allot resources to other cases.

2 Application by the court of the overriding objective

The court must seek to give effect to the overriding objective when it –

  (a) exercises any power given to it by these Rules; or
  (b) interprets any rule.

3 Duty of the parties

The parties are required to help the court to further the overriding objective.

4 Court's duty to manage cases

(1) The court must further the overriding objective by actively managing cases.

(2) Active case management includes –

  (a) encouraging the parties to co-operate with each other in the conduct of the proceedings;
  (b) identifying at an early stage –
     (i) the issues; and
     (ii) who should be a party to the proceedings;
  (c) deciding promptly –
     (i) which issues need full investigation and hearing and which do not; and
     (ii) the procedure to be followed in the case;
  (d) deciding the order in which issues are to be resolved;

(e) encouraging the parties to use an alternative dispute resolution procedure if the court considers that appropriate and facilitating the use of such procedure;
(f) helping the parties to settle the whole or part of the case;
(g) fixing timetables or otherwise controlling the progress of the case;
(h) considering whether the likely benefits of taking a particular step justify the cost of taking it;
(i) dealing with as many aspects of the case as it can on the same occasion;
(j) dealing with the case without the parties needing to attend at court;
(k) making use of technology; and
(l) giving directions to ensure that the case proceeds quickly and efficiently.

PART 2

INTERPRETATION AND APPLICATION OF OTHER RULES

5 Extent and application of other rules

(1) Unless the context otherwise requires, these Rules apply to proceedings in –

(a) the High Court;
(b) a county court; and
(c) a magistrates' court.

(2) Rule 35.15 of the CPR shall apply in detailed assessment proceedings in the High Court and a county court.

(3) Subject to paragraph (4), Parts 43, 44 (except rules 44.3(2) and (3) and 44.9 to 44.12A), 47 and 48 and rule 45.6 of the CPR apply to costs in proceedings, with the following modifications –

(a) in rule 43.2(1)(c)(ii), 'district judge' includes a district judge of the principal registry of the Family Division;
(b) after rule 43.2(1)(d)(iv), insert –
'or (v) a magistrates' court.'; and
(c) in rule 48.7(1) after 'section 51(6) of the Supreme Court Act 1981' insert 'or section 145A of the Magistrates' Courts Act 1980'.[1]

(4) Part 47 of the CPR does not apply to proceedings in a magistrates' court.

(5) Parts 50 and 70 to 74 of, and Schedules 1 and 2 to, the CPR apply, as far as they are relevant, to the enforcement of orders made in proceedings in the High Court and county courts with necessary modifications.

6 Interpretation

(1) In these Rules –

'the Act' means Part 1 of the Adoption and Children Act 2002;
'the 1989 Act' means the Children Act 1989;[2]

---

[1] 1980 c 43. Section 145A was inserted by s 112 of the Courts and Legal Services Act 1990 (c 41).
[2] 1989 c 41.

'adoption proceedings' means proceedings for the making of an adoption order under the Act;

'application notice' means a document in which the applicant states his intention to seek a court order in accordance with the procedure in Part 9;

'business day' means any day other than –
  (a) a Saturday, Sunday, Christmas Day or Good Friday; or
  (b) a bank holiday under the Banking and Financial Dealings Act 1971,[1] in England and Wales;

'Central Authority' means, in relation to England, the Secretary of State for Education and Skills, and in relation to Wales, the National Assembly for Wales;

'child' –
  (a) means, subject to paragraph (b), a person under the age of 18 years who is the subject of the proceedings; and
  (b) in adoption proceedings, also includes a person who has attained the age of 18 years before the proceedings are concluded;

'children and family reporter' means an officer of the Service or a Welsh family proceedings officer who prepares a report on matters relating to the welfare of the child;

'children's guardian' means an officer of the Service or a Welsh family proceedings officer appointed to act on behalf of a child who is a party to the proceedings with the duty of safeguarding the interests of the child;

'civil restraint order' means an order restraining a party –
  (a) from making any further applications in current proceedings (a limited civil restraint order);
  (b) from making certain applications in specified courts (an extended civil restraint order); or
  (c) from making any application in specified courts (a general civil restraint order);

'court officer' means, in the High Court and a county court, a member of court staff, and in a magistrates' court, the designated officer;

'CPR' means the Civil Procedure Rules 1998;[2]

'detailed assessment proceedings' means the procedure by which the amount of costs is decided in accordance with Part 47 of the CPR;

'filing', in relation to a document, means delivering it, by post or otherwise, to the court office;

'jurisdiction' means, unless the context requires otherwise, England and Wales and any part of the territorial waters of the United Kingdom adjoining England and Wales;

'legal representative' means a barrister or a solicitor, solicitor's employee or other authorised litigator (as defined in section 119 of the Courts and Legal Services Act 1990[3]) who has been instructed to act for a party in relation to an application;

'litigation friend' has the meaning given by section 1 of Part 7;

'non-subject child' means a person under the age of 18 years who is a party to the proceedings but is not the subject of the proceedings;

'officer of the Service' has the meaning given by section 11(3) of the Criminal Justice and Court Services Act 2000;[4]

'patient' means a party to proceedings who, by reason of mental disorder within the meaning of the Mental Health Act 1983,[5] is incapable of managing and administering his property and affairs;

---

1 1971 c 80.
2 SI 1998/3132.
3 1990 c 41.
4 2000 c 43.
5 1983 c 20.

'placement proceedings' means proceedings for the making, varying or revoking of a placement order under the Act;

'proceedings' means, unless the context otherwise requires, proceedings brought under the Act (whether at first instance or appeal) or proceedings for the purpose of enforcing an order made in any proceedings under that Act, as the case may be;

'provision for contact' means a contact order under section 8 or 34 of the 1989 Act or a contact order under section 26;

'reporting officer' means an officer of the Service or a Welsh family proceedings officer appointed to witness the documents which signify a parent or guardian's consent to the placing of the child for adoption or to the making of an adoption order or a section 84 order;

'section 84 order' means an order made by the High Court under section 84 giving parental responsibility prior to adoption abroad;

'section 88 direction' means a direction given by the High Court under section 88 that section 67(3) (status conferred by adoption) does not apply or does not apply to any extent specified in the direction;

'section 89 order' means an order made by the High Court under section 89 –
  (a) annulling a Convention adoption or Convention adoption order;
  (b) providing for an overseas adoption or determination under section 91 to cease to be valid; or
  (c) deciding the extent, if any, to which a determination under section 91 has been affected by a subsequent determination under that section;

'the Service Regulation' means Council Regulation (EC) No 1348/2000 of 29 May 2000 on the service in the Member States of judicial and extrajudicial documents in civil or commercial matters;

'Welsh family proceedings officer' has the meaning given by section 35(4) of the Children Act 2004.[1]

(2) A section or Schedule referred to by number alone means the section or Schedule so numbered in the Adoption and Children Act 2002.

(3) Any provision in these Rules –

(a) requiring or permitting directions to be given by the court is to be taken as including provision for such directions to be varied or revoked; and
(b) requiring or permitting a date to be set is to be taken as including provision for that date to be set aside.

7 Power to perform functions of the court

(1) Where these Rules or a practice direction provide for the court to perform any act then, except where any rule or practice direction, any other enactment, or the Family Proceedings (Allocation to Judiciary) Directions,[2] provides otherwise, that act may be performed –

(a) in relation to proceedings in the High Court or in a district registry, by any judge or district judge of that Court including a district judge of the principal registry of the Family Division;

---

[1] 2004 c 31.
[2] The Family Proceedings (Allocation to Judiciary) Directions [1999] 2 FLR 799 provides that circuit judges, deputy circuit judges, recorders (subject to certain exceptions), district judges and deputy district judges must be nominated as a judge to whom adoption proceedings may be allocated by the President of the Family Division.

(b) in relation to proceedings in a county court, by any judge or district judge including a district judge of the principal registry of the Family Division when the principal registry of the Family Division is treated as if it were a county court;[1] and
(c) in relation to proceedings in a magistrates' court –
  (i) by any family proceedings court constituted in accordance with sections 66 and 67 of the Magistrates' Courts Act 1980;[2] or
  (ii) by a single justice of the peace who is a member of the family panel –
    (aa) where an application without notice is made under section 41(2) (recovery orders); and
    (bb) in accordance with the relevant practice direction.

(The Justices' Clerks Rules 2005[3] make provision for a justices' clerk or assistant clerk to carry out certain functions of a single justice of the peace.)

(2) A deputy High Court judge and a district judge, including a district judge of the principal registry of the Family Division, may not try a claim for a declaration of incompatibility in accordance with section 4 of the Human Rights Act 1998.[4]

8 Court's discretion as to where it deals with cases

The court may deal with a case at any place that it considers appropriate.

9 Court documents

(1) A court officer must seal,[5] or otherwise authenticate with the stamp of the court, the following documents on issue –

(a) the application form;
(b) the order; and
(c) any other document which a rule or practice direction requires it to seal or stamp.

(2) The court officer may place the seal or the stamp on the document –

(a) by hand; or
(b) by printing a facsimile of the seal on the document whether electronically or otherwise.

(3) A document purporting to bear the court's seal or stamp will be admissible in evidence without further proof.

(4) The relevant practice direction contains provisions about court documents.

10 Computation of time

(1) This rule shows how to calculate any period of time for doing any act which is specified –

(a) by these Rules;
(b) by a practice direction; or

---

1   By virtue of art 19 of the Children (Allocation of Proceedings) Order 1991 (SI 1991/1677) the Principal Registry of the Family Division is treated as a county court.
2   1980 c 43. Section 67 was substituted by s 49 of the Courts Act 2003 (c 39).
3   SI 2005/545 (L 10), amended by SI 2005/2796 (L 23).
4   1998 c 42.
5   A seal is a mark which the court puts on a document to indicate that the document has been issued by the court.

(c) by a direction or order of the court.

(2) A period of time expressed as a number of days must be computed as clear days.

(3) In this rule 'clear days' means that in computing the numbers of days –

    (a) the day on which the period begins; and
    (b) if the end of the period is defined by reference to an event, the day on which that event occurs

are not included.

(4) Where the specified period is 7 days or less and would include a day which is not a business day, that day does not count.

(5) When the period specified –

    (a) by these Rules or a practice direction; or
    (b) by any direction or order of the court,

for doing any act at the court office ends on a day on which the office is closed, that act will be in time if done on the next day on which the court office is open.

11 Dates for compliance to be calendar dates and to include time of day

(1) Where the court makes an order or gives a direction which imposes a time limit for doing any act, the last date for compliance must, wherever practicable –

    (a) be expressed as a calendar date; and
    (b) include the time of day by which the act must be done.

(2) Where the date by which an act must be done is inserted in any document, the date must, wherever practicable, be expressed as a calendar date.

(3) Where 'month' occurs in any order, direction or other document, it means a calendar month.

PART 3
GENERAL CASE MANAGEMENT POWERS

12 The court's general powers of management

(1) The list of powers in this rule is in addition to any powers given to the court by any other rule or practice direction or by any other enactment or any powers it may otherwise have.

(2) Except where these Rules provide otherwise, the court may –

    (a) extend or shorten the time for compliance with any rule, practice direction or court direction (even if an application for extension is made after the time for compliance has expired);
    (b) adjourn or bring forward a hearing;
    (c) require a party or a party's legal representative to attend the court;
    (d) hold a hearing and receive evidence by telephone or by using any other method of direct oral communication;
    (e) direct that part of any proceedings be dealt with as separate proceedings;

(f) stay the whole or part of any proceedings or judgment either generally or until a specified date or event;
(g) consolidate proceedings;
(h) hear two or more applications on the same occasion;
(i) direct a separate hearing of any issue;
(j) decide the order in which issues are to be heard;
(k) exclude an issue from consideration;
(l) dismiss or give judgment on an application after a decision on a preliminary issue;
(m) direct any party to file and serve an estimate of costs; and
(n) take any other step or give any other direction for the purpose of managing the case and furthering the overriding objective.

(3) The court may not extend the period within which a section 89 order must be made.

(4) Paragraph (2)(f) does not apply to proceedings in a magistrates' court.

13 Exercise of powers of court's own initiative

(1) Except where an enactment provides otherwise, the court may exercise the powers in rule 12 on an application or of its own initiative.

(Part 9 sets out the procedure for making an application.)

(2) Where the court proposes to exercise its powers of its own initiative –

(a) it may give any person likely to be affected an opportunity to make representations; and
(b) where it does so it must specify the time by and the manner in which the representations must be made.

(3) Where the court proposes to hold a hearing to decide whether to exercise its powers of its own initiative it must give each party likely to be affected at least 3 days' notice of the hearing.

(4) The court may exercise its powers of its own initiative, without hearing the parties or giving them an opportunity to make representations.

(5) Where the court has exercised its powers under paragraph (4) –

(a) a party affected by the direction may apply to have it set aside or varied; and
(b) the direction must contain a statement of the right to make such an application.

(6) An application under paragraph (5)(a) must be made –

(a) within such period as may be specified by the court; or
(b) if the court does not specify a period, within 7 days beginning with the date on which the order was served on the party making the application.

(7) If the High Court or a county court of its own initiative dismisses an application (including an application for permission to appeal) and it considers that the application is totally without merit –

(a) the court's order must record that fact; and
(b) the court must at the same time consider whether it is appropriate to make a civil restraint order.

14 Court officer's power to refer to the court

Where these Rules require a step to be taken by a court officer –

(a) the court officer may consult the court before taking that step;
(b) the step may be taken by the court instead of the court officer.

15 General power of the court to rectify matters where there has been an error of procedure

Where there has been an error of procedure such as a failure to comply with a rule or practice direction –

(a) the error does not invalidate any step taken in the proceedings unless the court so orders; and
(b) the court may make an order to remedy the error.

16 Power of the court to make civil restraint orders

The relevant practice direction sets out –

(a) the circumstances in which the High Court or a county court has the power to make a civil restraint order against a party to proceedings;
(b) the procedure where a party applies for a civil restraint order against another party; and
(c) the consequences of the court making a civil restraint order.

PART 4
HOW TO START PROCEEDINGS

17 Forms

Subject to rule 28(2) and (3), the forms set out in the relevant practice direction or forms to the like effect must be used in the cases to which they apply.

18 Documents to be attached to the application form

The application form must have attached to it any documents referred to in the application form.

19 How to start proceedings

(1) Proceedings are started when a court officer issues an application at the request of the applicant.

(2) An application is issued on the date entered in the application form by the court officer.

(Restrictions on where proceedings may be started are set out in the Children (Allocation of Proceedings) Order 1991.)[1]

20 Application for a serial number

(1) This rule applies to any application in proceedings by a person who intends to adopt the child.

(2) If the applicant wishes his identity to be kept confidential in the proceedings, he may, before those proceedings have started, request a court officer to assign a serial number to him to identify him in connection with the proceedings, and a number will be assigned to him.

---

1   SI 1991/1677 amended by SI 2005/2797 (L 24); there are other amending instruments, but none is relevant.

(3) The court may at any time direct that a serial number identifying the applicant in the proceedings referred to in paragraph (2) must be removed.

(4) If a serial number has been assigned to a person under paragraph (2) –

(a) the court officer will ensure that any application form or application notice sent in accordance with these Rules does not contain information which discloses, or is likely to disclose, the identity of that person to any other party to that application who is not already aware of that person's identity; and
(b) the proceedings on the application will be conducted with a view to securing that the applicant is not seen by or made known to any party who is not already aware of his identity except with his consent.

21 Personal details

(1) Unless the court directs otherwise, a party is not required to reveal –

(a) the address or telephone number of their private residence;
(b) the address of the child;
(c) the name of a person with whom the child is living, if that person is not the applicant; or
(d) in relation to an application under section 28(2) (application for permission to change the child's surname), the proposed new surname of the child.

(2) Where a party does not wish to reveal any of the particulars in paragraph (1), he must give notice of those particulars to the court and the particulars will not be revealed to any person unless the court directs otherwise.

(3) Where a party changes his home address during the course of proceedings, he must give notice of the change to the court.

PART 5

PROCEDURE FOR APPLICATIONS IN ADOPTION, PLACEMENT AND RELATED PROCEEDINGS

22 Application of this Part

The rules in this Part apply to the following proceedings –

(a) adoption proceedings;
(b) placement proceedings; or
(c) proceedings for –
   (i) the making of a contact order under section 26;
   (ii) the variation or revocation of a contact order under section 27;
   (iii) an order giving permission to change a child's surname or remove a child from the United Kingdom under section 28(2) and (3);
   (iv) a section 84 order;
   (v) a section 88 direction;
   (vi) a section 89 order; or
   (vii) any other order that may be referred to in a practice direction.

(Parts 9 and 10 set out the procedure for making an application in proceedings not dealt with in this Part.)

23 Who the parties are

(1) In relation to the proceedings set out in column 1 of each of the following tables, column 2 of Table 1 sets out who the application may be made by and column 2 of Table 2 sets out who the respondents to those proceedings will be.

Table 1

Proceedings for	Applicants
An adoption order (section 46)	The prospective adopters (section 50 and 51).
A section 84 order	The prospective adopters asking for parental responsibility prior to adoption abroad.
A placement order (section 21)	A local authority (section 22).
An order varying a placement order (section 23)	The joint application of the local authority authorised by the placement order to place the child for adoption and the local authority which is to be substituted for that authority (section 23).
An order revoking a placement order (section 24)	The child;
	the local authority authorised to place the child for adoption; or
	where the child is not placed for adoption by the authority, any other person who has the permission of the court to apply (section 24).
A contact order (section 26)	The child;
	the adoption agency;
	any parent, guardian or relative;
	any person in whose favour there was provision for contact under the 1989 Act which ceased to have effect on an adoption agency being authorised to place a child for adoption, or placing a child for adoption who is less than six weeks old (section 26(1));
	a person in whose favour there was a residence order in force immediately before the adoption agency was authorised to place the child for adoption or placed the child for adoption at a time when he was less than six weeks old;
	a person who by virtue of an order made in the exercise of the High Court's inherent jurisdiction with respect to children had care of the child immediately before that time; or
	any person who has the permission of the court to make the application (section 26).

Proceedings for	Applicants
An order varying or revoking a contact order (section 27)	The child;
	the adoption agency; or
	any person named in the contact order (section 27(1)).
An order permitting the child's name to be changed or the removal of the child from the United Kingdom (section 28(2) and (3))	Any person including the adoption agency or the local authority authorised to place, or which has placed, the child for adoption (section 28(2)).
A section 88 direction	The adopted child;
	the adopters;
	any parent; or
	any other person.
A section 89 order	The adopters;
	the adopted person;
	any parent;
	the relevant Central Authority;
	the adoption agency;
	the local authority to whom notice under section 44 (notice of intention to adopt or apply for a section 84 order) has been given;
	the Secretary of State for the Home Department; or
	any other person.

Table 2

Proceedings for	Respondents
An adoption order (section 46) or a section 84 order	Each parent who has parental responsibility for the child or guardian of the child unless he has given notice under section 20(4)(a) (statement of wish not to be informed of any application for an adoption order) which has effect;
	any person in whose favour there is provision for contact;
	any adoption agency having parental responsibility for the child under section 25;
	any adoption agency which has taken part at any stage in the arrangements for adoption of the child;
	any local authority to whom notice under section 44 (notice of intention to adopt or apply for a section 84 order) has been given;
	any local authority or voluntary organisation which has parental responsibility for, is looking after, or is caring for, the child; and
	the child where – • permission has been granted to a parent or guardian to oppose the making of the adoption order (section 47(3) or 47(5)); • he opposes the making of an adoption order; • a children and family reporter recommends that it is in the best interests of the child to be a party to the proceedings and that recommendation is accepted by the court; • he is already an adopted child; • any party to the proceedings or the child is opposed to the arrangements for allowing any person contact with the child, or a person not being allowed contact with the child after the making of the adoption order; • the application is for a Convention adoption order or a section 84 order; • he has been brought into the United Kingdom in the circumstances where section 83(1) applies (restriction on bringing children in); • the application is for an adoption order other than a Convention adoption order and the prospective adopters intend the child to live in a country or territory outside the British Islands after the making of the adoption order; or • the prospective adopters are relatives of the child.

Proceedings for	Respondents
A placement order (section 21)	Each parent who has parental responsibility for the child or guardian of the child;
	any person in whose favour an order under the 1989 Act is in force in relation to the child;
	any adoption agency or voluntary organisation which has parental responsibility for, is looking after, or is caring for, the child;
	the child; and
	the parties or any persons who are or have been parties to proceedings for a care order in respect of the child where those proceedings have led to the application for the placement order.
An order varying a placement order (section 23)	The parties to the proceedings leading to the placement order which it is sought to have varied except the child who was the subject of those proceedings; and
	any person in whose favour there is provision for contact.
An order revoking a placement order (section 24)	The parties to the proceedings leading to the placement order which it is sought to have revoked; and
	any person in whose favour there is provision for contact.
A contact order (section 26)	The adoption agency authorised to place the child for adoption or which has placed the child for adoption;
	the person with whom the child lives or is to live;
	each parent with parental responsibility for the child or guardian of the child; and
	the child where – • the adoption agency authorised to place the child for adoption or which has placed the child for adoption or a parent with parental responsibility for the child opposes the making of the contact order under section 26; • he opposes the making of the contact order under section 26; • existing provision for contact is to be revoked; • relatives of the child do not agree to the arrangements for allowing any person contact with the child, or a person not being allowed contact with the child; or • he is suffering or is at risk of suffering harm within the meaning of the 1989 Act.
An order varying or revoking a contact order (section 27)	The parties to the proceedings leading to the contact order which it is sought to have varied or revoked; and
	any person named in the contact order.

Proceedings for	Respondents
An order permitting the child's name to be changed or the removal of the child from the United Kingdom (section 28(2) and (3))	The parties to proceedings leading to any placement order;
	the adoption agency authorised to place the child for adoption or which has placed the child for adoption;
	any prospective adopters with whom the child is living; and
	each parent with parental responsibility for the child or guardian of the child.
A section 88 direction	The adopters;
	the parents;
	the adoption agency;
	the local authority to whom notice under section 44 (notice of intention to apply for a section 84 order) has been given; and
	the Attorney-General.
A section 89 order	The adopters;
	the parents;
	the adoption agency; and
	the local authority to whom notice under section 44 (notice of intention to adopt or apply for a section 84 order) has been given.

(2) The court may at any time direct that a child, who is not already a respondent to proceedings, be made a respondent to proceedings where –

(a) the child –
 (i) wishes to make an application; or
 (ii) has evidence to give to the court or a legal submission to make which has not been given or made by any other party; or
(b) there are other special circumstances.

(3) The court may at any time direct that –

(a) any other person or body be made a respondent to proceedings; or
(b) a respondent be removed.

(4) If the court makes a direction for the addition or removal of a party, it may give consequential directions about –

(a) serving a copy of the application form on any new respondent;
(b) serving relevant documents on the new party; and
(c) the management of the proceedings.

24 What the court or a court officer will do when the application has been issued

(1) As soon as practicable after the application has been issued in proceedings –

(a) the court will –

- (i) if section 48(1) (restrictions on making adoption orders) applies, consider whether it is proper to hear the application;
- (ii) subject to paragraph (4), set a date for the first directions hearing;
- (iii) appoint a children's guardian in accordance with rule 59;
- (iv) appoint a reporting officer in accordance with rule 69;
- (v) consider whether a report relating to the welfare of the child is required, and if so, request such a report in accordance with rule 73;
- (vi) set a date for the hearing of the application; and
- (vii) do anything else that may be set out in a practice direction; and

(b) a court officer will –
- (i) subject to receiving confirmation in accordance with paragraph (2)(b)(ii), give notice of any directions hearing set by the court to the parties and to any children's guardian, reporting officer or children and family reporter;
- (ii) serve a copy of the application form (but, subject to sub-paragraphs (iii) and (iv), not the documents attached to it) on the persons referred to in the relevant practice direction;
- (iii) send a copy of the certified copy of the entry in the register of live-births or Adopted Children Register and any health report attached to an application for an adoption order to –
    - (aa) any children's guardian, reporting officer or children and family reporter; and
    - (bb) the local authority to whom notice under section 44 (notice of intention to adopt or apply for a section 84 order) has been given;
- (iv) if notice under rule 27 has been given (request to dispense with consent of parent or guardian), in accordance with that rule inform the parent or guardian of the request and send a copy of the statement of facts to –
    - (aa) the parent or guardian;
    - (bb) any children's guardian, reporting officer or children and family reporter;
    - (cc) any local authority to whom notice under section 44 (notice of intention to adopt or apply for a section 84 order) has been given; and
    - (dd) any adoption agency which has placed the child for adoption; and
- (v) do anything else that may be set out in a practice direction.

(2) In addition to the matters referred to in paragraph (1), as soon as practicable after an application for an adoption order or a section 84 order has been issued the court or the court officer will –

(a) where the child is not placed for adoption by an adoption agency –
- (i) ask either the Service or the Assembly to file any relevant form of consent to an adoption order or a section 84 order; and
- (ii) ask the local authority to prepare a report on the suitability of the prospective adopters if one has not already been prepared; and

(b) where the child is placed for adoption by an adoption agency, ask the adoption agency to –
- (i) file any relevant form of consent to –
    - (aa) the child being placed for adoption;
    - (bb) an adoption order;
    - (cc) a future adoption order under section 20; or
    - (dd) a section 84 order;
- (ii) confirm whether a statement has been made under section 20(4)(a) (statement of wish not to be informed of any application for an adoption order) and if so, to file that statement;
- (iii) file any statement made under section 20(4)(b) (withdrawal of wish not to be informed of any application for an adoption order) as soon as it is received by the adoption agency; and

(iv) prepare a report on the suitability of the prospective adopters if one has not already been prepared.

(3) In addition to the matters referred to in paragraph (1), as soon as practicable after an application for a placement order has been issued –

(a) the court will consider whether a report giving the local authority's reasons for placing the child for adoption is required, and if so, will direct the local authority to prepare such a report; and

(b) the court or the court officer will ask either the Service or the Assembly to file any form of consent to the child being placed for adoption.

(4) Where it considers it appropriate the court may, instead of setting a date for a first directions hearing, give the directions provided for by rule 26.

25 Date for first directions hearing

Unless the court directs otherwise, the first directions hearing must be within 4 weeks beginning with the date on which the application is issued.

26 The first directions hearing

(1) At the first directions hearing in the proceedings the court will –

(a) fix a timetable for the filing of –
   (i) any report relating to the suitability of the applicants to adopt a child;
   (ii) any report from the local authority;
   (iii) any report from a children's guardian, reporting officer or children and family reporter;
   (iv) if a statement of facts has been filed, any amended statement of facts;
   (v) any other evidence, and
give directions relating to the reports and other evidence;

(b) consider whether an alternative dispute resolution procedure is appropriate and, if so, give directions relating to the use of such procedure;

(c) consider whether the child or any other person should be a party to the proceedings and, if so, give directions in accordance with rule 23(2) or (3) joining that child or person as a party;

(d) give directions relating to the appointment of a litigation friend for any patient or non-subject child unless a litigation friend has already been appointed;

(e) consider whether the case needs to be transferred to another court and, if so, give directions to transfer the proceedings to another court in accordance with any order made by the Lord Chancellor under Part I of Schedule 11 to the 1989 Act;

(f) give directions about –
   (i) tracing parents or any other person the court considers to be relevant to the proceedings;
   (ii) service of documents;
   (iii) subject to paragraph (2), disclosure as soon as possible of information and evidence to the parties; and
   (iv) the final hearing; and

(2) Rule 77(2) applies to any direction given under paragraph (1)(f)(iii) as it applies to a direction given under rule 77(1).

(3) In addition to the matters referred to in paragraph (1), the court will give any of the directions listed in the relevant practice direction in proceedings for –

(a) a Convention adoption order;
(b) a section 84 order;
(c) a section 88 direction;
(d) a section 89 order; or
(e) an adoption order where section 83(1) applies (restriction on bringing children in).

(4) The parties or their legal representatives must attend the first directions hearing unless the court directs otherwise.

(5) Directions may also be given at any stage in the proceedings –

(a) of the court's own initiative; or
(b) on the application of a party or any children's guardian or, where the direction concerns a report by a reporting officer or children and family reporter, the reporting officer or children and family reporter.

(6) For the purposes of giving directions or for such purposes as the court directs –

(a) the court may set a date for a further directions hearing or other hearing; and
(b) the court officer will give notice of any date so fixed to the parties and to any children's guardian, reporting officer or children and family reporter.

(7) After the first directions hearing the court will monitor compliance with the court's timetable and directions by the parties.

27 Requesting the court to dispense with the consent of any parent or guardian

(1) The following paragraphs apply where the applicant wants to ask the court to dispense with the consent of any parent or guardian of a child to –

(a) the child being placed for adoption;
(b) the making of an adoption order except a Convention adoption order; or
(c) the making of a section 84 order.

(2) The applicant requesting the court to dispense with the consent must –

(a) give notice of the request in the application form or at any later stage by filing a written request setting out the reasons for the request; and
(b) file a statement of facts setting out a summary of the history of the case and any other facts to satisfy the court that –
    (i) the parent or guardian cannot be found or is incapable of giving consent; or
    (ii) the welfare of the child requires the consent to be dispensed with.

(3) If a serial number has been assigned to the applicant under rule 20, the statement of facts supplied under paragraph (2)(b) must be framed so that it does not disclose the identity of the applicant.

(4) On receipt of the notice of the request –

(a) a court officer will –
    (i) inform the parent or guardian of the request; and
    (ii) send a copy of the statement of facts filed in accordance with paragraph (2)(b) to –
        (aa) the parent or guardian;
        (bb) any children's guardian, reporting officer or children and family reporter;
        (cc) any local authority to whom notice under section 44 (notice of intention to adopt or apply for a section 84 order) has been given; and
        (dd) any adoption agency which has placed the child for adoption; and

(b) if the applicant considers that the parent or guardian is incapable of giving consent, the court will consider whether to –
   (i) appoint a litigation friend for the parent or guardian under rule 55(1); or
   (ii) give directions for an application to be made under rule 55(3),
unless a litigation friend is already appointed for that parent or guardian.

28 Consent

(1) Consent of any parent or guardian of a child –

(a) under section 19, to the child being placed for adoption; and
(b) under section 20, to the making of a future adoption order

must be given in the form required by the relevant practice direction or a form to the like effect.

(2) Subject to paragraph (3), consent –

(a) to the making of an adoption order; or
(b) to the making of a section 84 order,

may be given in the form required by the relevant practice direction or a form to the like effect.

(3) Any consent to a Convention adoption order must be in a form which complies with the internal law relating to adoption of the Convention country of which the child is habitually resident.

(4) Any form of consent executed in Scotland must be witnessed by a Justice of the Peace or a Sheriff.

(5) Any form of consent executed in Northern Ireland must be witnessed by a Justice of the Peace.

(6) Any form of consent executed outside the United Kingdom must be witnessed by –

(a) any person for the time being authorised by law in the place where the document is executed to administer an oath for any judicial or other legal purpose;
(b) a British Consular officer;
(c) a notary public; or
(d) if the person executing the document is serving in any of the regular armed forces of the Crown, an officer holding a commission in any of those forces.

29 Reports by the adoption agency or local authority

(1) The adoption agency or local authority must file the report on the suitability of the applicant to adopt a child within the timetable fixed by the court.

(2) A local authority that is directed to prepare a report on the placement of the child for adoption must file that report within the timetable fixed by the court.

(3) The reports must cover the matters specified in the relevant practice direction.

(4) The court may at any stage request a further report or ask the adoption agency or local authority to assist the court in any other manner.

(5) A court officer will send a copy of any report referred to in this rule to any children's guardian, reporting officer or children and family reporter.

(6) Any report to the court under this rule will be confidential.

30 Health reports

(1) Reports by a registered medical practitioner ('health reports') made not more than three months earlier on the health of the child and of each applicant must be attached to an application for an adoption order or a section 84 order except where –

(a) the child was placed for adoption with the applicant by an adoption agency;
(b) the applicant or one of the applicants is a parent of the child; or
(c) the applicant is the partner of a parent of the child.

(2) Health reports must contain the matters set out in the relevant practice direction.

(3) Any health report will be confidential.

31 Notice of final hearing

A court officer will give notice to the parties, any children's guardian, reporting officer or children and family reporter and to any other person that may be referred to in a practice direction –

(a) of the date and place where the application will be heard; and
(b) of the fact that, unless the person wishes or the court requires, the person need not attend.

32 The final hearing

(1) Any person who has been given notice in accordance with rule 31 may attend the final hearing and, subject to paragraph (2), be heard on the question of whether an order should be made.

(2) A person whose application for the permission of the court to oppose the making of an adoption order under section 47(3) or (5) has been refused is not entitled to be heard on the question of whether an order should be made.

(3) Any member or employee of a party which is a local authority, adoption agency or other body may address the court at the final hearing if he is authorised to do so.

(4) The court may direct that any person must attend a final hearing.

(5) Paragraphs (6) and (7) apply to –

(a) an adoption order;
(b) a section 84 order; or
(c) a section 89 order.

(6) Subject to paragraphs (7) and (8), the court cannot make an order unless the applicant and the child personally attend the final hearing.

(7) The court may direct that the applicant or the child need not attend the final hearing.

(8) In a case of adoption by a couple[1] under section 50 the court may make an adoption order after personal attendance of one only of the applicants if there are special circumstances.

(9) The court cannot make a placement order unless a legal representative of the applicant attends the final hearing.

---

1 A couple is defined in s 144(4) of the Adoption and Children Act 2002.

33 Proof of identity of the child

(1) Unless the contrary is shown, the child referred to in the application will be deemed to be the child referred to in the form of consent –

- (a) to the child being placed for adoption;
- (b) to the making of an adoption order; or
- (c) to the making of a section 84 order

where the conditions in paragraph (2) apply.

(2) The conditions are –

- (a) the application identifies the child by reference to a full certified copy of an entry in the registers of live-births;
- (b) the form of consent identifies the child by reference to a full certified copy of an entry in the registers of live-births attached to the form; and
- (c) the copy of the entry in the registers of live-births referred to in sub-paragraph (a) is the same or relates to the same entry in the registers of live-births as the copy of the entry in the registers of live-births attached to the form of consent.

(3) Where the child is already an adopted child paragraph (2) will have effect as if for the references to the registers of live-births there were substituted references to the Adopted Children Register.

(4) Subject to paragraph (7), where the precise date of the child's birth is not proved to the satisfaction of the court, the court will determine the probable date of birth.

(5) The probable date of the child's birth may be specified in the placement order, adoption order or section 84 order as the date of his birth.

(6) Subject to paragraph (7), where the child's place of birth cannot be proved to the satisfaction of the court –

- (a) he may be treated as having been born in the registration district of the court where it is probable that the child may have been born in –
  - (i) the United Kingdom;
  - (ii) the Channel Islands; or
  - (iii) the Isle of Man; or
- (b) in any other case, the particulars of the country of birth may be omitted from the placement order, adoption order or section 84 order.

(7) A placement order identifying the probable date and place of birth of the child will be sufficient proof of the date and place of birth of the child in adoption proceedings and proceedings for a section 84 order.

PART 6

SERVICE

Section 1
General rules about service

34 Scope of this Part

The rules in this Part apply to the service of documents, including a document that is required to be given or sent by these Rules or any practice direction, except where –

(a) any other enactment, a rule in another Part or a practice direction makes a different provision; or
(b) the court directs otherwise.

35 Methods of service

(1) Subject to paragraph (2), a document may be served –
  (a) where it is not known whether a solicitor is acting on behalf of a party –
    (i) by delivering it to the party personally; or
    (ii) by delivering it at, or by sending it by first class post to, the party's residence or last known residence; or
  (b) where a solicitor is known to be acting on behalf of a party –
    (i) by delivering the document at, or sending it by first class post to, the solicitor's address for service; or
    (ii) through a document exchange in accordance with the relevant practice direction.

(2) A notice of hearing must be served in accordance with paragraph (1)(a)(i) or (ii) irrespective of whether a solicitor is acting on behalf of a party.

(3) Where it appears to the court that there is a good reason to authorise service by a method not permitted by paragraph (1), the court may direct that service is effected by an alternative method.

(4) A direction that service is effected by an alternative method must specify –
  (a) the method of service; and
  (b) the date when the document will be deemed to be served.

36 Who is to serve

(1) A document which has been issued or prepared by a court officer will be served by the court officer except where –
  (a) a practice direction provides otherwise; or
  (b) the court directs otherwise.

(2) Where a court officer is to serve a document, it is for the court to decide which of the methods of service specified in rule 35(1) is to be used.

37 Service of documents on children and patients

(1) The following table shows the person on whom a document must be served if it is a document which would otherwise be served on a child, non-subject child or patient –

Nature of party	Type of document	Person to be served
Child who is not also a patient	Any document	The solicitor acting for the child;
		where there is no such solicitor, the children's guardian or the children and family reporter.

Nature of party	Type of document	Person to be served
Non-subject child who is not also a patient	Application form	One of the non-subject child's parents or guardians;
		if there is no parent or guardian, the person with whom the non-subject child resides or in whose care the non-subject child is.
Patient	Application form	The person authorised under Part VII of the Mental Health Act 1983[1] to conduct the proceedings in the name of the patient or on his behalf;
		if there is no person so authorised, the person with whom the patient resides or in whose care the patient is.
Non-subject child or patient	Application for an order appointing a litigation friend, where the non-subject child or patient has no litigation friend	See rule 57.
	Any other document	The litigation friend who is conducting proceedings on behalf of the non-subject child or patient.

(2) Where a child is directed by the court to serve a document, service is to be effected by –

- (a) the solicitor acting for the child;
- (b) where there is no such solicitor, the children's guardian;
- (c) where there is neither a solicitor or children's guardian, the litigation friend; or
- (d) where there is neither a solicitor, children's guardian, or litigation friend, a court officer.

(3) Where a non-subject child or patient is directed by the court to serve a document, service is to be effected by –

- (a) the solicitor acting for the non-subject child or patient; or
- (b) where there is no such solicitor, the litigation friend.

(4) The court may give directions permitting a document to be served on the child, non-subject child or patient, or on some other person other than the person specified in the table in this rule.

(5) The court may direct that, although a document has been served on someone other than the person specified in the table, the document is to be treated as if it had been properly served.

---

1   1983 c 20.

(6) This rule does not apply where a non-subject child is conducting proceedings without a litigation friend in accordance with rule 51.

38 Deemed service

(1) Unless the contrary is proved, a document which is served in accordance with these Rules or any relevant practice direction will be deemed to be served on the day shown in the following table –

Method of service	Deemed day of service
First class post	The second day after it was posted.
Document exchange	The second day after it was left at the document exchange.
Delivering the document to address	The day after the document was delivered to that address.

(2) If a document is served personally –

(a) after 5 p.m. on a business day; or

(b) at any time on a day which is not a business day

it will be treated as being served on the next business day.

39 Power of court to dispense with service

Where a rule or practice direction requires a document to be served, the court may direct that the requirement is dispensed with.

40 Certificate of service

(1) Where a rule, practice direction or court order requires a certificate of service, the certificate must state the details set out in the following table –

Method of service	Details to be certified
Post	Date of posting.
Personal	Date of personal service.
Document exchange	Date of delivery to the document exchange.
Delivery of document to address	Date when the document was delivered to the address.
Alternative method permitted by the court	As required by the court.

(2) Where an application form is to be served by the applicant he must file a certificate of service within 7 days beginning with the date on which the application form was served.

41 Notice of non-service

Where a person fails to serve any document under these Rules or as directed by the court he must file a certificate of non-service stating the reason why service has not been effected.

Section 2
Service out of the jurisdiction

42 Scope and definitions

(1) This Section contains rules about –

(a) service out of the jurisdiction; and
(b) the procedure for serving out of the jurisdiction.

(Rule 6 defines 'jurisdiction'.)

(2) In this Section –

'application form' includes application notice; and
'the Hague Convention' means the Convention on the service abroad of judicial and extra-judicial documents in civil or commercial matters signed at the Hague on 15 November 1965.[1]

43 Service of documents

(1) Any document to be served for the purposes of these Rules may be served out of the jurisdiction without the permission of the court.

(2) Subject to paragraph (4) or (5), any document served out of the jurisdiction in a country in which English is not the official language must be accompanied by a translation of the document –

(a) in the official language of the country in which the document is to be served; or
(b) if there is more than one official language of the country, in any one of those languages which is appropriate to the place in that country in which the document is to be served.

(3) Every translation filed under this rule must be signed by the translator to certify that the translation is accurate.

(4) Any document served out of the jurisdiction in a country in which English is not the official language need not be accompanied by a translation of the document where –

(a) the person on whom the document is to be served is able to read and understand English; and
(b) service of the document is to be effected directly on that person.

(5) Paragraphs (2) and (3) do not apply where service is to be effected in accordance with the Service Regulation.

44 Method of service – general provisions

(1) Where an application form is to be served out of the jurisdiction, it may be served by any method –

---

[1] Cmnd 3986.

(a) permitted by the law of the country in which it is to be served; or
(b) provided for by –
 (i) rule 45 (service through foreign governments, judicial authorities and British Consular authorities); or
 (ii) rule 47 (service in accordance with the Service Regulation).

(2) Nothing in this rule or in any court order will authorise or require any person to do anything in the country where the application form is to be served which is against the law of that country.

45 Service through foreign governments, judicial authorities and British Consular authorities

(1) Where an application form is to be served on a respondent in any country which is a party to the Hague Convention, the application form may be served –

(a) through the authority designated under the Hague Convention in respect of that country; or
(b) if the law of that country permits –
 (i) through the judicial authorities of that country; or
 (ii) through a British Consular authority in that country.

(2) Where an application form is to be served on a respondent in any country which is not a party to the Hague Convention, the application form may be served, if the law of that country so permits –

(a) through the government of that country, where that government is willing to serve it; or
(b) through a British Consular authority in that country.

(3) Paragraph (2) does not apply where the application form is to be served in –

(a) Scotland, Northern Ireland, the Isle of Man or the Channel Islands;
(b) any Commonwealth State; or
(c) any United Kingdom Overseas Territory listed in the relevant practice direction.

(4) This rule does not apply where service is to be effected in accordance with the Service Regulation.

46 Procedure where service is to be through foreign governments, judicial authorities and British Consular authorities

(1) This rule applies where the applicant wishes to serve the application form through –

(a) the judicial authorities of the country where the application form is to be served;
(b) a British Consular authority in that country;
(c) the authority designated under the Hague Convention in respect of that country; or
(d) the government of that country.

(2) Where this rule applies, the applicant must file –

(a) a request for service of the application form by the method in paragraph (1) that he has chosen;
(b) a copy of the application form;
(c) any translation required under rule 43; and
(d) any other documents, copies of documents or translations required by the relevant practice direction.

(3) When the applicant files the documents specified in paragraph (2), a court officer will –

   (a) seal, or otherwise authenticate with the stamp of the court, the copy of the application form; and
   (b) forward the documents to the Senior Master of the Queen's Bench Division.

(4) The Senior Master will send documents forwarded under this rule –

   (a) where the application form is being served through the authority designated under the Hague Convention, to that authority; or
   (b) in any other case, to the Foreign and Commonwealth Office with a request that it arranges for the application to be served by the method indicated in the request for service filed under paragraph (2) or, where that request indicates alternative methods, by the most convenient method.

(5) An official certificate will be evidence of the facts stated in the certificate if it –

   (a) states that the application form has been served in accordance with this rule either personally, or in accordance with the law of the country in which service was effected;
   (b) specifies the date on which the application form was served; and
   (c) is made by –
      (i) a British Consular authority in the country where the application form was served;
      (ii) the government or judicial authorities in that country; or
      (iii) any other authority designated in respect of that country under the Hague Convention.

(6) A document purporting to be an official certificate under paragraph (5) will be treated as such a certificate, unless it is proved not to be.

(7) This rule does not apply where service is to be effected in accordance with the Service Regulation.

47 Service in accordance with the Service Regulation

(1) This rule applies where an application form is to be served in accordance with the Service Regulation.

(2) The applicant must file the application form and any translations or other documents required by the Service Regulation.

(3) When the applicant files the documents referred to in paragraph (2), a court officer will –

   (a) seal, or otherwise authenticate with the stamp of the court, the copy of the application form; and
   (b) forward the documents to the Senior Master of the Queen's Bench Division.

(The Service Regulation is annexed to the relevant practice direction.)

48 Undertaking to be responsible for expenses of the Foreign and Commonwealth Office

Every request for service filed under rule 46 (service through foreign governments, judicial authorities etc.) must contain an undertaking by the person making the request –

   (a) to be responsible for all expenses incurred by the Foreign and Commonwealth Office or foreign judicial authority; and

(b) to pay those expenses to the Foreign and Commonwealth Office or foreign judicial authority on being informed of the amount.

PART 7

LITIGATION FRIEND, CHILDREN'S GUARDIAN, REPORTING OFFICER AND CHILDREN AND FAMILY REPORTER

Section 1
Litigation friend

49 Application of this Section

(1) This Section –

  (a) contains special provisions which apply in proceedings involving non-subject children and patients; and
  (b) sets out how a person becomes a litigation friend.

(2) The provisions of this Section also apply to a child who does not have a children's guardian, in which case, any reference to a 'non-subject child' in these Rules is to be taken as including a child.

50 Requirement for litigation friend in proceedings

(1) Subject to rule 51, a non-subject child must have a litigation friend to conduct proceedings on his behalf.

(2) A patient must have a litigation friend to conduct proceedings on his behalf.

51 Circumstances in which the non-subject child does not need a litigation friend

(1) A non-subject child may conduct proceedings without a litigation friend –

  (a) where he has obtained the court's permission to do so; or
  (b) where a solicitor –
     (i) considers that the non-subject child is able, having regard to his understanding, to give instructions in relation to the proceedings; and
     (ii) has accepted instructions from that child to act for him in the proceedings and, if the proceedings have begun, he is already acting.

(2) An application for permission under paragraph (1)(a) may be made by the non-subject child without notice.

(3) Where a non-subject child has a litigation friend in proceedings and he wishes to conduct the remaining stages of the proceedings without a litigation friend, the non-subject child may apply to the court, on notice to the litigation friend, for permission for that purpose and for the removal of the litigation friend.

(4) Where the court is considering whether to –

  (a) grant permission under paragraph (1)(a); or
  (b) grant permission under paragraph (3) and remove a litigation friend

it will grant the permission sought and, as the case may be, remove the litigation friend if it considers that the non-subject child concerned has sufficient understanding to conduct the proceedings concerned or proposed without a litigation friend.

(5) In exercising its powers under paragraph (4) the court may require the litigation friend to take such part in the proceedings as the court directs.

(6) The court may revoke any permission granted under paragraph (1)(a) where it considers that the non-subject child does not have sufficient understanding to participate as a party in the proceedings concerned without a litigation friend.

(7) Where a solicitor is acting for a non-subject child in proceedings without a litigation friend by virtue of paragraph (1)(b) and either of the conditions specified in paragraph (1)(b)(i) or (ii) cease to be fulfilled, he must inform the court immediately.

(8) Where –

(a) the court revokes any permission under paragraph (6); or
(b) either of the conditions specified in paragraph (1)(b)(i) or (ii) is no longer fulfilled

the court may, if it considers it necessary in order to protect the interests of the non-subject child concerned, appoint a person to be that child's litigation friend.

52 Stage of proceedings at which a litigation friend becomes necessary

(1) This rule does not apply where a non-subject child is conducting proceedings without a litigation friend in accordance with rule 51.

(2) A person may not without the permission of the court take any step in proceedings except –

(a) filing an application form; or
(b) applying for the appointment of a litigation friend under rule 55

until the non-subject child or patient has a litigation friend.

(3) If a party becomes a patient during proceedings, no party may take any step in proceedings without the permission of the court until the patient has a litigation friend.

53 Who may be a litigation friend for a patient without a court order

(1) This rule does not apply if the court has appointed a person to be a litigation friend.

(2) A person authorised under Part VII of the Mental Health Act 1983 to conduct legal proceedings in the name of a patient or on his behalf is entitled to be the litigation friend of the patient in any proceedings to which his authority extends.

(3) If nobody has been appointed by the court or, in the case of a patient, authorised under Part VII of the Mental Health Act 1983, a person may act as a litigation friend if he –

(a) can fairly and competently conduct proceedings on behalf of the non-subject child or patient;
(b) has no interest adverse to that of the non-subject child or patient; and
(c) subject to paragraph (4), undertakes to pay any costs which the non-subject child or patient may be ordered to pay in relation to the proceedings, subject to any right he may have to be repaid from the assets of the non-subject child or patient.

(4) Paragraph (3)(c) does not apply to the Official Solicitor, an officer of the Service or a Welsh family proceedings officer.

54 How a person becomes a litigation friend without a court order

(1) If the court has not appointed a litigation friend, a person who wishes to act as a litigation friend must follow the procedure set out in this rule.

(2) A person authorised under Part VII of the Mental Health Act 1983 must file an official copy[1] of the order or other document which constitutes his authorisation to act.

(3) Any other person must file a certificate of suitability stating that he satisfies the conditions specified in rule 53(3).

(4) A person who is to act as a litigation friend must file –

(a) the authorisation; or
(b) the certificate of suitability

at the time when he first takes a step in the proceedings on behalf of the non-subject child or patient.

(5) A court officer will send the certificate of suitability to every person on whom, in accordance with rule 37(1) (service on parent, guardian etc.), the application form should be served.

(6) This rule does not apply to the Official Solicitor, an officer of the Service or a Welsh family proceedings officer.

55 How a person becomes a litigation friend by court order

(1) The court may make an order appointing –

(a) the Official Solicitor;
(b) in the case of a non-subject child, an officer of the Service or a Welsh family proceedings officer (if he consents); or
(c) some other person (if he consents)

as a litigation friend.

(2) An order appointing a litigation friend may be made by the court of its own initiative or on the application of –

(a) a person who wishes to be a litigation friend; or
(b) a party to the proceedings.

(3) The court may at any time direct that a party make an application for an order under paragraph (2).

(4) An application for an order appointing a litigation friend must be supported by evidence.

(5) Unless the court directs otherwise, a person appointed under this rule to be a litigation friend for a non-subject child or patient will be treated as a party for the purpose of any provision in these Rules requiring a document to be served on, or sent to, or notice to be given to, a party to the proceedings.

(6) Subject to rule 53(4), the court may not appoint a litigation friend under this rule unless it is satisfied that the person to be appointed complies with the conditions specified in rule 53(3).

---

1 An official copy is a copy of an official document supplied and marked as such by the office that issued the original.

56 Court's power to change litigation friend and to prevent person acting as litigation friend

(1) The court may –

(a) direct that a person may not act as a litigation friend;
(b) terminate a litigation friend's appointment; or
(c) appoint a new litigation friend in substitution for an existing one.

(2) An application for an order under paragraph (1) must be supported by evidence.

(3) Subject to rule 53(4), the court may not appoint a litigation friend under this rule unless it is satisfied that the person to be appointed complies with the conditions specified in rule 53(3).

57 Appointment of litigation friend by court order – supplementary

(1) A copy of the application for an order under rule 55 or 56 must be sent by a court officer to every person on whom, in accordance with rule 37(1) (service on parent, guardian etc.), the application form should be served.

(2) Where an application for an order under rule 55 is in respect of a patient, the court officer must also send a copy of the application to the patient unless the court directs otherwise.

(3) A copy of an application for an order under rule 56 must also be sent to –

(a) the person who is the litigation friend, or who is purporting to act as the litigation friend, when the application is made; and
(b) the person who it is proposed should be the litigation friend, if he is not the applicant.

58 Procedure where appointment of litigation friend comes to an end

(1) When a non-subject child who is not a patient reaches the age of 18, a litigation friend's appointment comes to an end.

(2) When a party ceases to be a patient, the litigation friend's appointment continues until it is brought to an end by a court order.

(3) An application for an order under paragraph (2) may be made by –

(a) the former patient;
(b) the litigation friend; or
(c) a party.

(4) A court officer will send a notice to the other parties stating that the appointment of the non-subject child or patient's litigation friend to act has ended.

Section 2
Children's guardian

59 Appointment of children's guardian

(1) In proceedings to which Part 5 applies, the court will appoint a children's guardian where the child is a party to the proceedings unless it is satisfied that it is not necessary to do so to safeguard the interests of the child.

(2) At any stage in proceedings where the child is a party to the proceedings –

(a) a party may apply, without notice to the other parties unless the court directs otherwise, for the appointment of a children's guardian; or
(b) the court may of its own initiative appoint a children's guardian.

(3) The court will grant an application under paragraph (2)(a) unless it considers that such an appointment is not necessary to safeguard the interests of the child.

(4) When appointing a children's guardian the court will consider the appointment of anyone who has previously acted as a children's guardian of the same child.

60 What the court or a court officer will do once the court has made a decision about appointing a children's guardian

(1) Where the court refuses an application under rule 59(2)(a) it will give reasons for the refusal and the court or a court officer will –

(a) record the refusal and the reasons for it; and
(b) as soon as practicable, notify the parties and either the Service or the Assembly of a decision not to appoint a children's guardian.

(2) Where the court appoints a children's guardian under rule 59 a court officer will record the appointment and, as soon as practicable, will –

(a) inform the parties and either the Service or the Assembly; and
(b) unless it has already been sent, send the children's guardian a copy of the application and copies of any document filed with the court in the proceedings.

(3) A court officer also has a continuing duty to send the children's guardian a copy of any other document filed with the court during the course of the proceedings.

61 Termination of the appointment of the children's guardian

(1) The appointment of a children's guardian under rule 59 continues for such time as is specified in the appointment or until terminated by the court.

(2) When terminating an appointment in accordance with paragraph (1), the court will give reasons for doing so, a note of which will be taken by the court or a court officer.

62 Powers and duties of the children's guardian

(1) The children's guardian is to act on behalf of the child upon the hearing of any application in proceedings to which Part 5 applies with the duty of safeguarding the interests of the child.

(2) The children's guardian must also provide the court with such other assistance as it may require.

63 How the children's guardian exercises his duties – investigations and appointment of solicitor

(1) The children's guardian must make such investigations as are necessary for him to carry out his duties and must, in particular –

(a) contact or seek to interview such persons as he thinks appropriate or as the court directs; and
(b) obtain such professional assistance as is available to him which he thinks appropriate or which the court directs him to obtain.

(2) The children's guardian must –

(a) appoint a solicitor for the child unless a solicitor has already been appointed;
(b) give such advice to the child as is appropriate having regard to his understanding; and
(c) where appropriate instruct the solicitor representing the child on all matters relevant to the interests of the child, including possibilities for appeal, arising in the course of proceedings.

(3) Where the children's guardian is authorised in the terms mentioned by and in accordance with section 15(1) of the Criminal Justice and Court Services Act 2000[1] or section 37(1) of the Children Act 2004[2] (right of officer of the Service or Welsh family proceedings officer to conduct litigation or exercise a right of audience), paragraph (2)(a) will not apply if he intends to have conduct of the proceedings on behalf of the child unless –

(a) the child wishes to instruct a solicitor direct; and
(b) the children's guardian or the court considers that he is of sufficient understanding to do so.

64 Where the child instructs a solicitor or conducts proceedings on his own behalf

(1) Where it appears to the children's guardian that the child –

(a) is instructing his solicitor direct; or
(b) intends to conduct and is capable of conducting the proceedings on his own behalf

he must inform the court of that fact.

(2) Where paragraph (1) applies, the children's guardian –

(a) must perform the duties set out in rules 62, 63, 65 to 67 and this rule, other than those duties in rule 63(2)(a) and (c), and such other duties as the court may direct;
(b) must take such part in the proceedings as the court may direct; and
(c) may, with the permission of the court, have legal representation in the conduct of those duties.

65 How the children's guardian exercises his duties – attendance at court, advice to the court and reports

(1) The children's guardian or the solicitor appointed under section 41(3) of the 1989 Act or in accordance with rule 63(2)(a) must attend all directions hearings unless the court directs otherwise.

(2) The children's guardian must advise the court on the following matters –

(a) whether the child is of sufficient understanding for any purpose including the child's refusal to submit to a medical or psychiatric examination or other assessment that the court has the power to require, direct or order;
(b) the wishes of the child in respect of any matter relevant to the proceedings including his attendance at court;
(c) the appropriate forum for the proceedings;
(d) the appropriate timing of the proceedings or any part of them;

---

1   2000 c 43.
2   2004 c 31.

(e) the options available to it in respect of the child and the suitability of each such option including what order should be made in determining the application; and

(f) any other matter on which the court seeks his advice or on which he considers that the court should be informed.

(3) The advice given under paragraph (2) may, subject to any direction of the court, be given orally or in writing.

(4) The children's guardian must –

(a) unless the court directs otherwise, file a written report advising on the interests of the child in accordance with the timetable set by the court; and

(b) where practicable, notify any person the joining of whom as a party to those proceedings would be likely, in his opinion, to safeguard the interests of the child, of the court's power to join that person as a party under rule 23 and must inform the court –
   (i) of any notification;
   (ii) of anyone whom he attempted to notify under this paragraph but was unable to contact; and
   (iii) of anyone whom he believes may wish to be joined to the proceedings.

(5) Any report to the court under this rule will be confidential.

(Part 9 sets out the procedure for making an application to be joined as a party in proceedings.)

66 How the children's guardian exercises his duties – service of documents and inspection of records

(1) The children's guardian must –

(a) serve documents on behalf of the child in accordance with rule 37(2)(b); and

(b) accept service of documents on behalf of the child in accordance with the table in rule 37(1),

and, where the child has not himself been served and has sufficient understanding, advise the child of the contents of any document so served.

(2) Where the children's guardian inspects records of the kinds referred to in –

(a) section 42 of the 1989 Act (right to have access to local authority records); or

(b) section 103 (right to have access to adoption agency records)

he must bring all records and documents which may, in his opinion, assist in the proper determination of the proceedings to the attention of –
   (i) the court; and
   (ii) unless the court directs otherwise, the other parties to the proceedings.

67 How the children's guardian exercises his duties – communication of a court's decision to the child

The children's guardian must ensure that, in relation to a decision made by the court in the proceedings –

(a) if he considers it appropriate to the age and understanding of the child, the child is notified of that decision; and

(b) if the child is notified of the decision, it is explained to the child in a manner appropriate to his age and understanding.

68 Solicitor for child

(1) A solicitor appointed under section 41(3) of the 1989 Act or in accordance with rule 63(2)(a) must represent the child –

(a) in accordance with instructions received from the children's guardian unless the solicitor considers, having taken into account the views of the children's guardian and any direction of the court under rule 64(2) –
   (i) that the child wishes to give instructions which conflict with those of the children's guardian; and
   (ii) that he is able, having regard to his understanding, to give such instructions on his own behalf,
   in which case the solicitor must conduct the proceedings in accordance with instructions received from the child;
(b) where no children's guardian has been appointed and the condition in section 41(4)(b) of the 1989 Act is satisfied, in accordance with instructions received from the child; or
(c) in default of instructions under sub-paragraph (a) or (b), in furtherance of the best interests of the child.

(2) A solicitor appointed under section 41(3) of the 1989 Act or in accordance with rule 63(2)(a) must –

(a) serve documents on behalf of the child in accordance with rule 37(2)(a); and
(b) accept service of documents on behalf of the child in accordance with the table in rule 37(1),

and, where the child has not himself been served and has sufficient understanding, advise the child of the contents of any document so served.

(3) Where the child wishes an appointment of a solicitor under section 41(3) of the 1989 Act or in accordance with rule 63(2)(a) to be terminated –

(a) he may apply to the court for an order terminating the appointment; and
(b) the solicitor and the children's guardian will be given an opportunity to make representations.

(4) Where the children's guardian wishes an appointment of a solicitor under section 41(3) of the 1989 Act or in accordance with rule 63(2)(a) to be terminated –

(a) he may apply to the court for an order terminating the appointment; and
(b) the solicitor and, if he is of sufficient understanding, the child, will be given an opportunity to make representations.

(5) When terminating an appointment in accordance with paragraph (3) or (4), the court will give its reasons for so doing, a note of which will be taken by the court or a court officer.

(6) The court or a court officer will record the appointment under section 41(3) of the 1989 Act or in accordance with rule 63(2)(a) or the refusal to make the appointment.

Section 3
Reporting officer

69 When the court appoints a reporting officer

In proceedings to which Part 5 applies, the court will appoint a reporting officer where –

(a) it appears that a parent or guardian of the child is willing to consent to the placing of the child for adoption, to the making of an adoption order or to a section 84 order; and
(b) that parent or guardian is in England or Wales.

70 Appointment of the same reporting officer in respect of two or more parents or guardians

The same person may be appointed as the reporting officer for two or more parents or guardians of the child.

71 The duties of the reporting officer

The reporting officer must witness the signature by a parent or guardian on the document in which consent is given to –

(a) the placing of the child for adoption;
(b) the making of an adoption order; or
(c) the making of a section 84 order.

72 How the reporting officer exercises his duties

(1) The reporting officer must –

(a) ensure so far as reasonably practicable that the parent or guardian is –
 (i) giving consent unconditionally; and
 (ii) with full understanding of what is involved;
(b) investigate all the circumstances relevant to a parent's or guardian's consent to the placing of the child for adoption or to the making of an adoption order or a section 84 order; and
(c) on completing his investigations the reporting officer must –
 (i) make a report in writing to the court in accordance with the timetable set by the court, drawing attention to any matters which, in his opinion, may be of assistance to the court in considering the application; or
 (ii) make an interim report to the court if a parent or guardian of the child is unwilling to consent to the placing of the child for adoption or to the making of an adoption order or section 84 order.

(2) On receipt of an interim report under paragraph (1)(c)(ii) a court officer must inform the applicant that a parent or guardian of the child is unwilling to consent to the placing of the child for adoption or to the making of an adoption order or section 84 order.

(3) The reporting officer may at any time before the final hearing make an interim report to the court if he considers necessary and ask the court for directions.

(4) The reporting officer must attend all directions hearings unless the court directs otherwise.

(5) Any report to the court under this rule will be confidential.

Section 4
Children and family reporter

73 Request by court for a welfare report in respect of the child

(1) In proceedings to which Part 5 applies, where the court is considering an application for an order in proceedings the court may ask a children and family reporter to prepare a report on matters relating to the welfare of the child.

(2) It is the duty of a children and family reporter to –

(a) comply with any request for a report under this rule; and
(b) provide the court with such other assistance as it may require.

(3) Any report to the court under this rule will be confidential.

74 How the children and family reporter exercises his powers and duties

(1) The children and family reporter must make such investigations as may be necessary for him to perform his powers and duties and must, in particular –

(a) contact or seek to interview such persons as he thinks appropriate or as the court directs; and
(b) obtain such professional assistance as is available to him which he thinks appropriate or which the court directs him to obtain.

(2) The children and family reporter must –

(a) notify the child of such contents of his report (if any) as he considers appropriate to the age and understanding of the child, including any reference to the child's own views on the application and his recommendation; and
(b) if he does notify the child of any contents of his report, explain them to the child in a manner appropriate to his age and understanding.

(3) The children and family reporter must –

(a) attend all directions hearings unless the court directs otherwise;
(b) advise the court of the child's wishes and feelings;
(c) advise the court if he considers that the joining of a person as a party to the proceedings would be likely to safeguard the interests of the child;
(d) consider whether it is in the best interests of the child for the child to be made a party to the proceedings, and if so, notify the court of his opinion together with the reasons for that opinion; and
(e) where the court has directed that a written report be made, file the report in accordance with the timetable set by the court.

Section 5
Who can act as children's guardian, reporting officer and children and family reporter

75 Persons who may not be appointed as children's guardian, reporting officer or children and family reporter

(1) In adoption proceedings or proceedings for a section 84 order or a section 89 order, a person may not be appointed as a children's guardian, reporting officer or children and family reporter if he –

(a) is a member, officer or servant of a local authority which is a party to the proceedings;
(b) is, or has been, a member, officer or servant of a local authority or voluntary organisation who has been directly concerned in that capacity in arrangements relating to the care, accommodation or welfare of the child during the five years prior to the commencement of the proceedings; or

(c) is a serving probation officer who has, in that capacity, been previously concerned with the child or his family.

(2) In placement proceedings, a person described in paragraph (1)(b) or (c) may not be appointed as a children's guardian, reporting officer or children and family reporter.

76 Appointment of the same person as children's guardian, reporting officer and children and family reporter

The same person may be appointed to act as one or more of the following –

(a) the children's guardian;
(b) the reporting officer; and
(c) the children and family reporter.

PART 8

DOCUMENTS AND DISCLOSURE OF DOCUMENTS AND INFORMATION

77 Confidential reports to the court and disclosure to the parties

(1) The court will consider whether to give a direction that a confidential report be disclosed to each party to the proceedings.

(2) Before giving such a direction the court will consider whether any information should be deleted including information which –

(a) discloses, or is likely to disclose, the identity of a person who has been assigned a serial number under rule 20(2); or
(b) discloses the particulars referred to in rule 21(1) where a party has given notice under rule 21(2) (disclosure of personal details).

(3) The court may direct that the report will not be disclosed to a party.

78 Communication of information relating to proceedings

(1) For the purposes of the law relating to contempt of court, information (whether or not it is recorded in any form) relating to proceedings held in private may be communicated –

(a) where the court gives permission;
(b) unless the court directs otherwise, in accordance with the relevant practice direction; or
(c) where the communication is to –
  (i) a party;
  (ii) the legal representative of a party;
  (iii) a professional legal adviser;
  (iv) an officer of the Service or a Welsh family proceedings officer;
  (v) a welfare officer;
  (vi) the Legal Services Commission;
  (vii) an expert whose instruction by a party has been authorised by the court; or
  (viii) a professional acting in furtherance of the protection of children.

(2) In this rule –

'professional acting in furtherance of the protection of children' includes –

(a) an officer of a local authority exercising child protection functions;
(b) a police officer who is –
   (i) exercising powers under section 46 of the 1989 Act; or
   (ii) serving in a child protection unit or a paedophile unit of a police force;
(c) any professional person attending a child protection conference or review in relation to a child who is the subject of the proceedings to which the information relates; or
(d) an officer of the National Society for the Prevention of Cruelty to Children;

'professional legal adviser' means a barrister or a solicitor, solicitor's employee or other authorised litigator (as defined in section 119 of the Courts and Legal Services Act 1990[1]) who is providing advice to a party but is not instructed to represent that party in the proceedings;

'welfare officer' means a person who has been asked to prepare a report under section 7(1)(b) of the 1989 Act.

79 Orders for disclosure against a person not a party

(1) This rule applies where an application is made to the court under any Act for disclosure by a person who is not a party to the proceedings.[2]

(2) The application must be supported by evidence.

(3) The court may make an order under this rule only where –

(a) the documents of which disclosure is sought are likely to support the case of the applicant or adversely affect the case of one of the other parties to the proceedings; and
(b) disclosure is necessary in order to dispose fairly of the application or to save costs.

(4) An order under this rule must –

(a) specify the documents or the classes of documents which the respondent must disclose; and
(b) require the respondent, when making disclosure, to specify any of those documents –
   (i) which are no longer in his control; or
   (ii) in respect of which he claims a right or duty to withhold inspection.

(5) Such an order may –

(a) require the respondent to indicate what has happened to any documents which are no longer in his control; and
(b) specify the time and place for disclosure and inspection.

(6) This rule does not apply to proceedings in a magistrates' court.

80 Rules not to limit other powers of the court to order disclosure

(1) Rule 79 does not limit any other power which the court may have to order –

(a) disclosure before proceedings have started; and
(b) disclosure against a person who is not a party to proceedings.

(2) This rule does not apply to proceedings in a magistrates' court.

---

1   1990 c 41.
2   An application for disclosure against a person who is not a party to proceedings is permitted under s 34 of the Supreme Court Act 1981 (c 54) or s 53 of the County Courts Act 1984 (c 28).

81 Claim to withhold inspection or disclosure of a document

(1) A person may apply, without notice, for an order permitting him to withhold disclosure of a document on the ground that disclosure would damage the public interest.

(2) Unless the court orders otherwise, an order of the court under paragraph (1) –

   (a) must not be served on any other person; and
   (b) must not be open to inspection by any person.

(3) A person who wishes to claim that he has a right or a duty to withhold inspection of a document, or part of a document, must state in writing –

   (a) that he has such a right or duty; and
   (b) the grounds on which he claims that right or duty.

(4) The statement referred to in paragraph (3) must be made to the person wishing to inspect the document.

(5) A party may apply to the court to decide whether a claim made under paragraph (3) should be upheld.

(6) For the purpose of deciding an application under paragraph (1) (application to withhold disclosure) or paragraph (3) (claim to withhold inspection) the court may –

   (a) require the person seeking to withhold disclosure or inspection of a document to produce that document to the court; and
   (b) invite any person, whether or not a party, to make representations.

(7) An application under paragraph (1) or (5) must be supported by evidence.

(8) This rule does not affect any rule of law which permits or requires a document to be withheld from disclosure or inspection on the ground that its disclosure or inspection would damage the public interest.

(9) This rule does not apply to proceedings in a magistrates' court.

82 Custody of documents

All documents relating to proceedings under the Act must, while they are in the custody of the court, be kept in a place of special security.

83 Inspection and copies of documents

Subject to the provisions of these Rules, any practice direction or any direction given by the court –

   (a) no document or order held by the court in proceedings under the Act will be open to inspection by any person; and
   (b) no copy of any such document or order, or of an extract from any such document or order, will be taken by or given to any person.

84 Disclosing information to an adopted adult

(1) The adopted person has the right, at his request, to receive from the court which made the adoption order a copy of the following –

   (a) the application form for an adoption order (but not the documents attached to that form);

(b) the adoption order and any other orders relating to the adoption proceedings;
(c) orders allowing any person contact with the child after the adoption order was made; and
(d) any other document or order referred to in the relevant practice direction.

(2) The court will remove any protected information from any copy of a document or order referred to in paragraph (1) before the copies are given to the adopted person.

(3) This rule does not apply to an adopted person under the age of 18 years.

(4) In this rule 'protected information' means information which would be protected information under section 57(3) if the adoption agency gave the information and not the court.

85 Translation of documents

(1) Where a translation of any document is required for the purposes of proceedings for a Convention adoption order the translation must –

(a) unless the court directs otherwise, be provided by the applicant; and
(b) be signed by the translator to certify that the translation is accurate.

(2) This rule does not apply where the document is to be served in accordance with the Service Regulation.

PART 9

PROCEDURE FOR OTHER APPLICATIONS IN PROCEEDINGS

86 Types of application for which Part 9 procedure may be followed

(1) The Part 9 procedure is the procedure set out in this Part.

(2) An applicant may use the Part 9 procedure if the application is made –

(a) in the course of existing proceedings;
(b) to commence proceedings other than those to which Part 5 applies; or
(c) in connection with proceedings which have been concluded.

(Rule 22 lists the proceedings to which Part 5 applies.)

(3) Paragraph (2) does not apply –

(a) to applications made in accordance with –
   (i) section 60(3) (order to prevent disclosure of information to an adopted person);
   (ii) section 79(4) (order for Registrar General to give any information referred to in section 79(3));
   (iii) rule 27 (request to dispense with consent);
   (iv) rule 59(2) (appointment of children's guardian);
   (v) rule 84 (disclosure of information to adopted adult);
   (vi) rule 106 (withdrawal of application); or
   (vii) rule 107 (recovery orders); or
(b) if a practice direction provides that the Part 9 procedure may not be used in relation to the type of application in question.

(4) The following persons are to be respondents to an application under this Part –

(a) where there are existing proceedings or the proceedings have concluded, the parties to those proceedings;

(b) where there are no existing proceedings –
  (i) if notice has been given under section 44 (notice of intention to adopt or apply for a section 84 order), the local authority to whom notice has been given; and
  (ii) if an application is made in accordance with –
    (aa) section 26(3)(f) (permission to apply for contact order); or
    (bb) section 42(6) (permission to apply for adoption order),
  any person who, in accordance with rule 23, will be a party to the proceedings brought if permission is granted; and
(c) any other person as the court may direct.

87 Application notice to be filed

(1) Subject to paragraph (2), the applicant must file an application notice.

(2) An applicant may make an application without filing an application notice if –

(a) this is permitted by a rule or practice direction; or
(b) the court dispenses with the requirement for an application notice.

88 Notice of an application

(1) Subject to paragraph (2), a copy of the application notice will be served on each respondent.

(2) An application may be made without serving a copy of the application notice if this is permitted by –

(a) a rule;
(b) a practice direction; or
(c) the court.

(Rule 91 deals with service of a copy of the application notice.)

89 Time when an application is made

Where an application must be made within a specified time, it is so made if the court receives the application notice within that time.

90 What an application notice must include

(1) An application notice must state –

(a) what order the applicant is seeking; and
(b) briefly, why the applicant is seeking the order.

(2) The applicant may rely on the matters set out in his application notice as evidence if the application is verified by a statement of truth.

91 Service of a copy of an application notice

(1) A court officer will serve a copy of the application notice –

(a) as soon as practicable after it is filed; and
(b) in any event at least 7 days before the court is to deal with the application.

(2) The applicant must, when he files the application notice, file a copy of any written evidence in support.

(3) When a copy of an application notice is served by a court officer it will be accompanied by –

    (a) a notice of the date and place where the application will be heard;
    (b) a copy of any witness statement in support; and
    (c) a copy of any draft order which the applicant has attached to his application.

(4) If –

    (a) an application notice is served; but
    (b) the period of notice is shorter than the period required by these Rules or a practice direction,

the court may direct that, in the circumstances of the case, sufficient notice has been given and hear the application.

(5) This rule does not require written evidence –

    (a) to be filed if it has already been filed; or
    (b) to be served on a party on whom it has already been served.

92 Applications which may be dealt with without a hearing

The court may deal with an application without a hearing if –

    (a) the parties agree as to the terms of the order sought;
    (b) the parties agree that the court should dispose of the application without a hearing; or
    (c) the court does not consider that a hearing would be appropriate.

93 Service of application where application made without notice

(1) This rule applies where the court has disposed of an application which it permitted to be made without service of a copy of the application notice.

(2) Where the court makes an order, whether granting or dismissing the application, a copy of the application notice and any evidence in support will, unless the court directs otherwise, be served with the order on all the parties in the proceedings.

(3) The order must contain a statement of the right to make an application to set aside or vary the order under rule 94.

94 Application to set aside or vary order made without notice

(1) A person who was not served with a copy of the application notice before an order was made under rule 93 may apply to have the order set aside or varied.

(2) An application under this rule must be made within 7 days beginning with the date on which the order was served on the person making the application.

95 Power of the court to proceed in the absence of a party

(1) Where the applicant or any respondent fails to attend the hearing of an application, the court may proceed in his absence.

(2) Where –

    (a) the applicant or any respondent fails to attend the hearing of an application; and
    (b) the court makes an order at the hearing,

the court may, on application or of its own initiative, re-list the application.

96 Dismissal of totally without merit applications

If the High Court or a county court dismisses an application (including an application for permission to appeal) and it considers that the application is totally without merit –

(a) the court's order must record that fact; and
(b) the court must at the same time consider whether it is appropriate to make a civil restraint order.

PART 10

ALTERNATIVE PROCEDURE FOR APPLICATIONS

97 Types of application for which Part 10 procedure may be followed

(1) The Part 10 procedure is the procedure set out in this Part.

(2) An applicant may use the Part 10 procedure where the procedure set out in Part 9 does not apply and –

(a) there is no form prescribed by a rule or practice direction in which to make the application;
(b) he seeks the court's decision on a question which is unlikely to involve a substantial dispute of fact; or
(c) paragraph (5) applies.

(3) The court may at any stage direct that the application is to continue as if the applicant had not used the Part 10 procedure and, if it does so, the court may give any directions it considers appropriate.

(4) Paragraph (2) does not apply –

(a) to applications made in accordance with –
   (i) rule 27 (request to dispense with consent);
   (ii) rule 59(2) (appointment of children's guardian);
   (iii) rule 84 (disclosure of information to adopted adult);
   (iv) rule 106 (withdrawal of application); or
   (v) rule 107 (recovery orders); or
(b) if a practice direction provides that the Part 10 procedure may not be used in relation to the type of application in question.

(5) A rule or practice direction may, in relation to a specified type of proceedings –

(a) require or permit the use of the Part 10 procedure; and
(b) disapply or modify any of the rules set out in this Part as they apply to those proceedings.

98 Contents of the application

(1) In this Part 'application' means an application made under this Part.

(2) Where the applicant uses the Part 10 procedure the application must state –

(a) that this Part applies;
(b) (i) the question which the applicant wants the court to decide; or

(ii) the order which the applicant is seeking and the legal basis of the application for that order;
(c) if the application is being made under an enactment, what that enactment is;
(d) if the applicant is applying in a representative capacity, what that capacity is; and
(e) if the respondent appears or is to appear in a representative capacity, what that capacity is.

(3) A court officer will serve a copy of the application on the respondent.

99 Issue of application without naming respondents

(1) A practice direction may set out circumstances in which an application may be issued under this Part without naming a respondent.

(2) The practice direction may set out those cases in which an application for permission must be made before the application is issued.

(3) The application for permission –

(a) need not be served on any other person; and
(b) must be accompanied by a copy of the application that the applicant proposes to issue.

(4) Where the court gives permission it will give directions about the future management of the application.

100 Acknowledgement of service

(1) Subject to paragraph (2), each respondent must file an acknowledgement of service within 14 days beginning with the date on which the application is served.

(2) If the application is to be served out of the jurisdiction the respondent must file an acknowledgement of service within the period set out in the practice direction supplementing Part 6, section 2.

(3) A court officer will serve the acknowledgement of service on the applicant and any other party.

(4) The acknowledgement of service must –

(a) state whether the respondent contests the application;
(b) state, if the respondent seeks a different order from that set out in the application, what that order is; and
(c) be signed by the respondent or his legal representative.

101 Consequence of not filing an acknowledgement of service

(1) This rule applies where –

(a) the respondent has failed to file an acknowledgement of service; and
(b) the time period for doing so has expired.

(2) The respondent must attend the hearing of the application but may not take part in the hearing unless the court gives permission.

102 Filing and serving written evidence

(1) The applicant must file written evidence on which he intends to rely when he files his application.

(2) A court officer will serve the applicant's evidence on the respondent with the application.

(3) A respondent who wishes to rely on written evidence must file it when he files his acknowledgement of service.

(4) A court officer will serve the respondent's evidence, if any, on the other parties with the acknowledgement of service.

(5) The applicant may, within 14 days beginning with the date on which a respondent's evidence was served on him, file further written evidence in reply.

(6) If he does so, a court officer will serve a copy of that evidence on the other parties.

(7) The applicant may rely on the matters set out in his application as evidence under this rule if the application is verified by a statement of truth.

103 Evidence – general

(1) No written evidence may be relied on at the hearing of the application unless –
   (a) it has been served in accordance with rule 102; or
   (b) the court gives permission.

(2) The court may require or permit a party to give oral evidence at the hearing.

(3) The court may give directions requiring the attendance for cross-examination of a witness who has given written evidence.

104 Procedure where respondent objects to use of the Part 10 procedure

(1) Where a respondent contends that the Part 10 procedure should not be used because –
   (a) there is a substantial dispute of fact; and
   (b) the use of the Part 10 procedure is not required or permitted by a rule or practice direction,

he must state his reasons when he files his acknowledgement of service.

(2) When the court receives the acknowledgement of service and any written evidence it will give directions as to the future management of the case.

105 Applications under section 60(3) and 79(4) or rule 108

(1) The Part 10 procedure must be used in an application made in accordance with –
   (a) section 60(3) (order to prevent disclosure of information to an adopted person);
   (b) section 79(4) (order for Registrar General to give any information referred to in section 79(3)); and
   (c) rule 108 (directions of High Court regarding fathers without parental responsibility).

(2) The respondent to an application made in accordance with paragraph (1)(b) is the Registrar General.

PART 11
MISCELLANEOUS

106 Withdrawal of application

(1) An application may be withdrawn with the permission of the court.

(2) Subject to paragraph (3), a person seeking permission to withdraw an application must file a written request for permission setting out the reasons for the request.

(3) The request under paragraph (2) may be made orally to the court if the parties and any children's guardian, reporting officer or children and family reporter are present.

(4) A court officer will notify the other parties and any children's guardian, reporting officer or children and family reporter of a written request.

(5) The court may deal with a written request under paragraph (2) without a hearing if the other parties and any children's guardian, reporting officer or children and family reporter have had an opportunity to make written representations to the court about the request.

107 Application for recovery orders

(1) An application for any of the orders referred to in section 41(2) (recovery orders) may –

- (a) in the High Court or a county court, be made without notice in which case the applicant must file the application –
    - (i) where the application is made by telephone, the next business day after the making of the application; or
    - (ii) in any other case, at the time when the application is made; and
- (b) in a magistrates' court, be made, with the permission of the court, without notice in which case the applicant must file the application at the time when the application is made or as directed by the court.

(2) Where the court refuses to make an order on an application without notice it may direct that the application is made on notice in which case the application will proceed in accordance with Part 5.

(3) The respondents to an application under this rule are –

- (a) in a case where –
    - (i) placement proceedings;
    - (ii) adoption proceedings; or
    - (iii) proceedings for a section 84 order

    are pending, all parties to those proceedings;
- (b) any adoption agency authorised to place the child for adoption or which has placed the child for adoption;
- (c) any local authority to whom notice under section 44 (notice of intention to adopt or apply for a section 84 order) has been given;
- (d) any person having parental responsibility for the child;
- (e) any person in whose favour there is provision for contact;
- (f) any person who was caring for the child immediately prior to the making of the application; and
- (g) any person whom the applicant alleges to have effected or to have been or to be responsible for taking or keeping the child.

108 Inherent jurisdiction and fathers without parental responsibility

Where no proceedings have started an adoption agency or local authority may ask the High Court for directions on the need to give a father without parental responsibility notice of the intention to place a child for adoption.

109 Timing of applications for section 89 order

An application for a section 89 order must be made within 2 years beginning with the date on which –

(a) the Convention adoption or Convention adoption order; or
(b) the overseas adoption or determination under section 91

to which it relates was made.

110 Costs

The court may at any time make such order as to costs as it thinks just including an order relating to the payment of expenses incurred by any officer of the Service or a Welsh family proceedings officer.

(Rule 5(3) provides that Parts 43, 44 (except rules 44.3(2) and (3) and 44.9 to 44.12A), 47 and 48 and rule 45.6 of the CPR apply to costs in proceedings.)

111 Orders

(1) An order takes effect from the date when it is made, or such later date as the court may specify.

(2) In proceedings in Wales a party may request that an order be drawn up in Welsh as well as English.

112 Copies of orders

(1) Within 7 days beginning with the date on which the final order was made in proceedings or such shorter time as the court may direct a court officer will send –

(a) a copy of the order to the applicant;
(b) a copy, which is sealed, authenticated with the stamp of the court or certified as a true copy, of –
    (i) an adoption order;
    (ii) a section 89 order; or
    (iii) an order quashing or revoking an adoption order or allowing an appeal against an adoption order
    to the Registrar General;
(c) a copy of a Convention adoption order to the relevant Central Authority;
(d) a copy of a section 89 order relating to a Convention adoption order or a Convention adoption to the –
    (i) relevant Central Authority;
    (ii) adopters;
    (iii) adoption agency; and
    (iv) local authority;
(e) unless the court directs otherwise, a copy of a contact order or a variation or revocation of a contact order to the –
    (i) person with whom the child is living;
    (ii) adoption agency; and
    (iii) local authority; and
(f) a notice of the making or refusal of –
    (i) the final order; or

(ii) an order quashing or revoking an adoption order or allowing an appeal against an order in proceedings

to every respondent and, with the permission of the court, any other person.

(2) The court officer will also send notice of the making of an adoption order or a section 84 order to –

(a) any court in Great Britain which appears to him to have made any such order as is referred to in section 46(2) (order relating to parental responsibility for, and maintenance of, the child); and
(b) the principal registry of the Family Division, if it appears to him that a parental responsibility agreement has been recorded at the principal registry.

(3) A copy of any final order may be sent to any other person with the permission of the court.

(4) The court officer will send a copy of any order made during the course of the proceedings to all the parties to those proceedings unless the court directs otherwise.

(5) If an order has been drawn up in Welsh as well as English in accordance with rule 111(2) any reference in this rule to sending an order is to be taken as a reference to sending both the Welsh and English orders.

113 Amendment and revocation of orders

(1) Subject to paragraph (2), an application under –

(a) section 55 (revocation of adoptions on legitimation); or
(b) paragraph 4 of Schedule 1 (amendment of adoption order and revocation of direction)

may be made without serving a copy of the application notice.

(2) The court may direct that an application notice be served on such persons as it thinks fit.

(3) Where the court makes an order granting the application, a court officer will send the Registrar General a notice –

(a) specifying the amendments; or
(b) informing him of the revocation,

giving sufficient particulars of the order to enable the Registrar General to identify the case.

(4) The court may at any time correct an accidental slip or omission in an order.

(5) A party may apply for a correction under paragraph (4) without notice to the other parties.

114 Keeping of registers

(1) A magistrates' court officer will keep a register in which there will be entered a minute or memorandum of every adjudication of the court in proceedings to which these Rules apply.

(2) The register may be stored in electronic form on the court computer system and entries in the register will include, where relevant, the following particulars –

(a) the name and address of the applicant;
(b) the name of the child including, in adoption proceedings, the name of the child prior to, and after, adoption;
(c) the age and sex of the child;
(d) the nature of the application; and

(e) the minute of adjudication.

(3) The part of the register relating to adoption proceedings will be kept separately to any other part of the register and will –

(a) not contain particulars of any other proceedings; and
(b) be kept by the court in a place of special security.

PART 12

DISPUTING THE COURT'S JURISDICTION

115 Procedure for disputing the court's jurisdiction

(1) A respondent who wishes to –

(a) dispute the court's jurisdiction to hear the application; or
(b) argue that the court should not exercise its jurisdiction

may apply to the court for an order declaring that it has no such jurisdiction or should not exercise any jurisdiction which it may have.

(2) An application under this rule must –

(a) be made within 14 days beginning with the date on which the notice of the directions hearing is sent to the parties; and
(b) be supported by evidence.

(3) If the respondent does not make an application within the period specified in paragraph (2) he is to be treated as having accepted that the court has jurisdiction to hear the application.

(4) An order containing a declaration that the court has no jurisdiction or will not exercise its jurisdiction may also make further provision including –

(a) setting aside the application form;
(b) discharging any order made before the application was commenced or, where applicable, before the application form was served; and
(c) staying the proceedings.

(5) If a respondent makes an application under this rule, he must file his written evidence in support with the application notice, but he need not before the hearing of the application file any other written evidence.

(6) Paragraph (4) does not apply to proceedings in a magistrates' court.

PART 13

HUMAN RIGHTS

116 Human Rights Act 1998

(1) A party who seeks to rely on any provision of or right arising under the Human Rights Act 1998[1] or seeks a remedy available under that Act must inform the court in his application or otherwise in writing specifying –

---

1   1998 c 42.

(a) the Convention right which it is alleged has been infringed and details of the alleged infringement; and
(b) the relief sought and whether this includes a declaration of incompatibility.

(2) The High Court may not make a declaration of incompatibility unless 21 days' notice, or such other period of notice as the court directs, has been given to the Crown.

(3) Where notice has been given to the Crown, a Minister, or other person permitted by that Act, will be joined as a party on giving notice to the court.

(4) Where a claim is made under section 7(1) of the Human Rights Act 1998 (claim that public authority acted unlawfully) in respect of a judicial act –

(a) that claim must be set out in the application form or the appeal notice; and
(b) notice must be given to the Crown.

(5) Where paragraph (4) applies and the appropriate person (as defined in section 9(5) of the Human Rights Act 1998) has not applied within 21 days, or such other period as the court directs, beginning with the date on which the notice to be joined as a party was served, the court may join the appropriate person as a party.

(6) On any application concerning a committal order, if the court ordering the release of the person concludes that his Convention rights have been infringed by the making of the order to which the application or appeal relates, the judgment or order should so state, but if the court does not do so, that failure will not prevent another court from deciding the matter.

(7) Where by reason of a rule, practice direction or court order the Crown is permitted or required –

(a) to make a witness statement;
(b) to swear an affidavit;
(c) to verify a document by a statement of truth; or
(d) to discharge any other procedural obligation,

that function will be performed by an appropriate officer acting on behalf of the Crown, and the court may if necessary nominate an appropriate officer.

(8) In this rule –

'Convention right' has the same meaning as in the Human Rights Act 1998; and
'declaration of incompatibility' means a declaration of incompatibility under section 4 of the Human Rights Act 1998.

(A practice direction makes provision for the notices mentioned in this rule.)

PART 14

INTERIM INJUNCTIONS

117 Scope of this Part

The rules in this Part do not apply to proceedings in a magistrates' court.

118 Order for interim injunction

(1) The court may grant an interim injunction.

(2) Paragraph (1) does not limit any other power which the court may have to grant an injunction.

(3) The court may grant an interim injunction whether or not there has been an application.

119 Time when an order for an interim injunction may be made

(1) An order for an interim injunction may be made at any time, including –

(a) before proceedings are started; and
(b) after judgment has been given.

(Rule 19 provides that proceedings are started when the court issues an application form.)

(2) However –

(a) paragraph (1) is subject to any rule, practice direction or other enactment which provides otherwise; and
(b) the court may grant an interim injunction before an application has been made only if –
 (i) the matter is urgent; or
 (ii) it is otherwise desirable to do so in the interests of justice.

(3) Where the court grants an interim injunction before an application has been commenced, it may give directions requiring an application to be commenced.

120 How to apply for an interim injunction

(1) The court may grant an interim injunction on an application made without notice if it appears to the court that there are good reasons for not giving notice.

(2) An application for an interim injunction must be supported by evidence, unless the court orders otherwise.

(3) If the applicant makes an application without giving notice, the evidence in support of the application must state the reasons why notice has not been given.

(Rule 12 lists general case-management powers of the court.)

(Part 9 contains general rules about making an application.)

121 Interim injunction to cease if application is stayed

If –

(a) the court has granted an interim injunction; and
(b) the application is stayed other than by agreement between the parties,

the interim injunction shall be set aside unless the court orders that it should continue to have effect even though the application is stayed.

PART 15

ADMISSIONS AND EVIDENCE

122 Making an admission

(1) A party may admit the truth of the whole or any part of another party's case by giving notice in writing.

(2) The court may allow a party to amend or withdraw an admission.

123 Power of court to control evidence

(1) The court may control the evidence by giving directions as to –

    (a) the issues on which it requires evidence;
    (b) the nature of the evidence which it requires to decide those issues; and
    (c) the way in which the evidence is to be placed before the court.

(2) The court may use its power under this rule to exclude evidence that would otherwise be admissible.

(3) The court may limit cross-examination.

124 Evidence of witnesses – general rule

(1) The general rule is that any fact which needs to be proved by the evidence of witnesses is to be proved –

    (a) at final hearing, by their oral evidence; and
    (b) at any other hearing, by their evidence in writing.

(2) This is subject –

    (a) to any provision to the contrary contained in these Rules or elsewhere; or
    (b) to any order of the court.

125 Evidence by video link or other means

The court may allow a witness to give evidence through a video link or by other means.

126 Service of witness statements for use at final hearing

(1) A witness statement is a written statement signed by a person which contains the evidence which that person would be allowed to give orally.

(2) The court will give directions about the service of any witness statement of the oral evidence which a party intends to rely on in relation to any issues of fact to be decided at the final hearing on the other parties.

(3) The court may give directions as to –

    (a) the order in which witness statements are to be served; and
    (b) whether or not the witness statements are to be filed.

127 Use at final hearing of witness statements which have been served

(1) If –

    (a) a party has filed a witness statement which has been served on the other parties; and
    (b) he wishes to rely at the final hearing on the evidence of the witness who made the statement,

he must call the witness to give oral evidence unless the court directs otherwise or he puts the statement in as hearsay evidence.

(2) Where a witness is called to give oral evidence under paragraph (1), his witness statement shall stand as his evidence in chief unless the court directs otherwise.

(3) A witness giving oral evidence at final hearing may with the permission of the court –

(a) amplify his witness statement; and
(b) give evidence in relation to new matters which have arisen since the witness statement was served on the other parties.

(4) The court will give permission under paragraph (3) only if it considers that there is good reason not to confine the evidence of the witness to the contents of his witness statement.

(5) If a party who has filed a witness statement which has been served on the other parties does not –

(a) call the witness to give evidence at final hearing; or
(b) put the witness statement in as hearsay evidence, any other party may put the witness statement in as hearsay evidence.

128 Evidence in proceedings other than at final hearing

(1) Subject to paragraph (2), the general rule is that evidence at hearings other than the final hearing is to be by witness statement unless the court, a practice direction or any other enactment requires otherwise.

(2) At hearings other than the final hearing, a party may, rely on the matters set out in –

(a) his application form; or
(b) his application notice, if it is verified by a statement of truth.

129 Order for cross-examination

(1) Where, at a hearing other than the final hearing, evidence is given in writing, any party may apply to the court for permission to cross-examine the person giving the evidence.

(2) If the court gives permission under paragraph (1) but the person in question does not attend as required by the order, his evidence may not be used unless the court gives permission.

130 Form of witness statement

A witness statement must comply with the requirements set out in the relevant practice direction.

131 Witness summaries

(1) A party who –

(a) is required to file a witness statement for use at final hearing; but
(b) is unable to obtain one, may apply, without notice, for permission to file a witness summary instead.

(2) A witness summary is a summary of –

(a) the evidence, if known, which would otherwise be included in a witness statement; or
(b) if the evidence is not known, the matters about which the party filing the witness summary proposes to question the witness.

(3) Unless the court directs otherwise, a witness summary must include the name and address of the intended witness.

(4) Unless the court directs otherwise, a witness summary must be filed within the period in which a witness statement would have had to be filed.

(5) Where a party files a witness summary, so far as practicable, rules 126 (service of witness statements for use at final hearing), 127(3) (amplifying witness statements), and 130 (form of witness statement) shall apply to the summary.

132 Cross-examination on a witness statement

Where a witness is called to give evidence at final hearing, he may be cross-examined on his witness statement whether or not the statement or any part of it was referred to during the witness's evidence in chief.

133 False statements

(1) Proceedings for contempt of court may be brought against a person if he makes, or causes to be made, a false statement in a document verified by a statement of truth without an honest belief in its truth.

(2) Proceedings under this rule may be brought only –

  (a) by the Attorney General; or
  (b) with the permission of the court.

(3) This rule does not apply to proceedings in a magistrates' court.

134 Affidavit evidence

Evidence must be given by affidavit instead of or in addition to a witness statement if this is required by the court, a provision contained in any other rule, a practice direction or any other enactment.

135 Form of affidavit

An affidavit must comply with the requirements set out in the relevant practice direction.

136 Affidavit made outside the jurisdiction

A person may make an affidavit outside the jurisdiction in accordance with –

  (a) this Part; or
  (b) the law of the place where he makes the affidavit.

137 Notarial acts and instruments

A notarial act or instrument may be received in evidence without further proof as duly authenticated in accordance with the requirements of law unless the contrary is proved.

138 Use of plans, photographs and models as evidence

(1) This rule applies to evidence (such as a plan, photograph or model) which is not –

  (a) contained in a witness statement, affidavit or expert's report; and

(b) to be given orally at the final hearing.

(2) This rule includes documents which may be received in evidence without further proof under section 9 of the Civil Evidence Act 1995.[1]

(3) Unless the court orders otherwise the evidence shall not be receivable at the final hearing unless the party intending to put it in evidence has given notice to the court in accordance with this rule and the court will give directions about service of the notice on any other party.

(4) Where the party intends to use the evidence as evidence of any fact then, subject to paragraph (6), he must give notice not later than the latest date for filing witness statements.

(5) He must give notice at least 21 days before the hearing at which he proposes to put in the evidence, if –

(a) there are not to be witness statements; or

(b) he intends to put in the evidence solely in order to disprove an allegation made in a witness statement.

(6) Where the evidence forms part of expert evidence, he must give notice when the expert's report is filed.

(7) Where the evidence is being produced to the court for any reason other than as part of factual or expert evidence, he must give notice at least 21 days before the hearing at which he proposes to put in the evidence.

(8) Where a party has given notice that he intends to put in the evidence, the court may direct that every other party be given an opportunity to inspect it and to agree to its admission without further proof.

139 Evidence of finding on question of foreign law

(1) This rule sets out the procedure which must be followed by a party who intends to put in evidence a finding on a question of foreign law by virtue of section 4(2) of the Civil Evidence Act 1972.[2]

(2) He must give the court notice of his intention –

(a) if there are to be witness statements, not later than the latest date for filing them; or

(b) otherwise, not less than 21 days before the hearing at which he proposes to put the finding in evidence

and the court will give directions about service of the notice on any other party.

(3) The notice must –

(a) specify the question on which the finding was made; and

(b) enclose a copy of a document where it is reported or recorded.

---

1   1995 c 38. Section 9 of the Civil Evidence Act 1995 provides that documents forming part of the records of a business or public authority, as defined in that section, may be received in evidence without further proof.
2   1972 c 30.

PART 16

WITNESSES, DEPOSITIONS AND EVIDENCE FOR FOREIGN COURTS

Section 1
Witnesses and depositions

140 Scope of this Section

(1) This Section of this Part provides –

(a) for the circumstances in which a person may be required to attend court to give evidence or to produce a document; and

(b) for a party to obtain evidence before a hearing to be used at the hearing.

(2) This Section, except for rule 149(2) to (4), does not apply to proceedings in a magistrates' court.

(Section 97 of the Magistrates' Courts Act 1980[1] sets out the procedure for obtaining a witness summons in proceedings in a magistrates' court.)

141 Witness summonses

(1) A witness summons is a document issued by the court requiring a witness to –

(a) attend court to give evidence; or
(b) produce documents to the court.

(2) A witness summons must be in the relevant form.

(3) There must be a separate witness summons for each witness.

(4) A witness summons may require a witness to produce documents to the court either –

(a) on the date fixed for a hearing; or
(b) on such date as the court may direct.

(5) The only documents that a summons under this rule can require a person to produce before a hearing are documents which that person could be required to produce at the hearing.

142 Issue of a witness summons

(1) A witness summons is issued on the date entered on the summons by the court.

(2) A party must obtain permission from the court where he wishes to –

(a) have a summons issued less than 7 days before the date of the final hearing;
(b) have a summons issued for a witness to attend court to give evidence or to produce documents on any date except the date fixed for the final hearing; or
(c) have a summons issued for a witness to attend court to give evidence or to produce documents at any hearing except the final hearing.

---

1   1980 c 43.

(3) A witness summons must be issued by –

  (a) the court where the case is proceeding; or
  (b) the court where the hearing in question will be held.

(4) The court may set aside or vary a witness summons issued under this rule.

143 Time for serving a witness summons

(1) The general rule is that a witness summons is binding if it is served at least 7 days before the date on which the witness is required to attend before the court or tribunal.

(2) The court may direct that a witness summons shall be binding although it will be served less than 7 days before the date on which the witness is required to attend before the court or tribunal.

(3) A witness summons which is –

  (a) served in accordance with this rule; and
  (b) requires the witness to attend court to give evidence,

is binding until the conclusion of the hearing at which the attendance of the witness is required.

144 Who is to serve a witness summons

(1) Unless the court directs otherwise, a witness summons is to be served by the court.

(2) Where the court is to serve the witness summons, the party on whose behalf it is issued must deposit, in the court office, the money to be paid or offered to the witness under rule 145.

145 Right of witness to travelling expenses and compensation for loss of time

At the time of service of a witness summons the witness must be offered or paid –

  (a) a sum reasonably sufficient to cover his expenses in travelling to and from the court; and
  (b) such sum by way of compensation for loss of time as may be specified in the relevant practice direction.

146 Evidence by deposition

(1) A party may apply for an order for a person to be examined before the hearing takes place.

(2) A person from whom evidence is to be obtained following an order under this rule is referred to as a 'deponent' and the evidence is referred to as a 'deposition'.

(3) An order under this rule shall be for a deponent to be examined on oath before –

  (a) a judge or district judge, including a district judge of the principal registry of the Family Division;
  (b) an examiner of the court; or
  (c) such other person as the court appoints.

(4) The order may require the production of any document which the court considers is necessary for the purposes of the examination.

(5) The order must state the date, time and place of the examination.

(6) At the time of service of the order the deponent must be offered or paid –

(a) a sum reasonably sufficient to cover his expenses in travelling to and from the place of examination; and

(b) such sum by way of compensation for loss of time as may be specified in the relevant practice direction.

(7) Where the court makes an order for a deposition to be taken, it may also order the party who obtained the order to file a witness statement or witness summary in relation to the evidence to be given by the person to be examined.

(Part 15 contains the general rules about witness statements and witness summaries.)

147 Conduct of examination

(1) Subject to any directions contained in the order for examination, the examination must be conducted in the same way as if the witness were giving evidence at a final hearing.

(2) If all the parties are present, the examiner may conduct the examination of a person not named in the order for examination if all the parties and the person to be examined consent.

(3) The examiner will conduct the examination in private unless he considers it is not appropriate to do so.

(4) The examiner must ensure that the evidence given by the witness is recorded in full.

(5) The examiner must send a copy of the deposition –

(a) to the person who obtained the order for the examination of the witness; and

(b) to the court where the case is proceeding.

(6) The court will make directions as to the service of a copy of the deposition on the other parties.

148 Enforcing attendance of witness

(1) If a person served with an order to attend before an examiner –

(a) fails to attend; or

(b) refuses to be sworn for the purpose of the examination or to answer any lawful question or produce any document at the examination,

a certificate of his failure or refusal, signed by the examiner, must be filed by the party requiring the deposition.

(2) On the certificate being filed, the party requiring the deposition may apply to the court for an order requiring that person to attend or to be sworn or to answer any question or produce any document, as the case may be.

(3) An application for an order under this rule may be made without notice.

(4) The court may order the person against whom an order is made under this rule to pay any costs resulting from his failure or refusal.

149 Use of deposition at a hearing

(1) A deposition ordered under rule 146 may be given in evidence at a hearing unless the court orders otherwise.

(2) A party intending to put in evidence a deposition at a hearing must file notice of his intention to do so on the court and the court will make directions about serving the notice on every other party.

(3) He must file the notice at least 21 days before the day fixed for the hearing.

(4) The court may require a deponent to attend the hearing and give evidence orally.

150 Where a person to be examined is out of the jurisdiction – letter of request

(1) This rule applies where a party wishes to take a deposition from a person who is –

    (a) out of the jurisdiction; and
    (b) not in a Regulation State within the meaning of Section 2 of this Part.

(2) The High Court may order the issue of a letter of request to the judicial authorities of the country in which the proposed deponent is.

(3) A letter of request is a request to a judicial authority to take the evidence of that person, or arrange for it to be taken.

(4) The High Court may make an order under this rule in relation to county court proceedings.

(5) If the government of a country allows a person appointed by the High Court to examine a person in that country, the High Court may make an order appointing a special examiner for that purpose.

(6) A person may be examined under this rule on oath or affirmation or in accordance with any procedure permitted in the country in which the examination is to take place.

(7) If the High Court makes an order for the issue of a letter of request, the party who sought the order must file –

    (a) the following documents and, subject to paragraph (8), a translation of them –
        (i) a draft letter of request;
        (ii) a statement of the issues relevant to the proceedings; and
        (iii) a list of questions or the subject matter of questions to be put to the person to be examined; and
    (b) an undertaking to be responsible for the Secretary of State's expenses.

(8) There is no need to file a translation if –

    (a) English is one of the official languages of the country where the examination is to take place; or
    (b) a practice direction has specified that country as a country where no translation is necessary.

151 Fees and expenses of examiner of the court

(1) An examiner of the court may charge a fee for the examination.

(2) He need not send the deposition to the court unless the fee is paid.

(3) The examiner's fees and expenses must be paid by the party who obtained the order for examination.

(4) If the fees and expenses due to an examiner are not paid within a reasonable time, he may report that fact to the court.

(5) The court may order the party who obtained the order for examination to deposit in the court office a specified sum in respect of the examiner's fees and, where it does so, the examiner will not be asked to act until the sum has been deposited.

(6) An order under this rule does not affect any decision as to the party who is ultimately to bear the costs of the examination.

Section 2
Taking of evidence – Member States of the European Union

152 Interpretation

In this Section –

'designated court' has the meaning given in the relevant practice direction;
'Regulation State' has the same meaning as 'Member State' in the Taking of Evidence Regulation, that is all Member States except Denmark;
'the Taking of Evidence Regulation' means Council Regulation (EC) No. 1206/2001 of 28 May 2001 on co-operation between the courts of the Member States in the taking of evidence in civil and commercial matters.

153 Where a person to be examined is in another Regulation State

(1) This rule applies where a party wishes to take a deposition from a person who is in another Regulation State –

(a) outside the jurisdiction; and
(b) in a Regulation State.

(2) The court may order the issue of a request to a designated court ('the requested court') in the Regulation State in which the proposed deponent is.

(3) If the court makes an order for the issue of a request, the party who sought the order must file –

(a) a draft Form A as set out in the annex to the Taking of Evidence Regulation (request for the taking of evidence);
(b) subject to paragraph (4), a translation of the form;
(c) an undertaking to be responsible for costs sought by the requested court in relation to –
  (i) fees paid to experts and interpreters; and
  (ii) where requested by that party, the use of special procedures or communications technology; and
(d) an undertaking to be responsible for the court's expenses.

(4) There is no need to file a translation if –

(a) English is one of the official languages of the Regulation State where the examination is to take place; or
(b) the Regulation State has indicated, in accordance with the Taking of Evidence Regulation, that English is a language which it will accept.

(5) Where article 17 of the Taking of Evidence Regulation (direct taking of evidence by the requested court) allows evidence to be taken directly in another Regulation State, the court may make an order for the submission of a request in accordance with that article.

(6) If the court makes an order for the submission of a request under paragraph (5), the party who sought the order must file –

(a) a draft Form I as set out in the annex to the Taking of Evidence Regulation (request for direct taking of evidence);
(b) subject to paragraph (4), a translation of the form; and
(c) an undertaking to be responsible for the court's expenses.

PART 17

EXPERTS

154 Duty to restrict expert evidence

Expert evidence shall be restricted to that which is reasonably required to resolve the proceedings.

155 Interpretation

A reference to an 'expert' in this Part –

(a) is a reference to an expert who has been instructed to give or prepare evidence for the purpose of court proceedings; and
(b) does not include –
   (i) a person who is within a prescribed description for the purposes of section 94(1) of the Act (persons who may prepare a report for any person about the suitability of a child for adoption or of a person to adopt a child or about the adoption, or placement for adoption, of a child); or
   (ii) an officer of the Service or a Welsh family proceedings officer when acting in that capacity.

(Regulation 3 of the Restriction on the Preparation of Adoption Reports Regulations 2005 (SI 2005/1711) sets out which persons are within a prescribed description for the purposes of section 94(1) of the Act.)

156 Experts – overriding duty to the court

(1) It is the duty of an expert to help the court on the matters within his expertise.

(2) This duty overrides any obligation to the person from whom he has received instructions or by whom he is paid.

157 Court's power to restrict expert evidence

(1) No party may call an expert or put in evidence an expert's report without the court's permission.

(2) When a party applies for permission under this rule he must identify –

(a) the field in which he wishes to rely on expert evidence; and
(b) where practicable the expert in that field on whose evidence he wishes to rely.

(3) If permission is granted under this rule it shall be in relation only to the expert named or the field identified under paragraph (2).

(4) The court may limit the amount of the expert's fees and expenses that the party who wishes to rely on the expert may recover from any other party.

158 General requirement for expert evidence to be given in a written report

Expert evidence is to be given in a written report unless the court directs otherwise.

159 Written questions to experts

(1) A party may put to –

(a) an expert instructed by another party; or
(b) a single joint expert appointed under rule 160,

written questions about his report.

(2) Written questions under paragraph (1) –

(a) may be put once only;
(b) must be put within 5 days beginning with the date on which the expert's report was served; and
(c) must be for the purpose only of clarification of the report,

unless in any case –
  (i) the court gives permission;
  (ii) the other party agrees; or
  (iii) any practice direction provides otherwise.

(3) An expert's answers to questions put in accordance with paragraph (1) shall be treated as part of the expert's report.

(4) Where –

(a) a party has put a written question to an expert instructed by another party in accordance with this rule; and
(b) the expert does not answer that question,

the court may make one or both of the following orders in relation to the party who instructed the expert –
  (i) that the party may not rely on the evidence of that expert; or
  (ii) that the party may not recover the fees and expenses of that expert from any other party.

160 Court's power to direct that evidence is to be given by a single joint expert

(1) Where two or more parties wish to submit expert evidence on a particular issue, the court may direct that the evidence on that issue is to given by one expert only.

(2) The parties wishing to submit the expert evidence are called 'the instructing parties'.

(3) Where the instructing parties cannot agree who should be the expert, the court may –

(a) select the expert from a list prepared or identified by the instructing parties; or
(b) direct that the expert be selected in such other manner as the court may direct.

161 Instructions to a single joint expert

(1) Where the court gives a direction under rule 160 for a single joint expert to be used, each instructing party may give instructions to the expert.

(2) When an instructing party gives instructions to the expert he must, at the same time, send a copy of the instructions to the other instructing parties.

(3) The court may give directions about –

(a) the payment of the expert's fees and expenses; and
(b) any inspection, examination or experiments which the expert wishes to carry out.

(4) The court may, before an expert is instructed, limit the amount that can be paid by way of fees and expenses to the expert.

(5) Unless the court otherwise directs, the instructing parties are jointly and severally liable for the payment of the expert's fees and expenses.

162 Power of court to direct a party to provide information

(1) Where a party has access to information which is not reasonably available to the other party, the court may direct the party who has access to the information to prepare and file a document recording the information.

(2) A court officer will send a copy of that document to the other party.

163 Contents of report

(1) An expert's report must comply with the requirements set out in the relevant practice direction.

(2) At the end of an expert's report there must be a statement that –

(a) the expert understands his duty to the court; and
(b) he has complied with that duty.

(3) The expert's report must state the substance of all material instructions, whether written or oral, on the basis of which the report was written.

(4) The instructions referred to in paragraph (3) shall not be privileged against disclosure.

164 Use by one party of expert's report disclosed by another

Where a party has disclosed an expert's report, any party may use that expert's report as evidence at the final hearing.

165 Discussions between experts

(1) The court may, at any stage, direct a discussion between experts for the purpose of requiring the experts to –

(a) identify and discuss the expert issues in the proceedings; and
(b) where possible, reach an agreed opinion on those issues.

(2) The court may specify the issues which the experts must discuss.

(3) The court may direct that following a discussion between the experts they must prepare a statement for the court showing –

(a) those issues on which they agree; and
(b) those issues on which they disagree and a summary of their reasons for disagreeing.

166 Consequence of failure to disclose expert's report

A party who fails to disclose an expert's report may not use the report at the final hearing or call the expert to give evidence orally unless the court gives permission.

167 Expert's right to ask court for directions

(1) An expert may file a written request for directions to assist him in carrying out his function as an expert.

(2) An expert must, unless the court directs otherwise, provide a copy of any proposed request for directions under paragraph (1) –

(a) to the party instructing him, at least 7 days before he files the request; and
(b) to all other parties, at least 4 days before he files it.

(3) The court, when it gives directions, may also direct that a party be served with a copy of the directions.

PART 18
CHANGE OF SOLICITOR

168 Change of solicitor – duty to give notice

(1) This rule applies where –

(a) a party for whom a solicitor is acting wants to change his solicitor;
(b) a party, after having conducted the application in person, appoints a solicitor to act on his behalf (except where the solicitor is appointed only to act as an advocate for a hearing); or
(c) a party, after having conducted the application by a solicitor, intends to act in person.

(2) Where this rule applies, the party or his solicitor (where one is acting) must –

(a) file notice of the change; and
(b) where paragraph (1)(a) or (c) applies, serve notice of the change on the former solicitor.

(3) The court will give directions about serving notice of the change on every other party.

(4) The notice filed at court must state that notice has been served as required by paragraph (2)(b).

(5) Subject to paragraph (6), where a party has changed his solicitor or intends to act in person, the former solicitor will be considered to be the party's solicitor unless and until –

(a) notice is filed and served in accordance with paragraphs (2) and (3); or
(b) the court makes an order under rule 169 and the order is served as required by paragraph (3) of that rule.

(6) Where the certificate of a LSC funded client or an assisted person is revoked or discharged –

(a) the solicitor who acted for that person will cease to be the solicitor acting in the case as soon as his retainer is determined under regulation 4 of the Community Legal Service (Costs) Regulations 2000;[1] and

(b) if that person wishes to continue where he appoints a solicitor to act on his behalf, paragraph (2) will apply as if he had previously conducted the application in person;

(7) In this rule –

'assisted person' means an assisted person within the statutory provisions relating to legal aid;

'certificate' means a certificate issued under the Funding Code (approved under section 9 of the Access to Justice Act 1999[2]);

'LSC funded client' means an individual who receives services funded by the Legal Services Commission as part of the Community Legal Service within the meaning of Part I of the Access to Justice Act 1999.

169 Order that a solicitor has ceased to act

(1) A solicitor may apply for an order declaring that he has ceased to be the solicitor acting for a party.

(2) Where an application is made under this rule –

(a) notice of the application must be given to the party for whom the solicitor is acting, unless the court directs otherwise; and

(b) the application must be supported by evidence.

(3) Where the court makes an order that a solicitor has ceased to act –

(a) the court will give directions about serving the order on every party to the proceedings; and

(b) if it is served by a party or the solicitor, the party or the solicitor (as the case may be) must file a certificate of service.

170 Removal of solicitor who has ceased to act on application of another party

(1) Where –

(a) a solicitor who has acted for a party –
  (i) has died;
  (ii) has become bankrupt;
  (iii) has ceased to practice; or
  (iv) cannot be found; and
(b) the party has not given notice of a change of solicitor or notice of intention to act in person as required by rule 168(2),

any other party may apply for an order declaring that the solicitor has ceased to be the solicitor acting for the other party in the case.

(2) Where an application is made under this rule, notice of the application must be given to the party to whose solicitor the application relates unless the court directs otherwise.

---

1   SI 2000/441.
2   1999 c 22.

(3) Where the court makes an order made under this rule –

   (a) the court will give directions about serving the order on every party to the proceedings; and
   (b) where it is served by a party, that party must file a certificate of service.

PART 19
APPEALS

171 Scope and interpretation

(1) The rules in this Part apply to appeals to –

   (a) the High Court; and
   (b) a county court.

(2) This Part does not apply to an appeal in detailed assessment proceedings against a decision of an authorised court officer.

(Rules 47.20 to 47.23 of the CPR deal with appeals against a decision of an authorised court officer in detailed assessment proceedings.)

(3) In this Part –

   'appeal' includes an appeal by way of case stated;
   'appeal court' means the court to which an appeal is made;
   'appeal notice' means an appellant's or respondent's notice;
   'appellant' means a person who brings or seeks to bring an appeal;
   'lower court' means the court from whose decision an appeal is brought;
   'respondent' means –

   (a) a person other than the appellant who was a party to the proceedings in the lower court and who is affected by the appeal; and
   (b) a person who is permitted by the appeal court to be a party to the appeal.

(4) This Part is subject to any rule, enactment or practice direction which sets out special provisions with regard to any particular category of appeal.

172 Parties to comply with the practice direction

All parties to an appeal must comply with the relevant practice direction.

173 Permission

(1) An appellant or respondent requires permission to appeal –

   (a) against a decision in assessment proceedings relating to costs in proceedings where the decision appealed against was made by a district judge or a costs judge; or
   (b) as provided by the relevant practice direction.

(2) An application for permission to appeal may be made –

   (a) to the lower court, if that court is a county court or the High Court, at the hearing at which the decision to be appealed was made; or
   (b) to the appeal court in an appeal notice.

(Rule 174 sets out the time limits for filing an appellant's notice at the appeal court. Rule 175 sets out the time limits for filing a respondent's notice at the appeal court. Any application for permission to appeal to the appeal court must be made in the appeal notice (see rules 174(1) and 175(3).)

(3) Where the lower court refuses an application for permission to appeal, a further application for permission to appeal may be made to the appeal court.

(4) Where the appeal court, without a hearing, refuses permission to appeal, the person seeking permission may request the decision to be reconsidered at a hearing.

(5) A request under paragraph (4) must be filed within 7 days beginning with the date on which the notice that permission has been refused was served.

(6) Permission to appeal will only be given where –

   (a) the court considers that the appeal would have a real prospect of success; or
   (b) there is some other compelling reason why the appeal should be heard.

(7) An order giving permission may –

   (a) limit the issues to be heard; and
   (b) be made subject to conditions.

(8) In this rule 'costs judge' means a taxing master of the Supreme Court.

174 Appellant's notice

(1) Where the appellant seeks permission from the appeal court it must be requested in the appellant's notice.

(2) The appellant must file the appellant's notice at the appeal court within –

   (a) such period as may be directed by the lower court, if that court is a county court or the High Court; or
   (b) (i) where the lower court makes no such direction; or
       (ii) the lower court is a magistrates' court,
       14 days beginning with the date on which the decision of the lower court that the appellant wishes to appeal was made.

(3) Unless the appeal court directs otherwise, an appeal notice must be served on the persons referred to in paragraph (4) –

   (a) as soon as practicable; and
   (b) in any event not later than 7 days,

after it is filed.

(4) The persons referred to in paragraph (3) are –

   (a) each respondent;
   (b) any children's guardian, reporting officer or children and family reporter; and
   (c) where the appeal is from a magistrates' court, the court officer.

(5) Unless the appeal court directs otherwise, a court officer will serve the appeal notice.

175 Respondent's notice

(1) A respondent may file a respondent's notice.

(2) A respondent who –

    (a) is seeking permission to appeal from the appeal court; or

    (b) wishes to ask the appeal court to uphold the order of the lower court for reasons different from or additional to those given by the lower court,

must file a respondent's notice.

(3) Where the respondent seeks permission from the appeal court it must be requested in the respondent's notice.

(4) A respondent's notice must be filed within –

    (a) such period as may be directed by the lower court, if that court is a county court or the High Court; or

    (b) (i) where the lower court makes no such direction; or
        (ii) the lower court is a magistrates' court,
    14 days beginning with the date referred to in paragraph (5).

(5) The date referred to in paragraph (4) is –

    (a) the date on which the respondent is served with the appellant's notice where –
        (i) permission to appeal was given by the lower court; or
        (ii) permission to appeal is not required;

    (b) the date on which the respondent is served with notification that the appeal court has given the appellant permission to appeal; or

    (c) the date on which the respondent is served with notification that the application for permission to appeal and the appeal itself are to be heard together.

(6) Unless the appeal court directs otherwise, a respondent's notice must be served on the appellant and any other respondent –

    (a) as soon as practicable; and

    (b) in any event not later than 7 days,

after it is filed.

(7) Unless the appeal court directs otherwise, a court officer will serve a respondent's notice.

176 Variation of time

(1) An application to vary the time limit for filing an appeal notice must be made to the appeal court.

(2) The parties may not agree to extend any date or time limit set by –

    (a) these Rules;

    (b) the relevant practice direction; or

    (c) an order of the appeal court or the lower court.

(Rule 12(2)(a) provides that the court may extend or shorten the time for compliance with any rule, practice direction or court order (even if an application for extension is made after the time for compliance has expired).)

(Rule 12(2)(b) provides that the court may adjourn or bring forward a hearing.)

177 Stay

Unless the appeal court or the lower court, other than a magistrates' court, orders otherwise an appeal shall not operate as a stay of any order or decision of the lower court.

178 Amendment of appeal notice

An appeal notice may not be amended without the permission of the appeal court.

179 Striking out appeal notices and setting aside or imposing conditions on permission to appeal

(1) The appeal court may –

  (a) strike out the whole or part of an appeal notice;
  (b) set aside permission to appeal in whole or in part; or
  (c) impose or vary conditions upon which an appeal may be brought.

(2) The court will only exercise its powers under paragraph (1) where there is a compelling reason for doing so.

(3) Where a party was present at the hearing at which permission was given he may not subsequently apply for an order that the court exercise its powers under paragraphs (1)(b) or (c).

180 Appeal court's powers

(1) In relation to an appeal the appeal court has all the powers of the lower court.

(Rule 171(4) provides that this Part is subject to any enactment that sets out special provisions with regard to any particular category of appeal.)

(2) The appeal court has power to –

  (a) affirm, set aside or vary any order or judgment made or given by the lower court;
  (b) refer any application or issue for determination by the lower court;
  (c) order a new hearing;
  (d) make orders for the payment of interest; and
  (e) make a costs order.

(3) The appeal court may exercise its powers in relation to the whole or part of an order of the lower court.

(Rule 12 contains general rules about the court's case management powers.)

(4) If the appeal court –

  (a) refuses an application for permission to appeal;
  (b) strikes out an appellant's notice; or
  (c) dismisses an appeal,

and it considers that the application, the appellant's notice or the appeal is totally without merit, the provisions of paragraph (5) must be complied with.

(5) Where paragraph (4) applies –

  (a) the court's order must record the fact that it considers the application, the appellant's notice or the appeal to be totally without merit; and

(b) the court must at the same time consider whether it is appropriate to make a civil restraint order.

181 Hearing of appeals

(1) Every appeal will be limited to a review of the decision of the lower court unless –

(a) a practice direction makes different provision for a particular category of appeal; or
(b) the court considers that in the circumstances of an individual appeal it would be in the interests of justice to hold a re-hearing.

(2) Unless it orders otherwise, the appeal court will not receive –

(a) oral evidence; or
(b) evidence which was not before the lower court.

(3) The appeal court will allow an appeal where the decision of the lower court was –

(a) wrong; or
(b) unjust because of a serious procedural or other irregularity in the proceedings in the lower court.

(4) The appeal court may draw any inference of fact which it considers justified on the evidence.

(5) At the hearing of the appeal a party may not rely on a matter not contained in his appeal notice unless the appeal court gives permission.

182 Assignment of appeals to the Court of Appeal

(1) Where the court from or to which an appeal is made or from which permission to appeal is sought ('the relevant court') considers that –

(a) an appeal which is to be heard by a county court or the High Court would raise an important point of principle or practice; or
(b) there is some other compelling reason for the Court of Appeal to hear it,

the relevant court may order the appeal to be transferred to the Court of Appeal.

(2) This rule does not apply to proceedings in a magistrates' court.

183 Reopening of final appeals

(1) The High Court will not reopen a final determination of any appeal unless –

(a) it is necessary to do so in order to avoid real injustice;
(b) the circumstances are exceptional and make it appropriate to reopen the appeal; and
(c) there is no alternative effective remedy.

(2) In paragraphs (1), (3), (4) and (6), 'appeal' includes an application for permission to appeal.

(3) This rule does not apply to appeals to a county court.

(4) Permission is needed to make an application under this rule to reopen a final determination of an appeal.

(5) There is no right to an oral hearing of an application for permission unless, exceptionally, the judge so directs.

(6) The judge will not grant permission without directing the application to be served on the other party to the original appeal and giving him an opportunity to make representations.

(7) There is no right of appeal or review from the decision of the judge on the application for permission, which is final.

(8) The procedure for making an application for permission is set out in the practice direction.

EXPLANATORY NOTE

(This note is not part of these Rules)

These Rules govern the practice and procedure to be followed in proceedings under the Adoption and Children Act 2002 (c.38) in the High Court, county courts and magistrates' courts. They are the first Family Procedure Rules to be made by the Family Procedure Rule Committee.

Part 1 sets out the overriding objective of the Rules. Part 2 contains provisions for interpreting and applying the Rules. Part 3 contains the court's general case management powers. Part 4 sets out how to start proceedings including provisions on how to apply for a serial number or to keep personal details confidential.

Part 5 contains rules about the general procedure to be followed in relation to proceedings for –

(a) the making of an adoption order;

(b) the making, varying or revoking of a placement order;

(c) the making, varying or revoking of a contact order under sections 26 and 27 of the 2002 Act;

(d) an order giving permission to change a child's surname or remove a child from the United Kingdom under section 28(2) and (3) of that Act; or

(e) an order under section 84 or 89, or a direction under section 88, of that Act.

Part 6 contains rules about the service of documents including those required to be served out of the jurisdiction. Part 7 contains rules about the appointment of a litigation friend and officers of the Service and their powers and duties. Part 8 contains rules about documents particularly in relation to the custody, inspection and disclosure of documents and information obtained during the course of proceedings.

Part 9 contains rules about the procedure to be followed if an application is made –

(a) in the course of existing proceedings;

(b) to commence proceedings other than those to which Part 5 applies; or

(c) in connection with proceedings which have concluded.

Part 10 contains rules about the procedure to be followed in proceedings –

(a) under section 60(3) (order to prevent disclosure of information to an adopted person);

(b) under section 79(4) (order for Registrar General to given information referred to in section 79(3);

(c) in accordance with rule 108 (directions from the High Court regarding fathers without parental responsibility); and

(d) where –

   (i) Part 9 of the Rules does not apply;

(ii) there is no prescribed form to use in relation to the application; and
(iii) there is unlikely to be a substantial dispute of fact.

Part 11 contains miscellaneous provisions such as applications for recovery orders and seeking directions from the High Court regarding fathers without parental responsibility. Part 12 sets out the procedure for disputing the court's jurisdiction. Part 13 contains provisions about human rights. Part 14 makes provision for applications for interim injunctions. Parts 15 and 16 contain rules about evidence. Part 17 deals with experts, Part 18 with change of solicitor and Part 19 with appeals.

These Rules come into force on 30 December 2005.

Appendix D

PRACTICE DIRECTIONS

PRACTICE DIRECTION – HEARINGS BY A SINGLE JUSTICE OF THE PEACE

THIS PRACTICE DIRECTION SUPPLEMENTS PART 2, RULE 7(1)(C)(II)(BB) OF THE FAMILY PROCEDURE (ADOPTION) RULES 2005

Functions of the court that may be dealt with by a single justice of the peace

1.1 Rule 7(1)(c) provides that a single justice of the peace who is a member of the family panel may deal with an application under section 41(2) (recovery orders) made without notice.

1.2 A single justice of the peace who is a member of the family panel may also perform the functions of the court listed in –

(a) column 2 of Table 1 in accordance with the rules listed in column 1; and
(b) column 2 of Table 2 in accordance with the paragraph of the practice direction listed in column 1.

Table 1

Rule	Nature of function
12(2)(a) to (c), (e), (g), (i), (j), (m) and (n)	Case management powers, in accordance with rule 13 (except paragraphs (5) and (7), if exercised of own initiative).
14(b)	Step to be taken by court instead of court officer.
20(3)	Direction that serial number be removed.
21(1) and (2)	Direction to reveal personal details.
23(2)	Direction that child be made a respondent.
23(3)	Direction that any other person or body be made a respondent or cease to be a respondent.
23(4)	Consequential directions following the addition or removal of a party.
24(1)(a)(ii)	Set date for first directions hearing.
24(1)(a)(vi)	Set date for final hearing.
24(2)(a)(i)	Ask that relevant forms of consent to an adoption order or section 84 order be filed.

Rule	Nature of function
24(2)(a)(ii)	Ask that the local authority prepare a report on the suitability of the prospective adopters.
24(2)(b)(i)	Ask that the adoption agency file relevant forms of consent.
24(2)(b)(ii) and (iii)	Ask that any statements made under section 20(4)(a) or (b) be filed.
24(2)(b)(iv)	Ask that the adoption agency prepare a report on the suitability of the prospective adopters.
24(3)(a)	Direction that local authority prepare report giving their reasons for placing the child for adoption.
24(3)(b)	Ask that relevant forms of consent to the child being placed for adoption be filed.
24(4)	Giving directions instead of setting date for first directions hearing.
25	Direction that first directions hearing may be more than 4 weeks after the date on which the application is issued.
26(1) and (4)	Giving directions at first directions hearing.
26(5)	Giving directions at any stage of the proceedings.
26(6)(a)	Setting a date for a further directions hearing or other hearing.
26(7)	Monitoring compliance with timetable and directions given.
27(4)(b)(ii)	Direction that an application under rule 55(3) (litigation friend) be made.
29(4)	Request to adoption agency or local authority for further report or for assistance.
32(4)	Direction that person must attend final hearing.
32(7)	Direction that child or applicant need not attend final hearing.
34(b)	Direction that the provisions in Part 6 do not apply to the service of a document.
35(3)	Direction that service be effected by an alternative method.
36(1)(b)	Direction that document be served by someone other than court officer.
36(2)	Decision as to which method of service to use.
37(4)	Direction that document be served on child, patient or some other person other than person specified in table.
37(5)	Direction that, although document served on someone other than the person specified in table, it is to be treated as properly served.
39	Direction that service of a document is dispensed with.

Rule	Nature of function
55(3)	Direction that an application under rule 55(3) (litigation friend) be made by a party.
55(5)	Direction that person appointed as litigation friend will not be treated as a party for the purpose of any provision in the Rules regarding service.
57(2)	Direction that court officer need not send application to patient.
59	Appointment of children's guardian.
60(1)(a)	Recording reasons for refusal to appoint children's guardian.
61(1) and (2)	Terminating appointment of children's guardian and recording the reasons for doing so.
63(1)	Direction regarding investigations conducted by children's guardian.
63(3)(b)	Consideration that child of sufficient understanding to instruct a solicitor direct.
64(2)(a) and (b)	Directions about children's guardian performing duties and role in proceedings where child instructing solicitor direct.
64(2)(c)	Giving permission for children's guardian to have legal representation.
65(1)	Direction that children's guardian or solicitor need not attend directions hearing.
65(3)	Direction that advice from children's guardian to be given to the court in a particular way.
65(4)(a)	Direction that children's guardian need not file written report on the interests of the child.
66(2)(b)(ii)	Direction that children's guardian need not bring documents/records to attention of parties.
68(5)	Terminating appointment of solicitor and recording the reasons for doing so.
68(6)	Recording the appointment of or refusal to appoint a solicitor for the child.
69	Appointment of reporting officer.
72(4)	Direction that reporting officer need not attend directions hearing.
73(1)	Request to children and family reporter to prepare report on the welfare of the child.
74(1)	Direction regarding investigations conducted by children and family reporter.
74(3)(a)	Direction that children and family reporter need not attend directions hearing.

Rule	Nature of function
77	Direction that confidential report be disclosed to party.
78(1)(a)	Giving permission to communicate information relating to proceedings held in private.
78(1)(b)	Direction that information relating to proceedings held in private is not to be disclosed in accordance with the relevant practice direction.
83	Direction that document or order be open to inspection or given to any person.
84(2)	Removing protected information from document before disclosing to adopted adult.
85(1)(a)	Direction that translation of document may be provided by party other than the applicant.
86(4)(c)	Direction that other person be a respondent to Part 9 application.
87(2)(b)	Dispensing with requirement to file application notice.
88(2)(c)	Giving permission to make Part 9 application without serving copy of application notice.
92(c)	Direction that Part 9 application may be dealt with without hearing.
93(2)	Direction that copy application and evidence need not be served with order on parties.
97(3)	Direction that Part 10 application should continue as if the applicant had not used the Part 10 procedure and other directions as appropriate.
99(4)	Directions about future management of Part 10 application once permission given.
103(1)(b)	Giving permission to file and serve additional evidence before the hearing.
103(3)	Direction that witness who has given written evidence attend for cross-examination.
104(2)	Directions about future management of Part 10 application once acknowledgement of service received.
106	Giving permission to withdraw application.
107(1)(b)	Giving permission to make application for recovery order without notice and giving directions re filing of application.
107(2)	Direction that application for a recovery order be made on notice.
112(1)	Direction that final order be sent in less than 7 days.
112(1)(e)	Direction that contact order, or a variation or revocation of a contact order, is not sent.

Rule	Nature of function
112(1)(f)	Giving permission to send notice of final order to other person.
112(3)	Giving permission to send final order to other person.
112(4)	Direction that order made in the course of proceedings is not sent.
113(2)	Direction that application under rule 113 is served on particular person.
126(2)	Direction about the service of witness statements on other parties.
126(3)	Directions as to the order in which statements are to be served and whether or not witness statements are to be filed.
131(3)	Direction that witness summary does not need to contain name and address of witness.
131(4)	Direction that witness summary need not be filed within same period that witness statement is filed.
138(3)	Direction about the service of evidence on other parties.
138(8)	Direction that other parties be given opportunity to inspect evidence intended to be filed under rule 138.
139(2)	Direction about the service of notice of intention to file evidence on a question of foreign law on other parties.
149(2)	Direction about the service of notice to use deposition on other parties.
157(1)	Giving permission to call expert or put in evidence an expert's report.
158	Direction that expert's evidence need not be given in written report.
159(2)(c)(i)	Giving permission with regard to the written questions that can be put to expert.
160(1)	Direction that evidence on an issue be given by one joint expert.
160(3)	Selection of joint expert or direction that expert be selected in particular manner.
161(3)	Directions about expert's fees and inspection, examination or experiments expert wishes to carry out.
162(1)	Direction that party prepare, file and serve document recording information which other party has no access to.
165	Direction about discussions between experts.
167(2)	Direction that expert requesting directions from court need not provide request for directions to party instructing him and other parties.
167(3)	Direction about service, on parties, of directions given to expert.
168(3)	Direction about service of notice of change of solicitor on other parties.
169(2)(a)	Direction that notice of an application under rule 169 need not be given to party for whom the solicitor is acting.

Rule	Nature of function
169(3)(a)	Direction about service of order made under rule 169 on other parties.
170(2)	Direction that notice of an application under rule 170 need not be given to the party to whose solicitor the application relates.
170(3)(a)	Direction about service of order made under rule 170 on other parties.

Table 2

Paragraph	Nature of function
Practice Direction supplementing Part 2, rule 9(4)	
2.3	Direction that document need not be deposited in the office of court which ordered it to be lodged.
2.4	Giving permission for document to be taken out of the court office in which it was filed or lodged.
Practice Direction supplementing Part 5, rule 24(1)(b)(ii)	
1	Direction that application form be sent to any other person.
Practice Direction supplementing Part 8, rule 78	
1.2	Direction that information may not be communicated in accordance with the practice direction.
Practice Direction supplementing Part 9	
2.5, 2.6 and 8.2	Direction about filing of evidence.
2.9	Direction given when reviewing conduct of case.
4	Direction about service of application.
5.1	Direction that application or part of application be dealt with by telephone hearing and any directions about that hearing.
7	Recording brief details of proceedings before the court.
8.4	Direction about service of respondent's evidence.

Paragraph	Nature of function
8.5	Direction about service of any evidence applicant files in reply to respondent's evidence.
8.6	Direction about filing of exhibits.
Practice Direction supplementing Part 10	
4.1	Directions immediately Part 10 application issued.
4.2	Directions for disposal of Part 10 application.
4.4	Convening a directions hearing.
5.5	Giving extension of time to serve and file evidence under rule 102.
Practice Direction supplementing Part 15	
15.4	Directions about exhibits where they are unable to be served on account of their bulk.
25.1	Directions about bundles for hearings.
Annex 3	Direction that part of proceedings be dealt with by means of video conferencing and related directions.
Practice Direction supplementing Part 17	
4	Giving permission to cross-examine an expert on the contents of his instructions.

1.3 Where a directions hearing is being conducted by a single justice of the peace and that justice considers, for whatever reason, that it is inappropriate to give a direction on a particular matter, he shall refer the matter to the court which may give any appropriate direction.

PRACTICE DIRECTION – COURT DOCUMENTS

THIS PRACTICE DIRECTION SUPPLEMENTS PART 2, RULE 9(4) OF THE FAMILY PROCEDURE (ADOPTION) RULES 2005

Form of documents

1.1 Documents drafted by a legal representative should bear his/her signature and if they are drafted by a legal representative as a member or employee of a firm they should be signed in the name of the firm.

1.2 Every document prepared by a party for filing or use at the court must –

(1) unless the nature of the document renders it impracticable, be on A4 paper of durable quality having a margin, not less than 3.5 centimetres wide;

(2) be fully legible and should normally be typed;

(3) where possible be bound securely in a manner which would not hamper filing or otherwise each page should be endorsed with the case number;

(4) have the pages numbered consecutively;

(5) be divided into numbered paragraphs;

(6) have all numbers, including dates, expressed as figures; and

(7) give in the margin the reference of every document mentioned that has already been filed.

1.3 A document which is a copy produced by a colour photostat machine or other similar device may be filed at the court office provided that the coloured date seal of the court is not reproduced on the copy.

Documents for filing at court

2.1 The date on which a document was filed at court must be recorded on the document. This may be done by a seal or a receipt stamp.

2.2 Particulars of the date of delivery at a court office of any document for filing and the title of the proceedings in which the document is filed shall be entered in court records, on the court file or on a computer kept in the court office for the purpose. Except where a document has been delivered at the court office through the post, the time of delivery should also be recorded.

2.3 Where the court orders any document to be lodged in court, the document must, unless otherwise directed, be deposited in the office of that court.

2.4 A document filed, lodged or held in any court office shall not be taken out of that office without the permission of the court unless the proceedings are transferred to another court in accordance with the Children (Allocation of Proceedings) Order 1991.[1]

---

[1] SI 1991/1677.

PRACTICE DIRECTION – CIVIL RESTRAINT ORDERS
THIS PRACTICE DIRECTION SUPPLEMENTS PART 3, RULE 16 OF THE FAMILY PROCEDURE (ADOPTION) RULES 2005

Introduction

1 This practice direction applies where the court is considering whether to make –

(a) a limited civil restraint order;
(b) an extended civil restraint order; or
(c) a general civil restraint order,

against a party who has made applications which are totally without merit.

Rules 13(7) and 96 provide that where an application is dismissed and is totally without merit, the court order must specify that fact and the court must consider whether to make a civil restraint order. Rule 180(5) makes similar provision where the appeal court strikes out an appellant's notice or dismisses an appeal.

Limited civil restraint orders

2.1 A limited civil restraint order may be made by a judge or district judge (including a district judge of the principal registry of the Family Division) of the High Court or a county court where a party has made 2 or more applications which are totally without merit.

2.2 Where the court makes a limited civil restraint order, the party against whom the order is made –

(1) will be restrained from making any further applications in the proceedings in which the order is made without first obtaining the permission of a judge identified in the order;
(2) may apply for amendment or discharge of the order provided he has first obtained the permission of a judge identified in the order; and
(3) may apply for permission to appeal the order and if permission is granted, may appeal the order.

2.3 Where a party who is subject to a limited civil restraint order –

(1) makes a further application in the proceedings in which the order is made without first obtaining the permission of a judge identified in the order, such application will automatically be dismissed –
   (a) without the judge having to make any further order; and
   (b) without the need for the other party to respond to it; and
(2) repeatedly makes applications for permission pursuant to that order which are totally without merit, the court may direct that if the party makes any further application for permission which is totally without merit, the decision to dismiss the application will be final and there will be no right of appeal, unless the judge who refused permission grants permission to appeal.

2.4 Unless the court directs otherwise, a party who is subject to a limited civil restraint order may not make an application for permission under paragraphs 2.2(1) or (2) without first serving notice of the application on the other party in accordance with paragraph 2.5.

2.5 A notice under paragraph 2.4 must –

(1) set out the nature and grounds of the application; and

(2) provide the other party with at least 7 days within which to respond.

2.6 An application for permission under paragraphs 2.2(1) or (2) –

(1) must be made in writing;
(2) must include the other party's written response, if any, to the notice served under paragraph 2.4; and
(3) will be determined without a hearing.

2.7 An order under paragraph 2.3(2) may only be made by a High Court judge.

2.8 Where a party makes an application for permission under paragraphs 2.2(1) or (2) and permission is refused, any application for permission to appeal –

(1) must be made in writing; and
(2) will be determined without a hearing.

2.9 A limited civil restraint order –

(1) is limited to the particular proceedings in which it is made;
(2) will remain in effect for the duration of the proceedings in which it is made, unless the court otherwise orders; and
(3) must identify the judge or judges to whom an application for permission under paragraphs 2.2(1), 2.2(2) or 2.8 should be made.

Extended civil restraint orders

3.1 An extended civil restraint order may be made by a judge of the High Court where a party has persistently made applications which are totally without merit.

3.2 Unless the court otherwise orders, where the court makes an extended civil restraint order, the party against whom the order is made –

(1) will be restrained from making applications in any court concerning any matter involving or relating to or touching upon or leading to the proceedings in which the order is made without first obtaining the permission of a judge identified in the order;
(2) may apply for amendment or discharge of the order provided he has first obtained the permission of a judge identified in the order; and
(3) may apply for permission to appeal the order and if permission is granted, may appeal the order.

3.3 Where a party who is subject to an extended civil restraint order –

(1) makes an application in a court identified in the order concerning any matter involving or relating to or touching upon or leading to the proceedings in which the order is made without first obtaining the permission of a judge identified in the order, the application will automatically be struck out or dismissed –
   (a) without the judge having to make any further order; and
   (b) without the need for the other party to respond to it; and
(2) repeatedly makes applications for permission pursuant to that order which are totally without merit, the court may direct that if the party makes any further application for permission which is totally without merit, the decision to dismiss the application will be final and there will be no right of appeal, unless the judge who refused permission grants permission to appeal.

3.4 Unless the court otherwise directs, a party who is subject to an extended civil restraint order may not make an application for permission under paragraphs 3.2(1) or (2) without first serving notice of the application on the other party in accordance with paragraph 3.5.

3.5 A notice under paragraph 3.4 must –

(1) set out the nature and grounds of the application; and
(2) provide the other party with at least 7 days within which to respond.

3.6 An application for permission under paragraphs 3.2(1) or (2) –

(1) must be made in writing;
(2) must include the other party's written response, if any, to the notice served under paragraph 3.4; and
(3) will be determined without a hearing.

3.7 An order under paragraph 3.3(2) may only be made by a High Court judge.

3.8 Where a party makes an application for permission under paragraphs 3.2(1) or (2) and permission is refused, any application for permission to appeal –

(1) must be made in writing; and
(2) will be determined without a hearing.

3.9 An extended civil restraint order –

(1) will be made for a specified period not exceeding 2 years;
(2) must identify the courts in which the party against whom the order is made is restrained from making applications; and
(3) must identify the judge or judges to whom an application for permission under paragraphs 3.2(1), 3.2(2) or 3.8 should be made.

3.10 The court may extend the duration of an extended civil restraint order, if it considers it appropriate to do so, but it must not be extended for a period greater than 2 years on any given occasion.

General civil restraint orders

4.1 A general civil restraint order may be made by a judge of the High Court where, the party against whom the order is made persists in making applications which are totally without merit, in circumstances where an extended civil restraint order would not be sufficient or appropriate.

4.2 Unless the court otherwise orders, where the court makes a general civil restraint order, the party against whom the order is made –

(1) will be restrained from making any application in any court without first obtaining the permission of a judge identified in the order;
(2) may apply for amendment or discharge of the order provided he has first obtained the permission of a judge identified in the order; and
(3) may apply for permission to appeal the order and if permission is granted, may appeal the order.

4.3 Where a party who is subject to a general civil restraint order –

(1) makes an application in a court identified in the order without first obtaining the permission of a judge identified in the order, the application will automatically be struck out or dismissed –

   (a) without the judge having to make any further order; and

(b) without the need for the other party to respond to it; and

(2) repeatedly makes applications for permission pursuant to that order which are totally without merit, the court may direct that if the party makes any further application for permission which is totally without merit, the decision to dismiss that application will be final and there will be no right of appeal, unless the judge who refused permission grants permission to appeal.

4.4 Unless the court directs otherwise, a party who is subject to a general civil restraint order may not make an application for permission under paragraphs 4.2(1) or (2) without first serving notice of the application on the other party in accordance with paragraph 4.5.

4.5 A notice under paragraph 4.4 must –

(1) set out the nature and grounds of the application; and
(2) provide the other party with at least 7 days within which to respond.

4.6 An application for permission under paragraphs 4.2(1) or (2) –

(1) must be made in writing;
(2) must include the other party's written response, if any, to the notice served under paragraph 4.4; and
(3) will be determined without a hearing.

4.7 An order under paragraph 4.3(2) may only be made by a High Court judge.

4.8 Where a party makes an application for permission under paragraphs 4.2(1) or (2) and permission is refused, any application for permission to appeal –

(1) must be made in writing; and
(2) will be determined without a hearing.

4.9 A general civil restraint order –

(1) will be made for a specified period not exceeding 2 years;
(2) must identify the courts in which the party against whom the order is made is restrained from making applications; and
(3) must identify the judge or judges to whom an application for permission under paragraphs 4.2(1), 4.2(2) or 4.8 should be made.

4.10 The court may extend the duration of a general civil restraint order, if it considers it appropriate to do so, but it must not be extended for a period greater than 2 years on any given occasion.

General

5.1 The other party or parties to the proceedings may apply for any civil restraint order.

5.2 An application under paragraph 5.1 must be made using the procedure in Part 9 unless the court otherwise directs and the application must specify which type of civil restraint order is sought.

PRACTICE DIRECTION – FORMS

THIS PRACTICE DIRECTION SUPPLEMENTS PART 4, RULE 17 AND PART 5, RULE 28 OF THE FAMILY PROCEDURE (ADOPTION) RULES 2005

Scope of this Practice Direction

1.1 This Practice Direction lists the forms to be used in proceedings under the Act.

1.2 This Practice Direction contains two tables –

- Table 1 lists forms required or permitted by rule 17;
- Table 2 lists forms required by rule 28 (consent).

Table 1

No	Title
A50	Application for a placement order
A51	Application for variation of a placement order
A52	Application for revocation of a placement order
A53	Application for a contact order
A54	Application for variation or revocation of a contact order
A55	Application for permission to change a child's surname
A56	Application for permission to take a child out of the UK
A57	Application for a recovery order
A58	Application for an adoption order
A59	Application for an adoption order (Convention adoption)
A60	Application for an adoption order (foreign element)
A61	Application for an order under section 84 (parental responsibility prior to adoption abroad)
A62	Application for a direction under section 88
A63	Application for an order under section 89
A64	Application to receive information from court records
A65	Confidential information
FP1	Application under Part 10 of the Family Procedure (Adoption) Rules 2005
FP1A	Application under Part 10 of the Family Procedure (Adoption) Rules 2005 – notes for applicant
FP1B	Application under Part 10 of the Family Procedure (Adoption) Rules 2005 – notes for respondent
FP2	Application Notice Part 9 of the Family Procedure (Adoption) Rules 2005
FP3	Injunction application
FP5	Acknowledgement of service – Part 10 application
FP6	Certificate of service
FP8	Notice of change of solicitor
FP9	Certificate of suitability of litigation friend

No	Title
FP25	Witness summons

Table 2

No	Title
A100	Consent to placement for adoption with any prospective adopters
A101	Consent to placement for adoption with identified prospective adopters
A102	Consent to placement for adoption with identified prospective adopters and, if the placement breaks down, with any prospective adopters
A103	Advance consent to adoption
A104	Consent to adoption
A105	Consent to the making of an order under section 84
A106	Withdrawal of consent

PRACTICE DIRECTION – WHO RECEIVES A COPY OF THE APPLICATION FORM FOR ORDERS IN PROCEEDINGS

THIS PRACTICE DIRECTION SUPPLEMENTS PART 5, RULE 24(1)(B)(II) OF THE FAMILY PROCEDURE (ADOPTION) RULES 2005

Persons who receive copy of application form

1 In relation to each type of proceedings in column 1 of the following table, column 2 sets out which persons are to receive a copy of the application form –

Proceeding for	Who Receives a Copy of the Application Form
An adoption order (section 46 of the Act); or a section 84 order	• Any appointed children's guardian, children and family reporter and reporting officer; • the local authority to whom notice under section 44 (notice of intention to apply to adopt or apply for a section 84 order) has been given; • the adoption agency which placed the child for adoption with the applicants; • any other person directed by the court to receive a copy.
A placement order (section 21 of the Act); or an order varying a placement order (section 23 of the Act)	• Each parent with parental responsibility for the child or guardian of the child; • any appointed children's guardian, children and family reporter and reporting officer; • any other person directed by the court to receive a copy.
An order revoking a placement order (section 24 of the Act)	• Each parent with parental responsibility for the child or guardian of the child; • any appointed children's guardian and children and family reporter; • the local authority authorised by the placement order to place the child for adoption; • any other person directed by the court to receive a copy.

Proceeding for	Who Receives a Copy of the Application Form
A contact order (section 26 of the Act); an order varying or revoking a contact order (section 27 of the Act); an order permitting the child's name to be changed or the removal of the child from the United Kingdom (section 28(2) of the Act); a recovery order (section 41(2) of the Act); a section 89 order; and a section 88 direction	• All the parties; • any appointed children's guardian and children and family reporter; • any other person directed by the court to receive a copy.

PRACTICE DIRECTION – THE FIRST DIRECTIONS HEARING – ADOPTIONS WITH A FOREIGN ELEMENT

THIS PRACTICE DIRECTION SUPPLEMENTS PART 5, RULE 26(3) OF THE FAMILY PROCEDURE (ADOPTION) RULES 2005

Application

1 This Practice Direction applies to proceedings for –

(a) a Convention adoption order;
(b) a section 84 order;
(c) a section 88 direction;
(d) a section 89 order; and
(e) an adoption order where the child has been brought into the United Kingdom in the circumstances where section 83(1) of the Act applies.

The first directions hearing

2 At the first directions hearing the court will, in addition to any matters referred to in rule 26(1) –

(a) consider whether the requirements of the Act and the Adoptions with a Foreign Element Regulations 2005 (SI 2005/392) appear to have been complied with and, if not, consider whether or not it is appropriate to transfer the case to the High Court;
(b) consider whether all relevant documents are translated into English and, if not, fix a timetable for translating any outstanding documents;
(c) consider whether the applicant needs to file an affidavit setting out the full details of the circumstances in which the child was brought to the United Kingdom, of the attitude of the parents to the application and confirming compliance with the requirements of The Adoptions with A Foreign Element Regulations 2005;
(d) give directions about –
 (i) the production of the child's passport and visa;
 (ii) the need for the Official Solicitor and a representative of the Home Office to attend future hearings; and
 (iii) personal service on the parents (via the Central Authority in the case of an application for a Convention Adoption Order) including information about the role of the Official Solicitor and availability of legal aid to be represented within the proceedings; and
(e) consider fixing a further directions appointment no later than 6 weeks after the date of the first directions appointment and timetable a date by which the Official Solicitor should file an interim report in advance of that further appointment.

PRACTICE DIRECTION – REPORTS BY THE ADOPTION AGENCY OR LOCAL AUTHORITY

THIS PRACTICE DIRECTION SUPPLEMENTS PART 5, RULE 29(3) OF THE FAMILY PROCEDURE (ADOPTION) RULES 2005

Matters to be contained in reports

1.1 The matters to be covered in the report on the suitability of the applicant to adopt a child are set out in Annex A to this Practice Direction.

1.2 The matters to be covered in a report on the placement of the child for adoption are set out in Annex B to this Practice Direction.

1.3 Where a matter to be covered in the reports set out in Annex A and Annex B does not apply to the circumstances of a particular case, the reasons for not covering the matter should be given.

ANNEX A

REPORT TO THE COURT WHERE THERE HAS BEEN AN APPLICATION FOR AN ADOPTION ORDER OR AN APPLICATION FOR A SECTION 84 ORDER

Section A: The Report and Matters for the Proceedings

Section B: The Child and the Birth Family

Section C: The Prospective Adopter of the Child

Section D: The Placement

Section E: Recommendations

Section F: Further information for proceedings relating to Convention Adoption Orders, Convention adoptions, section 84 Orders or adoptions where section 83(1) of the 2002 Act applies.

Section A: The Report and Matters for the Proceedings

Part 1 The Report

For each of the principal author/s of the report:

  (i) name;
  (ii) role in relation to this case;
  (iii) sections completed in this report;
  (iv) qualifications and experience;
  (v) name and address of the adoption agency; and
  (vi) adoption agency case reference number.

Part 2 Matters for the Proceedings

(a) Whether the adoption agency considers that any other person should be made a respondent or a party to the proceedings, including the child.

(b) Whether any of the respondents is under the age of 18.
(c) Whether a respondent is a person who, by reason of mental disorder within the meaning of the Mental Health Act 1983, is incapable of managing and administering his or her property and affairs. If so, medical evidence should be provided with particular regard to the effect on that person's ability to make decisions in the proceedings.

Section B: The Child and the Birth Family

Part 1

(i) Information about the Child

(a) Name, sex, date and place of birth and address including local authority area.
(b) Photograph and physical description.
(c) Nationality.
(d) Racial origin and cultural and linguistic background.
(e) Religious persuasion (including details of baptism, confirmation or equivalent ceremonies).
(f) Details of any siblings, half-siblings and step-siblings, including dates of birth.
(g) Whether the child is looked after by a local authority.
(h) Whether the child has been placed for adoption with the prospective adopter by a UK adoption agency.
(i) Whether the child was being fostered by the prospective adopter.
(j) Whether the child was brought into the UK for adoption, including date of entry and whether an adoption order was made in the child's country of origin.
(k) Personality and social development, including emotional and behavioural development and any related needs.
(l) Details of interests, likes and dislikes.
(m) A summary, written by the agency's medical adviser, of the child's health history, his current state of health and any need for health care which is anticipated, and date of the most recent medical examination.
(n) Any known learning difficulties or known general medical or mental health factors which are likely to have, or may have, genetic implications.
(o) Names, addresses and types of nurseries or schools attended, with dates.
(p) Educational attainments.
(q) Any special needs in relation to the child (whether physical, learning, behavioural or any other) and his emotional and behavioural development.
(r) Whether the child is subject to a statement under the Education Act 1996.
(s) Previous orders concerning the child:
  (i) the name of the court;
  (ii) the order made; and
  (iii) the date of the order.
(t) Inheritance rights and any claim to damages under the Fatal Accidents Act 1976 the child stands to retain or lose if adopted.
(u) Any other relevant information which might assist the court.

(ii) Information about each Parent of the Child

(a) Name, date and place of birth and address (date on which last address was confirmed current) including local authority area.
(b) Photograph, if available, and physical description.
(c) Nationality.

(d) Racial origin and cultural and linguistic background.
(e) Whether the mother and father were married to each other at the time of the child's birth or have subsequently married.
(f) Where the parent has been previously married or entered into a civil partnership, dates of those marriages or civil partnerships.
(g) Where the mother and father are not married, whether the father has parental responsibility and, if so, how it was acquired.
(h) If the identity or whereabouts of the father are not known, the information about him that has been ascertained and from whom, and the steps that have been taken to establish paternity.
(i) Past and present relationship with the other parent.
(j) Other information about the parent, where available:
  (i) health, including any known learning difficulties or known general medical or mental health factors which are likely to have, or may have, genetic implications;
  (ii) religious persuasion;
  (iii) educational history;
  (iv) employment history; and
  (v) personality and interests.
(k) Any other relevant information which might assist the court.

Part 2 Relationships, contact arrangements and views

The Child

(a) If the child is in the care of a local authority or voluntary organisation, or has been, details (including dates) of any placements with foster parents, or other arrangements in respect of the care of the child, including particulars of the persons with whom the child has had his home and observations on the care provided.
(b) The child's wishes and feelings (if appropriate, having regard to the child's age and understanding) about adoption, the application and its consequences, including any wishes in respect of religious and cultural upbringing.
(c) The child's wishes and feelings in relation to contact (if appropriate, having regard to the child's age and understanding).
(d) The child's wishes and feelings recorded in any other proceedings.
(e) Date when the child's views were last ascertained.

The Child's Parents (or guardian) and relatives

(a) The parents' wishes and feelings before the placement, about the placement and about adoption, the application and its consequences, including any wishes in respect of the child's religious and cultural upbringing.
(b) Each parent's (or guardian's) wishes and feelings in relation to contact.
(c) Date/s when the views of each parent or guardian were last ascertained.
(d) Arrangements concerning any siblings, including half-siblings and step-siblings, and whether any are the subject of a parallel application or have been the subject of any orders. If so, for each case give:
  (i) the name of the court;
  (ii) the order made, or (if proceedings are pending) the order applied for; and
  (iii) the date of order, or date of next hearing if proceedings are pending.
(e) Extent of contact with the child's mother and father and, in each case, the nature of the relationship enjoyed.
(f) The relationship which the child has with relatives, and with any other person considered relevant, including:

(i) the likelihood of any such relationship continuing and the value to the child of its doing so; and
   (ii) the ability and willingness of any of the child's relatives, or of any such person, to provide the child with a secure environment in which the child can develop, and otherwise to meet the child's needs.
(g) The wishes and feelings of any of the child's relatives, or of any such person, regarding the child.
(h) Whether the parents (or members of the child's family) have met or are likely to meet the prospective adopter and, if they have met, the effect on all involved of such meeting.
(i) Dates when the views of members of the child's wider family and any other relevant person were last ascertained.

Part 3 A summary of the actions of the adoption agency

(a) Brief account of the agency's actions in the case, with particulars and dates of all written information and notices given to the child and his parents and any person with parental responsibility.
(b) If consent has been given for the child to be placed for adoption, and also consent for the child to be adopted, the names of those who gave consent and the date such consents were given. If such consents were subsequently withdrawn, the dates of these withdrawals.
(c) If any statement has been made under section 20(4)(a) of the Adoption and Children Act 2002 (the '2002 Act') that a parent or guardian does not wish to be informed of any application for an adoption order, the names of those who have made such statements and the dates the statements were made. If such statements were subsequently withdrawn, the dates of these withdrawals.
(d) Whether an order has been made under section 21 of the 2002 Act, section 18 of the Adoption (Scotland) Act 1978 or Article 17(1) or 18(1) of the Northern Ireland Order 1987.
(e) Details of the support and advice given to the parents and any services offered or taken up.
(f) If the father does not have parental responsibility, details of the steps taken to inform him of the application for an adoption order.
(g) Brief details and dates of assessments of the child's needs, including expert opinions.
(h) Reasons for considering that adoption would be in the child's best interests (with date of relevant decision and reasons for any delay in implementing the decision).

Section C: The Prospective Adopter of the Child

Part 1 Information about the Prospective Adopter, including suitability to adopt

(a) Name, date and place of birth and address (date on which last address was confirmed current) including local authority area.
(b) Photograph and physical description.
(c) Whether the prospective adopter is domiciled or habitually resident in a part of the British Islands and, if habitually resident, for how long they have been habitually resident.
(d) Racial origin and cultural and linguistic background.
(e) Marital status or civil partnership status, date and place of most recent marriage (if any) or civil partnership (if any).

(f) Details of any previous marriage, civil partnership, or relationship where the prospective adopter lived with another person as a partner in an enduring family relationship.
(g) Relationship (if any) to the child.
(h) Where adopters wish to adopt as a couple, the status of the relationship and an assessment of the stability and permanence of their relationship.
(i) If a married person or a civil partner is applying alone, the reasons for this.
(j) Description of how the prospective adopter relates to adults and children.
(k) Previous experience of caring for children (including as a step-parent, foster parent, child-minder or prospective adopter) and assessment of ability in this respect, together where appropriate with assessment of ability in bringing up the prospective adopter's own children.
(l) A summary, written by the agency's medical adviser, of the prospective adopter's health history, current state of health and any need for health care which is anticipated, and date of most recent medical examination.
(m) Assessment of ability and suitability to bring up the child throughout his childhood.
(n) Details of income and comments on the living standards of the household with particulars of the home and living conditions (and particulars of any home where the prospective adopter proposes to live with the child, if different).
(o) Details of other members of the household, including any children of the prospective adopter even if not resident in the household.
(p) Details of the parents and any siblings of the prospective adopter, with their ages or ages at death.
(q) Other information about the prospective adopter:
  (i) religious persuasion;
  (ii) educational history;
  (iii) employment history; and
  (iv) personality and interests.
(r) Confirmation that the applicants have not been convicted of, or cautioned for, a specified offence within the meaning of regulation 23(3) of the Adoption Agencies Regulations 2005 (S.I. 2005/389).
(s) Confirmation that the prospective adopter is still approved.
(t) Confirmation that any referees have been interviewed, with a report of their views and opinion of the weight to be placed thereon and whether they are still valid.
(u) Details of any previous family court proceedings in which the prospective adopter has been involved (which have not been referred to elsewhere in this report.)

Part 2 Wishes, views and contact arrangements

Prospective Adopter

(a) Whether the prospective adopter is willing to follow any wishes of the child or his parents or guardian in respect of the child's religious and cultural upbringing.
(b) The views of other members of the prospective adopter's household and wider family in relation to the proposed adoption.
(c) Reasons for the prospective adopter wishing to adopt the child and extent of understanding of the nature and effect of adoption. Whether the prospective adopter has discussed adoption with the child.
(d) Any hope and expectations the prospective adopter has for the child's future.
(e) The prospective adopter's wishes and feelings in relation to contact.

Part 3 Actions of the adoption agency

(a) Brief account of the Agency's actions in the case, with particulars and dates of all written information and notices given to the prospective adopter.
(b) The Agency's proposals for contact, including options for facilitating or achieving any indirect contact or direct contact.
(c) The Agency's opinion on the likely effect on the prospective adopter and on the security of the placement of any proposed contact.
(d) Where the prospective adopter has been approved by an agency as suitable to be an adoptive parent, the agency's reasons for considering that the prospective adopter is suitable to be an adoptive parent for this child (with dates of relevant decisions).

Section D: The Placement

(a) Where the child was placed for adoption by an adoption agency (section 18 of the 2002 Act), the date and circumstances of the child's placement with prospective adopter.
(b) Where the child is living with persons who have applied for the adoption order to be made (section 44 of the 2002 Act), the date when notice of intention to adopt was given.
(c) Where the placement is being provided with adoption support, this should be summarised and should include the plan and timescales for continuing the support beyond the making of the adoption order.
(d) Where the placement is not being provided with adoption support, the reasons why.
(e) A summary of the information obtained from the Agency's visits and reviews of the placement, including whether the child has been seen separately to the prospective adopter and whether there has been sufficient opportunity to see the family group and the child's interaction in the home environment.
(f) An assessment of the child's integration within the family of the prospective adopter and the likelihood of the child's full integration into the family and community.
(g) Any other relevant information that might assist the court.

Section E: Recommendations

(a) The relative merits of adoption and other orders with an assessment of whether the child's long term interests would be best met by an adoption order or by other orders (such as residence and special guardianship orders).
(b) Recommendations as to whether or not the order sought should be made (and, if not, alternative proposals).
(c) Recommendations as to whether there should be future contact arrangements (or not).

Section F: Further Information for Proceedings Relating to Convention Adoption Orders, Convention Adoptions, Section 84 Orders or an Adoption where Section 83(1) of the 2002 Act Applies

(a) The child's knowledge of their racial and cultural origin.
(b) The likelihood of the child's adaptation to living in the country he/she is to be placed.
(c) Where the UK is the State of origin, reasons for considering that, after possibilities for placement of the child within the UK have been given due consideration, intercountry adoption is in the child's best interests.
(d) Confirmation that the requirements of regulations made under sections 83(4), (5), (6) and (7) and 84(3) and (6) of the 2002 Act have been complied with.

(e) For a Convention adoption or a Convention Adoption Order where the United Kingdom is either the State of origin or the receiving State, confirmation that the Central Authorities of both States have agreed that the adoption may proceed.
(f) Where the State of origin is not the United Kingdom, the documents supplied by the Central Authority of the State of origin should be attached to the report, together with translation if necessary.
(g) Where a Convention adoption order is proposed, details of the arrangements which were made for the transfer of the child to the UK and that they were in accordance with the Adoptions with a Foreign Element Regulations 2005 (SI 2005/392).

ANNEX B

REPORT TO THE COURT WHERE THERE HAS BEEN AN APPLICATION FOR A PLACEMENT ORDER

Section A: The Report and Matters for the Proceedings

Section B: The Child and the Birth Family

Section C: Recommendations

Section A: The Report and Matters for the Proceedings

Part 1 The Report

For each of the principal author/s of the report:

(i) name;
(ii) role in relation to this case;
(iii) section completed in this report;
(iv) qualifications and experience;
(v) name and address of the adoption agency; and
(vi) adoption agency case reference number.

Part 2 Matters for the Proceedings

(a) Whether the adoption agency considers that any other person should be made a respondent or a party to the proceedings.
(b) Whether any of the respondents is under the age of 18.
(c) Whether a respondent is a person who, by reason of mental disorder within the meaning of the Mental Health Act 1983, is incapable of managing and administering his or her property and affairs. If so, medical evidence should be provided with particular regard to the effect on that person's ability to make decisions in the proceedings.

Section B: The Child and the Birth Family

Part 1

(i) Information about the Child

(a) Name, sex, date and place of birth and address including local authority area.
(b) Photograph and physical description.

(c) Nationality.
(d) Racial origin and cultural and linguistic background.
(e) Religious persuasion (including details of baptism, confirmation or equivalent ceremonies).
(f) Details of any siblings, half-siblings and step-siblings, including dates of birth.
(g) Whether the child is looked after by a local authority.
(h) Personality and social development, including emotional and behavioural development and any related needs.
(i) Details of interests, likes and dislikes.
(j) A summary, written by the agency's medical adviser, of the child's health history, his current state of health and any need for health care which is anticipated, and date of the most recent medical examination.
(k) Any known learning difficulties or known general medical or mental health factors which are likely to have, or may have, genetic implications.
(l) Names, addresses and types of nurseries or schools attended, with dates.
(m) Educational attainments.
(n) Any special needs in relation to the child (whether physical, learning, behavioural or any other) and his emotional and behavioural development.
(o) Whether the child is subject to a statement under the Education Act 1996.
(p) Previous orders concerning the child:
   (i) the name of the court;
   (ii) the order made; and
   (ii) the date of the order.
(q) Inheritance rights and any claim to damages under the Fatal Accidents Act 1976 the child stands to retain or lose if adopted.
(r) Any other relevant information which might assist the court.

(ii) Information about each Parent of the Child

(a) Name, date and place of birth and address (date on which last address was confirmed current) including local authority area.
(b) Photograph, if available, and physical description.
(c) Nationality.
(d) Racial origin and cultural and linguistic background.
(e) Whether the mother and father were married to each other at the time of the child's birth, or have subsequently married.
(f) Where the parent has been previously married or entered into a civil partnership, dates of those marriages or civil partnerships.
(g) Where the mother and father are not married, whether the father has parental responsibility and, if so, how it was acquired.
(h) If the identity or whereabouts of the father are not known, the information about him that has been ascertained and from whom, and the steps that have been taken to establish paternity.
(i) Past and present relationship with the other parent.
(j) Other information about the parent, where available:
   (i) health, including any known learning difficulties or known general medical or mental health factors which are likely to have, or may have, genetic implications;
   (ii) religious persuasion;
   (iii) educational history;
   (iv) employment history; and
   (v) personality and interests.
(k) Any other relevant information which might assist the court.

Part 2 Relationships, contact arrangements and views

The Child

(a) If the child is in the care of a local authority or voluntary organisation, or has been, details (including dates) of any placements with foster parents, or other arrangements in respect of the care of the child, including particulars of the persons with whom the child has had his home and observations on the care provided.
(b) The child's wishes and feelings (if appropriate, having regard to the child's age and understanding) about the application, its consequences, and adoption, including any wishes in respect of religious and cultural upbringing.
(c) The child's wishes and feelings in relation to contact (if appropriate, having regard to the child's age and understanding).
(d) The child's wishes and feelings recorded in any other proceedings.
(e) Date when the child's views were last ascertained.

The Child's Parents (or guardian) and relatives

(a) The parents' wishes and feelings about the application, its consequences, and adoption, including any wishes in respect of the child's religious and cultural upbringing.
(b) Each parent's (or guardian's) wishes and feelings in relation to contact.
(c) Date/s when the views of each parent or guardian were last ascertained.
(d) Arrangements concerning any siblings, including half-siblings and step-siblings, and whether any are the subject of a parallel application or have been the subject of any orders. If so, for each case give:
　(i) the name of the court;
　(ii) the order made, or (if proceedings are pending) the order applied for; and
　(iii) the date of order, or date of next hearing if proceedings are pending.
(e) Extent of contact with the child's mother and father and in each case the nature of the relationship enjoyed.
(f) The relationship which the child has with relatives, and with any other person considered relevant, including:
　(i) the likelihood of any such relationship continuing and the value to the child of its doing so; and
　(ii) the ability and willingness of any of the child's relatives, or of any such person, to provide the child with a secure environment in which the child can develop, and otherwise to meet the child's needs.
(g) The wishes and feelings of any of the child's relatives, or of any such person, regarding the child.
(h) Dates when the views of members of the child's wider family and any other relevant person were last ascertained.

Part 3 Summary of the actions of the adoption agency

(a) Brief account of the Agency's actions in the case, with particulars and dates of all written information and notices given to the child and his parents and any person with parental responsibility.
(b) If consent has been given for the child to be placed for adoption, and also consent for the child to be adopted, the names of those who gave consent and the date such consents were given. If such consents were subsequently withdrawn, the dates of these withdrawals.
(c) If any statement has been made under section 20(4)(a) of the 2002 Act that a parent or guardian does not wish to be informed of any application for an adoption order, the

names of those who have made such statements and the dates the statements were made. If such statements were subsequently withdrawn, the dates of these withdrawals.
(d) Details of the support and advice given to the parents and any services offered or taken up.
(e) If the father does not have parental responsibility, details of the steps taken to inform him of the application for a placement order.
(f) Brief details and dates of assessments of the child's needs, including expert opinions.
(g) Reasons for considering that adoption would be in the child's best interests (with date of relevant decision and reasons for any delay in implementing the decision).

Section C: Recommendations

(a) The relative merits of a placement order and other orders (such as a residence or special guardianship order) with an assessment of why the child's long term interests are likely to be best met by a placement order rather than by any other order.
(b) Recommendations as to whether there should be future contact arrangements (or not), including whether a contact order under section 26 of the 2002 Act should be made.

PRACTICE DIRECTION – REPORTS BY A REGISTERED MEDICAL PRACTITIONER ('HEALTH REPORTS')

THIS PRACTICE DIRECTION SUPPLEMENTS PART 5, RULE 30(2) OF THE FAMILY PROCEDURE (ADOPTION) RULES 2005

Matters to be contained in health reports

1.1 Rule 30(1) requires that health reports must be attached to an application for an adoption order or a section 84 order except where –

(a) the child was placed for adoption with the applicant by an adoption agency;
(b) the applicant or one of the applicants is a parent of the child; or
(c) the applicant is the partner of a parent of the child.

1.2 The matters to be contained in the health reports are set out in the Annex to this Practice Direction.

1.3 Where a matter to be contained in the health report does not apply to the circumstances of a particular case, the reasons for not covering the matter should be given.

ANNEX

CONTENTS OF HEALTH REPORTS

This information is required for reports on the health of children and their prospective adopter(s). Its purpose is to build up a full picture of each child's health history and current state of health, including strengths and weaknesses. This will enable local authorities' medical adviser to base their advice to the court on the fullest possible information when commenting on the health implications of the proposed adoption. The reports made by the examining doctor should cover, as far as practicable, the following matters.

1 The Child

Name, date of birth, sex, weight and height.

A A health history of each natural parent, so far as is possible, including:

(i) name, date of birth, sex, weight and height;
(ii) a family health history, covering the parents, the brothers and sisters and the other children of the natural parent, with details of any serious physical or mental illness and inherited and congenital disease;
(iii) past health history, including details of any serious physical or mental illness, disability, accident, hospital admission or attendance at an out-patient department, and in each case any treatment given;
(iv) a full obstetric history of the mother, including any problems in the ante-natal, labour and post-natal periods, with the results of any tests carried out during or immediately after pregnancy;
(v) details of any present illness including treatment and prognosis;
(vi) any other relevant information which might assist the medical adviser; and
(vii) the name and address of any doctor(s) who might be able to provide further information about any of the above matters.

B A neo-natal report on the child, including:

(i) details of the birth, and any complications;
(ii) results of a physical examination and screening tests;
(iii) details of any treatment given;
(iv) details of any problem in management and feeding;
(v) any other relevant information which might assist the medical adviser; and
(vi) the name and address of any doctor(s) who might be able to provide further information about any of the above matters.

C A full health history and examination of the child, including:

(i) details of any serious illness, disability, accident, hospital admission or attendance at an out-patient department, and in each case any treatment given;
(ii) details and dates of immunisations;
(iii) a physical and developmental assessment according to age, including an assessment of vision and hearing and of neurological, speech and language development and any evidence of emotional or conduct disorder;
(iv) details, if relevant, of the impact of any addiction or substance use on the part of the natural mother before, during or following the pregnancy, and its impact or likely future impact on the child;
(v) the impact, if any, on the child's development and likely future development of any past exposure to physical, emotional or sexual abuse or neglectful home conditions and/or any non-organic failure to thrive;
(vi) for a child of school age, the school health history (if available);
(vii) any other relevant information which might assist the medical adviser; and
(viii) the name and address of any doctor(s) who might be able to provide further information about any of the above matters.

D The signature, name, address and qualifications of the registered medical practitioner who prepared the report, and the date of the report and of the examinations carried out.

2 The Applicant

(If there is more than one applicant, a report on each applicant should be supplied covering all the matters listed below.)

A (i) name, date of birth, sex, weight and height;
(ii) a family health history, covering the parents, the brothers and sisters and the children of the applicant, with details of any serious physical or mental illness and inherited and congenital disease;
(iii) marital history, including (if applicable) reasons for inability to have children, and any history of domestic violence;
(iv) past health history, including details of any serious physical or mental illness, disability, accident, hospital admission or attendance at an out-patient department, and in each case any treatment given;
(v) obstetric history (if applicable);
(vi) details of any present illness, including treatment and prognosis;
(vii) a full medical examination;
(viii) details of any consumption of alcohol, tobacco and habit-forming drugs;
(ix) any other relevant information which might assist the medical adviser; and
(x) the name and address of any doctor(s) who might be able to provide further information about any of the above matters.

B The signature, name, address and qualifications of the registered medical practitioner who prepared the report, and the date of the report and of the examinations carried out.

PRACTICE DIRECTION – SERVICE

THIS PRACTICE DIRECTION SUPPLEMENTS PART 6, SECTION 1 OF THE FAMILY PROCEDURE (ADOPTION) RULES 2005

Methods of Service

1.1 The various methods of service are set out in rule 35.

1.2 The following provisions apply to the specific methods of service referred to.

Service by Document Exchange

2.1 Service by document exchange (DX) may take place only where:

(1) the legal representative's address for service includes a numbered box at a DX; or
(2) the writing paper of the legal representative sets out the DX box number; and
(3) the legal representative has not indicated in writing that they are unwilling to accept service by DX.

('Legal representative' is defined in rule 6)

2.2 Service by DX is effected by leaving the document addressed to the numbered box:

(1) at the DX of the legal representative; or
(2) at a DX which sends documents to that legal representative's DX every business day.

Service by the court

3 Where the court effects service of a document in accordance with rule 36, the method will normally be by first class post.

Service on members of HM Forces

4.1 Where a person to be served (the 'serviceman') is known to be serving or to have recently served as a member of H.M. Forces the applicant's legal representative may obtain the address for service of proceedings under the Adoption and Children Act 2002 from the appropriate officer of the Ministry of Defence as specified in the table in paragraph 4.7.

4.2 The letter of enquiry should in every case show that the writer is a legal representative and that the enquiry is made solely with a view to the service of legal documents in those proceedings.

4.3 In all cases the letter should give the full name, service number, rank or rating, and Ship, Arm or Trade, Regiment or Corps and Unit or as much of this information as is available. Failure to quote the service number and the rank or rating may result either in failure to identify the serviceman or in considerable delay.

4.4 The letter should contain an undertaking by the legal representative that if the address is given, it will be used solely for the purpose of issuing and serving documents in the proceedings and that so far as is possible the legal representative will disclose the address only to the court and not to the applicant or any other person, except in the normal course of the proceedings. A legal representative in the service of a public authority or private company should undertake that the address will be used solely for the purpose of issuing and serving documents in the proceedings and that the address will not be disclosed so far as is possible to any other part of his employing organisation or to any other person but only to the court. Normally on receipt of the required information and undertaking the appropriate office will give the service address.

4.5 If the legal representative does not give the undertaking, the only information he will receive will be whether the serviceman is at that time serving in England or Wales, Scotland, Northern Ireland or outside the United Kingdom.

4.6 It should be noted that a serviceman's address which ends with a British Forces Post Office address and reference (BFPO) will nearly always indicate that he is serving outside the United Kingdom.

4.7 The letter of enquiry should be addressed as follows –

Royal Navy Officers	The Naval Secretary Room 161 Victory Building HM Naval Base Portsmouth Hants PO1 3LS
RN Ratings	Commodore Naval Drafting Centurion Building Grange Road Gosport Hants PO13 9XA
RN Medical and Dental Officers	The Medical Director General (Naval) Room 114 Victory Building HM Naval Base Portsmouth Hants PO1 3LS
Officers of Queen Alexandra's Royal Naval Nursing Service	The Matron-in-Chief QARNNS Room 139 Victory Building HM Naval Base Portsmouth Hants PO1 3LS
Naval Chaplains	Director General Naval Chaplaincy Service Room 201 Victory Building HM Naval Base Portsmouth Hants PO1 3LS

Royal Marine Officers and Ranks	Personnel Section West Battery Whale Island Portsmouth Hants PO2 8DX
RM Ranks HQRM	(DRORM) West Battery Whale Island Portsmouth Hants PO2 8DX
Army Officers and other ranks	Army Personnel Centre Secretariat, Public Enquiries RM CD424 Kentigern House 65 Brown Street Glasgow G2 8EH
Royal Air Force Officers and Other Ranks	Personnel Management Agency (RAF) Building 248 RAF Innsworth Gloucester GL3 1EZ

4.8 Once the applicant's legal representative has learnt the serviceman's address, that address may be used for service by post, in cases where this method of service is allowed by the Rules.

PRACTICE DIRECTION – SERVICE OUT OF THE JURISDICTION
THIS PRACTICE DIRECTION SUPPLEMENTS PART 6, SECTION 2 OF THE FAMILY PROCEDURE (ADOPTION) RULES 2005

Service in other Member States of the European Union

1.1 Where service is to be effected in another Member of State of the European Union, Council Regulation (EC) 1348/2000 of 29 May 2000 on the service in the Member States of judicial and extrajudicial documents in civil or commercial matters ('the Service Regulation') applies.

1.2 The Service Regulation is annexed to this Practice Direction.

(Article 20(1) of the Service Regulation provides that the Regulation prevails over other provisions contained in bilateral or multilateral agreements or arrangements concluded by the Member of States and in particular Article IV of the protocol to the Brussels Convention of 1968 and the Hague Convention of 15 November 1965)

Originally published in the official languages of the European Community in the *Official Journal of the European Communities* by the Office for Official Publications of the European Communities

Documents to be filed under rule 46(2)(d)

2.1 A duplicate of the application form and of any translation required by rule 43 must be provided for each party to be served out of the jurisdiction.

2.2 The documents to be served in certain countries require legalisation and the Foreign Process Section (Room E02), Royal Courts of Justice will advise on request. Some countries require legalisation and some require a formal letter of request.

Service in Scotland, Northern Ireland, the Channel Islands, the Isle of Man, Commonwealth countries and United Kingdom Overseas Territories.

3.1 Where rule 45(3) applies, service should be effected by the applicant or his agent direct except in the case of a Commonwealth State where the judicial authorities have required service to be in accordance with rule 44(1)(b)(i). These are presently Malta and Singapore.

3.2 For the purposes of rule 45(3)(c), the following countries are United Kingdom Overseas Territories –

(a) Anguilla;
(b) Bermuda;
(c) British Antarctic Territory;
(d) British Indian Ocean Territory;
(e) Cayman Islands;
(f) Falkland Islands;
(g) Gibraltar;
(h) Montserrat;
(i) Pitcairn, Henderson, Ducie and Oeno;
(j) St Helena and Dependencies;
(k) South Georgia and the South Sandwich Islands;
(l) Sovereign Base Areas of Akrotiri and Dhekelia;
(m) Turks and Caicos Islands; and
(n) Virgin Islands.

Service of application notices and orders

4.1 The provisions of Section 2 of Part 6 (special provisions about service out of the jurisdiction) also apply to service out of the jurisdiction of an application notice or order.

4.2 Where an application notice is to be served out of the jurisdiction in accordance with Section 2 of Part 6 the court must have regard to the country in which the application notice is to be served in setting the date for the hearing of the application and giving any direction about service of the respondent's evidence.

Period for responding to an application

5 Where a Part 10 application needs to be served out of the jurisdiction, the period for responding to service is 7 days less than the number of days listed in the Table.

Table

Place or country	number of days
Abu Dhabi	22
Afghanistan	23
Albania	25
Algeria	22
Angola	22
Anguilla	31
Antigua	23
Antilles (Netherlands)	31
Argentina	22
Armenia	21
Ascension	31
Australia	25
Austria	21
Azores	23
Bahamas	22
Bahrain	22
Balearic Islands	21
Bangladesh	23
Barbados	23
Belarus	21
Belgium	21
Belize	23
Benin	25
Bermuda	31
Bhutan	28
Bolivia	23
Bosnia-Hercegovina	21

Place or country	number of days
Botswana	23
Brazil	22
Brunei	25
Bulgaria	23
Burkina Faso	23
Burma	23
Burundi	22
Cameroon	22
Canada	22
Canary Islands	22
Cape Verde Islands	25
Caroline Islands	31
Cayman Islands	31
Central African Republic	25
Chad	25
Chile	22
China	24
Christmas Island	27
Cocos (Keeling) Islands	41
Colombia	22
Comoros	23
Congo (People's Republic)	25
Corsica	21
Costa Rica	23
Croatia	21
Cuba	24
Cyprus	31
Cyrenaica (see Libya)	21
Czech Republic	21
Denmark	21
Djibouti	22
Dominica	23
Dominican Republic	23
Dubai	22
Ecuador	22
Egypt (Arab Republic)	22
El Salvador (Republic of)	25
Equatorial Guinea	23
Estonia	21

Place or country	number of days
Ethiopia	22
Falkland Islands and Dependencies	31
Faroe Islands	31
Fiji	23
Finland	24
France	21
French Guiana	31
French Polynesia	31
French West Indies	31
Gabon	25
Gambia	22
Georgia	21
Germany	21
Ghana	22
Gibraltar	31
Greece	21
Greenland	31
Grenada	24
Guatemala	24
Guernsey	18
Guyana	22
Haiti	23
Holland (Netherlands)	21
Honduras	24
Hong Kong	31
Hungary	22
Iceland	22
India	23
Indonesia	22
Iran	22
Iraq	22
Ireland (Republic of)	21
Ireland (Northern)	21
Isle of Man	18
Israel	22
Italy	21
Ivory Coast	22
Jamaica	22
Japan	23

Place or country	number of days
Jersey	18
Jordan	23
Kampuchea	38
Kazakhstan	21
Kenya	22
Kirgizstan	21
Korea (North)	28
Korea (South)	24
Kuwait	22
Laos	30
Latvia	21
Lebanon	22
Lesotho	23
Liberia	22
Libya	21
Liechtenstein	21
Lithuania	21
Luxembourg	21
Macau	31
Macedonia	21
Madagascar	23
Madeira	31
Malawi	23
Malaya	24
Maldive Islands	26
Mali	25
Malta	21
Mariana Islands	26
Marshall Islands	32
Mauritania	23
Mauritius	22
Mexico	23
Moldova	21
Monaco	21
Montserrat	31
Morocco	22
Mozambique	23
Nauru Island	36
Nepal	23

Place or country	number of days
Netherlands	21
Nevis	24
New Caledonia	31
New Hebrides (now Vanuatu)	29
New Zealand	26
New Zealand Island Territories	50
Nicaragua	24
Niger (Republic of)	25
Nigeria	22
Norfolk Island	31
Norway	21
Oman (Sultanate of)	22
Pakistan	23
Panama (Republic of)	26
Papua New Guinea	26
Paraguay	22
Peru	22
Philippines	23
Pitcairn Island	31
Poland	21
Portugal	21
Portuguese Timor	31
Puerto Rico	23
Qatar	23
Reunion	31
Romania	22
Russia	21
Rwanda	23
Sabah	23
St. Helena	31
St. Kitts–Nevis	24
St. Lucia	24
St. Pierre and Miquelon	31
St. Vincent and the Grenadines	24
Samoa (USA Territory) (See also Western Samoa)	30
Sarawak	28
Saudi Arabia	24
Scotland	21
Senegal	22

Place or country	number of days
Seychelles	22
Sharjah	24
Sierra Leone	22
Singapore	22
Slovakia	21
Slovenia	21
Society Islands (French Polynesia)	31
Solomon Islands	29
Somali Democratic Republic	22
South Africa (Republic of)	22
South Georgia (Falkland Island Dependencies)	31
South Orkneys	21
South Shetlands	21
Spain	21
Spanish Territories of North Africa	31
Sri Lanka	23
Sudan	22
Suriname	22
Swaziland	22
Sweden	21
Switzerland	21
Syria	23
Taiwan	23
Tajikistan	21
Tanzania	22
Thailand	23
Tibet	34
Tobago	23
Togo	22
Tonga	30
Tortola	31
Trinidad & Tobago	23
Tristan Da Cunha	31
Tunisia	22
Turkey	21
Turkmenistan	21
Turks & Caicos Islands	31
Uganda	22
Ukraine	21

Place or country	number of days
United States of America	22
Uruguay	22
Uzbekistan	21
Vanuatu	29
Vatican City State	21
Venezuela	22
Vietnam	28
Virgin Islands – British (Tortola)	31
Virgin Islands – USA	24
Wake Island	25
Western Samoa	34
Yemen (Republic of)	30
Yugoslavia (except for Bosnia-Hercegovina, Croatia, Macedonia and Slovenia)	21
Zaire	25
Zambia	23
Zimbabwe	22

Further information

6 Further information concerning service out of the jurisdiction can be obtained from the Foreign Process Section, Room E02, Royal Courts of Justice, Strand, London WC2A 2LL (telephone 020 7947 6691).

ANNEX

**Council regulation (EC) No 1348/2000
of 29 May 2000
on the service in the Member States of judicial and extrajudicial documents
in civil or commercial matters**

THE COUNCIL OF THE EUROPEAN UNION,

Having regard to the Treaty establishing the European Community, and in particular Article 61(c) and Article 67(1) thereof,

Having regard to the proposal from the Commission,[1]

Having regard to the opinion of the European Parliament,[2]

---

1 OJ C 247 E, 31.8.1999, p 11.
2 Opinion of 17 November 1999 (not yet published in the Official Journal).

Having regard to the opinion of the Economic and Social Committee,[1]

Whereas:

(1) The Union has set itself the objective of maintaining and developing the Union as an area of freedom, security and justice, in which the free movement of persons is assured. To establish such an area, the Community is to adopt, among others, the measures relating to judicial cooperation in civil matters needed for the proper functioning of the internal market.

(2) The proper functioning of the internal market entails the need to improve and expedite the transmission of judicial and extrajudicial documents in civil or commercial matters for service between the Member States.

(3) This is a subject now falling within the ambit of Article 65 of the Treaty.

(4) In accordance with the principles of subsidiarity and proportionality as set out in Article 5 of the Treaty, the objectives of this Regulation cannot be sufficiently achieved by the Member States and can therefore be better achieved by the Community. This Regulation does not go beyond what is necessary to achieve those objectives.

(5) The Council, by an Act dated 26 May 1997,[2] drew up a Convention on the service in the Member States of the European Union of judicial and extrajudicial documents in civil or commercial matters and recommended it for adoption by the Member States in accordance with their respective constitutional rules. That Convention has not entered into force. Continuity in the results of the negotiations for conclusion of the Convention should be ensured. The main content of this Regulation is substantially taken over from it.

(6) Efficiency and speed in judicial procedures in civil matters means that the transmission of judicial and extrajudicial documents is to be made direct and by rapid means between local bodies designated by the Member States. However, the Member States may indicate their intention of designating only one transmitting or receiving agency or one agency to perform both functions for a period of five years. This designation may, however, be renewed every five years.

(7) Speed in transmission warrants the use of all appropriate means, provided that certain conditions as to the legibility and reliability of the document received are observed. Security in transmission requires that the document to be transmitted be accompanied by a pre-printed form, to be completed in the language of the place where service is to be effected, or in another language accepted by the Member State in question.

(8) To secure the effectiveness of this Regulation, the possibility of refusing service of documents is confined to exceptional situations.

(9) Speed of transmission warrants documents being served within days of reception of the document. However, if service has not been effected after one month has elapsed, the receiving agency should inform the transmitting agency. The expiry of this period should not imply that the request be returned to the transmitting agency where it is clear that service is feasible within a reasonable period.

(10) For the protection of the addressee's interests, service should be effected in the official language or one of the official languages of the place where it is to be effected or in another language of the originating Member State which the addressee understands.

---

1   OJ C 368, 20.12.1999, p 47.
2   OJ C 261, 27.8.1997, p 1. On the same day as the Convention was drawn up the Council took note of the explanatory report on the Convention which is set out on page 26 of the aforementioned Official Journal.

(11) Given the differences between the Member States as regards their rules of procedure, the material date for the purposes of service varies from one Member State to another. Having regard to such situations and the possible difficulties that may arise, this Regulation should provide for a system where it is the law of the receiving Member State which determines the date of service. However, if the relevant documents in the context of proceedings to be brought or pending in the Member State of origin are to be served within a specified period, the date to be taken into consideration with respect to the applicant shall be that determined according to the law of the Member State of origin. A Member State is, however, authorised to derogate from the aforementioned provisions for a transitional period of five years, for appropriate reasons. Such a derogation may be renewed by a Member State at five-year intervals due to reasons related to its legal system.

(12) This Regulation prevails over the provisions contained in bilateral or multilateral agreements or arrangements having the same scope, concluded by the Member States, and in particular the Protocol annexed to the Brussels Convention of 27 September 1968[1] and the Hague Convention of 15 November 1965 in relations between the Member States party thereto. This Regulation does not preclude Member States from maintaining or concluding agreements or arrangements to expedite or simplify the transmission of documents, provided that they are compatible with the Regulation.

(13) The information transmitted pursuant to this Regulation should enjoy suitable protection. This matter falls within the scope of Directive 95/46/EC of the European Parliament and of the Council of 24 October 1995 on the protection of individuals with regard to the processing of personal data and on the free movement of such data,[2] and of Directive 97/66/EC of the European Parliament and of the Council of 15 December 1997 concerning the processing of personal data and the protection of privacy in the telecommunications sector.[3]

(14) The measures necessary for the implementation of this Regulation should be adopted in accordance with Council Decision 1999/468/EC of 28 June 1999 laying down the procedures for the exercise of implementing powers conferred on the Commission.[4]

(15) These measures also include drawing up and updating the manual using appropriate modern means.

(16) No later than three years after the date of entry into force of this Regulation, the Commission should review its application and propose such amendments as may appear necessary.

(17) The United Kingdom and Ireland, in accordance with Article 3 of the Protocol on the position of the United Kingdom and Ireland annexed to the Treaty on European Union and the Treaty establishing the European Community, have given notice of their wish to take part in the adoption and application of this Regulation.

(18) Denmark, in accordance with Articles 1 and 2 of the Protocol on the position of Denmark annexed to the Treaty on European Union and the Treaty establishing the European Community, is not participating in the adoption of this Regulation, and is therefore not bound by it nor subject to its application,

---

1   Brussels Convention of 27 September 1968 on Jurisdiction and the Enforcement of Judgments in Civil and Commercial Matters (OJ L 299, 13.12.1972, p 32; consolidated version, OJ C 27, 26.1.1998, p 1).
2   OJ L 281, 23.11.1995, p 31.
3   OJ L 24, 30.1.1998, p 1.
4   OJ L 184, 17.7.1999, p 23.

HAS ADOPTED THIS REGULATION:

Chapter I
General provisions

Article 1
Scope

1. This Regulation shall apply in civil and commercial matters where a judicial or extrajudicial document has to be transmitted from one Member State to another for service there.

2. This Regulation shall not apply where the address of the person to be served with the document is not known.

Article 2
Transmitting and receiving agencies

1. Each Member State shall designate the public officers, authorities or other persons, hereinafter referred to as 'transmitting agencies', competent for the transmission of judicial or extrajudicial documents to be served in another Member State.

2. Each Member State shall designate the public officers, authorities or other persons, hereinafter referred to as 'receiving agencies', competent for the receipt of judicial or extrajudicial documents from another Member State.

3. A Member State may designate one transmitting agency and one receiving agency or one agency to perform both functions. A federal State, a State in which several legal systems apply or a State with autonomous territorial units shall be free to designate more than one such agency. The designation shall have effect for a period of five years and may be renewed at five-year intervals.

4. Each Member State shall provide the Commission with the following information:

   (a) the names and addresses of the receiving agencies referred to in paragraphs 2 and 3;
   (b) the geographical areas in which they have jurisdiction;
   (c) the means of receipt of documents available to them; and
   (d) the languages that may be used for the completion of the standard form in the Annex.

Member States shall notify the Commission of any subsequent modification of such information.

Article 3
Central body

Each Member State shall designate a central body responsible for:

   (a) supplying information to the transmitting agencies;
   (b) seeking solutions to any difficulties which may arise during transmission of documents for service;
   (c) forwarding, in exceptional cases, at the request of a transmitting agency, a request for service to the competent receiving agency.

A federal State, a State in which several legal systems apply or a State with autonomous territorial units shall be free to designate more than one central body.

Chapter II
Judicial documents

SECTION 1
TRANSMISSION AND SERVICE OF JUDICIAL DOCUMENTS

Article 4
Transmission of documents

1. Judicial documents shall be transmitted directly and as soon as possible between the agencies designated on the basis of Article 2.

2. The transmission of documents, requests, confirmations, receipts, certificates and any other papers between transmitting agencies and receiving agencies may be carried out by any appropriate means, provided that the content of the document received is true and faithful to that of the document forwarded and that all information in it is easily legible.

3. The document to be transmitted shall be accompanied by a request drawn up using the standard form in the Annex. The form shall be completed in the official language of the Member State addressed or, if there are several official languages in that Member State, the official language or one of the official languages of the place where service is to be effected, or in another language which that Member State has indicated it can accept. Each Member State shall indicate the official language or languages of the European Union other than its own which is or are acceptable to it for completion of the form.

4. The documents and all papers that are transmitted shall be exempted from legalisation or any equivalent formality.

5. When the transmitting agency wishes a copy of the document to be returned together with the certificate referred to in Article 10, it shall send the document in duplicate.

Article 5
Translation of documents

1. The applicant shall be advised by the transmitting agency to which he or she forwards the document for transmission that the addressee may refuse to accept it if it is not in one of the languages provided for in Article 8.

2. The applicant shall bear any costs of translation prior to the transmission of the document, without prejudice to any possible subsequent decision by the court or competent authority on liability for such costs.

Article 6
Receipt of documents by receiving agency

1. On receipt of a document, a receiving agency shall, as soon as possible and in any event within seven days of receipt, send a receipt to the transmitting agency by the swiftest possible means of transmission using the standard form in the Annex.

2. Where the request for service cannot be fulfilled on the basis of the information or documents transmitted, the receiving agency shall contact the transmitting agency by the swiftest possible means in order to secure the missing information or documents.

3. If the request for service is manifestly outside the scope of this Regulation or if non-compliance with the formal conditions required makes service impossible, the request and

the documents transmitted shall be returned, on receipt, to the transmitting agency, together with the notice of return in the standard form in the Annex.

4. A receiving agency receiving a document for service but not having territorial jurisdiction to serve it shall forward it, as well as the request, to the receiving agency having territorial jurisdiction in the same Member State if the request complies with the conditions laid down in Article 4(3) and shall inform the transmitting agency accordingly, using the standard form in the Annex. That receiving agency shall inform the transmitting agency when it receives the document, in the manner provided for in paragraph 1.

Article 7
Service of documents

1. The receiving agency shall itself serve the document or have it served, either in accordance with the law of the Member State addressed or by a particular form requested by the transmitting agency, unless such a method is incompatible with the law of that Member State.

2. All steps required for service of the document shall be effected as soon as possible. In any event, if it has not been possible to effect service within one month of receipt, the receiving agency shall inform the transmitting agency by means of the certificate in the standard form in the Annex, which shall be drawn up under the conditions referred to in Article 10(2). The period shall be calculated in accordance with the law of the Member State addressed.

Article 8
Refusal to accept a document

1. The receiving agency shall inform the addressee that he or she may refuse to accept the document to be served if it is in a language other than either of the following languages:

(a) the official language of the Member State addressed or, if there are several official languages in that Member State, the official language or one of the official languages of the place where service is to be effected; or

(b) a language of the Member State of transmission which the addressee understands.

2. Where the receiving agency is informed that the addressee refuses to accept the document in accordance with paragraph 1, it shall immediately inform the transmitting agency by means of the certificate provided for in Article 10 and return the request and the documents of which a translation is requested.

Article 9
Date of service

1. Without prejudice to Article 8, the date of service of a document pursuant to Article 7 shall be the date on which it is served in accordance with the law of the Member State addressed.

2. However, where a document shall be served within a particular period in the context of proceedings to be brought or pending in the Member State of origin, the date to be taken into account with respect to the applicant shall be that fixed by the law of that Member State.

3. A Member State shall be authorised to derogate from the provisions of paragraphs 1 and 2 for a transitional period of five years, for appropriate reasons. This transitional period may be renewed by a Member State at five-yearly intervals due to reasons related to its legal system. That Member State shall inform the Commission of the content of such a derogation and the circumstances of the case.

Article 10
Certificate of service and copy of the document served

1. When the formalities concerning the service of the document have been completed, a certificate of completion of those formalities shall be drawn up in the standard form in the Annex and addressed to the transmitting agency, together with, where Article 4(5) applies, a copy of the document served.

2. The certificate shall be completed in the official language or one of the official languages of the Member State of origin or in another language which the Member State of origin has indicated that it can accept. Each Member State shall indicate the official language or languages of the European Union other than its own which is or are acceptable to it for completion of the form.

Article 11
Costs of service

1. The service of judicial documents coming from a Member State shall not give rise to any payment or reimbursement of taxes or costs for services rendered by the Member State addressed.

2. The applicant shall pay or reimburse the costs occasioned by:

   (a) the employment of a judicial officer or of a person competent under the law of the Member State addressed;
   (b) the use of a particular method of service.

SECTION 2
OTHER MEANS OF TRANSMISSION AND SERVICE OF JUDICIAL DOCUMENTS

Article 12
Transmission by consular or diplomatic channels

Each Member State shall be free, in exceptional circumstances, to use consular or diplomatic channels to forward judicial documents, for the purpose of service, to those agencies of another Member State which are designated pursuant to Article 2 or 3.

Article 13
Service by diplomatic or consular agents

1. Each Member State shall be free to effect service of judicial documents on persons residing in another Member State, without application of any compulsion, directly through its diplomatic or consular agents.

2. Any Member State may make it known, in accordance with Article 23(1), that it is opposed to such service within its territory, unless the documents are to be served on nationals of the Member State in which the documents originate.

Article 14
Service by post

1. Each Member State shall be free to effect service of judicial documents directly by post to persons residing in another Member State.

2. Any Member State may specify, in accordance with Article 23(1), the conditions under which it will accept service of judicial documents by post.

Article 15
Direct service

1. This Regulation shall not interfere with the freedom of any person interested in a judicial proceeding to effect service of judicial documents directly through the judicial officers, officials or other competent persons of the Member State addressed.

2. Any Member State may make it known, in accordance with Article 23(1), that it is opposed to the service of judicial documents in its territory pursuant to paragraph 1.

Chapter III
Extrajudicial documents

Article 16
Transmission

Extrajudicial documents may be transmitted for service in another Member State in accordance with the provisions of this Regulation.

Chapter IV
Final provisions

Article 17
Implementing rules

The measures necessary for the implementation of this Regulation relating to the matters referred to below shall be adopted in accordance with the advisory procedure referred to in Article 18(2):

(a) drawing up and annually updating a manual containing the information provided by Member States in accordance with Article 2(4);
(b) drawing up a glossary in the official languages of the European Union of documents which may be served under this Regulation;
(c) updating or making technical amendments to the standard form set out in the Annex.

Article 18
Committee

1. The Commission shall be assisted by a committee.

2. Where reference is made to this paragraph, Articles 3 and 7 of Decision 1999/468/EC shall apply.

3. The Committee shall adopt its rules of procedure.

Article 19
Defendant not entering an appearance

1. Where a writ of summons or an equivalent document has had to be transmitted to another Member State for the purpose of service, under the provisions of this Regulation, and the defendant has not appeared, judgment shall not be given until it is established that:

(a) the document was served by a method prescribed by the internal law of the Member State addressed for the service of documents in domestic actions upon persons who are within its territory; or
(b) the document was actually delivered to the defendant or to his residence by another method provided for by this Regulation;

and that in either of these cases the service or the delivery was effected in sufficient time to enable the defendant to defend.

2. Each Member State shall be free to make it known, in accordance with Article 23(1), that the judge, notwithstanding the provisions of paragraph 1, may give judgment even if no certificate of service or delivery has been received, if all the following conditions are fulfilled:

(a) the document was transmitted by one of the methods provided for in this Regulation;
(b) a period of time of not less than six months, considered adequate by the judge in the particular case, has elapsed since the date of the transmission of the document;
(c) no certificate of any kind has been received, even though every reasonable effort has been made to obtain it through the competent authorities or bodies of the Member State addressed.

3. Notwithstanding paragraphs 1 and 2, the judge may order, in case of urgency, any provisional or protective measures.

4. When a writ of summons or an equivalent document has had to be transmitted to another Member State for the purpose of service, under the provisions of this Regulation, and a judgment has been entered against a defendant who has not appeared, the judge shall have the power to relieve the defendant from the effects of the expiration of the time for appeal from the judgment if the following conditions are fulfilled:

(a) the defendant, without any fault on his part, did not have knowledge of the document in sufficient time to defend, or knowledge of the judgment in sufficient time to appeal; and
(b) the defendant has disclosed a prima facie defence to the action on the merits.

An application for relief may be filed only within a reasonable time after the defendant has knowledge of the judgment.

Each Member State may make it known, in accordance with Article 23(1), that such application will not be entertained if it is filed after the expiration of a time to be stated by it in that communication, but which shall in no case be less than one year following the date of the judgment.

5. Paragraph 4 shall not apply to judgments concerning status or capacity of persons.

Article 20
Relationship with agreements or arrangements to which Member States are Parties

1. This Regulation shall, in relation to matters to which it applies, prevail over other provisions contained in bilateral or multilateral agreements or arrangements concluded by the Member States, and in particular Article IV of the Protocol to the Brussels Convention of 1968 and the Hague Convention of 15 November 1965.

2. This Regulation shall not preclude individual Member States from maintaining or concluding agreements or arrangements to expedite further or simplify the transmission of documents, provided that they are compatible with this Regulation.

3. Member States shall send to the Commission:

(a) a copy of the agreements or arrangements referred to in paragraph 2 concluded between the Member States as well as drafts of such agreements or arrangements which they intend to adopt; and

(b) any denunciation of, or amendments to, these agreements or arrangements.

Article 21
Legal aid

This Regulation shall not affect the application of Article 23 of the Convention on Civil Procedure of 17 July 1905, Article 24 of the Convention on Civil Procedure of 1 March 1954 or Article 13 of the Convention on International Access to Justice of 25 October 1980 between the Member States Parties to these Conventions.

Article 22
Protection of information transmitted

1. Information, including in particular personal data, transmitted under this Regulation shall be used by the receiving agency only for the purpose for which it was transmitted.

2. Receiving agencies shall ensure the confidentiality of such information, in accordance with their national law.

3. Paragraphs 1 and 2 shall not affect national laws enabling data subjects to be informed of the use made of information transmitted under this Regulation.

4. This Regulation shall be without prejudice to Directives 95/46/EC and 97/66/EC.

Article 23
Communication and publication

1. Member States shall communicate to the Commission the information referred to in Articles 2, 3, 4, 9, 10, 13, 14, 15, 17(a) and 19.

2. The Commission shall publish in the Official Journal of the European Communities the information referred to in paragraph 1.

Article 24
Review

No later than 1 June 2004, and every five years thereafter, the Commission shall present to the European Parliament, the Council and the Economic and Social Committee a report on the application of this Regulation, paying special attention to the effectiveness of the bodies designated pursuant to Article 2 and to the practical application of point (c) of Article 3 and Article 9. The report shall be accompanied if need be by proposals for adaptations of this Regulation in line with the evolution of notification systems.

Article 25
Entry into force

This Regulation shall enter into force on 31 May 2001.

This Regulation shall be binding in its entirety and directly applicable in the Member States in accordance with the Treaty establishing the European Community.

Done at Brussels, 29 May 2000.

For the Council

The President

A Costa

PRACTICE DIRECTION – LITIGATION FRIENDS
THIS PRACTICE DIRECTION SUPPLEMENTS PART 7, SECTION 1 OF THE FAMILY PROCEDURE (ADOPTION) RULES 2005

General

1.1 In this Practice Direction 'non-subject child' means a person under 18 years old who is a party to the proceedings but is not the subject of the proceedings and 'patient' means a person who by reason of mental disorder within the meaning of the Mental Health Act 1983 is incapable of managing and administering his property and affairs.[1]

1.2 A patient must have a litigation friend to conduct proceedings on his behalf (see paragraph 2 for the definition of a litigation friend).

1.3 In the proceedings referred to in paragraph 1.2 the patient should be referred to in the title as 'A.B. (by C.D. his litigation friend)'.

1.4 A non-subject child must have a litigation friend to conduct proceedings on his behalf unless the rule 51 applies.

1.5 A child[2] who does not have a children's guardian must have a litigation friend to conduct proceedings on his behalf unless rule 51 applies and any reference to non-subject child in this Practice Direction is to be taken as including a child.

1.6 Where –

(1) the non-subject child has a litigation friend, he or she should be referred to in the title to proceedings as 'A.B. (a child by C.D. his litigation friend)'; and
(2) the non-subject child is conducting proceedings on his own behalf, he or she should be referred to in the title as 'A.B. (a child)'.

The litigation friend

2.1 It is the duty of a litigation friend fairly and competently to conduct proceedings on behalf of a non-subject child or patient. He must have no interest in the proceedings adverse to that of the non-subject child or patient and all steps and decisions he takes in the proceedings must be taken for the benefit of the non-subject child or patient.

2.2 A person may become a litigation friend of a non-subject child or a patient –

(a) without a court order under the provisions of rule 54; or
(b) by a court order under rule 55.

2.3 In order to become a litigation friend without a court order the person who wishes to act as litigation friend must –

(1) if he wishes to act on behalf of a patient, file an official copy of the order or other document which constitutes the authorisation to act under Part VII of the Mental Health Act 1983; or

---

1 See rule 49(1).
2 'Child' means a person under the age of 18 years who is the subject of the proceedings, and in adoption proceedings, also includes a person who has attained the age of 18 years before the proceedings are concluded.

(2) if he wishes to act on behalf of a non-subject child, or on behalf of a patient without the authorisation referred to in (1) above, file a certificate of suitability in form FP9 –[1]
   (a) stating that he consents to act;
   (b) stating that he knows or believes that the [applicant] [respondent] is a [non-subject child] [patient];
   (c) in the case of a patient, stating the grounds of his belief and if his belief is based upon medical opinion attaching any relevant document to the certificate;
   (d) stating that he can fairly and competently conduct proceedings on behalf of the non-subject child or patient and has no interest adverse to that of the non-subject child or patient;
   (e) undertaking to pay any costs which the non-subject child or patient may be ordered to pay in relation to the proceedings, subject to any right he may have to be repaid from the assets of the non-subject child or patient; and
   (f) which he has signed in verification of its contents.

2.4 Paragraph 2.3 does not apply to the Official Solicitor, an officer of the Service or a Welsh family proceedings officer.

2.5 The court officer will send the certificate of suitability –[2]

(1) in the case of a non-subject child (who is not also a patient) to one of the non-subject child's parents or guardians or if there is no parent or guardian, to the person with whom the non-subject child resides or in whose care the non-subject child is; and
(2) in the case of a patient to the person authorised under Part VII of the Mental Health Act 1983 to conduct proceedings on behalf of the patient or if there is no person so authorised, to the person with whom the patient resides or in whose care the patient is.

2.6 The court officer is not required to send the documents referred to in paragraph 2.3(2)(c) when he sends the certificate of suitability to the person to be served under paragraph 2.5.

2.7 The litigation friend must file either the certificate of suitability or the authority referred to in paragraph 2.3(1) at a time when he first takes a step in the proceedings on behalf of the non-subject child or patient.

Application for a court order appointing a litigation friend

3.1 Rule 55 sets out who may apply for an order appointing a litigation friend.

3.2 An application should be made in accordance with Part 9 and must be supported by evidence.

3.3 The court officer must serve the application notice –

(1) on the persons referred to in paragraph 2.5; and
(2) where the application is in respect of a patient, on the patient unless the court directs otherwise.

3.4 The evidence in support must satisfy the court that the proposed litigation friend –

(1) consents to act;
(2) can fairly and competently conduct proceedings on behalf of the non-subject child or patient;

---

1 See rule 54(4)(b).
2 See rule 54(5).

(3) has no interest adverse to that of the non-subject child or patient; and
(4) undertakes to pay any costs which the non-subject child or patient may be ordered to pay in relation to the proceedings, subject to any right he may have to be repaid from the assets of the non-subject child or patient.

3.5 Paragraph 3.4(4) does not apply to the Official Solicitor, an officer of the Service or a Welsh family proceedings officer.

3.6 The proposed litigation friend must satisfy the conditions in paragraphs 3.4(1), (2) and (3) and may be one of the persons referred to in paragraph 2.5 where appropriate, or otherwise may be the Official Solicitor, an officer of the Service or a Welsh family proceedings officer. Where it is sought to appoint the Official Solicitor, an officer of the Service or a Welsh family proceedings officer, provision should be made for payment of his charges.

Change of litigation friend and prevention of person acting as litigation friend

4.1 Rule 56(1) states that the court may –

(1) direct that a person may not act as a litigation friend;
(2) terminate a litigation friend's appointment; or
(3) substitute a new litigation friend for an existing one.

4.2 Where an application is made for an order under rule 56(1), the application notice must set out the reasons for seeking it. The application must be supported by evidence.

4.3 Subject to paragraph 3.5, if the order sought is the substitution of a new litigation friend for an existing one, the evidence must satisfy the court of the matters set out in paragraph 3.4.

4.4 The court officer will serve the application notice on –

(1) the persons referred to in paragraph 2.5; and
(2) the litigation friend or person purporting to act as litigation friend.

Procedure where the need for a litigation friend has come to an end

5.1 Rule 58 deals with the situation where the need for a litigation friend comes to an end during the proceedings because either –

(1) a non-subject child who is not also a patient reaches the age of 18 (full age) during the proceedings; or
(2) a patient ceases to be a patient (recovers).

5.2 The court officer will send a notice to the other parties informing them that the appointment of a non-subject child or patient's litigation friend has ceased.

5.3 A non-subject child who reaches full age will subsequently be described in the proceedings as 'A.B. (formerly a child but now of full age)'.

5.4 Where a patient recovers, an application under rule 58(3) must be made for an order under rule 58(2) that the litigation friend's appointment has ceased.

5.5 The application must be supported by the following evidence –

(1) a medical report indicating that the patient has recovered and that he is capable of managing and administering his property and affairs; and
(2) where the patient's affairs were under the control of the Court of Protection, a copy of the order or notice discharging the receiver.

PRACTICE DIRECTION – COMMUNICATION OF INFORMATION RELATING TO PROCEEDINGS

THIS PRACTICE DIRECTION SUPPLEMENTS PART 8, RULE 78(1)(B) OF THE FAMILY PROCEDURE (ADOPTION) RULES 2005

Communication of information relating to proceedings

1.1 Rule 78 deals with the communication of information (whether or not it is recorded in any form) relating to proceedings.

1.2 Subject to any direction of the court, information may be communicated for the purposes of the law relating to contempt in accordance with paragraphs 1.3 or 1.4.

1.3 A person specified in the first column of the following table may communicate to a person listed in the second column such information as is specified in the third column for the purpose or purposes specified in the fourth column.

Communication of information without permission of the court

Communicated by	To	Information	Purpose
A party	A lay adviser or a McKenzie Friend	Any information relating to the proceedings	To enable the party to obtain advice or assistance in relation to the proceedings.
A party	The party's spouse, civil partner, cohabitant or close family member		For the purpose of confidential discussions enabling the party to receive support from his spouse, civil partner, cohabitant or close family member.
A party	A health care professional or a person or body providing counselling services for children or families		To enable the party or any child of the party to obtain health care or counselling.

Communicated by	To	Information	Purpose
A party or any person lawfully in receipt of information	The Children's Commissioner or the Children's Commissioner for Wales		To refer an issue affecting the interests of children to the Children's Commissioner or the Children's Commissioner for Wales.
A party or a legal representative	A mediator		For the purpose of mediation in relation to the proceedings.
A party, any person lawfully in receipt of information or a proper officer	A person or body conducting an approved research project		For the purpose of an approved research project.
A party, a legal representative or a professional legal adviser	A person or body responsible for investigating or determining complaints in relation to legal representatives or professional legal advisers		For the purposes of making a complaint or the investigation or determination of a complaint in relation to a legal representative or a professional legal adviser.
A legal representative or a professional legal adviser	A person or body assessing quality assurance systems		To enable the legal representative or professional legal adviser to obtain a quality assurance assessment.
A legal representative or a professional legal adviser	An accreditation body	Any information relating to the proceedings providing that it does not, or is not likely to, identify any person involved in the proceedings	To enable the legal representative or professional legal adviser to obtain accreditation.

Communicated by	To	Information	Purpose
A party	An elected representative or peer	The text or summary of the whole or part of a judgment given in the proceedings	To enable the elected representative or peer to give advice, investigate any complaint or raise any question of policy or procedure.
A party	The General Medical Council		For the purpose of making a complaint to the General Medical Council.
A party	A police officer		For the purpose of a criminal investigation.
A party or any person lawfully in receipt of information	A member of the Crown Prosecution Service		To enable the Crown Prosecution Service to discharge its functions under any enactment.

1.4 A person in the second column of the table in paragraph 1.3 may only communicate information relating to the proceedings received from a person in the first column for the purpose or purposes –

(a) for which he received that information, or
(b) of professional development or training, providing that any communication does not, or is not likely to, identify any person involved in the proceedings without that person's consent.

1.5 In this Practice Direction –

(1) 'accreditation body' means –
    (a) The Law Society,
    (b) Resolution, or
    (c) The Legal Services Commission;
(2) 'approved research project' means a project of research –
    (a) approved in writing by a Secretary of State after consultation with the President of the Family Division,
    (b) approved in writing by the President of the Family Division, or
    (c) conducted under section 83 of the Act of 1989 or section 13 of the Criminal Justice and Court Services Act 2000;
(3) 'body assessing quality assurance systems' includes –
    (a) The Law Society,
    (b) The Legal Services Commission, or
    (c) The General Council of the Bar;
(4) 'body or person responsible for investigating or determining complaints in relation to legal representatives or professional legal advisers' means –
    (a) The Law Society,

(b) The General Council of the Bar,
(c) The Institute of Legal Executives, or
(d) The Legal Services Ombudsman;
(5) 'cohabitant' means one of two persons who are neither married to each other nor civil partners of each other but are living together as husband and wife or as if they were civil partners;
(6) 'criminal investigation' means an investigation conducted by police officers with a view to it being ascertained –
(a) whether a person should be charged with an offence, or
(b) whether a person charged with an offence is guilty of it;
(7) 'elected representative' means –
(a) a member of the House of Commons,
(b) a member of the National Assembly for Wales, or
(c) a member of the European Parliament elected in England and Wales;
(8) 'health care professional' means –
(a) a registered medical practitioner,
(b) a registered nurse or midwife,
(c) a clinical psychologist, or
(d) a child psychotherapist;
(9) 'lay adviser' means a non-professional person who gives lay advice on behalf of an organisation in the lay advice sector;
(10) 'McKenzie Friend' means any person permitted by the court to sit beside an unrepresented litigant in court to assist that litigant by prompting, taking notes and giving him advice;
(11) 'mediator' means a family mediator who is –
(a) undertaking, or has successfully completed, a family mediation training course approved by the United Kingdom College of Family Mediators, or
(b) a member of the Law Society's Family Mediation Panel;
(12) 'peer' means a member of the House of Lords as defined by the House of Lords Act 1999.

PRACTICE DIRECTION – DISCLOSING INFORMATION TO AN ADOPTED ADULT

THIS PRACTICE DIRECTION SUPPLEMENTS PART 8, RULE 84(1)(D) OF THE FAMILY PROCEDURE (ADOPTION) RULES 2005

How to request for information

1.1 Rule 84 states that an adopted person who is over the age of 18 has the right to receive from the court which made the adoption order a copy of –

(a) the application form for an adoption order (but not the documents attached to that form);
(b) the adoption order and any other orders relating to the adoption proceedings; and
(c) orders allowing any person contact with the child after the adoption order was made.

1.2 An application under rule 84 must be made in form A64 which is contained in the practice direction supplementing rule 17 and must have attached to it a full certified copy of the entry in the Adopted Children Register relating to the applicant.

1.3 The completed application form must be taken to the court which made the adoption order along with evidence of the applicant's identity showing a photograph and signature, such as a passport or driving licence.

Additional documents that the adopted person is also entitled to receive from the court

2 The adopted adult is also entitled to receive the following documents –

(a) any transcript or written reasons of the court's decision; and
(b) a report made to the court by –
   (i) a children's guardian, reporting officer or children and family reporter;
   (ii) a local authority; or
   (iii) an adoption agency.

Before the documents are sent to the adopted adult

3 The court will remove protected information from documents before they are sent to the adopted adult.

PRACTICE DIRECTION – OTHER APPLICATIONS IN PROCEEDINGS

THIS PRACTICE DIRECTION SUPPLEMENTS PART 9 OF THE FAMILY PROCEDURE (ADOPTION) RULES 2005

Application of Part 9

1 All applications for the court's permission should be made under this Part other than applications for permission to:

(a) change a child's surname; or
(b) remove a child from the jurisdiction,

which should be made by in accordance with Part 5.

Application notices

2.1 An application notice must, in addition to the matters set out in rule 90, be signed and include:

(a) the title of the case (if available);
(b) the reference number of the case (if available);
(c) the full name of the applicant;
(d) where the applicant is not already a party, his address including a postcode,[1] save that if the applicant does not wish his address to be revealed to any other party he may give his address to the court in a separate form prescribed for that purpose; and
(e) either a request for a hearing or a request that the application be dealt with without a hearing.

(Form FP2 may be used.)

2.2 In addition to the matters set out in rule 90 and paragraph 2.1, an application notice relating to an application under section 42(6) (permission to apply for an adoption order) must include:

(a) the child's name, sex, date of birth and nationality;
(b) in relation to each of the child's parents or guardian, their name, address and nationality;
(c) the length of time that the child has had his home with the applicant;
(d) the reason why the child has his home with the applicant;
(e) details of any local authority or adoption agency involved in placing the child in the applicant's home; and
(f) if there are or have been other court proceedings relating to the child, the nature of those proceedings, the name of the court in which they are being or have been dealt with, the date and type of any order made and, if the proceedings are still ongoing, the date of the next hearing.

2.3 On receipt of an application notice containing a request for a hearing, unless the court considers that the application is suitable for consideration without a hearing, the court officer will notify the applicant of the time and date fixed for the hearing of the application.

---

1 Postcode information may be obtained from www.royalmail.com or the Royal Mail Address Management Guide.

2.4 On receipt of an application notice containing a request that the application be dealt with without a hearing, the court will decide whether the application is suitable for consideration without a hearing.

2.5 Where the court considers that the application is suitable for consideration without a hearing, it may give directions for the filing of evidence and the court officer will inform the applicant and the respondent(s) of the court's decision. (Rules 93 and 94 enable a party to apply for an order made without a hearing to be set aside or varied.)

2.6 Where the court does not agree that the application is suitable for consideration without a hearing it may give directions as to the filing of evidence and the court officer will notify the applicant and the respondent of the time, date and place for the hearing of the application and any directions given.

2.7 Every application should be made as soon as it becomes apparent that it is necessary or desirable to make it.

2.8 Applications should wherever possible be made so that they can be considered at any directions hearing or other hearing for which a date has already been fixed or for which a date is about to be fixed.

2.9 The parties must anticipate that at any hearing (including any directions hearing) the court may wish to review the conduct of the case as a whole and give any necessary directions. They should be ready to assist the court in doing so and to answer questions the court may ask for this purpose.

2.10 Where a date for a hearing has been fixed and a party wishes to make an application at that hearing but he does not have sufficient time to file an application notice he should inform the court (if possible in writing) and, if possible, the other parties as soon as he can of the nature of the application and the reason for it. He should then make the application orally at the hearing.

Applications without service of application notice

3 An application may be made without the court officer serving an application notice only:

(1) where there is exceptional urgency;
(2) where the overriding objective is best furthered by doing so;
(3) by consent of all parties;
(4) with the permission of the court;
(5) where paragraph 2.10 applies; or
(6) where a rule or practice direction permits.

Giving notice of an application

4 Unless the court directs otherwise or paragraph 3 of this Practice Direction applies the application notice will be served, by a court officer, as soon as practicable after it has been issued and, if there is to be a hearing, at least 7 clear days before the hearing date.

Telephone hearings

5.1 The court may direct that an application or part of an application be dealt with by a telephone hearing.

5.2 The applicant should indicate on his application notice if he seeks a direction under paragraph 5.1. Where he has not done so but nevertheless wishes to seek an order the request should be made as early as possible.

5.3 A direction under 5.1 will not normally be made unless every party entitled to be given notice of the application and to be heard at the hearing has consented to the order.

5.4

(1) Where a party entitled to be heard at the hearing of the application is acting in person, the court –
   (a) may not make a direction under 5.1 except on condition that arrangements will be made for the party acting in person to be attended at the telephone hearing by a responsible person to whom the party acting in person is known and who can confirm to the court the identity of the party; and
   (b) may not give effect to a direction under 5.1 unless the party acting in person is accompanied by a responsible person who at the commencement of the hearing confirms to the court the identity of the party;

(2) the 'responsible person' may be a barrister, solicitor, legal executive, doctor, clergyman, police officer, prison officer or other person of comparable status; and

(3) if the court makes a direction under 5.1 it will give any directions necessary for a telephone hearing.

5.5 No representative of a party to an application being heard by telephone may attend the court in person while the application is being heard unless the other parties to the application have agreed that he may do so.

5.6 If an application is to be heard by telephone the following directions will apply, subject to any direction to the contrary:

(1) the applicant's legal representative must arrange the telephone conference for precisely the time fixed by the court. The telecommunications provider must be capable of connecting the parties and the court;

(2) he must tell the operator the telephone numbers of all those participating in the conference call and the sequence in which they are to be called;

(3) it is the responsibility of the applicant's legal representative to ascertain from all the other parties whether they have instructed counsel, and whether the legal representative and counsel will be on the same or different telephone numbers;

(4) the sequence in which they are to be called will be:
   (a) the applicant's legal representative and (if on a different number) his counsel
   (b) the legal representative (or counsel) for all other parties; and
   (c) the judge, district judge or justices, as the case may be;

(5) the applicant's legal representative must arrange for the conference to be recorded on tape by the telecommunications provider whose system is being used and must send the tape to the court;

(6) each speaker is to remain on the line after being called by the operator setting up the conference call. The call may be 2 or 3 minutes before the time fixed for the application;

(7) when the judge, district judge or justices have been connected the applicant's legal representative (or his counsel) will introduce the parties in the usual way;

(8) if the use of a 'speaker phone' by any party causes the court or any other party difficulty in hearing what is said the court may require the party to use a hand held telephone; and

(9) the telephone charges debited to the account of the party initiating the conference call will be treated as part of the costs of the application.

Video conferencing

6 Where the parties to a matter wish to use video conferencing facilities, and those facilities are available in the relevant court, they should apply to the court for directions.

(Paragraph 27 and Annex 3 of the practice direction supplementing Part 15 provide guidance on the use of video conferencing)

Note of proceedings

7   The court or court officer should keep, either by way of a note or a tape recording, brief details of all proceedings before the court, including the dates of the proceedings and a short statement of the decision taken at each hearing.

Evidence

8.1   The requirement for evidence in certain types of applications is set out in some of the rules and practice directions. Where there is no specific requirement to provide evidence it should be borne in mind that, as a practical matter, the court will often need to be satisfied by evidence of the facts that are relied on in support of or for opposing the application.

8.2   The court may give directions for the filing of evidence in support or opposing a particular application. The court may also give directions for the filing of evidence in relation to any hearing that it fixes on its own initiative. The directions may specify the form that evidence is to take and when it is to be served.

8.3   Where it is intended to rely on evidence which is not contained in the application itself, the evidence, if it has not already been served, should be served with the application.

8.4   Where a respondent to an application wishes to rely on evidence it must be filed in accordance with any directions the court may have given and a court officer will serve the evidence on the other parties, unless the court directs otherwise.

8.5   If it is necessary for the applicant to file any evidence in reply the court officer will serve it on the other parties, unless the court directs otherwise.

8.6   Evidence must be filed with the court as well as served on the parties. Exhibits should not be filed unless the court otherwise directs.

8.7   The contents of an application notice may be used as evidence provided that the contents have been verified by a statement of truth.

Consent orders

9.1   The parties to an application for a consent order must ensure that they provide the court with any material it needs to be satisfied that it is appropriate to make the order. Subject to any rule or practice direction a letter will generally be acceptable for this purpose.

9.2   Where a judgment or order has been agreed in respect of an application where a hearing date has been fixed, the parties must inform the court immediately.

Other applications considered without a hearing

10.1   Where rule 92(b) applies the parties should so inform the court in writing and each should confirm that all evidence and other material on which he relies has been disclosed to the other parties to the application.

10.2   Where rule 92(c) applies the court will treat the application as if it were proposing to make an order on its own initiative.

Miscellaneous

11.1 Except in the most simple application the applicant should bring to any hearing a draft of the order sought. If the case is proceeding in the High Court and the order is unusually long or complex it should also be supplied on disk for use by the court office.

11.2 Where rule 95 applies the power to re-list the application in rule 95(2) is in addition to any other powers of the court with regard to the order (for example to set aside, vary, discharge or suspend the order).

Costs

12. Attention is also drawn to rule 44.13(i) of the CPR which provides that if an order makes no mention of costs, none are payable in respect of the proceedings to which it relates.

PRACTICE DIRECTION – ALTERNATIVE PROCEDURE FOR APPLICATIONS

THIS PRACTICE DIRECTION SUPPLEMENTS PART 10 OF THE FAMILY PROCEDURE (ADOPTION) RULES 2005

Types of application in which Part 10 procedure may be used

1.1 An applicant must use the Part 10 procedure if the application is for an order under –

(a) section 60(3), to prevent disclosure of information to an adopted person;
(b) section 79(4), to require the Registrar General to provide information; or
(c) rule 108, to request directions of the High Court regarding fathers without parental responsibility.

1.2 An applicant may use the Part 10 procedure if Part 9 does not apply and if –

(a) there is no prescribed form in which to make the application; or
(b) he seeks the court's decision on a question which is unlikely to involve a substantial dispute of fact.

1.3 An applicant may also use the Part 10 procedure if a practice direction permits or requires its use for the type of proceedings concerned.

1.4 The practice directions referred to in paragraphs 1.3 may in some respects modify or disapply the Part 10 procedure and, where that is so, it is those practice directions that must be complied with.

1.5 The types of application for which the Part 10 procedure may be used include an application for an order or direction which is unopposed by each respondent before the commencement of proceedings and the sole purpose of the application is to obtain the approval of the court to the agreement.

1.6 The court may at any stage order the application to continue as if the applicant had not used the Part 10 procedure and, if it does so, the court will give such directions as it considers appropriate.

The application

2.1 Where an applicant uses the Part 10 procedure, application form FP1 should be used and must state the matters set out in rule 98 and, if paragraphs 1.3 or 1.4 apply, must comply with the practice direction in question. In particular, the application must state that Part 10 applies. A Part 10 application means an application which so states.

2.2 An application –

(a) in accordance with rule 108, to ask the High Court for directions on the need to give a father without parental responsibility notice of the intention to place a child for adoption; or
(b) under section 60(3), for an order to prevent disclosure of information to an adopted person

may be issued without naming a respondent.

Responding to the application

3.1 Where a respondent who wishes to respond to a Part 10 application is required to file an acknowledgement of service, that acknowledgement of service should be in form FP5 but can, alternatively, be given in an informal document such as a letter.

3.2 Rule 100 sets out provisions relating to an acknowledgement of service of a Part 10 application.

3.3 Rule 101 sets out the consequence of failing to file an acknowledgement of service.

3.4 Where a respondent believes that the Part 10 procedure should not be used because there is a substantial dispute of fact or, as the case may be, because its use is not authorised by any rule or practice direction, he must state his reasons in writing when he files his acknowledgement of service.

Managing the application

4.1 The court may give directions immediately a Part 10 application is issued either on the application of a party or on its own initiative. The directions may include fixing a hearing date where –

(a) there is no dispute; or
(b) where there may be a dispute but a hearing date could conveniently be given.

4.2 Where the court does not fix a hearing date when the application is issued, it will give directions for the disposal of the application as soon as practicable after each respondent has acknowledged service of the application or, as the case may be, after the period for acknowledging service has expired.

4.3 Certain applications may not require a hearing.

4.4 The court may convene a directions hearing before giving directions.

Evidence

5.1 An applicant wishing to rely on written evidence should file it with his Part 10 application (unless the evidence is contained in the application form itself).

5.2 Evidence will normally be in the form of a witness statement or an affidavit but an applicant may rely on the matters set out in the application provided that it has been verified by a statement of truth.

5.3 A respondent wishing to rely on written evidence should file it with his acknowledgement of service.

5.4 Rule 102 sets out the times and provisions for filing and serving written evidence.

5.5 The court may give a party an extension of time to serve and file evidence under rule 102 or may give permission to serve and file additional evidence under rule 103(1).

PRACTICE DIRECTION – HUMAN RIGHTS, JOINING THE CROWN

THIS PRACTICE DIRECTION SUPPLEMENTS PART 13 OF THE FAMILY PROCEDURE (ADOPTION) RULES 2005

Section 4 of the Human Rights Act 1998

1.1 Where a party has informed the court about –

(a) a claim for a declaration of incompatibility in accordance with section 4 of the Human Rights Act 1998; or

(b) an issue for the court to decide which may lead to the court considering making a declaration

then the court may at any time consider whether notice should be given to the Crown as required by that Act and give directions for the content and service of the notice. The rule allows a period of 21 days before the court will make the declaration but the court may vary this period of time.

1.2 The court will normally consider the issues and give the directions referred to in paragraph 1.1 at a directions hearing.

1.3 The notice must be served on the person named in the list published under section 17 of the Crown Proceedings Act 1947.

1.4 The notice will be in the form directed by the court and will normally include the directions given by the court. The notice will also be served on all the parties.

1.5 The court may require the parties to assist in the preparation of the notice.

1.6 Unless the court orders otherwise, the Minister or other person permitted by the Human Rights Act 1998 to be joined as a party must, if he wishes to be joined, give notice of his intention to be joined as a party to the court and every other party. Where the Minister has nominated a person to be joined as a party the notice must be accompanied by the written nomination.

(Section 5(2)(a) of the Human Rights Act 1998 permits a person nominated by a Minister of the Crown to be joined as a party. The nomination may be signed on behalf of the Minister.)

Section 9 of the Human Rights Act 1998

2.1 The procedure in paragraphs 1.1 to 1.6 also applies where a claim is made under sections 7(1)(a) and 9(3) of the Human Rights Act for damages in respect of a judicial act.

2.2 Notice must be given to the Lord Chancellor and should be served on the Treasury Solicitor on his behalf.

2.3 The notice will also give details of the judicial act, which is the subject of the claim for damages, and of the court that made it.

(Section 9(4) of the Human Rights Act 1998 provides that no award of damages may be made against the Crown as provided for in section 9(3) unless the appropriate person is joined in the proceedings. The appropriate person is the Minister responsible for the court concerned or a person or department nominated by him (section 9(5) of the Act).

PRACTICE DIRECTION – INTERIM INJUNCTIONS

THIS PRACTICE DIRECTION SUPPLEMENTS PART 14 OF THE FAMILY PROCEDURE (ADOPTION) RULES 2005

Making an application

2.1 The application notice must state –

(1) the order sought; and
(2) the date, time and place of the hearing.

2.2 Unless the court directs otherwise, the application notice and evidence in support must be served as soon as practicable after issue and in any event not less than 7 days before the court is due to hear the application.[1]

2.3 The applicant should file sufficient copies of the application notice and evidence in support for the court and for each respondent.

2.4 Whenever possible a draft of the order sought should be filed with the application notice and a disk containing the draft should also be available to the court in a format compatible with the word processing software used by the court. This will enable the court officer to arrange for any amendments to be incorporated and for the speedy preparation and sealing of the order.

Evidence

3.1 Applications for interim injunctions must be supported by evidence set out in either –

(1) a witness statement; or
(2) the application notice provided that it is verified by a statement of truth

unless the court, an Act, a rule or a practice direction requires evidence by affidavit.

3.2 The evidence must set out the facts on which the applicant relies for the application being made against the respondent, including all material facts of which the court should be made aware.

3.3 Where an application is made without notice to the respondent, the evidence must also set out why notice was not given.

(See Part 15 and the practice direction that supplements it for information about evidence.)

Urgent applications and applications without notice

4.1 These fall into two categories –

(1) applications where an application form in proceedings has already been issued; and
(2) applications where an application form in proceedings has not yet been issued;

and, in both cases, where notice of the application has not been given to the respondent.

4.2 These applications are normally dealt with at a court hearing but cases of extreme urgency may be dealt with by telephone.

4.3 Applications dealt with at a court hearing after issue of an application form –

---

1 See rule 91(1) and (2) and rule 91(4) (short notice).

(1) the application notice, evidence in support and a draft order (as in paragraph 2.4) should be filed with the court two hours before the hearing wherever possible;
(2) if an application is made before the application notice has been issued, a draft order (as in paragraph 2.4) should be provided at the hearing, and the application notice and evidence in support must be filed with the court on the same or next working day or as ordered by the court; and
(3) except in cases where secrecy is essential, the applicant should take steps to notify the respondent informally of the application.

4.4 Applications made before the issue of an application form –

(1) in addition to the provisions set out at paragraph 4.3, unless the court orders otherwise, either the applicant must undertake to the court to issue an application notice immediately or the court will give directions for the commencement of the application;[1] and
(2) an order made before the issue of an application form should state in the title after the names of the applicant and respondent 'the Applicant and Respondent in Intended Proceedings'.

4.5 Applications made outside normal working hours –

(1) where an application is made outside normal working hours the applicant should either –
   (a) telephone the Royal Courts of Justice on 020 7947 6000 where he will be put in contact with the clerk to the appropriate duty judge in the High Court (or the appropriate area Circuit Judge where known); or
   (b) the Urgent Court Business Officer of the appropriate Circuit who will contact the local duty judge;
(2) where the facility is available it is likely that the judge will require a draft order to be faxed to him;
(3) the application notice and evidence in support must be filed with the court on the same or next working day or as ordered, together with two copies of the order for sealing; and
(4) injunctions will be heard by telephone only where the applicant is acting by counsel or solicitors.

Orders for injunctions

5.1 Any order for an injunction, unless the court orders otherwise, must contain –

(1) an undertaking by the applicant to the court to pay any damages which the respondent(s) (or any other party served with or notified of the order) sustain which the court considers the applicant should pay;
(2) if made without notice to any other party, an undertaking by the applicant to the court to serve on the respondent the application notice, evidence in support and any order made as soon as practicable;
(3) if made without notice to any other party, a return date for a further hearing at which the other party can be present;
(4) if made before filing the application notice, an undertaking to file and pay the appropriate fee on the same or next working day, and
(5) if made before issue of an application form in proceedings –
   (a) an undertaking to issue and pay the appropriate fee on the same or next working day; or

---

1 See rule 119(3).

(b) directions for the commencement of the proceedings.

5.2 An order for an injunction made in the presence of all parties to be bound by it or made at a hearing of which they have had notice, may state that it is effective until final hearing or further order.

5.3 Any order for an injunction must set out clearly what the respondent must do or not do.

PRACTICE DIRECTION – EVIDENCE

THIS PRACTICE DIRECTION SUPPLEMENTS PART 15 OF THE FAMILY PROCEDURE (ADOPTION) RULES 2005

Evidence in general

1.1 Rule 124 sets out how evidence is to be given and facts are to be proved.

1.2 Evidence at a hearing other than the final hearing should normally be given by witness statement[1] (see paragraph 17 onwards).

1.3 Application forms and application notices[2] may also be used as evidence provided that their contents have been verified by a statement of truth.[3]

(For information regarding evidence by deposition see Part 16 and the practice direction which supplements it.)

1.4 Affidavits must be used as evidence in the following instances –

(1) where sworn evidence is required by an enactment, rule, order or practice direction;
(2) in any application for an order against anyone for alleged contempt of court.

1.5 If a party believes that sworn evidence is required by a court in another jurisdiction for any purpose connected with the proceedings, he may apply to the court for a direction that evidence shall be given only by affidavit on any applications to be heard before the final hearing.

1.6 The court may give a direction under rule 134 that evidence shall be given by affidavit instead of or in addition to a witness statement –

(1) on its own initiative; or
(2) after any party has applied to the court for such a direction.

1.7 An affidavit, where referred to in the Rules or a practice direction, also means an affirmation unless the context requires otherwise.

Affidavits

Deponent

2 A deponent is a person who gives evidence by affidavit or affirmation.

Heading

3.1 The affidavit should be headed with the title of the proceedings where the proceedings are between several parties with the same status it is sufficient to identify the parties, subject to paragraph 4.2, as follows –

Number –
A.B. (and others)
Applicants

---

1 See rule 128(1).
2 See Part 9 for information about making an application.
3 See rule 128(2).

C.D. (and others)
Respondents
(as appropriate)

3.2 Subject to paragraph 4.2, at the top right hand corner of the first page (and on the backsheet) there should be clearly written –

(1) the party on whose behalf it is made;
(2) the initials and surname of the deponent;
(3) the number of the affidavit in relation to that deponent;
(4) the identifying initials and number of each exhibit referred to; and
(5) the date sworn.

Body of Affidavit

4.1 Subject to paragraph 4.2 and rule 21, the affidavit must, if practicable, be in the deponent's own words, the affidavit should be expressed in the first person and the deponent should –

(1) commence 'I (*full name*) of (*address*) state on oath …';
(2) if giving evidence in his professional, business or other occupational capacity, give the address at which he works in (1) above, the position he holds and the name of his firm or employer;
(3) give his occupation or, if he has none, his description; and
(4) state if he is a party to the proceedings or employed by a party to the proceedings, if it be the case.

4.2 If a serial number has been assigned under rule 20, the affidavit must be framed so that it does not disclose the identity of the applicant.

(Rule 21 provides that unless the court directs otherwise, a party is not required to reveal the address of his private residence)

4.3 An affidavit must indicate –

(1) which of the statements in it are made from the deponent's own knowledge and which are matters of information or belief; and
(2) the source for any matters of information or belief.

4.4 Where a deponent –

(1) refers to an exhibit or exhibits, he should state 'there is now shown to me marked "…" the (*description of exhibit*)'; and
(2) makes more than one affidavit (to which there are exhibits) in the same proceedings; the numbering of the exhibits should run consecutively throughout and not start again with each affidavit.

Jurat

5.1 The jurat of an affidavit is a statement set out at the end of the document which authenticates the affidavit.

5.2 It must –

(1) be signed by all deponents;
(2) be completed and signed by the person before whom the affidavit was sworn whose name and qualification must be printed beneath his signature;
(3) contain the full address of the person before whom the affidavit was sworn; and

(4) follow immediately on from the text and not be put on a separate page.

5.3 If a serial number has been assigned under rule 20 or the name of the witness is not being revealed in accordance with rule 21, the signature of the deponent will be edited from the affidavit before it is served on any other party.

Format of Affidavits

6.1 An affidavit should –

   (1) be produced on durable quality A4 paper with a 3.5cm margin;
   (2) be fully legible and should normally be typed on one side of the paper only;
   (3) where possible, be bound securely in a manner which would not hamper filing, or otherwise each page should be endorsed with the case number and should bear the initials of the deponent and of the person before whom it was sworn;
   (4) have the pages numbered consecutively as a separate document (or as one of several documents contained in a file);
   (5) be divided into numbered paragraphs;
   (6) have all numbers, including dates, expressed in figures; and
   (7) give the reference to any document or documents mentioned either in the margin or in bold text in the body of the affidavit.

6.2 It is usually convenient for an affidavit to follow the chronological sequence of events or matters dealt with; each paragraph of an affidavit should as far as possible be confined to a distinct portion of the subject.

Inability of Deponent to read or sign Affidavit

7.1 Where an affidavit is sworn by a person who is unable to read or sign it, the person before whom the affidavit is sworn must certify in the jurat that –

   (1) he read the affidavit to the deponent;
   (2) the deponent appeared to understand it; and
   (3) the deponent signed or made his mark, in his presence.

7.2 If that certificate is not included in the jurat, the affidavit may not be used in evidence unless the court is satisfied that it was read to the deponent and that he appeared to understand it. Two versions of the form of jurat with the certificate are set out at Annex 1 to this practice direction.

Alterations to Affidavits

8.1 Any alteration to an affidavit must be initialled by both the deponent and the person before whom the affidavit was sworn.

8.2 An affidavit which contains an alteration that has not been initialled may be filed or used in evidence only with the permission of the court.

Who may administer oaths and take Affidavits

9.1 Only the following may administer oaths and take affidavits –

(1) Commissioners for oaths;[1]
(2) Practising solicitors;[2]
(3) other persons specified by statute;[3]
(4) certain officials of the Supreme Court;[4]
(5) a circuit judge or district judge;[5]
(6) any justice of the peace;[6] and
(7) certain officials of any county court appointed by the judge of that court for the purpose.[7]

9.2 An affidavit must be sworn before a person independent of the parties or their representatives.

Filing of Affidavits

10.1 If the court directs that an affidavit is to be filed,[8] it must be filed in the court or Division, or Office or Registry of the court or Division where the action in which it was or is to be used, is proceeding or will proceed.

10.2 Where an affidavit is in a foreign language –

(1) the party wishing to rely on it –
    (a) must have it translated; and
    (b) must file the foreign language affidavit with the court; and
(2) the translator must sign the translation to certify that it is accurate.

Exhibits

Manner of Exhibiting Documents

11.1 A document used in conjunction with an affidavit should be –

(1) produced to and verified by the deponent, and remain separate from the affidavit; and
(2) identified by a declaration of the person before whom the affidavit was sworn.

11.2 The declaration should be headed with the name of the proceedings in the same way as the affidavit.

11.3 The first page of each exhibit should be marked –

(1) as in paragraph 3.2; and
(2) with the exhibit mark referred to in the affidavit.

---

1 Commissioners for Oaths Acts 1889 and 1891.
2 Section 81 of the Solicitors Act 1974.
3 Section 65 of the Administration of Justice Act 1985, Courts and Legal Services Act 1990, s 113 and the Commissioners for Oaths (Prescribed Bodies) Regulations 1994 and 1995.
4 Section 2 of the Commissioners for Oaths Act 1889.
5 Section 58 of the County Courts Act 1984.
6 CCA 1984, s 58.
7 CCA 1984, s 58.
8 See rules 123(1) and 126(3)(b).

Letters

12.1 Copies of individual letters should be collected together and exhibited in a bundle or bundles. They should be arranged in chronological order with the earliest at the top, and firmly secured.

12.2 When a bundle of correspondence is exhibited, the exhibit should have a front page attached stating that the bundle consists of original letters and copies. They should be arranged and secured as above and numbered consecutively.

Other documents

13.1 Photocopies instead of original documents may be exhibited provided the originals are made available for inspection by the other parties before the hearing and by the court at the hearing.

13.2 Court documents must not be exhibited (official copies of such documents prove themselves).

13.3 Where an exhibit contains more than one document, a front page should be attached setting out a list of the documents contained in the exhibit; the list should contain the dates of the documents.

Exhibits other than documents

14.1 Items other than documents should be clearly marked with an exhibit number or letter in such a manner that the mark cannot become detached from the exhibit.

14.2 Small items may be placed in a container and the container appropriately marked.

General provisions

15.1 Where an exhibit contains more than one document –

(1) the bundle should not be stapled but should be securely fastened in a way that does not hinder the reading of the documents; and
(2) the pages should be numbered consecutively at bottom centre.

15.2 Every page of an exhibit should be clearly legible; typed copies of illegible documents should be included, paginated with 'a' numbers.

15.3 Where affidavits and exhibits have become numerous, they should be put into separate bundles and the pages numbered consecutively throughout.

15.4 Where on account of their bulk the service of exhibits or copies of exhibits on the other parties would be difficult or impracticable, the directions of the court should be sought as to arrangements for bringing the exhibits to the attention of the other parties and as to their custody pending final hearing.

Affirmations

16 All provisions in this or any other practice direction relating to affidavits apply to affirmations with the following exceptions –

(1) the deponent should commence 'I (*name*) of (*address*) do solemnly and sincerely affirm ...'; and
(2) in the jurat the word 'sworn' is replaced by the word 'affirmed'.

Witness statements

Heading

17.1 The witness statement should be headed with the title of the proceedings; where the proceedings are between several parties with the same status it is sufficient to identify the parties, subject to paragraph 18.2, as follows –

Number –
A.B. (and others)
Applicants
C.D. (and others)
Respondents
(as appropriate)

17.2 Subject to paragraph 18.2, at the top right hand corner of the first page there should be clearly written –

(1) the party on whose behalf it is made;
(2) the initials and surname of the witness;
(3) the number of the statement in relation to that witness;
(4) the identifying initials and number of each exhibit referred to; and
(5) the date the statement was made.

Body of Witness Statement

18.1 Subject to paragraph 18.2 and rule 21, the witness statement must, if practicable, be in the intended witness's own words, the statement should be expressed in the first person and should also state –

(1) the full name of the witness;
(2) his place of residence or, if he is making the statement in his professional, business or other occupational capacity, the address at which he works, the position he holds and the name of his firm or employer;
(3) his occupation, or if he has none, his description; and
(4) the fact that he is a party to the proceedings or is the employee of such a party if it be the case.

18.2 If a serial number has been assigned under rule 20, the witness statement must be framed so that it does not disclose the identity of the applicant.

(Rule 21 provides that unless the court directs otherwise, a party is not required to reveal the address of his private residence)

18.3 A witness statement must indicate –

(1) which of the statements in it are made from the witness's own knowledge and which are matters of information or belief; and
(2) the source for any matters of information or belief.

18.4 An exhibit used in conjunction with a witness statement should be verified and identified by the witness and remain separate from the witness statement.

18.5 Where a witness refers to an exhibit or exhibits, he should state 'I refer to the (*description of exhibit*) marked "…" '.

18.6 The provisions of paragraphs 11.3 to 15.4 (exhibits) apply similarly to witness statements as they do to affidavits.

18.7 Where a witness makes more than one witness statement to which there are exhibits, in the same proceedings, the numbering of the exhibits should run consecutively throughout and not start again with each witness statement.

Format of Witness Statement

19.1 A witness statement should –

(1) be produced on durable quality A4 paper with a 3.5cm margin;
(2) be fully legible and should normally be typed on one side of the paper only;
(3) where possible, be bound securely in a manner which would not hamper filing, or otherwise each page should be endorsed with the case number and should bear the initials of the witness;
(4) have the pages numbered consecutively as a separate statement (or as one of several statements contained in a file);
(5) be divided into numbered paragraphs;
(6) have all numbers, including dates, expressed in figures; and
(7) give the reference to any document or documents mentioned either in the margin or in bold text in the body of the statement.

19.2 It is usually convenient for a witness statement to follow the chronological sequence of the events or matters dealt with, each paragraph of a witness statement should as far as possible be confined to a distinct portion of the subject.

Statement of Truth

20.1 A witness statement is the equivalent of the oral evidence which that witness would, if called, give in evidence; it must include a statement by the intended witness that he believes the facts in it are true.

20.2 To verify a witness statement the statement of truth is as follows –

'I believe that the facts stated in this witness statement are true'.

20.3 Attention is drawn to rule 133 which sets out the consequences of verifying a witness statement containing a false statement without an honest belief in its truth.

20.4 If a serial number has been assigned under rule 20 or the name of the witness is not being revealed in accordance with rule 21, the signature of the witness will be edited from the affidavit before it is served on any other party.

Inability of witness to read or sign statement

21.1 Where a witness statement is made by a person who is unable to read or sign the witness statement, it must contain a certificate made by an authorised person.

21.2 An authorised person is a person able to administer oaths and take affidavits but need not be independent of the parties or their representatives.

21.3 The authorised person must certify –

(1) that the witness statement has been read to the witness;
(2) that the witness appeared to understand it and approved its content as accurate;

(3) that the declaration of truth has been read to the witness;
(4) that the witness appeared to understand the declaration and the consequences of making a false witness statement; and
(5) that the witness signed or made his mark in the presence of the authorised person.

21.4 The form of the certificate is set out at Annex 2 to this practice direction.

Alterations to witness statements

22.1 Any alteration to a witness statement must be initialled by the person making the statement or by the authorised person where appropriate (see paragraph 21.1).

22.2 A witness statement which contains an alteration that has not been initialled may be used in evidence only with the permission of the court.

Filing of witness statements

23.1 If the court directs that a witness statement is to be filed,[1] it must be filed in the court or Division, or Office or Registry of the court or Division where the action in which it was or is to be used, is proceeding or will proceed.

23.2 Where the court has directed that a witness statement in a foreign language is to be filed –

(1) the party wishing to rely on it must –
   (a) have it translated; and
   (b) file the foreign language witness statement with the court; and
(2) the translator must sign the translation to certify that it is accurate.

Defects in affidavits, witness statements and exhibits

24.1 Where –

(1) an affidavit;
(2) a witness statement; or
(3) an exhibit to either an affidavit or a witness statement;

does not comply with Part 15 or this practice direction in relation to its form, the court may refuse to admit it as evidence and may refuse to allow the costs arising from its preparation.

24.2 Permission to file a defective affidavit or witness statement or to use a defective exhibit may be obtained from the court where the case is proceeding.

Agreed bundles for hearings

25.1 The court may give directions requiring the parties to use their best endeavours to agree a bundle or bundles of documents for use at any hearing.

25.2 All documents contained in bundles which have been agreed for use at a hearing shall be admissible at that hearing as evidence of their contents, unless –

(1) the court directs otherwise; or
(2) a party gives written notice of objection to the admissibility of particular documents.

---

1 See rule 126(3)(b).

Penalty

26.1

(1) Where a party alleges that a statement of truth is false the party shall refer that allegation to the court dealing with the application in which the statement of truth has been made.

(2) the court may –

    (a) exercise any of its powers under the rules;

    (b) initiate steps to consider if there is a contempt of court and, where there is, to punish it;

(Order 52 of the Rules of the Supreme Court and Order 29 of the County Court Rules (Schedules 1 and 2 to the CPR) make provision where committal to prison is a possibility if contempt is proved)

    (c) direct the party making the allegation to refer the matter to the Attorney General with a request to him to consider whether he wishes to bring proceedings for contempt of court.

26.2

(1) An application to the Attorney General should be made to his chambers at 9 Buckingham Gate London SW1E 6JP in writing. The Attorney General will initially require a copy of the order recording the direction of the judge or district judge referring the matter to him and information which –

    (a) identifies the statement said to be false; and

    (b) explains –

        (i) why it is false; and

        (ii) why the maker knew it to be false at the time he made it; and

    (c) explains why contempt proceedings would be appropriate in the light of the overriding objective in Part 1.

(2) The practice of the Attorney General is to prefer an application that comes from the court, and so has received preliminary consideration by a judge or district judge, to one made direct to him by a party to the application in which the alleged contempt occurred without prior consideration by the court. An application to the Attorney General is not a way of appealing against, or reviewing, the decision of the judge or district judge.

26.3 Where a party makes an application to the court for permission for that party to commence proceedings for contempt of court, it must be supported by written evidence containing the information specified in paragraph 27.2(1) and the result of the application to the Attorney General made by the applicant.

26.4 The rules do not change the law of contempt or introduce new categories of contempt. A person applying to commence such proceedings should consider whether the incident complained of does amount to contempt of court and whether such proceedings would further the overriding objective in Part 1.

Video conferencing

27.1 Guidance on the use of video conferencing in courts is set out at Annex 3 to this practice direction.

27.2 A list of the sites which are available for video conferencing can be found on Her Majesty's Courts Service website at www.hmcourts-service.gov.uk.

ANNEX 1

Certificate to be used where a deponent to an affidavit is unable to read or sign it

Sworn at ...... this .... day of ...... Before me, I having first read over the contents of this affidavit to the deponent [*if there are exhibits, add* 'and explained the nature and effect of the exhibits referred to in it'] who appeared to understand it and approved its content as accurate, and made his mark on the affidavit in my presence.

Or, (after, *Before me*) the witness to the mark of the deponent having been first sworn that he had read over etc (*as above*) and that he saw him make his mark on the affidavit. (*Witness must sign.*)

Certificate to be used where a deponent to an affirmation is unable to read or sign it

Affirmed at ...... this .... day of ...... Before me, I having first read over the contents of this affirmation to the deponent [*if there are exhibits, add* 'and explained the nature and effect of the exhibits referred to in it'] who appeared to understand it and approved its content as accurate, and made his mark on the affirmation in my presence.

Or, (after, *Before me*) the witness to the mark of the deponent having been first sworn that he had read over etc (*as above*) and that he saw him make his mark on the affirmation. (*Witness must sign.*)

ANNEX 2

Certificate to be used where a witness is unable to read or sign a witness statement

I certify that I [*name and address of authorised person*] have read over the contents of this witness statement and the declaration of truth to the witness [*if there are exhibits, add* 'and explained the nature and effect of the exhibits referred to in it'] who appeared to understand (a) the statement and approved its content as accurate and (b) the declaration of truth and the consequences of making a false witness statement, and made his mark in my presence.

ANNEX 3

Video conferencing guide

This guidance is for the use of video conferencing (VCF) in proceedings to which the Rules apply. It is in part based, with permission, upon the protocol of the Federal Court of Australia. It is intended to provide a guide to all persons involved in the use of VCF, although it does not attempt to cover all the practical questions which might arise.

Any reference in this guide to a judge is to be taken as including a district judge or justices of the peace if the proceedings are before a magistrate' court.

Video conferencing generally

1. The guidance covers the use of VCF equipment both (a) in a courtroom, whether via equipment which is permanently placed there or via a mobile unit, and (b) in a separate studio or conference room. In either case, the location at which the judge sits is referred to as the 'local site'. The other site or sites to and from which transmission is made are referred to as 'the remote

site' and in any particular case any such site may be another courtroom. The guidance applies to cases where VCF is used for the taking of evidence and also to its use for other parts of any legal proceedings

2. VCF may be a convenient way of dealing with any part of proceedings – it can involve considerable savings in time and cost. Its use for the taking of evidence from overseas witnesses will, in particular, be likely to achieve a material saving of costs, and such savings may also be achieved by its use for taking domestic evidence. It is, however, inevitably not as ideal as having the witness physically present in court. Its convenience should not therefore be allowed to dictate its use. A judgment must be made in every case in which the use of VCF is being considered not only as to whether it will achieve an overall cost saving but as to whether its use will be likely to be beneficial to the efficient, fair and economic disposal of the litigation. In particular, it needs to be recognised that the degree of control a court can exercise over a witness at the remote site is or may be more limited than it can exercise over a witness physically before it.

3. When used for the taking of evidence, the objective should be to make the VCF session as close as possible to the usual practice in court where evidence is taken in open court. To gain the maximum benefit, several differences have to be taken into account. Some matters, which are taken for granted when evidence is taken in the conventional way, take on a different dimension when it is taken by VCF – for example, the administration of the oath, ensuring that the witness understands who is at the local site and what their various roles are, the raising of any objections to the evidence and the use of documents.

4. It should not be presumed that all foreign governments are willing to allow their nationals or others within their jurisdiction to be examined before a court in England or Wales by means of VCF. If there is any doubt about this, enquiries should be directed to the Foreign and Commonwealth Office (International Legal Matters Unit, Consular Division) with a view to ensuring that the country from which the evidence is to be taken raises no objection to it at diplomatic level. The party who is directed to be responsible for arranging the VCF (see paragraph 8) will be required to make all necessary inquiries about this well in advance of the VCF and must be able to inform the court what those inquiries were and of their outcome.

5. Time zone differences need to be considered when a witness abroad is to be examined in England or Wales by VCF. The convenience of the witness, the parties, their representatives and the court must all be taken into account. The cost of the use of a commercial studio is usually greater outside normal business hours.

6. Those involved with VCF need to be aware that, even with the most advanced systems currently available, there are the briefest of delays between the receipt of the picture and that of the accompanying sound. If due allowance is not made for this, there will be a tendency to 'speak over' the witness, whose voice will continue to be heard for a millisecond or so after he or she appears on the screen to have finished speaking.

7. With current technology, picture quality is good, but not as good as a television picture. The quality of the picture is enhanced if those appearing on VCF monitors keep their movements to a minimum.

Preliminary arrangements

8. The court's permission is required for any part of any proceedings to be dealt with by means of VCF. Before seeking a direction, the applicant should notify the listing officer, diary manager or other appropriate court officer of the intention to seek it, and should enquire as to the availability of court VCF equipment for the day or days of the proposed VCF. If all parties consent to a direction, permission can be sought by letter, fax or e-mail, although the court may

still require an oral hearing. All parties are entitled to be heard on whether or not such a direction should be given and as to its terms. If a witness at a remote site is to give evidence by an interpreter, consideration should be given at this stage as to whether the interpreter should be at the local site or the remote site. If a VCF direction is given, arrangements for the transmission will then need to be made. The court will ordinarily direct that the party seeking permission to use VCF is to be responsible for this. That party is hereafter referred to as 'the VCF arranging party'.

9. Subject to any order to the contrary, all costs of the transmission, including the costs of hiring equipment and technical personnel to operate it, will initially be the responsibility of, and must be met by, the VCF arranging party. All reasonable efforts should be made to keep the transmission to a minimum and so keep the costs down. All such costs will be considered to be part of the costs of the proceedings and the court will determine at such subsequent time as is convenient or appropriate who, as between the parties, should be responsible for them and (if appropriate) in what proportions.

10. The local site will, if practicable, be a courtroom but it may instead be an appropriate studio or conference room. The VCF arranging party must contact the listing officer, diary manager or other appropriate officer of the court which made the VCF direction and make arrangements for the VCF transmission. Details of the remote site, and of the equipment to be used both at the local site (if not being supplied by the court) and the remote site (including the number of ISDN lines and connection speed), together with all necessary contact names and telephone numbers, will have to be provided to the listing officer, diary manager or other court officer. The court will need to be satisfied that any equipment provided by the parties for use at the local site and also that at the remote site is of sufficient quality for a satisfactory transmission. The VCF arranging party must ensure that an appropriate person will be present at the local site to supervise the operation of the VCF throughout the transmission in order to deal with any technical problems. That party must also arrange for a technical assistant to be similarly present at the remote site for like purposes.

11. It is recommended that the judge, practitioners and witness should arrive at their respective VCF sites about 20 minutes prior to the scheduled commencement of the transmission.

12. If the local site is not a courtroom, but a conference room or studio, the judge will need to determine who is to sit where. The VCF arranging party must take care to ensure that the number of microphones is adequate for the speakers and that the panning of the camera for the practitioners' table encompasses all legal representatives so that the viewer can see everyone seated there.

14. In cases where the local site is a studio or conference room, the VCF arranging party should make arrangements, if practicable, for the royal coat of arms to be placed above the judge's seat.

15. In cases in which the VCF is to be used for the taking of evidence, the VCF arranging party must arrange for recording equipment to be provided by the court which made the VCF direction so that the evidence can be recorded. An associate will normally be present to operate the recording equipment when the local site is a courtroom. The VCF arranging party should take steps to ensure that an associate is present to do likewise when it is a studio or conference room. The equipment should be set up and tested before the VCF transmission. It will often be a valuable safeguard for the VCF arranging party also to arrange for the provision of recording equipment at the remote site. This will provide a useful back-up if there is any reduction in sound quality during the transmission. A direction from the court for the making of such a back-up recording must, however, be obtained first. This is because the proceedings are court proceedings and, save as directed by the court, no other recording of them must be made. The court will direct what is to happen to the back-up recording.

16. Some countries may require that any oath or affirmation to be taken by a witness accord with local custom rather than the usual form of oath or affirmation used in England and Wales. The VCF arranging party must make all appropriate prior inquiries and put in place all arrangements necessary to enable the oath or affirmation to be taken in accordance with any local custom. That party must be in a position to inform the court what those inquiries were, what their outcome was and what arrangements have been made. If the oath or affirmation can be administered in the manner normal in England and Wales, the VCF arranging party must arrange in advance to have the appropriate holy book at the remote site. The associate will normally administer the oath.

17. Consideration will need to be given in advance to the documents to which the witness is likely to be referred. The parties should endeavour to agree on this. It will usually be most convenient for a bundle of the copy documents to be prepared in advance, which the VCF arranging party should then send to the remote site.

18. Additional documents are sometimes quite properly introduced during the course of a witness's evidence. To cater for this, the VCF arranging party should ensure that equipment is available to enable documents to be transmitted between sites during the course of the VCF transmission. Consideration should be given to whether to use a document camera. If it is decided to use one, arrangements for its use will need to be established in advance. The panel operator will need to know the number and size of documents or objects if their images are to be sent by document camera. In many cases, a simpler and sufficient alternative will be to ensure that there are fax transmission and reception facilities at the participating sites.

The hearing

19. The procedure for conducting the transmission will be determined by the judge. He will determine who is to control the cameras. In cases where the VCF is being used for an application in the course of the proceedings, the judge will ordinarily not enter the local site until both sites are on line. Similarly, at the conclusion of the hearing, he will ordinarily leave the local site while both sites are still on line. The following paragraphs apply primarily to cases where the VCF is being used for the taking of the evidence of a witness at a remote site.

20. At the beginning of the transmission, the judge will probably wish to introduce himself and the advocates to the witness. He will probably want to know who is at the remote site and will invite the witness to introduce himself and anyone else who is with him. He may wish to give directions as to the seating arrangements at the remote site so that those present are visible at the local site during the taking of the evidence. He will probably wish to explain to the witness the method of taking the oath or of affirming, the manner in which the evidence will be taken, and who will be conducting the examination and cross-examination. He will probably also wish to inform the witness of the matters referred to in paragraphs 6 and 7 (co-ordination of picture with sound, and picture quality).

21. The examination of the witness at the remote site should follow as closely as possible the practice adopted when a witness is in the courtroom. During examination, cross-examination and re-examination, the witness must be able to see the legal representative asking the question and also any other person (whether another legal representative or the judge) making any statements in regard to the witness's evidence. It will in practice be most convenient if everyone remains seated throughout the transmission.

PRACTICE DIRECTION – DEPOSITION AND COURT ATTENDANCE BY WITNESSES

THIS PRACTICE DIRECTION SUPPLEMENTS PART 16 OF THE FAMILY PROCEDURE (ADOPTION) RULES 2005

Witness summonses

Issue of witness summons

1.1 A witness summons may require a witness to –

(1) attend court to give evidence;
(2) produce documents to the court; or
(3) both;

on either a date fixed for the hearing or such date as the court may direct.[1]

1.2 Two copies of the witness summons[2] should be filed with the court for sealing, one of which will be retained on the court file.

1.3 A mistake in the name or address of a person named in a witness summons may be corrected if the summons has not been served.

1.4 The corrected summons must be re-sealed by the court and marked 'Amended and Re-Sealed'.

Magistrates' courts proceedings

2.1 An application for the issue of a summons or warrant under section 97 of the Magistrates' courts Act 1980 may be made by the applicant in person or by his legal representative.

2.2 An application for the issue of such a summons may be made by delivering or sending the application in writing to the court officer for the magistrates' court.

Travelling expenses and compensation for loss of time

3.1 When a witness is served with a witness summons he must be offered a sum to cover his travelling expenses to and from the court and compensation for his loss of time.[3]

3.2 If the witness summons is to be served by the court, the party issuing the summons must deposit with the court –

(1) a sum sufficient to pay for the witness's expenses in travelling to the court and in returning to his home or place of work; and
(2) a sum in respect of the period during which earnings or benefit are lost, or such lesser sum as it may be proved that the witness will lose as a result of his attendance at court in answer to the witness summons.

---

1   Rule 141(4).
2   In Form FP25.
3   Rule 145.

3.3 The sum referred to in 3.2(2) is to be based on the sums payable to witnesses attending the Crown Court.[1]

Depositions

To be taken in England and Wales for use as evidence in proceedings in courts in England and Wales

4.1 A party may apply for an order for a person to be examined on oath before –

(1) a judge or district judge (including a district judge of the principal registry of the Family Division;
(2) an examiner of the court; or
(3) such other person as the court may appoint.[2]

4.2 The party who obtains an order for the examination of a deponent[3] before an examiner of the court must –

(1) apply to the Foreign Process Section of the Masters' Secretary's Department at the Royal Courts of Justice for the allocation of an examiner;
(2) when allocated, provide the examiner with copies of all documents in the proceedings necessary to inform the examiner of the issues; and
(3) pay the deponent a sum to cover his travelling expenses to and from the examination and compensation for his loss of time.[4]

4.3 In ensuring that the deponent's evidence is recorded in full, the court or the examiner may permit it to be recorded on audiotape or videotape, but the deposition[5] must always be recorded in writing by him or by a competent shorthand writer or stenographer.

4.4 If the deposition is not recorded word for word, it must contain, as nearly as may be, the statement of the deponent; the examiner may record word for word any particular questions and answers which appear to him to have special importance.

4.5 If a deponent objects to answering any question or where any objection is taken to any question, the examiner must –

(1) record in the deposition or a document attached to it –
    (a) the question;
    (b) the nature of and grounds for the objection; and
    (c) any answer given; and
(2) give his opinion as to the validity of the objection and must record it in the deposition or a document attached to it.

The court will decide as to the validity of the objection and any question of costs arising from it.

4.6 Documents and exhibits must –

(1) have an identifying number or letter marked on them by the examiner, and

---

1 Fixed pursuant to the Prosecution of Offences Act 1985 and the Costs in Criminal Cases (General) Regulations 1986.
2 Rule 146(3).
3 See rule 146(2) for explanation of 'deponent' and 'deposition'.
4 Rule 146(6).
5 See rule 146(2) for explanation of 'deponent' and 'deposition'.

(2) be preserved by the party or his legal representative[1] who obtained the order for the examination, or as the court or the examiner may direct.

4.7 The examiner may put any question to the deponent as to –

(1) the meaning of any of his answers; or
(2) any matter arising in the course of the examination.

4.8 Where a deponent –

(1) fails to attend the examination; or
(2) refuses to –
    (a) be sworn; or
    (b) answer any lawful question; or
    (c) produce any document;

the examiner will sign a certificate[2] of such failure or refusal and may include in his certificate any comment as to the conduct of the deponent or of any person attending the examination.

4.9 The party who obtained the order for the examination must file the certificate with the court and may apply for an order that the deponent attend for examination or produce any document, as the case may be.[3] The application may be made without notice.[4]

4.10 The court will make such order on the application as it thinks fit including an order for the deponent to pay any costs resulting from his failure or refusal.[5]

4.11 A deponent who wilfully refuses to obey an order made against him under Part 16 may be proceeded against for contempt of court.

4.12 A deposition must –

(1) be signed by the examiner;
(2) have any amendments to it initialled by the examiner and the deponent;
(3) be endorsed by the examiner with –
    (a) a statement of the time occupied by the examination; and
    (b) a record of any refusal by the deponent to sign the deposition and of his reasons for not doing so; and
(4) be sent by the examiner to the court where the proceedings are taking place for filing on the court file.

4.13 Rule 151 deals with the fees and expenses of an examiner.

Depositions to be taken abroad for use as evidence in proceedings before courts in England and Wales (where the Taking of Evidence Regulation does not apply)

5.1 Where a party wishes to take a deposition from a person outside the jurisdiction, the High Court may order the issue of a letter of request to the judicial authorities of the country in which the proposed deponent is.[6]

---

1   For the definition of legal representative see rule 6.
2   Rule 148.
3   Rule 148(2) and (3).
4   Rule 148(3).
5   Rule 148(4).
6   Rule 150(1) and (2).

5.2 An application for an order referred to in paragraph 5.1 should be made by application notice in accordance with Part 9.

5.3 The documents which a party applying for an order for the issue of a letter of request must file with his application notice are set out in rule 150(7). They are as follows –

(1) a draft letter of request in the form set out in Annex A to this practice direction;
(2) a statement of the issues relevant to the proceedings;
(3) a list of questions or the subject matter of questions to be put to the proposed deponent;
(4) a translation of the documents in (1), (2) and (3), unless the proposed deponent is in a country of which English is an official language; and
(5) an undertaking to be responsible for the expenses of the Secretary of State.

In addition to the documents listed above the party applying for the order must file a draft order.

5.4 The above documents should be filed with the Masters' Secretary in Room E214, Royal Courts of Justice, Strand, London WC2A 2LL.

5.5 The application will be dealt with by the Senior Master of the Queen's Bench Division of the High Court who will, if appropriate, sign the letter of request.

5.6 Attention is drawn to the provisions of rule 94 (application to vary or discharge an order made without notice).

5.7 If parties are in doubt as to whether a translation under paragraph 5.3(4) is required, they should seek guidance from the Foreign Process Section of the Masters' Secretary's Department.

5.8 A special examiner appointed under rule 150(5) may be the British Consul or the Consul-General or his deputy in the country where the evidence is to be taken if –

(1) there is in respect of that country a Civil Procedure Convention providing for the taking of evidence in that country for the assistance of proceedings in the High Court or other court in this country; or
(2) the Secretary of State has consented.

5.9 The provisions of paragraphs 4.1 to 4.12 apply to the depositions referred to in this paragraph.

Taking of evidence between EU Member States

Taking of Evidence Regulation

6.1 Where evidence is to be taken from a person in another Member State of the European Union for use as evidence in proceedings before courts in England and Wales Council Regulation (EC) No 1206/2001 of 28 May 2001 on co-operation between the courts of the Member States in the taking of evidence in civil or commercial matters ('the Taking of Evidence Regulation') applies.

6.2 The Taking of Evidence Regulation is annexed to this practice direction as Annex B.

6.3 The Taking of Evidence Regulation does not apply to Denmark. In relation to Denmark, therefore, rule 150 will continue to apply.

(Article 21(1) of the Taking of Evidence Regulation provides that the Regulation prevails over other provisions contained in bilateral or multilateral agreements or arrangements concluded by the Member States)

Originally published in the official languages of the European Community in the *Official Journal of the European Communities* by the Office for Official Publications of the European Communities.

Meaning of 'designated court'

7.1 In accordance with the Taking of Evidence Regulation, each Regulation State has prepared a list of courts competent to take evidence in accordance with the Regulation indicating the territorial and, where appropriate, special jurisdiction of those courts.

7.2 Where Part 16, Section 2 refers to a 'designated court' in relation to another Regulation State, the reference is to the court, referred to in the list of competent courts of that State, which is appropriate to the application in hand.

7.3 Where the reference is to the 'designated court' in England and Wales, the reference is to the appropriate competent court in the jurisdiction. The designated courts for England and Wales are listed in Annex C to this practice direction.

Central Body

8.1 The Taking of Evidence Regulation stipulates that each Regulation State must nominate a Central Body responsible for–

(a) supplying information to courts;
(b) seeking solutions to any difficulties which may arise in respect of a request; and
(c) forwarding, in exceptional cases, at the request of a requesting court, a request to the competent court.

8.2 The United Kingdom has nominated the Senior Master, Queen's Bench Division, to be the Central Body for England and Wales.

8.3 The Senior Master, as Central Body, has been designated responsible for taking decisions on requests pursuant to Article 17 of the Regulation. Article 17 allows a court to submit a request to the Central Body or a designated competent authority in another Regulation State to take evidence directly in that State.

Evidence to be taken in another Regulation State for use in England and Wales

9.1 Where a person wishes to take a deposition from a person in another Regulation State, the court where the proceedings are taking place may order the issue of a request to the designated court in the Regulation State (rule 153(2)). The form of request is prescribed as Form A in the Taking of Evidence Regulation.

9.2 An application to the court for an order under rule 153(2) should be made by application notice in accordance with Part 9.

9.3 Rule 153(3) provides that the party applying for the order must file a draft form of request in the prescribed form. Where completion of the form requires attachments or documents to accompany the form, these must also be filed.

9.4 If the court grants an order under rule 153(2), it will send the form of request directly to the designated court.

9.5 Where the taking of evidence requires the use of an expert, the designated court may require a deposit in advance towards the costs of that expert. The party who obtained the order is responsible for the payment of any such deposit which should be deposited with the court for onward transmission. Under the provisions of the Taking of Evidence Regulation, the designated court is not required to execute the request until such payment is received.

9.6 Article 17 permits the court where proceedings are taking place to take evidence directly from a deponent in another Regulation State if the conditions of the article are satisfied. Direct taking of evidence can only take place if evidence is given voluntarily without the need for coercive measures. Rule 153(5) provides for the court to make an order for the submission of a request to take evidence directly. The form of request is Form I annexed to the Taking of Evidence Regulation and rule 153(6) makes provision for a draft of this form to be filed by the party seeking the order. An application for an order under rule 153(5) should be by application notice in accordance with Part 9.

9.7 Attention is drawn to the provisions of rule 94 (application to vary or discharge an order made without notice).

ANNEX A

Draft letter of request (where the taking of evidence regulation does not apply)

To the Competent Judicial Authority of   in the   of

I [*name*] Senior Master of the Queen's Bench Division of the Supreme Court of England and Wales respectfully request the assistance of your court with regard to the following matters.

1 An application is now pending in the Division of the High Court of Justice in England and Wales entitled as follows [*set out full title and case number*] in which [*name*] of [*address*] is the applicant and [*name*] of [*address*] is the respondent.

2 The names and addresses of the representatives or agents of [*set out names and addresses of representatives of the parties*].

3 The application by the applicant is for –

(a) [set out the nature of the application]
(b) [the order sought, and]
(c) [a summary of the facts.]

4 It is necessary for the purposes of justice between the parties that you cause the following witnesses, who are resident within your jurisdiction, to be examined. The names and addresses of the witnesses are as follows –

5 The witnesses should be examined on oath or if that is not possible within your laws or is impossible of performance by reason of the internal practice and procedure of your court or by reason of practical difficulties, they should be examined in accordance with whatever procedure your laws provide for in these matters.

6 Either/

The witnesses should be examined in accordance with the list of questions annexed hereto.

Or/

The witnesses should be examined regarding [*set out full details of evidence sought*]

NB: Where the witness is required to produce documents, these should be clearly identified.

7 I would ask that you cause me, or the agents of the parties (if appointed), to be informed of the date and place where the examination is to take place.

8 Finally, I request that you will cause the evidence of the said witnesses to be reduced into writing and all documents produced on such examinations to be duly marked for identification and that you will further be pleased to authenticate such examinations by the seal of your court or in such other way as is in accordance with your procedure and return the written evidence and documents produced to me addressed as follows –

Senior Master of the Queen's Bench Division
Royal Courts of Justice
Strand
London
WC2A 2LL
England

ANNEX B

Council Regulation (EC) No 1206/2001 of 28 May 2001 on co-operation between the courts of the Member States in the taking of evidence in civil or commercial matters

THE COUNCIL OF THE EUROPEAN UNION,

Having regard to the Treaty establishing the European Community, and in particular Article 61(c) and Article 67(1) thereof,

Having regard to the initiative of the Federal Republic of Germany,[1]

Having regard to the opinion of the European Parliament,[2]

Having regard to the opinion of the Economic and Social Committee,[3]

Whereas –

(1) The European Union has set itself the objective of maintaining and developing the European Union as an area of freedom, security and justice in which the free movement of persons is ensured. For the gradual establishment of such an area, the Community is to adopt, among others, the measures relating to judicial cooperation in civil matters needed for the proper functioning of the internal market.

(2) For the purpose of the proper functioning of the internal market, cooperation between courts in the taking of evidence should be improved, and in particular simplified and accelerated.

(3) At its meeting in Tampere on 15 and 16 October 1999, the European Council recalled that new procedural legislation in cross-border cases, in particular on the taking of evidence, should be prepared.

(4) This area falls within the scope of Article 65 of the Treaty.

(5) The objectives of the proposed action, namely the improvement of cooperation between the courts on the taking of evidence in civil or commercial matters, cannot be sufficiently achieved by the Member States and can therefore be better achieved at Community level. The

---

1 OJ C 314, 3.11.2000, p 2.
2 Opinion delivered on 14 March 2001 (not yet published in the Official Journal).
3 Opinion delivered on 28 February 2001 (not yet published in the Official Journal).

Community may adopt measures in accordance with the principle of subsidiarity as set out in Article 5 of the Treaty. In accordance with the principle of proportionality, as set out in that Article, this Regulation does not go beyond what is necessary to achieve those objectives.

(6) To date, there is no binding instrument between all the Member States concerning the taking of evidence. The Hague Convention of 18 March 1970 on the taking of evidence abroad in civil or commercial matters applies between only 11 Member States of the European Union.

(7) As it is often essential for a decision in a civil or commercial matter pending before a court in a Member State to take evidence in another Member State, the Community's activity cannot be limited to the field of transmission of judicial and extrajudicial documents in civil or commercial matters which falls within the scope of Council Regulation (EC) 1348/2000 of 29 May 2000 on the serving in the Member States of judicial and extrajudicial documents in civil or commercial matters.[1] It is therefore necessary to continue the improvement of cooperation between courts of Member States in the field of taking of evidence.

(8) The efficiency of judicial procedures in civil or commercial matters requires that the transmission and execution of requests for the performance of taking of evidence is to be made directly and by the most rapid means possible between Member States' courts.

(9) Speed in transmission of requests for the performance of taking of evidence warrants the use of all appropriate means, provided that certain conditions as to the legibility and reliability of the document received are observed. So as to ensure the utmost clarity and legal certainty the request for the performance of taking of evidence must be transmitted on a form to be completed in the language of the Member State of the requested court or in another language accepted by that State. For the same reasons, forms should also be used as far as possible for further communication between the relevant courts.

(10) A request for the performance of the taking of evidence should be executed expeditiously. If it is not possible for the request to be executed within 90 days of receipt by the requested court, the latter should inform the requesting court accordingly, stating the reasons which prevent the request from being executed swiftly.

(11) To secure the effectiveness of this Regulation, the possibility of refusing to execute the request for the performance of taking of evidence should be confined to strictly limited exceptional situations.

(12) The requested court should execute the request in accordance with the law of its Member State.

(13) The parties and, if any, their representatives, should be able to be present at the performance of the taking of evidence, if that is provided for by the law of the Member State of the requesting court, in order to be able to follow the proceedings in a comparable way as if evidence were taken in the Member State of the requesting court. They should also have the right to request to participate in order to have a more active role in the performance of the taking of evidence. However, the conditions under which they may participate should be determined by the requested court in accordance with the law of its Member State.

(14) The representatives of the requesting court should be able to be present at the performance of the taking of evidence, if that is compatible with the law of the Member State of the requesting court, in order to have an improved possibility of evaluation of evidence. They should

---

1   OJ L 160, 30.6.2000, p 37.

also have the right to request to participate, under the conditions laid down by the requested court in accordance with the law of its Member State, in order to have a more active role in the performance of the taking of evidence.

(15) In order to facilitate the taking of evidence it should be possible for a court in a Member State, in accordance with the law of its Member State, to take evidence directly in another Member State, if accepted by the latter, and under the conditions determined by the central body or competent authority of the requested Member State.

(16) The execution of the request, according to Article 10, should not give rise to a claim for any reimbursement of taxes or costs. Nevertheless, if the requested court requires reimbursement, the fees paid to experts and interpreters, as well as the costs occasioned by the application of Article 10(3) and (4), should not be borne by that court. In such a case, the requesting court is to take the necessary measures to ensure reimbursement without delay. Where the opinion of an expert is required, the requested court may, before executing the request, ask the requesting court for an adequate deposit or advance towards the costs.

(17) This Regulation should prevail over the provisions applying to its field of application, contained in international conventions concluded by the Member States. Member States should be free to adopt agreements or arrangements to further facilitate cooperation in the taking of evidence.

(18) The information transmitted pursuant to this Regulation should enjoy protection. Since Directive 95/46/EC of the European Parliament and of the Council of 24 October 1995 on the protection of individuals with regard to the processing of personal data and on the free movement of such data,[1] and Directive 97/66/EC of the European Parliament and of the Council of 15 December 1997 concerning the processing of personal data and the protection of privacy in the telecommunications sector,[2] are applicable, there is no need for specific provisions on data protection in this Regulation.

(19) The measures necessary for the implementation of this Regulation should be adopted in accordance with Council Decision 1999/468/EC of 28 June 1999[3] laying down the procedures for the exercise of implementing powers conferred on the Commission.

(20) For the proper functioning of this Regulation, the Commission should review its application and propose such amendments as may appear necessary.

(21) The United Kingdom and Ireland, in accordance with Article 3 of the Protocol on the position of the United Kingdom and Ireland annexed to the Treaty on the European Union and to the Treaty establishing the European Community, have given notice of their wish to take part in the adoption and application of this Regulation.

(22) Denmark, in accordance with Articles 1 and 2 of the Protocol on the position of Denmark annexed to the Treaty on European Union and to the Treaty establishing the European Community, is not participating in the adoption of this Regulation, and is therefore not bound by it nor subject to its application,

HAS ADOPTED THIS REGULATION –

---

1 OJ L 281, 23.11.1995, p 31.
2 OJ L 24, 30.1.1998, p 1.
3 OJ L 184, 17.7.1999, p 23.

Chapter I
General provisions

Article 1
Scope

1. This Regulation shall apply in civil or commercial matters where the court of a Member State, in accordance with the provisions of the law of that State, requests –
   (a) the competent court of another Member State to take evidence; or
   (b) to take evidence directly in another Member State.

2. A request shall not be made to obtain evidence which is not intended for use in judicial proceedings, commenced or contemplated.

3. In this Regulation, the term 'Member State' shall mean Member States with the exception of Denmark.

Article 2
Direct transmission between the courts

1. Requests pursuant to Article 1(1)(a), hereinafter referred to as 'requests', shall be transmitted by the court before which the proceedings are commenced or contemplated, hereinafter referred to as the 'requesting court', directly to the competent court of another Member State, hereinafter referred to as the 'requested court', for the performance of the taking of evidence.

2. Each Member State shall draw up a list of the courts competent for the performance of taking of evidence according to this Regulation. The list shall also indicate the territorial and, where appropriate, the special jurisdiction of those courts.

Article 3
Central body

1. Each Member State shall designate a central body responsible for –
   (a) supplying information to the courts;
   (b) seeking solutions to any difficulties which may arise in respect of a request;
   (c) forwarding, in exceptional cases, at the request of a requesting court, a request to the competent court.

2. A federal State, a State in which several legal systems apply or a State with autonomous territorial entities shall be free to designate more than one central body.

3. Each Member State shall also designate the central body referred to in paragraph 1 or one or several competent authority(ies) to be responsible for taking decisions on requests pursuant to Article 17.

Chapter II
Transmission and execution of requests

Section 1
Transmission of the request

Article 4
Form and content of the request

1. The request shall be made using form A or, where appropriate, form I in the Annex. It shall contain the following details –

(a) the requesting and, where appropriate, the requested court;
(b) the names and addresses of the parties to the proceedings and their representatives, if any;
(c) the nature and subject matter of the case and a brief statement of the facts;
(d) a description of the taking of evidence to be performed;
(e) where the request is for the examination of a person –
    – the name(s) and address(es) of the person(s) to be examined,
    – the questions to be put to the person(s) to be examined or a statement of the facts about which he is (they are) to be examined,
    – where appropriate, a reference to a right to refuse to testify under the law of the Member State of the requesting court,
    – any requirement that the examination is to be carried out under oath or affirmation in lieu thereof, and any special form to be used,
    – where appropriate, any other information that the requesting court deems necessary;
(f) where the request is for any other form of taking of evidence, the documents or other objects to be inspected;
(g) where appropriate, any request pursuant to Article 10(3) and (4), and Articles 11 and 12 and any information necessary for the application thereof.

2. The request and all documents accompanying the request shall be exempted from authentication or any equivalent formality.

3. Documents which the requesting court deems it necessary to enclose for the execution of the request shall be accompanied by a translation into the language in which the request was written.

Article 5
Language

The request and communications pursuant to this Regulation shall be drawn up in the official language of the requested Member State or, if there are several official languages in that Member State, in the official language or one of the official languages of the place where the requested taking of evidence is to be performed, or in another language which the requested Member State has indicated it can accept. Each Member State shall indicate the official language or languages of the institutions of the European Community other than its own which is or are acceptable to it for completion of the forms.

Article 6
Transmission of requests and other communications

Requests and communications pursuant to this Regulation shall be transmitted by the swiftest possible means, which the requested Member State has indicated it can accept. The transmission may be carried out by any appropriate means, provided that the document received accurately reflects the content of the document forwarded and that all information in it is legible.

SECTION 2
RECEIPT OF REQUEST

Article 7
Receipt of request

1. Within seven days of receipt of the request, the requested competent court shall send an acknowledgement of receipt to the requesting court using form B in the Annex. Where the

request does not comply with the conditions laid down in Articles 5 and 6, the requested court shall enter a note to that effect in the acknowledgement of receipt.

2. Where the execution of a request made using form A in the Annex, which complies with the conditions laid down in Article 5, does not fall within the jurisdiction of the court to which it was transmitted, the latter shall forward the request to the competent court of its Member State and shall inform the requesting court thereof using form A in the Annex.

Article 8
Incomplete request

1. If a request cannot be executed because it does not contain all of the necessary information pursuant to Article 4, the requested court shall inform the requesting court thereof without delay and, at the latest, within 30 days of receipt of the request using form C in the Annex, and shall request it to send the missing information, which should be indicated as precisely as possible.

2. If a request cannot be executed because a deposit or advance is necessary in accordance with Article 18(3), the requested court shall inform the requesting court thereof without delay and, at the latest, within 30 days of receipt of the request using form C in the Annex and inform the requesting court how the deposit or advance should be made. The requested Court shall acknowledge receipt of the deposit or advance without delay, at the latest within 10 days of receipt of the deposit or the advance using form D.

Article 9
Completion of the request

1. If the requested court has noted on the acknowledgement of receipt pursuant to Article 7(1) that the request does not comply with the conditions laid down in Articles 5 and 6 or has informed the requesting court pursuant to Article 8 that the request cannot be executed because it does not contain all of the necessary information pursuant to Article 4, the time limit pursuant to Article 10 shall begin to run when the requested court received the request duly completed.

2. Where the requested court has asked for a deposit or advance in accordance with Article 18(3), this time limit shall begin to run when the deposit or the advance is made.

SECTION 3
TAKING OF EVIDENCE BY THE REQUESTED COURT

Article 10
General provisions on the execution of the request

1. The requested court shall execute the request without delay and, at the latest, within 90 days of receipt of the request.

2. The requested court shall execute the request in accordance with the law of its Member State.

3. The requesting court may call for the request to be executed in accordance with a special procedure provided for by the law of its Member State, using form A in the Annex. The requested court shall comply with such a requirement unless this procedure is incompatible with the law of the Member State of the requested court or by reason of major practical difficulties. If the requested court does not comply with the requirement for one of these reasons it shall inform the requesting court using form E in the Annex.

4. The requesting court may ask the requested court to use communications technology at the performance of the taking of evidence, in particular by using videoconference and teleconference.

The requested court shall comply with such a requirement unless this is incompatible with the law of the Member State of the requested court or by reason of major practical difficulties.

If the requested court does not comply with the requirement for one of these reasons, it shall inform the requesting court, using form E in the Annex.

If there is no access to the technical means referred to above in the requesting or in the requested court, such means may be made available by the courts by mutual agreement.

Article 11
Performance with the presence and participation of the parties

1. If it is provided for by the law of the Member State of the requesting court, the parties and, if any, their representatives, have the right to be present at the performance of the taking of evidence by the requested court.

2. The requesting court shall, in its request, inform the requested court that the parties and, if any, their representatives, will be present and, where appropriate, that their participation is requested, using form A in the Annex. This information may also be given at any other appropriate time.

3. If the participation of the parties and, if any, their representatives, is requested at the performance of the taking of evidence, the requested court shall determine, in accordance with Article 10, the conditions under which they may participate.

4. The requested court shall notify the parties and, if any, their representatives, of the time when, the place where, the proceedings will take place, and, where appropriate, the conditions under which they may participate, using form F in the Annex.

5. Paragraphs 1 to 4 shall not affect the possibility for the requested court of asking the parties and, if any their representatives, to be present at or to participate in the performance of the taking of evidence if that possibility is provided for by the law of its Member State.

Article 12
Performance with the presence and participation of representatives of the requesting court

1. If it is compatible with the law of the Member State of the requesting court, representatives of the requesting court have the right to be present in the performance of the taking of evidence by the requested court.

2. For the purpose of this Article, the term 'representative' shall include members of the judicial personnel designated by the requesting court, in accordance with the law of its Member State. The requesting court may also designate, in accordance with the law of its Member State, any other person, such as an expert.

3. The requesting court shall, in its request, inform the requested court that its representatives will be present and, where appropriate, that their participation is requested, using form A in the Annex. This information may also be given at any other appropriate time.

4. If the participation of the representatives of the requesting court is requested in the performance of the taking of evidence, the requested court shall determine, in accordance with Article 10, the conditions under which they may participate.

5. The requested court shall notify the requesting court, of the time when, and the place where, the proceedings will take place, and, where appropriate, the conditions under which the representatives may participate, using form F in the Annex.

Article 13
Coercive measures

Where necessary, in executing a request the requested court shall apply the appropriate coercive measures in the instances and to the extent as are provided for by the law of the Member State of the requested court for the execution of a request made for the same purpose by its national authorities or one of the parties concerned.

Article 14
Refusal to execute

1. A request for the hearing of a person shall not be executed when the person concerned claims the right to refuse to give evidence or to be prohibited from giving evidence,

   (a) under the law of the Member State of the requested court; or
   (b) under the law of the Member State of the requesting court, and such right has been specified in the request, or, if need be, at the instance of the requested court, has been confirmed by the requesting court.

2. In addition to the grounds referred to in paragraph 1, the execution of a request may be refused only if –

   (a) the request does not fall within the scope of this Regulation as set out in Article 1; or
   (b) the execution of the request under the law of the Member State of the requested court does not fall within the functions of the judiciary; or
   (c) the requesting court does not comply with the request of the requested court to complete the request pursuant to Article 8 within 30 days after the requested court asked it to do so; or
   (d) a deposit or advance asked for in accordance with Article 18(3) is not made within 60 days after the requested court asked for such a deposit or advance.

3. Execution may not be refused by the requested court solely on the ground that under the law of its Member State a court of that Member State has exclusive jurisdiction over the subject matter of the action or that the law of that Member State would not admit the right of action on it.

4. If execution of the request is refused on one of the grounds referred to in paragraph 2, the requested court shall notify the requesting court thereof within 60 days of receipt of the request by the requested court using form H in the Annex.

Article 15
Notification of delay

If the requested court is not in a position to execute the request within 90 days of receipt, it shall inform the requesting court thereof, using form G in the Annex. When it does so, the grounds for the delay shall be given as well as the estimated time that the requested court expects it will need to execute the request.

Article 16
Procedure after execution of the request

The requested court shall send without delay to the requesting court the documents establishing the execution of the request and, where appropriate, return the documents received from the requesting court. The documents shall be accompanied by a confirmation of execution using form H in the Annex.

SECTION 4
DIRECT TAKING OF EVIDENCE BY THE REQUESTING COURT

Article 17

1. Where a court requests to take evidence directly in another Member State, it shall submit a request to the central body or the competent authority referred to in Article 3(3) in that State, using form I in the Annex.

2. Direct taking of evidence may only take place if it can be performed on a voluntary basis without the need for coercive measures.

Where the direct taking of evidence implies that a person shall be heard, the requesting court shall inform that person that the performance shall take place on a voluntary basis.

3. The taking of evidence shall be performed by a member of the judicial personnel or by any other person such as an expert, who will be designated, in accordance with the law of the Member State of the requesting court.

4. Within 30 days of receiving the request, the central body or the competent authority of the requested Member State shall inform the requesting court if the request is accepted and, if necessary, under what conditions according to the law of its Member State such performance is to be carried out, using form J.

In particular, the central body or the competent authority may assign a court of its Member State to take part in the performance of the taking of evidence in order to ensure the proper application of this Article and the conditions that have been set out.

The central body or the competent authority shall encourage the use of communications technology, such as videoconferences and teleconferences.

5. The central body or the competent authority may refuse direct taking of evidence only if –

   (a) the request does not fall within the scope of this Regulation as set out in Article 1;
   (b) the request does not contain all of the necessary information pursuant to Article 4; or
   (c) the direct taking of evidence requested is contrary to fundamental principles of law in its Member State.

6. Without prejudice to the conditions laid down in accordance with paragraph 4, the requesting court shall execute the request in accordance with the law of its Member State.

SECTION 5
COSTS

Article 18

1. The execution of the request, in accordance with Article 10, shall not give rise to a claim for any reimbursement of taxes or costs.

2. Nevertheless, if the requested court so requires, the requesting court shall ensure the reimbursement, without delay, of –

- the fees paid to experts and interpreters, and
- the costs occasioned by the application of Article 10(3) and (4).

The duty for the parties to bear these fees or costs shall be governed by the law of the Member State of the requesting court.

3. Where the opinion of an expert is required, the requested court may, before executing the request, ask the requesting court for an adequate deposit or advance towards the requested costs. In all other cases, a deposit or advance shall not be a condition for the execution of a request.

The deposit or advance shall be made by the parties if that is provided for by the law of the Member State of the requesting court.

Chapter III
Final provisions

Article 19
Implementing rules

1. The Commission shall draw up and regularly update a manual, which shall also be available electronically, containing the information provided by the Member States in accordance with Article 22 and the agreements or arrangements in force, according to Article 21.

2. The updating or making of technical amendments to the standard forms set out in the Annex shall be carried out in accordance with the advisory procedure set out in Article 20(2).

Article 20
Committee

1. The Commission shall be assisted by a Committee.

2. Where reference is made to this paragraph, Articles 3 and 7 of Decision 1999/468/EC shall apply.

3. The Committee shall adopt its Rules of Procedure.

Article 21
Relationship with existing or future agreements or arrangements between Member States

1. This Regulation shall, in relation to matters to which it applies, prevail over other provisions contained in bilateral or multilateral agreements or arrangements concluded by the Member States and in particular the Hague Convention of 1 March 1954 on Civil Procedure and the Hague Convention of 18 March 1970 on the Taking of Evidence Abroad in Civil or Commercial Matters, in relations between the Member States party thereto.

2. This Regulation shall not preclude Member States from maintaining or concluding agreements or arrangements between two or more of them to further facilitate the taking of evidence, provided that they are compatible with this Regulation.

3. Member States shall send to the Commission –

(a) by 1 July 2003, a copy of the agreements or arrangements maintained between the Member States referred to in paragraph 2;

(b) a copy of the agreements or arrangements concluded between the Member States referred to in paragraph 2 as well as drafts of such agreements or arrangements which they intend to adopt; and

(c) any denunciation of, or amendments to, these agreements or arrangements.

Article 22
Communication

By 1 July 2003 each Member State shall communicate to the Commission the following –

(a) the list pursuant to Article 2(2) indicating the territorial and, where appropriate, the special jurisdiction of the courts;

(b) the names and addresses of the central bodies and competent authorities pursuant to Article 3, indicating their territorial jurisdiction;

(c) the technical means for the receipt of requests available to the courts on the list pursuant to Article 2(2);

(d) the languages accepted for the requests as referred to in Article 5.

Member States shall inform the Commission of any subsequent changes to this information.

Article 23
Review

No later than 1 January 2007, and every five years thereafter, the Commission shall present to the European Parliament, the Council and the Economic and Social Committee a report on the application of this Regulation, paying special attention to the practical application of Article 3(1)(c) and 3, and Articles 17 and 18.

Article 24
Entry into force

1. This Regulation shall enter into force on 1 July 2001.

2. This Regulation shall apply from 1 January 2004, except for Articles 19, 21 and 22, which shall apply from 1 July 2001.

This Regulation shall be binding in its entirety and directly applicable in the Member States in accordance with the Treaty establishing the European Community.

Done at Brussels, 28 May 2001.

For the Council

The President

T Bodström

ANNEX C

Designated courts in England and Wales under the Taking of Evidence Regulation (see paragraph 7)

Area	Designated court
London and South Eastern Circuit	Royal Courts of Justice (Queen's Bench Division)
Midland Circuit	Birmingham Civil Justice Centre
Western Circuit	Bristol County Court
Wales and Chester Circuit	Cardiff Civil Justice Centre
Northern Circuit	Manchester County Court
North Eastern Circuit	Leeds County Court

PRACTICE DIRECTION – EXPERTS

THIS PRACTICE DIRECTION SUPPLEMENTS PART 17 OF THE FAMILY PROCEDURE (ADOPTION) RULES 2005

Part 17 is intended to limit the use of oral expert evidence to that which is reasonably required. In addition, where possible, matters requiring expert evidence should be dealt with by a single expert. Permission of the court is always required either to call an expert or to put an expert's report in evidence.

Expert evidence – general requirements

1.1 It is the duty of an expert to help the court on matters within his own expertise: rule 156(1). This duty is paramount and overrides any obligation to the person from whom the expert has received instructions or by whom he is paid: rule 156(2).

1.2 Expert evidence should be the independent product of the expert uninfluenced by the pressures of litigation.

1.3 An expert should assist the court by providing objective, unbiased opinion on matters within his expertise, and should not assume the role of an advocate.

1.4 An expert should consider all material facts, including those which might detract from his opinion.

1.5 An expert should make it clear –

(a) when a question or issue falls outside his expertise; and
(b) when he is not able to reach a definite opinion, for example because he has insufficient information.

1.6 If, after producing a report, an expert changes his view on any material matter, such change of view should be communicated to all the parties without delay, and when appropriate to the court.

Form and content of expert's reports

2.1 An expert's report should be addressed to the court and not to the party from whom the expert has received his instructions.

2.2 An expert's report must –

(1) give details of the expert's qualifications;
(2) give details of any literature or other material which the expert has relied on in making the report;
(3) contain a statement setting out the substance of all facts and instructions given to the expert which are material to the opinions expressed in the report or upon which those opinions are based;
(4) make clear which of the facts stated in the report are within the expert's own knowledge;
(5) say who carried out any examination, measurement, test or experiment which the expert has used for the report, give the qualifications of that person, and say whether or not the test or experiment has been carried out under the expert's supervision;
(6) where there is a range of opinion on the matters dealt with in the report –
    (a) summarise the range of opinion, and
    (b) give reasons for his own opinion;
(7) contain a summary of the conclusions reached;

(8) if the expert is not able to give his opinion without qualification, state the qualification; and

(9) contain a statement that the expert understands his duty to the court, and has complied and will continue to comply with that duty.

2.3 An expert's report must be verified by a statement of truth as well as containing the statements required in paragraph 2.2(8) and (9).

2.4 The form of the statement of truth is as follows –

'I confirm that insofar as the facts stated in my report are within my own knowledge I have made clear which they are and I believe them to be true, and that the opinions I have expressed represent my true and complete professional opinion.'

2.5 Attention is drawn to rule 133 which sets out the consequences of verifying a document containing a false statement without an honest belief in its truth.

Information

3 Under rule 162 the court may direct a party with access to information which is not reasonably available to another party to prepare and file a document which records the information. A court officer will then send a copy of that document to the other party. The document must include sufficient details of all the facts, tests, experiments and assumptions which underlie any part of the information to enable the party on whom it is served to make, or to obtain, a proper interpretation of the information and an assessment of its significance.

Instructions

4 The instructions referred to in paragraph 2.2(3) will not be protected by privilege (see rule 163(4)). But cross-examination of the expert on the contents of his instructions will not be allowed unless the court permits it (or unless the party who gave the instructions consents to it). Before it gives permission the court must be satisfied that there are reasonable grounds to consider that the statement in the report of the substance of the instructions is inaccurate or incomplete. If the court is so satisfied, it will allow the cross-examination where it appears to be in the interests of justice to do so.

Questions to experts

5.1 Questions asked for the purpose of clarifying the expert's report (see rule 159) should be put, in writing, to the expert not later than 5 days after receipt of the expert's report (see paragraphs 1.2 to 1.5 as to verification).

5.2 Where a party sends a written question or questions direct to an expert, a copy of the questions should, at the same time, be sent to the court and, unless the court directs otherwise, a court officer will send them to the other party or parties.

5.3 The party or parties instructing the expert must pay any fees charged by that expert for answering questions put under rule 159. This does not affect any decision of the court as to the party who is ultimately to bear the expert's costs.

Single expert

6 Where the court has directed that the evidence on a particular issue is to be given by one expert only (rule 160) but there are a number of disciplines relevant to that issue, a leading expert in the dominant discipline should be identified as the single expert. He should prepare the general part of the report and be responsible for annexing or incorporating the contents of any reports from experts in other disciplines.

Orders

7 Where a direction requires an act to be done by an expert, or otherwise affects an expert, the party instructing that expert must serve a copy of the direction on the expert instructed by him. In the case of a jointly instructed expert, unless the court directs otherwise, the applicant must serve the direction.

PRACTICE DIRECTION – CHANGE OF SOLICITOR

THIS PRACTICE DIRECTION SUPPLEMENTS PART 18 OF THE FAMILY PROCEDURE (ADOPTION) RULES 2005

Solicitor acting for a party

1.2 Subject to rule 168(6) (where the certificate of a LSC funded client or assisted person is revoked or discharged), where a party has changed his solicitor or intends to act in person, the former solicitor will be considered to be the party's solicitor unless or until –

(1) a notice of the change is –
  (a) filed with the court;[1] and
  (b) served on the former solicitor;[2] and
  (c) served on every other party in accordance with directions of the court;[3] or
(2) the court makes an order under rule 169 and the order is served on the former solicitor and every other party in accordance with directions of the court.[4]

1.2 A solicitor appointed to represent a party only as an advocate at a hearing will not be considered to be acting for that party within the meaning of Part 18.

Notice of change of solicitor

2.1 Rule 168(1) sets out the circumstances following which a notice of the change must be filed and served.

2.2 A notice of the change must also be filed and served in accordance with the court's directions where, under rule 168(6) –

(1) the certificate of a LSC funded client or assisted person is revoked or discharged; and
(2) the LSC funded client or the assisted person wishes either to act in person or appoint another solicitor to act on his behalf.

2.3 Form FP8 should be used to give notice of any change. The notice should be filed in the court office in which the application is proceeding.

Application for an order that a solicitor has ceased to act

3.1 A solicitor may apply under rule 169 for an order declaring that he has ceased to be the solicitor acting for a party.

3.2 The application should be made in accordance with Part 9 and must be supported by evidence.[5] Unless the court directs otherwise the application notice must be served on the party.[6]

3.3 The court will give directions about serving an order made under rule 169 on every party. Where the order is not served by the court, the person serving must file a certificate of service in practice form FP6.

---

1 See rule 168(2)(a).
2 See rule 168(2)(b).
3 See rule 168(3).
4 See rule 168(5).
5 See Part 15 and the Practice Direction that supplements it.
6 See rule 169(2).

Application by another party to remove a solicitor

4.1 Rule 170 sets out circumstances in which any other party may apply for an order declaring that a solicitor has ceased to be the solicitor acting for another party in the proceedings.

4.2 The application should be made in accordance with Part 9 and must be supported by evidence. Unless the court directs otherwise the application notice must be served on the party to whose solicitor the application relates.

4.3 The court will give directions about serving an order made under rule 170 on every other party to the proceedings. Where the order is not served by the court, the person serving must file a certificate of service in practice form FP6.

PRACTICE DIRECTION – APPEALS

THIS PRACTICE DIRECTION SUPPLEMENTS PART 19 OF THE FAMILY PROCEDURE (ADOPTION) RULES 2005

1 This practice direction applies to all appeals to which Part 19 applies and in this practice direction a reference to a 'judge' includes a district judge, including a district judge of the principal registry of the Family Division.

Routes of appeal

2.1 The following table sets out to which court or judge an appeal is to be made (subject to obtaining any necessary permission) –

Decision of –	Appeal made to –
Magistrates' court	High Court
District judge of a county court	Circuit judge
District judge of the High Court	High Court judge
District judge of the principal registry of the Family Division	High Court judge
Costs judge	High Court judge
Circuit judge or recorder	Court of Appeal
High Court judge	Court of Appeal

(Section 16(1) of the Supreme Court Act 1981 (as amended); section 77(1) of the County Courts Act 1984 (as amended); section 94 of the Children Act 1989 (as amended) and the Access to Justice Act 1999 (Destination of Appeals) (Family Proceedings) Order 2005 set out the provisions governing routes of appeal.)

2.2 Where the decision to be appealed is a decision in a Part 10 application on a point of law in a case which did not involve any substantial dispute of fact, the court to which the appeal lies, where that court is the High Court or a county court and unless the appeal would lie to the Court of Appeal in any event, must consider whether to order the appeal to be transferred to the Court of Appeal under rule 182.

Grounds for appeal

3.1 Rule 181(3) sets out the circumstances in which the appeal court will allow an appeal.

3.2 The grounds of appeal should –

(1) set out clearly the reasons why rule 181(3)(a) or (b) is said to apply; and
(2) specify, in respect of each ground, whether the ground raises an appeal on a point of law or is an appeal against a finding of fact.

Permission to appeal

4.1 Rule 173 sets out the circumstances when permission to appeal is required.

(The requirement of permission to appeal may be imposed by a practice direction – see rule 173(1)(b).)

Court to which permission to appeal application should be made

4.2 An application for permission should be made orally at the hearing at which the decision to be appealed against is made, where that decision is made by the High Court or a county court.

4.3 Where –

(a) no application for permission to appeal is made at the hearing;
(b) the decision being appealed was made by a magistrates' court; or
(c) the lower court refuses permission to appeal,

an application for permission to appeal may be made to the appeal court in accordance with rules 173(2) and (3).

(Rule 171(3) defines 'lower court'.)

4.4 There is no appeal from a decision of the appeal court to allow or refuse permission to appeal to that court (although where the appeal court, without a hearing, refuses permission to appeal, the person seeking permission may request that decision to be reconsidered at a hearing). See section 54(4) of the Access to Justice Act 1999 and rule 173(2), (3), (4) and (5).

Consideration of Permission without a hearing

4.5 Applications for permission to appeal may be considered by the appeal court without a hearing.

4.6 If permission is granted without a hearing the parties will be notified of that decision and the procedure in paragraphs 6.1 to 6.8 will then apply.

4.7 If permission is refused without a hearing the parties will be notified of that decision with the reasons for it. The decision is subject to the appellant's right to have it reconsidered at an oral hearing. This may be before the same judge.

4.8 A request for the decision to be reconsidered at an oral hearing must be filed at the appeal court within 7 days after service of the notice that permission has been refused. A copy of the request must be served on the respondent. Unless the court directs otherwise, a court officer will effect service.

Permission hearing

4.9 Where an appellant, who is represented, makes a request for a decision to be reconsidered at an oral hearing, the appellant's advocate must, at least 4 days before the hearing, in a brief written statement –

(a) inform the court and the respondent of the points which he proposes to raise at the hearing;
(b) set out his reasons why permission should be granted notwithstanding the reasons given for the refusal of permission; and
(c) confirm, where applicable, that the requirements of paragraph 4.12 have been complied with (appellant in receipt of services funded by the Legal Services Commission).

4.10 Notice of a permission hearing will be given to the respondent but he is not required to attend unless the court requests him to do so.

4.11 If the court requests the respondent's attendance at the permission hearing, a copy of the appeal bundle will be supplied to the respondent (see paragraph 5.9) within 7 days of being notified of the request, or such other period as the court may direct. The costs of providing that bundle shall be borne by the appellant initially, but will form part of the costs of the permission application. Unless the court directs otherwise, a court officer will supply the appeal bundle.

Appellants in receipt of services funded by the Legal Services Commission applying for permission to appeal

4.12 Where the appellant is in receipt of services funded by the Legal Services Commission (or legally aided) and permission to appeal has been refused by the appeal court without a hearing, the appellant must send a copy of the reasons the appeal court gave for refusing permission to the relevant office of the Legal Services Commission as soon as it has been received from the court. The court will require confirmation that this has been done if a hearing is requested to re-consider the question of permission.

Limited permission

4.13 Where a court under rule 173(7) gives permission to appeal on some issues only, it will –

(1) refuse permission on any remaining issues; or
(2) reserve the question of permission to appeal on any remaining issues to the court hearing the appeal.

4.14 If the court reserves the question of permission under paragraph 4.13(2), the appellant must, within 14 days after service of the court's order, inform the appeal court in writing whether he intends to pursue the reserved issues. A court officer will inform the respondent whether the appellant intends to pursue the reserved issues. If the appellant does intend to pursue the reserved issues, the parties must include in any time estimate for the appeal hearing, their time estimate for the reserved issues.

4.15 If the appeal court refuses permission to appeal on the remaining issues without a hearing and the applicant wishes to have that decision reconsidered at an oral hearing, the time limit in rule 173(5) shall apply. Any application for an extension of this time limit should be made promptly. The court hearing the appeal on the issues for which permission has been granted will not normally grant, at the appeal hearing, an application to extend the time limit in rule 173(5) for the remaining issues.

4.16 If the appeal court refuses permission to appeal on remaining issues at or after an oral hearing, the application for permission to appeal on those issues cannot be renewed at the appeal hearing. See section 54(4) of the Access to Justice Act 1999.

Respondents' costs of permission applications

4.17 In most cases, applications for permission to appeal will be determined without the court requesting –

(1) submissions from; or
(2) if there is an oral hearing, attendance by,

the respondent.

4.18 Where the court does not request submissions from or attendance by the respondent, costs will not normally be allowed to a respondent who volunteers submissions or attendance.

4.19 Where the court does request –

(1) submissions from; or
(2) attendance by the respondent,

the court will normally allow the respondent his costs if permission is refused.

Appellant's notice

5.1 An appellant's notice must be filed and served in all cases. Where an application for permission to appeal is made to the appeal court it must be applied for in the appellant's notice.

Human Rights

5.2 Where the appellant seeks –

(a) to rely on any issue under the Human Rights Act 1998; or
(b) a remedy available under that Act,

for the first time in an appeal, he must include in his appeal notice the information required by rule 116(1).

5.3 The practice direction supplementing Part 13 shall apply as if references to the directions hearing were to the application for permission to appeal.

Extension of time for filing appellant's notice

5.4 If an appellant requires an extension of time for filing his notice the application must be made in the appellant's notice. The notice should state the reason for the delay and the steps taken prior to the application being made.

5.5 Where the appellant's notice includes an application for an extension of time and permission to appeal has been given or is not required the respondent has the right to be heard on that application. A copy of the appeal bundle must be served on the respondent (see paragraph 5.9). Unless the court directs otherwise, a court officer will effect service. However, a respondent who unreasonably opposes an extension of time runs the risk of being ordered to pay the appellant's costs of that application.

5.6 If an extension of time is given following such an application the procedure at paragraphs 6.1 to 6.8 applies.

Applications

5.7 Notice of an application to be made to the appeal court for a remedy incidental to the appeal (eg an interim injunction under rule 118) may be included in the appeal notice or in a Part 9 application notice.

(Paragraph 9 of this practice direction contains other provisions relating to applications.)

Documents

5.8 The appellant must file the following documents together with an appeal bundle (see paragraph 5.9) with his appellant's notice –

(a) two additional copies of the appellant's notice for the appeal court;
(b) one copy of the appellant's notice for each of the respondents;
(c) one copy of his skeleton argument for each copy of the appellant's notice that is filed (see paragraph 5.9);
(d) a sealed or stamped copy of the order being appealed or a copy of the notice of the making of an order;

(e) a copy of any order giving or refusing permission to appeal, together with a copy of the judge's reasons for allowing or refusing permission to appeal; and

(f) any witness statements or affidavits in support of any application included in the appellant's notice.

5.9 An appellant must include the following documents in his appeal bundle –

(a) a sealed or stamped copy of the appellant's notice;

(b) a sealed or stamped copy of the order being appealed, or a copy of the notice of the making of an order;

(c) a copy of any order giving or refusing permission to appeal, together with a copy of the judge's reasons for allowing or refusing permission to appeal;

(d) any affidavit or witness statement filed in support of any application included in the appellant's notice;

(e) a copy of his skeleton argument;

(f) a transcript or note of judgment or, in a magistrates' court, written reasons for the courts decision (see paragraph 5.23), and in cases where permission to appeal was given by the lower court or is not required those parts of any transcript of evidence which are directly relevant to any question at issue on the appeal;

(g) the application form;

(h) any application notice (or case management documentation) relevant to the subject of the appeal;

(i) any other documents which the appellant reasonably considers necessary to enable the appeal court to reach its decision on the hearing of the application or appeal; and

(j) such other documents as the court may direct.

5.10 All documents that are extraneous to the issues to be considered on the application or the appeal must be excluded. The appeal bundle may include affidavits, witness statements, summaries, experts' reports and exhibits but only where these are directly relevant to the subject matter of the appeal.

5.11 Where the appellant is represented, the appeal bundle must contain a certificate signed by his solicitor, counsel or other representative to the effect that he has read and understood paragraph 5.10 and that the composition of the appeal bundle complies with it.

5.12 Where it is not possible to file all the above documents, the appellant must indicate which documents have not yet been filed and the reasons why they are not currently available. The appellant must then provide a reasonable estimate of when the missing document or documents can be filed and file them as soon as reasonably practicable.

Skeleton arguments

5.13 The appellant's notice must, subject to paragraphs 5.14 and 5.15, be accompanied by a skeleton argument. Alternatively the skeleton argument may be included in the appellant's notice. Where the skeleton argument is so included it will not form part of the notice for the purposes of rule 178.

5.14 Where it is impracticable for the appellant's skeleton argument to accompany the appellant's notice it must be filed and served on all respondents within 14 days of filing the notice. Unless the court directs otherwise, a court officer will effect service.

5.15 An appellant who is not represented need not file a skeleton argument but is encouraged to do so since this will be helpful to the court.

5.16 A skeleton argument must contain a numbered list of the points which the party wishes to make. These should both define and confine the areas of controversy. Each point should be stated as concisely as the nature of the case allows.

5.17 A numbered point must be followed by a reference to any document on which the party wishes to rely.

5.18 A skeleton argument must state, in respect of each authority cited –

  (a) the proposition of law that the authority demonstrates; and
  (b) the parts of the authority (identified by page or paragraph references) that support the proposition.

5.19 If more than one authority is cited in support of a given proposition, the skeleton argument must briefly state the reason for taking that course.

5.20 The statement referred to in paragraph 5.19 should not materially add to the length of the skeleton argument but should be sufficient to demonstrate, in the context of the argument –

  (a) the relevance of the authority or authorities to that argument; and
  (b) that the citation is necessary for a proper presentation of that argument.

5.21 The cost of preparing a skeleton argument which –

  (a) does not comply with the requirements set out in this paragraph; or
  (b) was not filed within the time limits provided by this Practice Direction (or any further time granted by the court),

will not be allowed on assessment except to the extent that the court otherwise directs.

5.22 The appellant should consider what other information the appeal court will need. This may include a list of persons who feature in the case or glossaries of technical terms. A chronology of relevant events will be necessary in most appeals.

Suitable record of the judgment

5.23 Where the judgment to be appealed has been officially recorded by the court, an approved transcript of that record should accompany the appellant's notice. Photocopies will not be accepted for this purpose. However, where there is no officially recorded judgment, the following documents will be acceptable –

WRITTEN JUDGMENTS

Where the judgment was made in writing a copy of that judgment endorsed with the judge's signature.

WRITTEN REASONS

Where, in a magistrates' court, reasons for the court's decision are given in writing, a copy of those reasons.

NOTE OF JUDGMENT

When judgment was not officially recorded or made in writing a note of the judgment (agreed between the appellant's and respondent's advocates) should be submitted for approval to the judge whose decision is being appealed. If the parties cannot agree on a single note of the judgment, both versions should be provided to that judge with an explanatory letter. For the purpose of an application for permission to appeal the note need not be approved by the respondent or the lower court judge.

ADVOCATES' NOTES OF JUDGMENTS WHERE THE APPELLANT IS UNREPRESENTED

When the appellant was unrepresented in the lower court it is the duty of any advocate for the respondent to make his/her note of judgment promptly available, free of charge to the appellant where there is no officially recorded judgment or if the court so directs. Where the appellant was represented in the lower court it is the duty of his/her own former advocate to make his/her note available in these circumstances. The appellant should submit the note of judgment to the appeal court.

5.24 An appellant may not be able to obtain an official transcript or other suitable record of the lower court's decision within the time within which the appellant's notice must be filed. In such cases the appellant's notice must still be completed to the best of the appellant's ability on the basis of the documentation available. However it may be amended subsequently with the permission of the appeal court in accordance with rule 178.

Advocates' notes of judgments

5.25 Advocates' brief (or, where appropriate, refresher) fee includes –

(1) remuneration for taking a note of the judgment of the court;
(2) having the note transcribed accurately;
(3) attempting to agree the note with the other side if represented;
(4) submitting the note to the judge for approval where appropriate;
(5) revising it if so requested by the judge;
(6) providing any copies required for the appeal court, instructing solicitors and lay client; and
(7) providing a copy of his note to an unrepresented appellant.

Transcripts or Notes of Evidence

5.26 When the evidence is relevant to the appeal an official transcript of the relevant evidence must be obtained. Transcripts or notes of evidence are generally not needed for the purpose of determining an application for permission to appeal.

Notes of evidence

5.27 If evidence relevant to the appeal was not officially recorded, a typed version of the judge's or justices' clerk's/assistant clerk's notes of evidence must be obtained.

Transcripts at public expense

5.28 Where the lower court or the appeal court is satisfied that an unrepresented appellant is in such poor financial circumstances that the cost of a transcript would be an excessive burden the court may certify that the cost of obtaining one official transcript should be borne at public expense.

5.29 In the case of a request for an official transcript of evidence or proceedings to be paid for at public expense, the court must also be satisfied that there are reasonable grounds for appeal. Whenever possible a request for a transcript at public expense should be made to the lower court when asking for permission to appeal.

Filing and service of appellant's notice

5.30 Rule 174 sets out the procedure and time limits for filing and serving an appellant's notice. The appellant must file the appellant's notice at the appeal court within such period as may be directed by the lower court, where that court is the High Court or a county court, which should not normally exceed 28 days or, where the lower court directs no such period or the lower court is a magistrates' court, within 14 days of the date of the decision that the appellant wishes to appeal.

5.31 Where the lower court judge announces his decision and reserves the reasons for his judgment or order until a later date, he should, in the exercise of powers under rule 174(2)(a), fix a period for filing the appellant's notice at the appeal court that takes this into account.

5.32 Except where the appeal court orders otherwise a sealed or stamped copy of the appellant's notice, including any skeleton arguments must be served on all respondents in accordance with the timetable prescribed by rule 174(3) except where this requirement is modified by paragraph 5.14 in which case the skeleton argument should be served as soon as it is filed.

5.33 Except where the appeal court orders otherwise, a sealed or stamped copy of the appellant's notice, including any skeleton arguments, must also be served on –

  (a) any children's guardian, reporting officer or children and family reporter; and
  (b) where the appeal is from a magistrates' court, the court officer.

Unless the court directs otherwise, a court officer will effect service.

5.34 Unless the court otherwise directs a respondent need not take any action when served with an appellant's notice until such time as notification is given to him that permission to appeal has been given.

5.35 The court may dispense with the requirement for service of the notice on a respondent.

5.36 Where the appellant is applying for permission to appeal in his appellant's notice, his appellant's notice and skeleton argument (but not the appeal bundle) must be served on the respondents, unless the appeal court directs otherwise.

5.37 Where permission to appeal –

  (a) has been given by the lower court; or
  (b) is not required,

the appeal bundle must be served on the respondents and the persons mentioned in paragraph 5.33 with the appellant's notice. Unless the court directs otherwise, a court officer will effect service.

Amendment of Appeal Notice

5.38 An appeal notice may be amended with permission. Such an application to amend and any application in opposition will normally be dealt with at the hearing unless that course would cause unnecessary expense or delay in which case a request should be made for the application to amend to be heard in advance. If the application to amend relates to an appeal from a magistrates' court it may be heard by a district judge of the appeal court.

Procedure after permission is obtained

6.1 This paragraph sets out the procedure where –

  (1) permission to appeal is given by the appeal court; or

(2) the appellant's notice is filed in the appeal court and –
   (a) permission was given by the lower court; or
   (b) permission is not required.

6.2 If the appeal court gives permission to appeal, the appeal bundle must be served on each of the respondents within 7 days beginning with the date that the order giving permission to appeal is made. Unless the court directs otherwise, a court officer will effect service.

6.3 The appeal court will send the parties –

(1) notification of the date of the hearing or the period of time (the 'listing window') during which the appeal is likely to be heard;
(2) where permission is granted by the appeal court a copy of the order giving permission to appeal; and
(3) any other directions given by the court.

6.4 Where the appeal court grants permission to appeal, the appellant must add the following documents to the appeal bundle –

(a) the respondent's notice and skeleton argument (if any);
(b) those parts of the transcripts of evidence which are directly relevant to any question at issue on the appeal;
(c) the order granting permission to appeal and, where permission to appeal was granted at an oral hearing, the transcript (or note) of any judgment which was given; and
(d) any document which the appellant and respondent have agreed to add to the appeal bundle in accordance with paragraph 7.16.

6.5 Where permission to appeal has been refused on a particular issue, the appellant must remove from the appeal bundle all documents that are relevant only to that issue.

Time estimates

6.6 If the appellant is legally represented, the appeal court must be notified, in writing, of the advocate's time estimate for the hearing of the appeal.

6.7 The time estimate must be that of the advocate who will argue the appeal. It should exclude the time required by the court to give judgment.

6.8 A court officer will notify the respondent of the appellant's time estimate and if the respondent disagrees with the time estimate he must inform the court within 7 days of the notification. In the absence of such notification the respondent will be deemed to have accepted the estimate proposed on behalf of the appellant.

Respondent

7.1 A respondent who wishes to ask the appeal court to vary the order of the lower court in any way must appeal and permission will be required on the same basis as for an appellant.

(Paragraph 3.2 applies to grounds of appeal by a respondent.)

7.2 A respondent who wishes to appeal or who wishes to ask the appeal court to uphold the order of the lower court for reasons different from or additional to those given by the lower court must file a respondent's notice.

7.3 If the respondent does not file a respondent's notice, he will not be entitled, except with the permission of the court, to rely on any reason not relied on in the lower court.

7.4 Paragraphs 5.2 to 5.4 of this practice direction (Human Rights and extension for time for filing appellant's notice) also apply to a respondent and a respondent's notice.

Time limits

7.5 The time limits for filing a respondent's notice are set out in rule 175(4) and (5).

7.6 Where an extension of time is required the extension must be requested in the respondent's notice and the reasons why the respondent failed to act within the specified time must be included.

7.7 Except where paragraph 7.8 applies, the respondent must file a skeleton argument for the court in all cases where he proposes to address arguments to the court. The respondent's skeleton argument may be included within a respondent's notice. Where a skeleton argument is included within a respondent's notice it will not form part of the notice for the purposes of rule 178.

7.8 A respondent who –

(a) files a respondent's notice; but
(b) does not include his skeleton argument within that notice,

must file his skeleton argument within 14 days of filing the notice.

7.9 A respondent who does not file a respondent's notice but who files a skeleton argument must file that skeleton argument at least 7 days before the appeal hearing.

(Rule 175(4) sets out the period for filing a respondent's notice.)

7.10 A respondent who is not represented need not file a skeleton argument but is encouraged to do so in order to assist the court.

7.11 The respondent's skeleton argument must be served on –

(a) the appellant; and
(b) any other respondent.

Unless the court directs otherwise, a court officer will effect service.

7.12 A respondent's skeleton argument must conform to the directions at paragraphs 5.16 to 5.22 with any necessary modifications. It should, where appropriate, answer the arguments set out in the appellant's skeleton argument.

Applications within respondent's notices

7.13 A respondent may include an application within a respondent's notice in accordance with paragraph 5.7.

Filing respondent's notices and skeleton arguments

7.14 The respondent must file the following documents with his respondent's notice in every case –

(a) two additional copies of the respondent's notice for the appeal court; and
(b) one copy each for the appellant and any other respondents.

7.15 The respondent may file a skeleton argument with his respondent's notice and –

(a) where he does so he must file two copies; and

(b) where he does not do so he must comply with paragraph 7.8.

7.16 If the respondent wishes to rely on any documents which he reasonably considers necessary to enable the appeal court to reach its decision on the appeal in addition to those filed by the appellant, any amendments to the appeal bundle should be agreed with the appellant if possible.

7.17 If the representatives for the parties are unable to reach agreement, the respondent may prepare a supplemental bundle.

7.18 If the respondent prepares a supplemental bundle he must file it, together with the requisite number of copies for the appeal court, at the appeal court –
  (a) with the respondent's notice; or
  (b) if a respondent's notice is not filed, within 21 days after he is served with the appeal bundle.

7.19 The following documents must be served –
  (1) the respondent's notice;
  (2) his skeleton argument (if any); and
  (3) the supplemental bundle (if any),

on –
  (a) the appellant; and
  (b) any other respondent,

as soon as practicable and in any event not later than 7 days after the respondent's notice was filed. Unless the court directs otherwise, a court officer will effect service.

Appeals to the High Court

Application

8.1 This paragraph applies where an appeal lies to the High Court from the decision of a magistrates' court.

8.2 The appellant's notice must be filed in –
  (a) the principal registry of the Family Division; or
  (b) the district registry, being in the same place as an adoption centre or an intercountry adoption centre within the meaning of article 2(d) and (e) of the Children (Allocation of Proceedings) Order 1991 (SI 1991/1677), which is nearest to the court from which the appeal lies.

8.3 A respondent's notice must be filed at the court where the appellant's notice was filed.

8.4 In the case of appeals from district judges of the High Court, appeals, applications for permission and any other applications in the appeal may be heard and directions in the appeal may be given by a High Court Judge or by any person authorised under section 9 of the Supreme Court Act 1981 to act as a judge of the High Court.

Appeals to a judge of a county court from a district judge

8.5 The Designated Family Judge in consultation with the Family Division Liaison Judges has responsibility for allocating appeals from decisions of district judges to circuit judges.

Applications

9.1 Where a party to an appeal makes an application whether in an appeal notice or by Part 9 application notice, the provisions of Part 9 will apply.

9.2 The applicant must file the following documents with the notice –

(1) one additional copy of the application notice for the appeal court and one copy for each of the respondents;
(2) where applicable a sealed or stamped copy of the order which is the subject of the main appeal or a copy of the notice of the making of an order;
(3) a bundle of documents in support which should include –
   (a) the Part 9 application notice; and
   (b) any witness statements and affidavits filed in support of the application notice.

Disposing of applications or appeals by consent

10.1 Where an appellant does not wish to pursue an application or an appeal, he may request the appeal court for an order that his application or appeal be dismissed. Such a request must state whether the appellant is a child, non-subject child or patient.

10.2 The request must be accompanied by a consent signed by the other parties stating whether the respondent is a child, non-subject child or patient and consents to the dismissal of the application or appeal.

10.3 Where the application relates to an appeal from a magistrates' court, the application may be heard by a district judge of the appeal court.

Allowing unopposed appeals or applications on paper

11 The appeal court will not normally make an order allowing an appeal unless satisfied that the decision of the lower court was wrong, but the appeal court may set aside or vary the order of the lower court with consent and without determining the merits of the appeal, if it is satisfied that there are good and sufficient reasons for doing so. Where the appeal court is requested by all parties to allow an application or an appeal the court may consider the request on the papers. The request should state whether any of the parties is a child, non-subject child or patient and set out the relevant history of the proceedings and the matters relied on as justifying the proposed order and be accompanied by a copy of the proposed order.

Withdrawal of appeal

12 An application to withdraw an appeal from a decision of a magistrates' court may be heard by a district judge of the appeal court.

Summary assessment of costs

13.1 Costs are likely to be assessed by way of summary assessment at the following hearings –

(1) contested directions hearings;
(2) applications for permission to appeal at which the respondent is present;
(3) appeals from case management decisions or decisions made at directions hearings; and
(4) appeals listed for one day or less.

(Provision for summary assessment of costs is made by section 13 of the practice direction supplementing CPR Part 44.)

13.2 Parties attending any of the hearings referred to in paragraph 13.1 should be prepared to deal with the summary assessment.

Reopening of final appeals

14.1 This paragraph applies to applications under rule 183 for permission to reopen a final determination of an appeal.

14.2 In this paragraph, 'appeal' includes an application for permission to appeal.

14.3 Permission must be sought from the court whose decision the applicant wishes to reopen.

14.4 The application for permission must be made by application notice and supported by written evidence, verified by a statement of truth.

14.5 A copy of the application for permission must not be served on any other party to the original appeal unless the court so directs.

14.6 Where the court directs that the application for permission is to be served on another party, that party may within 14 days of the service on him of the copy of the application file a written statement either supporting or opposing the application which, unless the court directs otherwise, a court officer will serve on the other parties.

14.7 The application for permission, and any written statements supporting or opposing it, will be considered on paper by a single judge, and will be allowed to proceed only if the judge so directs.

Appendix E

FORMS

Application for a placement order
Section 22 Adoption and Children Act 2002

Name of court	
Case no.	
Date received by the court	
Date issued	

Notes to applicants
- Before filling in this form, please read the guidance notes on completion.
- Please complete every item. If any item does not apply to your application, or you do not have the necessary information, please say so.
- If there is not enough room for your reply to any question, please continue on a separate sheet. Please put the child's name, the Part and the number of the question at the head of the continuation sheet.
- Use black ink when filling in the form.

Part 1 About you

1) Title

☐ Mr   ☐ Mrs   ☐ Miss   ☐ Ms   ☐ Other _____

2) My name is

First name(s) in full

Last name

3) I am an authorised officer of (give name and address (including postcode) of local authority)

4) My telephone number is

5) My position in the local authority is

6) My solicitor in these proceedings is

Name of solicitor	
Name of firm	
Address (including postcode)	

Telephone no.		Fax no.	
DX no.			
E-mail address			

A50 Application for a placement order Section 22 Adoption and Children Act 2002 (12.05)   HMCS

Part 2 About this application

7) I apply for an order authorising the said local authority to place (give name of child) ◀ See Note 1
◀ See Note 2

First name(s) in full

The child's address is

Last name

for adoption and give the following particulars in support of this application.

Grounds for the application
8) The grounds for this application are that the local authority are satisfied that the child   ◀ See Note 3
should be placed for adoption and (please tick the further grounds that apply)

☐ the child is subject to a care order and the local authority is/is not authorised to place the child for adoption, or

☐ an application for a care order has been made and has not been disposed of, or

☐ the child was placed for adoption by the local authority on (give date)
or the child is being accommodated by the local authority and no adoption agency is authorised to place the child for adoption,

and

☐ the child has no parent or guardian, or

☐ the local authority consider that the conditions in section 31(2) of the Children Act 1989 are met because the child is suffering or is likely to suffer significant harm.

Please state below why you consider that the conditions in section 31(2) of the Children Act 1989 are met (continue on a separate sheet if necessary).

Part 3 About the child

9) The child is a
☐ Boy ☐ Girl
and has not been married.

10) The child was born on

and is the person to whom the attached certified copy of the entry in the Register of Live Births/Register of Adopted Children relates

or To the best of my/our knowledge the child was born on or about

in

◄ See Note 4

11) The child's nationality is

Care

12) ☐ No local authority or voluntary organisation has parental responsibility for the child

or

☐ The following local authority/voluntary organisation has parental responsibility for the child:

Name of local authority or voluntary organisation	
Address (including post code)	

Name of your contact in the authority/organisation	
Telephone no.	

Care proceedings

13) ☐ There are no concurrent or ongoing care proceedings in respect of the child

or

☐ The child is the subject of ongoing/concurrent care proceedings (give details below)

Name of court	
Case number	
Date of issue	
Date of any timetabled hearing, or pre-hearing review	
Name of any allocated judge or legal advisor	

Maintenance

14) ☐ No maintenance order/agreement or award of child support maintenance under the Child Support Act 1991 has been made in respect of the child

◄ See Note 5

or

☐ The following maintenance order/agreement/award of child support maintenance has been made

Person liable to pay maintenance	
Address (including post code)	

Court and date of order	
Date of maintenance agreement/child support maintenance award	

About other orders or proceedings that affect the child

15) ☐ To the best of my knowledge, no proceedings relating to the child (other than any maintenance order or care proceedings as given above) have been completed or commenced in any court

◄ See Note 6

or

☐ The following proceedings relating to the child have been completed/commenced (in addition to any maintenance order or care proceedings given above)

Type of order made (or applied for)	Date of order (or date of next hearing)	Name of court	Case number (or serial number)

Cases concerning a related child

16) ☐ To the best of my knowledge, no proceedings relating to a full, half or step brother or sister of the child have been completed or commenced in any court

or

☐ The following proceedings relating to a full, half or step brother or sister of the child have been completed/commenced (please give details below and, if you were a party to any proceedings that have been completed, attach a copy of the final order)

Relationship to child (eg. sister, half-brother)	Type of order made (or applied for)	Date of order (or date of next hearing)	Name of court	Case number (or serial number)

Part 4 About the child's parents or guardian

The child's mother

17) The name of the child's mother is

First name(s) in full

Last name

Her address is (if deceased, please write 'Deceased' in the address box)

Her nationality is

The child's father

◀ See Note 7

18) The name of the child's father is

First name(s) in full

Last name

His address is (if deceased, please write 'Deceased' in the address box)

His nationality is

Does he have parental responsibility for the child?   ◀ See Note 8

☐ Yes   ☐ No

If No, does he intend to apply for an order under section 4(1)(c) of the Children Act 1989 (a parental responsibility order) or a residence or contact order in respect of the child?

☐ Yes   ☐ No

The child's guardian

19) The name of the child's guardian is   ◀ See Note 9

First name(s) in full

Last name

His/Her address is

Part 5 Parent(s)/guardian(s) consent to placement for adoption

20) ☐ The child's parent(s) (or the child's guardians(s)) has/have consented to the child being placed for adoption ◀ See Note 10

or

the following parent(s) (or guardian(s)) of the child has/have not consented to the child being placed for adoption or has/have withdrawn their consent
(give name(s) below)

and I ask the court to dispense with his/her/their consent to the making of a placement order on the following grounds: (state the grounds for your request below) ◀ See Note 11

Note: You must attach to your application a brief statement of facts, and two copies, setting out a summary of the history of the case and any other facts to satisfy the court that the grounds for your request apply.

428   *Adoption – The Modern Procedure*

Part 6 Arrangements for contact with the child

Current contact arrangements
21) The current arrangements for contact with the child are as follows: ◄ See Note 12

Proposed contact arrangements
22) If the placement order is made, the following contact arrangements are proposed: ◄ See Note 13

Part 7 Statement of truth

*[I believe] [The applicant believes] that the facts stated in this application are true.
*I am duly authorised by the applicant to sign this statement.

Print full name

Signed

Date

*[Applicant] [Applicant's solicitor]

*delete as appropriate

If you attend the court for a hearing

1. Do you have a disability for which you require special assistance or special facilities? ◀ See Note 14

☐ Yes   ☐ No

If Yes, please say what your needs are below
(the court staff will get in touch with you about your requirements)

What to do now

Once you have completed and signed this form, you should take or send the form and **three copies** to the court, together with the court fee and the following documents:

- a certified copy of the full entry in the Register of Live Births that relates to the child or, where the child has been adopted, a certified copy of the entry in the Adopted Children Register;
- any written consent of the parent or guardian to the child being placed for adoption, and any notice of withdrawal of such consent;
- if you are asking the court to dispense with the consent of any parent or guardian to the child being placed for adoption, a brief statement of the facts relied on in support of the request, and **two copies** of the statement;
- a copy of any final care order relating to the child;
- if available, a copy of any parental responsibility order or parental responsibility agreement relating to the child;
- if the authority was a party to the proceedings, a copy of any other final order relating to the child that has effect and, if available, a copy of any maintenance agreement or maintenance award relating to the child;
- if the authority was a party to the proceedings, a copy of any final order relating to a full, half or step brother or sister of the child that has effect.

Application for a Placement Order (Form A50)
Notes on completing the form

Important

If you are attaching any order of the High Court or a county court to your application, it must be a sealed copy of the order (that is, a copy that has been stamped with the seal of the court). If you are attaching an order made by a magistrates' court, it must be a certified copy (a copy certified by the court officer to be a true copy of the original order), or a copy that bears the stamp of the originating court. An order issued by any other authority must be properly authenticated by that authority. If you are in any doubt about what is needed, please contact the court for assistance.

Take or send the completed application form, **and three copies,** to the court, together with the court fee and any documents you are attaching in support of your application. If you are attaching a statement of facts (see note 11 below), please supply two additional copies of the statement.

Notes on the application form

Note 1 ▶ Enter the child's first names(s) and last name exactly as they are shown on the certified copy of the full entry in the Register of Live Births (or, if the child has previously been adopted, the register of Adopted Children) you are sending with your application, otherwise enter the first name(s) and last name by which the child is known.

Note 2 ▶ If you do not want the child's address to be disclosed to any other party, **do not enter the details on this application form.** Instead you should give the details on Form A65, which you must file at the court with your application. The details will not then be disclosed to any person, except by order of the court.

Note 3 ▶ State the grounds on which the local authority is basing its application for a placement order. Note that a local authority **must** apply for a placement order if:

- the authority have placed the child for adoption, or are providing the child with accommodation; and

- no adoption agency is authorised to place the child for adoption; and

- the child has no parent or guardian, or the authority consider that the conditions in section 31(2) of the Children Act 1989 (conditions for making a care order) are met; and

- the authority are satisfied that the child ought to be placed for adoption; (Section 22(1) of the Adoption and Children Act 2002)

or

- the child is subject to a care order and the authority is not authorised to place the child for adoption, or an application for a care order has been made (and has not been disposed of), and

- the authority are satisfied that the child ought to be placed for adoption (section 22(2) of the Adoption and Children Act 2002)

The local authority **may** apply for a placement order if the child is subject to a care order and the authority are authorised to place the child for adoption under section 19 of the 2002 Act. (Section 22(3) of the Adoption and Children Act 2002)

The court cannot make a placement order in respect of a child unless –
- the child is subject to a care order; or

- the court is satisfied that the conditions in section 31(2) of the Children Act 1989 (conditions for making a care order) are met, or

- the child has no parent or guardian. (Section 21(2) of the Adoption and Children Act 2002)

Note 4 ▶ If the child has previously been adopted, a certified copy of the entry in the Adopted Children Register should be attached and not a certified copy of the entry in the Register of Live Births. Where you are unable to attach a certificate, enter the place (including the country) of birth, if known.

Note 5 ▶ This section should be completed where some person is liable to pay maintenance for the child under a court order or agreement, or child support maintenance awarded under the Child Support Act 1991. If possible, a copy of the court order or a copy of the maintenance agreement or maintenance award should be attached to the application.

Note 6 ▶ Enter details of any other earlier and concurrent court proceedings relating to the child. (Do not repeat the details of any concurrent/ongoing care proceedings or maintenance order/agreement you have entered at paragraphs 13 or 14.) In each case, give the name of the court, the nature of the proceedings and the date and effect of any order made. Please ensure that you include details of any final care order, and any contact order or other order under the Children Act 1989 that is currently in force in respect of the child. If the authority was a party to the proceedings, a copy of the final order should be attached to the application.

Note 7 ▶ If the child has previously been adopted, give the names of his/her adoptive parents and not those of his/her natural parents.

Note 8 ▶ If the child's parents were not married at the time of his/her birth, the child's father may have acquired parental responsibility

- by subsequent marriage to the child's mother;
- because he has a parental responsibility agreement with the mother, or has been granted a parental responsibility order, or
- because he registered the child's birth jointly with the child's mother (on or after 1 December 2003).

Give details of any court order or agreement in respect of parental responsibility in paragraph 15 (About other orders or proceedings that affect the child).

Note 9 ▶ If the child has no guardian, enter 'not applicable'. Otherwise, enter the details of any person appointed to be the child's guardian by deed or will or otherwise in writing in accordance with section 5(5) of the Children Act 1989, or by an order made under section 5(1) or 14A of that Act. If the child has more than one guardian, please give the name and address of any other guardian(s) on a separate sheet, putting the child's full name, the number of the Part and the paragraph reference at the head of the sheet.

Note 10 ▶ If any parent/guardian has given consent to the child being placed for adoption, please attach a copy of the signed and witnessed consent form(s). If any parent/guardian has given consent and has subsequently withdrawn that consent, please also attach a copy of the notice of withdrawal and any documentation attached to the notice of withdrawal.

Note 11 ▶ The court cannot dispense with the consent of any parent or guardian to the making of the placement order unless it is satisfied that:
- he or she cannot be found
- he or she is incapable of giving consent, or
- the welfare of the child requires his or her consent to be dispensed with.

If you are asking the court to dispense with the agreement of a parent or guardian, please state which of these three grounds applies. The court will also require from you a brief statement of facts setting out a summary of the history of the case and any other facts to satisfy the court that the grounds for your request apply. If a parent cannot be found, your statement of facts should give details of the steps taken to trace him/her.

You should attach your statement of facts, and two copies, to your application form. You should also attach any documents you are submitting in support of your statement of facts.

Note 12 ▶ Give the full name(s) of the parents, relatives and any significant others who currently have contact with the child. In each case, state their relationship to the child, whether contact is under a court order or by agreement, or pursuant to the duty of the local authority under the Children Act 1989 to promote contact. You should also give the nature, duration and frequency of contact (eg. whether supervised, by letter, monthly, weekly etc). For each contact order, the name of the court, date and case number should be entered at paragraph 15 (About other orders or proceedings that affect the child).

Note: A copy of your application will be sent to each parent or guardian of the child. If you do not want details of contact to be disclosed, you should apply to the court for directions.

Note 13 ▶ Give the name of each person who it is proposed will have contact with the child, their relationship to the child, and the nature, duration and frequency of the proposed contact. State in each case whether the proposed arrangements will apply both before and after the child is placed with any prospective adopters. If they will change when the child is placed, state what the differences will be.

Note: A copy of your application will be sent to each parent or guardian of the child. If you do not want details of contact to be disclosed, you should apply to the court for directions.

Special assistance or facilities for disability if you attend court

Note 14 ▶ If you need special assistance or special facilities for a disability or impairment, please set out your requirements in full. The court staff will need to know, for example, whether you want documents to be supplied in an alternative format, such as Braille or large print. They will also need to know about any specific requirements you may have on the day of the hearing, such as wheelchair access, a hearing loop, or a sign language interpreter.

The court staff will get in touch with you about your requirements. It is important that you make the court aware of all your needs. If you do not, the result may be that the hearing has to be adjourned.

Application for variation of a placement order
Section 23 Adoption and Children Act 2002

Name of court	
Case no.	
Date received by the court	
Date issued	

Notes to applicants
- Before filling in this form, please read the notes on completion.
- If there is not enough room on the form for your reply, please continue on a separate sheet. Put the full name of the child, the Part and the paragraph number at the head of the continuation sheet.
- Please use black ink when filling in this form.

Part 1 About you

◀ See Note 1

First applicant

1. Title
   ☐ Mr ☐ Mrs ☐ Miss
   ☐ Ms ☐ Other _____

2. My name is
   First name(s) in full

   Last name

3. I am an authorised officer of
   (give name and address (including postcode) of local authority)

4. My telephone number is

5. My position in the local authority is

Second applicant

1. Title
   ☐ Mr ☐ Mrs ☐ Miss
   ☐ Ms ☐ Other _____

2. My name is
   First name(s) in full

   Last name

3. I am an authorised officer of
   (give name and address (including postcode) of local authority)

4. My telephone number is

5. My position in the local authority is

A51 Application for variation of a placement order Section 23 Adoption and Children Act 2002 (12.05) HMCS

6. First applicant - My solicitor in these proceedings is

Name of solicitor	
Name of firm	
Address (including postcode)	

Telephone no.		Fax no.	
DX no.			
E-mail address			

Second applicant - My solicitor in these proceedings is

Name of solicitor	
Name of firm	
Address (including postcode)	

Telephone no.		Fax no.	
DX no.			
E-mail address			

Part 2 About this application

7. An order under section 21 of the Adoption and Children Act 2002 was made by
(give name of court)

on (give date)

authorising (give name of local authority)

to place (give name of child)   ◀ See Note 2

for adoption.

The child is a   ☐ Boy   ☐ Girl   The child was born on

A copy of the placement order is attached.

We apply for the order to be varied so that (give name of local authority)

is authorised to place the child for adoption.

8. The grounds for this application are ◀ See Note 3

About other orders or proceedings that affect the child

9. ☐ To the best of my knowledge, no proceedings relating to the child (other than the placement order given above) have been completed or commenced in any court

    or

    ☐ The following proceedings relating to the child have been completed/commenced (in addition to the placement order given above) ◀ See Note 4

Type of order made (or applied for)	Date of order (or date of next hearing)	Name of court	Case number (or serial number)

Cases concerning a related child

10. ☐ To the best of my knowledge, no proceedings relating to a full, half or step brother or sister of the child have been completed or commenced in any court

    or

    ☐ The following proceedings relating to a full, half or step brother or sister of the child have been completed/commenced (please give details below and, if either authority was a party to any proceedings that have been completed, **attach a copy of the final order**)

Relationship to child (eg. sister, half-brother)	Type of order made (or applied for)	Date of order (or date of next hearing)	Name of court	Case number (or serial number)

Part 3 About the child's parents or guardian

The child's mother
11. The name of the child's mother is

First name(s) in full

Last name

Her address is (if deceased, please write 'Deceased' in the address box)

The child's father
The name of the child's father is

First name(s) in full

Last name

His address is (if deceased, please write 'Deceased' in the address box)

◀ See Note 5

12. Does he have parental responsibility for the child?   ◀ See Note 6

☐ Yes   ☐ No

If No, does he intend to apply for an order under section 4(1)(c) of the Children Act 1989 (a parental responsibility order) or a residence or contact order in respect of the child?

☐ Yes   ☐ No

13. **The child's guardian**

The name of the child's guardian is   ◀ See Note 7

First name(s) in full

Last name

His/Her address is

Part 4 Arrangements for contact with the child

14. The current arrangements for contact with the child are as follows:　　　　　See Note 8

15. If this application is granted, the following changes to contact arrangements are proposed:　　　　　See Note 8

Part 5 Statement of truth

*[I believe] [The first applicant believes] that the facts stated in this application are true.

*I am duly authorised by the first applicant to sign this statement.

Print full name [   ]

Signed [   ] Date [   ]

*[First applicant] [First applicant's solicitor]

For (name of local authority) [   ]

*delete as appropriate

---

*[I believe] [The second applicant believes] that the facts stated in this application are true.

*I am duly authorised by the second applicant to sign this statement.

Print full name [   ]

Signed [   ] Date [   ]

*[Second applicant] [Second applicant's solicitor]

For (name of local authority) [   ]

*delete as appropriate

If you attend the court for a hearing

1. Does either of you have a disability for which you require special assistance or special facilities? ◀ See Note 9

   ☐ Yes   ☐ No

   If Yes, please say what your needs are below
   (the court staff will get in touch with you about your requirements)

   [   ]

What to do now

Once you have completed and signed this form, you should take or send the form and **three copies** to the court, together with the court fee and the following documents:

- a copy of the placement order you are asking the court to vary;
- if either authority was a party to the proceedings, a copy of any other final order relating to the child that has effect;
- if either authority was a party to the proceedings, a copy of any final order relating to a full, half or step brother or sister of the child that has effect.

Application for variation of a placement order (Form A51)
Notes on completing the form

Important

If you are attaching any order of the High Court or a county court to your application, it must be a sealed copy of the order (that is, a copy that has been stamped with the seal of the court). If you are attaching an order made by a magistrates' court, it must be a certified copy (a copy certified by the court officer to be a true copy of the original order), or a copy that bears the stamp of the originating court. An order issued by any other authority must be properly authenticated by that authority. If you are in any doubt about what is needed, please contact the court for assistance.

Take or send the completed application form, **and three copies,** to the court, together with the court fee and any documents you are attaching in support of your application.

Notes on the application form

Note 1 — The court may only vary a placement order so as to substitute another local authority for the local authority authorised by the order to place the child for adoption on the joint application of **both** the authorities involved. (Section 23(2) of the Adoption and Children Act 2002)

Note 2 — Enter the child's first names(s) and last name as they are shown on the placement order you are asking the court to vary. **You must attach a copy of the placement order to your application.**

Note 3 — Set out your reasons for applying for the transfer of responsibility between local authorities. State why the transfer would be in the best interests of the child, and any administrative reasons which make the transfer desirable.

Note 4 — Enter details of any other earlier and concurrent court proceedings relating to the child. Do not repeat the details of the placement order entered at paragraph 7. In each case, give the name of the court, the nature of the proceedings and the date and effect of any order made. If either authority was a party to any proceedings that have been completed, a copy of the final order should be attached to the application.

Note 5 — If the child has previously been adopted, give the names of his/her adoptive parents and not those of his/her natural parents.

Note 6 — If the child's parents were not married at the time of his/her birth, the child's father may have acquired parental responsibility
- by subsequent marriage to the child's mother;
- because he has a parental responsibility agreement with the mother, or has been granted a parental responsibility order, or
- because he registered the child's birth jointly with the child's mother (on or after 1 December 2003).

Give details of any court order or agreement in respect of parental responsibility in paragraph 9 (About other orders or proceedings that affect the child).

A51 Notes - Application for Variation of a Placement Order Section 23 Adoption and Children Act 2002 Notes on the application form (12.05)   HMCS

Note 7 ▶ If the child has no guardian, enter 'not applicable'. Otherwise, enter the details of any person appointed to be the child's guardian by deed or will or otherwise in writing in accordance with section 5(5) of the Children Act 1989, or by an order made under section 5(1) or 14A of that Act. If the child has more than one guardian, please give the name and address of any other guardian(s) on a separate sheet, putting the child's full name, the number of the Part and the paragraph reference at the head of the sheet.

Note 8 ▶ Give the full name(s) of the parents, relatives and any significant others who have contact with the child. In each case, state their relationship to the child, whether contact is under a court order or by agreement and the nature, duration and frequency of contact (eg. supervised, by letter, monthly, etc)

In paragraph 15 you should set out the details of any proposed changes to current contact arrangements if the application to vary the placement order is granted, and the reason for the changes. If no changes are proposed, please say so.

Note: A copy of your application will be sent to each parent or guardian of the child. If you do not want details of contact to be disclosed, you should apply to the court for directions.

Special assistance or facilities for disability if you attend court

Note 9 ▶ If you need special assistance or special facilities for a disability or impairment, please set out your requirements in full. The court staff will need to know, for example, whether you want documents to be supplied in an alternative format, such as Braille or large print. They will also need to know about any specific requirements you may have on the day of the hearing, such as wheelchair access, a hearing loop, or a sign language interpreter.

The court staff will get in touch with you about your requirements. It is important that you make the court aware of all your needs. If you do not, the result may be that the hearing has to be adjourned.

Application for revocation of a placement order
Section 24 Adoption and Children Act 2002

Name of court	
Case no./Serial no.	
Date received by the court	
Date issued	

Notes to applicants

- Before filling in this form, please read the guidance notes on completing the form.
- Please complete every Part. If any Part does not apply to you, or you are not sure of the answer to any question, please say so. If there is not enough room for your reply, please continue on a separate sheet. Put the child's name, the number of the Part and the paragraph reference at the top of the continuation sheet.
- Please use black ink when filling in the form.

Part 1 About you

◀ See Note 1

a) Title

☐ Mr   ☐ Mrs   ☐ Miss   ☐ Ms   ☐ Other _____

b) My name is

First name(s) in full

Last name

c) My address is (including post code)

d) My telephone number is

◀ See Note 2
◀ See Note 3

e) My solicitor in these proceedings is

Name of solicitor	
Name of firm	
Address (including postcode)	

Telephone no.		Fax no.	
DX no.			
E-mail address			

A52 Application for revocation of a placement order Section 24 Adoption and Children Act 2002 (12.05)   HMCS

f) I am
- [ ] the child named in the placement order
- [ ] an authorised representative of the local authority named in the placement order

(please state your position in the local authority)

[   ]

- [ ] the mother of the child named in the placement order
- [ ] the father of the child named in the placement order
- [ ] a guardian of the child named in the placement order
- [ ] none of the above. I am

[   ]

g) I am a prospective adopter of the child and wish to keep my identity confidential and apply for a serial number   ☐ Yes   ☐ No   ◀ See Note 4

Part 2 About the child

a) The name of the child is

First name(s) in full   Last name   ◀ See Note 5

[   ]   [   ]

b) The child is a   c) The child was born on
   ☐ Boy   ☐ Girl   [ ][ ][ ][ ][ ][ ][ ][ ]

d) The local authority authorised to place the child for adoption (give the name and address of the local authority and (if known) the name and telephone number of the adoption worker who deals with the child)

Name of local authority	
Address (including post code)	

Name of your contact in the authority	
Telephone no.	

About other orders or proceedings that affect the child

◀ See Note 6

e) ☐ To the best of my knowledge, no proceedings relating to the child (other than the placement order entered in Part 4 of this application) have been completed or commenced in any court

or

☐ The following proceedings relating to the child have been completed/commenced (in addition to placement order entered in Part 4 of this application)

Type of order made (or applied for)	Date of order (or date of next hearing)	Name of court	Case number (or serial number)

Cases concerning a related child

f) ☐ To the best of my knowledge, no proceedings relating to a full, half or step brother or sister of the child have been completed or commenced in any court

or

☐ The following proceedings relating to a full, half or step brother or sister of the child have been completed/commenced (please give details below and, if you were a party to any proceedings that have been completed, attach a copy of the final order)

Relationship to child (eg. sister, half-brother)	Type of order made (or applied for)	Date of order (or date of next hearing)	Name of court	Case number (or serial number)

Part 3 About the child's parents or guardian

The name(s) and address(es) of the child's parent(s) are:

◀ See Note 7

The child's mother

a) The name of the child's mother is

First name(s) in full

Last name

b) Her address is (if deceased, please write 'Deceased' in the address box)

The child's father

c) The name of the child's father is

First name(s) in full

Last name

d) His address is (if deceased, please write 'Deceased' in the address box)

e) Does he have parental responsibility for the child?

☐ Yes ☐ No

◀ See Note 8

If No, does he intend to apply for an order under section 4(1)(c) of the Children Act 1989 (a parental responsibility order) or a residence or contact order in respect of the child?

☐ Yes ☐ No

The child's guardian

f) The name of the child's guardian is

◀ See Note 9

First name(s) in full

Last name

g) His/Her address is

Part 4 About this application

a) I apply for revocation of the order made by (give name of court)

on (date)

authorising (give name of local authority)

to place (give name of child) ◀ See Note 5

for adoption.

A copy of the placement order is attached

b) The court's permission to make this application

☐ is not required
☐ has been given (give details below and attach a copy of the court order giving permission) ◀ See Note 1

c) The reasons for this application are: ◀ See Note 10

Part 5 Statement of truth

*[I believe] [The applicant believes] that the facts stated in this application are true.
*I am duly authorised by the applicant to sign this statement.

Print full name

Signed   Date

*[Applicant] [Applicant's solicitor] [Litigation friend]

*delete as appropriate

If you attend the court for a hearing

1. Do you have a disability for which you require special assistance or special facilities? ◄ See Note 11

   ☐ Yes   ☐ No

   If Yes, please say what your needs are below
   (the court staff will get in touch with you about your requirements)

2. Do you want to use the services of an interpreter?

   ☐ Yes   ☐ No

   If Yes, please specify which language
   (the court staff will get in touch with you about your requirements)

What to do now
Once you have completed and signed this form, you should take or send the form and **three copies** to the court, together with the court fee* and the following documents:
- a copy of the placement order you are asking the court to revoke;
- if you were a party to the proceedings, a copy of any other final order relating to the child that has effect;
- if you were a party to the proceedings, a copy of any final order relating to a full, half or step brother or sister of the child that has effect;
- a copy of any order giving you permission to apply for the placement order to be revoked.

* If you are not sure about the court fee payable for your application, or you think that you may be exempt from paying all or part of the fee, you should contact the court for information.

Application for revocation of a placement order (Form 52)
Notes on completing the form

Important

If you are attaching any order of the High Court or a county court to your application, it must be a sealed copy of the order (that is, a copy that has been stamped with the seal of the court). If you are attaching an order made by a magistrates' court, it must be a certified copy (a copy certified by the court officer to be a true copy of the original order), or a copy that bears the stamp of the originating court. An order issued by any other authority must be properly authenticated by that authority. If you are in any doubt about what is needed, please contact the court for assistance.

Take or send the completed application form, **and three copies,** to the court, together with the court fee and any documents you are attaching in support of your application. If you are not sure about the court fee payable for your application, or you think that you may be exempt from paying all or part of the fee, you should contact the court for information.

Notes on the application form

Note 1 Anyone may apply for a placement order to be revoked but, unless you are the child named in the order or the local authority authorised by the order to place the child for adoption:

- you will need the court's permission* to make the application, and
- you cannot apply for the placement order to be revoked if the local authority has already placed the child for adoption.

*Any application for permission must be made under Part 9 of the Family Procedure (Adoption) Rules 2005, using form FP2

Note 2 If you are a prospective adopter (that is, you will be making an application to adopt the child) please see Note 4 below. Otherwise, if you do not want your private address and telephone number to be disclosed to any other party, **do not enter those details on this application form.** Instead you should enter the details on Form A65, which you must file at the court with your application. The information will not then be disclosed to any other person, except by order of the court.

Note 3 If you are applying as an officer of the local authority that is named in the placement order, you should enter the name and address of the local authority and the telephone number on which you can be contacted during working hours.

Note 4 If you are a prospective adopter (that is, you will be making an application to adopt the child) and you do not want your identity to be made known to the parents or guardians of the child, the court will issue you with a serial number. Any documents sent to the other parties will show the serial number, not your personal details. If you are required to attend the same court hearing, the court will make arrangements to ensure that your identity is protected.

If a serial number has already been issued to you, please ensure that it is entered in Part 2 paragraph (e) (About other orders or proceedings that affect the child).

Note 5 Please give the name of the child as it appears on the placement order. **You must attach a copy of the placement order to your application.**

A52 Notes - Application for revocation of a placement order (Form 52) Notes on completing the form (12.05)   HMCS

Note 6 ▶ If there are any other earlier, or current, court proceedings relating to the child, give the name of the court, the nature of the proceedings and the date and effect of any order made. If you were a party to any proceedings that have been completed, you should attach a copy of the final order to your application. **You do not need to enter here the details of the placement order you are asking the court to revoke. Instead, you should enter those details in Part 4 'About this application'.**

Note 7 ▶ If the child has previously been adopted, give the names of his/her adoptive parents and not those of his natural parents.

Note 8 ▶ If the child's parents were not married at the time of his/her birth, the child's father may have acquired parental responsibility
- by subsequent marriage to the child's mother;
- because he has a parental responsibility agreement with the mother, or has been granted a parental responsibility order, or
- because he registered the child's birth jointly with the child's mother (on or after 1 December 2003).

Give details of any court order or agreement in respect of parental responsibility in paragraph (e) of Part 2 (About other orders or proceedings that affect the child).

Note 9 ▶ If the child has no guardian, enter 'not applicable'. Otherwise, enter the details of any person appointed to be the child's guardian by deed or will or otherwise in writing in accordance with section 5(5) of the Children Act 1989, or by an order made under section 5(1) or 14A of that Act. If the child has more than one guardian, please give the name and address of any other guardian(s) on a separate sheet, putting the child's full name, the number of the Part and the paragraph reference at the head of the sheet.

Note 10 ▶ Please set out the reasons for your application and why you believe that revocation of the placement order would be in the best interests of the child. If there is not enough room for your reply, please continue on a separate sheet. Put the child's name, the number of the Part and the paragraph reference at the head of the continuation sheet.

Important: If you are the prospective adopter and you already have a serial number or have asked for one to be issued, you should make sure that the reasons for your application do not include any information that could lead to your identity being disclosed. Any applicant who has withheld their address or telephone number, or the child's address or the name of the person with whom the child lives on the application form should make sure that they do not include any information that could lead to these details being disclosed.

Special assistance or facilities for disability if you attend court

Note 11 ▶ If you need special assistance or special facilities for a disability or impairment, please set out your requirements in full. The court staff will need to know, for example, whether you want documents to be supplied in an alternative format, such as Braille or large print. They will also need to know about any specific requirements you may have on the day of the hearing, such as wheelchair access, a hearing loop, or a sign language interpreter. The court staff will get in touch with you about your requirements. It is important that you make the court aware of all your needs. If you do not, the result may be that the hearing has to be adjourned.

Application for a contact order
Section 26 Adoption and Children Act 2002

Name of court	
Case no./Serial no.	
Date received by the court	
Date issued	

Notes to applicants
- This form is only for use if you are applying for a contact order under section 26 of the Adoption and Children Act 2002.
- Before filling in this form, please read the guidance notes on completing the form.
- Please complete every Part. If any question does not apply to your application, or you are not sure of the answer, please say so.
- If there is not enough room for your reply to any question, continue on a separate sheet. Please put the child's name, the number of the Part and the paragraph reference at the head of the continuation sheet.
- Please use black ink when filling in the form.

Part 1 About you

◀ See Note 1

a) Title
☐ Mr ☐ Mrs ☐ Miss ☐ Ms ☐ Other _____

b) My name is

First name(s) in full

Last name

c) My address is (including postcode)

d) My telephone number is

◀ See Note 2
◀ See Note 3

e) My date of birth is

f) My solicitor in these proceedings is

Name of solicitor	
Name of firm	
Address (including postcode)	

Telephone no.		Fax no.	
DX no.			
E-mail address			

A53 Application for a contact order (section 26 Adoption and Children Act 2002) (12.05)

HMCS

g) I am: (please tick the box that applies to you and give any additional information asked for)

☐ the child whom the adoption agency is authorised to place for adoption

☐ an officer of the adoption agency that is authorised to place the child for adoption/has placed the child (who is less than six weeks old) for adoption
(please state your position in the adoption agency)

[   ]

☐ the child's mother

☐ the child's father

☐ the child's guardian

☐ a relative of the child (please state your relationship to the child) ◀ See Note 1

[   ]

or

The following order in my favour was in force immediately before the adoption agency was authorised to place the child for adoption/placed the child (who is less than six weeks old) for adoption: ◀ See Note 4

☐ a contact order made under the Children Act 1989 (give details of the order below)

☐ a residence order (give details of the order below)

☐ an order of the High Court giving me care of the child (give details of the order below)

Name of court	
Case number	
Type of order	
Date of order	

(Please attach a copy of the order to your application)

or

☐ None of the above applies to me, my relationship to the child is

[   ]

and

☐ I am applying for permission to make this application, **or**

☐ I have been given permission to make this application (please give details below and attach a copy of the order to your application)

Name of court	
Case number	
Date permission granted	

h) I am a prospective adopter of the child and wish to keep my identity confidential and apply for a serial number   ☐ Yes   ☐ No   ◀ See Note 5

Part 2 About the child

a) The name of the child is

First name(s) in full

Last name

b) The child is a

☐ Boy ☐ Girl

c) The child was born on

d) The child's address is
(If you do not know the child's address, please enter 'Not known')

e) The child lives with
(If you do not know the name of the person with whom the child lives, please enter 'Not known')

◀ See Note 2

f) The adoption agency that is authorised to place the child for adoption/has placed the child (who is less than six weeks old) for adoption is: (give the name and address of the adoption agency and (if known) the name and telephone number of the adoption worker who deals with the child)

Name of adoption agency	
Address (including post code)	

Name of your contact in the agency	
Telephone no.	

g) The child is subject to a placement order

☐ Yes ☐ No

(If Yes, please give details below)

or

The child is the subject of ongoing placement proceedings

☐ Yes ☐ No

(If Yes, please give details below)

Name of court	
Case number	

Date of placement order	

or

Date of hearing if placement proceedings are current	

h) Date of placement (if known)

About other orders or proceedings that affect the child

i) ☐ To the best of my knowledge, no proceedings relating to the child (other than any order(s) already entered above) have been completed or commenced in any court

or

☐ The following proceedings relating to the child have been completed/commenced (in addition to any order(s) already entered above)   ◀ See Note 6

Type of order made (or applied for)	Date of order (or date of next hearing)	Name of court	Case number (or serial number)

Cases concerning a related child

j) ☐ To the best of my knowledge, no proceedings relating to a full, half or step brother or sister of the child have been completed or commenced in any court

or

☐ The following proceedings relating to a full, half or step brother or sister of the child have been completed/commenced (please give details below and, if you were a party to any proceedings that have been completed, attach a copy of the final order)

Relationship to child (eg. sister, half-brother)	Type of order made (or applied for)	Date of order (or date of next hearing)	Name of court	Case number (or serial number)

Part 3 About the child's parents or guardian

The child's mother

a) The name of the child's mother is

First name(s) in full

Last name

b) Her address is (if deceased, please write 'Deceased' in the address box)

The child's father   ◀ See Note 7

c) The name of the child's father is

First name(s) in full

Last name

d) His address is (if deceased, please write 'Deceased' in the address box)

e) Does he have parental responsibility for the child?   ◀ See Note 8

☐ Yes   ☐ No

The child's guardian

f) The name of the child's guardian is ◀ See Note 9

   First name(s) in full

   Last name

g) His/Her address is

Part 4 About this application

Give details of the contact order you wish the court to make and the reasons why: ◀ See Note 10

Part 5 Statement of truth

*[I believe] [The applicant believes] that the facts stated in this application are true.

*I am duly authorised by the applicant to sign this statement.

Print full name

Signed

Date

*[Applicant] [Applicant's solicitor] [Litigation friend]

*delete as appropriate

If you attend the court for a hearing

1. Do you have a disability for which you require special assistance or special facilities?   ◀ See Note 11

☐ Yes   ☐ No

If Yes, please say what your needs are below
(the court staff will get in touch with you about your requirements)

2. Do you want to use the services of an interpreter?

☐ Yes   ☐ No

If Yes, please specify which language
(court staff will get in touch with you about your requirements)

What to do now

Once you have completed and signed this form, you should take or send the form and **three copies** to the court, together with the court fee* and the following documents:

- a copy of any of the following orders that was in effect immediately before the adoption agency was authorised to place the child for adoption, or placed a child for adoption at a time when he/she was less than six weeks old:
    - an order for contact made under section 8 or section 34 of the Children Act 1989 in your favour;
    - a residence order made in your favour;
    - an order made in exercise of the High Court's jurisdiction with respect to children giving you care of the child.
- if you were a party to the proceedings, a copy of any other final order relating to the child that has effect;
- if you were a party to the proceedings, a copy of any final order relating to a full, half or step brother or sister of the child that has effect;
- a copy of any court order giving you permission to apply for the contact order.

* If you are not sure about the court fee payable for your application, or you think that you may be exempt from paying all or part of the fee, you should contact the court for information.

Application for a contact order under section 26 of the Adoption and Children Act 2002 (Form A53)

Notes on completing the form

Important

This form is for use only if you are applying for a contact order under Section 26 of the Adoption and Children Act 2002.

If you are attaching any order of the High Court or a county court to your application, it must be a sealed copy of the order (that is, a copy that has been stamped with the seal of the court). If you are attaching an order made by a magistrates' court, it must be a certified copy (a copy certified by the court officer to be a true copy of the original order), or a copy that bears the stamp of the originating court. An order issued by any other authority must be properly authenticated by that authority. If you are in any doubt about what is needed, please contact the court for assistance.

Take or send the completed application form, and **three copies**, to the court, together with the court fee and any documents you are attaching in support of your application. If you are not sure about the court fee payable for your application, or you think that you may be exempt from paying all or part of the fee, you should contact the court for information.

Notes on the application form

Note 1 ➤ Where a child under six weeks old has been placed for adoption under the Adoption and Children Act 2002 or an adoption agency is authorised to place a child for adoption under the Act, contact with the child may only be:

- by arrangement with the agency that has placed the child, or is authorised to do so, **or**
- by a court order made under section 26 of the Act.

Any existing provision for contact with the child made under the Children Act 1989 ceases to have effect (section 26(1) of the Adoption and Children Act 2002).

An application to the court for a contact order may be made by:

- the child;
- the adoption agency;
- any parent, guardian or relative;*
- any person in whose favour there was provision for contact under the Children Act 1989 which ceased to have effect by virtue of section 26(1) of the 2002 Act;
- a person who had the benefit of a residence order immediately before the adoption agency was authorised to place the child for adoption, or placed the child for adoption at a time when he/she was less than six weeks old;
- a person who by virtue of an order made in the exercise of the High Court's inherent jurisdiction with respect to children (wardship) had care of the child immediately before the adoption agency was authorised to place the child for adoption, or placed the child for adoption at a time when he/she was less than six weeks old; **or**
- any person who has the permission of the court to make the application. An application for the court's permission must be made under Part 9 of the Family Procedure (Adoption) Rules 2005, using form FP2.

*'relative' means a grandparent, brother, sister, uncle or aunt, whether of the full blood or half-blood, or by marriage or civil partnership.

A53 Notes Application for a contact order under section 26 of the Adoption and Children Act 2002 - Notes on completing the form (12.05)   HMCS

Note 2 ▶ If you are a prospective adopter (that is, you will be making an application to adopt the child) please see Note 5 below. Otherwise, if you do not want your private address and telephone number, or the child's address, or (if the child does not live with you) the name of the person with whom the child lives, to be disclosed to any other party, **do not enter those details on this application form.** Instead you should enter the details on Form A65, which you must file at the court with your application. The details will not then be disclosed to any person, except by order of the court.

Note 3 ▶ If you are applying as an officer of the adoption agency that is authorised to place the child for adoption, or has placed the child for adoption, you should enter the name and address of the adoption agency, and the telephone number on which you can be contacted during working hours.

Note 4 ▶ Give details of:
- any order for contact made under section 8 or section 34 of the Children Act 1989 that was made in your favour;
- any residence order that was made in your favour;
- any order made in exercise of the High Court's inherent jurisdiction with respect to children giving you care of the child,

which was in effect **immediately before** the adoption agency was authorised to place the child for adoption, or placed the child for adoption at a time when he/she was less than six weeks old. Please give the name of the court that made the order, the type of order, the date of the order and the case number.

Please attach a copy of the order to your application.

Note 5 ▶ If you are a prospective adopter (that is, you will be making an application to adopt the child) and you do not want your identity to be made known to the parents or guardians of the child, the court will issue you with a serial number. Any documents sent to the other parties will show the serial number, not your personal details. If you are required to attend the same court hearing, the court will make arrangements to ensure that your identity is protected.

If a serial number has already been issued to you, please ensure that it is entered in Part 2 paragraph (i) (About other orders or proceedings that affect the child).

Note 6 ▶ If there are any other earlier, or current, court proceedings relating to the child, give the name of the court, the nature of the proceedings and the date and effect of any order made. If you were a party to any proceedings that have been completed, you should attach a copy of the final order to your application. **You do not need to repeat any details of orders you have already given in Part 1 of the application form, or details of any placement proceedings you have given in paragraph (g) of Part 2.**

Note 7 ▶ If the child has previously been adopted, give the names of his/her adoptive parents and not those of his/her natural parents.

Note 8 ▶ If the child's parents were not married at the time of his/her birth, the child's father may have acquired parental responsibility

- by subsequent marriage to the child's mother;
- because he has a parental responsibility agreement with the mother, or has been granted a parental responsibility order, or
- because he registered the child's birth jointly with the child's mother (on or after 1 December 2003).

Give details of any court order or agreement in respect of parental responsibility in Part 2 About the child, paragraph (i).

Note 9 ▶ If the child does not have a guardian, enter 'not applicable'. Otherwise, enter the details of any person appointed to be the child's guardian by deed or will or otherwise in writing in accordance with section 5(5) of the Children Act 1989, or by an order made under section 5(1) or 14A of that Act. If the child has more than one guardian, please give the name and address of any other guardian(s) on a separate sheet, putting the child's full name, the number of the Part and the paragraph reference at the head of the sheet.

Note 10 ▶ If you are the prospective adopter and you already have a serial number or have asked for one to be issued, you should make sure that the reasons for your application do not include any information that could lead to your identity being disclosed. Any applicant who has withheld their address or telephone number, or the child's address or the name of the person with whom the child lives on the application form should make sure that they do not include any information that could lead to these details being disclosed.

Special assistance or facilities for disability if you attend the court

Note 11 ▶ If you need special assistance or special facilities for a disability or impairment, please set out your requirements in full. The court staff will need to know, for example, whether you want documents to be supplied in an alternative format, such as Braille or large print. They will also need to know about any specific requirements you may have on the day of the hearing, such as wheelchair access, a hearing loop, or a sign language interpreter.

The court staff will get in touch with you about your requirements. It is important that you make the court aware of all your needs. If you do not, the result may be that the hearing has to be adjourned.

Application for variation or revocation of a contact order
Section 27(1)(b) Adoption and Children Act 2002

Name of court	
Case no./Serial no.	
Date received by the court	
Date issued	

Notes to applicants
- This form is only for use if you are applying for variation or revocation of a contact order made under section 26 of the Adoption and Children Act 2002.
- Before filling in this form, please read the guidance notes on completing the form.
- If any question does not apply to your application, or you are not sure of the answer, please say so.
- If there is not enough room for your reply to any question, continue on a separate sheet. Please put the child's name, the number of the Part and the paragraph reference at the head of the continuation sheet.
- Please use black ink when filling in the form.

Part 1 About you ◀ See Note 1

a) Title

☐ Mr ☐ Mrs ☐ Miss ☐ Ms ☐ Other _____

b) My name is

First name(s) in full

Last name

c) My address is (including post code)

d) My telephone number is ◀ See Note 2 ◀ See Note 3

e) My solicitor in these proceedings is

Name of solicitor	
Name of firm	
Address (including postcode)	

Telephone no.		Fax no.	
DX no.			
E-mail address			

A54 Application for variation or revocation of a contact order Section 27(1)(b) Adoption and Children Act 2002 (12.05)   HMCS

f) I am: (please tick the box that applies to you)

☐ the child to whom the contact order relates

☐ a person named on the contact order

☐ an officer of the adoption agency that is authorised to place the child for adoption/has placed the child (who is less than six weeks old) for adoption
(please state your position in the adoption agency)

g) I am a prospective adopter of the child and wish to keep my identity confidential and apply for a serial number ☐ Yes ☐ No ◀ See Note 4

Part 2 About the child

a) The name of the child is

First name(s) in full

Last name

b) The child is a
☐ Boy   ☐ Girl

c) The child was born on

d) The child's address is
(If you do not know the child's address, please enter 'Not known')

e) The child lives with
(If you do not know the name of the person with whom the child lives, please enter 'Not known') ◀ See Note 2

f) The adoption agency that is authorised to place the child for adoption/has placed the child (who is less than six weeks old) for adoption is: (give the name and address of the adoption agency and (if known) the name and telephone number of the adoption worker who deals with the child)

Name of adoption agency	
Address (including post code)	

Name of your contact in the agency	
Telephone no.	

About other orders or proceedings that affect the child   ◀ See Note 5

g) ☐ To the best of my knowledge, no proceedings relating to the child (other than the contact order entered in Part 4 of this application) have been completed or commenced in any court

or

☐ The following proceedings relating to the child have been completed/commenced (in addition to the contact order entered in Part 4 of this application)

Type of order made (or applied for)	Date of order (or date of next hearing)	Name of court	Case number (or serial number)

Cases concerning a related child

h) ☐ To the best of my knowledge, no proceedings relating to a full, half or step brother or sister of the child have been completed or commenced in any court

or

☐ The following proceedings relating to a full, half or step brother or sister of the child have been completed/commenced (please give details below and, if you were a party to any proceedings that have been completed, attach a copy of the final order)

Relationship to child (eg. sister, half-brother)	Type of order made (or applied for)	Date of order (or date of next hearing)	Name of court	Case number (or serial number)

Part 3 About the child's parents or guardian

The name(s) and address(es) of the child's parent(s) are: ◀ See Note 6

The child's mother

a) The name of the child's mother is

First name(s) in full

[ ]

Last name

[ ]

b) Her address is (if deceased, please write 'Deceased' in the address box)

[ ]

The child's father

c) The name of the child's father is

First name(s) in full

[ ]

Last name

[ ]

d) His address is (if deceased, please write 'Deceased' in the address box)

[ ]

e) Does he have parental responsibility for the child? ◀ See Note 7

☐ Yes ☐ No

The child's guardian

f) The name of the child's guardian is ◀ See Note 8

First name(s) in full

[ ]

Last name

[ ]

g) His/Her address is

[ ]

Part 4 About this application

a) I request that the order made by this court on (give date)

[ ]

in favour of (give name of person(s) granted contact)

[ ]

requiring contact with (name of child)

[ ]

☐ be revoked

or

☐ be varied as follows:(please give details of the order you wish the court to make; continue on an additional sheet if necessary)

[ ]

b) My reasons for this application are as follows: (continue on additional sheet if necessary) ◀ See Note 9

[ ]

Important: you must attach a copy of the contact order you are asking the court to vary or revoke to your application

Part 5 Statement of truth

*[I believe] [The applicant believes] that the facts stated in this application are true.

*I am duly authorised by the applicant to sign this statement.

Print full name

Signed   Date

*[Applicant] [Applicant's solicitor] [Litigation friend]

*delete as appropriate

If you attend the court for a hearing

1. Do you have a disability for which you require special assistance or special facilities?   ◀ See Note 10

    ☐ Yes   ☐ No

    If Yes, please say what your needs are below
    (the court staff will get in touch with you about your requirements)

2. Do you want to use the services of an interpreter?

    ☐ Yes   ☐ No

    If Yes, please specify which language
    (court staff will get in touch with you about your requirements)

What to do now

Once you have completed and signed this form, you should take or send the form and **three copies** to the court, together with the court fee* and the following documents:

- a copy of the contact order you are asking the court to vary or revoke;
- if you were a party to the proceedings, a copy of any other final order relating to the child that has effect;
- if you were a party to the proceedings, a copy of any final order relating to a full, half or step brother or sister of the child that has effect.

*If you are not sure about the court fee payable for your application, or you think that you may be exempt from paying all or part of the fee, you should contact the court for information.

Application for variation or revocation of a contact order made under section 26 of the Adoption and Children Act 2002 (Form A54)
Notes on completing the form

Important

This form is for use only if you are asking the court to vary or revoke a contact order made under section 26 of the Adoption and Children Act 2002.

If you are attaching any order of the High Court or a county court to your application, it must be a **sealed** copy of the order (that is, a copy that has been stamped with the seal of the court). If you are attaching an order made by a magistrates' court, it must be a **certified copy** (a copy certified by the court officer to be a true copy of the original order) or a copy that bears the stamp of the originating court. An order issued by any other authority must be properly authenticated by that authority. If you are in any doubt about what is needed, the court staff will be able to advise you.

Take or send the completed application form, and **three copies**, to the court, together with the court fee and any documents you are attaching in support of your application. If you are not sure about the court fee payable for your application, or you think that you may be exempt from paying all or part of the fee, you should contact the court for information.

Notes on the application form

Note 1 ▶ To be eligible to apply for a variation or revocation of a contact order made under section 26 of the Adoption and Children Act 2002, you must be:

- the child to whom the contact order applies; or
- an officer of the adoption agency that is authorised to place, or has placed, for adoption the child named in the contact order; or
- a person named in the contact order to which your application applies.

You must attach a copy of the contact order to your application.

Note 2 ▶ If you are a prospective adopter (that is, you will be making an application to adopt the child), please see Note 4 below. Otherwise, if you do not want your private address and telephone number, or the child's address, or (if the child does not live with you) the name of the person with whom the child lives, to be disclosed to any other party, do not enter those details on this application form. Instead you should enter the details on Form A65, which you must file at the court with your application. The information will not then be disclosed to any person, except by order of the court.

Note 3 ▶ If you are applying as an officer of the adoption agency that is authorised to place the child for adoption, or has placed the child for adoption, you should enter the name and address of the adoption agency and the telephone number on which you can be contacted during working hours.

A54 Notes - Application for variation or revocation of a contact order made under section 26 of the Adoption and Children Act 2002
Notes on completing the form (12.05)

HMCS

Note 4 ▶ If you are a prospective adopter (that is, you will be making an application to adopt the child) and you do not want your identity to be made known to the parents or guardians of the child, the court will issue you with a serial number. Any documents sent to the other parties will show the serial number, not your personal details. if you are required to attend the same court hearing, the court will make arrangements to ensure that your identity is protected.

If a serial number has already been issued to you, please ensure that it is entered in Part 2, paragraph (g) (About other orders or proceedings that affect the child).

Note 5 ▶ If there are any other earlier, or current, court proceedings relating to the child, give the name of the court, the nature of the proceedings and the date and effect of any order made. If you were a party to any proceedings that have been completed, you should attach a copy of the final order to your application. You do not need to enter here the details of the contact order you are asking the court to vary or revoke. Instead, you should enter those details in Part 4 'About this application'.

Note 6 ▶ If the child has previously been adopted, give the names of his/her adoptive parents and not those of his/her natural parents.

Note 7 ▶ If the child's parents were not married at the time of his/her birth, the child's father may have acquired parental responsibility

- by subsequent marriage to the child's mother;
- because he has a parental responsibility agreement with the mother, or has been granted a parental responsibility order, or
- because he registered the child's birth jointly with the child's mother (on or after 1 December 2003).

Give details of any court order or agreement in respect of parental responsibility in Part 2 About the child, paragraph (g).

Note 8 ▶ If the child does not have a guardian, enter 'not applicable'. Otherwise, enter the details of any person appointed to be the child's guardian by deed or will or otherwise in writing in accordance with section 5(5) of the Children Act 1989, or by an order made under section 5(1) or 14A of that Act. If the child has more than one guardian, please give the name and address of any other guardian(s) on a separate sheet, putting the child's full name, the number of the Part and the paragraph reference at the head of the sheet.

Note 9 ▶ If you are a prospective adopter and you already have a serial number or have asked for one to be issued, you should make sure that the reasons for your application do not include any information that could lead to your identity being disclosed.

Any applicant who has withheld their address or telephone number, or the child's address or the name of the person with whom the child lives should make sure that they do not include any information that could lead to those details being disclosed.

Special assistance or facilities for disability if you attend the court

Note 10 ▶ If you need special assistance or special facilities for a disability or impairment, please set out your requirements in full. The court staff will need to know, for example, whether you want documents to be supplied in an alternative format, such as Braille or large print. They will also need to know about any specific requirements you may have on the day of the hearing, such as wheelchair access, a hearing loop, or a sign language interpreter.

The court staff will get in touch with you about your requirements. It is important that you make the court aware of all your needs. If you do not, the result may be that the hearing has to be adjourned.

Application for permission to change a child's surname
Section 28 Adoption and Children Act 2002

Name of court	
Case no./Serial no.	
Date received by the court	
Date issued	

Notes to applicants
- This form is only for use if you are applying for permission under section 28 of the Adoption and Children Act 2002 to change a child's surname.
- Before completing this form, please read the guidance notes carefully.
- Please complete every Part. If any question does not apply to your application, or you are not sure of the answer, please say so.
- If there is not enough room for your reply to any question, continue on a separate sheet. Please put the child's name, the number of the Part and the paragraph reference at the head of the continuation sheet.
- Please use black ink when filling in the form.

Part 1 About you

a) I am a prospective adopter of the child and wish to keep my identity confidential and apply for a serial number ☐ Yes ☐ No ◀ See Note 1

b) Title
☐ Mr ☐ Mrs ☐ Miss ☐ Ms ☐ Other _____ ◀ See Note 2

c) My name is

First name(s) in full

Last name

d) My address is (including postcode)

e) My telephone number is ◀ See Note 3 / See Note 4

f) My solicitor in these proceedings is

Name of solicitor	
Name of firm	
Address (including postcode)	

Telephone no.		Fax no.	
DX no.			
E-mail address			

g) My relationship to the child is ◀ See Note 5

A55 Application for permission to change a child's surname Section 28 Adoption and Children Act 2002 (12.05)   HMCS

Part 2 About the child

a) The name of the child is

First name(s) in full

Last name

b) The child is a
☐ Boy   ☐ Girl

c) The child was born on

d) The child's address is
(If you do not know the child's address, please enter 'Not known')

e) The child lives with
(If you do not know the name of the person with whom the child lives, please enter 'Not known')

◀ See Note 3

f) The adoption agency/local authority that has placed or is authorised to place the child for adoption is: (give the name and address of the adoption agency or local authority and (if known) the name and telephone number of the adoption worker who deals with the child)

Name of adoption agency/ local authority	
Address (including post code)	

Name of your contact in the agency	
Telephone no.	

g) The child

☐ is not the subject of a placement order

or

☐ is the subject of a placement order
(please give details and **attach a copy of the placement order**)

Name of court	
Case number	
Date of placement order	

About other orders or proceedings that affect the child

h) ☐ To the best of my knowledge, no proceedings relating to the child (other than any placement order entered above) have been completed or commenced in any court

or

☐ The following proceedings relating to the child have been completed/commenced (in addition to any placement order entered above) ◀ See Note 6

Type of order made (or applied for)	Date of order (or date of next hearing)	Name of court	Case number (or serial number)

Cases concerning a related child

i) ☐ To the best of my knowledge, no proceedings relating to a full, half or step brother or sister of the child have been completed or commenced in any court

or

☐ The following proceedings relating to a full, half or step brother or sister of the child have been completed/commenced (please give details below and, if you were a party to any proceedings that have been completed, **attach a copy of the final order**)

Relationship to child (eg. sister, half-brother)	Type of order made (or applied for)	Date of order (or date of next hearing)	Name of court	Case number (or serial number)

Part 3 About the child's parents or guardian

The name(s) and address(es) of the child's parent(s) are: ◀ See Note 7

The child's mother

a) The name of the child's mother is

First name(s) in full

Last name

b) Her address is (if deceased, please write 'Deceased' in the address box)

The child's father

c) The name of the child's father is

First name(s) in full

Last name

d) His address is (if deceased, please write 'Deceased' in the address box)

e) Does he have parental responsibility for the child? ◀ See Note 8

☐ Yes   ☐ No

The child's guardian

f) The name of the child's guardian is ◀ See Note 9

First name(s) in full

Last name

g) His/Her address is

Part 4 About this application

a) I wish the child's surname to be changed to ◀ See Note 10

b) My reasons for making this application are ◀ See Note 11

Part 5 Statement of truth

*[I believe] [The applicant believes] that the facts stated in this application are true.
*I am duly authorised by the applicant to sign this statement.

Print full name

Signed   Date

*[Applicant] [Applicant's solicitor] [Litigation friend]

*delete as appropriate

If you attend the court for a hearing

1. Do you have a disability for which you require special assistance or special facilities? ◀ See Note 12

    ☐ Yes   ☐ No

    If Yes, please say what your needs are below
    (the court staff will get in touch with you about your requirements)

2. Do you want to use the services of an interpreter?

    ☐ Yes   ☐ No

    If Yes, please specify which language
    (court staff will get in touch with you about your requirements)

What to do now

Once you have completed and signed this form, you should take or send the form and **three copies** to the court, together with the court fee* and the following documents:

- a copy of the placement order relating to the child;
- if you were a party to the proceedings, a copy of any other final order relating to the child that has effect;
- if you were a party to the proceedings, a copy of any final order relating to a full, half or step brother or sister of the child that has effect.

* If you are not sure about the court fee payable for your application, or you think that you may be exempt from paying all or part of the fee, you should contact the court for information.

Application for permission to change a child's surname (Form A55)
Notes on completing the form

Important

This form is for an application under Section 28 of the Adoption and Children Act 2002 for permission of the court to change a child's surname.

If you are attaching any order of the High Court or a county court to your application, it must be a sealed copy of the order (that is, a copy that has been stamped with the seal of the court). If you are attaching an order made by a magistrates' court, it must be a certified copy (a copy certified by the court officer to be a true copy of the original order), or a copy that bears the stamp of the originating court. An order issued by any other authority must be properly authenticated by that authority. If you are in any doubt about what is needed, please contact the court for assistance.

Take or send the completed application form, **and three copies,** to the court, together with the court fee and any documents you are attaching in support of your application. If you are not sure about the court fee payable for your application, or you think that you may be exempt from paying all or part of the fee, you should contact the court for information.

Notes on the application form

Note 1 If you are a prospective adopter (that is, you will be making an application to adopt the child) and you do not want your identity to be made known to the parents or guardians of the child, the court will issue you with a serial number. Any documents sent to the other parties will show the serial number, not your personal details. If you are required to attend the same court hearing, the court will make arrangements to ensure that your identity is protected.

If a serial number has already been issued to you, please ensure that it is entered in Part 2 paragraph (h) (About other orders or proceedings that affect the child).

Note 2 Where a child has been placed for adoption under section 19 of the Adoption and Children Act 2002, or an adoption agency is authorised to place a child for adoption under that section, or a placement order is in force in respect of the child, no one may cause the child to be known by a new surname unless each parent or guardian of the child gives written consent, or the court gives permission.

An application to the court for permission to change the child's surname may be made by any person, including the adoption agency or local authority authorised to place the child for adoption.

Note 3 If you are a prospective adopter, please see note 1 above. Otherwise, if you do not want your private address and telephone number, or the child's address, or (if the child does not live with you) the name of the person with whom the child lives, to be disclosed to any other party, do not enter those details on this application form. Instead you should enter the details on Form A65 which you must file at the court with your application. The information will not then be disclosed to any person, except by order of the court.

Note 4 If you are applying as an officer of the adoption agency or local authority that has placed or is authorised to place the child for adoption, you should enter the name and address of the agency/authority and the telephone number on which you can be contacted during working hours.

A55 Notes - Application for permission to change a child's surname - Notes on completing the form (12.05)   HMCS

Note 5 If you are applying as an officer of the adoption agency or local authority that has placed or is authorised to place the child for adoption, please say so and state your position in the agency/local authority.

Note 6 If there are earlier or current court proceedings relating to the child, give the name of the court, the nature of the proceedings and the date and effect of any order made. If you were a party to any proceedings that have been completed, you should attach a copy of the final order to your application. You do not need to repeat the details of any placement order you have already given.

Note 7 If the child has previously been adopted, give the names of his/her adoptive parents and not those of his/her natural parents.

Note 8 If the child's parents were not married at the time of his/her birth, the child's father may have acquired parental responsibility

- by subsequent marriage to the child's mother;
- because he has a parental responsibility agreement with the mother, or has been granted a parental responsibility order, or
- because he registered the child's birth jointly with the child's mother (on or after 1 December 2003).

Give details of any court order or agreement in respect of parental responsibility in Part 2 About the child, paragraph (h).

Note 9 If the child does not have a guardian, enter 'not applicable'. Otherwise, enter the details of any person appointed to be the child's guardian by deed or will or otherwise in writing in accordance with section 5(5) of the Children Act 1989, or by an order made under section 5(1) or 14A of that Act. If the child has more than one guardian, please give the name and address of any other guardian(s) on a separate sheet, putting the child's full name, the number of the Part and the paragraph reference at the head of the sheet.

Note 10 If you do not want the child's new name to be disclosed to any other party, do not enter it on this application form. Instead you should enter the name on Form A65, which you must file at the court with your application. The information will not then be disclosed to any person, except by order of the court.

Note 11 If you are the prospective adopter and you already have a serial number or have asked for one to be issued, you should make sure that the reasons for your application do not include any information that could lead to your identity being disclosed.

Any applicant who has withheld their address or telephone number, or the child's address or the name of the person with whom the child lives on the application form should make sure that they do not include any information that could lead to these details being disclosed.

Special assistance or facilities for disability if you attend the court

Note 12 If you need special assistance or special facilities for a disability or impairment, please set out your requirements in full. The court staff will need to know, for example, whether you want documents to be supplied in an alternative format, such as Braille or large print. They will also need to know about any specific requirements you may have on the day of the hearing, such as wheelchair access, a hearing loop, or a sign language interpreter.

The court staff will get in touch with you about your requirements. It is important that you make the court aware of all your needs. If you do not, the result may be that the hearing has to be adjourned.

Application for permission to remove a child from the United Kingdom

Section 28 Adoption and Children Act 2002

Name of court	
Case no./Serial no.	
Date received by the court	
Date issued	

Notes to applicants

- This form is only for use if you are applying for permission to remove a child from the United Kingdom under section 28 of the Adoption and Children Act 2002.
- Before completing this form, please read the guidance notes carefully.
- Please complete every Part. If any question does not apply to your application, or you are not sure of the answer, please say so.
- If there is not enough room for your reply to any question, continue on a separate sheet. Please put the child's name, the number of the Part and the paragraph reference at the head of the continuation sheet.
- Please use black ink when filling in the form.

Part 1 About you

a) I am a prospective adopter of the child and wish to keep my identity confidential and apply for a serial number ☐ Yes ☐ No ◀ **See Note 1**

b) Title

☐ Mr ☐ Mrs ☐ Miss ☐ Ms ☐ Other _____ ◀ **See Note 2**

c) My name is

First name(s) in full

Last name

d) My address is (including postcode)

e) My telephone number is ◀ **See Note 3** ◀ **See Note 4**

f) My solicitor in these proceedings is

Name of solicitor	
Name of firm	
Address (including postcode)	

Telephone no.		Fax no.	
DX no.			
E-mail address			

g) My relationship to the child is ◀ **See Note 5**

A56 Application for permission to remove a child from the United Kingdom Section 28 Adoption and Children Act 2002(12.05)   HMCS

Part 2 About the child

a) The name of the child is

First name(s) in full

Last name

b) The child is a

☐ Boy ☐ Girl

c) The child was born on

d) The child's address is
(If you do not know the child's address, please enter 'Not known')

e) The child lives with
(If you do not know the name of the person with whom the child lives, please enter 'Not known')

◀ See Note 3

f) The adoption agency/local authority that has placed or is authorised to place the child for adoption is: (give the name and address of the adoption agency/local authority and (if known) the name and telephone number of the adoption worker who deals with the child)

Name of adoption agency/ local authority	
Address (including post code)	

Name of your contact in the agency	
Telephone no.	

g) The child

☐ is not the subject of a placement order

or

☐ is the subject of a placement order
(please give details and **attach a copy of the placement order**)

Name of court	
Case number	
Date of placement order	

About other orders or proceedings that affect the child

h) ☐ To the best of my knowledge, no proceedings relating to the child (other than any placement order entered above) have been completed or commenced in any court

or

☐ The following proceedings relating to the child have been completed/commenced (in addition to any placement order already entered above)

◀ See Note 6

Type of order made (or applied for)	Date of order (or date of next hearing)	Name of court	Case number (or serial number)

Cases concerning a related child

i) ☐ To the best of my knowledge, no proceedings relating to a full, half or step brother or sister of the child have been completed or commenced in any court

or

☐ The following proceedings relating to a full, half or step brother or sister of the child have been completed/commenced (please give details below and, if you were a party to any proceedings that have been completed, **attach a copy of the final order**)

Relationship to child (eg. sister, half-brother)	Type of order made (or applied for)	Date of order (or date of next hearing)	Name of court	Case number (or serial number)

Part 3 About the child's parents or guardian

The name(s) and address(es) of the child's parent(s) are: ◀ See Note 7

The child's mother

a) The name of the child's mother is

First name(s) in full

Last name

b) Her address is (if deceased, please write 'Deceased' in the address box)

The child's father

c) The name of the child's father is

First name(s) in full

Last name

d) His address is (if deceased, please write 'Deceased' in the address box)

e) Does he have parental responsibility for the child? ◀ See Note 8

☐ Yes   ☐ No

The child's guardian

f) The name of the child's guardian is ◀ See Note 9

First name(s) in full

Last name

g) His/Her address is

Part 4 About this application

My reasons for this application are: (please give a brief statement of the reasons for your application; include full details of the country (or countries) of destination, the purpose and duration of stay and the child's address(es) (if known) while outside the United Kingdom)

◄ See Note 10

Part 5 Statement of truth

*[I believe] [The applicant believes] that the facts stated in this application are true.

*I am duly authorised by the applicant to sign this statement.

Print full name

Signed   Date

*[Applicant] [Applicant's solicitor] [Litigation friend]

*delete as appropriate

If you attend the court for a hearing

1. Do you have a disability for which you require special assistance or special facilities?

☐ Yes ☐ No

◀ See Note 11

If Yes, please say what your needs are below
(the court staff will get in touch with you about your requirements)

2. Do you want to use the services of an interpreter?

☐ Yes ☐ No

If Yes, please specify which language
(court staff will get in touch with you about your requirements)

What to do now

Once you have completed and signed this form, you should take or send the form and **three copies** to the court, together with the court fee* and the following documents:

- a copy of the placement order relating to the child;
- if you were a party to the proceedings, a copy of any other final order relating to the child that has effect;
- if you were a party to the proceedings, a copy of any final order relating to a full, half or step brother or sister of the child that has effect.

* If you are not sure about the court fee payable for your application, or you think that you may be exempt from paying all or part of the fee, you should contact the court for information.

Application for permission to remove a child from the United Kingdom (Form A56)
Notes on completing the form

Important

This form is for an application under Section 28 of the Adoption and Children Act 2002 for permission of the court to remove a child from the United Kingdom.

If you are attaching any order of the High Court or a county court to your application, it must be a sealed copy of the order (that is, a copy that has been stamped with the seal of the court). If you are attaching an order made by a magistrates' court, it must be a certified copy (a copy certified by the court officer to be a true copy of the original order), or a copy that bears the stamp of the originating court. An order issued by any other authority must be properly authenticated by that authority. If you are in any doubt about what is needed, please contact the court for assistance.

Take or send the completed application form, **and three copies,** to the court, together with the court fee and any documents you are attaching in support of your application. If you are not sure about the court fee payable for your application, or you think that you may be exempt from paying all or part of the fee, you should contact the court for information.

Notes on the application form

Note 1 If you are a prospective adopter (that is, you will be making an application to adopt the child) and you do not want your identity to be made known to the parents or guardians of the child, the court will issue you with a serial number. Any documents sent to the other parties will show the serial number, not your personal details. If you are required to attend the same court hearing, the court will make arrangements to ensure that your identity is protected.

If a serial number has already been issued to you, please ensure that it is entered in Part 2 paragraph (h) (About other orders or proceedings that affect the child).

Note 2 Where a child has been placed for adoption under section 19 of the Adoption and Children Act 2002, or an adoption agency is authorised to place a child for adoption under that section, or a placement order is in force in respect of the child, the child may not be removed from the United Kingdom unless:

- the removal is by a person who provides the child's home and is for a period of less than one month; or
- each parent or guardian of the child gives written consent, or
- the court gives permission.

An application to the court for permission to remove the child from the United Kingdom may be made by any person, including the adoption agency or local authority authorised to place the child for adoption.

Note 3 If you are a prospective adopter, please see note 1 above. Otherwise, if you do not want your private address and telephone number, or the child's address, or (if the child does not live with you) the name of the person with whom the child lives, to be disclosed to any other party, do not enter those details on this application form. Instead you should enter the details on Form A65, which you must file at the court with your application. The information will not then be disclosed to any person, except by order of the court.

Note 4 ▶ If you are applying as an officer of the adoption agency or local authority that has placed or is authorised to place the child for adoption, you should enter the name and address of the agency/authority and the telephone number on which you can be contacted during working hours.

Note 5 ▶ If you are applying as an officer of the adoption agency or local authority that has placed or is authorised to place the child for adoption, please say so and state your position in the agency/local authority.

Note 6 ▶ If there are earlier, or current, court proceedings relating to the child, give the name of the court, the nature of the proceedings and the date and effect of any order made. If you were a party to any proceedings that have been completed, you should attach a copy of the final order to your application. You do not need to repeat the details of any placement order you have already given.

Note 7 ▶ If the child has previously been adopted, give the names of his/her adoptive parents and not those of his/her natural parents.

Note 8 ▶ If the child's parents were not married at the time of his/her birth, the child's father may have acquired parental responsibility

- by subsequent marriage to the child's mother;
- because he has a parental responsibility agreement with the mother, or has been granted a parental responsibility order, or
- because he registered the child's birth jointly with the child's mother (on or after 1 December 2003).

Give details of any court order or agreement in respect of parental responsibility in Part 2 About the child, paragraph (h).

Note 9 ▶ If the child does not have a guardian, enter 'not applicable'. Otherwise, enter the details of any person appointed to be the child's guardian by deed or will or otherwise in writing in accordance with section 5(5) of the Children Act 1989, or by an order made under section 5(1) or 14A of that Act. If the child has more than one guardian, please give the name and address of any other guardians(s) on a separate sheet, putting the child's full name, the number of the Part and the paragraph reference at the head of the sheet.

Note 10 ▶ If you are the prospective adopter and already have a serial number or have asked for one, you should make sure that the information does not include any details which could lead to your identity being disclosed.

Any applicant who has withheld their address or telephone number, or the child's address or the name of the person with whom the child lives should make sure that they do not include anything which could lead to these details being disclosed.

If you do not want details of the proposed dates of travel, country (or countries) of destination and address(es) while outside the United Kingdom to be disclosed to any other party you should say so on the form and explain your reasons for wishing to keep the information confidential. The details of the proposed travel should be set out in a separate letter to the court, which you must attach to your application. The information will not be then disclosed to any person, except by order of the court.

Special assistance or facilities for disability if you attend the court

Note 11 ▶ If you need special assistance or special facilities for a disability or impairment, please set out your requirements in full. The court staff will need to know, for example, whether you want documents to be supplied in an alternative format, such as Braille or large print. They will also need to know about any specific requirements you may have on the day of the hearing, such as wheelchair access, a hearing loop, or a sign language interpreter.

The court staff will get in touch with you about your requirements. It is important that you make the court aware of all your needs. If you do not, the result may be that the hearing has to be adjourned.

Application for a recovery order
Section 41 Adoption and Children Act 2002

Name of court	
Case no./Serial no.	
Date received by the court	
Date issued	

Notes to applicants
- This form is only for use if you are applying for a recovery order under section 41 of the Adoption and Children Act 2002.
- Before filling in this form, please read the guidance notes on completing the form.
- Please complete all parts. If any part does not apply to your application, or you are not sure of the answer, please say so.
- If there is not enough room for your reply to any question, continue on a separate sheet. Please put the child's name, the part and question number at the head of the continuation sheet.
- Please use black ink when filling in the form.

Part 1 About you

a) I am a prospective adopter of the child and wish to keep my identity confidential and apply for a serial number ☐ Yes ☐ No ◄ See Note 1

b) Title
☐ Mr ☐ Mrs ☐ Miss ☐ Ms ☐ Other _____

c) My name is

First name(s) in full

Last name

d) My address is (including post code)

e) My telephone number is ◄ See Note 2 ◄ See Note 3

f) Are you applying as an officer of an adoption agency or local authority?
☐ Yes ☐ No

If Yes, please give below the name of the adoption agency/local authority and your position within the adoption agency/local authority

Name of adoption agency/local authority	
Your position within the agency/local authority	

If No, please give below your relationship to the child ◄ See Note 4

A57 Application for a recovery order Section 41 Adoption and Children Act 2002 (12.05)   HMCS

g) My solicitor in these proceedings is

Name of solicitor	
Name of firm	
Address (including postcode)	

Telephone no.		Fax no.	
DX no.			
E-mail address			

Part 2 About the child

a) The name of the child is

First name(s) in full

Last name

b) The child is a

☐ Boy   ☐ Girl

c) The child was born on

d) The child's usual address is

e) The child lives with (If you do not know the name of the person with whom the child lives with enter 'Not Known')

◄ See Note 2

f) If the child is or has been the subject of continuing or previous court proceedings please give the details of the case and the court in which the proceedings are taking place or took place

Type of order made (or applied for)	Date of order (or date of next hearing)	Name of court	Case number (or serial number)

Part 3 Reason for application

Please read thoroughly the Guidance Notes for Part 3, which explain the different grounds for applying for a recovery order. Please then tick the box(es) that apply to your application and give full details. It is important to give as much information as possible about the whereabouts of the child, the person or persons who may have this information and the names and addresses of anyone who has removed or not returned the child. In every case give the name and address of the person referred to, their relationship to the child, the circumstances in which the child comes to be with them and any other information you think the court requires.

◄ See Note 5

The child has:

☐ been removed by the person or persons whose name(s) and address(es) are given below in contravention of any of the provisions of sections 30 to 40 of the Adoption and Children Act 2002.

or

☐ not yet been removed, but there are reasonable grounds to believe that the person or persons whose name(s) and address(es) are given below intend(s) to remove the child in contravention of sections 30 to 40 of the Adoption and Children Act 2002.

or

☐ Prospective Adopters (whose details are given below or on form A65) have not returned the child to the adoption agency within 7 days of the agency giving them notice to return the child under section 31(4) or 35(2) of the Act

☐ Prospective Adopters (whose details are given below or on form A65) have not returned the child to the adoption agency within 14 days of the agency giving them notice to return the child under section 32(2) of the Act

☐ Prospective Adopters (whose details are given below or on form A65) have not returned the child to the local authority on the date set by the court under section 33(2) of the Act

☐ Prospective Adopters (whose details are given below or on form A65) have not returned the child to the local authority within the period determined by the Court under section 34(3) of the Act

Part 4 The order and directions applied for

Please indicate the type of order you will be asking the court to make:

☐ An order directing the person identified below or any person who is in a position to do so to produce the child to one of the following: (Please tick the box that applies)

  ☐ The person named in the order

  ☐ Any constable

  ☐ Any person authorised to exercise any power under the order by the adoption agency authorised to place the child for adoption

☐ An order that one of the following people do remove the child (please tick the box that applies):

  ☐ The person named in the order

  ☐ Any constable

  ☐ Any person authorised to exercise any power under the order by the adoption agency authorised to place the child for adoption.

  Please give information below about the whereabouts of the child

☐ An order requiring the person(s) identified below to disclose information as to the child's whereabouts to any constable or officer of the court

☐ An order authorising a constable to enter into the premises specified below to search for the child (Include your grounds for believing the child to be on the premises.)

Is this application being made without notice being given to another party?

  ☐ Yes   ☐ No

If Yes, please state why.

Statement of truth

*[I believe] [The applicant believes] that the facts stated in this application are true.

*I am duly authorised by the applicant to sign this statement.

Print full name

Signed   Date

*[Applicant] [Applicant's solicitor] [Litigation friend]

*delete as appropriate

If you attend the court for a hearing

1. Do you have a disability for which you require special assistance or special facilities?   ◀ See Note 6

   ☐ Yes   ☐ No

   If Yes, please say what your needs are below
   (the court staff will get in touch with you about your requirements)

2. Do you want to use the services of an interpreter?

   ☐ Yes   ☐ No

   If Yes, please specify which language
   (court staff will get in touch with you about your requirements)

What to do now

Once you have completed and signed this form, you should take or send the form and **three copies** to the court, together with the court fee* and the following documents:

- Copies of any relevant orders i.e. placement orders or contact orders.

  If you are attaching any order of the High Court or a county court to your application, it must be a sealed copy of the order (that is, a copy that has been stamped with the seal of the court). If you are attaching an order made by a magistrates' court, it must be a certified copy (a copy certified by the court officer to be a true copy of the original order), or a copy that bears the stamp of the originating court.

- Evidence of the basis on which a child is accommodated or placed

- Evidence as to how any necessary notices, requests or court orders have been served

- If appropriate, a recent photograph of the child which should be dated.

- If the application is being made without notice and it is not possible to obtain documents in advance, you will need to ask the court for directions when you make the application.

*If you are not sure about the court fee payable for your application, or you think that you may be exempt from paying all or part of the fee, you should contact the court for information.

Application for a recovery order (Form A57)
Notes on completing the form

Parts 1 and 2 About the applicant

Note 1 ▶ If you are a prospective adopter (that is, you will be making an application to adopt the child) and you do not want your identity to be made known to the parents or guardians of the child you are intending to adopt, the court will issue you with a serial number. Any documents sent to the other parties will show the serial number, not your personal details. If you are required to attend the same court hearing, the court will make arrangements to ensure that your identity is protected. If you already have a serial number issued to you, please ensure that it is entered in Part 2, paragraph f.

Note 2 ▶ If you are a prospective adopter see note 1 above. Otherwise, if you do not want your private address, postcode, and telephone number, or the child's address and the name of the person with whom the child lives, to be disclosed to any other party, do not enter them on this application form. Instead you should enter the details on Form A65, which you must file at the court with your application. The information will not then be disclosed to any person, except by order of the court.

Note 3 ▶ If you are applying as the authorised officer of a local authority/adoption agency the contact details should be those for the local authority/agency which the court can use.

Note 4 ▶ There are no restrictions on who may apply for a recovery order but the court will need a brief indication of how you come to be making the application and how you are related to or connected to the child.

Part 3 Reasons for application and evidence in support

Note 5 ▶ If you do not want the names and addresses given in this section to be disclosed to any other party, do not enter them on this application form. Instead you should enter the details on Form A65, which you must file at the court with your application. The information will not then be disclosed to any person, except by order of the court.

Important: If you are the **prospective adopter** and already have a serial number or have asked for one, you should make sure that the reasons for your application do not include any information that could lead to your identity being disclosed.

Any applicant who has withheld their address or telephone number or the child's address or the name of the person with whom the child lives should make sure that they do not include any information which could lead to these being disclosed.

A. **The child has been removed or there are reasonable grounds to believe that someone intends to remove the child in contravention of sections 30-40 of the Adoption and Children Act 2002 (sections 30-35 (agency cases) and sections 36-40 (non agency cases)).**

The detailed removal provisions are in sections 30-40. The following situations are examples only.

1. Where a child is placed by consent under section 19 of the 2002 Act, only an adoption agency can remove the child (section 30(1)), e.g. a parent cannot remove the child.

2. Where a child is in accommodation provided by the local authority and an application for a placement order has been made, the child may only be removed by a person who has the court's permission, or the local authority (section 30(2)), e.g. a parent can only remove the child with the court's permission.

3. Where a placement order is in force or has been revoked but a child is still with the prospective adopters or in accommodation provided by the local authority, only the local authority may remove the child (section 34(1)), e.g. a parent cannot remove the child.

4. Where a child under six weeks old has been placed for adoption but after 6 weeks the agency does not have authorisation under section 19 of the 2002 Act, only the adoption agency can remove the child from the placement (section 30(1)), e.g. a parent cannot remove the child.

5. Where a step-parent or partner has given notice of intention to apply to adopt and the child has had his or her home with the step-parent/partner for not less than 3 years out of the last 5 the child may be removed only by a person with the court's permission or a local authority or other person in exercise of statutory powers (section 39(2)), e.g. a parent can only remove the child with the court's permission.

6. Where a step-parent or partner has given notice of intention to adopt and the child has had his or her home with the step-parent/partner for less than 3 years, the child may only be removed by the child's parent or guardian, by a person with the court's permission or a local authority or other person in exercise of statutory powers (section 39(3)), e.g. a parent can remove the child.

7. Where local authority foster parents have given notice of intention to apply to adopt and the child has had his or her home with the foster parents for 5 years the child may be removed only by a person with the court's permission or a local authority or other person in exercise of statutory powers (other than under section 20(8) of the Children Act 1989) (section 38(2) and (3)), e.g. a parent can only remove the child with the court's permission.

8. Where local authority foster parents have applied to the court for permission to apply to adopt the child because the child has not had his home with them for a year before the application to adopt (and the permission application has not been dealt with) the child may be removed only by a person with the court's permission or a local authority or other person in exercise of statutory powers (other than under section 20(8) of the Children Act 1989), e.g. a parent can only remove the child with the court's permission.

9. If the child has had his or her home with the foster parents for a year and the foster parents have given notice of intention to adopt, the child may only be removed by a person who has the court's permission, by a local authority or other person in exercise of statutory powers, or a person with parental responsibility for the child who is exercising the power in section 20(8) of the Children Act 1989 (section 38(4) and (5)), e.g. a parent can only remove the child with the court's permission unless he or she has parental responsibility for the child and the foster parents are providing accommodation pursuant to section 20 of the 1989 Act.

B. Prospective adopters have failed to:

1. Return the child to the adoption agency within 7 days of the agency giving them notice to return the child where the child:

a) is placed for adoption by an adoption agency and is less than six weeks old, or the agency has not been authorised to place the child for adoption and

b) the child's parent(s) or guardian(s) has/have informed the agency that they want the child to be returned to them, and

c) there is no pending application for a placement order, and

d) the child is not subject to a care order (section 31(3) and (4)).

2. Return the child to the adoption agency within 14 days of the agency giving them notice to return the child where the child:

a) is placed for adoption by an adoption agency under section 19 of the Act and

b) consent to placement under section 19 has been withdrawn and

c) there is no pending application for a placement order and

d) the child is not subject to a care order and

e) prior to service of the notice no application for an adoption order, special guardianship order, residence order or for permission to apply for special guardianship or residence, was made to the court and remains to be dealt with.

(Note: if there is such an application the prospective adopters are not required to return the child unless the court orders otherwise (section 32)).

3. Return the child to the local authority on the date set by the court for return of the child where

a) the child is placed for adoption by a local authority under section 19;

b) an application for a placement order has been refused and the parent or guardian has told the local authority that he wants the child returned and

c) the child is not subject to a care order (section 33).

4. Return the child to the local authority within the time set by the court when the court has revoked a placement order and has determined that the child is not to remain with the prospective adopters (section 34(3)).

5. Return the child to the adoption agency within 7 days of the agency giving them notice to return the child where the child:

a) had been placed with prospective adopters by the agency

b) the agency is of the opinion that the child should not remain with them and

c) Prior to service of the notice no application for an adoption order, special guardianship order, residence order or for permission to apply for special guardianship or residence, was made to the court and remains to be dealt with.

(Note: if there is such an application the prospective adopters are not required to return the child unless the court orders otherwise (section 35(2)).

Part 4 the order and directions applied for

Indicate here the type of order you will be asking the court to make. Give as much detail as you can.

Note 6 ▶ **Special assistance or facilities for disability**

If you need special assistance or special facilities for a disability or impairment, please set out your requirement in full. The court staff will need to know, for example, whether you want documents to be supplied in an alternative format, such as Braille or large print. They will also need to know about any specific requirements you may have on the day of the hearing such as wheelchair access, a hearing loop, or a sign language interpreter.

The court staff will get in touch with you about your requirements. It is important that you make the court aware of all your needs. If you do not, the result may be that the hearing has to be adjourned.

Application for an adoption order
Section 46 Adoption and Children Act 2002

Name of court	
Case no./Serial no.	
Date received by the court	
Date issued	

Notes to applicants
- Do not use this form if the child you want to adopt is not habitually resident in the United Kingdom, the Channel Isles or the Isle of Man, or if you intend to apply for a Convention adoption order. Instead you should use Form A60 (Application for an adoption order (excluding a Convention adoption order) where the child has been brought into the UK for adoption) or Form A59 (Application for a Convention adoption order).
- Before filling in this form, please read the guidance notes on completing the form.
- Please complete every Part. If you are not sure of the answer to any question, or you do not think that it applies to you, please say so.
- If there is not enough room on the form for your reply, you may continue on a separate sheet. Please put the child's full name, the number of the Part and the paragraph reference at the head of the continuation sheet.
- Please use black ink when filling in the form.

I/We the undersigned _____
(and _____)
wish to adopt _____ ◀ See Note 1
and give the following details in support of my/our application

I/We want my/our identity to be kept confidential and
wish to apply for a serial number   ☐ Yes   ☐ No   ◀ See Note 2

Part 1 About you

First applicant
a) Title
☐ Mr   ☐ Mrs   ☐ Miss
☐ Ms   ☐ Other _____

b) My name is
First name(s) in full

Last name

Second applicant
a) Title
☐ Mr   ☐ Mrs   ☐ Miss
☐ Ms   ☐ Other _____

b) My name is   ◀ See Note 3
First name(s) in full

Last name

A58 Application for an adoption order section 46 Adoption and Children Act 2002 (12.05)   HMCS

c) My address is (including postcode)   c) My address is (including postcode)

d) My telephone number is   d) My telephone number is

e) My date of birth is   e) My date of birth is

f) My nationality is   f) My nationality is

g) My occupation is   g) My occupation is   ◀ See Note 4

h) I am   h) I am
☐ Male   ☐ Female   ☐ Male   ☐ Female

i) My relationship to the child is   i) My relationship to the child is   ◀ See Note 5

j) My/Our solicitor in these proceedings is

Name of solicitor	
Name of firm	
Address (including postcode)	

Telephone no.		Fax no.	
DX no.			
E-mail address			

Domicile and residence   ◀ See Note 6

k) ☐ I am/We are/One of us, namely [_____]

is domiciled in the United Kingdom, the Channel Islands or the Isle of Man.

or

☐ I have/We have both been habitually resident in the United Kingdom, the Channel Islands or the Isle of Man for a period of at least one year, ending with the date of this application.

Status

> If you are applying to adopt as a couple, please go straight to **Part 2 About the Child**. Paragraphs (l) to (r) do not apply to you
>
> If you are applying to adopt alone, please tick the box at (l) to (r) below that applies to you. **If you tick (l), (m), (q) or (r) please the give additional information asked for.**

l) ☐ I am the partner of the child's
  ☐ Father ☐ Mother

  If you have ticked box (l), please go straight to Part 2 About the Child. Paragraphs (m) to (r) do not apply to you. ◀ See Note 7

m) ☐ I am the partner (not the spouse or civil partner) of a person who is not the child's parent and I am applying to adopt alone because:

  If you have ticked box (m), please go straight to Part 2 About the Child. Paragraphs (n) to (r) do not apply to you. ◀ See Note 8

  (please give reasons below, continuing on a separate sheet if necessary)

  [ ]

n) ☐ I am not married/I do not have a civil partner ◀ See Note 9
  or
o) ☐ I am divorced/my civil partnership has been dissolved ◀ See Note 9
  or
p) ☐ I am a widow/a widower/a surviving civil partner ◀ See Note 9
  or
q) ☐ I am married/I have a civil partner, and I can satisfy the court that: ◀ See Note 10
   ☐ my husband/wife/civil partner cannot be found
     or
   ☐ I have separated from my husband/wife/civil partner, we are living apart and the separation is likely to be permanent
     or
   ☐ my husband/wife/civil partner is not capable of making an application due to ill-health
  or
r) ☐ I am applying alone for an adoption order in respect of my own child and I can satisfy the court that ◀ See Note 11
   ☐ the other natural parent has died
     or
   ☐ the other natural parent cannot be found
     or
   ☐ by virtue of section 28 of the Human Fertilisation and Embryology Act 1990, there is no other parent
     or
   ☐ the other natural parent's exclusion from this application is justified
     (please give reasons below)

  [ ]

Part 2 About the child

a) The child is a
    ☐ Boy   ☐ Girl

b) The child was born on
[ ][ ][ ][ ][ ][ ][ ][ ]

or To the best of my/our knowledge the child was born on or about ◀ See Note 12
[ ][ ][ ][ ][ ][ ][ ][ ]

and is the person to whom the attached certified copy of the entry in the Register of Live Births/Register of Adopted Children relates

in (give place and country of birth)

c) The child's nationality is

d) I/we confirm that the child is not and has never been married or a civil partner ◀ See Note 13
    ☐ Yes   ☐ No

e) The child has had his/her home with me/us continuously since
[ ][ ][ ][ ][ ][ ][ ][ ]

f) The child was placed with me/us for adoption by an adoption agency
    ☐ Yes (If you ticked this box, please complete paragraphs (g) and (h) and then go straight to paragraph (j). Paragraph (i) does not apply to you.)
    ☐ No (If you ticked this box, please go straight to paragraph (i). Paragraphs (g) and (h) do not apply to you.)

g) The child was placed with me/us for adoption on
[ ][ ][ ][ ][ ][ ][ ][ ] by

Name of adoption agency	
Address (including post code)	

Name of your contact in the agency	
Telephone no.	

h) ☐ No other adoption agency has been involved in placing the child
or
    ☐ The following adoption agency has also been involved in placing the child

Name of adoption agency	
Address (including post code)	

Name of your contact in the agency	
Telephone no.	

i) I/we have notified in writing my/our local authority of my/our intention to apply for an adoption order (give details) ◀ See Note 14

Name of local authority	
Address (including post code)	
Date notified	
Name of your contact in the local authority	
Telephone no.	

j) ☐ No placement order or freeing order has been made in respect of the child ◀ See Note 15
or
☐ The following placement order/freeing order has been made in respect of the child:

Name of court	
Case number	
Type of order	
Date of order	

Care

k) ☐ No local authority or voluntary organisation has parental responsibility for the child
or
☐ The following local authority/voluntary organisation has parental responsibility for the child:

Name of local authority or voluntary organisation	
Address (including post code)	
Name of your contact in the authority/organisation	
Telephone no.	

Maintenance

l) ☐ No maintenance order/agreement or award of child support maintenance under the Child Support Act 1991 has been made in respect of the child ◀ See Note 16
or
☐ The following maintenance order/agreement/award of child support maintenance has been made

Person liable to pay maintenance	
Address (including post code)	
Court and date of order	
Date of maintenance agreement/child support maintenance award	

About other orders or proceedings that affect the child

m) ☐ To the best of my/our knowledge, no proceedings relating to the child (other than any freeing or placement order, or any maintenance order as given above) have been completed or commenced in any court

◀ See Note 17

or

☐ The following proceedings relating to the child have been completed/commenced (in addition to any freeing or placement order, or maintenance order given above)

Type of order made (or applied for)	Date of order (or date of next hearing)	Name of court	Case number (or serial number)

Cases concerning a related child

n) ☐ To the best of my knowledge, no proceedings relating to a full, half or step brother or sister of the child have been completed or commenced in any court

or

☐ The following proceedings relating to a full, half or step brother or sister of the child have been completed/commenced (please give details below and, if you were a party to any proceedings that have been completed, attach a copy of the final order)

Relationship to child (eg. sister, half-brother)	Type of order made (or applied for)	Date of order (or date of next hearing)	Name of court	Case number (or serial number)

Part 3 About the child's parents or guardian

The child's mother

a) The name of the child's mother is

First name(s) in full

Last name

b) Her address is (if deceased, please write 'Deceased' in the address box)

c) Her nationality is

The child's father   ◀ See Note 18

d) The name of the child's father is

First name(s) in full

Last name

e) His address is (if deceased, please write 'Deceased' in the address box)

f) His nationality is

g) Does he have parental responsibility for the child?   ◀ See Note 19

☐ Yes   ☐ No

If No, does he intend to apply for an order under section 4(1)(c) of the Children Act 1989 (a parental responsibility order) or a residence or contact order in respect of the child?

☐ Yes   ☐ No

The child's guardian

h) The name of the child's guardian is   ◀ See Note 20

First name(s) in full

Last name

i) His/Her address is

Parent/guardian consent to adoption

◀ See Note 21
◀ See Note 22

> **Note:** You do not need to complete paragraph (j) if
> - the child you are applying to adopt is the subject of a current placement order, the adoption agency has placed the child with you, and no parent/guardian of the child opposes the making of an adoption order;
>
> **or**
>
> - the child you are applying to adopt is the subject of a current freeing order.
>
> Instead, go straight to Part 4 General. You should give the details of the placement order or freeing order in Part 2 About the Child above. Otherwise, please tick the box that applies to your circumstances and give any further information requested.

j) ☐ The child's parent(s)/guardian(s) has/have consented to the making of an adoption order

or

☐ The child's parent(s)/guardian(s) gave advance consent to the making of a future adoption order (and has/have not withdrawn that consent) and does/do not oppose the making of an adoption order

or

☐ The child was placed with me/us for adoption by an adoption agency with the consent of each parent/guardian (and the mother's consent was given when the child was at least 6 weeks old), and no parent/guardian opposes the making of an adoption order

or

☐ The following parent(s)/guardian(s) of the child has/have not consented to the making of an adoption order: (give name(s) below)

```
┌──────────────────────────────────────────────────┐
│                                                  │
│                                                  │
│                                                  │
│                                                  │
└──────────────────────────────────────────────────┘
```

and I/we ask the court to dispense with his/her/their consent on the following grounds:
(please tick the grounds that apply)

☐ he/she/they cannot be found

☐ he/she is/they are incapable of giving consent

☐ the welfare of the child requires it.

You must attach a brief statement of facts (and two copies of the statement) setting out a summary of the history of the case and any other facts to satisfy the court that the grounds for your request apply.

> **IMPORTANT:** The court will send a copy of your statement of facts to each parent or guardian of the child. If you intend to ask the court to keep your identity confidential, you should make sure that the statement of facts does not include any information that could identify you, where you live, or where the child goes to school or nursery.

Part 4 General

Child's name on the adoption order

◀ See Note 23

If the adoption order is made, I/We want the child to be known as

First name(s) in full

Last name

Health reports

◀ See Note 24

Separate reports on my/our health and the health of the child made by a registered medical practitioner on (give date(s))

are attached to this application.

Declarations

I/We have not received or given payment or reward in respect of the proposed adoption (except as follows:) (give details below)

To the best of my/our knowledge, only the person(s) or organisation(s) named in Part 2 of this application have taken part in the arrangements for the child's adoption.

Part 5 Statement of truth

I believe that the facts stated in this application are true.

I believe that the facts stated in this application are true.

Signature of first applicant

Signature of second applicant

Print full name

Print full name

Signed

Signed

Date

Date

If you attend the court for a hearing

1. Do you/either of you have a disability for which you require special assistance or special facilities?   ◀ See Note 25

   ☐ Yes   ☐ No

   If Yes, please say what your needs are below
   (the court staff will get in touch with you about your requirements)

   [   ]

2. Do you/either of you want to use the services of an interpreter?

   ☐ Yes   ☐ No

   If Yes, please specify which language
   (court staff will get in touch with you about your requirements)

   [   ]

3. Are there any dates on which you know you will not be able to attend the court, or any particular dates that would especially suit you? If so, please give details below

Unavailable dates	Preferred dates

   (Please note that, although the court will try to fit in with your preferences, it may not be always be possible to do so)

What to do now

Once you have completed and signed this form, you should take or send the form and **three copies** to the court, together with the court fee* and the following documents:

- a certified copy of the full entry in the Register of Live Births that relates to the child or, where the child has been adopted, a certified copy of the entry in the Adopted Children Register;
- if you are asking the court to dispense with the consent of any parent or guardian to the adoption, a brief statement of the facts relied on in support of the request, and **two copies** of the statement;
- a copy of any placement order or freeing order relating to the child;
- if you were a party to the proceedings, a copy of any other final order relating to the child that has effect and, if possible, a copy of any maintenance agreement or maintenance award relating to the child;
- if you were a party to the proceedings, a copy of any final order relating to a full, half or step brother or sister of the child that has effect;
- reports by a registered medical practitioner on the health of the child and the applicant(s) covering the matters specified in the Practice Direction 'Reports by a registered medical practitioner (health reports)', and **two copies** of the reports.
  Note: You do not have to supply health reports if:
    - the child was placed with you for adoption by an adoption agency, or
    - he/she is your child, or the child of the other applicant, or
    - you are applying alone as the partner (including the husband, wife or civil partner) of the child's mother or father;
- where a parent of the child has died, a certified copy of the entry in the Register of Deaths;
- if you are submitting evidence of marriage or civil partnership, a certified copy of the entry in the Register of Marriages or the Register of Civil Partnerships;
- where your husband, wife or civil partner has died, a certified copy of the entry in the Register of Deaths;
- a copy of any decree absolute of divorce or decree of nullity of your marriage;
- in relation to a civil partnership, a copy of any dissolution order or nullity order of your civil partnership;
- any documentary evidence supporting the reasons why you are applying to adopt the child without your husband, wife or civil partner, such as a decree of judicial separation;
- if your name as entered on the application form is different from the name shown on any evidence of marriage or civil partnership you are sending with your application, any documentary evidence to explain the difference.

*If you are not sure about the court fee payable for your application, or you think that you may be exempt from paying all or part of the fee, you should contact the court for information.

Application for an adoption order (Form A58)
Notes on completing the form

Important

Do not use this form if the child you want to adopt is habitually resident outside the United Kingdom, the Channel Islands or the Isle of Man, or if you intend to apply for a Convention adoption order. Instead you should use Form A60 (Application for an adoption order (excluding a Convention adoption order) where the child has been brought into the UK for adoption) or Form A59 (Application for a Convention adoption order).

In these notes, any reference to a birth certificate, death certificate, marriage certificate or certificate of civil partnership means a certified copy of the entry in the Register of Live Births, the Register of Deaths, the Register of Marriages or the Register of Civil Partnerships, as appropriate. A photocopy is not acceptable. The birth certificate you send to the court for the child you are applying to adopt must be a certified copy of the **full** entry in the Register of Live Births.

If you are attaching any order of the High Court or a county court to your application, it must be a sealed copy of the order (that is, a copy that has been stamped with the seal of the court). If you are attaching an order made by a magistrates' court, it must be a certified copy (a copy certified by the court officer to be a true copy of the original order), or a copy that bears the stamp of the originating court. An order issued by any other authority must be properly authenticated by that authority. If you are in any doubt about what is needed, please contact the court for assistance.

Take or send the completed application form, **and three copies,** to the court, together with the court fee and any documents you are attaching in support of your application. If you are not sure about the court fee payable for your application, or you think that you may be exempt from paying all or part of the fee, you should contact the court for information.

If you are attaching a statement of facts to your application (see note 22), please supply **two additional copies** of the statement. If you are attaching health reports (see note 24), please supply **two additional copies** of the reports.

Notes on the application form

Note 1 — Enter the name of the child you are applying to adopt, surname last. You must enter the full first name(s) and the surname of the child exactly as they are shown on the birth certificate (or, if the child has previously been adopted, the certified copy of the entry in the Adopted Children Register) you are sending with your application (see note 12).

Note 2 — If you do not want your identity to be made known to the parents or guardians of the child you are intending to adopt, the court will issue you with a serial number. Any documents sent to the parents/guardians will show the serial number, not your personal details. If you are required to attend the same court hearing, the court will make arrangements to ensure that your identity is protected.

Part 1 About You

Note 3 — If the name you have entered is different from your name as it is shown on any evidence of marriage or civil partnership you are sending with your application form (for example, because you have changed your name by deed), please attach a continuation sheet explaining the reason for the difference, and a copy of any supporting documents (such as the deed).

Note 4 ▸ The occupation you give here will appear on the adoption order and will subsequently be entered in the Adopted Children Register. Please note that failure to give full details may result in a delay in issuing the child's adoption certificate. It is important that you enter the full title of your occupation (or former occupation if you are retired), for example, 'secondary school teacher' or 'ballet teacher', not 'teacher'; 'self-employed carpenter', not 'self-employed'; 'retired police officer', not 'retired'. Abbreviations or general descriptions such as 'self-employed', 'part-time worker', or 'retired', cannot be accepted. Please note also that company names cannot be entered in the Register and it is not sufficient to enter that you are an 'employee' or 'worker' with any particular company; you must give your occupation. If you are unemployed or currently unable to work because of disability, you should give your last occupation. If you are a member of HM Forces, you should give your rank and/or profession.

Note 5 ▸ Enter your relationship to the child you are applying to adopt, for example, step-parent, foster parent, grandparent, aunt, uncle, other relative (please specify). If you do not currently have any relationship to the child other than as prospective adopter, please enter 'none'.

Note 6 ▸ An adoption order cannot be made unless:

- you are (in the case of two applicants, at least one of you is) domiciled in the United Kingdom, the Channel Islands or the Isle of Man; **or**
- you (in the case of two applicants, both of you) have been habitually resident in the United Kingdom, the Channel Islands or the Isle of Man for a period of at least one year, ending with the date of your application. The United Kingdom means England, Wales, Scotland and Northern Ireland.

'Domicile' is normally taken to mean the place where you have your permanent home. 'Habitual residence' is normally taken to refer to usual, or customary, residence in a particular place. **If you are in any doubt as to whether you meet these conditions, you should seek legal advice.**

Note 7 ▸ If you are applying to adopt alone and you are the partner (including husband, wife or civil partner) of the child's father or mother, you should complete paragraph (l) and then go straight to Part 2 About the Child. Paragraphs (m) to (r) do not apply to you.

Note 8 ▸ If you are applying to adopt alone and you are the partner (but not the husband, wife or civil partner) of a person who is not the parent of the child you wish to adopt, you should complete paragraph (m). Please give your reasons for applying to adopt alone. If there is not enough room for your reply, you may continue on a separate sheet. You should then go straight to Part 2 About the Child. Paragraphs (n) to (r) do not apply to you.

Note 9 ▸ If you are applying to adopt alone and

- you have never been married/ had a civil partner, please complete paragraph (n);
- you are divorced, or your civil partnership has been dissolved, please complete paragraph (o) and attach a copy of the Decree Absolute or the Dissolution Order to your application;
- you are a widow or widower or a surviving civil partner, please complete paragraph (p) and attach the death certificate of your deceased husband, wife or civil partner to your application.

Forms 503

Note 10 ▶ If you are applying to adopt alone and you are married or you have a civil partner, you will need to satisfy the court that:

- your husband/wife or civil partner cannot be found, **or**
- you have separated from your husband/wife or civil partner, you are living apart, and the separation is likely to be permanent, **or**
- your husband/wife or civil partner is incapable of making an application due to physical or mental ill-health.

You must show on the application form which of these three grounds applies in your case by ticking the appropriate box.

You should attach your marriage certificate (or other evidence of marriage) or certificate of civil partnership (or other evidence of civil partnership) to your application, together with any other documentary evidence on which you propose to rely, such as a decree of official separation, or medical evidence of incapacity. You should also supply the name and address (if known) of your husband/wife or civil partner.

Note 11 ▶ If you are applying alone for an adoption order in respect of your own child you will need to satisfy the court that:

- the other natural parent has died, **or**
- the other natural parent cannot be found, **or**
- by virtue of section 28 of the Human Fertilisation and Embryology Act 1990, there is no other parent, **or**
- there is some other reason (which you must set out on your application form) justifying the other parent's exclusion from your application.

You must show on the application form which of these grounds applies in your case by ticking the appropriate box.

You should also attach to your application any documentary evidence on which you propose to rely, such as the death certificate.

Part 2 About the Child

Note 12 ▶ If the child has previously been adopted, a certified copy of the entry in the Adopted Children Register should be attached and not a certified copy of the full entry in the Register of Live Births. Where you are unable to attach a certificate, enter the place (including the country) of the child's birth, if known.

No application may be made in respect of a person who is aged 18 or more at the time of the application.

Note 13 ▶ The court cannot make an adoption order in relation to any person who is or has been married, or any person who is or has been a civil partner.

Note 14 ▶ If the child you wish to adopt was not placed with you for adoption by an adoption agency, you must notify in writing the local authority for the area in which you live of your intention to apply for an adoption order. You must give the local authority notice of your intention not more than 2 years, and not less than 3 months, before the date of your application to the court.

Note 15 Give details of the name of the court that made the placement or freeing order, the nature of the order, the case number and the date the order was made.

You should attach a copy of the placement or freeing order to your application.

Note 16 If some person or body is liable to pay maintenance for the child under a court order, or a maintenance agreement or child support maintenance awarded under the Child Support Act 1991, give the name and address of the person or body liable to pay. In the case of a maintenance order, give the name of the court and the date the order was made; otherwise, give the date of the maintenance agreement or child support maintenance award.

If possible, you should attach a copy of any maintenance order or a copy of the maintenance agreement or maintenance award to your application.

Note 17 If there are earlier, or current, court proceedings relating to the child you are applying to adopt (for example, proceedings for a care order, a contact order, a parental responsibility order or a residence order), give the name of the court, the nature of the proceedings and the date and effect of any order made, or the date of the next hearing if proceedings are current. You do not need to repeat the details of any placement order, freeing order, or maintenance order or agreement you have already given.

If you were a party to any proceedings that have been completed, you should attach a copy of the final order to your application.

Important: if you have previously applied for an adoption order in respect of the same child and the order was refused, you will need to satisfy the court that there has been a change of circumstances since you last applied, or that there is some other reason why the court should hear your current application. Please set out your reasons for making this application on a separate sheet, explaining why you think the application should be heard. Please put the child's full name, the number of the Part and the paragraph reference at the head of the sheet and attach it to your application form.

Part 3 About the child's parent(s) or guardian

Note 18 If the child has previously been adopted, give the names of his/her adoptive parents, not those of his/her natural parents.

Note 19 If the child's parents were not married to each other at the time of his/her birth, the child's father may have parental responsibility

- because he and the child's mother have married since the child was born;
- because he has a parental responsibility agreement with the mother, or has been granted a parental responsibility order, or
- because he registered the child's birth jointly with the child's mother (since 1 December 2003).

Give details of any court order or agreement in respect of parental responsibility in paragraph (m) of Part 2 About the Child.

Note 20 If the child has no guardian, enter 'not applicable'. Otherwise, enter the details of any person appointed to be the child's guardian by deed or will or otherwise in writing in accordance with section 5(5) of the Children Act 1989, or by an order made under section 5(1) or 14A of that Act. If the child has more than one guardian, please give the name and address of any other guardian(s) on a separate sheet, putting the child's full name, the number of the Part and the paragraph reference at the head of the sheet.

Forms

Note 21 ▶ If the child you are applying to adopt is already the subject of a current placement order, the adoption agency has placed the child with you and no parent or guardian opposes the making of the adoption order, you do not need to ask the court to dispense with the consent of the child's parent(s) or guardian(s) to your application. You do not have to complete paragraph (j), but please ensure that you have entered the details of the placement order in Part 2, About the Child.

If the child you are applying to adopt is already the subject of a current freeing order, you do not need to ask the court to dispense with the consent of the child's parent(s) or guardian(s) to your application. You do not have to complete paragraph (j), but please ensure that you have entered the details of the freeing order in Part 2, About the Child.

You do not need to ask the court to dispense with the consent of the child's parent(s) or guardian(s) to your application if:

- the child's parent(s)/guardian(s) has/have consented to the making of an adoption order; **or**
- the child's parent(s)/guardian(s) gave advance consent to the making of a future adoption order (and they have not withdrawn that consent) and they do not oppose the making of an adoption order; **or**
- the child was placed with you for adoption by an adoption agency with the consent of each parent/guardian (and the mother's consent was given when the child was at least 6 weeks old), and no parent/guardian opposes the making of an adoption order.

Please complete paragraph (j) showing which of these conditions applies in your case.

If the child's father does not have parental responsibility for the child, you do not need his consent to your application for an adoption order.

Note 22 ▶ If you are asking the court to dispense with the consent of any parent or guardian, the court can only dispense with that person's consent if it is satisfied that:

- he or she cannot be found; **or**
- he or she is incapable of giving consent; **or**
- the welfare of the child requires it.

You must complete paragraph (j) indicating which of these three grounds applies to your request. The court will also require from you a brief statement setting out a summary of the history of the case and any other facts to satisfy the court that the grounds for your request apply. This statement is known as a 'statement of facts'. If a parent cannot be found, your statement of facts should give details of the steps taken to trace him/her. The statement of facts must be signed by your solicitor, or by you (both of you) if you do not have a solicitor.

You should attach your statement of facts, **and two copies of the statement,** to your application form. You should also attach any documents you are submitting in support of your statement.

Important: The court will send a copy of your statement of facts to each parent or guardian of the child. If you intend to ask the court to keep your identity confidential, you should make certain that the statement of facts does not include any information that could identify you, where you live, or where the child goes to school or nursery.

Part 4 General

Note 23 ▶ Please enter the name by which you want the child to be known following the adoption. This is the name that will be entered on the Adopted Children Register. You may wish the child to have a new name following the adoption, but there is no obligation to change the child's name if you do not want to do so.

Note 24 ▶ You do not need to send a medical report on your health (or the health of the other applicant, if there is one) or the health of the child with your application if:

- the child was placed with you for adoption by an adoption agency; **or**
- he/she is your child, or the child of the other applicant; **or**
- you are applying alone as the partner (including the husband, wife or civil partner) of the child's mother or father.

In any other case you must attach separate health reports in respect of each applicant and the child, **and two copies of the reports.** The health reports should cover the matters set out in the Practice Direction 'Reports by a registered medical practitioner (health reports)', and must have been made no more than three months before the date of your application for an adoption order.

Special assistance or facilities for disability if you attend the court

Note 25 ▶ If you/either of you need special assistance or special facilities for a disability or impairment, please set out your requirements in full. The court staff will need to know, for example, whether you want documents to be supplied in an alternative format, such as Braille or large print. They will also need to know about any specific requirements you may have on the day of the hearing, such as wheelchair access, a hearing loop, or a sign language interpreter.

The court staff will get in touch with you about your requirements. It is important that you make the court aware of all your needs. If you do not, the result may be that the hearing has to be adjourned.

Application for a
Convention adoption order
Section 46 Adoption and Children Act 2002

Name of court	
Case no./Serial no.	
Date received by the court	
Date issued	

Notes to applicants
- This form should only be used if you wish to apply for a Convention adoption order.
- You shall need to complete Form A61 (Application for parental responsibility prior to adoption abroad) if you intend to adopt a child who is habitually resident in the United Kingdom (or who is a Commonwealth citizen) in a place outside of the British Islands (and provided you do not already have an order to remove the child under the Adoption (Scotland) Act 1978 or the Adoption (Northern Ireland) Order 1987, even if you will be applying for a Convention adoption order in a place outside the British Islands.
- Before filling in this form, please read the guidance notes on completing the form.
- Please complete every Part. If you are not sure of the answer to any question, or you do not think that it applies to you, please say so.
- If there is not enough room on the form for your reply, you may continue on a separate sheet. Please put the child's full name, the number of the Part and the paragraph reference at the head of the continuation sheet.
- Please use black ink when filling in the form.

I/We the undersigned _____

(and _____)

wish to adopt _____ ◄ See Note 1

and give the following details in support of my/our application

---

I/We want my/our identity to be kept confidential and
wish to apply for a serial number   ☐ Yes   ☐ No   ◄ See Note 2

Part 1 About you

First applicant

a) Title
☐ Mr   ☐ Mrs   ☐ Miss
☐ Ms   ☐ Other _____

b) My name is

First name(s) in full

[   ]

Last name

[   ]

Second applicant

a) Title
☐ Mr   ☐ Mrs   ☐ Miss
☐ Ms   ☐ Other _____

b) My name is   ◄ See Note 3

First name(s) in full

[   ]

Last name

[   ]

A59 Application for a Convention adoption order (12.05)   HMCS

c) My address is (including postcode)

c) My address is (including postcode)

d) My telephone number is

d) My telephone number is

e) My date of birth is

e) My date of birth is

f) My nationality is

f) My nationality is

Habitual Residence

◀ See Note 4

Please indicate whether the United Kingdom is the receiving State or State of origin by ticking the relevant box and the statement that applies to you (or both of you):

☐ The United Kingdom is the receiving State and [I (in the case of an application by one person)][both of us] have been habitually resident in a part of the British Islands for a period of not less than one year ending with the date of the application.

☐ The United Kingdom is the State of origin and [I am (in the case of an application by one person)][both of us are] habitually resident in a Convention country outside the British Islands on the date of the application.

Note: If the United Kingdom is the receiving State and you are (or if you are applying as a couple, either of you is) not a British citizen, please complete the following statement. Otherwise delete the following statement:

The First Applicant/the Second Applicant is not a British citizen, but the Home Office has confirmed that the child is authorised to enter and reside permanently in the United Kingdom. Evidence of the authorisation from the Home Office is attached.

g) My occupation is

g) My occupation is

◀ See Note 5

h) I am ☐ Male ☐ Female

h) I am ☐ Male ☐ Female

i) My relationship to the child is

i) My relationship to the child is

◀ See Note 6

j) My/Our solicitor in these proceedings is

Name of solicitor	
Name of firm	
Address (including postcode)	

Telephone no.		Fax no.	
DX no.			
E-mail address			

Status

If you are applying to adopt as a couple, please go straight to **Part 2 About the Child**. Paragraphs (k) to (p) do not apply to you

If you are applying to adopt alone, please tick the box at (k) to (p) below that applies to your circumstances. **If you tick (k), (l) or (p), please give the additional information asked for.**

k) ☐ I am the partner of the child's
☐ Father ☐ Mother

If you have ticked box (k), please go straight to Part 2 About the Child. Paragraphs (l) to (p) do not apply to you.

◀ See Note 7

l) ☐ I am the partner (not the spouse or civil partner) of a person who is not the child's parent and I am applying to adopt alone because:

If you have ticked box (l), please go straight to Part 2 About the Child. Paragraphs (m) to (p) do not apply to you.

◀ See Note 8

(please give reasons below, continuing on a separate sheet if necessary)

m) ☐ I am not married/I do not have a civil partner ◀ See Note 9
or
n) ☐ I am divorced/my civil partnership has been dissolved ◀ See Note 9
or
o) ☐ I am a widow/a widower/a surviving civil partner ◀ See Note 9
or
p) ☐ I am married/I have a civil partner, and I can satisfy the court that: ◀ See Note 10
☐ my husband/wife/civil partner cannot be found
or
☐ I have separated from my husband/wife/civil partner, we are living apart and the separation is likely to be permanent
or
☐ my husband/wife/civil partner is not capable of making an application due to ill-health

Part 2 About the child

a) The child is a

☐ Boy   ☐ Girl

b) The child was born on

[ ][ ][ ][ ][ ][ ][ ][ ]

and is the person to whom the attached certified copy of the child's orginal birth certificate, or other evidence attached regarding the child's identity relates.

or To the best of my/our knowledge the child was born on or about

[ ][ ][ ][ ][ ][ ][ ][ ] ◀ See Note 11

in (give place and country of birth)

c) The child's nationality is

d) I/we confirm that the child is not and has never been married or a civil partner   ◀ See Note 12

☐ Yes   ☐ No

e) The child has had his/her home with me/us continuously since

[ ][ ][ ][ ][ ][ ][ ][ ]

Habitual Residence

Please indicate whether the United Kingdom is the receiving State or the State of origin by ticking the relevant box and the statement that applies to the child:

☐ The United Kingdom is the receiving State and the child to be adopted was, on the date on which the Article 17(c) agreement was made, habitually resident in a Convention country outside the British Islands.

☐ The United Kingdom is the State of origin and the child to be adopted was, on the date on which the agreement under Article 17(c) was made, habitually resident in a part of the British Islands.

f) The child was placed with me/us for adoption by an adoption agency

☐ Yes   (If you ticked this box, please complete paragraphs (g) and (h) and then go straight to paragraph (j). Paragraph (i) does not apply to you.)

☐ No   (If you ticked this box, please go straight to paragraph (i). Paragraphs (g) and (h) do not apply to you.)

g) The child was placed with me/us for adoption on

[ ][ ][ ][ ][ ][ ][ ][ ] by

Name of adoption agency	
Address (including post code)	

Name of your contact in the agency	
Telephone no.	

h) ☐ No other adoption agency has been involved in placing the child
   or
   ☐ The following adoption agency has also been involved in placing the child

Name of adoption agency	
Address (including post code)	

Name of your contact in the agency	
Telephone no.	

i) I/we have notified in writing my/our local authority of my/our intention to apply for an adoption order (give details) ◀ See Note 13

Name of local authority	
Address (including post code)	
Date notified	
Name of your contact in the local authority	
Telephone no.	

Care

j) ☐ No local authority or voluntary organisation has parental responsibility for the child
   or
   ☐ The following local authority/voluntary organisation has parental responsibility for the child:

Name of local authority or voluntary organisation	
Address (including post code)	

Name of your contact in the authority/organisation	
Telephone no.	

Maintenance

k) ☐ No maintenance order/agreement or award of child support maintenance under the Child Support Act 1991 has been made in respect of the child

or

☐ The following maintenance order/agreement/award of child support maintenance has been made ◀ See Note 14

Person liable to pay maintenance	
Address (including post code)	

Court and date of order	
Date of maintenance agreement/child support maintenance award	

About other orders or proceedings that affect the child

l) ☐ To the best of my/our knowledge, no proceedings relating to the child (other than any maintenance order given above) have been completed or commenced in any court, whether in the United Kingdom or elsewhere

or

☐ The following proceedings relating to the child have been completed/commenced (in addition to any maintenance order given above) ◀ See Note 15

Type of order made (or applied for)	Date of order (or date of next hearing)	Name of court (and country if not in the UK)	Case number (or serial number)

Cases concerning a related child

m) ☐ To the best of my knowledge, no proceedings relating to a full, half or step brother or sister of the child have been completed or commenced in any court, whether in the United Kingdom or elsewhere

or

☐ The following proceedings relating to a full, half or step brother or sister of the child have been completed/commenced (please give details below and, if you were a party to any proceedings that have been completed, attach a copy of the final order)

Relationship to child (eg. sister, half-brother)	Type of order made (or applied for)	Date of order (or date of next hearing)	Name of court (and country if not in the UK)	Case number (or serial number)

Part 3 About the child's parents or guardian

The child's mother

a) The name of the child's mother is

First name(s) in full

Last name

b) Her address is (if deceased, please write 'Deceased' in the address box)

c) Her nationality is

The child's father ◀ See Note 16

d) The name of the child's father is

First name(s) in full

Last name

e) His address is (if deceased, please write 'Deceased' in the address box)

f) His nationality is

g) Does he have parental responsibility for the child? ◀ See Note 17

☐ Yes ☐ No

If No, does he intend to apply for an order under section 4(1)(c) of the Children Act 1989 (a parental responsibility order) or a residence or contact order in respect of the child?

☐ Yes ☐ No

The child's guardian

h) The name of the child's guardian is

First name(s) in full

Last name

i) His/Her address is ◀ See Note 18

Parent/guardian consent to adoption ◀ See Note 19
The child's parent(s)/guardians has/have consented to a Convention adoption order being made.

Part 4 General
Child's name on adoption

If the adoption order is made, I/We want the child to be known as

◀ See Note 20

First name(s) in full

Last name

Declarations

I/We have not received or given payment or reward in respect of the proposed adoption (except as follows:) (give details below)

To the best of my/our knowledge, only the person(s) or organisation(s) named in Part 2 of this application have taken part in the arrangements for the child's adoption.

Part 5 Statement of truth

I believe that the facts stated in this application are true.

I believe that the facts stated in this application are true.

Signature of first applicant

Signature of second applicant

Print full name

Print full name

Signed

Signed

Date

Date

If you attend the court for a hearing

1. Do you/either of you have a disability for which you require special assistance or special facilities? ◀ See Note 21

   ☐ Yes   ☐ No

   If Yes, please say what your needs are below
   (the court staff will get in touch with you about your requirements)

   ┌───┐
   │   │
   │   │
   │   │
   └───┘

2. Do you/either of you want to use the services of an interpreter?

   ☐ Yes   ☐ No

   If Yes, please specify which language
   (court staff will get in touch with you about your requirements)

   ┌─────────────────────┐
   │   │
   └─────────────────────┘

3. Are there any dates on which you know you will not be able to attend the court, or any particular dates that would especially suit you? If so, please give details below

Unavailable dates	Preferred dates

   (Please note that, although the court will try to fit in with your preferences, it may not be always be possible to do so)

What to do now

Once you have completed and signed this form, you should take or send the form and three copies to the court, together with the court fee* and the following documents:

- where the UK is the State of origin, a certified copy of the full entry in the Register of Live Births that relates to the child or, where the child has been adopted, a certified copy of the entry in the Adopted Children Register;
- where the UK is the receiving State, a certified copy of the child's original birth certificate, any abandonment certificate/declaration, or where the child has been adopted, a certified copy of the entry in the register of adoptions as recognised in the State of origin or a certified copy of the adoption certificate;
- if you were a party to the proceedings, a copy of any final order relating to the child that has effect and, if possible, a copy of any maintenance agreement or maintenance award relating to the child;
- if you were a party to the proceedings, a copy of any final order relating to a full, half or step brother or sister of the child that has effect;
- where a parent of the child has died, a certified copy of the entry in the Register of Deaths;
- if you are submitting evidence of marriage or civil partnership, a certified copy of the entry in the Register of Marriages or the Register of Civil Partnerships;
- where your husband, wife or civil partner has died, a certified copy of the entry in the Register of Deaths;
- a copy of any decree absolute of divorce or decree of nullity of your marriage;
- in relation to a civil partnership, a copy of any dissolution order or nullity order of your civil partnership;
- any documentary evidence supporting the reasons why you are applying to adopt the child without your husband, wife or civil partner, such as a decree of judicial separation;
- where the UK is the receiving State and the applicant (or in the case of a couple, either or both of the applicants) is not a British citizen, the child's passport containing confirmation the Home Office authorisation for the child to enter and reside permanently in the United Kingdom;
- if your name as entered on the application form is different from the name shown on any evidence of marriage or civil partnership you are sending with your application, any documentary evidence to explain the difference.

*If you are not sure about the court fee payable for your application, or think that you may be exempt from paying all or part of the fee, you should contact the court for information.

Application for a Convention adoption order (Form A59)
Notes on completing the form

Important
This form should only be used if you wish to apply for a Convention adoption order.

You need to complete Form A61 (Application for parental responsibility prior to adoption abroad) if you are applying for a Convention adoption order but intend to adopt a child who is habitually resident in the United Kingdom (or who is a Commonwealth citizen) in a place outside of the British Islands (and provided you do not already have an order to remove the child under Adoption (Scotland) Act 1978 or the Adoption (Northern Ireland) Order 1987) even if you will be applying for a Convention adoption order in a place outside the British Islands.

'Convention adoption order' means an adoption order which, by virtue of regulations under section 1 of the Adoption (Intercountry Aspects) Act 1999, is made as a Convention adoption order.

'the Convention' means the Convention on Protection of Children and Co-operation in respect of Intercountry Adoption, concluded at the Hague on 29th May 1993.

In these notes, any reference to a birth certificate, death certificate, marriage certificate or certificate of civil partnership obtained in England and Wales means a certified copy of the entry in the Register of Live Births, the Register of Deaths, the Register of Marriages or the Register of Civil Partnerships, as appropriate. A photocopy is not acceptable. Where the United Kingdom is the State of origin the birth certificate you send to the court for the child you are applying to adopt must be a certified copy of the full entry in the Register of Live Births.

If you are attaching any order of the High Court or a county court to your application, it must be a sealed copy of the order (that is, a copy that has been stamped with the seal of the court). If you are attaching an order made by a magistrates' court, it must be a certified copy (a copy certified by the court officer to be a true copy of the original order), or a copy that bears the stamp of the originating court. An order issued by any other authority must be properly authenticated by that authority. If you are in any doubt about what is needed, please contact the court for assistance.

Take or send the completed application form, **and three copies,** to the court, together with the court fee and any documents you are attaching in support of your application. If you are not sure about the court fee payable for your application, or you think that you may be exempt from paying all or part of the fee, you should contact the court for information.

Notes on the application form

Note 1
Enter the name of the child you are applying to adopt, surname last.

Where the UK is the State of origin you must enter the full first name(s) and the surname of the child exactly as they are shown on the birth certificate (or, if the child has previously been adopted, the certified copy of the entry in the Adopted Children Register) you are sending with your application (see note 11 below).

Where the UK is the receiving State you must enter the full first name(s) and the surname of the child exactly as they are shown on the certified copy of the child's original birth certificate, any abandonment certificate/declaration, or where the child has been adopted, the certified copy of the entry in the register of adoptions as recognised in the State of origin or a certified copy of the adoption certificate (see note 11 below).

Note 2 — If you do not want your identity to be made known to the parents or guardians of the child you are intending to adopt, the court will issue you with a serial number. Any documents sent to the parents/guardians will show the serial number, not your personal details. If you are required to attend the same court hearing, the court will make arrangements to ensure that your identity is protected.

Part 1 About you

Note 3 — If the name you have entered is different from your name as it is shown on any evidence of marriage or civil partnership you are sending with your application form (for example, because you have changed your name by deed), please attach a continuation sheet explaining the reason for the difference, and a copy of any supporting documents (such as the deed).

Note 4 — A Convention adoption order cannot be made unless:

- Where the United Kingdom is the receiving State, you (or in the case of two applicants, both of you) have been habitually resident in a part of the British Islands for a period of not less than one year ending with the date of the application, or

- Where the United Kingdom is the State of origin, you (or in the case of two applicants, both of you) have been habitually resident in a Convention country outside the British Islands on the date of the application.

The United Kingdom means England, Wales, Scotland and Northern Ireland.

'Habitual residence' is normally taken to refer to usual, or customary, residence in a particular place. If you are in any doubt as to whether you meet these conditions, you should seek legal advice.

If the United Kingdom is the receiving State and you are (or in the case a couple, either of you is) not a British citizen, you must obtain confirmation from the Home Office that the child is authorised to enter and reside permanently in the United Kingdom. You should attach the child's passport containing the Home Office authorisation to your application.

Note 5 — The occupation you give here will appear on the Convention adoption order and will subsequently be entered in the Adopted Children Register. Please note that failure to give full details may result in a delay in issuing the child's adoption certificate. It is important that you enter the full title of your occupation (or former occupation if you are retired), for example, 'secondary school teacher' or 'ballet teacher', not 'teacher'; 'self-employed carpenter', not 'self-employed'; 'retired police officer', not 'retired'. Abbreviations or general descriptions such as 'self-employed', 'part-time worker', or 'retired', cannot be accepted. Please note also that company names cannot be entered in the Register and it is not sufficient to enter that you are an 'employee' or 'worker' with any particular company, you must give your occupation. If you are unemployed or currently unable to work because of disability, you should give your last occupation. If you are a member of HM Forces, you should give your rank and/or profession.

Note 6 — Enter your relationship to the child you are applying to adopt, for example, step-parent, foster parent, grandparent, aunt, uncle, other relative (please specify). If you do not currently have any relationship to the child, other than as prospective adopter, please enter 'none'.

Note 7 — If you are applying to adopt alone and you are the partner (including husband, wife or civil partner) of the child's father or mother, you should complete paragraph (k) and then go straight to Part 2 About the Child. Paragraphs (l) to (p) do not apply to you.

Note 8 — If you are applying to adopt alone and you are the partner (but not the husband, wife or civil partner) of a person who is not the parent of the child you wish to adopt, you should complete paragraph (l). Please give your reasons for applying to adopt alone. If there is not enough room for your reply, you may continue on a separate sheet. You should then go straight to Part 2 About the Child. Paragraphs (m) to (p) do not apply to you.

Forms 519

Note 9 ▶ If you are applying to adopt alone and
- you have never been married/ had a civil partner, please complete paragraph (m);
- you are divorced, or your civil partnership has been dissolved, please complete paragraph (n) and attach a copy of the Decree Absolute or the Dissolution Order to your application;
- you are a widow or widower or a surviving civil partner, please complete paragraph (o) and attach the death certificate of your deceased husband, wife or civil partner to your application.

Note 10 ▶ If you are applying to adopt alone and you are married or you have a civil partner, you will need to satisfy the court that:
- your husband/wife or civil partner cannot be found, or
- you have separated from your husband/wife or civil partner, you are living apart, and the separation is likely to be permanent, or
- your husband/wife or civil partner is incapable of making an application due to physical or mental ill-health.

You must show on the application form which of these three grounds applies in your case by ticking the appropriate box.

You should attach your marriage certificate (or other evidence of marriage) or certificate of civil partnership (or other evidence of civil partnership) to your application, together with any other documentary evidence on which you propose to rely, such as a decree of official separation, or medical evidence of incapacity. You should also supply the name and address (if known) of your husband/wife or civil partner.

Part 2 About the Child

Note 11 ▶ Where the UK is the State of origin, if the child has previously been adopted a certified copy of the entry in the Adopted Children Register should be attached and not a certified copy of the full entry in the Register of Live Births.

Where the UK is the receiving State a certified copy of the child's original birth certificate, any abandonment certificate/declaration, or where the child has been adopted, a certified copy of the entry in the register of adoptions as recognised in the State of origin or a certified copy of the adoption certificate, should be attached.

Where you are unable to attach a certificate, enter the place (including the country) of the child's birth, if known.

No application may be made in respect of a person who is aged 18 or more at the time of the application.

Note 12 ▶ The court cannot make a Convention adoption order in relation to any person who is or has been married, or any person who is or has been a civil partner.

Note 13 ▶ Where the United Kingdom is the receiving state you must give notice of your intention to apply for a Convention adoption order to the local authority where you have your home or last had your home within 14 days beginning with the date on which the child enters the United Kingdom.

Note 14 ▶ If some person or body is liable to pay maintenance for the child under a court order, or a maintenance agreement or child support maintenance awarded under the Child Support Act 1991, give the name and address of the person or body liable to pay. In the case of a maintenance order, give the name of the court and the date the order was made; otherwise, give the date of the maintenance agreement or child support maintenance award.

If possible, you should attach a copy of any maintenance order or a copy of the maintenance agreement or maintenance award to your application.

Note 15 If there are earlier, or current, court proceedings relating to the child you are applying to adopt (for example, proceedings for a care order, a contact order, a parental responsibility order or a residence order), give the name of the court, the nature of the proceedings and the date and effect of any order made, or the date of the next hearing if proceedings are current. You do not need to repeat the details of any maintenance order or agreement you have already given.

If you were a party to any proceedings that have been completed, you should attach a copy of the final order to your application.

Important: if you have previously applied for an adoption order in respect of the same child and the order was refused, you will need to satisfy the court that there has been a change of circumstances since you last applied, or that there is some other reason why the court should hear your current application. Please set out your reasons for making this application on a separate sheet, explaining why you think the application should be heard. Please put the child's full name, the number of the Part and the paragraph reference at the head of the sheet and attach it to your application form.

Part 3 About the child's parent(s) or guardian

Note 16 If the child has previously been adopted, give the names of his/her adoptive parents, not those of his/her natural parents.

Note 17 Where England and Wales is the State of origin, if the child's parents were not married to each other at the time of his/her birth, the child's father may have parental responsibility
- because he and the child's mother have married since the child was born;
- because he has a parental responsibility agreement with the mother, or has been granted a parental responsibility order, or
- because he registered the child's birth jointly with the child's mother (since 1 December 2003).

Give details of any court order or agreement in respect of parental responsibility in paragraph (l) of Part 2 About the Child.

Note 18 If the child has no guardian, enter 'not applicable'. Otherwise, enter the details of any person appointed to be the child's guardian by deed or will or otherwise in writing in accordance with section 5(5) of the Children Act 1989, or by an order made under section 5(1) or 14A of that Act. Where the United Kingdom is the receiving State please enter the name of any person who is regarded as the child's guardian by the Convention country. If the child has more than one guardian, please give the name and address of any other guardian(s) on a separate sheet, putting the child's full name, the number of the Part and the paragraph reference at the head of the sheet.

Note 19 In the case of an application for a Convention adoption order the consents of the persons, institutions and authorities whose consents are necessary for adoption, must be obtained prior to the child entering the United Kingdom. Confirmation of this should be included in the Article 16 information received from the Central Authority of the child's State of origin.

Part 4 General

Note 20 ▶ Please enter the name by which you want the child to be known following the adoption. This is the name that will be entered on the Adopted Children Register. You may wish the child to have a new name following the adoption, but there is no obligation to change the child's name if you do not want to do so.

Special assistance or facilities for disability if you attend the court

Note 21 ▶ If you/either of you need special assistance or special facilities for a disability or impairment, please set out your requirements in full. The court staff will need to know, for example, whether you want documents to be supplied in an alternative format, such as Braille or large print. They will also need to know about any specific requirements you may have on the day of the hearing, such as wheelchair access, a hearing loop, or a sign language interpreter.

The court staff will get in touch with you about your requirements. It is important that you make the court aware of all your needs. If you do not, the result may be that the hearing has to be adjourned.

Application for an adoption order (excluding a Convention adoption order) where the child is habitually resident outside the British Islands and is brought into the United Kingdom for the purposes of adoption

Section 46 Adoption and Children Act 2002

Name of court	
Case no./Serial no.	
Date received by the court	
Date issued	

Notes to applicants
This form can be used where:
- a child who is habitually resident outside the British Islands is brought into the United Kingdom for the purpose of adoption by a British resident; or
- a child adopted by a British resident under the law of any country or territory outside the British Islands is brought into the United Kingdom and the British resident wants to apply for an adoption order, and the application is not for a Convention adoption order.

You will need to complete Form A61 (Application for parental responsibility prior to adoption abroad) if you intend to adopt a child who is habitually resident in the United Kingdom (or who is a Commonwealth citizen) in a place outside of the British Islands (and provided you do not already have an order to remove the child under the Adoption (Scotland) Act 1978 or the Adoption (Northern Ireland) Order 1987).

Before filling in this form, please read the guidance notes on completing the form.

Please complete every Part. If you are not sure of the answer to any question, or you do not think that it applies to you, please say so.

If there is not enough room on the form for your reply, you may continue on a separate sheet. Please put the child's full name, the number of the Part and the paragraph reference at the head of the continuation sheet.

Please use black ink when filling in the form.

I/We the undersigned _____
(and _____)
wish to adopt _____ ◀ See Note 1
and give the following details in support of my/our application

I/We want my/our identity to be kept confidential and
wish to apply for a serial number   ☐ Yes   ☐ No   ◀ See Note 2

A60 Application for an adoption order (excluding a Convention adoption order) (12.05)   HMCS

Part 1 About you

First applicant

a) Title
☐ Mr ☐ Mrs ☐ Miss
☐ Ms ☐ Other _____

b) My name is

First name(s) in full

Last name

c) My address is (including postcode)

d) My telephone number is

e) My date of birth is

f) My nationality is

g) My occupation is

h) I am
☐ Male ☐ Female

i) My relationship to the child is

Second applicant

a) Title
☐ Mr ☐ Mrs ☐ Miss
☐ Ms ☐ Other _____

b) My name is ◄ See Note 3

First name(s) in full

Last name

c) My address is (including postcode)

d) My telephone number is

e) My date of birth is

f) My nationality is

g) My occupation is ◄ See Note 4

h) I am
☐ Male ☐ Female

i) My relationship to the child is ◄ See Note 5

j) My/Our solicitor in these proceedings is

Name of solicitor	
Name of firm	
Address (including postcode)	

Telephone no.		Fax no.	
DX no.			
E-mail address			

Domicile and residence   ◄ See Note 6

k) ☐ I am/We are/One of us, namely [_____]

is domiciled in the United Kingdom, the Channel Islands or the Isle of Man.

or

☐ I have/We have both been habitually resident in the United Kingdom, the Channel Islands or the Isle of Man for a period of at least one year, ending with the date of this application.

Status

> If you are applying to adopt as a couple, please go straight to **Part 2 About the Child**. Paragraphs (l) to (r) do not apply to you
>
> If you are applying to adopt alone, please tick the box at (l) to (r) below that applies to your circumstances. **If you tick (l), (m), (q) or (r), please give the additional information asked for.**

l) ☐ I am the partner of the child's   If you have ticked box (l), please go straight to   ◄ See Note 7
   ☐ Father   ☐ Mother   Part 2 About the Child. Paragraphs (m) to (r) do
                                                 not apply to you.

m) ☐ I am the partner (not the spouse or   If you have ticked box (m), please go straight to   ◄ See Note 8
   civil partner) of a person who is not   Part 2 About the Child. Paragraphs (n) to (r) do
   the child's parent and I am applying   not apply to you.
   to adopt alone because:

(please give reasons below, continuing on a separate sheet if necessary)

[

]

n) ☐ I am not married/I do not have a civil partner ◀ See Note 9
   or
o) ☐ I am divorced/my civil partnership has been dissolved ◀ See Note 9
   or
p) ☐ I am a widow/a widower/a surviving civil partner ◀ See Note 9
   or
q) ☐ I am married/I have a civil partner, and I can satisfy the court that: ◀ See Note 10
   ☐ my husband/wife/civil partner cannot be found
      or
   ☐ I have separated from my husband/wife/civil partner, we are living apart and the separation is likely to be permanent
      or
   ☐ my husband/wife/civil partner is not capable of making an application due to ill-health
   or
r) ☐ I am applying alone for an adoption order in respect of my own child and I can satisfy the court that ◀ See Note 11
   ☐ the other natural parent has died
      or
   ☐ the other natural parent cannot be found
      or
   ☐ by virtue of section 28 of the Human Fertilisation and Embryology Act 1990, there is no other parent
      or
   ☐ the other natural parent's exclusion from this application is justified
      (please give reasons below)

Part 2 About the child

a) The child is a
   ☐ Boy   ☐ Girl

b) The child was born on   or To the best of my/our knowledge the child ◀ See Note 12
   ☐☐☐☐☐☐☐   was born on or about
                                                ☐☐☐☐☐☐☐
   and is the person to whom the attached
   certified copy of the entry in the Register   in (give place and country of birth)
   of Live Births/Register of Adopted
   Children relates

c) The child's nationality is

Note: Please complete the following statements. Otherwise delete the following statements: ◀ See Note 13

☐ The Child is habitually resident in a country outside the British Islands

☐ The Child is not a British citizen, however, the Department for Education and Skills has certified to the foreign authority that the child is authorised to enter and will be authorised to reside permanently in the United Kingdom if an adoption order is made.

☐ I attach a copy of the relevant notification letter from the Department for Education and Skills.

d) I/we confirm that the child is not and has never been married or a civil partner ◀ See Note 14
☐ Yes ☐ No

e) The child has had his/her home with me/us continuously since ◀ See Note 15

☐☐☐☐☐☐☐☐

f) I/we have notified in writing my/our local authority of my/our intention to apply for an adoption order (give details below) ◀ See Note 16

Name of local authority	
Address (including post code)	
Date notified	
Name of your contact in the local authority	
Telephone no.	

Care

g) ☐ No local authority or voluntary organisation has parental responsibility for the child
or
☐ The following local authority/voluntary organisation has parental responsibility for the child:

Name of local authority or voluntary organisation	
Address (including post code)	
Name of your contact in the authority/organisation	
Telephone no.	

Maintenance

h) ☐ No maintenance order/agreement or award of child support maintenance under the Child Support Act 1991 has been made in respect of the child ◀ See Note 17

or

☐ The following maintenance order/agreement/award of child support maintenance has been made

Person liable to pay maintenance	
Address (including post code)	

Court and date of order	
Date of maintenance agreement/child support maintenance award	

About other orders or proceedings that affect the child

i) ☐ To the best of my/our knowledge, no proceedings relating to the child (other than any maintenance order as given above) have been completed or commenced in any court, whether in the United Kingdom or elsewhere ◀ See Note 18

or

☐ The following proceedings relating to the child have been completed/commenced (in addition to any maintenance order given above)

Type of order made (or applied for)	Date of order (or date of next hearing)	Name of court (and country, if not in the UK)	Case number (or serial number)

Cases concerning a related child

j) ☐ To the best of my knowledge, no proceedings relating to a full, half or step brother or sister of the child have been completed or commenced in any court, whether in the United Kingdom or elsewhere.

or

☐ The following proceedings relating to a full, half or step brother or sister of the child have been completed/commenced (please give details below and, if you were a party to any proceedings that have been completed, attach a copy of the final order)

Relationship to child (eg. sister, half-brother)	Type of order made (or applied for)	Date of order (or date of next hearing)	Name of court (and country, if not in the UK)	Case number (or serial number)

Part 3 About the child's parents or guardian

The child's mother

a) The name of the child's mother is

First name(s) in full

Last name

b) Her address is (if deceased, please write 'Deceased' in the address box)

c) Her nationality is

The child's father
 ◀ See Note 19

d) The name of the child's father is

First name(s) in full

Last name

e) His address is (if deceased, please write 'Deceased' in the address box)

f) His nationality is

The child's guardian

g) The name of the child's guardian is ◀ See Note 20

First name(s) in full

Last name

h) His/Her address is

Parent/guardian consent to adoption

◄ See Note 21
◄ See Note 22

i) ☐ The child's parent(s)/guardian(s) has/have consented to the making of an adoption order

or

☐ The following parent(s)/guardian(s) of the child has/have not consented to the making of an adoption order (give name(s) below)

```


```

and I/we ask the court to dispense with his/her/their consent on the following grounds: (please tick the grounds that apply)

☐ he/she/they cannot be found

☐ he/she is/they are incapable of giving consent

☐ the welfare of the child requires it.

You must attach a brief statement of facts (and two copies of the statement) setting out a summary of the history of the case and any other facts to satisfy the court that the grounds for your request apply.

IMPORTANT: The court will send a copy of your statement of facts to each parent or guardian of the child. If you intend to ask the court to keep your identity confidential, you should make sure that the statement of facts does not include any information that could identify you, where you live, or where the child goes to school or nursery.

Part 4 General

Child's name on adoption
◀ See Note 23

If the adoption order is made, I/We want the child to be known as

First name(s) in full

Last name

Health reports
◀ See Note 24

Separate reports on my/our health and the health of the child made by a registered medical practitioner on (give date(s))

are attached to this application.

Declarations

I/We have not received or given payment or reward in respect of the proposed adoption (except as follows:) (give details below)

To the best of my/our knowledge, only the person(s) or organisation(s) named in Part 2 of this application have taken part in the arrangements for the child's adoption.

Part 5 Statement of truth

I believe that the facts stated in this application are true.

I believe that the facts stated in this application are true.

Signature of first applicant

Signature of second applicant

Print full name

Print full name

Signed

Signed

Date

Date

If you attend the court for a hearing

1. Do you/either of you have a disability for which you require special assistance or special facilities? ◀ See Note 25

   ☐ Yes   ☐ No

   If Yes, please say what your needs are below
   (the court staff will get in touch with you about your requirements)

2. Do you/either of you want to use the services of an interpreter?

   ☐ Yes   ☐ No

   If Yes, please specify which language
   (court staff will get in touch with you about your requirements)

3. Are there any dates on which you know you will not be able to attend the court, or any particular dates that would especially suit you? If so, please give details below

Unavailable dates	Preferred dates

   (Please note that, although the court will try to fit in with your preferences, it may not be always be possible to do so)

What to do now

Once you have completed and signed this form, you should take or send the form **and three copies** to the court, together with the court fee* and the following documents:

- a certified copy of the child's original birth certificate, any abandonment certificate, or where the child has been adopted, a certified copy of the entry in the register of adoptions as recognised in the State of origin or a certified copy of the adoption certificate;
- if you are asking the court to dispense with the consent of any parent or guardian to the adoption, a brief statement of facts relied on in support of the request, **and two copies** of the statement;
- if you were a party to the proceedings, a copy of any final order relating to the child that has effect and, if possible, a copy of any maintenance agreement or maintenance award relating to the child;
- if you were a party to the proceedings, a copy of any final order relating to a full, half or step brother or sister of the child that has effect;
- reports by a registered medical practitioner on the health of the child and the applicant(s) covering the matters specified in the Practice Direction 'Reports by a registered medical practitioner ("health reports")', **and two copies** of the reports.
  Note: you do not have to supply health reports if:
    - the child was placed with you for adoption by an adoption agency, or
    - he/she is your child, or the child of the other applicant, or
    - you are applying alone as the partner (including the husband, wife or civil partner) of the child's mother or father;
- where a parent of the child has died, a certified copy of the entry in the Register of Deaths;
- if you are submitting evidence of marriage or civil partnership, a certified copy of the entry in the Register of Marriages or the Register of Civil Partnerships;
- where your husband, wife or civil partner has died, a certified copy of the entry in the Register of Deaths;
- a copy of any decree absolute of divorce or decree of nullity of your marriage;
- in relation to a civil partnership, a copy of any dissolution order or nullity order of your civil partnership;
- any documentary evidence supporting the reasons why you are applying to adopt the child without your husband, wife or civil partner, such as a decree of judicial separation;
- the notification letter from the Department for Education and Skills that they have issued a "certificate of eligibility" to the foreign authority and that the child is authorised to enter and remain and will be authorised to reside permanently in the United Kingdom if an adoption order is made;
- if your name as entered on the application form is different from the name shown on any evidence of marriage or civil partnership you are sending with your application, any documentary evidence to explain the difference.

*If you are not sure about the court fee payable for your application, or think that you may be exempt from paying all or part of the fee, you should contact the court for information.

Application for an adoption order (excluding a Convention adoption order) where the child is habitually resident outside the British Islands and is brought into the United Kingdom for the purposes of adoption (Form A60)

Notes on completing the form

Important

In these notes, any reference to a birth certificate, death certificate, marriage certificate or certificate of civil partnership obtained in England and Wales means a certified copy of the entry in the Register of Live Births, the Register of Deaths, the Register of Marriages or the Register of Civil Partnerships, as appropriate. A photocopy is not acceptable.

If you are attaching any order of the High Court or a county court to your application, it must be a sealed copy of the order (that is, a copy that has been stamped with the seal of the court). If you are attaching an order made by a magistrates' court, it must be a certified copy (a copy certified by the court officer to be a true copy of the original order), or a copy that bears the stamp of the originating court. An order issued by any other authority must be properly authenticated by that authority. If you are in any doubt about what is needed, please contact the court for assistance.

Take or send the completed application form, and three copies, to the court, together with the court fee and any documents you are attaching in support of your application. If you are not sure about the court fee payable for your application, or you think that you may be exempt from paying all or part of the fee, you should contact the court for information.

If you are attaching a statement of facts to your application (see note 22 below), please supply two additional copies of the statement. If you are attaching health reports (see note 24 below), please supply two additional copies of the reports.

Notes on the application form

Note 1 ▶ Enter the name of the child you are applying to adopt, surname last. You must enter the full first name(s) and the surname of the child exactly as they are shown on the certified copy of the child's original birth certificate, any abandonment certificate/declaration, or where the child has been adopted, the certified copy of the entry in the register of adoptions as recognised in the State of origin or a certified copy of the adoption certificate (see note 12 below).

Note 2 ▶ If you do not want your identity to be made known to the parents or guardians of the child you are intending to adopt, the court will issue you with a serial number. Any documents sent to the parents/guardians will show the serial number, not your personal details. If you are required to attend the same court hearing, the court will make arrangements to ensure that your identity is protected.

Part 1 About You

Note 3 ▶ If the name you have entered is different from your name as it is shown on any evidence of marriage or civil partnership you are sending with your application form (for example, because you have changed your name by deed), please attach a continuation sheet explaining the reason for the difference, and a copy of any supporting documents (such as the deed).

Note 4 ▶ The occupation you give here will appear on the adoption order and will subsequently be entered in the Adopted Children Register. Please note that failure to give full details may result in a delay in issuing the child's adoption certificate. It is important that you enter the full title of your occupation (or former occupation if you are retired), for example, 'secondary school teacher' or 'ballet teacher', not 'teacher'; 'self-employed carpenter', not 'self-employed'; 'retired police officer', not 'retired'. Abbreviations or general descriptions such as 'self-employed', 'part-time worker', or 'retired', cannot be accepted. Please note also that company names cannot be entered in the Register and it is not sufficient to enter that you are an 'employee' or 'worker' with any particular company, you must give your occupation. If you are unemployed or currently unable to work because of disability, you should give your last occupation. If you are a member of HM Forces, you should give your rank and/or profession.

Note 5 ▶ Enter your relationship to the child you are applying to adopt, for example, step-parent, foster parent, grandparent, aunt, uncle, other relative (please specify). If you do not currently have any relationship to the child, other than as prospective adopter, please enter 'none'.

Note 6 ▶ An adoption order cannot be made unless

- you are (in the case of two applicants, at least one of you is) domiciled in the United Kingdom, the Channel Islands or the Isle of Man; or

- you (in the case of two applicants, both of you) have been habitually resident in the United Kingdom, the Channel Islands or the Isle of Man for a period of at least one year, ending with the date of your application.

The United Kingdom means England, Wales, Scotland and Northern Ireland

'Domicile' is normally taken to mean the place where you have your permanent home. 'Habitual residence' is normally taken to refer to usual, or customary, residence in a particular place. If you are in any doubt as to whether you meet these conditions, you should seek legal advice.

Note 7 ▶ If you are applying to adopt alone and you are the partner (including husband, wife or civil partner) of the child's father or mother, you should complete paragraph (l) and then go straight to Part 2 About the Child. Paragraphs (m) to (r) do not apply to you.

Note 8 ▶ If you are applying to adopt alone and you are the partner (but not the husband, wife or civil partner) of a person who is not the parent of the child you wish to adopt, you should complete paragraph (m). Please give your reasons for applying to adopt alone. If there is not enough room for your reply, you may continue on a separate sheet. You should then go straight to Part 2 About the Child. Paragraphs (n) to (r) do not apply to you.

Note 9 ▶ If you are applying to adopt alone and

- you have never been married/ had a civil partner, please complete paragraph (n);

- you are divorced, or your civil partnership has been dissolved, please complete paragraph (o) and attach a copy of the Decree Absolute or the Dissolution Order to your application;

- you are a widow or widower or a surviving civil partner, please complete paragraph (p) and attach the death certificate of your deceased husband, wife or civil partner to your application.

Note 10 ▶ If you are applying to adopt alone and you are married or you have a civil partner, you will need to satisfy the court that:

- your husband/wife or civil partner cannot be found, or
- you have separated from your husband/wife or civil partner, you are living apart, and the separation is likely to be permanent, or
- your husband/wife or civil partner is incapable of making an application due to physical or mental ill-health.

You must show on the application form which of these three grounds applies in your case by ticking the appropriate box.

You should attach your marriage certificate (or other evidence of marriage) or certificate of civil partnership (or other evidence of civil partnership) to your application, together with any other documentary evidence on which you propose to rely, such as a decree of official separation, or medical evidence of incapacity. You should also supply the name and address (if known) of your husband/wife or civil partner.

Note 11 ▶ If you are applying alone for an adoption order in respect of your own child you will need to satisfy the court that

- the other natural parent has died, or
- the other natural parent cannot be found, or
- by virtue of section 28 of the Human Fertilisation and Embryology Act 1990, there is no other parent, or
- there is some other reason (which you must set out on your application form) justifying the other parent's exclusion from your application.

You must show on the application form which of these grounds applies in your case by ticking the appropriate box.

You should attach to your application any documentary evidence on which you propose to rely, such as the death certificate.

Part 2 About the Child

Note 12 ▶ A certified copy of the child's original birth certificate, any abandonment certificate, or where the child has been adopted, a certified copy of the entry in the register of adoptions as recognised in the State of origin or a certified copy of the adoption certificate, should be attached.

Where you are unable to attach a birth certificate, enter the place (including the country) of the child's birth, if known.

No application may be made in respect of a person who is aged 18 or more at the time of the application.

Note 13 ▶ Where the child is habitually resident in a country outside the British Islands and is brought into the United Kingdom for the purposes of adoption by a British resident, prior to the child's entry into the United Kingdom the Department for Education and Skills (DfES) issue a certificate usually referred to as a 'certificate of eligibility' to the State of origin.

This certificate confirms to the foreign authority that the individual, or as the case may be the couple, have been assessed and approved to adopt and that the correct procedures have been followed. The certificate also refers to entry clearance procedures having to be complied with as well. The prospective adopter(s) is/are sent a letter notifying them that the certificate of eligibility has been issued. You should attach a copy of the notification letter from the DfES to this application.

Note 14 ▶ The court cannot make an adoption order in relation to any person who is or has been married, or any person who is or has been a civil partner.

Note 15 ▶ Where the requirements imposed by section 83(4) of the Adoption and Children Act 2002 have been complied with and the conditions required by section 83(5) have been met (i.e. you have complied with the Adoptions with a Foreign Element Regulations 2005) the child must have had his/her home with you or, in the case of an application by a couple, with one or both of you, for not less than six months preceding the application.

Where the requirements imposed by section 83(4) of the Act have **not** been complied with and the conditions required by section 83(5) have not been met (i.e. you have not complied with the Adoptions with a Foreign Element Regulations 2005) the child must have had his/her home with you or, in the case of an application by a couple with one or both of you, for not less than twelve months preceding the application.

Note 16 ▶ You must notify in writing the local authority where you have your home or last had your home of your intention to apply for an adoption order within 14 days beginning with the date on which the child is brought into the United Kingdom.

Note 17 ▶ If some person or body is liable to pay maintenance for the child under a court order, or a maintenance agreement or child support maintenance awarded under the Child Support Act 1991, give the name and address of the person or body liable to pay. In the case of a maintenance order, give the name of the court and the date the order was made; otherwise, give the date of the maintenance agreement or child support maintenance award.

If possible, you should attach a copy of any maintenance order or a copy of the maintenance agreement or maintenance award to your application.

Note 18 ▶ If there are earlier, or current, court proceedings relating to the child you are applying to adopt (for example, proceedings for a care order, a contact order, a parental responsibility order or a residence order), give the name of the court, the nature of the proceedings and the date and effect of any order made, or the date of the next hearing if proceedings are current. You do not need to repeat the details of any maintenance order or agreement you have already given.

If you were a party to any proceedings that have been completed, you should attach a copy of the final order to your application.

Important: if you have previously applied for an adoption order in respect of the same child and the order was refused, you will need to satisfy the court that there has been a change of circumstances since you last applied, or that there is some other reason why the court should hear your current application. Please set out your reasons for making this application on a separate sheet, explaining why you think the application should be heard. Please put the child's full name, the number of the Part and the paragraph reference at the head of the sheet and attach it to your application form.

Part 3 About the child's parent(s) or guardian

Note 19 ▶ If the child has previously been adopted, give the names of his/her adoptive parents, not those of his/her natural parents.

Note 20 ▶ If the child has no guardian, enter 'not applicable'. Otherwise please enter the name of any person who may be regarded as the child's guardian in the country where the child is habitually resident. If the child has more than one guardian, please give the name and address of any other guardian(s) on a separate sheet, putting the child's full name, the number of the Part and the paragraph reference at the head of the sheet.

Note 21 ▶ Copies of the consents of the persons, institutions and authorities whose consents are necessary for adoption in the place where the child is habitually resident and being brought from should where possible be attached.

You do not need to ask the court to dispense with the consent of the child's parent(s) or guardian(s) to your application if the child's parent(s)/guardian(s) has/have consented to the making of an adoption order.

Please complete paragraph (i) showing that this condition applies in your case.

Note 22 ▶ If you are asking the court to dispense with the consent of any parent or guardian, the court can only dispense with that person's consent if it is satisfied that:
- he or she cannot be found, or
- he or she is incapable of giving consent; or
- the welfare of the child requires it.

You must complete paragraph (i) indicating which of these three grounds applies to your request. The court will also require from you a brief statement setting out a summary of the history of the case and any other facts to satisfy the court that the grounds for your request apply. This statement is known as a 'statement of facts'. If a parent cannot be found, your statement of facts should give details of the steps taken to trace him/her. The statement of facts must be signed by your solicitor, or by you (both of you) if you do not have a solicitor.

You should attach your statement of facts, and two copies of the statement, to your application form. You should also attach any documents you are submitting in support of your statement.

Important: The court will send a copy of your statement of facts to each parent or guardian of the child. If you intend to ask the court to keep your identity confidential, you should make certain that the statement of facts does not include any information that could identify you, where you live, or where the child goes to school or nursery.

Part 4 General

Note 23 ▶ Please enter the name by which you want the child to be known following the adoption. This is the name that will be entered on the Adopted Children Register. You may wish the child to have a new name following the adoption, but there is no obligation to change the child's name if you do not want to do so.

Note 24 ▶ You do not need to send a report on your health (or the health of the other applicant, if there is one) or the health of the child with your application if:
- he/she is your child, or the child of the other applicant, or
- you are applying alone as the partner (including the husband, wife or civil partner) of the child's mother or father.

In any other case you must attach separate health reports in respect of each applicant and the child, and two copies of the reports. The health reports should cover the matters set out in the Practice Direction 'Reports by a registered medical practitioner ("health reports")', and must have been made no more than three months before the date of your application for an adoption order.

Special assistance or facilities for disability if you attend the court

Note 25 ▶ If you/either of you need special assistance or special facilities for a disability or impairment, please set out your requirements in full. The court staff will need to know, for example, whether you want documents to be supplied in an alternative format, such as Braille or large print. They will also need to know about any specific requirements you may have on the day of the hearing, such as wheelchair access, a hearing loop, or a sign language interpreter.

The court staff will get in touch with you about your requirements. It is important that you make the court aware of all your needs. If you do not, the result may be that the hearing has to be adjourned.

Application for an order for parental responsibility prior to adoption abroad
Section 84 Adoption and Children Act 2002

Name of court	
Case no./Serial no.	
Date received by the court	
Date issued	

Notes to applicants

- Do not use this form if you intend to apply to a court in England and Wales for an adoption order including a Convention adoption order.
- Before filling in this form, please read the guidance notes on completing the form.
- Please complete every Part. If you are not sure of the answer to any question, or you do not think that it applies to you, please say so.
- If there is not enough room on the form for your reply, you may continue on a separate sheet. Please put the child's full name, the number of the Part and the paragraph reference at the head of the continuation sheet.
- Please use black ink when filling in the form.

I/We the undersigned _____
(and _____)
intend to adopt _____ ◀ See Note 1

under the law of a country or territory outside the British Islands and therefore want to be given parental responsibility prior to adoption abroad and give the following details in support of my/our application.

I/We want my/our identity to be kept confidential and wish to apply for a serial number   ☐ Yes   ☐ No   ◀ See Note 2

Part 1 About you

First applicant

a) Title
☐ Mr   ☐ Mrs   ☐ Miss
☐ Ms   ☐ Other _____

b) My name is
First name(s) in full

Last name

Second applicant

a) Title
☐ Mr   ☐ Mrs   ☐ Miss
☐ Ms   ☐ Other _____

b) My name is   ◀ See Note 3
First name(s) in full

Last name

A61 Application for an order for parental responsibility prior to adoption abroad (12.05)   HMCS

c) My address is (including postcode)   c) My address is (including postcode)

d) My telephone number is   d) My telephone number is

e) My date of birth is   e) My date of birth is

f) My nationality is   f) My nationality is

g) My occupation is   g) My occupation is   ◀ See Note 4

h) I am   ☐ Male   ☐ Female   h) I am   ☐ Male   ☐ Female

i) My relationship to the child is   i) My relationship to the child is   ◀ See Note 5

j) My/Our solicitor in these proceedings is

Name of solicitor	
Name of firm	
Address (including postcode)	

Telephone no.		Fax no.	
DX no.			
E-mail address			

Domicile and residence   ◀ See Note 6

k) ☐ I am not /Neither of us is domiciled in the United Kingdom, the Channel Islands or the Isle of Man.

   and

   ☐ I have not /Neither of us has been habitually resident in the United Kingdom, the Channel Islands or the Isle of Man for a period of at least one year, ending with the date of this application.

Status

> If you are applying for an order for parental responsibility prior to adoption abroad as a couple, please go straight to **Part 2 About the Child.** Paragraphs (l) to (r) do not apply to you

If you are applying to adopt for an order for parental responsibility prior to adoption abroad alone, please tick the box at (l) to (r) below that applies to your circumstances. **If you have ticked (l), (m), (q) or (r), please give the additional information asked for.**

l) ☐ I am the partner of the child's
   ☐ Father ☐ Mother

   If you have ticked box (l), please go straight to Part 2 About the Child. Paragraphs (m) to (r) do not apply to you. ◀ See Note 7

m) ☐ I am the partner (not the spouse or civil partner) of a person who is not the child's parent and I am applying alone for an order for parental responsibility prior to adoption abroad because:

   If you have ticked box (m), please go straight to Part 2 About the Child. Paragraphs (n) to (r) do not apply to you. ◀ See Note 8

   (please give reasons below, continuing on a separate sheet if necessary)

   [   ]

n) ☐ I am not married/I do not have a civil partner ◀ See Note 9
   or
o) ☐ I am divorced/my civil partnership has been dissolved ◀ See Note 9
   or
p) ☐ I am a widow/a widower/a surviving civil partner ◀ See Note 9
   or
q) ☐ I am married/I have a civil partner, and I can satisfy the court that: ◀ See Note 10
   ☐ my husband/wife/civil partner cannot be found
      or
   ☐ I have separated from my husband/wife/civil partner, we are living apart and the separation is likely to be permanent
      or
   ☐ my husband/wife/civil partner is not capable of making an application due to ill-health
   or
r) ☐ I am applying alone for an order for parental responsibility prior to adoption abroad in respect of my own child and I can satisfy the court that ◀ See Note 11
   ☐ the other natural parent has died
      or
   ☐ the other natural parent cannot be found
      or
   ☐ by virtue of section 28 of the Human Fertilisation and Embryology Act 1990, there is no other parent
      or
   ☐ the other natural parent's exclusion from this application is justified
      (please give reasons below)

   [   ]

Part 2 About the child

a) The child is a
  ☐ Boy ☐ Girl

b) The child was born on ☐☐☐☐☐☐☐☐

and is the person to whom the attached certified copy of the entry in the Register of Live Births/Register of Adopted Children relates

or To the best of my/our knowledge the child was born on or about ☐☐☐☐☐☐☐☐

in (give place and country of birth)

◀ See Note 12

c) The child's nationality is

d) I/we confirm that the child is not and has never been married or a civil partner
  ☐ Yes ☐ No

◀ See Note 13

e) The child has had his/her home with me/us continuously since ☐☐☐☐☐☐☐☐

f) The child was placed with me/us for adoption by an adoption agency

  ☐ Yes (If you ticked this box, please complete paragraphs (g) and (h) and then go straight to paragraph (j). Paragraph (i) does not apply to you.)

  ☐ No (If you ticked this box, please go straight to paragraph (i). Paragraphs (g) and (h) do not apply to you.)

g) The child was placed with me/us for adoption on ☐☐☐☐☐☐☐☐ by

Name of adoption agency	
Address (including post code)	
Name of your contact in the agency	
Telephone no.	

h) ☐ No other adoption agency has been involved in placing the child
  or
  ☐ The following adoption agency has also been involved in placing the child

Name of adoption agency	
Address (including post code)	
Name of your contact in the agency	
Telephone no.	

i) I/we have notified in writing my/our local authority of my/our intention to apply for an order for parental responsibility prior to adoption abroad (give details) ◀ See Note 14

Name of local authority	
Address (including post code)	
Date notified	
Name of your contact in the local authority	
Telephone no.	

j) ☐ No placement order or freeing order has been made in respect of the child ◀ See Note 15
or
☐ The following placement order/freeing order has been made in respect of the child:

Name of court	
Case number	
Type of order	
Date of order	

Care

k) ☐ No local authority or voluntary organisation has parental responsibility for the child
or
☐ The following local authority/voluntary organisation has parental responsibility for the child:

Name of local authority or voluntary organisation	
Address (including post code)	

Name of your contact in the authority/organisation	
Telephone no.	

Maintenance

l) ☐ No maintenance order/agreement or award of child support maintenance under the Child Support Act 1991 has been made in respect of the child ◀ See Note 16
or
☐ The following maintenance order/agreement/award of child support maintenance has been made

Person liable to pay maintenance	
Address (including post code)	

Court and date of order	
Date of maintenance agreement/child support maintenance award	

About other orders or proceedings that affect the child

m) ☐ To the best of my/our knowledge, no proceedings relating to the child (other than any maintenance order as given above) have been completed or commenced in any court ◀ See Note 17

or

☐ The following proceedings relating to the child have been completed/commenced (in addition to any maintenance order given above)

Type of order made (or applied for)	Date of order (or date of next hearing)	Name of court	Case number (or serial number)

Cases concerning a related child

n) ☐ To the best of my knowledge, no proceedings relating to a full, half or step brother or sister of the child have been completed or commenced in any court

or

☐ The following proceedings relating to a full, half or step brother or sister of the child have been completed/commenced (please give details below and, if you were a party to any proceedings that have been completed, attach a copy of the final order)

Relationship to child (eg. sister, half-brother)	Type of order made (or applied for)	Date of order (or date of next hearing)	Name of court	Case number (or serial number)

Part 3 About the child's parents or guardian

The child's mother

a) The name of the child's mother is

First name(s) in full

Last name

b) Her address is (if deceased, please write 'Deceased' in the address box)

c) Her nationality is

The child's father ◀ See Note 18

d) The name of the child's father is

First name(s) in full

Last name

e) His address is (if deceased, please write 'Deceased' in the address box)

f) His nationality is

g) Does he have parental responsibility for the child? ◀ See Note 19

☐ Yes   ☐ No

If No, does he intend to apply for an order under section 4(1)(c) of the Children Act 1989 (a parental responsibility order) or a residence or contact order in respect of the child?

☐ Yes   ☐ No

The child's guardian ◀ See Note 20

h) The name of the child's guardian is

First name(s) in full

Last name

i) His/Her address is

Parent/guardian consent to adoption

> ◀ See Note 21
> ◀ See Note 22

> **Note:** You do not need to complete paragraph (j) if
> - the child you intend to take abroad for adoption is the subject of a current placement order, the adoption agency has placed the child with you, and no parent/guardian of the child opposes the making of an order for parental responsibility adoption abroad;
>
> **or**
>
> - the child you intend to take abroad for adoption is the subject of a current freeing order.
>
> Instead, go straight to Part 4 General. You should give the details of the placement order or freeing order in Part 2 About the Child above. Otherwise, please tick the box that applies to your circumstances and give any further information requested.

j) ☐ The child's parent(s)/guardian(s) has/have consented to the making of an order for parental responsibility prior to adoption abroad

  or

  ☐ The child was placed with me/us for adoption by an adoption agency with the consent of each parent/guardian (and the mother's consent was given when the child was at least 6 weeks old), and no parent/guardian opposes the making of an order for parental responsibility prior to adoption abroad

  or

  ☐ The following parent(s)/guardian(s) of the child has/have not consented to the making of an order for parental responsibility prior to adoption abroad:
  (give name(s) below)

  [   ]

and I/we ask the court to dispense with his/her/their consent on the following grounds:
(please tick the grounds that apply)

  ☐ he/she/they cannot be found

  ☐ he/she is/they are incapable of giving consent

  ☐ the welfare of the child requires it.

You must attach a brief statement of facts (and two copies of the statement) setting out a summary of the history of the case and any other facts to satisfy the court that the grounds for your request apply.

> **IMPORTANT:** The court will send a copy of your statement of facts to each parent or guardian of the child. If you intend to ask the court to keep your identity confidential, you should make sure that the statement of facts does not include any information that could identify you, where you live, or where the child goes to school or nursery.

Part 4 General
Child's name on making of the order

◀ See Note 23

If the order for parental responsibility prior to adoption abroad is made,
I/We want the child to be known as

First name(s) in full

Last name

Health reports

◀ See Note 24

Separate reports on my/our health and the
health of the child made by a registered
medical practitioner on (give date(s))

are attached to this application.

Declarations
I/We have not received or given payment or reward in respect of the proposed adoption
(except as follows:) (give details below)

To the best of my/our knowledge, only the person(s) or organisation(s) named in Part 2 of
this application have taken part in the arrangements for the child's adoption.

Part 5 Statement of truth

I believe that the facts stated in this
application are true.

I believe that the facts stated in this
application are true.

Signature of first applicant

Signature of second applicant

Print full name

Print full name

Signed

Signed

Date

Date

If you attend the court for a hearing

1. Do you/either of you have a disability for which you require special assistance or special facilities?   ◀ See Note 25

　　　　☐ Yes　　☐ No

    If Yes, please say what your needs are below
    (the court staff will get in touch with you about your requirements)

    [   ]

2. Do you/either of you want to use the services of an interpreter?

　　　　☐ Yes　　☐ No

    If Yes, please specify which language
    (court staff will get in touch with you about your requirements)

    [   ]

3. Are there any dates on which you know you will not be able to attend the court, or any particular dates that would especially suit you? If so, please give details below

Unavailable dates	Preferred dates

(Please note that, although the court will try to fit in with your preferences, it may not be always be possible to do so)

What to do now

Once you have completed and signed this form, you should take or send the form **and three copies** to the court, together with the court fee* and the following documents:

- a certified copy of the full entry in the Register of Live Births that relates to the child or, where the child has been adopted, a certified copy of the entry in the Adopted Children Register;
- if you are asking the court to dispense with the consent of any parent or guardian, a brief statement of the facts relied on in support of the request **and two copies of the statement;**
- a copy of any placement order or freeing order relating to the child;
- if you were a party to the proceedings, a copy of any other final order relating to the child that has effect and if possible, a copy of any maintenance agreement or maintenance award relating to the child;
- if you were a party to the proceedings, a copy of any final order relating to a full, half or step brother or sister of the child that has effect;
- reports by a registered medical practitioner on the health of the child and the applicant(s) covering the matters specified in the Practice Direction 'Reports by a registered medical practitioner ("health reports")', **and two copies** of the reports.
  Note: you do not have to supply health reports if:
    - the child was placed with you for adoption by an adoption agency, or
    - he/she is your child, or the child of the other applicant, or
    - you are applying alone as the partner (including the husband, wife or civil partner) of the child's mother or father;
- where a parent of the child has died, a certified copy of the entry in the Register of Deaths;
- if you are submitting evidence of marriage or civil partnership, a certified copy of the entry in the Register of Marriages or the Register of Civil Partnerships;
- where your husband, wife or civil partner has died, a certified copy of the entry in the Register of Deaths;
- a copy of any decree absolute of divorce or decree of nullity of your marriage;
- in relation to a civil partnership, a copy of any dissolution order or nullity order of your civil partnership;
- any documentary evidence supporting the reasons why you are applying to for parental responsibility prior to adopting the child abroad without your husband, wife or civil partner, such as a decree of judicial separation;
- if your name as entered on the application form is different from the name shown on any evidence of marriage or civil partnership you are sending with your application, any documentary evidence to explain the difference.

*If you are not sure about the court fee payable for your application, or you think that you may be exempt from paying all or part of the fee, you should contact the court for information.

Application for an order for parental responsibility prior to adoption abroad (Form A61)
Notes on completing the form

Important
Do not use this form if the child you intend to take abroad for adoption is habitually resident outside the United Kingdom, the Channel Islands or the Isle of Man.

In these notes, any reference to a birth certificate, death certificate, marriage certificate or certificate of civil partnership means a certified copy of the entry in the Register of Live Births, the Register of Deaths, the Register of Marriages or the Register of Civil Partnerships, as appropriate. A photocopy is not acceptable. The birth certificate you send to the court for the child you are intending to take abroad for adoption must be a certified copy of the full entry in the Register of Live Births.

If you are attaching any order of the High Court or a county court to your application, it must be a sealed copy of the order (that is, a copy that has been stamped with the seal of the court). If you are attaching an order made by a magistrates' court, it must be a certified copy (a copy certified by the court officer to be a true copy of the original order), or a copy that bears the stamp of the originating court. An order issued by any other authority must be properly authenticated by that authority. If you are in any doubt about what is needed, please contact the court for assistance.

Take or send the completed application form, **and three copies,** to the court, together with the court fee and any documents you are attaching in support of your application. If you are not sure about the court fee payable for your application, or you think that you may be exempt from paying all or part of the fee, you should contact the court for information.

If you are attaching a statement of facts to your application (see note 22 below), please supply **two additional copies of the statement.** If you are attaching health reports (see note 24 below), please supply **two additional copies of the reports.**

Notes on the application form

Note 1
Enter the name of the child you are intending to take abroad for adoption, surname last. You must enter the full first name(s) and the surname of the child exactly as they are shown on the birth certificate (or, if the child has previously been adopted, the certified copy of the entry in the Adopted Children Register) you are sending with your application (see note 12 below).

Note 2
If you do not want your identity to be made known to the parents or guardians of the child you are intending to take abroad for adoption, the court will issue you with a serial number. Any documents sent to the parents/guardians will show the serial number, not your personal details. If you are required to attend the same court hearing, the court will make arrangements to ensure that your identity is protected.

Part 1 About you

Note 3
If the name you have entered is different from your name as it is shown on any evidence of marriage or civil partnership you are sending with your application form (for example, because you have changed your name by deed), please attach a continuation sheet explaining the reason for the difference, and a copy of any supporting documents (such as the deed).

Note 4 ▶ The occupation you give here will appear on the order for parental responsibility prior to adoption abroad. It is important that you enter the full title of your occupation (or former occupation if you are retired), for example, 'secondary school teacher' or 'ballet teacher', not 'teacher'; 'self-employed carpenter', not 'self-employed'; 'retired police officer', not 'retired'. Abbreviations or general descriptions such as 'self-employed', 'part-time worker', or 'retired', cannot be accepted. Please note also that it is not sufficient to enter that you are an 'employee' or 'worker' with any particular company, you must give your occupation. If you are unemployed or currently unable to work because of disability, you should give your last occupation. If you are a member of HM Forces, you should give your rank and/or profession.

Note 5 ▶ Enter your relationship to the child you are intending to take abroad for adoption, for example, step-parent, foster parent, grandparent, aunt, uncle, other relative (please specify). If you do not currently have any relationship to the child, other than as prospective adopter, please enter 'none'.

Note 6 ▶ An order for parental responsibility prior to adoption abroad cannot be made if
- you are (in the case of two applicants, at least one of you is) domiciled in the United Kingdom, the Channel Islands or the Isle of Man; or
- you (in the case of two applicants, both of you) have been habitually resident in the United Kingdom, the Channel Islands or the Isle of Man for a period of at least one year, ending with the date of your application.

The United Kingdom means England, Wales, Scotland and Northern Ireland

'Domicile' is normally taken to mean the place where you have your permanent home. 'Habitual residence' is normally taken to refer to usual, or customary, residence in a particular place. If you are in any doubt as to whether you meet these conditions, you should seek legal advice.

Note 7 ▶ If you are applying alone for an order for parental responsibility prior to adoption abroad and you are the partner (including husband, wife or civil partner) of the child's father or mother, you should complete paragraph (l) and then go straight to Part 2 About the Child. Paragraphs (m) to (r) do not apply to you.

Note 8 ▶ If you are applying for an order for parental responsibility prior to adoption abroad alone and you are the partner (but not the husband, wife or civil partner) of a person who is not the parent of the child you intend to take abroad for adoption, you should complete paragraph (m). Please give your reasons for applying alone. If there is not enough room for your reply, you may continue on a separate sheet. You should then go straight to Part 2 About the Child. Paragraphs (n) to (r) do not apply to you.

Note 9 ▶ If you are applying for an order for parental responsibility prior to adoption abroad alone and
- you have never been married/ had a civil partner, please complete paragraph (n);
- you are divorced, or your civil partnership has been dissolved, please complete paragraph (o) and attach a sealed copy of the Decree Absolute or the Dissolution Order to your application;
- you are a widow or widower or a surviving civil partner, please complete paragraph (p) and attach the death certificate of your deceased husband, wife or civil partner to your application.

Note 10 ▶ If you are applying alone for an order for parental responsibility prior to adoption abroad and you are married or you have a civil partner, you will need to satisfy the court that:
- your husband/wife or civil partner cannot be found, or
- you have separated from your husband/wife or civil partner, you are living apart, and the separation is likely to be permanent, or
- your husband/wife or civil partner is incapable of making an application due to physical or mental ill-health.

You must show on the application form which of these three grounds applies in your case by ticking the appropriate box.

You should attach your marriage certificate (or other evidence of marriage) or certificate of civil partnership (or other evidence of civil partnership) to your application, together with any other documentary evidence on which you propose to rely, such as a decree of official separation, or medical evidence of incapacity. You should also supply the name and address (if known) of your husband/wife or civil partner.

Note 11 ▶ If you are applying alone for an order for parental responsibility prior to adoption abroad in respect of your own child you will need to satisfy the court that
- the other natural parent has died, or
- the other natural parent cannot be found, or
- by virtue of section 28 of the Human Fertilisation and Embryology Act 1990, there is no other parent, or
- there is some other reason (which you must set out on your application form) justifying the other parent's exclusion from your application.

You must show on the application form which of these grounds applies in your case by ticking the appropriate box.

You should attach to your application any documentary evidence on which you propose to rely, such as the death certificate.

Part 2 About the child

Note 12 ▶ If the child has previously been adopted, a certified copy of the entry in the Adopted Children Register should be attached and not a certified copy of the full entry in the Register of Live Births. Where you are unable to attach a certificate, enter the place (including the country) of the child's birth, if known.

No application may be made in respect of a person who is aged 18 or more at the time of the application.

Note 13 ▶ The court cannot make an order for parental responsibility prior to adoption abroad in relation to any person who is or has been married, or any person who is or has been a civil partner.

Note 14 ▶ If the child you intend to take abroad for adoption was not placed with you for adoption by an adoption agency, you must notify in writing the local authority for the area in which you live of your intention to apply for an order for parental responsibility prior to adoption abroad. You must give the local authority notice of your intention not more than 2 years, and not less than 3 months, before the date of your application to the court.

Note 15 ▶ Give details of the name of the court that made the placement or freeing order, the nature of the order, the case number and the date the order was made.

You should attach a copy of the court order to your application.

Note 16 ▶ If some person or body is liable to pay maintenance for the child under a court order, or a maintenance agreement or child support maintenance awarded under the Child Support Act 1991, give the name and address of the person or body liable to pay. In the case of a maintenance order, give the name of the court and the date the order was made; otherwise, give the date of the maintenance agreement or child support maintenance award.

If possible, you should attach a copy of any maintenance order or a copy of the maintenance agreement or maintenance award to your application.

Note 17 ▶ If there are earlier, or current, court proceedings relating to the child you are intending to take abroad for adoption (for example, proceedings for a care order, a contact order, a parental responsibility order or a residence order), give the name of the court, the nature of the proceedings and the date and effect of any order made, or the date of the next hearing if proceedings are current. You do not need to repeat the details of any placement order, freeing order, or maintenance order or agreement you have already given.

If you were a party to any proceedings that have been completed, you should attach a copy of the final order to your application.

Important: if you have previously applied for an adoption order in respect of the same child and the order was refused, you will need to satisfy the court that there has been a change of circumstances since you last applied, or that there is some other reason why the court should hear your current application. Please set out your reasons for making this application on a separate sheet, explaining why you think the application should be heard. Please put the child's full name, the number of the Part and the paragraph reference at the head of the sheet and attach it to your application form.

Part 3 About the child's parent(s) or guardian

Note 18 ▶ If the child has previously been adopted, give the names of his/her adoptive parents, not those of his/her natural parents.

Note 19 ▶ If the child's parents were not married to each other at the time of his/her birth, the child's father may have parental responsibility

- because he and the child's mother have married since the child was born;
- because he has a parental responsibility agreement with the mother, or has been granted a parental responsibility order, or
- because he registered the child's birth jointly with the child's mother (since 1 December 2003).

Give details of any court order or agreement in respect of parental responsibility in paragraph (m) of Part 2 About the Child.

Note 20 ▶ If the child has no guardian, enter 'not applicable'. Otherwise, enter the details of any person appointed to be the child's guardian by deed or will or otherwise in writing in accordance with section 5(5) of the Children Act 1989, or by an order made under section 5(1) or 14A of that Act. If the child has more than one guardian, please give the name and address of any other guardian(s) on a separate sheet, putting the child's full name, the number of the Part and the paragraph reference at the head of the sheet.

Note 21 ▶ If the child you are intending to adopt abroad is already the subject of a current placement order, the adoption agency has placed the child with you and no parent or guardian opposes the making of the order for parental responsibility prior to adoption abroad, you do not need to ask the court to dispense with the consent of the child's parent(s) or guardian(s) to your application. You do not have to complete paragraph (j), but please ensure that you have entered the details of the placement order in Part 2, About the Child.

If the child you are intending to take abroad for adoption is already the subject of a current freeing order, you do not need to ask the court to dispense with the consent of the child's parent(s) or guardian(s) to your application. You do not have to complete paragraph (j), but please ensure that you have entered the details of the freeing order in Part 2, About the Child.

You do not need to ask the court to dispense with the consent of the child's parent(s) or guardian(s) to your application if:
- the child's parent(s)/guardian(s) has/have consented to the making of an order for parental responsibility prior to adoption abroad, or
- the child was placed with you for adoption by an adoption agency with the consent of each parent/guardian (and the mother's consent was given when the child was at least 6 weeks old), and no parent/guardian opposes the making of an order for parental responsibility prior to adoption abroad.

Please complete paragraph (j) showing which of these conditions applies in your case.

If the child's father does not have parental responsibility for the child, you do not need his consent to your application for an order for parental responsibility prior to adoption abroad.

Note 22 ▶ If you are asking the court to dispense with the consent of any parent or guardian, the court can only dispense with that person's consent if it is satisfied that:
- he or she cannot be found, or
- he or she is incapable of giving consent; or
- the welfare of the child requires it.

You must complete paragraph (j) indicating which of these three grounds applies to your request. The court will also require from you a brief statement setting out a summary of the history of the case and any other facts to satisfy the court that the grounds for your request apply. This statement is known as a 'statement of facts'. If a parent cannot be found, your statement of facts should give details of the steps taken to trace him/her. The statement of facts must be signed by your solicitor, or by you (both of you) if you do not have a solicitor.

You should attach your statement of facts, **and two copies of the statement,** to your application form. You should also attach any documents you are submitting in support of your statement.

Important: The court will send a copy of your statement of facts to each parent or guardian of the child. If you intend to ask the court to keep your identity confidential, you should make certain that the statement of facts does not include any information that could identify you, where you live, or where the child goes to school or nursery.

Part 4 General

Note 23 ▶ Please enter the name by which you want the child to be known following the adoption abroad.

Note 24 ▶ You do not need to send a report on your health (or the health of the other applicant, if there is one) or the health of the child with your application if:
- the child was placed with you for adoption by an adoption agency, or
- he/she is your child, or the child of the other applicant, or
- you are applying alone as the partner (including the husband, wife or civil partner) of the child's mother or father.

In any other case you must attach separate health reports in respect of each applicant and the child, **and two copies of the reports.** The health reports should cover the matters set out in the Practice Direction 'Reports by a registered medical practitioner ("health reports")', and must have been made no more than three months before the date of your application for an adoption order.

Special assistance or facilities for disability if you attend the court

Note 25 ▶ If you/either of you need special assistance or special facilities for a disability or impairment, please set out your requirements in full. The court staff will need to know, for example, whether you want documents to be supplied in an alternative format, such as Braille or large print. They will also need to know about any specific requirements you may have on the day of the hearing, such as wheelchair access, a hearing loop, or a sign language interpreter.

The court staff will get in touch with you about your requirements. It is important that you make the court aware of all your needs. If you do not, the result may be that the hearing has to be adjourned.

Application for a direction under section 88(1) of the Adoption and Children Act 2002

Name of court	
Case no.	
Date received by the court	
Date issued	

Notes to applicants

- Before filling in this form, please read the guidance notes on completing the form.
- Please complete every Part. If you are not sure of the answer to any question, or you do not think that it applies to you, please say so.
- If there is not enough room on the form for your reply, you may continue on a separate sheet. Put the child's full name, the number of the Part and the paragraph reference at the top of the continuation sheet.
- Please use black ink when filling in the form.

Part 1 About you

◀ See Note 1

First applicant

a) Title
- [ ] Mr   [ ] Mrs   [ ] Miss
- [ ] Ms   [ ] Other _____

b) My name is

First name(s) in full

Last name

c) My address is

d) My telephone number is

e) My relationship to the child is

Second applicant

a) Title
- [ ] Mr   [ ] Mrs   [ ] Miss
- [ ] Ms   [ ] Other _____

b) My name is

First name(s) in full

Last name

c) My address is

◀ See Note 2

d) My telephone number is

e) My relationship to the child is

◀ See Note 3

A62 Application for a direction under section 88(1) of the Adoption and Children Act 2002 (12.05)   HMCS

f) My/our solicitor in these proceedings is

Name of solicitor	
Name of firm	
Address (including postcode)	

Telephone no.		Fax no.	
DX no.			
E-mail address			

Part 2 About the child

◀ See Note 4

a) The name of the child is

First name(s) in full

Last name

b) The child is a

☐ Boy   ☐ Girl

c) The child was born on

Part 3 About the respondents

◀ See Note 5

a) The Child's Adopters
   The name of the child's adoptive parent(s) is/are:

First adoptive parent

Title
☐ Mr   ☐ Mrs   ☐ Miss
☐ Ms   ☐ Other _____

First name(s) in full

Last name

Address

Second adoptive parent

Title
☐ Mr   ☐ Mrs   ☐ Miss
☐ Ms   ☐ Other _____

First name(s) in full

Last name

Address

b) **The Child's parents**
   The name of the child's parent(s) is/are:

First parent
   Title
   ☐ Mr   ☐ Mrs   ☐ Miss
   ☐ Ms   ☐ Other _____

   First name(s) in full
   [   ]

   Last name
   [   ]

   Address
   [   ]

Second parent
   Title
   ☐ Mr   ☐ Mrs   ☐ Miss
   ☐ Ms   ☐ Other _____

   First name(s) in full
   [   ]

   Last name
   [   ]

   Address
   [   ]

c) **The adoption agency** (only complete where the child was placed for adoption by an adoption agency)   ◄ See Note 6

Name of adoption agency	
Address (including post code)	

Name of your contact in the agency	
Telephone no.	

d) The local authority to whom notice under section 44 (notice of intention to apply for an order for parental responsibility prior to adoption abroad) has been given is:

Name of local authority	
Address (including post code)	

Name of your contact in the authority	
Telephone no.	

e) **The Attorney General**   ◄ See Note 5

Part 4 About this application

◀ See Note 7

I/we apply for a direction that, in respect of the child (insert name of child)

◀ See Note 4

☐ a) section 67(3) of the Adoption and Children Act 2002 shall not apply

or

☐ b) section 67(3) of the Adoption and Children Act 2002 shall apply with the following modifications:

(c) The reasons for this application are

◀ See Note 8

Part 5 Declarations

I/we certify that a Convention adoption which was authorised on ⬅ See Note 9

[   ]

at

[   ]

by which

[   ]

and

[   ]

adopted (insert the name of the child) ⬅ See Note 4

[   ]

was not, under the law of the country in which the adoption was effected, a full adoption ⬅ See Note 10

and

☐ that the consents referred to in Articles 4(c) and (d) of the Convention have not been given for a full adoption ⬅ See Note 11

or

☐ that the United Kingdom is not the receiving State within the meaning of Article 2 of the Convention ⬅ See Note 11

and that it would be more favourable for (insert name of child) ⬅ See Note 4

[   ]

if a direction under section 88(1) of the Adoption and Children Act 2002 was given.

A copy of the Convention adoption is attached

Part 6 Statement of truth

*[I believe] [The first applicant believes] that the facts stated in this application are true.
*I am duly authorised by the first applicant to sign this statement.

Print full name

Signed   Date

*[First applicant] [First applicant's solicitor] [First applicant's litigation friend]

*delete as appropriate

*[I believe] [The second applicant believes] that the facts stated in this application are true.
*I am duly authorised by the second applicant to sign this statement.

Print full name

Signed   Date

*[Second applicant] [Second applicant's solicitor] [Second applicant's litigation friend]

*delete as appropriate

If you attend the court for a hearing

1. Do you/either of you have a disability for which you require special assistance or special facilities?   ◀ See Note 12

   ☐ Yes   ☐ No

   If Yes, please say what your needs are below
   (the court staff will get in touch with you about your requirements)

2. Do you/either of you want to use the services of an interpreter?

   ☐ Yes   ☐ No

   If Yes, please specify which language
   (court staff will get in touch with you about your requirements)

What to do now

Once you have completed and signed this form, you should take or send the form and **three copies** to the High Court, together with the court fee and a copy of the Convention adoption. If you are not sure about the court fee payable for your application, or you think that you may be exempt from paying all or part of the fee, you should contact the court for information.

Application for a direction under section 88(1) of the Adoption and Children Act 2002 (Form A62)
Notes on completing the form

Important

This application form may be used to make an application to the High Court for a direction under section 88(1) of the Adoption and Children Act 2002 that, subject to the conditions which must be met, in the case of a Convention adoption section 67(3) does not apply, or does not apply to the extent specified in the direction.

If you are attaching any order of the High Court or a county court to your application, it must be a sealed copy of the order (that is, a copy that has been stamped with the seal of the court). An order issued by any other authority must be properly authenticated by that authority. If you are in any doubt about what is needed, please contact the court for assistance.

Take or send the completed application form, **and three copies,** to the High Court, together with the court fee and any documents you are attaching in support of your application. If you are not sure about the court fee payable for your application, or you think that you may be exempt from paying all or part of the fee, you should contact the court for information.

Notes on the application form

Note 1 The following persons may make this application:
- The adopted child;
- The adopters;
- Any parent;
- Any other person.

Note 2 If you do not want your private address and telephone number to be disclosed to any other party, do not enter those details on this application form. Instead you should enter the details on Form A65, which you must file at the court with your application. The information will not then be disclosed to any other person, except by order of the court.

Note 3 Enter your relationship to the child, for example, adopter, parent. If you are the child enter 'subject child'. If you do not have a relationship to the child enter 'none'.

Note 4 Please give the name of the child as it appears on the Convention adoption. **You must attach a copy of the order to your application.**

Note 5 The following people and institutions may be respondents to this application:
- The child's adopters;
- The child's parents
- The adoption agency;
- The local authority to whom notice under section 44 (notice of intention to apply for an order for parental responsibility prior to adoption abroad) has been given.

Please fill in their details as fully as possible.

The Attorney General will also be a respondent to these proceedings. The court already has the address for service on the Attorney General.

A62 Notes Application for a direction under section 88(1) of the Adoption and Children Act 2002 (Form A62) Notes on completing the form (12.05)
HMCS

Note 6 ▶ Only complete this part if the child was placed by an adoption agency. This is only likely to be relevant where the United Kingdom was the State of origin in the Convention adoption proceedings.

Note 7 ▶ In Part 4 of the application please indicate the order you are asking the court to make and complete the relevant additional details required, for example, please insert the details of the extent to which section 67(3) of the Adoption and Children Act 2002 should not apply.

Note 8 ▶ Please set out the reasons for your application. If there is not enough room for your reply, please continue on a separate sheet. Put the child's name, the number of the Part and the paragraph reference at the head of the continuation sheet.

If you have withheld your address or telephone number on the application form, you should make sure that the reasons you give for your application do not include any information that could lead to those details being disclosed.

Note 9 ▶ Enter the date on which the Convention adoption was authorised and by whom (e.g. which Court or Authority), together with the details of the adopters and the child adopted.

Note 10 ▶ A full adoption is an adoption following which the child is to be treated in law as not being the child of any person other than the adopters or adopter.

Note 11 ▶ The Convention means the Convention on Protection of Children and Co-operation in respect of Intercountry Adoption, concluded at the Hague on 29th May 1993.

Special assistance or facilities for disability if you attend court

Note 12 ▶ If you/either of you need special assistance or special facilities for a disability or impairment, please set out your requirements in full. The court staff will need to know, for example, whether you want documents to be supplied in an alternative format, such as Braille or large print. They will also need to know about any specific requirements you may have on the day of the hearing, such as wheelchair access, a hearing loop, or a sign language interpreter. The court staff will get in touch with you about your requirements. It is important that you make the court aware of all your needs. If you do not, the result may be that the hearing has to be adjourned.

Application for an order to annul a Convention adoption or Convention adoption order or for an overseas adoption or determination under section 91 to cease to be valid

Section 89 Adoption and Children Act 2002

Name of court	
Case no.	
Date received by the court	
Date issued	

Notes to applicants

- Before filling in this form, please read the guidance notes on completing the form.
- Please complete every Part. If you are not sure of the answer to any question, or you do not think that it applies to you, please say so.
- If there is not enough room on the form for your reply, you may continue on a separate sheet. Put the child's full name, the number of the Part and the paragraph reference at the top of the continuation sheet.
- Please use black ink when filling in the form.

Part 1 About you

◀ See Note 1

First applicant

a) Title
- ☐ Mr ☐ Mrs ☐ Miss
- ☐ Ms ☐ Other _____

b) My name is

First name(s) in full

Last name

c) My address is

d) My telephone number is

e) My relationship to the child is

Second applicant

a) Title
- ☐ Mr ☐ Mrs ☐ Miss
- ☐ Ms ☐ Other _____

b) My name is

First name(s) in full

Last name

c) My address is   ◀ See Note 2

d) My telephone number is   ◀ See Note 2

e) My relationship to the child is   ◀ See Note 3

A63 Application for an order to annul a Convention adoption, etc. (12.05)   HMCS

f) My solicitor in these proceedings is

Name of solicitor	
Name of firm	
Address (including postcode)	

Telephone no.		Fax no.	
DX no.			
E-mail address			

Part 2 About the child

◀ See Note 4

a) The name of the child is

First name(s) in full

Last name

b) The child is a   ☐ Boy   ☐ Girl

c) The child was born on

About other orders or proceedings that affect the child

◀ See Note 5

d) ☐ To the best of my/our knowledge, no proceedings relating to the child (other than the Convention adoption, Convention adoption order or other overseas adoption or determination under section 91 of the Adoption and Children Act 2002 entered in Part 4 of this application) have been completed or commenced in any court

or

☐ The following proceedings relating to the child have been completed/commenced (in addition to the Convention adoption, Convention adoption order or other overseas adoption or determination by an overseas authority under section 91 of the Adoption and Children Act 2002 entered in Part 4 of this application)

Type of order made (or applied for)	Date of order (or date of next hearing)	Name of court	Case number (or serial number)

Cases concerning a related child

e) ☐ To the best of my/our knowledge, no proceedings relating to a full, half or step brother or sister of the child have been completed or commenced in any court

or

☐ The following proceedings relating to a full, half or step brother or sister of the child have been completed/commenced (please give details below and, if you were a party to any proceedings that have been completed, **attach a copy of the final order**)

Relationship to child (eg. sister, half-brother)	Type of order made (or applied for)	Date of order (or date of next hearing)	Name of court	Case number (or serial number)

Part 3 About the child's adopters

The name(s) and address(es) of the child's adopter(s) is/are:

◀ See Note 6

First adoptive parent

a) First name(s) in full

Last name

b) Address is (if deceased, please write 'Deceased' in the address box)

Second adoptive parent

c) First name(s) in full

Last name

d) Address is (if deceased, please write 'Deceased' in the address box)

Part 4 About this application

◀ See Note 7

a) I/we apply for annulment of the

☐ Convention adoption   ☐ Convention adoption order

made by (give name of court or authority that made the order)

made on (date)

on the ground that the adoption is contrary to public policy.

◀ See Note 7

☐ I/we confirm that the [person adopted is] [adopter(s) are] habitually resident in England and Wales immediately prior to the making of this application.

◀ See Note 8

A copy of the Convention adoption or Convention adoption order is attached

b) I/we apply for an order that the [overseas adoption] [determination under section 91 of the Adoption and Children Act 2002]

made on (date)

cease to be valid on the ground that:

☐ the adoption or determination is contrary to public policy

or

☐ that the authority which purported to authorise the adoption or make the determination was not competent to entertain the case

◀ See Note 7

A copy of the overseas adoption or determination under section 91 of the Adoption and Children Act 2002 is attached

c) I/we apply for an order deciding the extent, if any, to which a determination under section 91 has been affected by a subsequent determination

◀ See Note 7

A copy of the determination under section 91 is attached

d) The reasons for this application are:

◀ See Note 9

Part 5 Statement of truth

First applicant

*[I believe] [The first applicant believes] that the facts stated in this application are true.

*I am duly authorised by the first applicant to sign this statement.

Print full name

Signed   Date

*[First applicant] [First applicant's solicitor] [First applicant's litigation friend]

*delete as appropriate

Second applicant

*[I believe] [The second applicant believes] that the facts stated in this application are true.

*I am duly authorised by the second applicant to sign this statement.

Print full name

Signed   Date

*[Second applicant] [Second applicant's solicitor] [Second applicant's litigation friend]

*delete as appropriate

If you attend the court for a hearing

1. Do you/either of you have a disability for which you require special assistance or special facilities? ◀ See Note 10

☐ Yes ☐ No

If Yes, please say what your needs are below
(the court staff will get in touch with you about your requirements)

[ ]

2. Do you/either of you want to use the services of an interpreter?

☐ Yes ☐ No

If Yes, please specify which language
(court staff will get in touch with you about your requirements)

[ ]

What to do now

Once you have completed and signed this form, you should take or send the form **and three copies** to the High Court, together with the court fee* and the following documents:

- a copy of the Convention adoption, Convention adoption order or other overseas adoption order or determination under section 91 you are asking the court to annul or declare invalid;
- a copy of any other determinations under section 91;
- if you were a party to the proceedings, a copy of any final order relating to the child that has effect;
- if you were a party to the proceedings, a copy of any final order relating to a full, half or step brother or sister of the child that has effect;
- a copy of any court order giving you permission to apply for the Convention adoption, Convention adoption order or other overseas order to be annulled.

*If you are not sure about the court fee payable for your application, or you think that you may be exempt from paying all or part of the fee, you should contact the court for information.

Application for an order to annul a Convention adoption or Convention adoption order or for an overseas adoption or determination under section 91 to cease to be valid (Form A63)

Notes on completing the form

Important

If you are attaching any order of the High Court or a county court to your application, it must be a sealed copy of the order (that is, a copy that has been stamped with the seal of the court). If you are attaching an order made by a magistrates' court, it must be a certified copy (a copy certified by the court officer to be a true copy of the original order), or a copy that bears the stamp of the originating court. An order issued by any other authority must be properly authenticated by that authority. If you are in any doubt about what is needed, please contact the court for assistance.

Take or send the completed application form, **and three copies,** to the High Court, together with the court fee and any documents you are attaching in support of your application. If you are not sure about the court fee payable for your application, or you think you may be exempt from paying all or part of the fee, you should contact the court for information.

Notes on the application form

Note 1 ▶ An application may be made to the High Court under section 89 of the Adoption and Children Act 2002 for:

- An order to annul a Convention adoption or Convention adoption order on the ground that the adoption is contrary to public policy;

- An order that an overseas adoption or a determination under section 91 cease to be valid on the ground that the adoption or determination is contrary to public policy or that the authority which purported to authorise the adoption or make the determination was not competent to entertain the case; or

- A decision about the extent, if any, to which a determination under section 91 has been affected by a subsequent determination under that section.

An 'overseas adoption' is one occurring in a place, under the law of that place, listed in the Schedule to the Adoption (Designation of Overseas Adoptions) Order 1973.

Note 2 ▶ If you do not want your private address and telephone number to be disclosed to any other party, do not enter those details on this application form. Instead you should enter the details on Form A65, which you must file at the court with your application. The information will not then be disclosed to any other person, except by order of the court.

Note 3 ▶ Enter your relationship to the child, for example, adopter, parent. If you are the child enter 'subject child'. If you do not have a relationship to the child enter 'none'.

Note 4 ▶ Please give the name of the child as it appears on the Convention adoption, Convention adoption order or other overseas adoption order or determination under section 91. **You must attach a copy of the order (or determination) to your application.**

Note 5 ▶ If there are any other earlier, or current, court proceedings relating to the child, give the name of the court, the nature of the proceedings and the date and effect of any order made. You should attach a copy of any court order to the application. You do not need to enter here the details of the Convention adoption, Convention adoption order or other overseas adoption order or determination under section 91 you are asking the court to annul or declare invalid. Instead, you should enter those details in Part 4 'About this application'.

A63 Notes - Application for an order to annul a Convention adoption, etc. (12.05)　　　　　　　　　　　　　HMCS

If you were a party to any proceedings that have been completed, you should attach a copy of the final order to your application.

If there are earlier, or current, court proceedings relating to a full, half or step brother or sister of the child, give the name of the court, the nature of the proceedings and the date and effect of any order made, or the date of the next hearing if proceedings are current.

If you were a party to any proceedings that have been completed, you should attach a copy of the final order to your application.

Note 6 ▶ Give the names of the child's adoptive parents.

Note 7 ▶ In Part 4 of the application please indicate the order(s) you are asking the court to make and complete the relevant additional details required. **You should ensure you attach a copy of the order (or determination) to this application.**

If you are applying for an order to annul the Convention adoption or Convention adoption order complete paragraph (a) in Part 4. You should then give your reasons for believing that the Convention adoption or Convention adoption order is contrary to public policy in paragraph (d).

If you are applying for an order that the overseas adoption or determination under section 91 should cease to be valid please complete paragraph (b) in Part 4. You should tick the appropriate box to indicate whether this is because:
- you believe the overseas adoption or determination to be contrary to public policy or
- the authority which purported to authorise the adoption or determination was not competent to do so;

and give your reason(s) for this in paragraph (d).

If you are asking the court to decide the extent to which a determination under section 91 has been affected by a subsequent determination under that section, complete paragraph (c) of Part 4. You should then give your reasons for the application in paragraph (d).

Note 8 ▶ An application to annul a Convention adoption or Convention adoption order can only be made if immediately before an application is made the person adopted or the adopter(s) were habitually resident in England and Wales. Please confirm that this is the case by ticking the appropriate box in paragraph (a) of Part 4.

Note 9 ▶ Please set out the reasons for your application. If there is not enough room for your reply, please continue on a separate sheet. Put the child's name, the number of the Part and the paragraph reference at the head of the continuation sheet.

If you have withheld your address or telephone number on the application form, you should make sure that the reasons you give for your application do not include any information that could lead to those details being disclosed.

Special assistance or facilities for disability if you attend court

Note 10 ▶ If you/either of you need special assistance or special facilities for a disability or impairment, please set out your requirements in full. The court staff will need to know, for example, whether you want documents to be supplied in an alternative format, such as Braille or large print. They will also need to know about any specific requirements you may have on the day of the hearing, such as wheelchair access, a hearing loop, or a sign language interpreter. The court staff will get in touch with you about your requirements. It is important that you make the court aware of all your needs. If you do not, the result may be that the hearing has to be adjourned.

Application to receive information from court records
Section 60(4) Adoption and Children Act 2002

Name of court
Case no. (If known)

Part 1 About you

1) Title
   ☐ Mr   ☐ Mrs   ☐ Miss   ☐ Ms   ☐ Other _____

2) My name is

   First name(s) in full

   Last name

3) My address is

4) My date of birth is

5) My name on adoption (if different from your name above)

   First name(s) in full

   Last name

6) My name at birth (if known)

   First name(s) in full

   Last name

7) The names of my adoptive parent(s)

   First name(s) in full

   Last name

   First name(s) in full

   Last name

8) The date of my adoption (if known):

A64 Application to receive information from court records (12.05)

HMCS

Part 2 The application

I apply for a copy of the following documents:

- [ ] The application form for an adoption order (this will not include the documents attached to that form)
- [ ] The adoption order or any other order relating to the adoption proceedings
- [ ] Order(s) allowing any person contact with the child after the adoption order was made
- [ ] Any transcript or written reasons of the court's decision
- [ ] A report made to the court by:
    - [ ] a children's guardian, reporting officer or children and family reporter
    - [ ] a local authority
    - [ ] an adoption agency

Part 3 Signature of applicant

I certify that I am the person to whom the attached certified copy of the entry in the Adopted Children Register relates.

Print full name

Signed   Date

To be completed by the court	
Proof of Identity	
Seen by (court officer)	

Guidance Notes: Application for information from court records

You should attach a full certified copy of the entry in the Register of Adopted Children which relates to you.

When you have completed the form you should take it in person to the court which made the adoption order along with evidence of your identity showing a photograph and signature, such as a passport or driving licence.

The court will check the evidence of your identity, make a note of it on the application form and return it to you.

What happens next

The court will locate the court records relevant to your application and send copies of the documents you have requested to your home address. The court may edit the documents before they are sent to you.

Confidential information

Name of court	
Case no./Serial no.	
Date received by the court	

Notes

- This form is for use if you are a party in proceedings under the Adoption and Children Act 2002, and you want the court to keep certain details about you or the child confidential.
- Before filling in this form, please read carefully the guidance notes on completion.
- Please use black ink when filling in the form.

Part 1 Your name and the name of the child

First applicant/respondent

Title
☐ Mr ☐ Mrs ☐ Miss
☐ Ms ☐ Other _____

My name is

First name(s) in full

Last name

Second applicant/respondent

Title
☐ Mr ☐ Mrs ☐ Miss
☐ Ms ☐ Other _____

My name is

First name(s) in full

Last name

Child's name

First name(s) in full

Last name

Part 2 Information to be kept confidential

Your address and telephone number

If you want your private address and telephone number to be kept confidential, please complete the details below:

My address is (including postcode)

My telephone number is

A65 Confidential information (12.05)

HMCS

The child's address

If you want the address of the child named in the application to be kept confidential, please complete the details below:

The child's address is

[ ]

Person the child lives with

If you want the name of the person with whom the child lives to be kept confidential, please complete the details below:

Title

☐ Mr ☐ Mrs ☐ Miss

☐ Ms ☐ Other _____

First name(s) in full

[ ]

Last name

[ ]

Change of surname

If you are applying to the court for permission to change the child's surname and you want the proposed new name to be kept confidential, please complete the details below:

[ ]

Notes on completing the form

Form A65 is for use if you are a party in proceedings under the Adoption and Children Act 2002 and you want the court to keep any of the following details confidential:
- your private address and telephone number;
- the address of the child;
- the name of the person with whom the child lives (Note: this does not apply to you if you are making an application and the child lives with you. In those circumstances your name will remain confidential only if you proposing to adopt the child and you are entitled to be assigned a serial number and a number has been assigned to you);
- if you are making an application under section 28(2) for permission to change the child's surname, the new surname proposed for the child.

If you are making the application to the court, do not enter the information you wish to be kept confidential on the application form. Instead, give the information on Form A65 and attach it to your application. If you are a respondent in the court proceedings, when you receive notice of the hearing you should complete the form and send it to the court, together with your acknowledgment of the notice. Information entered on Form A65 will not be revealed to any person, unless it is by order of the Court.

Part 1 (the full name(s) of the applicant(s)/respondent(s) and the name of the child) **must** be completed in all cases.

Application under Part 10 of the Family Procedure (Adoption) Rules 2005

Name of court	
Case no./ Serial no.	
Name of child	
Date issued	

Applicant

Respondent(s)

If you are acting by solicitor in these proceedings, your solicitor's name and address:

Name of solicitor	
Name of firm	
Address (including postcode)	

Telephone no.		Fax no.	
DX no.			
E-mail address			

Does your application include any issues under the Human Rights Act 1998? ☐ Yes ☐ No

Details of application *(continue over the page)*

FP1 - Application under Part 10 of the Family Procedure (Adoption) Rules 2005 (12.05)

HMCS

Case no./ Serial no.	

Details of application *(continued)*

Statement of truth

*(I believe)(The applicant believes) that the facts stated in this application are true.
* I am duly authorised by the applicant to sign this statement

Print full name _____

Signed _____
       *(Applicant)(Litigation friend)(Applicant's solicitor)

*(*Delete as appropriate)*

Application under Part 10 of the Family Procedure (Adoption) Rules 2005
Notes for applicant on completing the application (Form FP1)

- Please read all of these guidance notes before you begin completing the application. The notes follow the order in which information is required on the application.
- Court staff can help you fill in the application and give information about procedure once it has been issued, but they cannot give legal advice. If you need legal advice, for example, about the likely success of your application or the evidence you need to support it, you should contact a solicitor or a Citizens Advice Bureau.
- If you are filling in the application by hand, please use black ink and write in block capitals.
- You must file any written evidence to support your application either in or with the application. Your written evidence must be verified by a statement of truth.
- Copy the completed application, the respondent's notes for guidance and your written evidence so that you have a copy for yourself, one copy for the court and one copy for each respondent. Send or take the applications and evidence to the court office with the appropriate fee. The court will tell you how much this is.

Notes on completing the application

Applicant and Respondent details
As the person making the application, you are called the 'applicant'; any other party is called a 'respondent'. Applicants who are under 18 years old (unless otherwise permitted by the court) and patients within the meaning of the Mental Health Act 1983 must have a litigation friend to make the application and conduct court proceedings on their behalf. Court staff will tell you more about what you need to do if this applies to you.

You must provide the following information about yourself and each respondent (if known): -
- all known forenames and surname;
- whether Mr, Mrs, Miss, Ms or Other (e.g. Dr)
- residential address (including postcode and telephone number).

Where the person is:
- under 18, write ("a child, by 'Mr Joe Bloggs' his/her litigation friend")
- a patient within the meaning of the Mental Health Act 1983, write (", by Mr Joe Bloggs, his/her litigation friend")
- appearing in a representative capacity, you must say what that capacity is, eg. "Mr Joe Bloggs as the representative of Mrs Sharon Bloggs"

Your solicitor's name and address
If you are acting by solicitor in these proceedings, enter in this box your solicitor's full name and address, and other contact details as requested.

Details of application
Under this heading you must set out either:
- the question(s) you wish the court to decide; or
- the order you are seeking and the legal basis for your application; and
- if your application is being made under a specific rule or practice direction, you must state which.

Statement of truth
This must be signed by you, by your solicitor or your litigation friend, as appropriate.

FP1A - Application under Part 10 of the Family Procedure (Adoption) Rules 2005 Notes for applicant on completing the application (Form FP1) (12.05)

Application under Part 10 of the Family Procedure (Adoption) Rules 2005

Notes for respondent

Please read these notes carefully – they will help you to decide what to do about this application.

- You have 14 days from the date on which you were served with the application to respond to the application.
- If you **do not return** the acknowledgment of service, you will be allowed to attend any hearing of this application, but you will **not** be allowed to take part in the hearing unless the court gives you permission to do so.
- Court staff can tell you about procedures, but they cannot give legal advice. If you need legal advice, you should contact a solicitor or Citizens Advice Bureau immediately.

Time for responding

The completed acknowledgment of service must be returned to the court office within 14 days of the date on which the application was served on you. If the application was:

- sent by post, the 14 days begins 2 days from the date of the postmark on the envelope.
- delivered to your address, the 14 days begins the day after it was delivered.
- handed to you personally, the 14 days begins on the day it was given to you.

Completing the acknowledgment of service

You should complete sections A- F as appropriate. In all cases you must complete sections G and H.

Section A – not contesting the application

If you do not wish to contest the application, you should complete section A. In some cases the applicant may only be seeking the court's directions as to how to act, rather than seeking a specific order. In these circumstances, if you wish the court to direct the applicant to act in a certain way, give brief details.

Section B – contesting the application

If you do wish to contest the application, you should complete section B. If you seek an order different from that sought by the applicant, you should give brief details in the space provided.

Section C – disputing the court's jurisdiction

You should indicate your intention by completing section C and filing an application disputing the court's jurisdiction within 14 days of filing your acknowledgment of service at the court. The court will arrange a hearing date for the application and tell you and the applicant when and where to attend.

Section D – objecting to use of procedure

If you believe that the applicant should not have issued the application under Part 10 of the Family Procedure (Adoption) Rules 2005 because:

- there is a substantial dispute of fact involved; and
- you do not agree that the rule or practice direction stated does provide for the applicant to use this procedure

you should complete section D, setting out your reasons in the space provided.

Section E – written evidence

Complete this section if you wish to rely on written evidence. You must send your written evidence to the court with your acknowledgment of service. It must be verified by a statement of truth or the court may disallow it.

Section F – name and address of solicitor

If you are acting by solicitor in these proceedings, give your solicitor's full name and address and other contact details as requested.

Section G – name of respondent

Print your full name, or the full name of the respondent on whose behalf you are completing this form.

Serving other parties

You must file your completed acknowledgment of service and any written evidence with the court, together with one copy for each party named on the application.

What happens next

The applicant may, within 14 days of receiving your written evidence from the court, file further evidence in reply. On receipt of your acknowledgment of service, the court file will be referred to the court for directions for the disposal of the application. The court will contact you and tell you what to do next.

Statement of truth

This must be signed by you, by your solicitor or by your litigation friend, as appropriate.

FP1B - Application under Part 10 of the Family Procedure (Adoption) Rules 2005 Notes for respondent (12.05)   HMCS

Application notice
Part 9 of the Family Procedure (Adoption) Rules 2005

Name of court	
Case no./ Serial no.	
Name of child	
Date issued	

Notes to applicants
- Before filling in this form, please read the guidance notes on completion.
- You must complete Parts A **and** B, **and** Part C if applicable.

Part A

I (We) [_____] ◀ Note 1

and [_____]

of [_____] ◀ Note 2

intend to apply for an order (a draft of which is attached) that: ◀ Note 3

[_____]

because: ◀ Note 4

[_____]

Part B

I (We) wish to rely on: *(tick one box)*

☐ the attached (witness statement)(affidavit)

☐ evidence in Part C in support of this application

*(I am)(We are) intending to adopt the child who is the subject of this application and ◀ Note 5

☐ wish to keep my/our identity confidential and apply for a serial number

☐ have already been assigned a serial number, which is [_____]

(delete if not applicable)

*I/We wish the court to deal with this application without a hearing
(delete if not applicable)

FP2 - Application Notice Part 9 of the Family Procedure (Adoption) Rules 2005 (12.05)   HMCS

My/our solicitor's name and address is:

Name of solicitor	
Name of firm	
Address (including postcode)	

Telephone no.		Fax no.	
DX no.			
E-mail address			

First applicant

Print full name _____

Signed _____ Date _____
*(Applicant)(Solicitor)(Applicant's litigation friend)
(*Delete as appropriate)

Second applicant

Print full name _____

Signed _____ Date _____
*(Applicant)(Solicitor)(Applicant's litigation friend)
(*Delete as appropriate)

	Case no./ Serial no.	

Part C

I (We) wish to rely on the following evidence in support of this application:

Statement of Truth - First applicant

*(I believe)(The applicant believes) that the facts stated in Part C are true.

Print full name _____

Signed _____ Date _____
       *(Applicant)(Solicitor)(Applicant's litigation friend)

(*Delete as appropriate)

Statement of Truth - Second applicant

*(I believe)(The applicant believes) that the facts stated in Part C are true.

Print full name _____

Signed _____ Date _____
       *(Applicant)(Solicitor)(Applicant's litigation friend)

(*Delete as appropriate)

Application notice
Part 9 of the Family Procedure (Adoption) Rules 2005
Notes on completion

Note 1 → **Your name(s)**

Enter your full name (in the case of two applicants, the full name of both applicants), surname last.

Note 2 → **Your address**

If you do not want your address to be disclosed to any other party, do not enter it on this application notice. Instead you should enter the details on Form A65, which you must file at the court with your application notice. The information will not then be disclosed to any other person, except by order of the court.

If you withhold your address on the application notice, you should make sure that the reason you give for your application, any evidence set out in Part C, and any draft order or witness statement attached to your application does not include information that could lead to your address being disclosed.

Important: if you are intending to adopt the child to whom your application relates, please see note 5 below.

Note 3 → **The order you are asking the court to make**

State clearly what order you are seeking and, if possible, attach a draft.

Important:
- if you are making an application under section 26(3)(f) of the Adoption and Children Act 2002 (seeking an order giving permission to apply for contact with a child who an adoption agency has placed for adoption or is authorised to place for adoption), **you must also attach a draft of your application form for a contact order (Form A53);**
- if you are making an application under section 42(6) of the Adoption and Children Act 2002 (seeking an order giving permission to apply for an adoption order before the child you are intending to adopt has lived with you for the period required under the Act) **you must also attach to your application notice an additional sheet giving the details required in paragraph 2.2 of the Practice Direction to Part 9 of the Family Procedure (Adoption) Rules 2005.**

Note 4 → **Reasons for your application**

Briefly set out why you are seeking the order. Include material facts on which you rely, identifying any rule or statutory provision.

Note 5 → **Prospective adopters**

If you are intending to adopt the child to whom your application relates and you do not want your identity to be made known to the child's parents or guardians, the court will issue you with a serial number. Any documents sent to the parents/guardians will show the serial number, not your personal details. If you are required to attend the same court hearing, the court will make arrangements to ensure that your identity is protected.

If you have already been given a serial number in other proceedings relating to the child, please enter the serial number in the space provided.

You should still give the details of your address on this application notice, as they will be needed by the court.

If you wish your identity to be kept confidential, you should make sure that the reason you give for your application, any evidence set out in Part C, and any draft order or witness statement attached to your application does not include information that could lead to your identity being disclosed.

Application for injunction
(General form)

Name of court	
Case no.	
Applicant's name or serial no.	
Respondent's name and ref.	

☐ By application in pending proceedings
☐ Under Statutory provision _____

Tick whichever box applies and specify legislation where appropriate

Does this application raise issues under the Human Rights Act 1998? ☐ Yes ☐ No

The applicant[1] _____

(1) Enter the full name of the person making the application

applies to the court for an injunction order in the following terms:

That the respondent[2] _____

(2) Enter the full name of the person the injunction is to be directed to

be forbidden (whether by himself or by instructing or encouraging any other person[3])

(3) Set out here the proposed terms of the injunction order

And that the respondent[4]

(4) Set out here any proposed mandatory orders requiring acts to be done

And that[5]

(5) Set out here any further terms asked for including provision for costs

The grounds of this application are set out in the written evidence of[6]

(6) Enter the names of all persons who have sworn affidavits or signed a statement in support of this application

sworn (signed) on

FP3 - Application for injunction (General form) (12.05) HMCS

This written evidence is served with this application.

This application is to be served upon [7]

> [7] Enter the names and addresses of all persons upon whom it is intended to serve this application.

This application is filed by [8]

(the solicitors for) the applicant whose address for service is

> [8] Enter the full name and address for service and delete as required.

Signed _____ Dated _____

This section to be completed by the court

To*

of

* Name and address of the person application is directed to

This application will be heard by the (District) Judge

at

on (date)   Time

If you do not attend at the time shown the court may make an injunction order in your absence

If you do not fully understand this application you should go to a Solicitor, Legal Advice Centre or a Citizen's Advice Bureau

Acknowledgment of service
Application under Part 10 of the Family Procedure (Adoption) Rules

Name of court	
Case no./ Serial no.	
Name of child	

You should read the 'notes for respondent' attached to the application form which will tell you how to complete this form, and when and where to send it.

Tick and complete sections A - F as appropriate.
In all cases you must complete sections G and H

Section A

☐ I **do not** intend to contest this application

Give details of any order, direction, etc. you are seeking from the court.

Section B

☐ I intend to contest this application

Give brief details of any different remedy you are seeking.

Section C

☐ I intend to dispute the court's jurisdiction
(Please note, any application must be filed within 14 days of the date on which you file this acknowledgment of service)

FP5 Acknowledgment of service (12.05)   HMCS

	Case no./ serial no.	

Section D

☐ I object to the applicant issuing under this procedure

My reasons for objecting are:

Section E

☐ I intend to rely on written evidence, which is filed with this form.

Section F

The name and address of my solicitor is

Name of solicitor	
Name of firm	
Address (including postcode)	

Telephone no.		Fax no.	
DX no.			
E-mail address			

Section G

Full name of respondent
filing this acknowledgment _____

Section H

Signed
(To be signed by you or by your solicitor or litigation friend)

*(I believe)(The respondent believes) that the facts stated in this form are true.
*I am duly authorised by the respondent to sign this statement.

*delete as appropriate

Date

Certificate of service

Name of court	
Case no./ Serial no.	
Name of child	

On the .... *(insert date)*

the .... *(insert title or description of documents served)*

a copy of which is attached to this notice was served on
(insert name of person served, including position e.g. manager, director, if appropriate)

....

Tick as appropriate

- [ ] by first class post
- [ ] by Document Exchange
- [ ] by delivering at the address given below *(see notes overleaf)*
- [ ] by personally handing it to *(please specify)*
- [ ] by other means permitted by the court *(please specify)*

at *(insert address where service effected, include DX number)*

being the [ ] applicant's [ ] respondent's [ ] solicitor's [ ] litigation friend's:

- [ ] usual residence
- [ ] last known residence
- [ ] place of business
- [ ] principal place of business
- [ ] principal office of the company
- [ ] other *(please specify)*

The date of service is therefore deemed to be .... *(insert date - see overleaf for guidance)*

I believe that the facts stated in this Certificate are true.

Print full name

Signed
(Applicant)(Respondent)('s solicitor)('s litigation friend)

Position or office held
(if signing on behalf of firm or company)

Date

FP6 Certificate of service (12.05)   HMCS

Certificate of service - Notes for guidance

Please note that these notes are only a guide and are not exhaustive.
If you are in doubt you should refer to Part 6 of the Family Procedure (Adoption) Rules 2005.

Where to serve

Nature of party to be served	Place of service
Individual	Usual or last known residence
Legal representative	Usual place of business or last known place of business
Corporation (incorporated in England and Wales) other than a company	Principal office of the corporation
Company registered in England and Wales	Principal office of the company; or any place of business of the company within the jurisdiction which has a real connection with the case

Personal Service – A document is served personally on an individual by leaving it with that individual. Where a legal representative is authorised to accept service on behalf of a party, sevice must be effected on the legal representative, unless otherwise ordered.

Deemed Service – (Part 6 of the Family Procedure (Adoption) Rules 2005). A document which is served in accordance with these rules or any relevant practice direction shall be deemed to be served on the day shown in the following table.

Method of service	Deemed day of service
First class post	The second day after it was posted
Document exchange	The second day after it was left at the document exchange
Delivering the document to, or leaving it at, an address	The day after it was delivered to or left at the address

- If a document (other than an application form) is served personally after 5 p.m. on a business day, or at any time on a Saturday, Sunday or a bank holiday, the document shall, for the purpose of calculating any period of time after service of the document, be treated as having been served on the next business day.

- In this context 'business day' means any day except Saturday, Sunday or a bank holiday; and 'bank holiday' includes Christmas Day and Good Friday.

Service of documents on children and patients – The rules relating to service on children and patients are contained in Part 6 of the Family Procedure (Adoption) Rules 2005.

Notice of change of solicitor

Note: You should tick either box **A** or **B** as appropriate. Complete details as necessary.

Name of court	
Case no.	
Name of applicant or serial no.	
Respondent	

I (We) give notice that

A ☐ my solicitor (insert name and address)

has ceased to act for me and I shall now be acting in person.

B ☐ we (insert name of solicitor)

have been instructed to act on behalf of the (applicant)(respondent) in this application
(in place of (insert name and address of previous solicitors))

Solicitor's address to which documents should be sent (including any reference)

Name of solicitor	
Name of firm	
Address (including postcode)	

Telephone no.		Fax no.	
DX no.			
E-mail address			

Signed		Position or office held	
(Applicant)(Respondent)('s solicitor)('s litigation friend)		If signing on behalf of firm	

Dated

FP8 Notice of change of solicitor (12.05)   HMCS

Certificate of suitability of litigation friend

Name of court	
Case no.	
Serial no.	

If you are acting
- **for a child**, you must serve a copy of the completed form on a parent or guardian of the child, or if there is no parent or guardian, the carer or the person with whom the child lives.
- **for a patient**, you must serve a copy of the completed form on the person authorised under Part VII of the Mental Health Act 1983 or, if no person is authorised, the carer or person with whom the patient lives unless you **are** that person. You must also complete a certificate of service (obtainable from the court office).

You should send the completed form to the court when you take the first step in the proceedings on behalf of the child or patient, together with the certificate of service (if applicable).

You do not need to complete this form if you do have an authorisation under Part VII of the Mental Health Act 1983 to conduct legal proceedings on the person's behalf.

I consent to act as litigation friend for

_____

the (applicant) (respondent)

I believe that the above named person is a

☐ child   ☐ patient *(give your reasons overleaf and attach a copy of any medical evidence in support)*

I am able to conduct proceedings on behalf of the above named person competently and fairly and I have no interests adverse to those of the above named person.

I undertake to pay any costs which the above named person may be ordered to pay in these proceedings, subject to any right I may have to be repaid from the assets of that person.

☐ Mr   ☐ Mrs   ☐ Miss
☐ Ms   ☐ Other _____

Please write your name in capital letters

Surname

_____

Forenames

_____

Address to which documents in this case are to be sent.

I certify that the information given in this form is correct

Signed _____

Dated _____

FP9 Certificate of suitability of litigation friend (12.05)   HMCS

Case no.	
Serial no.	

My reasons for believing that the (applicant)(respondent) is a patient are:-

Witness Summons

Name of court	
Case no.	
Applicant's name or serial no.	
Respondent's name and ref.	
Date issued	

To

You are summoned to attend at *(court address)*

on ☐ of ☐ at ☐ (am)(pm)

(and each following day of the hearing until the court tells you that you are no longer required.)

☐ to give evidence in respect of the above case

☐ to produce the following document(s) *(give details)*

The sum of £ ☐ is paid or offered to you with this summons. This is to cover your travelling expenses to and from court and includes an amount by way of compensation for loss of time.

This summons was issued on the application of the applicant (respondent) or the applicant's (respondent's) solicitor whose name, address and reference number is:

Do not ignore this summons

If you were offered money for travel expenses and compensation for loss of time, at the time it was served on you, you must –

- attend court on the date and time shown and/or produce documents as required by the summons; and
- take an oath or affirm as required for the purposes of answering questions about your evidence or the documents you have been asked to produce.

If you do not comply with this summons you will be liable, in county court proceedings, to a fine. In the High Court, disobedience of a witness summons is a contempt of court and you may be fined or imprisoned for contempt. You may also be liable to pay any wasted costs that arise because of your non-compliance.

If you wish to set aside or vary this witness summons, you may make an application to the court that issued it.

FP25 Witness Summons (12.05)   HMCS

Certificate of service

Case no.	
Serial no.	

I certify that the summons of which this is a true copy was served by posting to

_____ (the witness)

on _____ at the address stated on the summons in accordance with the request of the applicant or his/her solicitor.

I enclosed a payable order for £ _____ for the witness's expenses and compensation for loss of time.

Signed _____
      Officer of the Court

Parental Responsibility Agreement
Section 4(1)(b) Children Act 1989

Keep this form in a safe place
Date recorded at the Principal Registry of the Family Division:

Read the notes on the other side before you make this agreement.

This is a Parental Responsibility Agreement regarding

the Child   Full Name _____

                         Boy or Girl   Date of birth   Date of 18th birthday

Between
    the Mother   Name

                      Address

and   the Father   Name

                      Address

We declare that   we are the mother and father of the above child and we agree that the child's father shall have parental responsibility for the child (in addition to the mother having parental responsibility).

Signed **(Mother)**   Signed **(Father)**

Date   Date

Certificate of witness

The following evidence of identity was produced by the person signing above:

The following evidence of identity was produced by the person signing above:

Signed in the presence of:
Name of Witness

Signed in the presence of:
Name of Witness

Address

Address

Signature of Witness

Signature of Witness

[A Justice of the Peace] [Justices' Clerk] [An assistant to a justices' clerk] [An officer of the court authorised by the judge to administer oaths]

[A Justice of the Peace] [Justices' Clerk] [An assistant to a justices' clerk] [An Officer of the Court authorised by the judge to administer oaths]

C(PRA1) (12.05)   HMCS

Notes about the Parental Responsibility Agreement

Read these notes before you make the agreement.

About the Parental Responsibility Agreement

The making of this agreement will affect the legal position of the mother and the father. You should both seek legal advice before you make the Agreement. You can obtain the name and address of a solicitor from the Children Panel (020 7242 1222)

or from
- your local family proceedings court, or county court
- a Citizens Advice Bureau
- a Law Centre
- a local library.

You may be eligible for public funding.

When you fill in the Agreement

Please use black ink (the Agreement will be copied). Put the name of one child only. If the father is to have parental responsibility for more than one child, fill in a separate form for each child. **Do not sign the Agreement.**

When you have filled in the Agreement

Take it to a local family proceedings court, or county court, or the Principal Registry of the Family Division (the address is below).

A justice of the peace, a justices' clerk, an assistant to a justices' clerk, or a court official who is authorised by the judge to administer oaths, will witness your signature and he or she will sign the certificate of the witness. **A solicitor cannot witness your signature.**

To the mother: When you make the declaration you will have to prove that you are the child's mother so take to the court the child's full birth certificate.

You will also need evidence of your identity showing a photograph and signature (for example, a photocard, official pass or passport). **Please note that the child's birth certificate cannot be accepted as sufficient proof of your identity.**

To the father: You will need evidence of your identity showing a photograph and signature (for example, a photocard, official pass or passport).

When the Certificate has been signed and witnessed

Make 2 copies of the Agreement form. You do not need to copy these notes.

Take, or send, this form and the copies to **The Principal Registry of the Family Division, First Avenue House, 42-49 High Holborn, London, WC1V 6NP.**

The Registry will record the Agreement and keep this form. The copies will be stamped and sent back to each parent at the address on the Agreement. The Agreement will not take effect until it has been received and recorded at the Principal Registry of the Family Division.

Ending the Agreement

Once a parental responsibility agreement has been made it can only end
- by an order of the court made on the application of any person who has parental responsibility for the child
- by an order of the court made on the application of the child with permission of the court
- When the child reaches the age of 18.

C(PRA1) (Notes) (12.05)

… Forms

Step-Parent Parental Responsibility Agreement
Section 4A(1)(a) Children Act 1989

Keep this form in a safe place
Date recorded at the Principal Registry of the Family Division:

Read the notes on the other side before you make this agreement.

This is a Step-Parent Parental Responsibility Agreement regarding

the Child *Full Name* _____

Boy or Girl _____ *Date of birth* _____ *Date of 18th birthday* _____

Between
Parent A *Name* _____

Address _____

and
*****the other parent** *Name* _____
(with parental responsibility)
Address _____

and
the step-parent *Name* _____

Address _____

We declare that we are the parents and step-parent of the above child and we agree that the above mentioned step-parent shall have parental responsibility for the child (in addition to those already having parental responsibility).

Signed **(Parent A)**	*Signed **(Other Parent)**	Signed **(Step-Parent)**
Date	Date	Date

Certificate of witness

The following evidence of identity was produced by the person signing above:	The following evidence of identity was produced by the person signing above:	The following evidence of identity was produced by the person signing above:
Signed in the presence of: *Name of Witness*	Signed in the presence of: *Name of Witness*	Signed in the presence of: *Name of Witness*
Address	Address	Address
Signature of Witness	Signature of Witness	Signature of Witness
[A Justice of the Peace] [Justices' Clerk] [An assistant to a justices' clerk] [An Officer of the Court authorised by the judge to administer oaths]	[A Justice of the Peace] [Justices' Clerk] [An assistant to a justices' clerk] [An Officer of the Court authorised by the judge to administer oaths]	[A Justice of the Peace] [Justices' Clerk] [An assistant to a justices' clerk] [An Officer of the Court authorised by the judge to administer oaths]

*****If there is only one parent with parental responsibility, please delete this section.**

C(PRA2) (12.05)　　　　　　　　　　　　　　　　　　　　　　　　　　　　　　HMCS

Notes about the Step-Parent Parental Responsibility Form
Read these notes before you make the Agreement

About the Step-Parent Parental Responsibility Agreement

The making of this agreement will affect the legal position of the parent(s) and the step-parent. You should seek legal advice before you make the Agreement. You can obtain the name and address of a solicitor from the Children Panel (020 7242 1222) or from:

- your local family proceedings court, or county court,
- a Citizens Advice Bureau,
- a Law Centre,
- a local library.

You may be eligible for public funding.

When you fill in the Agreement

Please use black ink (the Agreement will be copied). Put the name of one child only. If the step-parent is to have parental responsibility for more than one child, fill in a separate form for each child. **Do not sign the Agreement.**

When you have filled in the Agreement

Take it to a local family proceedings court, or county court, or the Principal Registry of the Family Division (the address is below).

A justice of the peace, a justices' clerk, an assistant to a justices' clerk, or a court official who is authorised by the judge to administer oaths, will witness your signature and he or she will sign the certificate of the witness. **A solicitor cannot witness your signature.**

To Parent A and the Other Parent with parental responsibility:

When you make the declaration you will have to prove that you have parental responsibility for the child. You should therefore take with you to the court one of the following documents:

- the child's full birth certificate and a marriage certificate to show that the parents were married to each other at the time of birth or subsequently,
- a court order granting parental responsibility,
- a registered Parental Responsibility Agreement Form between the child's mother and father,
- if the birth was registered after the 1 December 2003, the child's full birth certificate showing that the parents jointly registered the child's birth.

C(PRA2) (Notes) (12.05)

You will also require evidence of your (both parents') identity showing a photograph and signature (for example, a photocard, official pass or passport) **(Please note that the child's birth certificate cannot be accepted as sufficient proof of your identity.)**

To the step-parent: When you make the declaration you will have to prove that you are married to, or the civil partner of, a parent of the child so take to the court your marriage certificate or certificate of civil partnership.

You will also need evidence of your identity showing a photograph and signature (for example, a photocard, official pass or passport).

When the Certificate has been signed and witnessed

Make sufficient copies of the Agreement Form for each person who has signed the form. You do not need to copy these notes.

Take, or send, the original form and the copies to:
The Principal Registry of the Family Division, First Avenue House, 42-49 High Holborn, London, WC1V 6NP.

The Registry will record the Agreement and retain the original form. The copies will be stamped with the seal of the court and sent back to every person with parental responsibility who has signed the Agreement Form and to the step-parent. The Agreement will not take effect until it has been received and recorded at the Principal Registry of the Family Division.

Ending the Agreement

Once a step-parent parental responsibility agreement has been made it can only end:

- by an order of the court made on the application of any person who has parental responsibility for the child,
- by an order of the court made on the application of the child with permission of the court,
- when the child reaches the age of 18.

Supplement for an application for a Special Guardianship Order
Section 14A Children Act 1989

Name of court	
Case no.	
Date issued	

Full name(s) of the child(ren)	Child(ren's) number(s)

1. Your relationship to the child(ren)

State whether
- you are a guardian
- you are a person in whose favour a residence order is in force (Section 14A (5)(b))
- you are a person with whom the child has lived for 3 out of the last 5 years
- you are a person who:
    - if a residence order is in force, has the consent of every person in whose favour the order was made
    - if the child is in the care of the local authority, the consent of that authority
    - in any other case, has the consent of every person with parental responsibility
- you are a local authority foster parent with whom the child has lived for a period of at least one year immediately preceding the application (Section 14A(5)(d))
- you are applying to the court for permission to make this application; or
- the court gave permission for you to apply for a special guardianship order. In this case please state the name of the court and the date of the order.

2. Notification to the Local Authority

Please state below the name of the local authority (if the child is looked after by a local authority, give details of that authority otherwise give the details of the local authority where you normally live). Give the date on which you notified them of your intention to make an application to the court for a special guardianship order (Section 14A(7)).

If you notified the local authority less than three months before making this application please state whether an application to adopt the child named above has been made; the name of the court in which the application is proceeding and, where known, the court case number.

C13A Supplement for an application for a Special Guardianship Order (12.05) HMCS

3. The reason(s) for the application:

State briefly your reasons for applying. Please only provide brief details, including brief details of any request you have made or will be making to the local authority for special guardianship support services. You may be asked to provide a full statement later.

4. Your plans for the child(ren)

Include
- details of any existing arrangements or arrangements you intend to make to allow the child(ren) contact with a parent, relative or other person (Section 14B(1)(a))
- details of any existing residence, contact, prohibited steps or specific issues order which you would like the court to vary or discharge (Section 14B(1)(b))
- any condition you will invite the court to impose pursuant to Section 14E(5) of the Children Act 1989

Signed _____   Date _____
(Applicant)

Appendix F

ADOPTION SUPPORT SERVICES REGULATIONS 2005, SI 2005/691

PART 1
INTRODUCTORY

1 Citation, commencement and application

(1) These Regulations may be cited as the Adoption Support Services Regulations 2005 and shall come into force on 30 December 2005.

(2) These Regulations apply to England only.

2 Interpretation

(1) In these Regulations –

'the Act' means the Adoption and Children Act 2002;
'adoptive child' means –
  (a) a child who has been adopted or in respect of whom a person has given notice of his intention to adopt under section 44 of the Act; or
  (b) a child whom an adoption agency has matched with a prospective adopter or placed for adoption;
'adoptive parent' means –
  (a) a person who has adopted a child or has given notice under section 44 of the Act of his intention to adopt a child; or
  (b) a person with whom an adoption agency has matched a child or has placed a child for adoption;
'agency adoptive child' means –
  (a) a child who has been adopted after having been placed for adoption by an adoption agency; or
  (b) a child whom an adoption agency has matched with a prospective adopter or placed for adoption;
  (c) a child whose adoptive parent has been a local authority foster parent in relation to him (unless the local authority oppose the adoption);
'child' means (subject to paragraph (2)) a person who has not attained the age of 18;
'income support' means income support under Part VII of the Social Security Contributions and Benefits Act 1992;
'jobseeker's allowance' has the same meaning as in the Jobseekers Act 1995;
'local authority foster parent' has the same meaning as in the Children Act 1989;
'local education authority' has the same meaning as in the Education Act 1996;
'Local Health Board' means a Local Health Board established by the National Assembly for Wales under section 16BA of the National Health Service Act 1977;

'Primary Care Trust' means a Primary Care Trust established under section 16A of the National Health Service Act 1977;

'related person' in relation to an adoptive child means –
  (a) a relative within the meaning of section 144(1) of the Act; or
  (b) any person with whom the adoptive child has a relationship which appears to the local authority to be beneficial to the welfare of the child having regard to the matters referred to in sub-paragraphs (i) to (iii) of section 1(4)(f) of the Act;

'tax credit' has the same meaning as in the Tax Credits Act 2002;

(2) In any case where –
  (a) a person has attained the age of 18 years and is in full-time education or training; and
  (b) immediately before he attained the age of 18 years –
    (i) he was an adoptive child; and
    (ii) financial support was payable in relation to him,

the definition of 'child' shall, for the purposes of the continued provision of financial support and any review of financial support, have effect in relation to him as if he had not attained the age of 18 years.

(3) For the purposes of these Regulations a child has been matched with a prospective adopter if an adoption agency is considering placing the child for adoption with that person.

PART 2

PROVISION OF ADOPTION SUPPORT SERVICES

3 Prescribed services

(1) For the purposes of section 2(6)(b) of the Act the following services are prescribed as adoption support services (in addition to counselling, advice and information) –

  (a) financial support payable under Part 3;
  (b) services to enable groups of adoptive children, adoptive parents and natural parents or former guardians of an adoptive child to discuss matters relating to adoption;
  (c) assistance, including mediation services, in relation to arrangements for contact between an adoptive child and a natural parent, natural sibling, former guardian or a related person of the adoptive child;
  (d) services in relation to the therapeutic needs of an adoptive child;
  (e) assistance for the purpose of ensuring the continuance of the relationship between an adoptive child and his adoptive parent, including –
    (i) training for adoptive parents for the purpose of meeting any special needs of the child; and
    (ii) subject to paragraph (4), respite care;
  (f) assistance where disruption of an adoptive placement, or of an adoption arrangement following the making of an adoption order, has occurred or is in danger of occurring, including –
    (i) making arrangements for the provision of mediation services; and
    (ii) organising and running meetings to discuss disruptions in such placements or arrangements.

(2) The services prescribed in paragraph (1) do not include any services that might be provided in the case of an adoption of a child by his natural parent or the partner of his natural parent.

(3) The services prescribed in paragraph (1)(b) to (f) may include giving assistance in cash.

(4) For the purposes of paragraph (1)(e)(ii) respite care that consists of the provision of accommodation must be accommodation provided by or on behalf of a local authority under section 23 of the Children Act 1989 (accommodation of looked after children) or by a voluntary organisation under section 59 of that Act.

4 Persons to whom adoption support services must be extended

(1) This regulation prescribes, for the purposes of section 3(3)(a) of the Act, the description of persons to whom the provision of adoption support services must be extended.

(2) Counselling, advice and information must extend to –

   (a) children who may be adopted, their parents and guardians;
   (b) persons wishing to adopt a child;
   (c) adopted persons, their parents, natural parents and former guardians;
   (d) children of adoptive parents (whether or not adopted);
   (e) children who are natural siblings (whether full or half-blood) of an adoptive child;
   (f) related persons in relation to adoptive children.

(3) Financial support under Part 3 must extend to an adoptive parent of an agency adoptive child.

(4) The services mentioned in regulation 3(1)(b) (services to enable discussion) must extend to –

   (a) an adoptive parent of an agency adoptive child;
   (b) an agency adoptive child;
   (c) a natural parent or former guardian of an agency adoptive child.

(5) The services mentioned in regulation 3(1)(c) (contact) must extend to –

   (a) an adoptive parent of an agency adoptive child;
   (b) an agency adoptive child;
   (c) a child who is the natural sibling (whether full or half-blood) of an adoptive child;
   (d) a natural parent, former guardian or related person in relation to an agency adoptive child.

(6) The services mentioned in regulation 3(1)(d) (therapeutic services) must extend to –

   (a) an agency adoptive child;
   (b) an adoptive child in circumstances where the restrictions in section 83 of the Act (restrictions on bringing children in) apply;
   (c) an adoptive child in the case of a Convention adoption.

(7) The services mentioned in regulation 3(1)(e) to (f) (services to ensure continuation of a relationship and services to assist in cases of disruption) must extend to –

   (a) a child mentioned in paragraph (6);
   (b) an adoptive parent of such a child;
   (c) a child of such an adoptive parent (whether or not adopted).

5 Arrangement for securing provision of services

(1) The following persons are prescribed for the purposes of section 3(4)(b) of the Act (persons other than registered adoption societies who may provide the requisite facilities) in relation to the provision of adoption support services –

(a) another local authority;
(b) a registered adoption support agency;
(c) a Local Health Board or Primary Care Trust; and
(d) a local education authority.

(2) In paragraph (1) 'registered adoption support agency' means an adoption support agency in respect of which a person is registered under Part 2 of the Care Standards Act 2000.

6 Adoption support services adviser

(1) The local authority must appoint a person (an 'adoption support services adviser') to carry out the functions specified in paragraph (2).

(2) The functions of the adoption support services adviser are to –

(a) give advice and information to persons who may be affected by the adoption or proposed adoption of a child, including as to –
  (i) services that may be appropriate to those persons; and
  (ii) how those services may be made available to them;
(b) give advice, information and assistance to the local authority which appointed him, including as to –
  (i) the assessment of needs for adoption support services in accordance with Part 4;
  (ii) the availability of adoption support services;
  (iii) the preparation of plans required under section 4(5) of the Act; and
(c) consult with, and give advice, information and assistance to, another local authority where appropriate.

(3) The local authority must not appoint a person as an adoption support services adviser unless they are satisfied that his knowledge and experience of –

(a) the process of adoption; and
(b) the effect of the adoption of a child on persons likely to be affected by the adoption, is sufficient for the purposes of the work that he is to perform.

7 Services for persons outside the area

(1) Section 4 of the Act applies to a local authority in respect of the following persons who are outside the authority's area –

(a) an agency adoptive child whom the authority has placed for adoption or who has been adopted after being placed for adoption by the authority;
(b) an adoptive parent of such a child;
(c) a child of such an adoptive parent (whether or not adopted).

(2) But section 4 ceases to apply at the end of the period of three years from the date of the adoption order except in relation to any financial support provided by the local authority where the decision to provide that support was made before the adoption.

(3) Nothing in this regulation prevents a local authority from providing adoption support services to persons outside their area where they consider it appropriate to do so.

PART 3

PROVISION OF FINANCIAL SUPPORT

8 Circumstances in which financial support is payable

(1) Financial support is payable under this Part to an adoptive parent for the purpose of supporting the placement of the adoptive child or the continuation of adoption arrangements after an adoption order is made.

(2) Such support is payable only in the following circumstances –

   (a) where it is necessary to ensure that the adoptive parent can look after the child;
   (b) where the child needs special care which requires greater expenditure of resources by reason of illness, disability, emotional or behavioural difficulties or the continuing consequences of past abuse or neglect;
   (c) where it is necessary for the local authority to make any special arrangements to facilitate the placement or the adoption by reason of –
      (i) the age or ethnic origin of the child; or
      (ii) the desirability of the child being placed with the same adoptive parent as his brother or sister (whether of full or half-blood) or with a child with whom he previously shared a home;
   (d) where such support is to meet recurring costs in respect of travel for the purpose of visits between the child and a related person;
   (e) where the local authority consider it appropriate to make a contribution to meet the following kinds of expenditure –
      (i) expenditure on legal costs, including fees payable to a court in relation to an adoption;
      (ii) expenditure for the purpose of introducing an adoptive child to his adoptive parent;
      (iii) expenditure necessary for the purpose of accommodating and maintaining the child, including the provision of furniture and domestic equipment, alterations to and adaptations of the home, provision of means of transport and provision of clothing, toys and other items necessary for the purpose of looking after the child.

9 Remuneration for former foster parents

(1) Financial support under this Part may include an element of remuneration but only where the decision to include it is taken before the adoption order is made and the local authority consider it to be necessary to facilitate the adoption in a case where –

   (a) the adoptive parent has been a local authority foster parent in respect of the child; and
   (b) an element of remuneration was included in the payments made by the local authority to the adoptive parent in relation to his fostering the child.

(2) But that element of remuneration ceases to be payable at the end of the period of two years from the adoption order unless the local authority consider its continuation to be necessary having regard to the exceptional needs of the child or any other exceptional circumstances.

10 Payment of financial support

Financial support under this Part may be paid –

   (a) periodically, if it is provided to meet a need which is likely to give rise to recurring expenditure; or

(b) in any other case, by a single payment or, if the local authority and adoptive parent agree, by instalments.

11 Cessation of financial support

Financial support ceases to be payable to an adoptive parent if –

(a) the child ceases to have a home with him;
(b) the child ceases full-time education or training and commences employment;
(c) the child qualifies for income support or jobseeker's allowance in his own right; or
(d) the child attains the age of 18 unless he continues in full-time education or training, when it may continue until the end of the course or training he is then undertaking.

12 Conditions

(1) Where financial support is to be paid periodically, it is not payable until the adoptive parent or, in the case of adoption by a couple, each adoptive parent, has agreed to the following conditions –

(a) that he will inform the local authority immediately if –
   (i) he changes his address;
   (ii) the child dies;
   (iii) any of the changes mentioned in regulation 11 (cessation of financial support) occurs; or
   (iv) there is a change in his financial circumstances or the financial needs or resources of the child which may affect the amount of financial support payable to him,
and, where the information is given orally, that he will confirm it in writing within seven days;
(b) that he will complete and supply the local authority with an annual statement as to the following matters –
   (i) his financial circumstances;
   (ii) the financial needs and resources of the child;
   (iii) his address and whether the child still has a home with him.

(2) The local authority may provide financial support subject to any other conditions they consider appropriate, including the timescale within which and purposes for which any payment of financial support should be utilised.

(3) Subject to paragraph (4), where any condition imposed in accordance with this regulation is not complied with, the local authority may –

(a) suspend or terminate payment of financial support; and
(b) seek to recover all or part of the financial support they have paid.

(4) Where the condition not complied with is a failure to provide an annual statement in accordance with an agreement referred to in paragraph (1), the local authority shall not take any steps under paragraph (3) until –

(a) they have sent to the person who entered into the agreement a written reminder of the need to provide an annual statement; and
(b) 28 days have expired since the date on which that notice was sent.

PART 4

ASSESSMENTS AND PLANS

13 Request for assessment

(1) The following persons are prescribed for the purposes of section 4(1)(b) of the Act (persons at whose request an assessment must be carried out) –

- (a) a child of an adoptive parent (whether or not adopted);
- (b) a child who is the natural sibling (whether full or half-blood) of an adoptive child;
- (c) a related person in relation to an adoptive child.

(2) Where the request of a person falling within section 4(1)(a) of the Act or paragraph (1) for an assessment relates to a particular adoption support service, or it appears to the local authority that the person's needs for adoption support services may be adequately assessed by reference to a particular adoption support service, the local authority may carry out the assessment by reference only to that service.

(3) In assessing a person's needs for adoption support services the local authority are not required to assess the person's need for a service if he is not within the description of persons to whom provision of the service must be extended by virtue of regulation 4.

14 Procedure for assessment

(1) Where the local authority carry out an assessment of a person's needs for adoption support services they must have regard to such of the following considerations as are relevant to the assessment –

- (a) the needs of the person being assessed and how these might be met;
- (b) the needs of the adoptive family and how these might be met;
- (c) the needs, including developmental needs, of the adoptive child and how these might be met;
- (d) the parenting capacity of the adoptive parent;
- (e) wider family and environmental factors;
- (f) in the case of a child who is, or was, placed for adoption or matched for adoption, the circumstances that led to the child being so placed or matched; and
- (g) any previous assessment of needs for adoption support services undertaken in relation to the person in question.

(2) In paragraph (1) 'adoptive family' means the family consisting of the adoptive child, the adoptive parents and any other child of the adoptive parents (whether or not adopted).

(3) The local authority must –

- (a) where they consider it appropriate to do so, interview the person and, where the person is an adoptive child, his adoptive parents; and
- (b) prepare a written report of the assessment.

(4) Where it appears to the local authority that the person may have a need for services from a Primary Care Trust, a Local Health Board or a local education authority, the local authority shall, as part of the assessment, consult that Primary Care Trust, Local Health Board or local education authority.

15 Assessment for financial support

(1) This regulation applies where the local authority carry out an assessment of a person's needs for financial support.

(2) In determining the amount of financial support, the local authority must take account of any other grant, benefit, allowance or resource which is available to the person in respect of his needs as a result of the adoption of the child.

(3) Subject to paragraphs (4) and (5) the local authority must also take account of the following considerations –

(a) the person's financial resources, including any tax credit or benefit, which would be available to him if the child lived with him;
(b) the amount required by the person in respect of his reasonable outgoings and commitments (excluding outgoings in respect of the child);
(c) the financial needs and resources of the child.

(4) The local authority must disregard the considerations in paragraph (3) where they are considering providing financial support in respect of –

(a) legal costs, including fees payable to a court, where an adoption order is applied for in respect of an agency adoptive child; or
(b) expenditure for the purpose of introducing an agency adoptive child to his adoptive parents.

(5) The local authority may disregard any of the considerations in paragraph (3) –

(a) where they are considering providing financial support in respect of –
   (i) initial costs of accommodating an agency adoptive child;
   (ii) recurring costs in respect of travel for the purpose of visits between the child and a related person; or
   (iii) any special arrangements or special care referred to in regulation 8(2)(b) or (c) in relation to an agency adoptive child; or
(b) where they are considering including an element of remuneration under regulation 9.

16 Plan

(1) This regulation applies in relation to the requirement in section 4(5) of the Act for the local authority to prepare a plan in accordance with which adoption support services are to be provided.

(2) The local authority must prepare a plan if they propose to provide adoption support services to a person on more than one occasion and the services are not limited to the provision of advice or information.

(3) Where it appears to the local authority that the person may have a need for services from a Primary Care Trust, a Local Health Board or a local education authority, they must consult that Primary Care Trust, Local Health Board or local education authority before preparing the plan.

(4) The local authority must nominate a person to monitor the provision of the services in accordance with the plan.

17 Notice of proposal to provide adoption support services

(1) Before making any decision under section 4(4) of the Act as to whether to provide adoption support services, the local authority must allow the person an opportunity to make representations in accordance with this regulation.

(2) The local authority must first give the person notice of the proposed decision and the time allowed for making representations.

(3) The notice must contain the following information –

(a) a statement as to the person's needs for adoption support services;
(b) where the assessment relates to his need for financial support, the basis upon which financial support is determined;
(c) whether the local authority propose to provide him with adoption support services;
(d) the services (if any) that are proposed to be provided to him;
(e) if financial support is to be paid to him, the proposed amount that would be payable; and
(f) any proposed conditions under regulation 12(2).

(4) In a case where the local authority propose to provide adoption support services and are required to prepare a plan under section 4(5) of the Act, the notice must be accompanied by a draft of that plan.

(5) The local authority shall not make a decision until –

(a) the person has made representations to the local authority or notified the local authority that he is satisfied with the proposed decision and, where applicable, the draft plan; or
(b) the period of time for making representations has expired.

18 Notification of decision as to adoption support services

(1) After making their decision under section 4(4) of the Act as to whether to provide adoption support services to a person, the local authority must give the person notice of that decision, including the reasons for it.

(2) Where the local authority are required to prepare a plan under section 4(5) of the Act, the notice must include details of that plan and the person nominated under regulation 16(4).

(3) If the local authority decide that financial support is to be provided, notice given under paragraph (1) must include the following information –

(a) the method of the determination of the amount of financial support;
(b) where financial support is to be paid in instalments or periodically –
    (i) the amount of financial support;
    (ii) the frequency with which the payment will be made;
    (iii) the period for which financial support is to be paid;
    (iv) when the first payment of financial support is to be made.
(c) where financial support is to be paid as a single payment, when the payment is to be made;
(d) where financial support is to be paid subject to any conditions imposed in accordance with regulation 12, those conditions, the date (if any) by which the conditions are to be met and the consequences of failing to meet the conditions;
(e) the arrangements and procedure for review, variation and termination of financial support;
(f) the responsibilities of –
    (i) the local authority under Part 5 (reviews); and
    (ii) the adoptive parent pursuant to any agreement mentioned in regulation 12.

PART 5
REVIEWS

19 Reviews: general procedure

(1) This regulation applies where the local authority provide adoption support services for a person other than financial support payable periodically.

(2) The local authority must review the provision of such services –

(a) if any change in the person's circumstances which may affect the provision of adoption support services comes to their notice;
(b) at such stage in the implementation of the plan as they consider appropriate;
(c) in any event, at least annually.

(3) Regulations 14 and 15 apply in relation to a review under this regulation as they apply in relation to an assessment under Part 4.

(4) If the local authority propose to vary or terminate the provision of adoption support services to any person, before making any decision as a result of the review, they must give the person an opportunity to make representations and for that purpose they must give him notice of the proposed decision and the time allowed for making representations.

(5) The notice must contain the information mentioned in regulation 17(3) and, if the local authority propose to revise the plan, a draft of the revised plan.

(6) The local authority shall, having regard to the review and after considering any representations received within the period specified in the notice –

(a) decide whether to vary or terminate the provision of adoption support services for the person; and
(b) where appropriate, revise the plan.

(7) The local authority must give the person notice of their decision (including the reasons for it) and, if applicable, details of the revised plan.

20 Review of financial support payable periodically

(1) This regulation applies where the local authority provide financial support payable periodically.

(2) The local authority shall review the financial support –

(a) annually, on receipt of the statement from the adoptive parent mentioned in regulation 12;
(b) if any relevant change of circumstances or any breach of a condition mentioned in regulation 12 comes to their notice;
(c) at any stage in the implementation of the plan that they consider appropriate.

(3) In paragraph (2) a relevant change of circumstances is any of the changes that the adoptive parent has agreed to notify under regulation 12.

(4) Regulations 14 and 15 apply in relation to a review under this regulation as they apply in relation to an assessment under Part 4.

(5) If the local authority propose, as a result of the review, to reduce or terminate financial support or revise the plan, before making that decision the local authority must give the person

an opportunity to make representations and for that purpose they must give the person notice of the proposed decision and the time allowed for making representations.

(6) But paragraph (5) does not prevent the local authority from suspending financial support pending that decision.

(7) The notice must contain the information mentioned in regulation 17(3) and, if applicable, a draft of the revised plan.

(8) The local authority must, having regard to the review, and after considering any representations received within the period specified in the notice –

   (a) decide whether to vary or terminate payment of the financial support or whether to seek to recover all or part of any financial support that has been paid; and
   (b) where appropriate, revise the plan.

(9) The local authority must give the person notice of their decision including the reasons for it and, if applicable, the revised plan.

PART 6

MISCELLANEOUS

21 Urgent cases

Where any requirement applicable to the local authority under these Regulations in relation to carrying out an assessment, preparing a plan or giving notice would delay the provision of a service in a case of urgency, that requirement does not apply.

22 Notices

(1) Any notice required to be given under these Regulations must be given in writing.

(2) If the person to whom notice is to be given is a child and –

   (a) it appears to the local authority that the child is not of sufficient age and understanding for it to be appropriate to give him such notice; or
   (b) in all the circumstances it is not appropriate to give him such notice,

the notice must be given to his adoptive parent or to the adult that the local authority consider most appropriate.

23 Recovery of expenses between local authorities

(1) Subject to paragraph (2), where a local authority ('the recovering authority') provide adoption support services to any person following a request under section 4(10) of the Act from another local authority ('the paying authority'), the recovering authority may recover the expenses of providing those services from the paying authority.

(2) Paragraph (1) shall not apply where –

   (a) the recovering authority are, by virtue of regulation 7, a local authority to which section 4 of the Act applies in respect of the person referred to in paragraph (1); or
   (b) the service provided by the recovering authority is advice or information under section 2(6)(a) of the Act.

24 Revocations and transitional provision

(1) Subject to paragraph (3), the Adoption Allowance Regulations 1991 and the Adoption Support Services (Local Authorities) (England) Regulations 2003 ('the 2003 Regulations') shall be revoked.

(2) This paragraph applies where immediately before the date on which these Regulations come into force –

(a) an assessment had been requested, was being prepared or was in place;
(b) a plan was being prepared or was in place;
(c) a review was being arranged or was underway; or
(d) an adoption support service was being provided,

under the 2003 Regulations.

(3) Where paragraph (2) applies, the assessment, plan, review or adoption support service referred to in that paragraph shall, from the date these Regulations come into force, be treated as an assessment, plan, review or adoption support service under these Regulations.

EXPLANATORY NOTE

(This note is not part of the Regulations)

These Regulations make provision for local authorities in England to provide adoption support services as part of the service maintained by them under section 3(1) of the Adoption and Children Act 2002 ('The Act').

Part 2 deals with the provision of adoption support services, which are defined by section 2(6) of the Act as counselling, advice and information, and other services prescribed by regulations, in relation to adoption. Such services are prescribed by regulation 3 and include financial support (as required by section 2(7) of the Act). The services must be extended to the classes of person specified in regulation 4 and their provision may be secured from the persons specified in regulation 5. Local authorities are required to appoint an adoption support services adviser to give advice and information to them and to persons who may be affected by the adoption of a child (regulation 6). Regulation 7 provides for services to persons outside the local authority's area.

Part 3 deals with financial support. It may only be paid in the circumstances specified in regulation 8. It may only include a remuneration element where paid to a former local authority foster parent (regulation 9). Regulations 10 to 12 provide for payment of financial support, circumstances in which financial support ceases and conditions that may be imposed.

Part 4 deals with the assessment of a person's needs for adoption support services, plans for provision of services and notifications of proposals and decisions in relation to the provision of services.

Part 5 deals with reviews of adoption support services.

Part 6 contains miscellaneous provisions, including a general exception from giving notice etc. in cases of urgency (regulation 21), service of notices (regulation 22) and recovery of expenses between authorities (regulation 23). Regulation 24 revokes the Adoption Allowance Regulations 1991 and the Adoption Support Services (Local Authorities) (England) Regulations 2003 and makes transitional provision.

A Regulatory Impact Assessment has been carried out for these Regulations and a copy has been placed in the library of each House of Parliament. Copies of the Regulatory Impact Assessment can be obtained from the Department for Education and Skills' website http://www.dfes.gov.uk/ria/.

Appendix G

THE INDEPENDENT REVIEW OF DETERMINATIONS (ADOPTION) REGULATIONS 2005, SI 2005/3332

PART 1
GENERAL

1 Citation, commencement and application

(1) These Regulations may be cited as the Independent Review of Determinations (Adoption) Regulations 2005 and shall come into force on 30 December 2005.

(2) These Regulations apply to England only.

2 Interpretation

In these Regulations –

'the Act' means the Adoption and Children Act 2002;
'the Agencies Regulations' means the Adoption Agencies Regulations 2005;
'adoption panel' means a panel constituted in accordance with regulation 3 of the Agencies Regulations;
'applicant' means –
  (a) in the case of a suitability determination, a prospective adopter;
  (b) in the case of a disclosure determination, a relevant person within the meaning of regulation 15(7) of the Disclosure Regulations;
'the central list' shall be construed in accordance with regulation 4;
'disclosure determination' means a qualifying determination described in regulation 15(1) of the Disclosure Regulations;
'the Disclosure Regulations' means the Disclosure of Adoption Information (Post-Commencement Adoptions) Regulations 2005;
'panel' means a panel constituted in accordance with regulation 4(1);
'prospective adopter's report' means a report prepared in accordance with regulation 25 of the Agencies Regulations;
'qualifying determination' means a determination described in regulation 3 of these Regulations or regulation 15(1) of the Disclosure Regulations for the purposes of section 12(2) of the Act;
'review meeting' means a meeting convened in accordance with regulation 11 for the purposes of reviewing a qualifying determination;
'social worker' means a person who is registered as a social worker in a register maintained by the General Social Care Council or the Care Council for Wales under section 56 of the Care Standards Act 2000 or in a corresponding register maintained under the law of Scotland or Northern Ireland; and

'suitability determination' means a qualifying determination described in regulation 3.

3 Qualifying determination for the purposes of section 12(2) of the Act

A determination made by an adoption agency in accordance with regulation 27(4) of the Agencies Regulations that the adoption agency does not propose to approve a prospective adopter as suitable to adopt a child is a qualifying determination for the purposes of section 12(2) of the Act.

PART 2

PANELS

4 Constitution and membership of panels

(1) The Secretary of State shall, on receipt of an application made by an applicant in accordance with regulation 10, constitute a panel for the purpose of reviewing the qualifying determination.

(2) The members of the panel shall be appointed by the Secretary of State from a list of persons ('the central list') kept by the Secretary of State.

(3) The members of the central list shall include –

(a) social workers who have at least three years' post-qualifying experience in child care social work, including direct experience in adoption work;
(b) registered medical practitioners; and
(c) other persons who are considered by the Secretary of State to be suitable as members including, where reasonably practicable, persons with personal experience of adoption.

(4) Where the qualifying determination being reviewed is a suitability determination, the maximum number of people who may be appointed to a panel is ten and the panel shall include at least –

(a) two persons falling within paragraph (3)(a);
(b) one person falling within paragraph (3)(b); and
(c) four other persons falling within paragraph (3)(c) including where reasonably practicable at least two persons with personal experience of adoption.

(5) Where the qualifying determination being reviewed is a disclosure determination, the number of people who shall be appointed to a panel is three and the panel shall include at least two persons falling within paragraph (3)(a).

(6) The Secretary of State shall –

(a) appoint to chair the panel a person who has the skills and experience necessary for chairing a panel; and
(b) in the case of a panel constituted to review a suitability determination, appoint one of the members of the panel as vice chair to act as chair if the person appointed to chair the panel is absent or if the office of chair is vacant.

(7) A person shall not be appointed to a panel if –

(a) he is a member of the adoption panel of the adoption agency that made the qualifying determination;
(b) where the adoption agency which made the qualifying determination is a local authority

he is, or has been within the period of one year prior to the date on which the qualifying determination was made, employed by that authority in their children and family social services or a member of that authority;
(c) where the adoption agency which made the qualifying determination is a registered adoption society he is, or has been within the period of one year prior to the date on which the qualifying determination was made, an employee or a trustee of that agency;
(d) he is related to a person falling within sub-paragraph (a), (b) or (c);
(e) he has had a child placed for adoption with him by the adoption agency which made the qualifying determination;
(f) in the case of an adopted person, the adoption agency which made the qualifying determination was the adoption agency which arranged his adoption;
(g) he was approved as a prospective adopter by the adoption agency that made the qualifying determination; or
(h) he knows the applicant in a personal or professional capacity.

(8) In this regulation –

(a) 'employed' includes employed whether or not for payment and whether under a contract of service or a contract for services or as a volunteer; and
(b) a person ('person A') is related to another person ('person B') if person A is –
   (i) a member of the household of, or married to or the civil partner of, person B;
   (ii) the son, daughter, mother, father, sister or brother of person B; or
   (iii) the son, daughter, mother, father, sister or brother of the person to whom person B is married or with whom person B has formed a civil partnership.

5 Functions of panel constituted to review a suitability determination

(1) This regulation applies where the qualifying determination being reviewed is a suitability determination.

(2) A panel constituted under regulation 4(4) shall review the suitability determination and –

(a) where paragraph (3) applies, make to the adoption agency that made the suitability determination a recommendation as to whether or not the prospective adopter is suitable to adopt a child; or
(b) where paragraph (4) applies, make to the adoption agency that made the suitability determination a recommendation that –
   (i) it should prepare a prospective adopter's report in accordance with paragraph (5) of regulation 25 of the Agencies Regulations to include all of the information required by that regulation; or
   (ii) the prospective adopter is not suitable to adopt a child.

(3) This paragraph applies where the prospective adopter's report included all of the information required by regulation 25 of the Agencies Regulations.

(4) This paragraph applies where the prospective adopter's report, in accordance with regulation 25(7) of the Agencies Regulations, did not include all of the information required by regulation 25 of the Agencies Regulations.

(5) In considering what recommendation to make, the panel –

(a) must consider and take into account all of the information passed to it in accordance with regulation 28 of the Agencies Regulations;
(b) may request the adoption agency to obtain any other relevant information which the panel considers necessary or to provide such other assistance as the panel may request; and

(c) may obtain such legal advice as it considers necessary in relation to the case.

6 Functions of panel constituted to review a disclosure determination

(1) This regulation applies where the qualifying determination being reviewed is a disclosure determination.

(2) A panel constituted under regulation 4(5) shall review the disclosure determination and make to the adoption agency that made the disclosure determination a recommendation as to whether or not the agency should proceed with its original determination.

(3) In considering what recommendation to make, the panel –

(a) must consider and take into account all of the information passed to it in accordance with regulation 15(3) of the Disclosure Regulations;
(b) may request the adoption agency to obtain any other relevant information which the panel considers necessary or to provide such other assistance as the panel may request; and
(c) may obtain such legal advice or advice from a registered medical practitioner included in the central list as it considers necessary in relation to the case.

7 Fees of panel members

The Secretary of State may pay to any member of a panel such fees as the Secretary of State considers to be reasonable.

8 Meetings of panels

(1) Where the qualifying determination being reviewed is a suitability determination, the proceedings of the panel will be invalidated unless at least five of its members including the chair or vice chair and a person falling within regulation 4(3)(a) are present.

(2) Where the qualifying determination being reviewed is a disclosure determination, the proceedings of the panel will be invalidated unless all three members are present.

9 Records

The Secretary of State shall ensure that a written record of a panel's review of a qualifying determination, including the reasons for its recommendation and whether the recommendation was unanimous or that of a majority, is retained –

(a) for a period of 12 months from the date on which the recommendation is made; and
(b) in conditions of appropriate security.

PART 3

PROCEDURE

10 Application for review of qualifying determination

An application to the Secretary of State for a review of a qualifying determination must be made by the applicant in writing and include the grounds of the application.

11 Appointment of panel and conduct of review

Upon receipt of an application which has been made in accordance with regulation 10, the Secretary of State shall –

(a) notify the adoption agency which made the qualifying determination that the application has been made by sending to the agency a copy of the application;
(b) send a written acknowledgment of the application to the applicant and notify him of the steps taken under sub-paragraph (a);
(c) constitute a panel in accordance with regulation 4;
(d) fix a date, time and venue for the panel to meet for the purposes of a review meeting;
(e) after taking the steps prescribed in sub-paragraph (d), inform in writing the applicant and the adoption agency which made the qualifying determination of –
   (i) the appointment of the panel; and
   (ii) the date, time and venue of the review meeting; and
(f) inform the applicant in writing that he may, if he wishes, provide to the panel further details of the grounds of his application in writing in the period up to two weeks before the review meeting and orally at the review meeting.

12 Recommendation of panel

(1) The panel's recommendation may be that of the majority.

(2) The recommendation and the reasons for it and whether it was unanimous or that of a majority must be recorded without delay in a document signed and dated by the chair.

(3) The panel must without delay send a copy of the recommendation and the reasons for it to the applicant and to the adoption agency which made the qualifying determination.

13 Order for payment of costs

The panel may make an order for the payment by the adoption agency by which the qualifying determination reviewed was made of such costs as the panel considers reasonable.

EXPLANATORY NOTE

(This note is not part of the Regulations)

These Regulations are made under the Adoption and Children Act 2002 ('the Act'). They apply to England only. They make provision for the review by an independent panel in two types of case. First, a determination made by an adoption agency under the Adoption Agencies Regulations 2005 that it does not propose to approve a prospective adopter as suitable to adopt a child. Such a determination is specified in regulation 3 of these Regulations as a qualifying determination for the purposes of section 12(2) of the Act. Secondly, determinations made by an adoption agency under the Disclosure of Adoption Information (Post-Commencement Adoptions) Regulations 2005. These determinations are specified in regulation 15(1) of those Regulations as qualifying determinations for the purposes of section 12(2) of the Act.

Part 2 makes provision for the constitution and membership of panels, their functions and the payment of fees, meetings and record keeping of the panels which are appointed by the Secretary of State to review qualifying determinations.

Part 3 makes provision for the procedure to be followed when a review of a qualifying determination by a panel constituted under Part 2 is sought.

Appendix H

THE DISCLOSURE OF ADOPTION INFORMATION (POST-COMMENCEMENT ADOPTIONS) REGULATIONS 2005, SI 2005/888

PART 1

GENERAL

1 Citation, commencement and application

(1) These Regulations may be cited as the Disclosure of Adoption Information (Post-Commencement Adoptions) Regulations 2005 and shall come into force on 30 December 2005.

(2) These Regulations apply to England only.

(3) These Regulations apply only in relation to adoptions on or after 30 December 2005.

2 Interpretation

In these Regulations –

'the Act' means the Adoption and Children Act 2002;
'appropriate adoption agency' has the same meaning as in section 65(1) of the Act;
'independent review panel' means a panel constituted under section 12 of the Act;
'registered adoption support agency' means an adoption support agency in respect of which a person is registered under Part 2 of the Care Standards Act 2000;
'the registration authority' means the Commission for Social Care Inspection;
'relative' in relation to an adopted person means a person who, but for the adoption, would be related to him by blood (including half-blood) or marriage;
'section 56 information' means the information prescribed by regulation 4.

PART 2

KEEPING OF INFORMATION ABOUT ADOPTIONS

3 Application of this Part

The requirements of this Part in relation to the keeping of information about a person's adoption apply –

(a) to the adoption agency that placed the person for adoption; or
(b) to an adoption agency to which the case record in respect of the adopted person (or any information mentioned in regulation 4(3)) has been transferred.

4 Information to be kept about a person's adoption

(1) Paragraphs (2) and (3) prescribe, for the purposes of section 56 of the Act, the information that an adoption agency must keep in relation to a person's adoption ('section 56 information').

(2) The adoption agency must continue to keep the case record that was set up in respect of the adopted person under Part 3 of the Adoption Agencies Regulations 2005 or under the Adoption Agencies Regulations 1983.

(3) Subject to paragraph (4) the adoption agency must also keep –

   (a) any information that has been supplied by a natural parent or relative or other significant person in the adopted person's life, with the intention that the adopted person may, should he wish to, be given that information;
   (b) any information supplied by the adoptive parents or other persons which is relevant to matters arising after the making of the adoption order;
   (c) any information that the adopted person has requested should be kept;
   (d) any information given to the adoption agency in respect of an adopted person by the Registrar General under section 79(5) of the Act (information that would enable an adopted person to obtain a certified copy of the record of his birth);
   (e) any information disclosed to the adoption agency about an entry relating to the adopted person on the Adoption Contact Register;
   (f) any information required to be recorded in accordance with regulation 10, 14 or 18;
   (g) the record of any agreement under regulation 11.

(4) The adoption agency is not required to keep any information falling within paragraph (3)(a) to (c) if the adoption agency considers –

   (a) that it would be prejudicial to the adopted person's welfare to keep it; or
   (b) that it would not be reasonably practicable to keep it.

5 Storage and manner of keeping of section 56 information

The adoption agency must ensure that section 56 information in relation to a person's adoption is at all times kept in secure conditions and in particular that all appropriate measures are taken to prevent theft, unauthorised disclosure, damage, loss or destruction.

6 Preservation of section 56 information

The adoption agency must keep section 56 information in relation to a person's adoption for at least 100 years from the date of the adoption order.

7 Transfer of section 56 information

(1) Where a registered adoption society intends to cease to act or exist as such, it must transfer any section 56 information which it holds in relation to a person's adoption –

   (a) to another adoption agency, having first obtained the approval of the registration authority for such transfer;
   (b) to the local authority in whose area the society's principal office is situated; or
   (c) in the case of a society which amalgamates with another registered adoption society to form a new registered adoption society, to the new body.

(2) A registered adoption society that transfers its records to another adoption agency by virtue of paragraph (1) must, if its activities were principally based in the area of a single local authority, give written notification of the transfer to that authority.

(3) An adoption agency to which records are transferred by virtue of paragraph (1) must give written notification of the transfer to the registration authority.

PART 3

DISCLOSURE OF INFORMATION – GENERAL

8 Disclosure for purposes of agency's functions or for research

(1) An adoption agency may disclose section 56 information that is not protected information as it thinks fit for the purposes of carrying out its functions as an adoption agency.

(2) An adoption agency may disclose section 56 information (including protected information) to –

- (a) a registered adoption support agency or another adoption agency which provides services to the adoption agency in connection with any of its functions under section 61 or 62 of the Act (disclosing protected information about adults or about children); or
- (b) a person who is authorised in writing by the Secretary of State to obtain information for the purposes of research.

9 Disclosure required for purposes of inquiries, inspection etc

An adoption agency must disclose section 56 information (including protected information) as may be required –

- (a) to those holding an inquiry under section 17 of the Act or section 81 of the Children Act 1989 for the purposes of such an inquiry;
- (b) to the Secretary of State;
- (c) to the registration authority;
- (d) subject to the provisions of section 29(7) and 32(3) of the Local Government Act 1974 (investigations and disclosure), to the Commission for Local Administration in England, for the purposes of any investigation conducted in accordance with Part 3 of that Act;
- (e) to any person appointed by the adoption agency for the purposes of the consideration by the agency of any representations (including complaints);
- (f) to a panel constituted under section 12 of the Act to consider a qualifying determination in relation to the disclosure of section 56 information;
- (g) to a court having power to make an order under the Act or under the Children Act 1989.

10 Requirements relating to disclosure

The adoption agency must make a written record of any disclosure made under regulation 8 or 9, which must include –

- (a) a description of the information disclosed;
- (b) the date on which the information is disclosed;
- (c) the person to whom the information is disclosed;
- (d) the reason for disclosure.

11 Agreements for the disclosure of protected information

(1) A prescribed agreement for the purposes of section 57(5) of the Act is –

(a) an agreement made between the adoption agency and a person aged 18 or over at the time the agreement is made as to the disclosure of protected information about him; or
(b) an agreement made between the adoption agency and each of the following persons as to the disclosure of protected information about them or about the adopted person –
   (i) the adoptive parent, or in the case of adoption by a couple, both adoptive parents, of the adopted person;
   (ii) each person who, before the adoption order was made, was a parent with parental responsibility for the adopted person.

(2) The adoption agency must keep a written record of any such agreement and that record must include –

(a) the full names and signatures of the persons who are parties;
(b) the date on which it is made;
(c) the reasons for making it;
(d) the information that may be disclosed in accordance with the agreement;
(e) any agreed restrictions on the circumstances in which information may be disclosed.

PART 4

APPLICATIONS FOR DISCLOSURE OF PROTECTED INFORMATION

12 Manner of application

An application to an adoption agency for the disclosure of protected information under section 61 or 62 of the Act must be in writing and must state the reasons for the application.

13 Duties of agency on receipt of application

On receipt of an application for the disclosure of protected information under section 61 or 62 of the Act an adoption agency must take reasonable steps to confirm –

(a) the identity of the applicant or of any person acting on his behalf; and
(b) that any person acting on behalf of the applicant is authorised to do so.

14 Record of views

An adoption agency must ensure that any views obtained under section 61(3) or 62(3) or (4) of the Act are recorded in writing.

15 Independent review

(1) The following determinations by the appropriate adoption agency in relation to an application under section 61 of the Act are qualifying determinations for the purposes of section 12 of the Act (independent review of determinations) –

(a) not to proceed with an application from any person for disclosure of protected information;
(b) to disclose information against the express views of the person the information is about;
(c) not to disclose information about a person to the applicant where that person has expressed the view that the information should be disclosed.

(2) The adoption agency must give the relevant person written notification of the determination, which must –

(a) state the reasons for it; and
(b) advise the relevant person that he may apply to the Secretary of State within 40 working days, beginning with the date on which the notification was sent, for a review by an independent review panel of the qualifying determination.

(3) If the adoption agency receives notification from the Secretary of State that the relevant person has applied for a review by an independent review panel of the qualifying determination, the agency must, within 10 working days of receipt of that notification, send to the Secretary of State –

(a) a copy of the application for disclosure of information;
(b) a copy of the notification given under paragraph (2);
(c) the record of any views obtained by the agency under section 61(3) of the Act; and
(d) any additional information requested by the panel.

(4) The adoption agency must not take any action in accordance with its original determination before –

(a) the independent review panel has made its recommendation; or
(b) if the person has not applied for a review within that 40 day period, the end of that period.

(5) The adoption agency must have regard to any recommendation of the independent review panel in deciding whether to proceed with its original determination.

(6) In paragraph (3) –

(a) the reference to an independent review panel is to a panel constituted for the purposes of section 12 of the Act; and
(b) 'working day' means any day other than a Saturday or Sunday, Christmas Day, Good Friday or a day which is a bank holiday within the meaning of the Banking and Financial Dealings Act 1971.

(7) In this regulation 'the relevant person' is –

(a) in the case of a qualifying determination mentioned in paragraph (1)(a) or (c), the applicant;
(b) in the case of a qualifying determination mentioned in paragraph (1)(b), the person the protected information is about.

PART 5

COUNSELLING

16 Information about the availability of counselling

(1) An adoption agency must provide written information about the availability of counselling to any person –

(a) who is seeking information under section 60, 61 or 62 of the Act;
(b) whose views have been sought as to the disclosure of information about him under section 61(3) or 62(3) or (4) of the Act;
(c) who enters into, or is considering entering into, an agreement with the agency under regulation 11.

(2) The information provided under paragraph (1) must include information about the fees that may be charged by persons providing counselling.

17 Duty to secure counselling

(1) Where a person mentioned in regulation 16(1) requests that counselling be provided for him, the adoption agency must make arrangements to secure counselling for that person.

(2) The adoption agency may provide the counselling itself or make arrangements with any of the following persons for provision of counselling –

   (a) if the person is in England or Wales, another adoption agency or a registered adoption support agency;
   (b) if the person is in Scotland, a Scottish adoption agency;
   (c) if the person is in Northern Ireland, an adoption society which is registered under Article 4 of the Adoption (Northern Ireland) Order 1987 or any Board; or
   (d) if the person is outside the United Kingdom, any person or body outside the United Kingdom who appears to the agency to correspond in its functions to a body mentioned in paragraphs (a) to (c).

(3) In this regulation 'Board' means a Health and Social Services Board established under Article 16 of the Health and Personal Social Services (Northern Ireland) Order 1972 or, where the functions of a Board are exercisable by a Health and Social Services Trust, that Trust.

18 Disclosure of information for the purposes of counselling

(1) An adoption agency may disclose any information (which may include protected information) which is required for the purposes of providing counselling to any person with whom it has made arrangements to provide counselling.

(2) An adoption agency must make a written record of any disclosure made by virtue of this regulation.

PART 6

THE REGISTRAR GENERAL

19 Seeking information from the Registrar General

(1) Where –

   (a) an adopted person who has attained the age of 18 years requests information from an adoption agency under section 60(2)(a) of the Act that would enable him to obtain a certified copy of the record of his birth; and
   (b) the agency does not have that information,

the agency must seek that information from the Registrar General.

(2) Where an adoption agency seeks information from the Registrar General under paragraph (1) the agency must provide him in writing with the following information, so far as it is known –

   (a) the name, date of birth and country of birth of the adopted person;
   (b) the names of that person's adoptive father and mother;
   (c) the date of the adoption order.

20 Registrar General to disclose information regarding the appropriate adoption agency and the Adoption Contact Register

(1) The Registrar General must –

(a) disclose to any person (including an adopted person) at his request any information that the person requires to assist him to make contact with the adoption agency which is the appropriate adoption agency in the case of the person specified in the request (or, as the case may be, in the applicant's case); and

(b) disclose to the appropriate adoption agency any information that the agency requires, in relation to an application under section 60, 61 or 62 of the Act, about any entry relating to an adopted person on the Adoption Contact Register.

(2) The appropriate adoption agency must pay any fee that the Registrar General determines is reasonable for the disclosure of information under paragraph (1)(b).

PART 7
MISCELLANEOUS

21 Offence

A registered adoption society which discloses any information in contravention of section 57 of the Act (restrictions on disclosure etc. of information) is guilty of an offence and is liable on summary conviction to a fine not exceeding level 5 on the standard scale.

22 Fees charged by adoption agencies

(1) Subject to paragraph (2) an adoption agency may charge a fee which it determines to be a reasonable fee –

(a) in respect of the disclosure of information under section 61 or 62 of the Act;
(b) for providing counselling in connection with the disclosure of information under those sections; or
(c) for making arrangements to secure counselling in accordance with regulation 17 where the counselling is provided by a person outside the United Kingdom.

(2) No fee shall be payable by an adopted person in respect of any information disclosed to him under section 60, 61 or 62 of the Act in relation to any relative of his or for any counselling provided to him in connection with any such disclosure.

(3) An adoption agency must, before providing a service to any person for which it may charge a fee under this regulation, give the person information about its fees.

EXPLANATORY NOTE

(This note is not part of the Regulations)

These Regulations prescribe certain matters for the purposes of the regime set out in sections 56 to 65 of the Adoption and Children Act 2002 ('the Act'). The regime provides for adoption agencies to keep information about each adoption and to deal with applications for disclosure of such information. The regime will apply in relation to persons adopted on or after 30th December 2005. In relation to persons adopted before that day, the Adoption Agencies Regulations 1983 (SI 1983/1964) will continue to have effect.

Part 2 provides for the keeping of information in relation to persons adopted on or after 30 December 2005. Regulation 4 prescribes the information that must be kept ('section 56 information'). Part 2 also deals with storage and transfer of section 56 information. Regulation 6 requires that section 56 information be kept for at least 100 years from the date of the adoption order.

Part 3 makes general provision for the disclosure of section 56 information and protected information (which is defined in section 57(3) of the Act). Under regulation 8 an adoption agency may disclose section 56 information that is not protected information as necessary for the purpose of its functions or for research. It may also disclose any section 56 information, including protected information, to persons providing services in relation to its functions under section 61 or 62 of the Act (for example a registered adoption support agency carrying out enquiries on its behalf). Regulation 9 provides for disclosure of information to specified persons including persons holding inquiries, the Commission for Social Care Inspection and the Secretary of State. Regulation 10 requires a written record to be kept of any disclosure. Regulation 11 prescribes the requirements for an agreement under section 57(5) of the Act.

Part 4 relates to applications for disclosure of protected information under section 61 (information about adults) and 62 (information about children). Regulations 12 to 14 deal with procedural matters in relation to such applications. Regulation 15 makes provision for independent review of certain decisions of the adoption agency in relation to applications under section 61.

Part 5 makes provision for counselling. Regulation 16 requires adoption agencies to provide information about availability of counselling for persons seeking information about an adoption or persons about whom information is being sought. Regulation 17 requires adoption agencies to secure counselling where requested by persons seeking information.

Part 6 relates to the Registrar General. Adopted adults have a right under section 60 of the Act to request information about their birth records. They must first approach the appropriate adoption agency, which then requests the information from the Registrar General (who is obliged to provide it by virtue of section 79(5) of the Act). Regulation 19 requires the appropriate adoption agency to seek that information and prescribes the manner of the application for it. Regulation 20 requires the Registrar General to disclose information to any person that may assist the person in making contact with the adoption agency that holds the records of his adoption. Regulation 20 also requires the Registrar General to disclose information from the Adoption Contact Register where requested by the appropriate adoption agency in connection with an application under section 60, 61 or 62.

Part 6 deals with miscellaneous matters. It creates an offence of disclosing information in contravention of section 57 of the Act. Regulation 22 prescribes fees that may be charged by adoption agencies in relation to disclosure of information and counselling.

A Regulatory Impact Assessment has been carried out for these Regulations and a copy has been placed in the library of each House of Parliament. Copies of the Regulatory Impact Assessment can be obtained from the Department for Education and Skills' website http://www.dfes.gov.uk/ria/.

Appendix I

THE ADOPTION INFORMATION AND INTERMEDIARY SERVICES (PRE-COMMENCEMENT ADOPTIONS) REGULATIONS 2005, SI 2005/890

PART 1
INTRODUCTORY

1 Citation, commencement and application

(1) These Regulations may be cited as the Adoption Information and Intermediary Services (Pre-Commencement Adoptions) Regulations 2005 and shall come into force on 30 December 2005.

(2) These Regulations apply to England only.

2 Interpretation

In these Regulations –

'the Act' means the Adoption and Children Act 2002;
'applicant' means an adopted person or a relative of an adopted person who makes an application under regulation 5;
'the appropriate adoption agency' has the same meaning as in section 65(1) of the Act;
'identifying information' has the meaning given in regulation 7;
'intermediary agency' and 'intermediary service' have the meaning given in regulation 4;
'registered adoption support agency' means an adoption support agency in respect of which a person is registered under Part 2 of the Care Standards Act 2000;
'relative', in relation to an adopted person, has the same meaning as in section 98 of the Act;
'subject', in relation to an application under regulation 5, is a person with whom the applicant seeks contact.

3 Provision of intermediary services

(1) A registered adoption support agency or an adoption agency may provide an intermediary service.

(2) The service must be provided in accordance with these Regulations.

(3) An intermediary service is an adoption support service for the purposes of section 2(6) of the Act.

4 Meaning of 'intermediary service' and 'intermediary agency'

(1) For the purposes of these Regulations an intermediary service is a service provided for the purposes of –

(a) assisting adopted persons aged 18 or over, who were adopted before 30th December 2005, to obtain information in relation to their adoption; and
(b) facilitating contact between such persons and their relatives.

(2) But an adoption agency does not provide an intermediary service for the purposes of these Regulations if it is the appropriate adoption agency in relation to an adopted person and only provides information in relation to that person's adoption.

(3) A registered adoption support agency or an adoption agency that provides an intermediary service is referred to in these Regulations as an 'intermediary agency'.

PART 2
APPLICATIONS FOR INTERMEDIARY SERVICES

5 Applications that may be accepted

(1) Subject to paragraphs (2) and (3) an intermediary agency may accept an application –

(a) from a person adopted before 30 December 2005 for assistance in contacting a relative of his; or
(b) from a relative of a person adopted before 30 December 2005 for assistance in contacting that person.

(2) Where the intermediary agency has limited capacity to deal with such applications, it must give priority to applications in respect of adoptions before 12 November 1975.

(3) The applicant and the person with whom the applicant seeks contact ('the subject') must be aged 18 or over.

6 No obligation to proceed if not appropriate

(1) An intermediary agency that accepts an application under these Regulations is not required to proceed with it, or having begun to proceed with it is not required to continue, if the intermediary agency considers that it would not be appropriate to do so.

(2) In deciding whether it is appropriate to proceed (or continue proceeding) with an application the intermediary agency must have regard to –

(a) the welfare of –
   (i) the applicant;
   (ii) the subject; and
   (iii) any other persons who may be identified or otherwise affected by the application;
(b) any views of the appropriate adoption agency obtained under regulation 12;
(c) any information obtained from the Adoption Contact Register under regulation 13,

and all the other circumstances of the case.

(3) In relation to any decision under paragraph (2) the intermediary agency must have particular regard to the welfare of any person mentioned in paragraph (2)(a)(iii) who is under the age of 18.

(4) If, at any time, the intermediary agency ascertains that the subject of an application is under the age of 18 it must not proceed further with the application in relation to that subject.

7 Consent of subject to disclosure etc

(1) Subject to paragraph (2) an intermediary agency must not disclose to the applicant any identifying information about the subject without the subject's consent.

(2) If the subject has died or the agency determines that he is incapable of giving informed consent, the agency may disclose such identifying information about him to the applicant as it considers appropriate, having regard to the matters referred to in regulation 6(2).

(3) The agency must take all reasonable steps to ensure that any person whose consent to disclosure is required under this regulation has sufficient information to make an informed decision as to whether to give his consent.

(4) In this regulation and in regulations 9 and 12, 'identifying information' means information which, whether taken on its own or together with other information possessed by the applicant, enables the subject to be identified or traced.

8 Veto by an adopted person

(1) A veto applies in relation to an application under regulation 5 where –

  (a) the subject is the adopted person; and
  (b) that person has notified the appropriate adoption agency in writing –
   (i) that he does not wish to be contacted by an intermediary agency in relation to an application under these Regulations; or
   (ii) that he only wishes to be contacted in specified circumstances.

(2) Where the appropriate adoption agency is notified of a veto under paragraph (1) it must keep a written record of it on the adopted person's case record and ensure that it is made known to any intermediary agency that contacts it in relation to an application under these Regulations.

(3) Where an intermediary agency is aware that a veto applies, it must not proceed with the application except in the circumstances referred to in paragraph (1)(b)(ii).

9 Provision of background information where consent refused etc

In a case where the consent of the subject is refused or cannot be obtained under regulation 7 or a veto applies under regulation 8, nothing in those regulations prevents the intermediary agency from disclosing to the applicant any information about the subject that is not identifying information and that the agency considers it appropriate to disclose.

10 Counselling

(1) An intermediary agency must provide written information about the availability of counselling to any person who –

  (a) makes an application to it under these Regulations; or
  (b) is the subject of such an application and is considering whether to consent to disclosure of information about himself to the applicant.

(2) The information provided under paragraph (1) must include details of –

  (a) persons offering counselling; and
  (b) fees that may be charged by such persons.

(3) If a person mentioned in paragraph (1) requests that counselling be provided for him, the intermediary agency must secure the provision of counselling for that person.

(4) The intermediary agency may provide the counselling itself or make arrangements with any of the following persons for provision of counselling –

(a) if the person is in England or Wales, another adoption agency or a registered adoption support agency;
(b) if the person is in Scotland, a Scottish adoption agency;
(c) if the person is in Northern Ireland, an adoption society which is registered under Article 4 of the Adoption (Northern Ireland) Order 1987 or any Board; or
(d) if the person is outside the United Kingdom, any person or body outside the United Kingdom who appears to the agency to correspond in its functions to a body mentioned in paragraphs (a) to (c).

(5) In this regulation 'Board' means a Health and Social Services Board established under Article 16 of the Health and Personal Social Services (Northern Ireland) Order 1972 or where the functions of a Board are exercisable by a Health and Social Services Trust, that Trust.

PART 3

PROCEDURE FOR HANDLING APPLICATIONS

11 Procedure on receipt of application

The intermediary agency must, on receipt of an application under regulation 5, take reasonable steps to confirm –

(a) the identity of the applicant or of any person acting on his behalf;
(b) the age of the applicant;
(c) that any person acting on behalf of the applicant is authorised to do so;
(d) in the case of an application by a relative of the adopted person, that the applicant is related to that person.

12 Contacting the appropriate adoption agency

(1) The intermediary agency must (unless it is the appropriate adoption agency) take reasonable steps to establish whether an adoption agency was involved in the adoption and, if so, to identify the appropriate adoption agency.

(2) The steps referred to in paragraph (1) include –

(a) requesting that information in writing from the Registrar General;
(b) if the Registrar General certifies that he does not have that information, requesting it in writing from the court that made the adoption order;
(c) making enquiries of the local authority for the area where the adoption took place.

(3) Where the appropriate adoption agency has been identified, the intermediary agency must contact that agency in order to –

(a) ascertain whether a veto under regulation 8 exists;
(b) if no veto exists –
    (i) ascertain whether the subject has, at any time, expressed his views to the agency about future contact with any relative of his or about his being approached with regard to such contact;

(ii) ascertain the agency's views as to whether the application is appropriate having regard to the matters mentioned in regulation 6; and
(c) seek any other information required for the following purposes –
  (i) tracing the subject;
  (ii) enabling the subject to make an informed decision as to whether he consents to the disclosure of identifying information about him or to contact with the applicant;
  (iii) counselling the subject in relation to that decision;
  (iv) counselling the applicant.

(4) Unless a veto under regulation 8 applies, the appropriate adoption agency must take reasonable steps to provide the information sought from it under paragraph (3) and may disclose to the intermediary agency such information (including identifying information) as is necessary for that purpose.

13 Obtaining information from the Registrar General

(1) If, in any of the cases mentioned in paragraph (2), the intermediary agency has not obtained from the appropriate adoption agency sufficient information for the purposes mentioned in regulation 12(3)(c), the intermediary agency may make a request in writing to the Registrar General for such of the following information as may assist it for those purposes –

(a) information he may hold that would enable an application to be made for a certificate from the Adopted Children Register;
(b) information from the Adoption Contact Register.

(2) The cases mentioned in paragraph (1) are –

(a) where the intermediary agency is unable to identify the appropriate adoption agency or ascertains that no adoption agency was involved in the adoption;
(b) where the intermediary agency contacts the appropriate adoption agency and ascertains that it does not hold the necessary information.

(3) Where the intermediary agency is the appropriate adoption agency and does not hold sufficient information for the purpose mentioned in regulation 12(3)(c)(i) it may request from the Registrar General such of the information mentioned in paragraph (1)(a) and (b) as may assist it for those purposes.

14 Registrar General to comply with request

(1) The Registrar General must take reasonable steps to comply with a written request for information from an intermediary agency under regulation 12 or 13.

(2) If the Registrar General does not have the information about the appropriate adoption agency requested under regulation 12 he must provide the intermediary agency with written confirmation of that fact together with details of the court that made the adoption order.

15 Court to comply with request

(1) The court must disclose any information requested in writing by the intermediary agency under regulation 12(2)(b) that is contained in court records.

(2) If the court does not have the information requested under regulation 12(2)(b) it must inform the intermediary agency of that fact in writing, specifying the searches made of court records and, if the court considers that the information may be found in the records of another court, provide the intermediary agency with details of that court.

16 Authorised disclosures

An intermediary agency must treat information obtained or held for the purposes of these Regulations as confidential, but may disclose such information (including information that identifies any person) as is necessary –

(a) to the Registrar General or to the court for the purpose of obtaining information under regulation 12 or 13;
(b) to the appropriate adoption agency for the purposes of ascertaining its views or seeking information under regulation 12;
(c) to the subject to enable him to make an informed decision under regulation 7;
(d) to a person providing counselling in connection with an application under these Regulations.

PART 4
MISCELLANEOUS

17 Offence

An intermediary agency that discloses information in contravention of regulation 7 without reasonable excuse is guilty of an offence and is liable on summary conviction to a fine not exceeding level 5 on the standard scale.

18 Fees

(1) An intermediary agency may charge the applicant any fee it determines is reasonable in connection with the processing of an application under these Regulations.

(2) An intermediary agency may charge a person mentioned in regulation 10(1) such fee as it determines is reasonable in respect of –

(a) the provision of counselling services for that person; or
(b) making arrangements to secure counselling where the counselling is provided by a person outside the United Kingdom.

(3) The Registrar General may charge a fee of £10 for providing information under regulation 14.

(4) An adoption agency may charge an intermediary agency such fee as it determines is reasonable for providing information or giving its views in accordance with a request under regulation 12.

(5) A court may charge an intermediary agency a fee not exceeding £20 for providing information under regulation 15.

EXPLANATORY NOTE

(This note is not part of the Regulations)

These Regulations make provision under section 98 of the Adoption and Children Act 2002 ('the Act') for the purposes of assisting persons adopted before 30th December 2005 to obtain information about their adoption and to facilitate contact between those persons and their birth relatives. The regime for disclosure of information about adoptions on or after 30 December 2005 is set out in sections 56 to 65 of the Act and regulations under those sections.

Part 1 confers functions on registered adoption support agencies and adoption agencies ('intermediary agencies') that are willing to provide intermediary services in respect of adoptions before 30 December 2005. Agencies providing such services are required to do so in accordance with these Regulations.

Part 2 deals generally with applications for intermediary services. An intermediary agency may accept an application for an intermediary service from an adopted person or a relative of an adopted person in respect of any adoption before 30 December 2005 but they must give priority to applications in respect of adoptions before 12 November 1975. The intermediary agency is not required to proceed with an application where it does not consider that it would be appropriate. Regulation 6 sets out the factors that the intermediary agency should take into account in making that decision. Regulation 7 requires the intermediary agency to obtain the informed consent of the subject of the application before disclosing information about him that would identify him to the applicant or enable him to be traced. Regulation 8 enables the adopted person to register a veto with the appropriate adoption agency in relation to an application under these Regulations. Regulation 10 requires the intermediary agency to provide information about counselling and secure counselling services in relation to applications for intermediary services.

Part 3 sets out the procedure to be followed by the intermediary agency in processing an application. The first steps include confirming the identity of the applicant and establishing that he is related to the subject. The intermediary agency should then identify the adoption agency that holds the records relating to the adoption (seeking assistance where appropriate from the Registrar General and the court). It should then contact that agency to seek its views on the application and to seek such information as may be necessary to trace the subject of the application (regulation 12). Where that information cannot be obtained from the adoption agency, the intermediary agency may seek such information from the Registrar General as may assist in processing the application (regulation 14). Regulations 14 and 15 require the Registrar General and the court to provide information when requested. Regulation 16 authorises certain disclosures for the purpose of an application under these Regulations.

Part 4 deals with miscellaneous matters. Regulation 17 creates an offence of disclosure of information in contravention of Regulation 7. Regulation 18 provides for fees that may be charged by intermediary agencies, adoption agencies, the Registrar General and the court in relation to applications under these Regulations.

A Regulatory Impact Assessment has been carried out for these Regulations and a copy has been placed in the library of each House of Parliament. Copies of the Regulatory Impact Assessment can be obtained from the Department for Education and Skills' website http://www.dfes.gov.uk/ria/.

Appendix J

THE ADOPTION AGENCIES REGULATIONS 2005, SI 2005/389

PART 1
GENERAL

1 Citation, commencement and application

(1) These Regulations may be cited as the Adoption Agencies Regulations 2005 and shall come into force on 30 December 2005.

(2) These Regulations apply to England only.

2 Interpretation

In these Regulations –

'the Act' means the Adoption and Children Act 2002;
'the 1989 Act' means the Children Act 1989;
'adoption panel' means a panel established in accordance with regulation 3;
'adoption placement plan' has the meaning given in regulation 35(2);
'adoption placement report' means the report prepared by the adoption agency in accordance with regulation 31(2)(d);
'adoption support services' has the meaning given in section 2(6)(a) of the Act and in any regulations made under section 2(6)(b) of the Act;
'adoptive family' has the meaning given in regulation 31(2)(a);
'CAFCASS' means the Children and Family Court Advisory and Support Service;
'child's case record' has the meaning given in regulation 12;
'child's health report' means the report obtained in accordance with regulation 15(2)(b);
'child's permanence report' means the report prepared by the adoption agency in accordance with regulation 17(1);
'independent member' in relation to an adoption panel has the meaning given in regulation 3(3)(e);
'independent review panel' means a panel constituted under section 12 of the Act;
'joint adoption panel' means an adoption panel established in accordance with regulation 3(5);
'medical adviser' means the person appointed as the medical adviser by the adoption agency in accordance with regulation 9(1);
'proposed placement' has the meaning given in regulation 31(1);
'prospective adopter's case record' has the meaning given in regulation 22(1);
'prospective adopter's report' means the report prepared by the adoption agency in accordance with regulation 25(5);
'prospective adopter's review report' means the report prepared by the adoption agency in accordance with regulation 29(4)(a);
'qualifying determination' has the meaning given in regulation 27(4)(a);

'registration authority' means the Commission for Social Care Inspection;

'relevant foreign authority' means a person, outside the British Islands performing functions in the country in which the child is, or in which the prospective adopter is, habitually resident which correspond to the functions of an adoption agency or to the functions of the Secretary of State in respect of adoptions with a foreign element;

'relevant post-qualifying experience' means post-qualifying experience in child care social work including direct experience in adoption work;

'section 83 case' means a case where a person who is habitually resident in the British Islands intends to bring, or to cause another to bring, a child into the United Kingdom in circumstances where section 83 of the Act (restriction on bringing children into the United Kingdom) applies;

'social worker' means a person who is registered as a social worker in a register maintained by the General Social Care Council or the Care Council for Wales under section 56 of the Care Standards Act 2000 or in a corresponding register maintained under the law of Scotland or Northern Ireland;

'vice chair' has the meaning given in regulation 3(4) or, as the case may be, (5)(c);

'working day' means any day other than a Saturday, Sunday, Christmas Day, Good Friday or a day which is a bank holiday within the meaning of the Banking and Financial Dealings Act 1971.

PART 2

ADOPTION AGENCY – ARRANGEMENTS FOR ADOPTION WORK

3 Establishment of adoption panel

(1) Subject to paragraph (5), an adoption agency must establish at least one panel, to be known as an adoption panel, in accordance with this regulation.

(2) The adoption agency must appoint to chair the panel a person, not being a disqualified person, who has the skills and experience necessary for chairing an adoption panel.

(3) Subject to paragraph (5), the adoption panel shall consist of no more than ten members, including the person appointed under paragraph (2), and shall include –

(a) two social workers each with at least three years' relevant post-qualifying experience;
(b) in the case of a registered adoption society, one person who is a director, manager or other officer and is concerned in the management of that society;
(c) in the case of a local authority, one member of that authority;
(d) the medical adviser to the adoption agency (or one of them if more than one medical adviser is appointed);
(e) at least three other persons (in this regulation referred to as 'independent members') including where reasonably practicable at least two persons with personal experience of adoption.

(4) The adoption agency must appoint one member of the adoption panel as vice chair ('vice chair') who shall act as chair if the person appointed to chair the panel is absent or his office is vacant.

(5) An adoption panel may be established jointly by any two or more local authorities ('joint adoption panel') and if a joint adoption panel is established –

(a) the maximum number of members who may be appointed to that panel is eleven;
(b) by agreement between the local authorities there shall be appointed to that panel –

(i) a person to chair the panel, not being a disqualified person, who has the skills and experience necessary for chairing an adoption panel;
(ii) two social workers each with at least three years' relevant post-qualifying experience;
(iii) one member of any of the local authorities;
(iv) the medical adviser to one of the local authorities; and
(v) at least three independent members including where reasonably practicable at least two persons with personal experience of adoption;

(c) by agreement the local authorities must appoint one member of the panel as vice chair ('vice chair') who shall act as chair if the person appointed to chair the panel is absent or his office is vacant.

(6) A person shall not be appointed as an independent member of an adoption panel if –

(a) in the case of a registered adoption society, he is or has been within the last year a trustee or employee, or is related to an employee, of that society;
(b) in the case of a local authority, he –
   (i) is or has been within the last year employed by that authority in their children and family social services;
   (ii) is related to a person falling within head (i); or
   (iii) is or has been within the last year a member of that authority; or
(c) he is the adoptive parent of a child who was –
   (i) placed for adoption with him by the adoption agency ('agency A'); or
   (ii) placed for adoption with him by another adoption agency where he had been approved as suitable to be an adoptive parent by agency A,

unless at least twelve months has elapsed since the adoption order was made in respect of the child.

(7) For the purposes of regulation 3(2) and (5)(b)(i) a person is a disqualified person if –

(a) in the case of a registered adoption society, he is or has been within the last year a trustee or employee, or is related to an employee, of that society; or
(b) in the case of a local authority, he is or has been within the last year a member or employee, or is related to an employee, of that authority.

(8) For the purposes of paragraphs (6)(a) and (b)(ii) and (7) a person ('person A') is related to another person ('person B') if person A is –

(a) a member of the household of, or married to or the civil partner of, person B;
(b) the son, daughter, mother, father, sister or brother of person B; or
(c) the son, daughter, mother, father, sister or brother of the person to whom person B is married or with whom B has formed a civil partnership.

4 Tenure of office of members of the adoption panel

(1) Subject to the provisions of this regulation and regulation 10, a member of an adoption panel shall hold office for a term not exceeding three years, and may not hold office for the adoption panel of the same adoption agency for more than three terms in total.

(2) The medical adviser member of the adoption panel shall hold office only for so long as he is the medical adviser.

(3) A member of an adoption panel may resign his office at any time by giving one month's notice in writing to the adoption agency.

(4) Where an adoption agency is of the opinion that any member of the adoption panel is unsuitable or unable to remain in office, it may terminate his office at any time by giving him notice in writing with reasons.

(5) If the member whose appointment is to be terminated under paragraph (4) is a member of a joint adoption panel, his appointment may only be terminated with the agreement of all the local authorities whose panel it is.

5 Meetings of adoption panel

(1) Subject to paragraph (2), no business shall be conducted by the adoption panel unless at least five of its members, including the person appointed to chair the panel or the vice chair and at least one of the social workers and one of the independent members, meet as the panel.

(2) In the case of a joint adoption panel, no business shall be conducted unless at least six of its members, including the person appointed to chair the panel or the vice chair and at least one of the social workers and one of the independent members, meet as the panel.

(3) An adoption panel must make a written record of its proceedings, its recommendations and the reasons for its recommendations.

6 Payment of fees to member of local authority adoption panel

A local authority may pay to any member of their adoption panel such fee as they may determine, being a fee of a reasonable amount.

7 Adoption agency arrangements for adoption work

An adoption agency must, in consultation with the adoption panel and, to the extent specified in regulation 9(2) with the agency's medical adviser, prepare and implement written policy and procedural instructions governing the exercise of the functions of the agency and the adoption panel in relation to adoption and such instructions shall be kept under review and, where appropriate, revised by the agency.

8 Requirement to appoint an agency adviser to the adoption panel

(1) The adoption agency must appoint a senior member of staff, or in the case of a joint adoption panel the local authorities whose panel it is must by agreement appoint a senior member of staff of one of them, (referred to in this regulation as the 'agency adviser') –

(a) to assist the agency with the appointment (including re-appointment), termination and review of appointment of members of the adoption panel;

(b) to be responsible for the induction and training of members of the adoption panel;

(c) to be responsible for liaison between the agency and the adoption panel, monitoring the performance of members of the adoption panel and the administration of the adoption panel; and

(d) to give such advice to the adoption panel as the panel may request in relation to any case or generally.

(2) The agency adviser must be a social worker and have at least five years' relevant post-qualifying experience and, in the opinion of the adoption agency, relevant management experience.

9 Requirement to appoint a medical adviser

(1) The adoption agency must appoint at least one registered medical practitioner to be the agency's medical adviser.

(2) The medical adviser shall be consulted in relation to the arrangements for access to, and disclosure of, health information which is required or permitted by virtue of these Regulations.

10 Establishment of new adoption panels on 30 December 2005

(1) All members of an adoption panel established before 30 December 2005 (referred to in this regulation as the 'old adoption panel') shall cease to hold office on that date.

(2) With effect from 30 December 2005 an adoption agency shall establish a new adoption panel in accordance with regulations 3 and 4.

(3) This paragraph applies where the term of office of a member of the old adoption panel was extended by the adoption agency in accordance with regulation 5A(1A) of the Adoption Agencies Regulations 1983.

(4) This paragraph applies where a member of the old adoption panel was in his first term of office as a member of the old adoption panel.

(5) A member of the old adoption panel who holds office immediately before 30 December 2005 may not hold office as a member of the new adoption panel of the same adoption agency –

(a) where paragraph (3) applies, for more than one term, not exceeding one year;
(b) where paragraph (4) applies, for more than two terms, each term not exceeding three years;
(c) in any other case, for more than one term, not exceeding three years.

PART 3

DUTIES OF ADOPTION AGENCY WHERE THE AGENCY IS CONSIDERING ADOPTION FOR A CHILD

11 Application of regulations 11 to 17

Regulations 11 to 17 apply where the adoption agency is considering adoption for a child.

12 Requirement to open the child's case record

(1) The adoption agency must set up a case record ('the child's case record') in respect of the child and place on it –

(a) the information and reports obtained by the agency by virtue of this Part;
(b) the child's permanence report;
(c) the written record of the proceedings of the adoption panel under regulation 18, its recommendation and the reasons for its recommendation and any advice given by the panel to the agency;
(d) the record of the agency's decision and any notification of that decision under regulation 19;
(e) any consent to placement for adoption under section 19 of the Act (placing children with parental consent);
(f) any consent to the making of a future adoption order under section 20 of the Act (advance consent to adoption);

(g) any form or notice withdrawing consent under section 19 or 20 of the Act or notice under section 20(4)(a) or (b) of the Act;
(h) a copy of any placement order in respect of the child; and
(i) any other documents or information obtained by the agency which it considers should be included in that case record.

(2) Where an adoption agency places on the child's case record a notice under section 20(4)(a) or (b) of the Act, the agency must send a copy of that notice to a court which has given the agency notice of the issue of an application for an adoption order.

13 Requirement to provide counselling and information for, and ascertain wishes and feelings of, the child

(1) The adoption agency must, so far as is reasonably practicable –

(a) provide a counselling service for the child;
(b) explain to the child in an appropriate manner the procedure in relation to, and the legal implications of, adoption for the child and provide him with appropriate written information about these matters; and
(c) ascertain the child's wishes and feelings regarding –
   (i) the possibility of placement for adoption with a new family and his adoption;
   (ii) his religious and cultural upbringing; and
   (iii) contact with his parent or guardian or other relative or with any other person the agency considers relevant.

(2) Paragraph (1) does not apply if the adoption agency is satisfied that the requirements of that paragraph have been carried out in respect of the child by another adoption agency.

14 Requirement to provide counselling and information for, and ascertain wishes and feelings of, the parent or guardian of the child and others

(1) The adoption agency must, so far as is reasonably practicable –

(a) provide a counselling service for the parent or guardian of the child;
(b) explain to him –
   (i) the procedure in relation to both placement for adoption and adoption;
   (ii) the legal implications of –
      (aa) giving consent to placement for adoption under section 19 of the Act;
      (bb) giving consent to the making of a future adoption order under section 20 of the Act; and
      (cc) a placement order; and
   (iii) the legal implications of adoption,
and provide him with written information about these matters; and
(c) ascertain the wishes and feelings of the parent or guardian of the child and, of any other person the agency considers relevant, regarding –
   (i) the child;
   (ii) the placement of the child for adoption and his adoption, including any wishes and feelings about the child's religious and cultural upbringing; and
   (iii) contact with the child if the child is authorised to be placed for adoption or the child is adopted.

(2) Paragraph (1) does not apply if the agency is satisfied that the requirements of that paragraph have been carried out in respect of the parent or guardian and any other person the agency considers relevant by another adoption agency.

(3) This paragraph applies where the father of the child does not have parental responsibility for the child and the father's identity is known to the adoption agency.

(4) Where paragraph (3) applies and the adoption agency is satisfied it is appropriate to do so, the agency must –

- (a) carry out in respect of the father the requirements of paragraph (1)(a), (b)(i) and (iii) and (c) as if they applied to him unless the agency is satisfied that the requirements have been carried out in respect of the father by another agency; and
- (b) ascertain so far as possible whether the father –
    - (i) wishes to acquire parental responsibility for the child under section 4 of the 1989 Act (acquisition of parental responsibility by father); or
    - (ii) intends to apply for a residence order or contact order with respect to the child under section 8 of the 1989 Act (residence, contact and other orders with respect to children) or, where the child is subject to a care order, an order under section 34 of the 1989 Act (parental contact etc. with children in care).

15 Requirement to obtain information about the child

(1) The adoption agency must obtain, so far as is reasonably practicable, the information about the child which is specified in Part 1 of Schedule 1.

(2) Subject to paragraph (4), the adoption agency must –

- (a) make arrangements for the child to be examined by a registered medical practitioner; and
- (b) obtain from that practitioner a written report ('the child's health report') on the state of the child's health which shall include any treatment which the child is receiving, any need for health care and the matters specified in Part 2 of Schedule 1,

unless the agency has received advice from the medical adviser that such an examination and report is unnecessary.

(3) Subject to paragraph (4), the adoption agency must make arrangements –

- (a) for such other medical and psychiatric examinations of, and other tests on, the child to be carried out as are recommended by the agency's medical adviser; and
- (b) for written reports of such examinations and tests to be obtained.

(4) Paragraphs (2) and (3) do not apply if the child is of sufficient understanding to make an informed decision and refuses to submit to the examinations or other tests.

16 Requirement to obtain information about the child's family

(1) The adoption agency must obtain, so far as is reasonably practicable, the information about the child's family which is specified in Part 3 of Schedule 1.

(2) The adoption agency must obtain, so far as is reasonably practicable, the information about the health of each of the child's natural parents and his brothers and sisters (of the full blood or half-blood) which is specified in Part 4 of Schedule 1.

17 Requirement to prepare child's permanence report for the adoption panel

(1) The adoption agency must prepare a written report ('the child's permanence report') which shall include –

- (a) the information about the child and his family as specified in Parts 1 and 3 of Schedule 1;

(b) a summary, written by the agency's medical adviser, of the state of the child's health, his health history and any need for health care which might arise in the future;
(c) the wishes and feelings of the child regarding the matters set out in regulation 13(1)(c);
(d) the wishes and feelings of the child's parent or guardian, and where regulation 14(4)(a) applies, his father, and any other person the agency considers relevant, regarding the matters set out in regulation 14(1)(c);
(e) the views of the agency about the child's need for contact with his parent or guardian or other relative or with any other person the agency considers relevant and the arrangements the agency proposes to make for allowing any person contact with the child;
(f) an assessment of the child's emotional and behavioural development and any related needs;
(g) an assessment of the parenting capacity of the child's parent or guardian and, where regulation 14(4)(a) applies, his father;
(h) a chronology of the decisions and actions taken by the agency with respect to the child;
(i) an analysis of the options for the future care of the child which have been considered by the agency and why placement for adoption is considered the preferred option; and
(j) any other information which the agency considers relevant.

(2) The adoption agency must send –

(a) the child's permanence report;
(b) the child's health report and any other reports referred to in regulation 15; and
(c) the information relating to the health of each of the child's natural parents,

to the adoption panel.

(3) The adoption agency must obtain, so far as is reasonably practicable, any other relevant information which may be requested by the adoption panel and send that information to the panel.

18 Function of the adoption panel in relation to a child referred by the adoption agency

(1) The adoption panel must consider the case of every child referred to it by the adoption agency and make a recommendation to the agency as to whether the child should be placed for adoption.

(2) In considering what recommendation to make the adoption panel must have regard to the duties imposed on the adoption agency under section 1(2), (4), (5) and (6) of the Act (considerations applying to the exercise of powers in relation to the adoption of a child) and –

(a) must consider and take into account the reports and any other information passed to it in accordance with regulation 17;
(b) may request the agency to obtain any other relevant information which the panel considers necessary; and
(c) must obtain legal advice in relation to the case.

(3) Where the adoption panel makes a recommendation to the adoption agency that the child should be placed for adoption, it must consider and may at the same time give advice to the agency about –

(a) the arrangements which the agency proposes to make for allowing any person contact with the child; and
(b) where the agency is a local authority, whether an application should be made by the authority for a placement order in respect of the child.

19 Adoption agency decision and notification

(1) The adoption agency must take into account the recommendation of the adoption panel in coming to a decision about whether the child should be placed for adoption.

(2) No member of the adoption panel shall take part in any decision made by the adoption agency under paragraph (1).

(3) The adoption agency must, if their whereabouts are known to the agency, notify in writing the parent or guardian and, where regulation 14(3) applies and the agency considers it is appropriate, the father of the child of its decision.

20 Request to appoint an officer of the Service or a Welsh family proceedings officer

Where the parent or guardian of the child is prepared to consent to the placement of the child for adoption under section 19 of the Act and, as the case may be, to consent to the making of a future adoption order under section 20 of the Act, the adoption agency must request the CAFCASS to appoint an officer of the Service or the National Assembly for Wales to appoint a Welsh family proceedings officer for the purposes of the signification by that officer of the consent to placement or to adoption by that parent or guardian and send with that request the information specified in Schedule 2.

PART 4

DUTIES OF ADOPTION AGENCY IN RESPECT OF A PROSPECTIVE ADOPTER

21 Requirement to provide counselling and information

(1) Where an adoption agency is considering a person's suitability to adopt a child, the agency must –

(a) provide a counselling service for the prospective adopter;
(b) in a section 83 case, explain to the prospective adopter the procedure in relation to, and the legal implications of, adopting a child from the country from which the prospective adopter wishes to adopt;
(c) in any other case, explain to him the procedure in relation to, and the legal implications of, placement for adoption and adoption; and
(d) provide him with written information about the matters referred to in sub-paragraph (b) or, as the case may be, (c).

(2) Paragraph (1) does not apply if the adoption agency is satisfied that the requirements set out in that paragraph have been carried out in respect of the prospective adopter by another adoption agency.

22 Requirement to consider application for an assessment of suitability to adopt a child

(1) Where the adoption agency, following the procedures referred to in regulation 21, receives an application in writing in the form provided by the agency from a prospective adopter for an assessment of his suitability to adopt a child, the agency must set up a case record in respect of that prospective adopter ('the prospective adopter's case record') and consider his suitability to adopt a child.

(2) The adoption agency may ask the prospective adopter to provide any further information in writing the agency may reasonably require.

(3) The adoption agency must place on the prospective adopter's case record –

- (a) the application by the prospective adopter for an assessment of his suitability to adopt a child referred to in paragraph (1);
- (b) the information and reports obtained by the agency by virtue of this Part;
- (c) the prospective adopter's report and his observations on that report;
- (d) the written record of the proceedings of the adoption panel under regulation 26 (and, where applicable, regulation 27(6)), its recommendation and the reasons for its recommendation and any advice given by the panel to the agency;
- (e) the record of the agency's decision under regulation 27(3), (5) or, as the case may be, (9);
- (f) where the prospective adopter applied to the Secretary of State for a review by an independent review panel the recommendation of that review panel;
- (g) where applicable, the prospective adopter's review report and his observations on that report; and
- (h) any other documents or information obtained by the agency which it considers should be included in that case record.

23 Requirement to carry out police checks

(1) An adoption agency must take steps to obtain –

- (a) in respect of the prospective adopter, an enhanced criminal record certificate within the meaning of section 115 of the Police Act 1997 including the matters specified in subsection (6A) of that section; and
- (b) in respect of any other member of his household aged 18 or over, an enhanced criminal record certificate under section 115 of that Act including the matters specified in subsection (6A) of that section.

(2) An adoption agency may not consider a person suitable to adopt a child if he or any member of his household aged 18 or over –

- (a) has been convicted of a specified offence committed at the age of 18 or over; or
- (b) has been cautioned by a constable in respect of any such offence which, at the time the caution was given, he admitted.

(3) In paragraph (2), 'specified offence' means –

- (a) an offence against a child;
- (b) an offence specified in Part 1 of Schedule 3;
- (c) an offence contrary to section 170 of the Customs and Excise Management Act 1979 in relation to goods prohibited to be imported under section 42 of the Customs Consolidation Act 1876 (prohibitions and restrictions relating to pornography) where the prohibited goods included indecent photographs of children under the age of 16;
- (d) any other offence involving bodily injury to a child, other than an offence of common assault or battery,

and the expression 'offence against a child' has the meaning given to it by section 26(1) of the Criminal Justice and Court Services Act 2000 except that it does not include an offence contrary to section 9 of the Sexual Offences Act 2003 (sexual activity with a child) in a case where the offender was under the age of 20 and the child was aged 13 or over at the time the offence was committed.

(4) An adoption agency may not consider a person suitable to adopt a child if he or any member of his household aged 18 or over –

(a) has been convicted of an offence specified in paragraph 1 of Part 2 of Schedule 3 committed at the age of 18 or over or has been cautioned by a constable in respect of any such offence which, at the time the caution was given, was admitted; or

(b) falls within paragraph 2 or 3 of Part 2 of Schedule 3,

notwithstanding that the statutory offences specified in Part 2 of Schedule 3 have been repealed.

(5) Where an adoption agency becomes aware that a prospective adopter or a member of his household falls within paragraph (2) or (4), the agency must notify the prospective adopter as soon as possible that he cannot be considered suitable to adopt a child.

24 Requirement to provide preparation for adoption

(1) Where an adoption agency is considering a person's suitability to adopt a child, the agency must make arrangements for the prospective adopter to receive such preparation for adoption as the agency considers appropriate.

(2) In paragraph (1) 'preparation for adoption' includes the provision of information to the prospective adopter about –

(a) the age range, sex, likely needs and background of children who may be placed for adoption by the adoption agency;
(b) the significance of adoption for a child and his family;
(c) contact between a child and his parent or guardian or other relatives where a child is authorised to be placed for adoption or is adopted;
(d) the skills which are necessary for an adoptive parent;
(e) the adoption agency's procedures in relation to the assessment of a prospective adopter and the placement of a child for adoption; and
(f) the procedure in relation to placement for adoption and adoption.

(3) Paragraph (1) does not apply if the adoption agency is satisfied that the requirements set out in that paragraph have been carried out in respect of the prospective adopter by another adoption agency.

25 Prospective adopter's report

(1) This regulation applies where the adoption agency, following the procedures referred to in regulations 23 and 24, consider the prospective adopter may be suitable to adopt a child.

(2) The adoption agency must obtain the information about the prospective adopter which is specified in Part 1 of Schedule 4.

(3) The adoption agency must obtain –

(a) a written report from a registered medical practitioner about the health of the prospective adopter following a full examination which must include matters specified in Part 2 of Schedule 4 unless the agency has received advice from its medical adviser that such an examination and report is unnecessary; and

(b) a written report of each of the interviews with the persons nominated by the prospective adopter to provide personal references for him.

(4) The adoption agency must ascertain whether the local authority in whose area the prospective adopter has his home have any information about the prospective adopter which may be relevant to the assessment and if so obtain from that authority a written report setting out that information.

(5) The adoption agency must prepare a written report ('the prospective adopter's report') which shall include –

   (a) the information about the prospective adopter and his family which is specified in Part 1 of Schedule 4;
   (b) a summary, written by the agency's medical adviser, of the state of health of the prospective adopter;
   (c) any relevant information the agency obtains under paragraph (4);
   (d) any observations of the agency on the matters referred to in regulations 21, 23 and 24;
   (e) the agency's assessment of the prospective adopter's suitability to adopt a child; and
   (f) any other information which the agency considers to be relevant.

(6) In a section 83 case, the prospective adopter's report shall also include –

   (a) the name of the country from which the prospective adopter wishes to adopt ('country of origin');
   (b) confirmation that the prospective adopter meets the eligibility requirements to adopt from the country of origin;
   (c) additional information obtained as a consequence of the requirements of the country of origin; and
   (d) the agency's assessment of the prospective adopter's suitability to adopt a child who is habitually resident outside the British Islands.

(7) Where the adoption agency receives information under paragraph (2), (3) or (4) or other information in relation to the assessment of the prospective adopter and is of the opinion that a prospective adopter is unlikely to be considered suitable to adopt a child, it may make the prospective adopter's report under paragraph (5) notwithstanding that the agency may not have obtained all the information about the prospective adopter which may be required by this regulation.

(8) The adoption agency must notify the prospective adopter that his application is to be referred to the adoption panel and give him a copy of the prospective adopter's report, inviting him to send any observations in writing to the agency within 10 working days, beginning with the date on which the notification is sent.

(9) At the end of the period of 10 working days referred to in paragraph (8) (or earlier if any observations made by the prospective adopter are received before that period has expired) the adoption agency must send –

   (a) the prospective adopter's report and the prospective adopter's observations;
   (b) the written reports referred to in paragraphs (3) and (4); and
   (c) any other relevant information obtained by the agency,

to the adoption panel.

(10) The adoption agency must obtain, so far as is reasonably practicable, any other relevant information which may be required by the adoption panel and send that information to the panel.

26 Function of the adoption panel

(1) Subject to paragraph (2), the adoption panel must consider the case of the prospective adopter referred to it by the adoption agency and make a recommendation to the agency as to whether the prospective adopter is suitable to adopt a child.

(2) In considering what recommendation to make the adoption panel –

(a) must consider and take into account all the information and reports passed to it in accordance with regulation 25;
(b) may request the adoption agency to obtain any other relevant information which the panel considers necessary; and
(c) may obtain legal advice as it considers necessary in relation to the case.

(3) Where the adoption panel makes a recommendation to the adoption agency that the prospective adopter is suitable to adopt a child, the panel may consider and give advice to the agency about the number of children the prospective adopter may be suitable to adopt, their age range, sex, likely needs and background.

(4) Before making any recommendation, the adoption panel must invite the prospective adopters to attend a meeting of the panel.

27 Adoption agency decision and notification

(1) The adoption agency must make a decision about whether the prospective adopter is suitable to adopt a child.

(2) No member of the adoption panel shall take part in any decision made by the adoption agency under paragraph (1).

(3) Where the adoption agency decides to approve the prospective adopter as suitable to adopt a child, it must notify him in writing of its decision.

(4) Where the adoption agency considers that the prospective adopter is not suitable to adopt a child, it must –

(a) notify the prospective adopter in writing that it proposes not to approve him as suitable to adopt a child ('qualifying determination');
(b) send with that notification its reasons together with a copy of the recommendation of the adoption panel if that recommendation is different;
(c) advise the prospective adopter that within 40 working days beginning with the date on which the notification was sent he may –
   (i) submit any representations he wishes to make to the agency; or
   (ii) apply to the Secretary of State for a review by an independent review panel of the qualifying determination.

(5) If, within the period of 40 working days referred to in paragraph (4), the prospective adopter has not made any representations or applied to the Secretary of State for a review by an independent review panel, the adoption agency shall proceed to make its decision and shall notify the prospective adopter in writing of its decision together with the reasons for that decision.

(6) If, within the period of 40 working days referred to in paragraph (4), the adoption agency receives further representations from the prospective adopter, it may refer the case together with all the relevant information to the adoption panel for further consideration.

(7) The adoption panel must consider any case referred to it under paragraph (6) and make a fresh recommendation to the adoption agency as to whether the prospective adopter is suitable to adopt a child.

(8) The adoption agency must make a decision on the case but –

(a) if the case has been referred to the adoption panel under paragraph (6), the agency must make the decision only after taking into account the recommendations of the adoption panel made under both paragraph (7) and regulation 26; or

(b) if the prospective adopter has applied to the Secretary of State for a review by an independent review panel of the qualifying determination, the agency must make the decision only after taking into account the recommendation of the independent review panel and the recommendation of the adoption panel made under regulation 26.

(9) As soon as possible after making its decision under paragraph (8), the adoption agency must notify the prospective adopter in writing of its decision stating its reasons for that decision if they do not consider the prospective adopter suitable to adopt a child, and of the adoption panel's recommendation under paragraph (7), if this is different from the agency's decision.

(10) In a case where an independent review panel has made a recommendation, the adoption agency shall send to the Secretary of State a copy of the notification referred to in paragraph (9).

28 Information to be sent to the independent review panel

(1) If the adoption agency receives notification from the Secretary of State that a prospective adopter has applied for a review by an independent review panel of the qualifying determination, the agency must, within 10 working days of receipt of that notification, send to the Secretary of State the information specified in paragraph (2).

(2) The following information is specified for the purposes of paragraph (1) –

(a) all of the documents and information which were passed to the adoption panel in accordance with regulation 25;

(b) any relevant information in relation to the prospective adopter which was obtained by the agency after the date on which the documents and information referred to in sub-paragraph (a) were passed to the adoption panel; and

(c) the documents referred to in regulation 27(4)(a) and (b).

29 Review and termination of approval

(1) The adoption agency must review the approval of each prospective adopter in accordance with this regulation, unless –

(a) in a section 83 case, the prospective adopter has visited the child in the country in which the child is habitually resident and has confirmed in writing that he wishes to proceed with the adoption; and

(b) in any other case, a child is placed for adoption with the prospective adopter.

(2) A review must take place whenever the adoption agency considers it necessary but otherwise not more than one year after approval and thereafter at intervals of not more than a year.

(3) When undertaking such a review the adoption agency must –

(a) make such enquiries and obtain such information as it considers necessary in order to review whether the prospective adopter continues to be suitable to adopt a child; and

(b) seek and take into account the views of the prospective adopter.

(4) If at the conclusion of the review, the adoption agency considers that the prospective adopter may no longer be suitable to adopt a child, it must –

   (a) prepare a written report ('the prospective adopter's review report') which shall include the agency's reasons;
   (b) notify the prospective adopter that his case is to be referred to the adoption panel; and
   (c) give him a copy of the report inviting him to send any observations to the agency within 10 working days beginning with the date on which that report is sent.

(5) At the end of the period of 10 working days referred to in paragraph (4)(c) (or earlier if the prospective adopter's comments are received before that period has expired), the adoption agency must send the prospective adopter's review report together with the prospective adopter's observations to the adoption panel.

(6) The adoption agency must obtain, so far as is reasonably practicable, any other relevant information which may be required by the adoption panel and send that information to the panel.

(7) The adoption panel must consider the prospective adopter's review report, the prospective adopter's observations and any other information passed to it by the adoption agency and make a recommendation to the agency as to whether the prospective adopter continues to be suitable to adopt a child.

(8) The adoption agency must make a decision as to whether the prospective adopter continues to be suitable to adopt a child and regulation 27(2) to (10) shall apply in relation to that decision by the agency.

30 Duties of the adoption agency in a section 83 case

Where the adoption agency decides in a section 83 case to approve a prospective adopter as suitable to adopt a child, the agency must send to the Secretary of State –

   (a) written confirmation of the decision and any recommendation the agency may make in relation to the number of children the prospective adopter may be suitable to adopt, their age range, sex, likely needs and background;
   (b) all the documents and information which were passed to the adoption panel in accordance with regulation 25;
   (c) the record of the proceedings of the adoption panel, its recommendation and the reasons for its recommendation;
   (d) if the prospective adopter applied to the Secretary of State for a review by an independent review panel of a qualifying determination, the record of the proceedings of that panel, its recommendation and the reasons for its recommendation; and
   (e) any other information relating to the case which the Secretary of State or the relevant foreign authority may require.

PART 5

DUTIES OF ADOPTION AGENCY IN RESPECT OF PROPOSED PLACEMENT OF CHILD WITH PROSPECTIVE ADOPTER

31 Proposed placement

(1) Where an adoption agency is considering placing a child for adoption with a particular prospective adopter ('the proposed placement') the agency must –

(a) provide the prospective adopter with a copy of the child's permanence report and any other information the agency considers relevant;
(b) meet with the prospective adopter to discuss the proposed placement;
(c) ascertain the views of the prospective adopter about –
    (i) the proposed placement; and
    (ii) the arrangements the agency proposes to make for allowing any person contact with the child; and
(d) provide a counselling service for, and any further information to, the prospective adopter as may be required.

(2) Where the adoption agency considers that the proposed placement should proceed, the agency must –

(a) where the agency is a local authority, carry out an assessment of the needs of the child and the prospective adopter and any children of the prospective adopter ('the adoptive family') for adoption support services in accordance with regulations made under section 4(6) of the Act;
(b) where the agency is a registered adoption society, notify the prospective adopter that he may request the local authority in whose area he has his home ('the relevant authority') to carry out an assessment of his needs for adoption support services under section 4(1) of the Act and pass to the relevant authority, at their request, a copy of the child's permanence report and a copy of the prospective adopter's report;
(c) consider the arrangements for allowing any person contact with the child; and
(d) prepare a written report ('the adoption placement report') which shall include –
    (i) the agency's reasons for proposing the placement;
    (ii) the information obtained by the agency by virtue of paragraph (1);
    (iii) where the agency is a local authority, their proposals for the provision of adoption support services for the adoptive family;
    (iv) the arrangements the agency proposes to make for allowing any person contact with the child; and
    (v) any other relevant information.

(3) The adoption agency must notify the prospective adopter that the proposed placement is to be referred to the adoption panel and give him a copy of the adoption placement report, inviting him to send any observations in writing to the agency within 10 working days, beginning with the date on which the notification is sent.

(4) At the end of the period of 10 working days referred to in paragraph (3) (or earlier if observations are received before the 10 working days has expired) the adoption agency must send –

(a) the adoption placement report;
(b) the child's permanence report; and
(c) the prospective adopter's report and his observations,

to the adoption panel.

(5) The adoption agency must obtain so far as is reasonably practicable any other relevant information which may be requested by the adoption panel in connection with the proposed placement and send that information to the panel.

(6) This paragraph applies where an adoption agency ('agency A') intends to refer a proposed placement to the adoption panel and another agency ('agency B') made the decision (in accordance with these Regulations) that –

(a) the child should be placed for adoption; or

(b) the prospective adopter is suitable to be an adoptive parent.

(7) Where paragraph (6) applies agency A may only refer the proposed placement to the adoption panel if it has consulted agency B about the proposed placement.

(8) Agency A must –

(a) where paragraph (6)(a) applies, open a child's case record; or
(b) where paragraph (6)(b) applies, open a prospective adopter's case record,

and place on the appropriate record, the information and documents received from agency B.

32 Function of the adoption panel in relation to proposed placement

(1) The adoption panel must consider the proposed placement referred to it by the adoption agency and make a recommendation to the agency as to whether the child should be placed for adoption with that particular prospective adopter.

(2) In considering what recommendation to make the adoption panel shall have regard to the duties imposed on the adoption agency under section 1(2), (4) and (5) of the Act (considerations applying to the exercise of powers in relation to the adoption of a child) and –

(a) must consider and take into account all information and the reports passed to it in accordance with regulation 31;
(b) may request the agency to obtain any other relevant information which the panel considers necessary; and
(c) may obtain legal advice as it considers necessary in relation to the case.

(3) The adoption panel must consider –

(a) in a case where the adoption agency is a local authority, the authority's proposals for the provision of adoption support services for the adoptive family;
(b) the arrangements the adoption agency proposes to make for allowing any person contact with the child; and
(c) whether the parental responsibility of any parent or guardian or the prospective adopter should be restricted and if so the extent of any such restriction.

(4) Where the adoption panel makes a recommendation to the adoption agency that the child should be placed for adoption with the particular prospective adopter, the panel may at the same time give advice to the agency about any of the matters set out in paragraph (3).

(5) An adoption panel may only make the recommendation referred to in paragraph (1) if –

(a) that recommendation is to be made at the same meeting of the adoption panel at which a recommendation has been made that the child should be placed for adoption; or
(b) the adoption agency, or another adoption agency, has already made a decision in accordance with regulation 19 that the child should be placed for adoption,

and in either case that recommendation is to be made at the same meeting of the panel at which a recommendation has been made that the prospective adopter is suitable to adopt a child or the adoption agency, or another adoption agency, has made a decision in accordance with regulation 27 that the prospective adopter is suitable to adopt a child.

33 Adoption agency decision in relation to proposed placement

(1) The adoption agency must take into account the recommendation of the adoption panel in coming to a decision about whether the child should be placed for adoption with the particular prospective adopter.

(2) No member of the adoption panel shall take part in any decision made by the adoption agency under paragraph (1).

(3) As soon as possible after making its decision the adoption agency must notify in writing –

(a) the prospective adopter of its decision; and
(b) if their whereabouts are known to the agency, the parent or guardian and, where regulation 14(3) applies and the agency considers it is appropriate, the father of the child, of the fact that the child is to be placed for adoption.

(4) If the adoption agency decides that the proposed placement should proceed, the agency must, in an appropriate manner and having regard to the child's age and understanding, explain its decision to the child.

(5) The adoption agency must place on the child's case record –

(a) the prospective adopter's report;
(b) the adoption placement report and the prospective adopter's observations on that report;
(c) the written record of the proceedings of the adoption panel under regulation 32, its recommendation, the reasons for its recommendation and any advice given by the panel to the agency; and
(d) the record and notification of the agency's decision under this regulation.

34 Function of the adoption agency in a section 83 case

(1) This paragraph applies where in a section 83 case the adoption agency receives from the relevant foreign authority information about a child to be adopted by a prospective adopter.

(2) Where paragraph (1) applies, the adoption agency must –

(a) send a copy of the information referred to in paragraph (1) to the prospective adopter unless it is aware that the prospective adopter has received a copy;
(b) consider that information and meet with the prospective adopter to discuss the information; and
(c) if appropriate, provide a counselling service for, and any further information to, the prospective adopter as may be required.

PART 6
PLACEMENT AND REVIEWS

35 Requirements imposed on the adoption agency before the child may be placed for adoption

(1) This paragraph applies where the adoption agency –

(a) has decided in accordance with regulation 33 to place a child for adoption with a particular prospective adopter; and
(b) has met with the prospective adopter to consider the arrangements it proposes to make for the placement of the child with him.

(2) Where paragraph (1) applies, the adoption agency must, as soon as possible, send the prospective adopter a placement plan in respect of the child which covers the matters specified in Schedule 5 ('the adoption placement plan').

(3) Where the prospective adopter notifies the adoption agency that he wishes to proceed with the placement and the agency is authorised to place the child for adoption or, subject to paragraph (4), the child is less than 6 weeks old, the agency may place the child for adoption with the prospective adopter.

(4) Unless there is a placement order in respect of the child, the adoption agency may not place for adoption a child who is less than six weeks old unless the parent or guardian of the child has agreed in writing with the agency that the child may be placed for adoption.

(5) Where the child already has his home with the prospective adopter, the adoption agency must notify the prospective adopter in writing of the date on which the child is placed for adoption with him by that agency.

(6) The adoption agency must before the child is placed for adoption with the prospective adopter –

- (a) send to the prospective adopter's general practitioner written notification of the proposed placement and send with that notification a written report of the child's health history and current state of health;
- (b) send to the local authority (if that authority is not the adoption agency) and Primary Care Trust or Local Health Board (Wales), in whose area the prospective adopter has his home, written notification of the proposed placement; and
- (c) where the child is of compulsory school age, send to the local education authority, in whose area the prospective adopter has his home, written notification of the proposed placement and information about the child's educational history and whether he has been or is likely to be assessed for special educational needs under the Education Act 1996.

(7) The adoption agency must notify the prospective adopter in writing of any change to the adoption placement plan.

(8) The adoption agency must place on the child's case record –

- (a) in the case of a child who is less than 6 weeks old and in respect of whom there is no placement order, a copy of the agreement referred to in paragraph (4); and
- (b) a copy of the adoption placement plan and any changes to that plan.

36 Reviews

(1) Where an adoption agency is authorised to place a child for adoption but the child is not for the time being placed for adoption the agency must carry out a review of the child's case –

- (a) not more than 3 months after the date on which the agency first has authority to place; and
- (b) thereafter not more than 6 months after the date of the previous review ('6 months review'),

until the child is placed for adoption.

(2) Paragraphs (3) and (4) apply where a child is placed for adoption.

(3) The adoption agency must carry out a review of the child's case –

- (a) not more than 4 weeks after the date on which the child is placed for adoption ('the first review');
- (b) not more than 3 months after the first review; and
- (c) thereafter not more than 6 months after the date of the previous review,

unless the child is returned to the agency by the prospective adopter or an adoption order is made.

(4) The adoption agency must –

(a) ensure that the child and the prospective adopter are visited within one week of the placement and thereafter at least once a week until the first review and thereafter at such frequency as the agency decides at each review;
(b) ensure that written reports are made of such visits; and
(c) provide such advice and assistance to the prospective adopter as the agency considers necessary.

(5) When carrying out a review the adoption agency must consider each of the matters set out in paragraph (6) and must, so far as is reasonably practicable, ascertain the views of –

(a) the child, having regard to his age and understanding;
(b) if the child is placed for adoption, the prospective adopter; and
(c) any other person the agency considers relevant,

in relation to such of the matters set out in paragraph (6) as the agency considers appropriate.

(6) The matters referred to in paragraph (5) are –

(a) whether the adoption agency remains satisfied that the child should be placed for adoption;
(b) the child's needs, welfare and development, and whether any changes need to be made to meet his needs or assist his development;
(c) the existing arrangements for contact, and whether they should continue or be altered;
(d) where the child is placed for adoption, the arrangements in relation to the exercise of parental responsibility for the child, and whether they should continue or be altered;
(e) the arrangements for the provision of adoption support services for the adoptive family and whether there should be any re-assessment of the need for those services;
(f) in consultation with the appropriate agencies, the arrangements for assessing and meeting the child's health care and educational needs;
(g) subject to paragraphs (1) and (3), the frequency of the reviews.

(7) Where the child is subject to a placement order and has not been placed for adoption at the time of the first 6 months review, the local authority must at that review –

(a) establish why the child has not been placed for adoption and consider what further steps the authority should take in relation to the placement of the child for adoption; and
(b) consider whether it remains satisfied that the child should be placed for adoption.

(8) The adoption agency must, so far as is reasonably practicable, notify –

(a) the child, where the agency considers he is of sufficient age and understanding;
(b) the prospective adopter; and
(c) any other person whom the agency considers relevant,

of the outcome of a review and of any decision taken by the agency in consequence of that review.

(9) The adoption agency must ensure that –

(a) the information obtained in the course of a review or visit in respect of a child's case including the views expressed by the child;
(b) the details of the proceedings of any meeting arranged by the agency to consider any aspect of the review of the case; and

(c) details of any decision made in the course of or as a result of the review,

are recorded in writing and placed on the child's case record.

(10) Where the child is returned to the adoption agency in accordance with section 35(1) or (2) of the Act, the agency must conduct a review of the child's case no earlier than 28 days, or later than 42 days, after the date on which the child is returned to the agency and when carrying out that review the agency must consider the matters set out in paragraph (6)(a), (b), (c) and (f).

37 Independent reviewing officers

(1) An adoption agency which is –

- (a) a local authority; or
- (b) a registered adoption society which is a voluntary organisation who provide accommodation for a child,

must appoint a person ('the independent reviewing officer') in respect of the case of each child authorised to be placed for adoption by the agency to carry out the functions mentioned in section 26(2A) of the 1989 Act.

(2) The independent reviewing officer must be registered as a social worker in a register maintained by the General Social Care Council or by the Care Council for Wales under section 56 of the Care Standards Act 2000 or in a corresponding register maintained under the law of Scotland or Northern Ireland.

(3) The independent reviewing officer must, in the opinion of the adoption agency, have sufficient relevant social work experience to undertake the functions referred to in paragraph (1) in relation to the case.

(4) A person who is an employee of the adoption agency may not be appointed as an independent reviewing officer in a case if he is involved in the management of the case or is under the direct management of –

- (a) a person involved in the management of the case;
- (b) a person with management responsibilities in relation to a person mentioned in sub-paragraph (a); or
- (c) a person with control over the resources allocated to the case.

(5) The independent reviewing officer must –

- (a) as far as is reasonably practicable attend any meeting held in connection with the review of the child's case; and
- (b) chair any such meeting that he attends.

(6) The independent reviewing officer must, as far as is reasonably practicable, take steps to ensure that the review is conducted in accordance with regulation 36 and in particular to ensure –

- (a) that the child's views are understood and taken into account;
- (b) that the persons responsible for implementing any decision taken in consequence of the review are identified; and
- (c) that any failure to review the case in accordance with regulation 36 or to take proper steps to make the arrangements agreed at the review is brought to the attention of persons at an appropriate level of seniority within the adoption agency.

(7) If the child whose case is reviewed wishes to take proceedings on his own account, for example, to apply to the court for revocation of a placement order, it is the function of the independent reviewing officer –

(a) to assist the child to obtain legal advice; or
(b) to establish whether an appropriate adult is able and willing to provide such assistance or bring the proceedings on the child's behalf.

(8) The adoption agency must inform the independent reviewing officer of –

(a) any significant failure to make the arrangements agreed at a review; and
(b) any significant change in the child's circumstances after a review.

38 Withdrawal of consent

(1) This paragraph applies where consent given under section 19 or 20 of the Act in respect of a child is withdrawn in accordance with section 52(8) of the Act.

(2) Where paragraph (1) applies and the adoption agency is a local authority, on receipt of the form or notice given in accordance with section 52(8) of the Act the authority must immediately review their decision to place the child for adoption and where, in accordance with section 22(1) to (3) of the Act, the authority decide to apply for a placement order in respect of the child, they must notify as soon as possible –

(a) the parent or guardian of the child;
(b) where regulation 14(3) applies and the agency considers it is appropriate, the child's father; and
(c) if the child is placed for adoption, the prospective adopter with whom the child is placed.

(3) Where paragraph (1) applies and the adoption agency is a registered adoption society, the agency must immediately consider whether it is appropriate to inform the local authority in whose area the child is living.

PART 7

CASE RECORDS

39 Storage of case records

The adoption agency must ensure that the child's case record and the prospective adopter's case record and the contents of those case records are at all times kept in secure conditions and in particular that all appropriate measures are taken to prevent the theft, unauthorised disclosure, loss or destruction of, or damage to, the case record or its contents.

40 Preservation of case records

An adoption agency must keep the child's case record and the prospective adopter's case record for such period as it considers appropriate.

41 Confidentiality of case records

Subject to regulation 42, the contents of the child's case record and the prospective adopter's case record shall be treated by the adoption agency as confidential.

42 Access to case records and disclosure of information

(1) Subject to paragraph (3), an adoption agency shall provide such access to its case records and disclose such information in its possession, as may be required –

(a) to those holding an inquiry under section 81 of the 1989 Act (inquiries) or section 17 of the Act (inquiries) for the purposes of such an inquiry;
(b) to the Secretary of State;
(c) to the registration authority;
(d) subject to the provisions of sections 29(7) and 32(3) of the Local Government Act 1974 (investigations and disclosure), to the Commission for Local Administration in England, for the purposes of any investigation conducted in accordance with Part 3 of that Act;
(e) to any person appointed by the agency for the purposes of the consideration by the agency of any representations (including complaints);
(f) by and to the extent specified in these Regulations;
(g) to an officer of the Service or a Welsh family proceedings officer for the purposes of the discharge of his duties under the Act; and
(h) to a court having power to make an order under the Act or the 1989 Act.

(2) Subject to paragraph (3), an adoption agency may provide such access to its case records and disclose such information in its possession, as it thinks fit for the purposes of carrying out its functions as an adoption agency.

(3) A written record shall be kept by an adoption agency of any access provided or disclosure made by virtue of this regulation.

43 Transfer of case records

(1) An adoption agency may transfer a copy of a child's case record or prospective adopter's case record (or part of that record) to another adoption agency when it considers this to be in the interests of the child or prospective adopter to whom the record relates, and a written record shall be kept of any such transfer.

(2) Subject to paragraph (3), a registered adoption society which intends to cease to act or exist as such shall forthwith either transfer its case records to another adoption agency having first obtained the registration authority's approval for such transfer, or transfer its case records –

(a) to the local authority in whose area the society's principal office is situated; or
(b) in the case of a society which amalgamates with another registered adoption society to form a new registered adoption society, to the new body.

(3) An adoption agency to which case records are transferred by virtue of paragraph (2)(a) or (b) shall notify the registration authority in writing of such transfer.

44 Application of regulations 40 to 42

Nothing in this Part applies to the information which an adoption agency must keep in relation to an adopted person by virtue of regulations made under section 56 of the Act.

PART 8

MISCELLANEOUS

45 Modification of 1989 Act in relation to adoption

(1) This paragraph applies where –

(a) a local authority are authorised to place a child for adoption; or
(b) a child who has been placed for adoption by a local authority is less than 6 weeks old.

(2) Where paragraph (1) applies –

(a) section 22(4)(b) of the 1989 Act shall not apply;
(b) section 22(4)(c) of the 1989 Act shall apply as if for that sub-paragraph there were inserted '(c) any prospective adopter with whom the local authority has placed the child for adoption.';
(c) section 22(5)(b) of the 1989 Act shall apply as if for the words '(4)(b) to (d)' there were inserted '(4)(c) and (d)'; and
(d) paragraphs 15 and 21 of Schedule 2 to the 1989 Act shall not apply.

(3) This paragraph applies where a registered adoption society is authorised to place a child for adoption or a child who has been placed for adoption by a registered adoption society is less than 6 weeks old.

(4) Where paragraph (3) applies –

(a) section 61(2)(a) of the 1989 Act is to have effect in relation to the child whether or not he is accommodated by or on behalf of the society;
(b) section 61(2)(b) of the 1989 Act shall not apply; and
(c) section 61(2)(c) of the 1989 Act shall apply as if for that sub-paragraph there were inserted '(c) any prospective adopter with whom the registered adoption society has placed the child for adoption.'.

46 Contact

(1) This paragraph applies where an adoption agency decides that a child should be placed for adoption.

(2) Where paragraph (1) applies and subject to paragraph (3), the adoption agency must consider what arrangements it should make for allowing any person contact with the child once the agency is authorised to place the child for adoption ('the contact arrangements').

(3) The adoption agency must –

(a) take into account the wishes and feelings of the parent or guardian of the child and, where regulation 14(3) applies and the agency considers it is appropriate, the father of the child;
(b) take into account any advice given by the adoption panel in accordance with regulation 18(3); and
(c) have regard to the considerations set out in section 1(2) and (4) of the Act,

in coming to a decision in relation to the contact arrangements.

(4) The adoption agency must notify –

(a) the child, if the agency considers he is of sufficient age and understanding;
(b) if their whereabouts are known to the agency, the parent or guardian, and, where regulation 14(3) applies and the agency considers it is appropriate, the father of the child;
(c) any person in whose favour there was a provision for contact under the 1989 Act which ceased to have effect by virtue of section 26(1) of the Act; and
(d) any other person the agency considers relevant,

of the contact arrangements.

(5) Where an adoption agency decides that a child should be placed for adoption with a particular prospective adopter, the agency must review the contact arrangements in light of the views of the prospective adopter and any advice given by the adoption panel in accordance with regulation 32(3).

(6) If the adoption agency proposes to make any change to the contact arrangements which affects any person mentioned in paragraph (4), it must seek the views of that person and take those views into account in deciding what arrangements it should make for allowing any person contact with the child while he is placed for adoption with the prospective adopter.

(7) The adoption agency must –

(a) set out the contact arrangements in the placement plan; and
(b) keep the contact arrangements under review.

47 Contact: supplementary

(1) Where an adoption agency has decided under section 27(2) of the Act to refuse to allow the contact that would otherwise be required by virtue of an order under section 26 of the Act, the agency must, as soon as the decision is made, inform the persons specified in paragraph (3) and notify them of the decision, the date of the decision, the reasons for the decision and the duration of the period.

(2) The terms of an order under section 26 of the Act may be departed from by agreement between the adoption agency and any person for whose contact with the child the order provides subject to the following conditions –

(a) where the child is of sufficient age and understanding, subject to his agreement;
(b) where the child is placed for adoption, subject to consultation before the agreement is reached, with the prospective adopter with whom the child is placed for adoption; and
(c) written confirmation by the agency to the persons specified in paragraph (3) of the terms of that agreement.

(3) The following persons are specified for the purposes of paragraphs (1) and (2) –

(a) the child, if the adoption agency considers he is of sufficient age and understanding;
(b) the person in whose favour the order under section 26 was made; and
(c) if the child is placed for adoption, the prospective adopter.

SCHEDULE 1

INFORMATION

Part 1

Regulation 15(1)

Information about the child

1 Name, sex, date and place of birth and address including the local authority area.

2 A photograph and physical description.

3 Nationality.

4 Racial origin and cultural and linguistic background.

5 Religious persuasion (including details of baptism, confirmation or equivalent ceremonies).

6 Whether the child is looked after or is provided with accommodation under section 59(1) of the 1989 Act.

7 Details of any order made by a court with respect to the child under the 1989 Act including the name of the court, the order made and the date on which the order was made.

8 Whether the child has any rights to, or interest in, property or any claim to damages under the Fatal Accidents Act 1976 or otherwise which he stands to retain or lose if he is adopted.

9 A chronology of the child's care since birth.

10 A description of the child's personality, his social development and his emotional and behavioural development.

11 Whether the child has any difficulties with activities such as feeding, washing and dressing himself.

12 The educational history of the child including –

(a) the names, addresses and types of nurseries or schools attended with dates;
(b) a summary of his progress and attainments;
(c) whether he is subject to a statement of special educational needs under the Education Act 1996;
(d) any special needs he has in relation to learning; and
(e) where he is looked after, details of his personal education plan prepared by the local authority.

13 Information about –

(a) the child's relationship with –
  (i) his parent or guardian;
  (ii) any brothers or sisters or other relatives he may have; and
  (iii) any other person the agency considers relevant;
(b) the likelihood of any such relationship continuing and the value to the child of its doing so; and
(c) the ability and willingness of the child's parent or guardian or any other person the agency considers relevant, to provide the child with a secure environment in which he can develop, and otherwise to meet his needs.

14 The current arrangements for and the type of contact between the child's parent or guardian or other person with parental responsibility for him, his father, and any relative, friend or other person.

15 A description of the child's interests, likes and dislikes.

16 Any other relevant information which might assist the adoption panel and the adoption agency.

17 In this Part 'parent' includes the child's father whether or not he has parental responsibility for the child.

Part 2

Regulation 15(2)

Matters to be included in the child's health report

1 Name, date of birth, sex, weight and height.

2 A neo-natal report on the child, including –

(a) details of his birth and any complications;
(b) the results of a physical examination and screening tests;
(c) details of any treatment given;
(d) details of any problem in management and feeding;
(e) any other relevant information which may assist the adoption panel and the adoption agency; and
(f) the name and address of any registered medical practitioner who may be able to provide further information about any of the above matters.

3 A full health history of the child, including –

(a) details of any serious illness, disability, accident, hospital admission or attendance at an out-patient department, and in each case any treatment given;
(b) details and dates of immunisations;
(c) a physical and developmental assessment according to age, including an assessment of vision and hearing and of neurological, speech and language development and any evidence of emotional disorder;
(d) for a child over five years of age, the school health history (if available);
(e) how his physical and mental health and medical history have affected his physical, intellectual, emotional, social or behavioural development; and
(f) any other relevant information which may assist the adoption panel and the adoption agency.

Part 3

Regulation 16(1)

Information about the child's family and others

Information about each parent of the child

1 Name, sex, date and place of birth and address including the local authority area.

2 A photograph, if available, and physical description.

3 Nationality.

4 Racial origin and cultural and linguistic background.

5 Religious persuasion.

6 A description of their personality and interests.

Information about the child's brothers and sisters

7 Name, sex, and date and place of birth.

8 A photograph, if available, and physical description.

9 Nationality.

10 Address, if appropriate.

11 If the brother or sister is under the age of 18 –

(a) where and with whom he or she is living;

(b) whether he or she is looked after or is provided with accommodation under section 59(1) of the 1989 Act;
(c) details of any court order made with respect to him or her under the 1989 Act, including the name of the court, the order made, and the date on which the order was made; and
(d) whether he or she is also being considered for adoption.

Information about the child's other relatives and any other person the agency considers relevant

12 Name, sex and date and place of birth.

13 Nationality.

14 Address, if appropriate.

Family history and relationships

15 Whether the child's parents were married to each other at the time of the child's birth (or have subsequently married) and if so, the date and place of marriage and whether they are divorced or separated.

16 Where the child's parents are not married, whether the father has parental responsibility for the child and if so how it was acquired.

17 If the identity or whereabouts of the child's father are not known, the information about him that has been ascertained and from whom, and the steps that have been taken to establish paternity.

18 Where the child's parents have been previously married or formed a civil partnership, the date of the marriage or, as the case may be, the date and place of registration of the civil partnership.

19 So far as is possible, a family tree with details of the child's grandparents, parents and aunts and uncles with their age (or ages at death).

20 Where it is reasonably practicable, a chronology of each of the child's parents from birth.

21 The observations of the child's parents about their own experiences of being parented and how this has influenced them.

22 The past and present relationship of the child's parents.

23 Details of the wider family and their role and importance to –
   (a) the child's parents; and
   (b) any brothers or sisters of the child.

Other information about each parent of the child

24 Information about their home and the neighbourhood in which they live.

25 Details of their educational history.

26 Details of their employment history.

27 Information about the parenting capacity of the child's parents, particularly their ability and willingness to parent the child.

28 Any other relevant information which might assist the adoption panel and the adoption agency.

29 In this Part 'parent' includes the father of the child whether or not he has parental responsibility for the child.

Part 4

Regulation 16(2)

Information relating to the health of the child's natural parents and brothers and sisters

1 Name, date of birth, sex, weight and height of each natural parent.

2 A health history of each of the child's natural parents, including details of any serious physical or mental illness, any hereditary disease or disorder, drug or alcohol misuse, disability, accident or hospital admission and in each case any treatment given where the agency consider such information to be relevant.

3 A health history of the child's brothers and sisters (of the full blood or half-blood), and the other children of each parent with details of any serious physical or mental illness and any hereditary disease or disorder.

4 A summary of the mother's obstetric history, including any problems in the ante-natal, labour and post-natal periods, with the results of any tests carried out during or immediately after the pregnancy.

5 Details of any present illness, including treatment and prognosis.

6 Any other relevant information which the adoption agency considers may assist the adoption panel and the agency.

SCHEDULE 2

INFORMATION AND DOCUMENTS TO BE PROVIDED TO THE CAFCASS OR THE NATIONAL ASSEMBLY FOR WALES

Regulation 20

1 A certified copy of the child's birth certificate.

2 Name and address of the child's parent or guardian.

3 A chronology of the actions and decisions taken by the adoption agency with respect to the child.

4 Confirmation by the adoption agency that it has counselled, and explained to the parent or guardian the legal implications of both consent to placement under section 19 of the Act and, as the case may be, to the making of a future adoption order under section 20 of the Act and provided the parent or guardian with written information about this together with a copy of the written information provided to him.

5 Such information about the parent or guardian or other information as the adoption agency considers the officer of the Service or the Welsh family proceedings officer may need to know.

SCHEDULE 3

Part 1

Regulation 23(3)

Offences specified for the purposes of regulation 23(3)(b)

Offences in England and Wales

1 Any of the following offences against an adult –

(a) an offence of rape under section 1 of the Sexual Offences Act 2003;
(b) an offence of assault by penetration under section 2 of that Act;
(c) an offence of causing a person to engage in sexual activity without consent under section 4 of that Act, if the activity fell within subsection (4) of that section;
(d) an offence of sexual activity with a person with a mental disorder impeding choice under section 30 of that Act, if the touching fell within subsection (3) of that section;
(e) an offence of causing or inciting a person with mental disorder impeding choice to engage in sexual activity under section 31of that Act, if the activity caused or incited fell within subsection (3) of that section;
(f) an offence of inducement, threat or deception to procure sexual activity with a person with a mental disorder under section 34 of that Act, if the touching involved fell within subsection (2) of that section; and
(g) an offence of causing a person with a mental disorder to engage in or agree to engage in sexual activity by inducement, threat or deception under section 35 of that Act, if the activity fell within subsection (2) of that section.

Offences in Scotland

2 An offence of rape.

3 An offence specified in Schedule 1 to the Criminal Procedure (Scotland) Act 1995 except, in a case where the offender was under the age of 20 at the time the offence was committed, an offence contrary to section 5 of the Criminal Law (Consolidation) (Scotland) Act 1995 (intercourse with a girl under 16), an offence of shameless indecency between men or an offence of sodomy.

4 An offence of plagium (theft of a child below the age of puberty).

5 Section 52 or 52A of the Civil Government (Scotland) Act 1982 (indecent photographs of children).

6 An offence under section 3 of the Sexual Offences (Amendment) Act 2000 (abuse of trust).

Offences in Northern Ireland

7 An offence of rape.

8 An offence specified in Schedule 1 to the Children and Young Person Act (Northern Ireland) 1968, except offences of common assault or battery or in the case where the offender was under the age of 20 at the time the offence was committed, an offence contrary to section 5 or 11 of the Criminal Law Amendment Act 1885 (unlawful carnal knowledge of a girl under 17 and gross indecency between males).

9 An offence under Article 3 of the Protection of Children (Northern Ireland) Order 1978 (indecent photographs).

10 An offence under Article 9 of the Criminal Justice (Northern Ireland) Order 1980 (inciting girl under 16 to have incestuous sexual intercourse).

11 An offence contrary to Article 15 of the Criminal Justice (Evidence, Etc.) (Northern Ireland) Order 1988 (possession of indecent photographs of children).

Part 2

Regulation 23(4)

Repealed statutory offences

1 (1) An offence under any of the following sections of the Sexual Offences Act 1956 –

- (a) section 1 (rape);
- (b) section 5 (intercourse with a girl under 13);
- (c) subject to paragraph 4, section 6 (intercourse with a girl under 16);
- (d) section 19 or 20 (abduction of girl under 18 or 16);
- (e) section 25 or 26 of that Act (permitting girl under 13, or between 13 and 16, to use premises for intercourse); and
- (f) section 28 (causing or encouraging prostitution of, intercourse with or indecent assault on, girl under 16).

(2) An offence under section 1 of the Indecency with Children Act 1960 (indecent conduct towards young child).

(3) An offence under section 54 of the Criminal Law Act 1977 (inciting girl under sixteen to incest).

(4) An offence under section 3 of the Sexual Offences (Amendment) Act 2000 (abuse of trust).

2 A person falls within this paragraph if he has been convicted of any of the following offences against a child committed at the age of 18 or over or has been cautioned by a constable in respect of any such offence which, at the time the caution was given, he admitted –

- (a) an offence under section 2 or 3 of the Sexual Offences Act 1956 Act (procurement of woman by threats or false pretences);
- (b) an offence under section 4 of that Act (administering drugs to obtain or facilitate intercourse);
- (c) an offence under section 14 or 15 of that Act (indecent assault);
- (d) an offence under section 16 of that Act (assault with intent to commit buggery);
- (e) an offence under section 17 of that Act (abduction of woman by force or for the sake of her property); and
- (f) an offence under section 24 of that Act (detention of woman in brothel or other premises).

3 A person falls within this paragraph if he has been convicted of any of the following offences committed at the age of 18 or over or has been cautioned by a constable in respect of any such offence which, at the time the caution was given, he admitted –

- (a) an offence under section 7 of the Sexual Offences Act 1956 (intercourse with defective) by having sexual intercourse with a child;

(b) an offence under section 9 of that Act (procurement of defective) by procuring a child to have sexual intercourse;
(c) an offence under section 10 of that Act (incest by a man) by having sexual intercourse with a child;
(d) an offence under section 11 of that Act (incest by a woman) by allowing a child to have sexual intercourse with her;
(e) subject to paragraph 4, an offence under section 12 of that Act by committing buggery with a child under the age of 16;
(f) subject to paragraph 4, an offence under section 13 of that Act by committing an act of gross indecency with a child;
(g) an offence under section 21 of that Act (abduction of defective from parent or guardian) by taking a child out of the possession of her parent or guardian;
(h) an offence under section 22 of that Act (causing prostitution of women) in relation to a child;
(i) an offence under section 23 of that Act (procuration of girl under 21) by procuring a child to have sexual intercourse with a third person;
(j) an offence under section 27 of that Act (permitting defective to use premise for intercourse) by inducing or suffering a child to resort to or be on premises for the purpose of having sexual intercourse;
(k) an offence under section 29 of that Act (causing or encouraging prostitution of defective) by causing or encouraging the prostitution of a child;
(l) an offence under section 30 of that Act (man living on earnings of prostitution) in a case where the prostitute is a child;
(m) an offence under section 31 of that Act (woman exercising control over prostitute) in a case where the prostitute is a child;
(n) an offence under section 128 of the Mental Health Act 1959 (sexual intercourse with patients) by having sexual intercourse with a child;
(o) an offence under section 4 of the Sexual Offences Act 1967 (procuring others to commit homosexual acts) by –
   (i) procuring a child to commit an act of buggery with any person; or
   (ii) procuring any person to commit an act of buggery with a child;
(p) an offence under section 5 of that Act (living on earnings of male prostitution) by living wholly or in part on the earnings of prostitution of a child; and
(q) an offence under section 9(1)(a) of the Theft Act 1968 (burglary), by entering a building or part of a building with intent to rape a child.

4 Paragraphs 1(c) and 3(e) and (f) do not include offences in a case where the offender was under the age of 20 at the time the offence was committed.

SCHEDULE 4

Part 1

Regulation 25(2)

Information about the prospective adopter

Information about the prospective adopter

1 Name, sex, date and place of birth and address including the local authority area.

2 A photograph and physical description.

3 Whether the prospective adopter is domiciled or habitually resident in a part of the British Islands and if habitually resident for how long he has been habitually resident.

4 Racial origin and cultural and linguistic background.

5 Religious persuasion.

6 Relationship (if any) to the child.

7 A description of his personality and interests.

8 If the prospective adopter is married or has formed a civil partnership and is applying alone for an assessment of his suitability to adopt, the reasons for this.

9 Details of any previous family court proceedings in which the prospective adopter has been involved.

10 Names and addresses of three referees who will give personal references on the prospective adopter, not more than one of whom may be a relative.

11 Name and address of the prospective adopter's registered medical practitioner.

12 If the prospective adopter is –

 (a) married, the date and place of marriage;
 (b) has formed a civil partnership, the date and place of registration of that partnership; or
 (c) has a partner, details of that relationship.

13 Details of any previous marriage, civil partnership or relationship.

14 A family tree with details of the prospective adopter, his siblings and any children of the prospective adopter, with their ages (or ages at death).

15 A chronology of the prospective adopter from birth.

16 The observations of the prospective adopter about his own experience of being parented and how this has influenced him.

17 Details of any experience the prospective adopter has had of caring for children (including as a parent, step-parent, foster parent, child minder or prospective adopter) and an assessment of his ability in this respect.

18 Any other information which indicates how the prospective adopter and anybody else living in his household is likely to relate to a child placed for adoption with the prospective adopter.

Wider family

19 A description of the wider family of the prospective adopter and their role and importance to the prospective adopter and their likely role and importance to a child placed for adoption with the prospective adopter.

Information about the home etc of the prospective adopter

20 Information about the prospective adopter's home and the neighbourhood in which he lives.

21 Details of other members of the prospective adopter's household (including any children of the prospective adopter whether or not resident in the household).

22 Information about the local community of the prospective adopter, including the degree of the family's integration with its peer groups, friendships and social networks.

Education and employment

23 Details of the prospective adopter's educational history and attainments and his views about how this has influenced him.

24 Details of his employment history and the observations of the prospective adopter about how this has influenced him.

25 The current employment of the prospective adopter and his views about achieving a balance between employment and child care.

Income

26 Details of the prospective adopter's income and expenditure.

Other information

27 Information about the prospective adopter's capacity to –

 (a) provide for a child's needs, particularly emotional and behavioural development needs;
 (b) share a child's history and associated emotional issues; and
 (c) understand and support a child through possible feelings of loss and trauma.

28 The prospective adopter's –

 (a) reasons for wishing to adopt a child;
 (b) views and feelings about adoption and its significance;
 (c) views about his parenting capacity;
 (d) views about parental responsibility and what it means;
 (e) views about a suitable home environment for a child;
 (f) views about the importance and value of education;
 (g) views and feelings about the importance of a child's religious and cultural upbringing; and
 (h) views and feelings about contact.

29 The views of other members of the prospective adopter's household and wider family in relation to adoption.

30 Any other relevant information which might assist the adoption panel or the adoption agency.

Part 2

Regulation 25(3)(a)

Report on the health of the prospective adopter

1 Name, date of birth, sex, weight and height.

2 A family health history of the parents, any brothers and sisters and the children of the prospective adopter, with details of any serious physical or mental illness and hereditary disease or disorder.

3 Infertility or reasons for deciding not to have children (if applicable).

4 Past health history, including details of any serious physical or mental illness, disability, accident, hospital admission or attendance at an out-patient department, and in each case any treatment given.

5 Obstetric history (if applicable).

6 Details of any present illness, including treatment and prognosis.

7 Details of any consumption of alcohol that may give cause for concern or whether the prospective adopter smokes or uses habit-forming drugs.

8 Any other relevant information which the adoption agency considers may assist the adoption panel and the adoption agency.

SCHEDULE 5
ADOPTION PLACEMENT PLAN

Regulation 35(2)

1 Whether placed under a placement order or with the consent of the parent or guardian.

2 The arrangements for preparing the child and the prospective adopter for the placement.

3 Date on which it is proposed to place the child for adoption with the prospective adopter.

4 The arrangements for review of the placement.

5 Whether parental responsibility of the prospective adopter for the child is to be restricted, and if so, the extent to which it is to be restricted.

6 Where the local authority has decided to provide adoption support services for the adoptive family, how these will be provided and by whom.

7 The arrangements which the adoption agency has made for allowing any person contact with the child, the form of contact, the arrangements for supporting contact and the name and contact details of the person responsible for facilitating the contact arrangements (if applicable).

8 The dates on which the child's life story book and later life letter are to be passed by the adoption agency to the prospective adopter.

9 Details of any other arrangements that need to be made.

10 Contact details of the child's social worker, the prospective adopter's social worker and out of hours contacts.

EXPLANATORY NOTE

(This note is not part of the Regulations)

These Regulations make provision relating to the exercise by adoption agencies (local authorities and registered adoption societies) of their functions in relation to adoption under the Adoption and Children Act 2002 ('the Act').

Part 2 makes provision for the arrangements for adoption work which adoption agencies ('agencies') must put in place. Regulation 3 requires agencies to set up adoption panels and regulations 4 and 5 make provision in relation to the tenure of panel members and the proceedings of adoption panels. Agencies are required to appoint an adoption adviser to the adoption panel and medical adviser (regulations 8 and 9) and regulation 10 provides for the establishment of new panels on 30 December 2005 (the date on which these Regulations come into force).

Part 3 applies where an agency is considering adoption for a child. Regulation 12 requires the agency to open a case record in respect of the child. Regulations 13 and 14 require the agency to provide counselling and information for, and ascertain the wishes and feelings of, the child, his parent or guardian and others. Regulation 14(3) and (4) make provision for the father of a child who does not have parental responsibility for the child and whose identity is known. If the agency considers it is appropriate it must counsel etc. the father. Regulations 15 and 16 impose duties on an agency to obtain information about the child and his family and others which is specified in Schedule 1. Regulation 17 requires the agency to prepare a written report about the child ('the child's permanence report'). The child's permanence report and certain other information must be sent to the adoption panel. Regulation 18 provides that the adoption panel have to make a recommendation to the agency as to whether the child should be placed for adoption. The agency must take into account that recommendation in coming to a decision about whether the child should be placed for adoption (regulation 19). Regulation 20 provides that the agency must request CAFCASS to appoint an officer of the Service or the National Assembly for Wales to appoint a Welsh family proceedings officer to witness consent to placement under section 19 of the Act and, as the case may be, to the making of a future adoption order under section 20 of the Act. The information to be provided to CAFCASS is specified in Schedule 2.

Part 4 makes provision for the assessment of prospective adopters. Regulation 21 requires the agency to provide counselling and information for a prospective adopter. The agency must consider an application by a prospective adopter for an assessment of his suitability to adopt a child (regulation 22). Regulation 23 requires the agency to carry out police checks and provides that an agency may not consider a person suitable to adopt a child if he or any member of his household aged 18 or over has been convicted of, or cautioned for, certain specified offences. The agency must arrange for the prospective adopter to receive preparation for adoption (regulation 24). The agency must obtain certain information and reports in respect of the prospective adopter and prepare a written report (regulation 25 and Schedule 4). The prospective adopter's case must be submitted to the adoption panel who must make a recommendation to the agency as to whether the prospective adopter is suitable to adopt a child (regulation 26). The agency must then make a decision about whether the prospective adopter is suitable to adopt a child (regulation 27). Regulation 29 makes provision for the review and termination of a prospective adopter's approval.

Part 5 makes provision in relation to the duties of the agency in respect of the placement of a child with a prospective adopter. The agency must provide the prospective adopter with the child's permanence report and meet with him to discuss the proposed placement (regulation 31). The proposed placement must be referred to the adoption panel who must consider the proposed placement and make a recommendation to the agency as to whether the child should be placed for adoption with the particular prospective adopter and the agency must take into account that recommendation when coming to its decision (regulations 32 and 33).

Part 6 makes provision in relation to placements and reviews. Regulation 36 provides that the agency must provide the prospective adopter with a placement plan (which must cover the matters specified in Schedule 5) and before the child is placed for adoption send certain information to the persons specified in regulation 35(6). Regulation 36 imposes a duty on the agency to carry out reviews. Regulation 37 requires an agency to appoint an independent reviewing officer. Regulation 38 makes provision in relation to what is to happen when a parent withdraws consent given under section 19 or 20 of the Act.

Part 7 makes general provision in relation to case records.

Part 8 makes miscellaneous provision including modifications to provisions in the Children Act 1989.

A Regulatory Impact Assessment has been prepared for these Regulations and a copy has been placed in the library of each House of Parliament. Copies of the Regulatory Impact Assessment can be obtained from the Department for Education and Skills' website http://www.dfes.gov.uk.ria/.

Appendix K

THE SUITABILITY OF ADOPTERS REGULATIONS 2005, SI 2005/1712

1 Citation, commencement and application

(1) These Regulations may be cited as the Suitability of Adopters Regulations 2005 and shall come into force on 30 December 2005.

(2) These Regulations apply to England only.

2 Interpretation

(1) In these Regulations, 'the Foreign Element Regulations' means the Adoptions with a Foreign Element Regulations 2005.

(2) In these Regulations, unless the context otherwise requires, a reference to a regulation is to the regulation bearing that number in the Adoption Agencies Regulations 2005.

3 Making reports in respect of the suitability to adopt a child

Subject to regulation 5 of these Regulations, in making any report in respect of the suitability of any person to adopt a child in accordance with regulations 25(5) (the prospective adopter's report) and 29(4) (the prospective adopter's review report), the matters to be taken into account by an adoption agency are –

(a) any information obtained as a consequence of providing a counselling service for the prospective adopter in accordance with –
   (i) regulation 21; or
   (ii) regulation 14(1) of the Foreign Element Regulations;
(b) any information obtained as a consequence of the preparation for adoption required in accordance with regulation 24;
(c) any information received as a consequence of obtaining an enhanced criminal record certificate in accordance with regulation 23(1)(a) and (b);
(d) the information about the prospective adopter obtained as a consequence of regulation 25(2);
(e) in a case where regulation 12 of the Foreign Element Regulations applies (Convention adoptions), any additional information obtained about the prospective adopter as a consequence of regulation 15(4) of those Regulations; and
(f) the written report –
   (i) obtained from the registered medical practitioner about the health of the prospective adopter in accordance with regulation 25(3)(a);
   (ii) of each of the interviews with the persons nominated by the prospective adopter to provide personal references for him in accordance with regulation 25(3)(b); and
   (iii) obtained from the local authority in whose area the prospective adopter has his home in accordance with regulation 25(4).

4 Determining the suitability to adopt a child

(1) Subject to regulation 5 of these Regulations, in determining the suitability of any person to adopt a child in accordance with regulation 27 (adoption agency decision and notification), the matters to be taken into account by an adoption agency are –

    (a)   the prospective adopter's report prepared in accordance with regulation 25(5);
    (b)   the written report obtained in accordance with regulation 25(3)(a) (medical report);
    (c)   the written report of each of the interviews in accordance with regulation 25(3)(b) (personal references);
    (d)   the recommendation of the adoption panel made in accordance with regulation 26(1);
    (e)   any other relevant information obtained by the adoption agency as a consequence of regulation 26(2)(b); and
    (f)   in a case of a person falling within regulation 12 of the Foreign Element Regulations, any additional information obtained as a consequence of Chapter 1 of Part 3 of those Regulations.

(2) An adoption agency shall, in determining the suitability of a couple to adopt a child, have proper regard to the need for stability and permanence in their relationship.

5 Cases in which a person is unlikely to be suitable to adopt a child

In a case where regulation 25(7) applies, the matters to be taken into account by the adoption agency in determining, or making any report in respect of, the suitability of any person to adopt a child may be limited to any information received under regulation 25(2), (3) or (4), or other information received as a consequence of which the agency is of the opinion that the prospective adopter is unlikely to be considered to be suitable to adopt a child.

EXPLANATORY NOTE

(This note is not part of the Regulations)

These Regulations are made under the Adoption and Children Act 2002. They apply in respect of adoption agencies in England only.

Regulations 3 and 4 make provision as to the matters to be taken into account by an adoption agency in determining, or making any report in respect of, the suitability of any person to adopt a child. Regulation 4(2) requires the adoption agency in determining the suitability of a couple to have proper regard to the need for stability and permanence in their relationship.

Regulation 5 provides for the matters to be taken into account in determining, or making a report on, suitability in a case where the adoption agency receives information and is of the opinion that the prospective adopter is unlikely to be considered suitable to adopt a child notwithstanding that the agency may not have obtained all the information required under regulation 25 of the Adoption Agencies Regulations 2005.

A Regulatory Impact Assessment has been prepared for these Regulations and a copy has been placed in the library of each House of Parliament. Copies of the Regulatory Impact Assessment can be obtained from the Department for Education and Skills' website http://www.dfes.gov.uk/ria/.

Appendix L

THE SPECIAL GUARDIANSHIP REGULATIONS 2005, SI 2005/1109

PART 1
INTRODUCTORY

1 Citation, commencement and application

(1) These Regulations may be cited as the Special Guardianship Regulations 2005 and shall come into force on 30 December 2005.

(2) These Regulations apply to England only.

2 Interpretation

(1) In these Regulations –

'the Act' means the Children Act 1989;
'couple' has the same meaning as in section 144(4) of the Adoption and Children Act 2002;
'Local Health Board' means a Local Health Board established by the National Assembly for Wales under section 16BA of the National Health Service Act 1977;
'prospective special guardian' means a person –
    (a) who has given notice to a local authority under section 14A(7) of the Act of his intention to make an application for a special guardianship order in accordance with section 14A(3) of the Act; or
    (b) in respect of whom a court has requested that a local authority conduct an investigation and prepare a report pursuant to section 14A(9) of the Act;
'relevant child' means a child in respect of whom –
    (a) a special guardianship order is in force;
    (b) a person has given notice to a local authority under section 14A(7) of the Act of his intention to make an application for a special guardianship order in accordance with section 14A(3) of the Act; or
    (c) a court is considering whether a special guardianship order should be made and has asked a local authority to conduct an investigation and prepare a report pursuant to section 14A(9) of the Act.

(2) In any case where –

    (a) a person aged 18 or over is in full-time education or training; and
    (b) immediately before he reached the age of 18, financial support was payable in relation to him under Chapter 2 of Part 2 of these Regulations,

then, for the purposes of the continued provision of financial support and any review of financial support, these Regulations shall have effect in relation to him as if he were still a child.

PART 2

SPECIAL GUARDIANSHIP SUPPORT SERVICES

Chapter 1
Provision of services

3 Prescribed services

(1) For the purposes of section 14F(1)(b) of the Act the following services are prescribed as special guardianship support services (in addition to counselling, advice and information) –

   (a) financial support payable under Chapter 2;
   (b) services to enable groups of –
      (i) relevant children;
      (ii) special guardians;
      (iii) prospective special guardians; and
      (iv) parents of relevant children,
to discuss matters relating to special guardianship;
   (c) assistance, including mediation services, in relation to arrangements for contact between a relevant child and –
      (i) his parent or a relative of his; or
      (ii) any other person with whom such a child has a relationship which appears to the local authority to be beneficial to the welfare of the child having regard to the factors specified in section 1(3) of the Act;
   (d) services in relation to the therapeutic needs of a relevant child;
   (e) assistance for the purpose of ensuring the continuance of the relationship between a relevant child and a special guardian or prospective special guardian, including –
      (i) training for that person to meet any special needs of that child;
      (ii) subject to paragraph (3), respite care;
      (iii) mediation in relation to matters relating to special guardianship orders.

(2) The services prescribed in paragraph (1)(b) to (e) may include giving assistance in cash.

(3) For the purposes of paragraph (1)(e)(ii) respite care that consists of the provision of accommodation must be accommodation provided by or on behalf of a local authority under section 23 of the Act (accommodation of looked after children) or by a voluntary organisation under section 59 of the Act.

4 Arrangements for securing provision of services

(1) The following are prescribed for the purposes of section 14F(9)(b) of the Act (persons who may provide special guardianship support services) –

   (a) a registered adoption society;
   (b) a registered adoption support agency;
   (c) a registered fostering agency;
   (d) a Local Health Board or Primary Care Trust;
   (e) a local education authority.

(2) In paragraph (1) –

   (a) 'registered adoption society' has the same meaning as in the Adoption and Children Act 2002;

(b) 'adoption support agency' has the same meaning as in the Adoption and Children Act 2002 and 'fostering agency' has the same meaning as in the Care Standards Act 2000 and 'registered' in relation to any such agency means that a person is registered in respect of it under Part 2 of the Care Standards Act 2000.

5 Services for persons outside the area

(1) Section 14F of the Act (special guardianship support services) applies to a local authority in respect of the following persons who are outside the authority's area –

(a) a relevant child who is looked after by the local authority or was looked after by the local authority immediately before the making of a special guardianship order;
(b) a special guardian or prospective special guardian of such a child;
(c) a child of a special guardian or prospective special guardian mentioned in sub-paragraph (b).

(2) But section 14F ceases to apply at the end of the period of three years from the date of the special guardianship order except in a case where the local authority are providing financial support under Chapter 2 and the decision to provide that support was made before the making of the order.

(3) Nothing in this regulation prevents a local authority from providing special guardianship support services to persons outside their area where they consider it appropriate to do so.

Chapter 2
Provision of financial support

6 Circumstances in which financial support is payable

(1) Financial support is payable under this Chapter to a special guardian or prospective special guardian –

(a) to facilitate arrangements for a person to become the special guardian of a child where the local authority consider such arrangements to be beneficial to the child's welfare; or
(b) to support the continuation of such arrangements after a special guardianship order is made.

(2) Such support is payable only in the following circumstances –

(a) where the local authority consider that it is necessary to ensure that the special guardian or prospective special guardian can look after the child;
(b) where the local authority consider that the child needs special care which requires a greater expenditure of resources than would otherwise be the case because of his illness, disability, emotional or behavioural difficulties or the consequences of his past abuse or neglect;
(c) where the local authority consider that it is appropriate to contribute to any legal costs, including court fees, of a special guardian or prospective special guardian, as the case may be, associated with –
 (i) the making of a special guardianship order or any application to vary or discharge such an order;
 (ii) an application for an order under section 8 of the Act;
 (iii) an order for financial provision to be made to or for the benefit of the child; or
(d) where the local authority consider that it is appropriate to contribute to the expenditure necessary for the purposes of accommodating and maintaining the child, including the

provision of furniture and domestic equipment, alterations to and adaptations of the home, provision of means of transport and provision of clothing, toys and other items necessary for the purpose of looking after the child.

7 Remuneration for former foster parents

(1) Financial support under this Chapter may include an element of remuneration but only where the decision to include it is taken before the special guardianship order is made and the local authority consider it to be necessary in order to facilitate arrangements for a person to become a special guardian in a case where –

    (a) the special guardian or prospective special guardian has been a local authority foster parent in respect of the child; and

    (b) an element of remuneration was included in the payments made by the local authority to that person in relation to his fostering the child.

(2) But that element of remuneration ceases to be payable after the expiry of the period of two years from the making of the special guardianship order unless the local authority consider its continuation to be necessary having regard to the exceptional needs of the child or any other exceptional circumstances.

8 Payment of financial support

Financial support under this Chapter may be paid –

    (a) periodically, if it is provided to meet a need which is likely to give rise to recurring expenditure; or

    (b) in any other case by a single payment or, if the local authority and the special guardian or prospective special guardian agree, by instalments.

9 Cessation of financial support

Financial support ceases to be payable to a special guardian or prospective special guardian if –

    (a) the child ceases to have a home with him;
    (b) the child ceases full-time education or training and commences employment;
    (c) the child qualifies for income support or jobseeker's allowance in his own right; or
    (d) the child attains the age of 18 unless he continues in full-time education or training, when it may continue until the end of the course or training he is then undertaking.

10 Conditions

(1) Where financial support is to be paid periodically it is not payable until the special guardian or prospective special guardian agrees to the following conditions –

    (a) that he will inform the local authority immediately if –
        (i) he changes his address;
        (ii) the child dies;
        (iii) any of the changes mentioned in regulation 9 (cessation of financial support) occurs; or
        (iv) there is a change in his financial circumstances or the financial needs or resources of the child which may affect the amount of financial support payable to him,
    and, where the information is given orally, to confirm it in writing within seven days;
    (b) that he will complete and supply the local authority with an annual statement as to the following matters –

(i) his financial circumstances;
(ii) the financial needs and resources of the child;
(iii) his address and whether the child still has a home with him.

(2) The local authority may provide financial support subject to any other conditions they consider appropriate, including the timescale within which, and purposes for which, any payment of financial support should be utilised.

(3) Subject to paragraph (4), where any condition imposed in accordance with this regulation is not complied with, the local authority may –

(a) suspend or terminate payment of financial support; and
(b) seek to recover all or part of the financial support they have paid.

(4) Where the condition not complied with is a failure to provide an annual statement in accordance with an agreement referred to in paragraph (1), the local authority shall not take any steps under paragraph (3) until –

(a) they have sent to the person who entered into the agreement a written reminder of the need to provide an annual statement; and
(b) 28 days have expired since the date on which that reminder was sent.

Chapter 3
Assessment and plans

11 Request for assessment

(1) The following persons are prescribed for the purposes of section 14F(3) of the Act (persons at whose request an assessment must be carried out) –

(a) a relevant child who is looked after by the local authority or was looked after by the local authority immediately before the making of a special guardianship order;
(b) a special guardian or prospective special guardian of such a child;
(c) a parent of such a child.

(2) Paragraph (3) applies if the local authority receive a written request from or, in the case of a child, on behalf of any of the following persons (not being a person falling within paragraph (1)) for an assessment of his needs for special guardianship support services –

(a) a person mentioned in section 14F(3)(a) to (c) of the Act;
(b) a child of a special guardian;
(c) any person whom the local authority consider to have a significant and ongoing relationship with a relevant child.

(3) The local authority must, if they are minded not to carry out an assessment, give the person notice of the proposed decision (including the reasons for it) and must allow him a reasonable opportunity to make representations in relation to that decision.

(4) Where the request of a person for an assessment relates to a particular special guardianship support service, or it appears to the local authority that a person's needs for special guardianship support services may be adequately assessed by reference to a particular special guardianship support service, the local authority may carry out the assessment by reference to that service only.

12 Procedure for assessment

(1) Where the local authority carry out an assessment of a person's needs for special guardianship support services they must have regard to such of the following considerations as are relevant to the assessment –

- (a) the developmental needs of the child;
- (b) the parenting capacity of the special guardian or prospective special guardian, as the case may be;
- (c) the family and environmental factors that have shaped the life of the child;
- (d) what the life of the child might be like with the person falling within sub-paragraph (b);
- (e) any previous assessments undertaken in relation to the child or a person falling within sub-paragraph (b);
- (f) the needs of a person falling within sub-paragraph (b) and of that person's family;
- (g) where it appears to the local authority that there is a pre-existing relationship between a person falling within sub-paragraph (b) and the parent of the child, the likely impact of the special guardianship order on the relationships between that person, that child and that parent.

(2) The local authority must, where they consider it appropriate to do so –

- (a) interview the person whose needs for special guardianship support services are being assessed;
- (b) where the person falling within sub-paragraph (a) is a child, interview –
    - (i) any special guardian or prospective special guardian, as the case may be, of the child; or
    - (ii) any adult the local authority consider it appropriate to interview.

(3) Where it appears to the local authority that the person may have a need for services from a Local Health Board, Primary Care Trust or local education authority, they must, as part of the assessment, consult that Local Health Board, Primary Care Trust or local education authority.

(4) After undertaking an assessment, the local authority must prepare a written report of the assessment.

13 Assessment of need for financial support

(1) This regulation applies where the local authority carry out an assessment of a person's need for financial support.

(2) In determining the amount of financial support, the local authority must take account of any other grant, benefit, allowance or resource which is available to the person in respect of his needs as a result of becoming a special guardian of the child.

(3) Subject to paragraphs (4) and (5) the local authority must also take account of the following considerations –

- (a) the person's financial resources, including any tax credit or benefit, which would be available to him if the child lived with him;
- (b) the amount required by the person in respect of his reasonable outgoings and commitments (excluding outgoings in respect of the child);
- (c) the financial needs and resources of the child.

(4) The local authority must disregard the considerations in paragraph (3) where they are considering providing financial support in respect of legal costs, including court fees, in a case where a special guardianship order is applied for in respect of a child who is looked after by the

local authority and the authority support the making of the order or an application is made to vary or discharge a special guardianship order in respect of such a child.

(5) The local authority may disregard any of the considerations in paragraph (3) –

- (a) where they are considering providing financial support in respect of –
  - (i) initial costs of accommodating a child who has been looked after by the local authority;
  - (ii) recurring costs in respect of travel for the purpose of visits between the child and a related person; or
  - (iii) any special care referred to in regulation 6(2)(b) in relation to a child who has been looked after by the local authority; or
- (b) where they are considering including an element of remuneration under regulation 7.

(6) In paragraph (5)(a)(ii) 'related person' means a relative of the child or any other person with whom the child has a relationship which appears to the local authority to be beneficial to the welfare of the child having regard to the factors specified in section 1(3) of the Act.

14 Plan

(1) This regulation applies in relation to the requirement in section 14F(6) of the Act for the local authority to prepare a plan in accordance with which special guardianship support services are to be provided.

(2) The local authority must prepare a plan if –

- (a) they propose to provide special guardianship support services to a person on more than one occasion; and
- (b) the services are not limited to the provision of advice or information.

(3) Where it appears to the local authority that the person may have a need for services from a Local Health Board, Primary Care Trust or a local education authority, they must consult that Local Health Board, Primary Care Trust or local education authority before preparing the plan.

(4) The local authority must nominate a person to monitor the provision of the services in accordance with the plan.

15 Notice of proposal as to special guardianship support services

(1) Before making any decision under section 14F(5) of the Act as to a person's needs for special guardianship support services, the local authority must allow the person an opportunity to make representations in accordance with this regulation.

(2) The local authority must first give the person notice of the proposed decision and the time allowed for making representations.

(3) The notice must contain the following information –

- (a) a statement as to the person's needs for special guardianship support services;
- (b) where the assessment relates to his need for financial support, the basis upon which financial support is determined;
- (c) whether the local authority propose to provide him with special guardianship support services;
- (d) the services (if any) that are proposed to be provided to him;
- (e) if financial support is to be paid to him, the proposed amount that would be payable; and
- (f) any proposed conditions under regulation 10(2).

(4) In a case where the local authority propose to provide special guardianship support services and are required to prepare a plan under section 14F(6) of the Act, the notice must be accompanied by a draft of that plan.

(5) The local authority shall not make a decision until –

(a) the person has made representations to the local authority or notified the local authority that he is satisfied with the proposed decision and, where applicable, the draft plan; or
(b) the period of time for making representations has expired.

16 Notification of decision as to special guardianship support services

(1) After making their decision under section 14F(5) of the Act as to whether to provide special guardianship support services to a person, the local authority must give the person notice of that decision, including the reasons for it.

(2) Where the local authority are required to prepare a plan under section 14F(6) of the Act, the notice must include details of that plan and the person nominated under regulation 14(4).

(3) If the local authority decide that financial support is to be provided, the notice given under paragraph (1) must include the following information –

(a) the method of the determination of the amount of financial support;
(b) where financial support is to be paid in instalments or periodically –
    (i) the amount of financial support;
    (ii) the frequency with which the payment will be made;
    (iii) the period for which financial support is to be paid;
    (iv) when payment will commence;
(c) where financial support is to be paid as a single payment, when the payment is to be made;
(d) where financial support is to be paid subject to any conditions imposed in accordance with regulation 10(2), those conditions, the date (if any) by which the conditions are to be met and the consequences of failing to meet the conditions;
(e) the arrangements and procedure for review, variation and termination of financial support;
(f) the responsibilities of –
    (i) the local authority under regulations 17 and 18 (reviews); and
    (ii) the special guardian or prospective special guardian pursuant to any agreement mentioned in regulation 10.

Chapter 4
Reviews

17 Reviews: general procedure

(1) This regulation applies where the local authority provide special guardianship support services for a person other than financial support payable periodically.

(2) The local authority must review the provision of such services –

(a) if any change in the person's circumstances which may affect the provision of special guardianship support services comes to their notice;
(b) at such stage in the implementation of the plan as they consider appropriate; and
(c) in any event, at least annually.

(3) Regulations 12 and 13 apply in relation to a review under this regulation as they apply in relation to an assessment under Chapter 3 of this Part.

(4) If the local authority propose to vary or terminate the provision of special guardianship support services to any person, before making any decision as a result of the review they must give the person an opportunity to make representations and for that purpose they must give him notice of the proposed decision and the time allowed for making representations.

(5) The notice must contain the information mentioned in regulation 15(3) and, if the local authority propose to revise the plan, a draft of the revised plan.

(6) The local authority must, having regard to the review and after considering any representations received within the period specified in the notice –

(a) decide whether to vary or terminate the provision of special guardianship support services for the person; and
(b) where appropriate, revise the plan.

(7) The local authority must give the person notice of their decision (including the reasons for it) and, if applicable, details of the revised plan.

18 Review of financial support payable periodically

(1) This regulation applies where the local authority provide financial support for a person payable periodically.

(2) The local authority must review the financial support –

(a) on receipt of the annual statement mentioned in regulation 10;
(b) if any relevant change of circumstances or any breach of a condition mentioned in regulation 10 comes to their notice; and
(c) at any stage in the implementation of the plan that they consider appropriate.

(3) In paragraph (2) a relevant change of circumstances is any of the changes that the person has agreed to notify under regulation 10.

(4) Regulations 12 and 13 apply in relation to a review under this regulation as they apply in relation to an assessment under Chapter 3 of this Part.

(5) If the local authority propose, as a result of the review, to reduce or terminate financial support or revise the plan, before making that decision, the local authority must give the person an opportunity to make representations and for that purpose they must give the person notice of the proposed decision and the time allowed for making representations.

(6) But paragraph (5) does not prevent the local authority from suspending payment of financial support pending that decision.

(7) The notice must contain the information mentioned in regulation 15(3) and, if applicable, a draft of the revised plan.

(8) The local authority must, having regard to the review, and after considering any representations received within the period specified in the notice –

(a) decide whether to vary or terminate payment of the financial support or whether to seek to recover all or part of any financial support that has been paid; and
(b) where appropriate, revise the plan.

(9) The local authority must give the person notice of their decision, including the reasons for it, and, if applicable, the revised plan.

Chapter 5
Urgent cases and notices

19 Urgent cases

Where any requirement applicable to the local authority in this Part in relation to carrying out an assessment, preparing a plan or giving notice would delay the provision of a service in a case of urgency, that requirement does not apply.

20 Notices

(1) Any notice required to be given under this Part must be given in writing.

(2) If the person to whom notice is to be given is a child and –

   (a) it appears to the local authority that the child is not of sufficient age and understanding for it to be appropriate to give him such notice; or
   (b) in all the circumstances it is not appropriate to give him such notice,

the notice must be given to his special guardian or prospective special guardian (where applicable) or otherwise to the adult the local authority consider most appropriate.

PART 3

MISCELLANEOUS PROVISIONS IN RELATION TO SPECIAL GUARDIANSHIP

21 Court report

The matters specified in the Schedule are the matters prescribed for the purposes of section 14A(8)(b) of the Act (matters to be dealt with in report for the court).

22 Relevant authority for the purposes of section 24(5)(za) of the Act

For the purposes of section 24(5)(za) of the Act (persons qualifying for advice and assistance) the relevant authority shall be the local authority which last looked after the person.

SCHEDULE

MATTERS TO BE DEALT WITH IN REPORT FOR THE COURT

Regulation 21

The following matters are prescribed for the purposes of section 14A(8)(b) of the Act.

1 In respect of the child –

   (a) name, sex, date and place of birth and address including local authority area;
   (b) a photograph and physical description;
   (c) nationality (and immigration status where appropriate);
   (d) racial origin and cultural and linguistic background;
   (e) religious persuasion (including details of baptism, confirmation or equivalent ceremonies);
   (f) details of any siblings including their dates of birth;

- (g) the extent of the child's contact with his relatives and any other person the local authority consider relevant;
- (h) whether the child is or has been looked after by a local authority or is or has been provided with accommodation by a voluntary organisation and details (including dates) of placements by the authority or organisation;
- (i) whether the prospective special guardian is a local authority foster parent of the child;
- (j) a description of the child's personality, his social development and his emotional and behavioural development and any related needs;
- (k) details of the child's interests, likes and dislikes;
- (l) a health history and a description of the state of the child's health which shall include any treatment the child is receiving;
- (m) names, addresses and types of nurseries or schools attended with dates;
- (n) the child's educational attainments;
- (o) whether the child is subject to a statement of special educational needs under the Education Act 1996; and
- (p) details of any order made by a court with respect to the child under the Act including –
  - (i) the name of the court;
  - (ii) the order made; and
  - (iii) the date on which the order was made.

2 In respect of the child's family –

- (a) name, date and place of birth and address (and the date on which their last address was confirmed) including local authority area of each parent of the child and his siblings under the age of 18;
- (b) a photograph, if available, and physical description of each parent;
- (c) nationality (and immigration status where appropriate) of each parent;
- (d) racial origin and cultural and linguistic background of each parent;
- (e) whether the child's parents were married to each other at the time of the child's birth or have subsequently married and whether they are divorced or separated;
- (f) where the child's parents have been previously married or formed a civil partnership, the date of the marriage or civil partnership;
- (g) where the child's parents are not married, whether the father has parental responsibility and, if so, how it was acquired;
- (h) if the identity or whereabouts of the father are not known, the information about him that has been ascertained and from whom, and the steps that have been taken to establish paternity;
- (i) the past and present relationship of the child's parents;
- (j) where available, the following information in respect of each parent –
  - (i) health history, including details of any serious physical or mental illness, any hereditary disease or disorder or disability;
  - (ii) religious persuasion;
  - (iii) educational history;
  - (iv) employment history;
  - (v) personality and interests;
- (k) in respect of the child's siblings under the age of 18 –
  - (i) the person with whom the sibling is living;
  - (ii) whether the sibling is looked after by a local authority or provided with accommodation by a voluntary organisation; and
  - (iii) details of any court order made with respect to the sibling under the Act, including the name of the court, the order made and the date on which the order was made.

3 In respect of the wishes and feelings of the child and others –

(a) an assessment of the child's wishes and feelings (considered in light of his age and understanding) regarding –
    (i) special guardianship;
    (ii) his religious and cultural upbringing; and
    (iii) contact with his relatives and any other person the local authority consider relevant,
    and the date on which the child's wishes and feelings were last ascertained.
(b) the wishes and feelings of each parent regarding –
    (i) special guardianship;
    (ii) the child's religious and cultural upbringing; and
    (iii) contact with the child,
    and the date on which the wishes and feelings of each parent were last ascertained; and
(c) the wishes and feelings of any of the child's relatives, or any other person the local authority consider relevant regarding the child and the dates on which those wishes and feelings were last ascertained.

4 In respect of the prospective special guardian or, where two or more persons are jointly prospective special guardians, each of them –

(a) name, date and place of birth and address including local authority area;
(b) a photograph and physical description;
(c) nationality (and immigration status where appropriate);
(d) racial origin and cultural and linguistic background;
(e) if the prospective special guardian is –
    (i) married, the date and place of marriage;
    (ii) has formed a civil partnership, the date and place of registration of the civil partnership; or
    (iii) has a partner, details of that relationship;
(f) details of any previous marriage, civil partnership, or relationship;
(g) where the prospective special guardians wish to apply jointly, the nature of their relationship and an assessment of the stability of that relationship;
(h) if the prospective special guardian is a member of a couple and is applying alone for a special guardianship order, the reasons for this;
(i) whether the prospective special guardian is a relative of the child;
(j) prospective special guardian's relationship with the child;
(k) a health history of the prospective special guardian including details of any serious physical or mental illness, any hereditary disease or disorder or disability;
(l) a description of how the prospective special guardian relates to adults and children;
(m) previous experience of caring for children;
(n) parenting capacity, to include an assessment of the prospective special guardian's ability and suitability to bring up the child;
(o) where there have been any past assessments as a prospective adopter, foster parent or special guardian, relevant details as appropriate;
(p) details of income and expenditure;
(q) information about the prospective special guardian's home and the neighbourhood in which he lives;
(r) details of other members of the household and details of any children of the prospective special guardian even if not resident in the household;
(s) details of the parents and any siblings of the prospective special guardian, with their ages or ages at death;
(t) the following information –
    (i) religious persuasion;

(ii) educational history;
(iii) employment history; and
(iv) personality and interests;
(u) details of any previous family court proceedings in which the prospective special guardian has been involved (which have not been referred to elsewhere in this report);
(v) a report of each of the interviews with the three persons nominated by the prospective special guardian to provide personal references for him;
(w) whether the prospective special guardian is willing to follow any wishes of the child or his parents in respect of the child's religious and cultural upbringing;
(x) the views of other members of the prospective special guardian's household and wider family in relation to the proposed special guardianship order;
(y) an assessment of the child's current and future relationship with the family of the prospective special guardian;
(z) reasons for applying for a special guardianship order and extent of understanding of the nature and effect of special guardianship and whether the prospective special guardian has discussed special guardianship with the child;
(aa) any hopes and expectations the prospective special guardian has for the child's future; and
(bb) the prospective special guardian's wishes and feelings in relation to contact between the child and his relatives or any other person the local authority considers relevant.

5 In respect of the local authority which completed the report –

(a) name and address;
(b) details of any past involvement of the local authority with the prospective special guardian, including any past preparation for that person to be a local authority foster parent or adoptive parent or special guardian;
(c) where section 14A(7)(a) of the Act applies and the prospective special guardian lives in the area of another local authority, details of the local authority's enquiries of that other local authority about the prospective special guardian;
(d) a summary of any special guardianship support services provided by the authority for the prospective special guardian, the child or the child's parent and the period for which those services are to be provided; and
(e) where the local authority has decided not to provide special guardianship support services, the reasons why.

6 A summary prepared by the medical professional who provided the information referred to in paragraphs 1(l) and 4(k).

7 The implications of the making of a special guardianship order for –

(a) the child;
(b) the child's parent;
(c) the prospective special guardian and his family; and
(d) any other person the local authority considers relevant.

8 The relative merits of special guardianship and other orders which may be made under the Act or the Adoption and Children Act 2002 with an assessment of whether the child's long term interests would be best met by a special guardianship order.

9 A recommendation as to whether or not the special guardianship order sought should be made in respect of the child and, if not, any alternative proposal in respect of the child.

10 A recommendation as to what arrangements there should be for contact between the child and his relatives or any person the local authority consider relevant.

EXPLANATORY NOTE

(This note is not part of the Regulations)

These Regulations make provision in relation to special guardianship orders which are provided for in sections 14A to 14G of the Children Act 1989 ('the Act').

Part 2 relates to the requirement in section 14F(1) of the Act for local authorities in England to make arrangements for provision of special guardianship support services. Special guardianship support services are defined by section 14F(1) of the Act as counselling, advice and information, and other services prescribed by regulations, in relation to special guardianship.

Chapter 1 of Part 2 deals with the provision of services. Such services are prescribed by regulation 3 and include financial support (as required by section 14F(2)). The provision of services may be secured from the persons specified in regulation 4. Regulation 5 provides for services to persons outside the local authority's area.

Chapter 2 of Part 2 deals with financial support. It may only be paid in the circumstances specified in regulation 6. It may include a remuneration element where it is paid to a former local authority foster parent under regulation 7. Regulations 8 to 10 provide for payment of financial support, including conditions that may be imposed.

Chapter 3 of Part 2 deals with assessment of a person's needs for special guardianship support services, plans for provision of services and notifications of proposals and decisions in relation to the provision of services.

Chapter 4 of Part 2 deals with reviews of special guardianship support services.

Chapter 5 of Part 2 contains miscellaneous provision in relation to special guardianship support services, including a general exemption from the requirements in relation to assessments, giving of notice etc. in cases of urgency (regulation 19) and provision as to service of notices (regulation 20).

Part 3 contains miscellaneous provisions. Regulation 21 and the Schedule prescribe the matters that must be included in a report to the court where a person gives notice of an application to be made a special guardian. Regulation 22 specifies for the purposes of sections 24A and 24B of the Act the relevant authority in relation to a child in respect of whom a special guardianship order is in force and who was immediately before the making of that order looked after by a local authority.

A Regulatory Impact Assessment has been carried out for these Regulations and a copy has been placed in the library of each House of Parliament. Copies of the Regulatory Impact Assessment can be obtained from the Department for Education and Skills' website http://www.dfes.gov.uk/ria/.

Appendix M

THE ADOPTIONS WITH A FOREIGN ELEMENT REGULATIONS 2005, SI 2005/392

PART 1
GENERAL

1 Citation, commencement and application

(1) These Regulations may be cited as the Adoptions with a Foreign Element Regulations 2005 and shall come into force on 30 December 2005.

(2) These Regulations apply to England and Wales.

2 Interpretation

In these Regulations –

'the Act' means the Adoption and Children Act 2002;
'adoption support services' has the meaning given in section 2(6)(a) of the Act and any regulations made under section 2(6)(b) of the Act;
'adoptive family' has the same meaning as in regulation 31(2)(a) of the Agencies Regulations or corresponding Welsh provision;
'adoption panel' means a panel established in accordance with regulation 3 of the Agencies Regulations or corresponding Welsh provision;
'the Agencies Regulations' means the Adoption Agencies Regulations 2005;
'child's case record' has the same meaning as in regulation 12 of the Agencies Regulations or corresponding Welsh provision;
'CA of the receiving State' means, in relation to a Convention country other than the United Kingdom, the Central Authority of the receiving State;
'CA of the State of origin' means, in relation to a Convention country other than the United Kingdom, the Central Authority of the State of origin;
'Convention adoption' is given a meaning by virtue of section 66(1)(c) of the Act;
'Convention country' has the same meaning as in section 144(1) of the Act;
'Convention list' means –
  (a) in relation to a relevant Central Authority, a list of children notified to that Authority in accordance with regulation 40; or
  (b) in relation to any other Central Authority within the British Islands, a list of children notified to that Authority in accordance with provisions, which correspond to regulation 40.
'corresponding Welsh provision' in relation to a Part or a regulation of the Agencies Regulations means the provision of regulations made by the Assembly under section 9 of the Act which corresponds to that Part or regulation;
'prospective adopter's case record' has the same meaning as in regulation 22(1) of the Agencies Regulations or corresponding Welsh provision;

'prospective adopter's report' has the same meaning as in regulation 25(5) of the Agencies Regulations or corresponding Welsh provisions;
'receiving State' has the same meaning as in Article 2 of the Convention;
'relevant Central Authority' means –
- (c) in Chapter 1 of Part 3, in relation to a prospective adopter who is habitually resident in –
  - (i) England, the Secretary of State; and
  - (ii) Wales, the National Assembly for Wales; and
- (d) in Chapter 2 of Part 3 in relation to a local authority in –
  - (i) England, the Secretary of State; and
  - (ii) Wales, the National Assembly for Wales;

'relevant local authority' means in relation to a prospective adopter –
- (a) the local authority within whose area he has his home; or
- (b) in the case where he no longer has a home in England or Wales, the local authority for the area in which he last had his home;

'relevant foreign authority' means a person, outside the British Islands performing functions in the country in which the child is, or in which the prospective adopter is, habitually resident which correspond to the functions of an adoption agency or to the functions of the Secretary of State in respect of adoptions with a foreign element;
'State of origin' has the same meaning as in Article 2 of the Convention.

PART 2

BRINGING CHILDREN INTO AND OUT OF THE UNITED KINGDOM

Chapter 1
Bringing children into the United Kingdom

3 Requirements applicable in respect of bringing or causing a child to be brought into the United Kingdom

A person intending to bring, or to cause another to bring, a child into the United Kingdom in circumstances where section 83(1) of the Act applies must –

- (a) apply in writing to an adoption agency for an assessment of his suitability to adopt a child; and
- (b) give the adoption agency any information it may require for the purpose of the assessment.

4 Conditions applicable in respect of a child brought into the United Kingdom

(1) This regulation prescribes the conditions for the purposes of section 83(5) of the Act in respect of a child brought into the United Kingdom in circumstances where section 83 applies.

(2) Prior to the child's entry into the United Kingdom, the prospective adopter must –

- (a) receive in writing, notification from the Secretary of State that she has issued a certificate confirming to the relevant foreign authority –
  - (i) that the person has been assessed and approved as eligible and suitable to be an adoptive parent in accordance with Part 4 of the Agencies Regulations or corresponding Welsh provision; and

(ii) that if entry clearance and leave to enter and remain, as may be necessary, is granted and not revoked or curtailed, and an adoption order is made or an overseas adoption is effected, the child will be authorised to enter and reside permanently in the United Kingdom;
(b) before visiting the child in the State of origin –
   (i) notify the adoption agency of the details of the child to be adopted;
   (ii) provide the adoption agency with any information and reports received from the relevant foreign authority; and
   (iii) meet with the adoption agency to discuss the proposed adoption and information received from the relevant foreign authority;
(c) visit the child in the State of origin (and where the prospective adopters are a couple each of them); and
(d) after that visit –
   (i) confirm in writing to the adoption agency that he has done so and wishes to proceed with the adoption;
   (ii) provide the adoption agency with any additional reports and information received on or after that visit; and
   (iii) notify the adoption agency of his expected date of entry into the United Kingdom with the child.

(3) The prospective adopter must accompany the child on entering the United Kingdom unless, in the case of a couple, the adoption agency and the relevant foreign authority have agreed that it is necessary for only one of them to do so.

(4) Except where an overseas adoption is or is to be effected, the prospective adopter must within the period of 14 days beginning with the date on which the child is brought into the United Kingdom give notice to the relevant local authority –

(a) of the child's arrival in the United Kingdom; and
(b) of his intention –
   (i) to apply for an adoption order in accordance with section 44(2) of the Act; or
   (ii) not to give the child a home.

(5) In a case where a prospective adopter has given notice in accordance with paragraph (4) and subsequently moves his home into the area of another local authority, he must within 14 days of that move confirm in writing to that authority, the child's entry into the United Kingdom and that notice of his intention –

(a) to apply for an adoption order in accordance with section 44(2) of the Act has been given to another local authority; or
(b) not to give the child a home,

has been given.

5 Functions imposed on the local authority

(1) Where notice of intention to adopt has been given to the local authority, that authority must –

(a) if it has not already done so, set up a case record in respect of the child and place on it any information received from the –
   (i) relevant foreign authority;
   (ii) adoption agency, if it is not the local authority;
   (iii) prospective adopter;
   (iv) entry clearance officer; and

(v) Secretary of State, or as the case may be, the Assembly;
(b) send the prospective adopter's general practitioner written notification of the arrival in England or Wales of the child and send with that notification a written report of the child's health history and current state of health, so far as is known;
(c) send to the Primary Care Trust or Local Health Board (Wales), in whose area the prospective adopter has his home, written notification of the arrival in England or Wales of the child;
(d) where the child is of compulsory school age, send to the local education authority, in whose area the prospective adopter has his home, written notification of the arrival of the child in England or Wales and information, if known, about the child's educational history and whether he is likely to be assessed for special educational needs under the Education Act 1996;
(e) ensure that the child and the prospective adopter are visited within one week of receipt of the notice of intention to adopt and thereafter not less than once a week until the review referred to in sub-paragraph (f) and thereafter at such frequency as the authority may decide;
(f) carry out a review of the child's case not more than 4 weeks after receipt of the notice of intention to adopt and –
  (i) visit and, if necessary, review not more than 3 months after that initial review; and
  (ii) thereafter not more than 6 months after the date of the previous visit,
unless the child no longer has his home with the prospective adopter or an adoption order is made;
(g) when carrying out a review consider –
  (i) the child's needs, welfare and development, and whether any changes need to be made to meet his needs or assist his development;
  (ii) the arrangements for the provision of adoption support services and whether there should be any re-assessment of the need for those services; and
  (iii) the need for further visits and reviews; and
(h) ensure that –
  (i) advice is given as to the child's needs, welfare and development;
  (ii) written reports are made of all visits and reviews of the case and placed on the child's case record; and
  (iii) on such visits, where appropriate, advice is given as to the availability of adoption support services.

(2) Part 7 of the Agencies Regulations or corresponding Welsh provision (case records) shall apply to the case record set up in respect of the child as a consequence of this regulation as if that record had been set up under the Agencies Regulations or corresponding Welsh provision.

(3) In a case where the prospective adopter fails to make an application under section 50 or 51 of the Act within two years of the receipt by a local authority of the notice of intention to adopt the local authority must review the case.

(4) For the purposes of the review referred to in paragraph (3), the local authority must consider –

(a) the child's needs, welfare and development, and whether any changes need to be made to meet his needs or assist his development;
(b) the arrangements, if any, in relation to the exercise of parental responsibility for the child;
(c) the terms upon which leave to enter the United Kingdom is granted and the immigration status of the child;
(d) the arrangements for the provision of adoption support services for the adoptive family and whether there should be any re-assessment of the need for those services; and

(e) in conjunction with the appropriate agencies, the arrangements for meeting the child's health care and educational needs.

(5) In a case where the local authority to which notice of intention to adopt is given ('the original authority') is notified by the prospective adopter that he intends to move or has moved his home into the area of another local authority, the original authority must notify the local authority into whose area the prospective adopter intends to move or has moved, within 14 days of receiving information in respect of that move, of –

(a) the name, sex, date and place of birth of child;
(b) the prospective adopter's name, sex and date of birth;
(c) the date on which the child entered the United Kingdom;
(d) where the original authority received notification of intention to adopt, the date of receipt of such notification whether an application for an adoption order has been made and the stage of those proceedings; and
(e) any other relevant information.

6 Application of Chapter 3 of the Act

In the case of a child brought into the United Kingdom for adoption in circumstances where section 83 of the Act applies –

(a) the modifications in regulations 7 to 9 apply;
(b) section 36(2) and (5) (restrictions on removal) and section 39(3)(a) (partners of parents) of the Act shall not apply.

7 Change of name and removal from the United Kingdom

Section 28(2) of the Act (further consequences of placement) shall apply as if from the words 'is placed' to 'then', there is substituted 'enters the United Kingdom in the circumstances where section 83(1)(a) of this Act applies'.

8 Return of the child

(1) Section 35 of the Act (return of child) shall apply with the following modifications.

(2) Subsections (1), (2) and (3) shall apply as if in each place where –

(a) the words 'is placed for adoption by an adoption agency' occur there were substituted 'enters the United Kingdom in circumstances where section 83(1) applies';
(b) the words 'the agency' occur there were substituted the words 'the local authority'; and
(c) the words 'any parent or guardian of the child' occur there were substituted 'the Secretary of State or, as the case may be, the Assembly'.

(3) Subsection (5) shall apply as if for the words 'an adoption agency' or 'the agency' there were substituted the words 'the local authority'.

9 Child to live with adopters before application

(1) In a case where the requirements imposed by section 83(4) of the Act have been complied with and the conditions required by section 83(5) of the Act have been met, section 42 shall apply as if –

(a) subsection (3) is omitted; and
(b) in subsection (5) the words from 'three years' to 'preceding' there were substituted 'six months'.

(2) In a case where the requirements imposed by section 83(4) of the Act have not been complied with or the conditions required by section 83(5) have not been met, section 42 shall apply as if –

(a) subsection (3) is omitted; and
(b) in subsection (5) the words from 'three years' to 'preceding' there were substituted 'twelve months'.

Chapter 2
Taking children out of the United Kingdom

10 Requirements applicable in respect of giving parental responsibility prior to adoption abroad

The prescribed requirements for the purposes of section 84(3) of the Act (requirements to be satisfied prior to the making of an order) are that –

(a) in the case of a child placed by an adoption agency, that agency has –
   (i) confirmed to the court that it has complied with the requirements imposed in accordance with Part 3 of the Agencies Regulations or corresponding Welsh provision;
   (ii) submitted to the court –
      (aa) the reports and information referred to in regulation 17(2) and (3) of the Agencies Regulations or corresponding Welsh provision;
      (bb) the recommendations made by the adoption panel in accordance with regulations 18 (placing child for adoption) and 33 (proposed placement) of the Agencies Regulations or corresponding Welsh provision;
      (cc) the adoption placement report prepared in accordance with regulation 31(2)(d) of the Agencies Regulations or corresponding Welsh provision;
      (dd) the reports of and information obtained in respect of the visits and reviews referred to in regulation 36 of the Agencies Regulations or corresponding Welsh provision; and
      (ee) the report referred to in section 43 of the Act as modified by regulation 11;
(b) in the case of a child placed by an adoption agency the relevant foreign authority has –
   (i) confirmed in writing to that agency that the prospective adopter has been counselled and the legal implications of adoption have been explained to him;
   (ii) prepared a report on the suitability of the prospective adopter to be an adoptive parent;
   (iii) determined and confirmed in writing to that agency that he is eligible and suitable to adopt in the country or territory in which the adoption is to be effected; and
   (iv) confirmed in writing to that agency that the child is or will be authorised to enter and reside permanently in that foreign country or territory; and
(c) in the case of a child placed by an adoption agency the prospective adopter has confirmed in writing to the adoption agency that he will accompany the child on taking him out of the United Kingdom and entering the country or territory where the adoption is to be effected, or in the case of a couple, the agency and relevant foreign authority have confirmed that it is necessary for only one of them to do so.

11 Application of the Act in respect of orders under section 84

(1) The following provisions of the Act which refer to adoption orders shall apply to orders under section 84 as if in each place where the words 'adoption order' appear there were substituted 'order under section 84' –

(a) section 1(7)(a) (coming to a decision relating to adoption of a child);
(b) section 18(4) (placement for adoption by agencies);
(c) section 21(4)(b) (placement orders);
(d) section 22(5)(a) and (b) (application for placement orders);
(e) section 24(4) (revoking placement orders);
(f) section 28(1) (further consequences of placement);
(g) section 29(4)(a) and (5)(a) (further consequences of placement orders);
(h) section 32(5) (recovery by parent etc where child placed and consent withdrawn);
(i) section 42(7) (sufficient opportunity for adoption agency to see the child);
(j) section 43 (reports where child placed by agency);
(k) section 44(2) (notice of intention to adopt);
(l) section 47(1) to (5), (8) and (9) (conditions for making orders);
(m) section 48(1) (restrictions on making applications);
(n) section 50(1) and (2) (adoption by a couple);
(o) section 51(1) to (4) (adoption by one person);
(p) section 52(1) to (4) (parental etc. consent);
(q) section 53(5) (contribution towards maintenance); and
(r) section 141(3) and (4)(c) (rules of procedure).

(2) Section 35(5) of the Act (return of child in other cases) shall apply to orders under section 84 of that Act as if in paragraph (b) of that subsection –

(a) for the first reference to 'adoption order' there were substituted 'order under section 84(1)'; and
(b) the words in brackets were omitted.

PART 3

ADOPTIONS UNDER THE CONVENTION

Chapter 1
Requirements, procedure, recognition and effect of adoptions where the United Kingdom is the receiving state

12 Application of Chapter 1

The provisions in this Chapter shall apply where a couple or a person, habitually resident in the British Islands, wishes to adopt a child who is habitually resident in a Convention country outside the British Islands in accordance with the Convention.

13 Requirements applicable in respect of eligibility and suitability

(1) A couple or a person who wishes to adopt a child habitually resident in a Convention country outside the British Islands shall –

(a) apply in writing to an adoption agency for a determination of eligibility, and an assessment of his suitability, to adopt; and
(b) give the agency any information it may require for the purposes of the assessment.

(2) An adoption agency may not consider an application under paragraph (1) unless at the date of that application –

(a) in the case of an application by a couple, they have both –
   (i) attained the age of 21 years; and
   (ii) been habitually resident in a part of the British Islands for a period of not less than one year ending with the date of application; and
(b) in the case of an application by one person, he has –
   (i) attained the age of 21 years; and
   (ii) been habitually resident in a part of the British Islands for a period of not less than one year ending with the date of application.

14 Counselling and information

(1) An adoption agency must provide a counselling service in accordance with regulation 21(1)(a) of the Agencies Regulations or corresponding Welsh provision and must –

(a) explain to the prospective adopter the procedure in relation to, and the legal implications of, adopting a child from the State of origin from which the prospective adopter wishes to adopt in accordance with the Convention; and
(b) provide him with written information about the matters referred to in sub-paragraph (a).

(2) Paragraph (1) does not apply if the adoption agency is satisfied that the requirements set out in that paragraph have been carried out in respect of the prospective adopter by another agency.

15 Procedure in respect of carrying out an assessment

(1) Regulation 22 of the Agencies Regulations (requirement to consider application for an assessment of suitability) or corresponding Welsh provision shall apply as if the reference to an application in those Regulations or corresponding Welsh provision was to an application made in accordance with regulation 13.

(2) Where the adoption agency is satisfied that the requirements in –

(a) regulation 14; and
(b) regulations 23 (police checks) and 24 (preparation for adoption) of the Agencies Regulations or corresponding Welsh provision,

have been meet, regulations 25 (prospective adopter's report) and 26 (adoption panel) of the Agencies Regulations or corresponding Welsh provisions shall apply.

(3) The adoption agency must place on the prospective adopter's case record any information obtained as a consequence of this Chapter.

(4) The adoption agency must include in the prospective adopter's report –

(a) the State of origin from which the prospective adopter wishes to adopt a child;
(b) confirmation that the prospective adopter is eligible to adopt a child under the law of that State;
(c) any additional information obtained as a consequence of the requirements of that State; and
(d) the agency's assessment of the prospective adopter's suitability to adopt a child who is habitually resident in that State.

(5) The references to information in regulations 25(5) and 26(2) of the Agencies Regulations or corresponding Welsh provisions shall include information obtained by the adoption agency or adoption panel as a consequence of this regulation.

16 Adoption agency decision and notification

The adoption agency must make a decision about whether the prospective adopter is suitable to adopt a child in accordance with regulation 27 of the Agencies Regulations and regulations made under section 45 of the Act, or corresponding Welsh provisions.

17 Review and termination of approval

The adoption agency must review the approval of each prospective adopter in accordance with regulation 29 of the Agencies Regulations or corresponding Welsh provision unless the agency has received written notification from the relevant Central Authority that the agreement under Article 17(c) of the Convention has been made.

18 Procedure following decision as to suitability to adopt

(1) Where an adoption agency has made a decision that the prospective adopter is suitable to adopt a child in accordance with regulation 16, it must send to the relevant Central Authority –

(a) written confirmation of the decision and any recommendation the agency may make in relation to the number of children the prospective adopter may be suitable to adopt, their age range, sex, likely needs and background;

(b) the enhanced criminal record certificate obtained under regulation 23 of the Agencies Regulations or corresponding Welsh provision;

(c) all the documents and information which were passed to the adoption panel in accordance with regulation 25(9) of the Agencies Regulations or corresponding Welsh provision;

(d) the record of the proceedings of the adoption panel, its recommendation and the reasons for its recommendation; and

(e) any other information relating to the case as the relevant Central Authority or the CA of the State of origin may require.

(2) If the relevant Central Authority is satisfied that the adoption agency has complied with the duties and procedures imposed by the Agencies Regulations or corresponding Welsh provision, and that all the relevant information has been supplied by that agency, the Authority must send to the CA of the State of origin –

(a) the prospective adopter's report prepared in accordance with regulation 25 of the Agencies Regulations or corresponding Welsh provision;

(b) the enhanced criminal record certificate;

(c) a copy of the adoption agency's decision and the adoption panel's recommendation;

(d) any other information that the CA of the State of origin may require; and

(e) a certificate in the form set out in Schedule 1 confirming that the –

   (i) prospective adopter is eligible to adopt;
   (ii) prospective adopter has been assessed in accordance with this Chapter;
   (iii) prospective adopter has been approved as suitable to adopt a child; and
   (iv) child will be authorised to enter and reside permanently in the United Kingdom if entry clearance, and leave to enter or remain as may be necessary, is granted and not revoked or curtailed and a Convention adoption order or Convention adoption is made.

(3) The relevant Central Authority must notify the adoption agency and the prospective adopter in writing that the certificate and the documents referred to in paragraph (2) have been sent to the CA of the State of origin.

19 Procedure following receipt of the Article 16 Information from the CA of the State of origin

(1) Where the relevant Central Authority receives from the CA of the State of origin, the Article 16 Information relating to the child whom the CA of the State of origin considers should be placed for adoption with the prospective adopter, the relevant Central Authority must send that Information to the adoption agency.

(2) The adoption agency must consider the Article 16 Information and –

(a) send that Information to the prospective adopter;
(b) meet with him to discuss –
   (i) that Information;
   (ii) the proposed placement;
   (iii) the availability of adoption support services; and
(c) if appropriate, offer a counselling service and further information as required.

(3) Where –

(a) the procedure in paragraph (2) has been followed;
(b) the prospective adopter (and where the prospective adopters are a couple each of them) has visited the child in the State of origin; and
(c) after that visit to the child, the prospective adopter has confirmed in writing to the adoption agency that –
   (i) he has visited the child;
   (ii) he has provided the adoption agency with additional reports and information received on or after that visit; and
   (iii) he wishes to proceed to adopt that child,

the agency must notify the relevant Central Authority in writing that the requirements specified in sub-paragraphs (a) to (c) have been satisfied and at the same time it must confirm that it is content for the adoption to proceed.

(4) Where the relevant Central Authority has received notification from the adoption agency under paragraph (3), the relevant Central Authority shall –

(a) notify the CA of the State of origin that –
   (i) the prospective adopter wishes to proceed to adopt the child;
   (ii) it is prepared to agree with the CA of the State of origin that the adoption may proceed; and
(b) confirm to the CA of the State of origin that –
   (i) in the case where the requirements specified in section 1(5A) of the British Nationality Act 1981 are met that the child will be authorised to enter and reside permanently in the United Kingdom; or
   (ii) in any other case, if entry clearance and leave to enter and remain, as may be necessary, is granted and not revoked or curtailed and a Convention adoption order or a Convention adoption is made, the child will be authorised to enter and reside permanently in the United Kingdom.

(5) The relevant Central Authority must inform the adoption agency and the prospective adopter when the agreement under Article 17(c) of the Convention has been made.

(6) For the purposes of this regulation and regulation 20 'the Article 16 Information' means –

  (a) the report referred to in Article 16(1) of the Convention including information about the child's identity, adoptability, background, social environment, family history, medical history including that of the child's family and any special needs of the child;
  (b) proof of confirmation that the consents of the persons, institutions and authorities whose consents are necessary for adoption have been obtained in accordance with Article 4 of the Convention; and
  (c) the reasons for the CA of the State of origin's determination on the placement.

20 Procedure where proposed adoption is not to proceed

(1) If, at any stage before the agreement under Article 17(c) of the Convention is made, the CA of the State of origin notifies the relevant Central Authority that it has decided the proposed placement should not proceed –

  (a) the relevant Central Authority must inform the adoption agency of the CA of the State of origin's decision;
  (b) the agency must then inform the prospective adopter and return the Article 16 Information to the relevant Central Authority; and
  (c) the relevant Central Authority must then return those documents to the CA of the State of origin.

(2) Where at any stage before the adoption agency receives notification of the agreement under Article 17(c) of the Convention the approval of the prospective adopter is reviewed under regulation 29 of the Agencies Regulations or corresponding Welsh provision, and as a consequence, the agency determines that the prospective adopter is no longer suitable to adopt a child –

  (a) the agency must inform the relevant Central Authority and return the documents referred to in regulation 19(1);
  (b) the relevant Central Authority must notify the CA of the State of origin and return those documents.

(3) If, at any stage before the child is placed with him, the prospective adopter notifies the adoption agency that he does not wish to proceed with the adoption of the child –

  (a) that agency must inform the relevant Central Authority and return the documents to that Authority; and
  (b) the relevant Central Authority must notify the CA of the State of origin of the prospective adopter's decision and return the documents to the CA of the State of origin.

21 Applicable requirements in respect of prospective adopter entering the United Kingdom with a child

Following any agreement under Article 17(c) of the Convention, the prospective adopter must –

  (a) notify the adoption agency of his expected date of entry into the United Kingdom with the child;
  (b) confirm to the adoption agency when the child is placed with him by the competent authority in the State of origin; and
  (c) accompany the child on entering the United Kingdom unless, in the case of a couple, the adoption agency and the CA of the State of origin have agreed that it is necessary for only one of them to do so.

22 Applicable requirements in respect of an adoption agency before the child enters the United Kingdom

Where the adoption agency is informed by the relevant Central Authority that the agreement under Article 17(c) of the Convention has been made and the adoption may proceed, before the child enters the United Kingdom that agency must –

(a) send the prospective adopter's general practitioner written notification of the proposed placement and send with that notification a written report of the child's health history and current state of health, so far as it is known;

(b) send the local authority (if that authority is not the adoption agency) and the Primary Care Trust or Local Health Board (Wales), in whose area the prospective adopter has his home, written notification of the proposed arrival of the child into England or Wales; and

(c) where the child is of compulsory school age, send the local education authority, in whose area the prospective adopter has his home, written notification of the proposed arrival of the child into England or Wales and information about the child's educational history if known and whether he is likely to be assessed for special educational needs under the Education Act 1996.

23 Applicable provisions following the child's entry into the United Kingdom where no Convention adoption is made

Regulations 24 to 27 apply where –

(a) following the agreement between the relevant Central Authority and the CA of the State of origin under Article 17(c) of the Convention that the adoption may proceed, no Convention adoption is made, or applied for, in the State of origin; and

(b) the child is placed with the prospective adopter in the State of origin who then returns to England or Wales with that child.

24 Applicable requirements in respect of prospective adopter following child's entry into the United Kingdom

(1) A prospective adopter must within the period of 14 days beginning with the date on which the child enters the United Kingdom give notice to the relevant local authority –

(a) of the child's arrival in the United Kingdom; and
(b) of his intention –
    (i) to apply for an adoption order in accordance with section 44(2) of the Act; or
    (ii) not to give the child a home.

(2) In a case where a prospective adopter has given notice in accordance with paragraph (1) and he subsequently moves his home into the area of another local authority, he must within 14 days of that move confirm to that authority in writing the child's entry into the United Kingdom and that notice of his intention –

(a) to apply for an adoption order in accordance with section 44(2) of the Act has been given to another local authority; or
(b) not to give the child a home,

has been given.

25 Functions imposed on the local authority following the child's entry into the United Kingdom

(1) Where notice is given to a local authority in accordance with regulation 24, the functions imposed on the local authority by virtue of regulation 5 shall apply subject to the modifications in paragraph (2).

(2) Paragraph (1) of regulation 5 shall apply as if –

(a) in sub-paragraph (a) –
 (i) in head (i) for the words 'relevant foreign authority' there is substituted 'CA of the State of origin and competent foreign authority';
 (ii) in head (v) there is substituted 'the relevant Central Authority'; and
(b) sub-paragraphs (b) to (d) were omitted.

26 Prospective adopter unable to proceed with adoption

Where the prospective adopter gives notice to the relevant local authority that he does not wish to proceed with the adoption and no longer wishes to give the child a home, that authority must –

(a) receive the child from him before the end of the period of seven days beginning with the giving of the notice; and
(b) give notice to the relevant Central Authority of the decision of the prospective adopter not to proceed with the adoption.

27 Withdrawal of child from prospective adopter

(1) Where the relevant local authority are of the opinion that the continued placement of the child is not in the child's best interests –

(a) that authority must give notice to the prospective adopter of their opinion and request the return of the child to them; and
(b) subject to paragraph (3), the prospective adopter must, not later than the end of the period of seven days beginning with the date on which notice was given, return the child to that authority.

(2) Where the relevant local authority has given notice under paragraph (1), that authority must at the same time notify the relevant Central Authority that they have requested the return of the child.

(3) Where notice is given under paragraph (1) but –

(a) an application for a Convention adoption order was made prior to the giving of that notice; and
(b) the application has not been disposed of,

the prospective adopter is not required by virtue of paragraph (1) to return the child unless the court so orders.

(4) This regulation does not affect the exercise by any local authority or other person of any power conferred by any enactment or the exercise of any power of arrest.

28 Breakdown of placement

(1) This regulation applies where –

(a) notification is given by the prospective adopter under regulation 26 (unable to proceed with adoption);

(b) the child is withdrawn from the prospective adopter under regulation 27 (withdrawal of child from prospective adopter);

(c) an application for a Convention adoption order is refused;

(d) a Convention adoption which is subject to a probationary period cannot be made; or

(e) a Convention adoption order or a Convention adoption is annulled pursuant to section 89(1) of the Act.

(2) Where the relevant local authority are satisfied that it would be in the child's best interests to be placed for adoption with another prospective adopter habitually resident in the United Kingdom they must take the necessary measures to identify a suitable adoptive parent for that child.

(3) Where the relevant local authority have identified and approved another prospective adopter who is eligible, and has been assessed as suitable, to adopt in accordance with these Regulations –

(a) that authority must notify the relevant Central Authority in writing that –
 (i) another prospective adopter has been identified; and
 (ii) the provisions in regulations 14, 15 and 16 have been complied with; and

(b) the requirements specified in regulations 18 and 19 have been complied with.

(4) Where the relevant Central Authority has been notified in accordance with paragraph (3)(a) –

(a) it shall inform the CA of the State of origin of the proposed placement; and

(b) it shall agree the placement with the CA of the State of origin in accordance with the provisions in this Chapter.

(5) Subject to paragraph (2), where the relevant local authority is not satisfied it would be in the child's best interests to be placed for adoption with another prospective adopter in England or Wales, it must liaise with the relevant Central Authority to arrange for the return of the child to his State of origin.

(6) Before coming to any decision under this regulation, the relevant local authority must have regard to the wishes and feelings of the child, having regard to his age and understanding, and where appropriate, obtain his consent in relation to measures to be taken under this regulation.

29 Convention adoptions subject to a probationary period

(1) This regulation applies where –

(a) the child has been placed with the prospective adopters by the competent authority in the State of origin and a Convention adoption has been applied for by the prospective adopters in the State of origin but the child's placement with the prospective adopter is subject to a probationary period before the Convention adoption is made; and

(b) the prospective adopter returns to England or Wales with the child before that probationary period is completed and the Convention adoption is made in the State of origin.

(2) The relevant local authority must, if requested by the competent authority of the State of origin, submit a report about the placement to that authority and such a report must be prepared within such timescales and contain such information as the competent authority may reasonably require.

30 Report of local authority investigation

The report of the investigation which a local authority must submit to the court in accordance with section 44(5) of the Act must include –

(a) confirmation that the Certificate of eligibility and approval has been sent to the CA of the State of origin in accordance with regulation 18;
(b) the date on which the agreement under Article 17(c) of the Convention was made; and
(c) details of the reports of the visits and reviews made in accordance with regulation 5 as modified by regulation 25.

31 Convention adoption order

An adoption order shall not be made as a Convention adoption order unless –

(a) in the case of –
   (i) an application by a couple, both members of the couple have been habitually resident in any part of the British Islands for a period of not less than one year ending with the date of the application; or
   (ii) an application by one person, the applicant has been habitually resident in any part of the British Islands for a period of not less than one year ending with the date of the application;
(b) the child to be adopted was, on the date on which the agreement under Article 17(c) of the Convention was made, habitually resident in a Convention country outside the British Islands; and
(c) in a case where one member of a couple (in the case of an application by a couple) or the applicant (in the case of an application by one person) is not a British citizen, the Home Office has confirmed that the child is authorised to enter and reside permanently in the United Kingdom.

32 Requirements following a Convention adoption order or Convention adoption

(1) Where the relevant Central Authority receives a copy of a Convention adoption order made by a court in England or Wales that Authority must issue a certificate in the form set out in Schedule 2 certifying that the adoption has been made in accordance with the Convention.

(2) A copy of the certificate issued under paragraph (1) must be sent to the –

(a) CA of the State of origin;
(b) adoptive parent; and
(c) adoption agency and, if different, the relevant local authority.

(3) Where a Convention adoption is made and the relevant Central Authority receives a certificate under Article 23 of the Convention in respect of that Convention adoption, the relevant Central Authority must send a copy of that certificate to the –

(a) adoptive parent; and
(b) adoption agency and, if different, the relevant local authority.

33 Refusal of a court in England or Wales to make a Convention adoption order

Where an application for a Convention adoption order is refused by the court or is withdrawn, the prospective adopter must return the child to the relevant local authority within the period determined by the court.

34 Annulment of a Convention adoption order or a Convention adoption

Where a Convention adoption order or a Convention adoption is annulled under section 89(1) of the Act and the relevant Central Authority receives a copy of the order from the court, it must forward a copy of that order to the CA of the State of origin.

Chapter 2
Requirements, procedure, recognition and effect of adoptions in England and Wales where the United Kingdom is the state of origin

35 Application of Chapter 2

The provisions in this Chapter shall apply where a couple or a person habitually resident in a Convention country outside the British Islands, wishes to adopt a child who is habitually resident in the British Islands in accordance with the Convention.

36 Counselling and information for the child

(1) Where an adoption agency is considering whether a child is suitable for an adoption in accordance with the Convention, it must provide a counselling service for and information to that child in accordance with regulation 13 of the Agencies Regulations or corresponding Welsh provision and it must –

(a) explain to the child in an appropriate manner the procedure in relation to, and the legal implications of, adoption under the Convention for that child by a prospective adopter habitually resident in the receiving State; and
(b) provide him with written information about the matters referred to in sub-paragraph (a).

(2) Paragraph (1) does not apply if the adoption agency is satisfied that the requirements set out in that paragraph have been carried out in respect of the prospective adopter by another agency.

37 Counselling and information for the parent or guardian of the child etc

(1) An adoption agency must provide a counselling service and information in accordance with regulation 14 of the Agencies Regulations or corresponding Welsh provision for the parent or guardian of the child and, where regulation 14(4) of the Agencies Regulations or corresponding Welsh provision applies, for the father.

(2) The adoption agency must also –

(a) explain to the parent or guardian, and, where regulation 14(4) of the Agencies Regulations or corresponding Welsh provision applies, the father the procedure in relation to, and the legal implications of, adoption under the Convention by a prospective adopter in a receiving State; and
(b) provide him with written information about the matters referred to in sub-paragraph (a).

(3) Paragraphs (1) and (2) do not apply if the adoption agency is satisfied that the requirements set out in that paragraph have been carried out in respect of the prospective adopter by another agency.

38 Requirements in respect of the child's permanence report and information for the adoption panel

(1) The child's permanence report which the adoption agency is required to prepare in accordance with regulation 17 of the Agencies Regulations or corresponding Welsh provision must include –

(a) a summary of the possibilities for placement of the child within the United Kingdom; and
(b) an assessment of whether an adoption by a person in a particular receiving State is in the child's best interests.

(2) The adoption agency must send –

(a) if received, the Article 15 Report; and
(b) their observations on that Report,

together with the reports and information referred to in regulation 17(2) of the Agencies Regulations or corresponding Welsh provision to the adoption panel.

39 Recommendation of adoption panel

Where an adoption panel make a recommendation in accordance with regulation 18(1) of the Agencies Regulations or corresponding Welsh provision it must consider and take into account the Article 15 Report, if available, and the observations thereon together with the information passed to it as a consequence of regulation 38.

40 Adoption agency decision and notification

Where the adoption agency decides in accordance with regulation 19 of the Agencies Regulations or corresponding Welsh provision that the child should be placed for an adoption in accordance with the Convention it must notify the relevant Central Authority of –

(a) the name, sex and age of the child;
(b) the reasons why they consider that the child may be suitable for such an adoption;
(c) whether a prospective adopter has been identified and, if so, provide any relevant information; and
(d) any other information that Authority may require.

41 Convention list

(1) The relevant Central Authority is to maintain a Convention list of children who are notified to that Authority under regulation 40 and shall make the contents of that list available for consultation by other Authorities within the British Islands.

(2) Where an adoption agency –

(a) places for adoption a child whose details have been notified to the relevant Central Authority under regulation 40; or
(b) determines that an adoption in accordance with the Convention is no longer in the best interests of the child,

it must notify the relevant Central Authority accordingly and that Authority must remove the details relating to that child from the Convention list.

42 Receipt of the Article 15 Report from the CA of the receiving State

(1) This regulation applies where –

(a) the relevant Central Authority receives a report from the CA of the receiving State which has been prepared for the purposes of Article 15 of the Convention ('the Article 15 Report');
(b) the Article 15 Report relates to a prospective adopter who is habitually resident in that receiving State; and

(c) the prospective adopter named in the Article 15 Report wishes to adopt a child who is habitually resident in the British Islands.

(2) Subject to paragraph (3), if the relevant Central Authority is satisfied the prospective adopter meets the following requirements –

(a) the age requirements as specified in section 50 of the Act in the case of adoption by a couple, or section 51 of the Act in the case of adoption by one person; and
(b) in the case of a couple, both are, or in the case of adoption by one person, that person is habitually resident in a Convention country outside the British Islands,

that Authority must consult the Convention list and may, if the Authority considers it appropriate, consult any Convention list maintained by another Central Authority within the British Islands.

(3) Where a prospective adopter has already been identified in relation to a proposed adoption of a particular child and the relevant Central Authority is satisfied that prospective adopter meets the requirements referred to in paragraph (2)(a) and (b), that Authority –

(a) need not consult the Convention list; and
(b) must send the Article 15 Report to the local authority which referred the child's details to the Authority.

(4) The relevant Central Authority may pass a copy of the Article 15 Report to any other Central Authority within the British Islands for the purposes of enabling that Authority to consult its Convention list.

(5) Where the relevant Central Authority identifies a child on the Convention list who may be suitable for adoption by the prospective adopter, that Authority must send the Article 15 Report to the local authority which referred the child's details to that Authority.

43 Proposed placement and referral to adoption panel

(1) Where the adoption agency is considering whether a proposed placement should proceed in accordance with the procedure provided for in regulation 31 of the Agencies Regulations or corresponding Welsh provision it must take into account the Article 15 Report.

(2) Where the adoption agency refers the proposal to place the child with the particular prospective adopter to the adoption panel in accordance with regulation 31 of the Agencies Regulations or corresponding Welsh provision, it must also send the Article 15 Report to the panel.

44 Consideration by adoption panel

The adoption panel must take into account when considering what recommendation to make in accordance with regulation 32(1) of the Agencies Regulations or corresponding Welsh provision the Article 15 Report and any other information passed to it as a consequence of the provisions in this Chapter.

45 Adoption agency's decision in relation to the proposed placement

(1) Regulation 33 of the Agencies Regulations or corresponding Welsh provision shall apply as if paragraph (3) of that regulation or corresponding Welsh provision was omitted.

(2) As soon as possible after the agency makes its decision, it must notify the relevant Central Authority of its decision.

(3) If the proposed placement is not to proceed –

(a) the adoption agency must return the Article 15 Report and any other documents or information sent to it by the relevant Central Authority to that Authority; and
(b) the relevant Central Authority must then send that Report, any such documents or such information to the CA of the receiving State.

46 Preparation of the Article 16 Information

(1) If the adoption agency decides that the proposed placement should proceed, it must prepare a report for the purposes of Article 16(1) of the Convention which must include –

(a) the information about the child which is specified in Schedule 1 to the Agencies Regulations or corresponding Welsh provision; and
(b) the reasons for their decision.

(2) The adoption agency must send the following to the relevant Central Authority –

(a) the report referred to in paragraph (1);
(b) details of any placement order or other orders, if any, made by the courts; and
(c) confirmation that the parent or guardian consents to the proposed adoption.

(3) The relevant Central Authority must then send the documents referred to in paragraph (2) to the CA of the receiving State.

47 Requirements to be met before the child is placed for adoption with prospective adopter

(1) The relevant Central Authority may notify the CA of the receiving State that it is prepared to agree that the adoption may proceed provided that CA has confirmed that –

(a) the prospective adopter has agreed to adopt the child and has received such counselling as may be necessary;
(b) the prospective adopter has confirmed that he will accompany the child to the receiving State, unless in the case of a couple, the adoption agency and the CA of the receiving State have agreed that it is only necessary for one of them to do so;
(c) it is content for the adoption to proceed;
(d) in the case where a Convention adoption is to be effected, it has explained to the prospective adopter the need to make an application under section 84(1) of the Act; and
(e) the child is or will be authorised to enter and reside permanently in the Convention country if a Convention adoption is effected or a Convention adoption order is made.

(2) The relevant Central Authority may not make an agreement under Article 17(c) of the Convention with the CA of the receiving State unless –

(a) confirmation has been received in respect of the matters referred to in paragraph (1); and
(b) the adoption agency has confirmed to the relevant Central Authority that –
   (i) it has met the prospective adopter and explained the requirement to make an application for an order under section 84 of the Act before the child can be removed from the United Kingdom;
   (ii) the prospective adopter has visited the child; and
   (iii) the prospective adopter is content for the adoption to proceed.

(3) An adoption agency may not place a child for adoption unless the agreement under Article 17(c) of the Convention has been made and the relevant Central Authority must advise that agency when that agreement has been made.

(4) In this regulation, the reference to 'prospective adopter' means in the case of a couple, both of them.

48 Requirements in respect of giving parental responsibility prior to a proposed Convention adoption

In the case of a proposed Convention adoption, the prescribed requirements for the purposes of section 84(3) of the Act (requirements to be satisfied prior to making an order) are –

(a) the competent authorities of the receiving State have –
   (i) prepared a report for the purposes of Article 15 of the Convention;
   (ii) determined and confirmed in writing that the prospective adoptive parent is eligible and suitable to adopt;
   (iii) ensured and confirmed in writing that the prospective adoptive parent has been counselled as may be necessary; and
   (iv) determined and confirmed in writing that the child is or will be authorised to enter and reside permanently in that State;
(b) the report required for the purposes of Article 16(1) of the Convention has been prepared by the adoption agency;
(c) the adoption agency confirms in writing that it has complied with the requirements imposed upon it under Part 3 of the Agencies Regulations or corresponding Welsh provision and this Chapter;
(d) the adoption agency has obtained and made available to the court –
   (i) the reports and information referred to in regulation 17(1) and (2) of the Agencies Regulations or corresponding Welsh provision;
   (ii) the recommendation made by the adoption panel in accordance with regulations 18 and 33 of the Agencies Regulations or corresponding Welsh provisions; and
   (iii) the adoption placement report prepared in accordance with regulation 31(2) of the Agencies Regulations or corresponding Welsh provision;
(e) the adoption agency includes in their report submitted to the court in accordance with section 43(a) or 44(5) of the Act as modified respectively by regulation 11, details of any reviews and visits carried out as consequence of Part 6 of the Agencies Regulations or corresponding Welsh provision; and
(f) the prospective adopter has confirmed in writing that he will accompany the child on taking the child out of the United Kingdom to travel to the receiving State or in the case of a couple the agency and competent foreign authority have confirmed that it is necessary for only one of them to do so.

49 Local authority report

In the case of a proposed application for a Convention adoption order, the report which a local authority must submit to the court in accordance with section 43(a) or 44(5) of the Act must include a copy of the –

(a) Article 15 Report;
(b) report prepared for the purposes of Article 16(1); and
(c) written confirmation of the agreement under Article 17(c) of the Convention.

50 Convention adoption order

An adoption order shall not be made as a Convention adoption order unless –

(a) in the case of –
   (i) an application by a couple, both members of the couple have been habitually resident in a Convention country outside the British Islands for a period of not less than one year ending with the date of the application; or
   (ii) an application by one person, the applicant has been habitually resident in a Convention country outside the British Islands for a period of not less than one year ending with the date of the application;
(b) the child to be adopted was, on the date on which the agreement under Article 17(c) of the Convention was made, habitually resident in any part of the British Islands; and
(c) the competent authority has confirmed that the child is authorised to enter and remain permanently in the Convention country in which the applicant is habitually resident.

51 Requirements following a Convention adoption order or Convention adoption

(1) Where the relevant Central Authority receives a copy of a Convention adoption order made by a court in England or Wales, that Authority must issue a certificate in the form set out in Schedule 2 certifying that the adoption has been made in accordance with the Convention.

(2) A copy of the certificate must be sent to the –

(a) CA of the receiving State; and
(b) the relevant local authority.

(3) Where a Convention adoption is made and the Central Authority receives a certificate under Article 23 in respect of that Convention adoption, the relevant Central Authority must send a copy of that certificate to the relevant local authority.

Chapter 3
Miscellaneous provisions

52 Application, with or without modifications, of the Act

(1) Subject to the modifications provided for in this Chapter, the provisions of the Act shall apply to adoptions within the scope of the Convention so far as the nature of the provision permits and unless the contrary intention is shown.

53 Change of name and removal from the United Kingdom

In a case falling within Chapter 1 of this Part, section 28(2) of the Act shall apply as if –

(a) at the end of paragraph (a), 'or' was omitted;
(b) at the end of paragraph (b) there were inserted 'or (c) a child is placed by a competent foreign authority for the purposes of an adoption under the Convention,'; and
(c) at the end of subsection (2) there were inserted 'or the competent foreign authority consents to a change of surname.'.

54 Removal of children

(1) In a case falling within Chapter 1 of this Part, sections 36 to 40 of the Act shall not apply.

(2) In a case falling within Chapter 2 of this Part –

(a) section 36 of the Act shall apply, as if –

(i) for the words 'an adoption order' in paragraphs (a) and (c) in subsection (1) there were substituted 'a Convention adoption order'; and
(ii) subsection (2) was omitted; and
(b) section 39 of the Act shall apply as if subsection (3)(a) was omitted.

55 Modifications of the Act in respect of orders under section 84 where child is to be adopted under the Convention

The modifications set out in regulation 11 shall apply in the case where a couple or person habitually resident in a Convention country outside the British Islands intend to adopt a child who is habitually resident in England or Wales in accordance with the Convention.

56 Child to live with adopters before application for a Convention adoption order

Section 42 of the Act shall apply as if –

(a) subsections (1)(b) and (3) to (6) were omitted; and
(b) in subsection (2) from the word 'If' to the end of paragraph (b) there were substituted 'In the case of an adoption under the Convention,'.

57 Notice of intention to adopt

Section 44 of the Act shall apply as if subsection (3) was omitted.

58 Application for Convention adoption order

Section 49 of the Act shall apply as if –

(a) in subsection (1), the words from 'but only' to the end were omitted;
(b) subsections (2) and (3) were omitted.

59 Offences

Any person who contravenes or fails to comply with –

(a) regulation 26 (requirement to notify relevant local authority);
(b) regulation 27 (withdrawal of child by local authority); and
(c) regulation 33 (refusal of court to make Convention adoption order)

is guilty of an offence and liable on summary conviction to imprisonment for a term not exceeding three months, or a fine not exceeding level 5 on the standard scale, or both.

SCHEDULE 1

Regulation 18

CERTIFICATE OF ELIGIBILITY AND APPROVAL

To the Central Authority of the State of origin

Re .... [name of applicant]

In accordance with Article 5 of the Convention, I hereby certify on behalf of the Central Authority for [England] [Wales] that .... [name of applicant] has been counselled, is eligible to adopt and has been assessed and approved as suitable to adopt a child from .... [State of origin] by .... [public authority or accredited body for the purposes of the Convention].

The attached report has been prepared in accordance with Article 15 of the Convention for presentation to the competent authority in .... [State of origin].

This certificate of eligibility and approval and the report under Article 15 of the Convention are provided on the condition that a Convention adoption or Convention adoption order will not be made until the agreement under Article 17(c) of the Convention has been made.

I confirm on behalf of the Central Authority that if following the agreement under Article 17(c) of the Convention that –

[in the case, where the requirements specified in section 1(5A) of the British Nationality Act 1981 are met that the child .... [name] will be authorised to enter and reside permanently in the United Kingdom]; or

[in any other case, if entry clearance and leave to enter and remain, as may be necessary, is granted and not revoked, or curtailed and a Convention adoption order or Convention adoption is made, the child .... [name] will be authorised to enter and reside permanently in the United Kingdom.]

Name

[On behalf of the Secretary of State, the Central Authority for England]

Date

[the National Assembly for Wales, the Central Authority for Wales]

SCHEDULE 2

Regulations 32 and 51

CERTIFICATE THAT THE CONVENTION ADOPTION ORDER HAS BEEN MADE IN ACCORDANCE WITH THE CONVENTION

1. The Central Authority as the competent authority for [England] [Wales] being the country in which the Convention adoption order was made hereby certifies, in accordance with Article 23(1) of the Convention, that the child:

(a) name: .... [name on birth certificate, also known as/now known as ....]

   sex: ....
   date and place of birth: ....
   habitual residence at the time of adoption: ....
   State of origin: ....

(b) was adopted on: ....

   by order made by: .... court in [England] [Wales]

(c) by the following person(s):

   (i) family name and first name(s): ....
       sex: ....
       date and place of birth: ....
       habitual residence at the time adoption order made: ....

(ii) family name and first name(s): ....
    sex: ....
    date and place of birth: ....
    habitual residence at the time adoption order made: ....

2. The competent authority for [England] [Wales] in pursuance of Article 23(1) of the Convention hereby certifies that the adoption was made in accordance with the Convention and that the agreement under Article 17(c) was given by:

(a) name and address of the Central Authority in State of origin: ....

    date of the agreement: ....

(b) name and address of the Central Authority of receiving State: ....

    date of the agreement: ....

Signed

Date

EXPLANATORY NOTE

(This note is not part of the Regulations)

These Regulations make provision relating to adoptions with a foreign element under the Adoption (Intercountry Aspects) Act 1999 and the Adoption and Children Act 2002.

Part 2 makes provision in relation to bringing children into and out of the United Kingdom. Chapter 1 applies where a person intends to bring a child into the United Kingdom for the purposes of adoption or under an external adoption order effected within the period of six months of the making of the adoption. Regulations 3 and 4 provide for the procedure and impose conditions and requirements that must be met before a child is brought into the United Kingdom. Regulation 5 imposes functions on the local authority in respect of bringing a child into the United Kingdom and after the child has entered the United Kingdom. Chapter 2 makes provision in respect of a child being taken out of the United Kingdom for the purposes of adoption.

Part 3 provides for adoptions under the 1993 Hague Convention on Protection of Children and Co-operation in respect of Intercountry Adoption that was concluded at the Hague on 29 May 1993 ('the Convention'). Chapter 1 sets out the requirements, procedure, recognition and effect of adoptions where a couple or person habitually resident in the British Islands wish to adopt child who is habitually resident in a Convention country outside the British Islands in accordance with the Convention. Chapter 2 sets out the requirements, procedure, recognition and the effect of adoptions in England and Wales where a couple or a person habitually resident in a Convention country outside the British Islands wish to adopt a child who is habitually resident in the British Islands in accordance with the Convention. Chapter 3 makes miscellaneous provisions. Regulations 52 to 58 provide for the modification of the Adoption and Children Act 2002 in respect of adoptions under the Convention. Regulation 59 makes it an offence where a person fails to comply with regulation 26 (requirement to notify relevant local authority), regulation 27 (withdrawal of child by local authority) and regulation 33 (refusal of court to make Convention adoption order).

A Regulatory Impact Assessment has been prepared for these Regulations and a copy has been placed in the library of each House of Parliament. Copies of the Regulatory Impact Assessment can be obtained from the Department for Education and Skills' website http://www.dfes.gov.uk/ria/

Appendix N

THE ADOPTION AND CHILDREN ACT 2002 (COMMENCEMENT NO 10 TRANSITIONAL AND SAVINGS PROVISIONS) ORDER 2005, SI 2005/2897

PART 1
INTRODUCTORY

1 Citation and interpretation

(1) This Order may be cited as the Adoption and Children Act 2002 (Commencement No 10 Transitional and Savings Provisions) Order 2005.

(2) In this Order –

'the 1976 Act' means the Adoption Act 1976;
'the 2002 Act' means the Adoption and Children Act 2002;
'the Agencies Regulations 1983' means the Adoption Agencies Regulations 1983;
'the Agencies Regulations 2005' means the Adoption Agencies Regulations 2005;
'the appointed day' means 30 December 2005;
'the Foreign Element Regulations' means the Adoptions with a Foreign Element Regulations 2005;
'the Hague Convention Regulations' means the Intercountry Adoption (Hague Convention) Regulations 2003;
'the Private Fostering Regulations' means the Children (Private Arrangements for Fostering) Regulations 2005;
'working day' means any day other than a Saturday, Sunday, Christmas Day, Good Friday or a day which is a bank holiday within the meaning of the Banking and Financial Dealings Act 1971.

(3) A reference in this Order to 'the corresponding Welsh provision' in relation to a provision in regulations that apply only in relation to England, is to the corresponding provision in regulations that apply only in relation to Wales.

PART 2
COMMENCEMENT

2 Appointed day

30 December 2005 is the day appointed by the Secretary of State for the coming into force of the following provisions of the 2002 Act –

(a) paragraphs 1, 2, 6 to 8, 17 to 22 of Schedule 4 and section 139(2) in so far as it relates to those paragraphs; and

(b) section 139(3) and Schedule 5 except in so far as they as the relate to any of the following provisions –
   (i) sections 50, 52, 53(2) and 65(1) of the Adoption (Scotland) Act 1978;
   (ii) section 40(2)(a) of the Matrimonial and Family Proceedings Act 1984; and
   (iii) section 14 of the Adoption (Intercountry Aspects) Act 1999.

PART 3

TRANSITIONAL ARRANGEMENTS

3 Cases in progress under the Agencies Regulations 1983 on the appointed day

(1) In relation to a case that is still in progress on the appointed day, the general rule is that any action or decision taken before the appointed day under a provision of the Agencies Regulations 1983 shall, on or after the appointed day, be treated as if it were an action or decision under the corresponding provision of the Agencies Regulations 2005 or the Adoption Agencies (Wales) Regulations 2005.

(2) That rule is subject to the following exceptions.

(3) Where, before the appointed day, an adoption panel has considered –

(a) whether adoption is in the best interests of the child;
(b) whether a prospective adopter is suitable to adopt a child; or
(c) whether a child should be placed for adoption with a particular prospective adopter,

and no decision on that question has been made by the adoption agency before the appointed day, the Agencies Regulations 1983 shall continue to apply for the purposes of making that decision.

(4) Where an adoption agency is minded to make a decision under the Agencies Regulations 1983 (whether before the appointed day or, by virtue of paragraph (3), on or after that day) as to whether a prospective adopter is suitable to adopt a child, the Agencies Regulations 1983 and the Independent Review of Determinations (Adoption) Regulations 2004 shall continue to apply for the purposes of making representations or reviewing any qualifying determination in relation to that decision.

(5) Where paragraph (4) applies the periods of 28 days and 7 days specified in regulation 11A of the Agencies Regulations 1983 shall be increased to 40 working days and 10 working days respectively.

(6) Where an adoption agency has made a decision under the Agencies Regulations 1983 (whether before the appointed day or, by virtue of paragraph (3), on or after that day) that a prospective adopter is suitable to adopt a particular child –

(a) the Agencies Regulations 1983 shall continue to apply for the purposes of placing the child with that prospective adopter and section 18 of the 2002 Act (placement for adoption by agencies) shall not apply to any such placement; and
(b) any such placement shall be treated as if it were made under the Agencies Regulations 2005 or the Adoption Agencies (Wales) Regulations 2005.

(7) Where a child is placed for adoption by an adoption agency before the appointed day or paragraph (6) applies, section 22 of the 2002 Act (applications for placement orders) shall not apply.

4 Case of child free for adoption

Where on or after the appointed day a child is free for adoption by virtue of a freeing order made under section 18 of the 1976 Act (freeing child for adoption) but is not placed for adoption –

(a) the adoption agency may place the child for adoption and sections 18 (placement for adoption by agencies) and 22 (applications for placement orders) of the 2002 Act shall not apply; and

(b) regulation 36 of the Agencies Regulations 2005 (placement and reviews) or the corresponding Welsh provision shall apply as if –

   (i) the adoption agency was authorised to place the child for adoption but the child is not for the time being placed for adoption; and

   (ii) the child was subject to a placement order.

5 Child ceasing to be a protected child

(1) This article applies where, in consequence of the repeal of sections 32 to 36 of the 1976 Act (protected children), a child ceases to be a protected child and becomes a privately fostered child within the meaning of section 66 of the Children Act 1989.

(2) If the person who is fostering the child privately is disqualified from doing so by regulations under section 68 of that Act, he shall be treated for the purposes of those regulations as having obtained the consent of the local authority until such time as the local authority notify him that such consent is refused.

(3) The person who is fostering the child privately shall not be taken to be in breach of regulation 5 of the Private Fostering Regulations (notification by person already fostering a child privately) or the corresponding Welsh provision if –

(a) he has already provided the local authority with the information required under that regulation (whether by way of a notice of intention to adopt or otherwise); or

(b) he has not provided that information, but does so no later than 30 January 2006.

(4) The local authority must, in so far as they have not already done so, discharge their functions under regulation 7 of the Private Fostering Regulations (action to be taken by local authority on receipt of notification about a child being fostered privately) or the corresponding Welsh provision no later than 7th February 2006.

(5) For the purposes of regulation 8 of the Private Fostering Regulations (subsequent visits) and the corresponding Welsh provision the private fostering arrangement shall be treated as beginning on the appointed day.

6 Hague Convention cases in progress on the appointed day

(1) In relation to a case that is still in progress on the appointed day the general rule is that any action or decision taken before the appointed day under a provision of the Hague Convention Regulations shall, on or after the appointed day, be treated as if it were an action or decision taken under the corresponding provision of Part 3 of the Foreign Element Regulations.

(2) That rule is subject to the following exceptions.

(3) Where, before the appointed day, an adoption panel has considered –

(a) whether or not adoption by a person habitually resident in a Convention country outside the British Islands is in the best interests of the child; or

(b) whether a prospective adopter is suitable to adopt a child, and no decision on that question has been made by the adoption agency before the appointed day, the Hague Convention Regulations shall continue to apply for the purposes of making that decision.

(4) Where an adoption agency is minded to make a decision under the Hague Convention Regulations (whether before the appointed day or, by virtue of paragraph (3), on or after that day) as to whether a prospective adopter is suitable to adopt a child, the Hague Convention Regulations and the Independent Review of Determinations (Adoption) Regulations 2004 shall continue to apply for the purposes of making representations or reviewing any qualifying determination in relation to that decision and the periods of 28 days and 7 days specified in regulation 10 of the Hague Convention Regulations shall be increased to 40 working days and 10 working days respectively.

7 Non-Convention adoptions – conditions to be met by prospective adopters under section 83(5) of the 2002 Act

(1) This paragraph applies in a case where, before the appointed day, the prospective adopter received notification from the Secretary of State that she had issued the certificate referred to in regulation 5(a) of the Adoption (Bringing Children into the United Kingdom) Regulations 2003.

(2) Where paragraph (1) applies and the prospective adopter has visited the child but the child has not entered the United Kingdom before the appointed day, regulation 4(2)(b) to (d) of the Foreign Element Regulations shall not apply.

(3) Where paragraph (1) applies and the child has entered the United Kingdom but the prospective adopter had not, before the appointed day, given notice of intention to adopt pursuant to regulation 5(b) of the Adoption (Bringing Children into the United Kingdom) Regulations 2003, regulation 4(2)(b) to (d) and (3) of the Foreign Element Regulations shall not apply.

8 Non-Convention and Hague Convention cases – functions imposed on the local authority following receipt of notice of intention to adopt

(1) In a case where notice of intention to adopt is given before the appointed day by a prospective adopter as a consequence of regulation 5(b) of the Adoption (Bringing Children into the United Kingdom) Regulations 2003 or regulation 15 of the Hague Convention Regulations, regulation 5 of the Foreign Element Regulations shall apply subject to paragraphs (2) and (3).

(2) Where the local authority have not visited the child and prospective adopter prior to the appointed day and more than one week has elapsed since the receipt of the notice of intention to adopt, 30 December 2005 shall be treated as the date of receipt of that notice for the purposes of regulation 5(1)(e) and (f) of the Foreign Element Regulations.

(3) Where the local authority have visited the child and prospective adopter prior to the appointed day –

    (a) the authority must, if they have not already done so, carry out the functions in respect of reviews and frequency of visits imposed by regulation 5(e) to (h) of the Foreign Element Regulations; and

    (b) in the case where the review considering the matters referred to in regulation 5(1)(g) of the Foreign Element Regulations has not taken place before the appointed day, 30 December 2005 shall be treated as the date of receipt of the notice of intention to adopt for the purposes of regulation 5(1)(f).

9 Restrictions on removal of children – pending applications for adoption and freeing orders

Notwithstanding the repeal of the provisions in the 1976 Act set out in Schedule 5 to the 2002 Act, sections 27 and 29 of the 1976 Act shall continue to have effect where –

(a) an application for an adoption order under section 12 of the 1976 Act (adoption orders); or

(b) an application for an order under section 18 of the 1976 Act (freeing for adoption),

has been made and has not been disposed of immediately before the appointed day.

10 Pending applications for freeing orders

Nothing in the 2002 Act affects any application for an order under section 18 of the 1976 Act (freeing for adoption) where –

(a) the application has been made and has not been disposed of immediately before the appointed day; and

(b) the child in relation to whom the application is made is not immediately before the appointed day placed for adoption by the adoption agency.

11 Pending applications for adoption orders in non-agency cases

Nothing in the 2002 Act affects any application for an adoption order under section 12 of the 1976 Act (adoption orders) in relation to a child in respect of whom –

(a) notice has been given to the local authority by virtue of section 22 of the 1976 Act; and

(b) the application has been made and has not been disposed of immediately before the appointed day.

12 Pending applications under section 53 or 55 of the 1976 Act

Nothing in the 2002 Act affects any application under section 53 (annulment, etc of overseas adoptions) or 55 (adoption of children abroad) of the 1976 Act, where the application has been made and has not been disposed of immediately before the appointed day.

PART 4

SAVINGS PROVISIONS

13 Records and disclosure of adoption information

Notwithstanding the repeal of the provisions of the 1976 Act set out in Schedule 5 to the 2002 Act, in the case of a person adopted before the appointed day –

(a) the Agencies Regulations 1983 shall continue to have effect in so far as they relate to the retention, storage, transfer and disclosure of information in relation to that person's adoption; and

(b) section 9 of the 1976 Act shall continue to have effect for the purposes of amending or revoking those Regulations.

14 Parental orders

(1) Notwithstanding the repeal of the provisions of the 1976 Act set out in Schedule 5 to the 2002 Act, the 1976 Act shall continue to have effect for the purpose of its application, with such modifications (if any) as may be specified in regulations under section 30(9) of the Human Fertilisation and Embryology Act 1990, in relation to orders under section 30 of that Act and applications for such orders.

(2) In regulation 2 (application of Adoption Act 1976 provisions with modifications to parental orders and applications for such orders) of the Parental Orders (Human Fertilisation and Embryology) Regulations 1994, for 'as they have effect' substitute 'as they had effect, prior to 30 December 2005,'.

(3) In article 2(o) of the Adoption and Children Act 2002 (Commencement No. 9) Order 2005, for '67 to 81' substitute '67 to 78, 80, 81'.

15 Local Authority Adoption Service

The repeal of the provisions of the 1976 Act set out in Schedule 5 to the 2002 Act shall not affect the operation of the Local Authority Adoption Service (England) Regulations 2003.

16 Voluntary Adoption Agencies

The repeal of the provisions of the 1976 Act set out in Schedule 5 to the 2002 Act shall not affect the operation of Parts 1 to 4 of the Voluntary Adoption Agencies and Adoption Agencies (Miscellaneous Amendments) Regulations 2003.

EXPLANATORY NOTE

(This note is not part of the Order)

This Order is the tenth Commencement Order made under the Adoption and Children Act 2002 ('the Act'). In addition to bringing into force further provisions of the Act, it makes a number of transitional and savings provisions.

Article 2 brings into force on 30 December 2005 a number of provisions of the Act.

Article 2(a) brings into force paragraphs 1, 2, 6 to 8, and 17 to 22 of Schedule 4 and section 139(2) in so far as it relates to those paragraphs. Schedule 4 is concerned with transitional and transitory provisions and savings and section 139(2) gives effect to it. Paragraph 1 of Schedule 4 sets out the general rules for continuity while paragraph 2 makes a general rule for old savings. Paragraphs 6, 7 and 8 are concerned, respectively, with pending applications for freeing orders, freeing orders and pending applications for adoption orders. Paragraphs 17 to 19 are concerned with the status of adopted children, paragraph 20 with the registration of adoptions, 21 with the effect on the application of the Child Abduction Act 1984 and 22 with the effect on the application of the Courts and Legal Services Act 1990.

Article 2(b) brings into force section 139(3) and Schedule 5 (repeals) except in so far as they relate to –

sections 50, 52, 53(2) and 65(1) of the Adoption (Scotland) Act 1978;
section 40(2)(a) of the Matrimonial and Family Proceedings Act 1984; and
section 14 of the Adoption (Intercountry Aspects) Act 1999.

All the provisions set out in Schedule 5 are repealed save for those listed above.

Part 3 of the Order is concerned with transitional arrangements.

Article 3 sets out, with exceptions, the general rule for how cases in progress under the Adoption Agencies Regulations 1983 on 30 December 2005 should be dealt with. Article 4 makes transitional provision for the case of a child free for adoption by virtue of a freeing order made under section 18 of the Adoption Act 1976 ('the 1976 Act').

Article 5 is concerned with the transitional arrangements in the case of a child who because of the repeal of sections 32 to 36 of the 1976 Act ceases to be a protected child and so becomes a privately fostered child.

Articles 6 to 8 make transitional arrangements in relation to intercountry adoption cases. Article 6 sets out a general rule, with exceptions, for Hague Convention cases in progress on 30 December 2005. Article 7 makes transitional provision concerning the conditions to be met by prospective adopters in non-Convention cases; article 8 regarding the functions on local authorities after receiving a notice of intention to adopt, in both non-Convention and Hague Convention cases.

Article 9 is concerned with restrictions on removal of children when an application for an order under section 12 (adoption orders) or section 18 (freeing for adoption) of the 1976 Act is pending on 30 December; article 10 is about applications for freeing orders pending on 30 December 2005; article 11 about pending application for adoption orders in non-agency cases; and article 12 is concerned with applications under section 53 (annulment, etc. of overseas adoptions) or 55 (adoption of children abroad) of the 1976 Act which have been made but not disposed of immediately before 30 December 2005.

Part 4 of the Order makes savings provisions in relation to records and the disclosure of adoption information (article 13); parental orders under section 30 of the Human Fertilisation and Embryology Act 1990 (article 14); the Local Authority Adoption Service (England) Regulations 2003 (article 15); and voluntary adoption agencies (article 16).

NOTE AS TO EARLIER COMMENCEMENT ORDERS

(*This note is not part of the Order*)

The following provisions of the Act have been or will be brought into force by Commencement Orders made before the date of this Order –

Provision	*Date of Commencement*	*SI No*
Section 1	30 December 2005	2005/2213 (C.92)
Section 2(1) to (5), (7) and (8)	7 December 2004	2004/3203 (C.139)
Section 2(6) in relation to England	7 December 2004	2004/3203 (C.139)
Section 2(6), (7) and (8) partially, in relation to England	6 October 2003	2003/366 (C.24)
Section 2(6) in relation to Wales	7 February 2004	2004/252 (W.27) (C.9)
Section 2(7) and (8) partially, in relation to Wales	28 November 2003	2003/3079 (C.117)
Section 3(1), (2), (5) and (6)	30 December 2005	2005/2213 (C.92)

Provision	Date of Commencement	SI No
Section 3(3) and (4) partially, in relation to England	7 December 2004	2004/3203 (C.139)
Section 3(3) and (4) in relation to Wales	6 June 2005	2005/1206 (W.78) (C.54)
Section 3(3) and (4) in relation to England	30 December 2005	2005/2213 (C.92)
Section 4(1)(a) in relation to England	30 December 2005	2005/2213 (C.92)
Section 4(1)(b) and (5) partially in relation to Wales	7 February 2004	2004/252 (W.27) (C.9)
Section 4(1)(b) and (5) partially, in relation to England	7 December 2004	2004/3203 (C.139)
Section 4(1)(b) and (5) in relation to England	30 December 2005	2005/2213 (C.92)
Section 4(2) to (4) in relation to England	30 December 2005	2005/2213 (C.92)
Section 4(6) and (7)(b) to (i) partially, in relation to England	10 March 2003	2003/366 (C.24)
Section 4(6) and (7)(b) to (i) partially, in relation to England	6 October 2003	2003/366 (C.24)
Section 4(6) and (7)(b) to (i) in relation to England	7 December 2004	2004/3203 (C.139)
Section 4(7)(a) in relation to England	7 December 2004	2003/3203 (C.139)
Section 4(6) and (7) in relation to Wales	7 February 2004	2004/252 (W.27) (C.9)
Section 4(8) to (11) in relation to England	30 December 2005	2005/2213 (C.92)
Section 6 in relation to England	30 December 2005	2005/ 2213(C.92)
Section 7 in relation to England	30 December 2005	2005/2213 (C.92)
Section 8 partially, in relation to England	7 December 2004	2004/3203 (C.139)
Section 8 in relation to England	30 December 2005	2005/2213 (C.92)
Section 9 in relation to Wales	7 February 2004	2004/252 (W.27) (C.9)
Section 9 in relation to England	7 December 2004	2004/3203 (C.139)
Section 10 in relation to Wales	7 February 2004	2004/252 (W.27) (C.9)

Provision	Date of Commencement	SI No
Section 10 in relation to England	7 December 2004	2004/3203 (C.139)
Section 11 in relation to Wales	7 February 2004	2004/252 (W.27) (C.9)
Section 11 in relation to England	7 December 2004	2004/3203 (C.139)
Section 12(1) to (3) in relation to Wales	7 February 2004	2004/252 (W.27) (C.9)
Section 12(1) to (3) partially, in relation to England	7 December 2004	2004/3203 (C.139)
Section 12 in relation to England	30 December 2005	2005/2213 (C.92)
Sections 13 to 15 in relation to England	30 December 2005	2005/2213 (C.92)
Section 16 in relation to Wales	1 February 2003	2003/181 (W.31) (C.9)
Section 16 partially, in relation to England	25 February 2003	2003/366 (C.24)
Section 16 partially, in relation to England	30 April 2003	2003/366 (C.24)
Section 16 in relation to England	30 December 2005	2005/2213 (C.92)
Section 18 to 26	30 December 2005	2005/2213 (C.92)
Section 27(1), (2), (4) and (5)	30 December 2005	2005/2213 (C.9)
Section 27(3) in relation to Wales	7 February 2004	2004/252 (W.27) (C.9)
Section 27(3) in relation to England	7 December 2004	2004/3203 (C.139)
Sections 28 to 43	30 December 2005	2005/2213 (C.92)
Section 44 partially	7 December 2004	2004/3203 (C.139)
Section 44	30 December 2005	2005/2213 (C.92)
Section 45	7 December 2004	2004/3203 (C.139)
Sections 46 to 52	30 December 2005	2005/2213 (C.92)
Section 53(1) to (3) in relation to Wales	7 February 2004	2004/252 (W.27) (C.9)
Section 53(1) to (3) in relation to England	7 December 2004	2004/3203 (C.139)
Section 53(4) to (6)	30 December 2005	2005/2213 (C.92)
Section 54 in relation to Wales	7 February 2004	2004/252 (W.27) (C.9)
Section 54 in relation to England	7 December 2004	2004/3203 (C.139)
Section 55	30 December 2005	2005/2213 (C.92)

Provision	Date of Commencement	SI No
Section 56(1) and (3) in relation to Wales	7 February 2004	2004/252 (W.27) (C.9)
Section 56 partially, in relation to England	7 December 2004	2004/3203 (C.139)
Section 56 in relation to England	30 December 2005	2005/2213 (C.92)
Section 57 partially, in relation to England	7 December 2004	2004/3203 (C.139)
Section 57 in relation to England	30 December 2005	2005/2213 (C.92)
Section 57(5) partially, in relation to Wales	7 February 2004	2004/252 (W.27) (C.9)
Section 57(6) in relation to Wales	7 February 2004	2004/252 (W.27) (C.9)
Section 58 partially, in relation to England	7 December 2004	2004/3203 (C.139)
Section 58 in relation to England	30 December 2005	2005/2213 (C.92)
Section 58(2) and (3) partially, in relation to Wales	7 February 2004	2004/252 (W.27) (C.9)
Section 59 in relation to Wales	7 February 2004	2004/252 (W.27) (C.9)
Section 59 partially, in relation to England	7 December 2004	2004/3203 (C.139)
Section 59 in relation to England	30 December 2005	2005/2213 (C.92)
Section 60(1), (3) and (5) in relation to England	30 December 2005	2005/2213 (C.92)
Section 60(2) and (4) partially, in relation to Wales	7 February 2004	2004/252 (W.27) (C.9)
Section 60(2) and (4) partially, in relation England	7 December 2004	2004/3203 (C.139)
Section 60(2) and (4) in relation to England	30 December 2005	2005/2213 (C.92)
Section 61(1) to (4) and (6) in relation to England	30 December 2005	2005/2213 (C.92)
Section 61(5) partially, in relation to England	7 December 2004	2004/3203 (C.139)
Section 61(5) in relation to England	30 December 2005	2005/2213 (C.92)
Section 61(5)(c) partially, in relation to Wales	7 February 2004	2004/252 (W.27) (C.9)

Provision	Date of Commencement	SI No
Section 62(1) to (6) and (8) in relation to England	30 December 2005	2005/2213 (C.92)
Section 62(7) partially, in relation to England	7 December 2004	2004/3203 (C.139)
Section 62(7) in relation to England	30 December 2005	2005/2213 (C.92)
Section 62(7)(c) partially, in relation to Wales	7 February 2004	2004/252 (W.27) (C.9)
Section 63 in relation to Wales	7 February 2004	2004/252 (W.27) (C.9)
Section 63 in relation to England and as respect subsections (2) to (5) in relation to Scotland and Northern Ireland	7 December 2004	2004/3203 (C.139)
Section 64 in relation to Wales	7 February 2004	2004/252 (W.27) (C.9)
Section 64 in relation to England	7 December 2004	2004/3203 (C.139)
Section 65 in relation to Wales	7 February 2004	2004/252 (W.27) (C.9)
Section 65 in relation to England and as respect subsections (2)(a) and (3) in relation to Scotland and (2)(b) and (3) in relation to Northern Ireland	7 December 2004	2004/3203 (C.139)
Sections 66 to 76	30 December 2005	2005/2213 (C.92)
Section 77(1), (2) and (4) to (6)	30 December 2005	2005/2213 (C.92)
Section 77(3) partially	7 December 2004	2004/3203 (C.139)
Section 77(3)	30 December 2005	2005/2213 (C.92)
Section 78(1), (2) and (4)	30 December 2005	2005/2213(C.92)
Section 78(3) partially	7 December 2004	2004/3203 (C.139)
Section 78(3)	30 December 2005	2005/2213 (C.92)
Section 80(1),(3) and (5)	30 December 2005	2005/2213 (C.92)
Section 80(2), (4) and (6) partially	7 December 2004	2004/3203 (C.139)
Section 80(2), (4) and (6)	30 December 2005	2005/2213 (C.92)
Section 81(1) to (3)	30 December 2005	2005/2213 (C.92)
Section 81(4)	7 December 2004	2004/3203 (C.139)
Section 82	30 December 2005	2005/2213 (C.92)
Section 83(1) to (7) and (9) partially	7 December 2004	2004/3203 (C.139)
Section 83(1) to (7) and (9)	30 December 2005	2005/2213 (C.92)

Provision	Date of Commencement	SI No
Section 83(8)	30 December 2005	2005/2213 (C.92)
Section 84 partially	7 December 2004	2004/3203 (C.139)
Section 84	30 December 2005	2005/2213 (C.92)
Section 85	30 December 2005	2005/2213 (C.92)
Section 86 partially	7 December 2004	2004/3203 (C.139)
Section 86	30 December 2005	2005/2213 (C.92)
Section 87(1)(a), (2), (5) and (6) partially	7 December 2004	2004/3203 (C.139)
Section 87(1)(a), (2), (5) and (6)	30 December 2005	2005/2213 (C.92)
Section 87(1)(b) and (4)	1 June 2003	2003/366 (C.24)
Section 87(3)	30 December 2005	2005/2213 (C.92)
Sections 88 to 91	30 December 2005	2005/2213 (C.92)
Section 92 partially	7 December 2004	2004/3203 (C.139)
Section 92	30 December 2005	2005/2213 (C.92)
Section 93	30 December 2005	2005/2213 (C.92)
Section 94(1) partially	7 December 2004	2004/3203 (C.139)
Section 94(1)	30 December 2005	2005/2213 (C.92)
Section 94(2) to (5)	30 December 2005	2005/2213 (C.92)
Sections 95, 96 and 97	30 December 2005	2005/2213 (C.92)
Section 98 in relation to Wales	7 February 2004	2004/252 (W.27) (C.9)
Section 98 in relation to England	7 December 2004	2004/3203 (C.139)
Sections 99 to 107	30 December 2005	2005/2213 (C.92)
Section 108	7 December 2004	2004/3203 (C.139)
Sections 109 and 110	30 December 2005	2005/ 2213(C.92)
Section 111	1 December 2003	2003/3079 (C.117)
Sections 112 to 115	30 December 2005	2005/2213 (C.92)
Section 117 partially	7 December 2004	2004/3203 (C.139)
Section 117	30 December 2005	2005/2213 (C.92)
Section 118	21 May 2004	2004/1403 (C.56)
Section 119	1 April 2004	2003/3079 (C.117)
Section 120	31 January 2005	2004/3203 (C.139)

Provision	Date of Commencement	SI No
Section 121 partially	7 December 2004	2004/3203 (C.139)
Section 121	30 December 2005	2005/2213 (C.92)
Section 122(1)(a)	30 December 2005	2005/2213 (C.92)
Section 122(1)(b) and (2)	7 December 2004	2004/3203 (C.139)
Sections 123 and 124 in relation to England, Wales, Scotland and Northern Ireland	30 December 2005	2005/2213 (C.92)
Section 135	1 June 2003	2003/366 (C.24)
Section 137	30 December 2005	2005/2213 (C.92)
Section 138 in relation to England, Wales and Scotland	30 December 2005	2005/2213 (C.92)
Section 139(1) partially, in relation to Northern Ireland	3 February 2003	2003/288 (C.14)
Partially, in relation England	25 February 2003	2003/366 (C.24)
Partially, in relation England	30 April 2003	2003/366 (C.24)
Partially, in relation to Wales	28 November 2003	2003/3079 (C.117)
Partially	1 December 2003	2003/3079 (C.117)
Partially	7 December 2004	2004/3203 (C.139)
Partially	30 December 2005	2005/2213 (C.139)
Section 139(2) partially	3 February 2003	2003/288 (C.14)
Partially	25 February 2003	2003/366 (C.24)
Partially, in relation to England	10 March 2003	2003/366 (C.24)
Partially	1 April 2003	2003/366 (C.24)
Partially	1 June 2003	2003/366 (C.24)
Partially, in relation to England	6 October 2003	2003/366 (C.24)
Partially, in relation to England	1 December 2003	2003/3079 (C.117)
Partially, in relation to England	1 April 2004	2004/3079 (C.117)
Partially, in relation to Wales	7 February 2004	2004/252 (W.27) (C.9)
Section 139(3) partially	28 November 2003	2003/3079 (C.117)
Partially	30 December 2005	2005/2213 (C.92)
Partially, in relation to England	30 December 2005	2005/2213 (C.92)

Provision	Date of Commencement	SI No
Schedule 1		
Paragraphs 1 and 3 partially	7 December 2004	2004/3203 (C.139)
Paragraphs 1 and 3	30 December 2005	2005/2213 (C.92)
Paragraphs 2 and 4 to 6	30 December 2005	2005/2213 (C.92)
Schedule 2		
Paragraph 1 partially	7 December 2004	2004/3203 (C.139)
Paragraph 1	30 December 2005	2005/2213 (C.92)
Paragraphs 2 to 4	30 December 2005	2005/2213 (C.92)
Schedule 3		
Paragraphs 1 to 5	30 December 2005	2005/2213(C.92)
Paragraphs 6 and 7	1 December 2003	2003/3079 (C.117)
Paragraphs 9 to 12	30 December 2005	2005/ 3079 (C.92)
Paragraph 13 in relation to England	30 December 2005	2005/2213 (C.92)
Paragraphs 14 to 20	30 December 2005	2005/2213 (C.92)
Paragraphs 36 to 43	30 December 2005	2005/2213 (C.92)
Paragraphs 45 to 52	30 December 2005	2005/2214 (C.92)
Paragraph 53	3 February 2003	2003/288 (C.14)
Paragraphs 54 to 59	30 December 2005	2005/2213 (C.92)
Paragraph 60 partially	7 December 2004	2004/3203 (C.139)
Paragraph 60	30 December 2005	2005/2213 (C.92)
Paragraphs 61 to 64	30 December 2005	2005/2213 (C.92)
Paragraph 65 in relation to England	30 December 2005	2005/2213 (C.92)
Paragraphs 67 to 81	30 December 2005	2005/2213 (C.92)
Paragraphs 85 to 93	30 December 2005	2005/2213 (C.92)
Paragraphs 95 to 99	30 December 2005	2005/2213 (C.92)
Paragraphs 101 and 102	30 December 2005	2005/2213 (C.92)
Paragraph 103 partially, in relation to England	25 February 2003	2003/366 (C.24)
Paragraph 103 partially, in relation to England	30 April 2003	2003/366 (C.24)
Paragraph 103 in relation to Wales	28 November 2003	2003/3079 (C.117)

Provision	Date of Commencement	SI No
Paragraph 103 in relation to England	30 December 2005	2005/2213 (C.92)
Paragraph 104	30 December 2005	2005/2213 (C.92)
Paragraph 105 in relation England	30 April 2003	2003/366 (C.24)
Paragraph 105 in relation Wales	28 November 2003	2003/3079 (C.117)
Paragraph 106 in relation England	30 April 2003	2003/366 (C.24)
Paragraph 106 in relation Wales	28 November 2003	2003/3079 (C.117)
Paragraphs 107 to 109	30 December 2005	2005/2213 (C.92)
Paragraph 110 partially, in relation to England	30 April 2003	2003/366 (C.24)
Paragraph 110 partially, in relation to Wales	28 November 2003	2003/3079 (C.117)
Paragraph 110	30 December 2005	2005/2213 (C.92)
Paragraphs 111 to 113 in relation to England	30 December 2005	2005/2213 (C.92)
Paragraphs 114 to 117	30 December 2005	2005/2213 (C.92)
Paragraph 118	28 November 2003	2003/3079 (C.117)
Schedule 4		
Paragraph 3 in relation to England	6 October 2003	2003/288 (C.14)
Paragraph 3 in relation to Wales	7 February 2004	2004/252 (W.27) (C.9)
Paragraph 4(1)	3 February 2003	2003/288 (C.14)
Paragraph 4(2)	25 February 2003	2003/366 (C.24)
Paragraph 5 in relation to England	1 April 2004	2003/3079 (C.117)
Paragraph 5 in relation to Wales	7 February 2004	2004/252 (W.27) (C.9)
Paragraph 10	1 June 2003	2003/366 (C.24)
Paragraph 11 partially	1 June 2003	2003/366 (C.24)
Paragraph 12 partially	1 April 2003	2003/366 (C.24)
Paragraph 12 partially	1 June 2003	2003/366 (C.24)
Paragraph 13	1 June 2003	2003/366 (C.24)
Paragraph 14	1 June 2003	2003/366 (C.24)
Schedule 5		
Partially	1 June 2003	2003/366 (C.24)

Provision	Date of Commencement	SI No
Partially	28 November 2003	2003/3079 (C.117)
Partially	1 December 2003	2003/3079 (C.117)
Partially	30 December 2005	2005/2213 (C.92)

Appendix O

THE LOCAL AUTHORITY (ADOPTION) (MISCELLANEOUS PROVISIONS) REGULATIONS 2005, SI 2005/3390

1 Citation, commencement and application

(1) These Regulations may be cited as the Local Authority (Adoption) (Miscellaneous Provisions) Regulations 2005 and come into force on 30 December 2005.

(2) These Regulations apply to England only.

2 Interpretation

In these Regulations –

'the Act' means the Adoption and Children Act 2002;
'the Agencies Regulations' means the Adoption Agencies Regulations 2005;
'the Foreign Element Regulations' means the Adoptions with a Foreign Element Regulations 2005;
'proposed adopter' has the same meaning as in section 44(1) of the Act; and
'social worker' means a person who is registered in –
  (a) the register for social workers maintained in accordance with section 56 of the Care Standards Act 2000;
  (b) the register maintained by the Scottish Social Services Council under section 44 of the Regulation of Care (Scotland) Act 2001; or
  (c) the register maintained by the Northern Ireland Social Care Council under section 3 of the Health and Personal Social Services Act (Northern Ireland) 2001.

3 Prescribed local authorities

(1) For the purposes of section 44(9)(a) of the Act, the following local authorities are prescribed in the following cases.

(2) In the case of the proposed adoption by one person who no longer has his home in England, the prescribed local authority is the local authority for the area in which that person's last home in England was situated.

(3) In the case of the proposed adoption by a couple who no longer have their home in England and who shared together the last home they had in England, the prescribed local authority is the local authority for the area in which that home in England was situated.

(4) In the case of the proposed adoption by a couple who no longer have their home in England and who did not share together the last home each had in England, the prescribed local authority is the local authority which the couple nominate, being the local authority for the area in which the last home in England of one of them was situated.

(5) In the case of the proposed adoption by a couple only one of whom ever had his home in England, the prescribed local authority is the local authority for the area in which that person's last home in England was situated.

4 Requirement to take steps to obtain police checks

For the purposes of an investigation arranged under section 44(5) of the Act, the local authority must take steps to obtain in respect of –

(a) the proposed adopters; and
(b) any other member of their household aged 18 or over,

an enhanced criminal record certificate within the meaning of section 115 of the Police Act 1997 including the matters specified in subsection (6A) of that section.

5 Fees for facilities provided in connection with adoption with a foreign element

(1) For the purposes of section 11(2) of the Act (fees), the fee which may be charged by a local authority must be reasonable and not exceed the local authority's costs and expenses properly incurred in providing the facilities.

(2) The fee may not include any element in respect of costs and expenses incurred by the local authority in connection with –

(a) a review of a qualifying determination within the meaning of section 12 of the Act; or
(b) the receipt and consideration of representations made by a prospective adopter under regulation 27 of the Agencies Regulations.

(3) Each local authority must, at the reasonable request of the person charged a fee under section 11(2), provide details of the method by which the fee was calculated.

(4) For the purposes of section 11(2) of the Act, prescribed facilities are facilities provided by local authorities –

(a) in the discharge by them of any function imposed on them under Part 4 of the Agencies Regulations (duties of adoption agency in respect of a prospective adopter), save for facilities provided under regulation 21 of those Regulations (requirement to provide counselling and information) or under regulations 15, 16 and 17 of the Foreign Element Regulations (assessment of prospective adopters – adoptions under the Convention); and
(b) in relation to the preparation of –
  (i) pre-adoption reports; and
  (ii) post-adoption reports.

(5) In this regulation –

'post-adoption report' means a report prepared otherwise than in accordance with the Agencies Regulations at the request of a relevant foreign authority following the adoption of a child from the country in which that authority performs its functions;

'pre-adoption report' means a report prepared otherwise than in accordance with the Agencies Regulations at the request of a relevant foreign authority following the placement for adoption of a child from the country in which that authority performs its functions and prior to that child's adoption but does not include a report prepared in accordance with regulation 29(2) of the Foreign Element Regulations or a report required before an overseas adoption is effected; and

'relevant foreign authority' has the meaning given in regulation 2 of the Foreign Element Regulations.

6 Local authority provision of facilities

For the purposes of section 3(4)(b) of the Act (maintenance of adoption service) a local authority may provide any of the requisite facilities by securing their provision by a social worker who has at least three years' post-qualifying experience in child care social work, including direct experience of adoption work.

EXPLANATORY NOTE

(This note is not part of the Regulations)

These Regulations make provision for when people wish to adopt a child who is not placed for adoption with them by an adoption agency, and enable local authorities to charge for services provided in connection with adoptions with a foreign element and to use people who are not their employees in the exercise of their functions.

These Regulations apply to England only and come into force on 30 December 2005.

Regulation 3 prescribes, for the purposes of section 44 of the Adoption and Children Act 2002 ('the Act'), the appropriate local authority where the proposed adopters are living overseas and wish to give notice of intention to apply for an adoption order. In four cases it prescribes the local authority to which proposed adopters have to give notice of intention to adopt and which has other functions under section 44 of the Act.

Regulation 4 requires the local authority, for the propose of the investigation which it is required to arrange under section 44(5) of the Act, to take steps to obtain enhanced criminal record certificates in respect of both the proposed adopters and other members of their household who are aged 18 or over.

Regulation 5 prescribes the facilities for which a local authority may charge, and the level of the fee, where the facilities are provided in connection with the adoption of a child brought into the United Kingdom for the purpose of adoption, or in connection with an adoption under the Hague Convention, an overseas adoption or an adoption effected under the law of a country outside the British Islands.

Regulation 6 allows local authorities to provide any of the requisite facilities for the purpose of maintaining an Adoption Service through an independent social worker who has the prescribed qualifications and experience.

Appendix P

NATIONAL ADOPTION STANDARDS FOR ENGLAND

INTRODUCTION

The Adoption Standards have been written to ensure that looked after children, birth families, prospective adopters and the general public understand what they can expect from the adoption service. The service will best meet its objectives if people know that they will be treated with courtesy and respect and receive a fair and equal service wherever they live. The values statement below explains the important principles which underpin these standards. The standards apply only to domestic adoptions through adoption agencies, however similar standards will be developed for step-parent and inter-country adoptions.

Values

- Children are entitled to grow up as part of a loving family which can meet their needs during childhood and beyond.
- It is best for children where possible to be brought up by their own birth family.
- The child's welfare, safety and needs will be at the centre of the adoption process.
- The child's wishes and feelings will be actively sought and fully taken into account at all stages.
- Delays in adoption can have a severe impact on the health and development of children and should be avoided wherever possible.
- Children's ethnic origin, cultural background, religion and language will be fully recognised and positively valued and promoted when decisions are made.
- The particular needs of disabled children will be fully recognised and taken into account when decisions are made.
- The role of adoptive parents in offering a permanent family to a child who cannot live with their birth family will be valued and respected.
- Adoption has lifelong implications for all involved and requires lifelong commitment from many different organisations, professions and individuals who have to work together to meet the needs for services of those affected by adoption.
- Government will work in partnership with local government, other statutory agencies and voluntary adoption agencies to ensure that these standards are delivered.

A. CHILDREN

The needs and wishes, welfare and safety of the looked after child are at the centre of the adoption process.

1 Children whose birth family cannot provide them with a secure, stable and permanent home are entitled to have adoption considered for them.

2 Whenever plans for permanence are being considered, they will be made on the basis of the needs of each looked after child, and within the following timescales:

(a) The child's need for a permanent home will be addressed at the four month review and a plan for permanence made;

(b) Clear timescales will be set for achieving the plan, which will be appropriately monitored and considered at every subsequent review;

(c) Where adoption has been identified as the plan for the child at a review, the adoption panel will make its recommendation within 2 months.

Where adoption is the plan:

3 The timescales below will be followed, taking account of the individual child's needs:

(a) A match with suitable adoptive parents will be identified and approved by panel within 6 months of the agency agreeing that adoption is in the child's best interest;

(b) In care proceedings, where the plan is adoption, a match with suitable adoptive parents will be identified and approved by panel within 6 months of the court's decision;

(c) Where a parent has requested that a child aged under 6 months be placed for adoption, a match with suitable adoptive parents will be identified and approved by panel within 3 months of the agency agreeing that adoption is in the child's best interest.

4 Every child will have his or her wishes and feelings listened to, recorded and taken into account. Where they are not acted upon, the reasons for not doing so will be explained to the child and properly recorded.

5 All children will have a named social worker who will be responsible for them throughout the adoption process.

6 Children will be given clear explanations and information about adoption, covering what happens at each stage (including at court), and how long each stage is likely to take in their individual case.

7 Children will be well prepared before joining a new family. This will include clear appropriate information on their birth family and life before adoption, and information about the adopters and their family. Children are entitled to information provided by their birth families, which will be kept safe both by agencies and adopters. It will be provided to adopted children, or adults, at a time and in a manner that reflects their age and understanding, as well as the nature of the information concerned.

8 Children will be matched with families who can best meet their needs. They will not be left waiting indefinitely for a 'perfect family'.

9 Every effort will be made to recruit sufficient adopters from diverse backgrounds, so that each child can be found an adoptive family within the timescales in **3** above, which best meets their needs, and in particular:

(a) which reflects their ethnic origin, cultural background, religion and language;

(b) which allows them to live with brothers and sisters unless this will not meet their individually assessed needs. Where this is the case, a clear explanation will be given to them and recorded.

10 The child's needs, wishes and feelings, and their welfare and safety are the most important concerns when considering links or contact with birth parents, wider birth family members and other people who are significant to them.

11 Adoption plans will include details of the arrangements for maintaining links (including contact) with birth parents, wider birth family members and other people who are significant to the child and how and when these arrangements will be reviewed.

12 Children are entitled to support services that meet their assessed needs. These include advice and counselling, health, education, leisure, and cultural services, and practical and financial help when needed. Information from agency records will be made available to the child when they are of an age and level of understanding to comprehend it.

13 Where there are difficulties arising from an adoption or a proposed adoption, or where an adoption or proposed adoption breaks down, a child will receive support and information without delay.

14 Children placed for adoption and adopted children will be informed of their right to make representations and complaints and will be helped to do so if this is required.

B. PROSPECTIVE ADOPTERS

People who are interested in becoming adoptive parents will be welcomed without prejudice, responded to promptly and given clear information about recruitment, assessment and approval. They will be treated fairly, openly and with respect throughout the adoption process.

1 Information on becoming an adoptive parent will be provided, including what is expected of adopters. Applicants will be given the opportunity to hear about preparation and support services available to adopters, and to talk to others who have adopted children.

2 Clear information will be given about children locally and across the country who need families to help prospective adopters decide whether to proceed further.

3 Written eligibility criteria and details of the assessment and approval process will be provided.

   (a) Applicants will be considered in terms of their capacity to look after children in a safe and responsible way that meets their developmental needs. Where agencies have specific eligibility criteria, eg because the agency has particular religious beliefs, applicants will be told what these are and, if necessary, be referred to another agency. People will not be automatically excluded on the grounds of age, health or other factors, except in the case of certain criminal convictions.

   (b) The assessment and approval process will be comprehensive, thorough and fair. An explanation will be given of the need for status checks and enquiries to be made about prospective adopters and members of their household.

4 There will be clear written timescales for each stage. Applicants can expect:

   (a) Written information sent in response to their enquiry within 5 working days.
   (b) Follow up interviews/invitation to an information meeting within 2 months
   (c) Agencies will prioritise applications that are more likely to meet the needs of children waiting for adoption. Where agencies and applicants decide to proceed, a decision on the outcome will be made by the agency following the Adoption Panel within six months of the receipt of the formal application. Where the agency decides not to proceed applicants will be informed in writing and advised of the options open to them.
   (d) If (b) and (c) follow each other without a gap, the whole process from enquiry to decision should not take more than 8 months. Panels will record reasons for delays.

5 Foster carers who make a formal application to adopt children in their care will be entitled to the same information and preparation as other adopters and be assessed within four months.

6 Applicants will be kept informed of progress throughout. They will receive a copy of the assessment report at least 28 days before an adoption panel and have the opportunity to comment on the report, and, if they wish, to attend the adoption panel and be heard.

7 Prospective adopters will be informed of their right to make representations and complaints.

C. ADOPTIVE PARENTS

Children will be matched with approved adopters who can offer them a stable and permanent home and help and support will be provided to achieve a successful and lasting placement.

1 Approved adopters will be given clear written information about the matching, introduction and placement process, as well as any support to facilitate this that they may need. This will include the role of the Adoption Register for England and Wales.

2 Before a match is agreed, adopters will be given full written information to help them understand the needs and background of the child and an opportunity to discuss this and the implications for them and their family.

3 There will be access to a range of multi-agency support services before, during and after adoption. Support services will include practical help, professional advice, financial assistance where needed and information about local and national support groups and services.

4 Adoptive parents will be involved in discussions as to how they can best maintain any links, including contact, with birth relatives and significant others identified in the adoption plan.

5 Adoptive parents will be encouraged to keep safe any information provided by birth families via agencies and to provide this to the adopted child on request, or as they feel appropriate.

6 Adoptive parents whose adopted child has decided to explore their birth heritage will be supported to deal with the impact of this decision.

7 Where there are difficulties with the placement or the adoption breaks down the agencies involved will cooperate to provide support and information to the adoptive parents and the child without delay.

8 Agencies will ask adoptive parents whether they are prepared to agree to notify the agency if an adopted child dies during childhood or soon afterwards.

9 Adoptive parents will be informed of their right to make representations and complaints.

D. BIRTH PARENTS AND BIRTH FAMILIES (INCLUDING GRANDPARENTS, BROTHERS, SISTERS AND OTHER PEOPLE WHO ARE SIGNIFICANT TO THE CHILD)

Birth parents and birth families are entitled to services that recognise the lifelong implications of adoption. They will be treated fairly, openly and with respect throughout the adoption process.

1 Agencies will work with birth parents and significant birth family members to enable effective plans to be made and implemented for their child(ren).

2 Every effort will be made to ensure that birth parents and significant birth family members have a full understanding of the adoption process, the legal implications, and their rights.

3 Birth parents will have access to a support worker independent of the child's social worker from the time adoption is identified as the plan for the child.

4 Birth parents and birth families (including siblings) will have access to a range of support services both before and after adoption, including information about local and national support groups and services.

5 Birth parents will have the opportunity to give their account of events, and to see and comment on what is written about them in reports for the adoption panel, and in information passed to the adopters.

6 Birth parents and families will be supported to provide information that the adopted child needs. This will include information about the adopted child's birth and early life, the birth family's views about adoption and contact and up-to-date information about themselves and their situation.

7 Where it is in the child's best interest for there to be ongoing links, including contact, with birth parents and families (including siblings separated by adoption), birth families will be involved in discussions about how best to achieve this and helped to fulfil agreed plans, e.g. through practical or financial support.

8 Where adoptive parents have agreed to inform the agency of the death of the adopted child or the breakdown of the adoption, birth parents or the 'next of kin' at adoption will, if they wish, be informed by the adoption agency.

9 Birth parents and birth families will be informed of their right to make representations and complaints.

E. COUNCILS

Corporate and senior management responsibilities

A comprehensive adoption service to meet the needs of children, birth families, adoptive parents and adopted adults will be planned corporately and provided in collaboration with other relevant agencies.

1 Councils will plan and deliver adoption services with local health and education bodies (including schools), voluntary adoption agencies, the local courts and other relevant agencies, including, where applicable, other councils.

2 There will be clear policies for adoption, including post-adoption services, which are set out in Children and Young People's Strategic Plans or equivalent local plans.

3 Councillors will carry out their responsibilities as corporate parents and receive regular information on the management and outcomes of the service they are responsible for providing.

4 Senior managers, with a clear management link to Director level, will ensure that adoption is an integral part of the council services for children, and will be involved in the strategic planning, delivery and monitoring of the adoption service.

5 A senior manager will have direct operational responsibility for all parts of the adoption service including planning, management and delivery of the adoption service, and performance management through quality assurance systems. This includes making sure that:

(a) Each child has a named social worker and an agreed care plan;
(b) Timescales for planning, decision making and adoptive placements are met;
(c) Staff are subject to the necessary safeguard checks;
(d) Staff have the necessary skills and knowledge, or access to them, and are supervised;
(e) Managers, councillors and panel members have access to necessary training and skills development;

(f) Procedures, guidance and sound professional practice are followed;
(g) Quality standards are set and consistently maintained;
(h) Management information systems inform service provision.

6 Councils, with the relevant agencies listed in **1**, will provide or commission a comprehensive range of pre- and post-adoption services consistent with any national framework or regulation. These will facilitate and support adoption and meet the needs of children who move between local authority areas. Criteria for access to services will be clear, concise and understandable.

F. ADOPTION AGENCIES AND SERVICES – COUNCIL AND VOLUNTARY

Each council and voluntary adoption agency will provide a high quality adoption service.

1 Children's welfare and safety will be put first, and their rights, needs and wishes, elicited, recorded and taken into account at all times.

2 Agencies will agree, and follow, policies and procedures for adoption which are clear, concise and easily understood. They will be made available to those affected by adoption, staff and the general public.

3 Councils and voluntary adoption agencies will work together to plan and deliver a co-ordinated package of services to meet the needs of the child.

4 The second and every subsequent review of a looked after child will consider permanence. Where adoption is the plan, reviews will evaluate the success of the plan in meeting the child's needs and specify any new objectives required to meet those needs.

5 Timescales will be met, taking account of the individual child's needs. The senior manager will monitor performance against timescales.

6 Agencies will plan, implement and evaluate effective strategies to recruit sufficient adopters to meet the needs of children waiting for adoption locally and nationally, especially those from diverse ethnic and cultural backgrounds and disabled children.

7 Agencies will have thorough and timely assessment processes in accordance with Sections A, B and C using the dimensions in the Framework for the Assessment of Children in Need and their Families. Children and adults will be prepared for adoption in accordance with Sections A and C.

8 Careful and thorough checks will be made on prospective adopters, members of their households and agency staff.

Adoption panels:

9 Agencies will arrange enough adoption panels to avoid any delays in considering children for adoption, approval of adopters and matching, and to meet the following timescales:

(a) Panels will receive all necessary information from agencies no later than 6 weeks from the completion of the assessment report;
(b) Where a review has agreed that adoption is the plan, the adoption panel will make its recommendation within 2 months;
(c) Panel recommendations will be conveyed orally to applicants, children and birth parents within 24 hours.

Agency decision making:

10 Agencies will ensure that timely decisions are taken on panel recommendations and to meet the following timescales:

(a) Decisions will be taken within 7 working days of the adoption panel recommendation;
(b) Decisions will be conveyed orally to the applicants, the child and the birth parents within 24 hours;
(c) Decisions will be confirmed in writing within 7 working days.

11 Where an adoption is at risk of breaking down, all agencies involved in the placement will cooperate to provide support and information to all parties without delay.

12 When an adoption has broken down all agencies involved will cooperate to provide support to the child and the adoptive parents, and ensure that the birth parents are informed.

13 Agencies will have effective systems for managing and keeping safe information from all the people affected by adoption.

14 Agencies will have representations and complaints procedures that comply with regulations and guidance.

Appendix Q

ADOPTION AND CHILDREN ACT 2002 GUIDANCE – ANNEX I: TRANSITIONAL ARRANGEMENTS

INTRODUCTION

1 This guidance explains how adoption agencies should manage ongoing adoption cases during the transfer from the 1976 Act to the 2002 Act. It should be read alongside the Adoption and Children Act 2002 (Commencement No 10, Transitional and Savings Provisions) Order 2005 (the transitionals Order), the main body of this guidance and the 2002 Act itself.

2 Notwithstanding the statement in paragraph 8 of the Introduction to the main body of this guidance, this annex has the status of statutory guidance. It is issued under Section 7 of the Local Authority Social Services Act 1970, which requires local authorities in their social services functions to act under the general guidance of the Secretary of State. As such, the document does not have the full force of statute, but should be complied with unless local circumstances indicate exceptional reasons which justify a variation. Like the rest of the guidance it applies to England only.

3 This annex will cease to be relevant and can be discarded when all of an agency's ongoing adoption cases that were being managed before 30 December 2005 have completed their transition to the new system. It is anticipated that this will be within two years of implementation.

What is a transitional case?

4 Any ongoing case an adoption agency is managing before the 2002 Act is implemented on 30 December 2005 is a transitional case. However, not all transitional cases will require special treatment. Many cases can simply be transferred to the new system on 30 December. Others will be handled under the old system as a result either of the provisions included in Schedule 4 to the 2002 Act or the transitionals Order. This guidance identifies where specific provisions have been put into place and where they have not.

What are the old and new systems?

5 When this guidance refers to 'the old system' it means the arrangements made under the 1976 Act and the regulations made under it. The phrase 'the new system' is used to describe the arrangements made under the 2002 Act and the regulations made under it.

General handling

6 The expectation is that the 2002 Act and the Regulations made under it will apply to all new cases plus to any new actions that take place on or after 30 December 2005 unless alternative arrangements have been put in place by the transitionals Order. To facilitate the transfer from the old to the new system, paragraph 1 of Schedule 4 to the 2002 Act allows for some references and actions under the 1976 Act to be treated as if they were references and actions under the 2002 Act.

7 Paragraph 1(1) of Schedule 4 to the 2002 Act provides that any reference in Part 1 of the 2002 Act or in any other enactment, instrument or document to any provision in Part 1 or things done or required to be done under Part 1, should be construed as including a reference to any corresponding provision repealed by the 2002 Act so far as the nature of the reference permits. So for example:

- Where notice of intention to adopt a child has been given to a local authority under Section 22(1) of the 1976 Act prior to 30 December is treated as being given under Section 44(1) of the 2002 Act after 30 December.
- An application in writing for an assessment as a prospective adopter made in accordance with the requirements of the Adoption (Bringing Children into the UK) Regulations 2003 made under the 1976 Act may be treated as an application made under the FER.
- An agency decision that an individual is suitable to adopt under the AAR 1983 may be treated as a decision made under the AAR.

8 Paragraph 1(2) of Schedule 4 to the 2002 Act provides that any reference in any enactment, instrument or document to a provision repealed by the 2002 Act, or things done or required to be done under a repealed provision, is to be construed as a reference to the corresponding provision in the 2002 Act or to the things done or required to be done under the corresponding provision so far as the nature of the reference permits. So for example:

- A reference to a child placed for adoption in an agency document dated prior to 30 December could be construed to be a child placed for adoption under the 2002 Act.
- A reference to a certificate of eligibility being issued by the Secretary of State in accordance with the requirements of the Adoption (Bringing Children into the UK) Regulations 2003 may be construed as a reference to a certificate of eligibility issued by the Secretary of State under the FER.

9 In the light of this, when managing ongoing adoption cases during the transition from the old system to the new system there are a number of general principles agencies should apply:

- Cases should continue to be handled in the usual way in the run up to implementation.
- When providing information about the adoption process in the run up to implementation, agencies should make clear that from 30 December 2005 a new system will apply. They should also provide information about how this may affect the child's or prospective adopter's case and the impact on natural families.
- The transfer should not require previous work to be redone.
- Decisions that have already been taken should stand and should not usually be reopened except in the specific circumstances set out in this guidance (or if they would have been reviewed regardless of the implementation of the 2002 Act).
- Existing adoption and freeing orders are not affected by the implementation of the 2002 Act.
- Local authorities will continue to be required to supply the Court reports that meet the requirements of the 1976 Act where pending applications for adoption orders and freeing orders continue to be considered.
- Some cases must continue to be handled using the old system until they reach a particular point in the process where the case may then be processed under the new system. This is explained below.
- Limited additional checks or information may be needed to allow some cases to be processed under the new system. The guidance that follows provides advice on handling.

COURT ORDERS

Freeing Orders

10 Key points to note:

- Freeing orders will remain in place unless they are revoked (see paragraph 7 of Schedule 4 to the 2002 Act).
- Any application to vary or revoke a freeing order will continue to be dealt with by the Court using the provisions of the 1976 Act and the Adoption Rules 1984 or the Magistrates Courts (Adoption) Rules 1984.
- Where an application has been made for a freeing order before 30 December 2005 and is pending on that date, the child has been placed for adoption by the adoption agency, and the child is living with the prospective adopters, the application will be considered by the Court under the 1976 Act by virtue of paragraph 6 of Schedule 4 to the 2002 Act.
- Where an application has been made for a freeing order before 30 December 2005 and is pending on that date and the child is not placed for adoption the application will be considered by the Court under the 1976 Act by virtue of article 10 of the transitionals Order.
- Applications cannot be made for a freeing order on or after 30 December 2005 even if this was in the local authority's original plans.
- Where a child is free for adoption by virtue of a freeing order, the third of the conditions for making an adoption order under Section 47 the 2002 Act is treated as satisfied. (See paragraph 7(3) of Schedule 4).
- Where a child is free for adoption but not yet placed the local authority may place the child for adoption within the requirements of the 2002 Act by virtue of article 4 of the transitionals Order.
- Where a child is free for adoption but not yet placed, AAR 36 applies as if the child is subject to a placement order by virtue of article 4 of the transitionals Order. This means that the child's case must be reviewed by the local authority not longer than 3 months after 30 December 2005 and thereafter not less than once every 6 months until they are placed for adoption.
- Where a child is free for adoption it will not be possible for the prospective adopters to exercise parental responsibility prior to any adoption order being made. The adoption agency will have parental responsibility for the child.
- Where a child has not been placed for adoption, and a freeing order application is pending on 30 December 2005, unless a proposed placement has been considered by panel prior to 30 December and the placement goes ahead under the AAR 1983 (see paragraph 26 below), the local authority will not be able to place the child until a freeing order is made or an alternative authority to place is obtained.

Adoption Orders

11 Key points to note:

- Adoption orders made before 30 December will not be affected by the implementation of the 2002 Act. A child adopted under the 1976 Act will continue to derive their adoptive status from Chapter 4 of the 1976 Act which has not been repealed.
- All adoption order applications made before 30 December will be dealt with by the Court under the provisions of the Adoption Act 1976 and the Adoption Rules 1984 or the Magistrates' Courts (Adoption) Rules 1984, as appropriate. Any order will be made using the powers in the Adoption Act 1976. (See paragraph 8 of Schedule 4 and article 11 of the transitionals Order).

- Applications for adoption orders made on or after 30 December must be made in accordance with the 2002 Act and will be considered against the requirements of that Act. Any order will be made under Part 1 of the 2002 Act. Where parents have agreed to their child being adopted prior to 30 December it will be for the Court to determine whether or not this meets the requirements of the 2002 Act.
- Where one member of an unmarried couple or a civil partnership has applied for an adoption order and that application is pending on 30 December the agency may wish to discuss with the prospective adopter whether or not it would be appropriate to withdraw the application and make a new joint application with their partner under the 2002 Act. To apply jointly both partners must have been assessed as suitable to adopt by the agency.
- The disclosure regime in Sections 56 to 65 of the 2002 Act and the AIR will apply in any case where an adoption order is made on or after 30 December. This applies regardless of whether the adoption order is made under the 1976 Act or the 2002 Act.

Removal and Recovery of Children

12 Article 9 of the transitionals order saves Sections 27 and 29 of the 1976 Act where there is a pending application for a freeing order or an adoption order on 30 December 2005. This means that restrictions on the removal of a child from a placement in the circumstances set out in Section 27 will continue to apply until such a time as the application for a freeing order is disposed of and that applications may continue to be made for the return of a child taken away in breach of Section 27 using Section 29.

Parental Responsibility Prior to Adoption Abroad Orders

13 Key points to note:

- Existing orders made under Section 55 of the 1976 Act (adoption of children abroad) will not be affected by the implementation of the 2002 Act.
- Applications made under Section 55 of the 1976 Act that have not been disposed of by 30 December 2005 will continue to be considered by the Court under the provisions of the 1976 Act and the Adoption Rules 1984. (See article 12 of the transitionals Order).
- Applications for orders giving parental responsibility prior to adoption abroad made on or after 30 December 2005 will be considered under Section 84 of the 2002 Act and the Family Proceedings (Adoption) Rules 2005.

Special Guardianship Orders

14 As Special Guardianship Orders will not be introduced until 30 December 2005 there will not be any pending cases or the need for any transitional arrangements. However, if local authorities are approached before 30 December by potential special guardians they may wish to provide information on the availability of such orders from 30 December. They may also wish to consider the possibility of special guardianship being appropriate in any case they are reviewing in advance of 30 December.

Residence Orders

15 The power of the court to direct (on request) that a residence order continues in force until the child reaches the age 18 applies to all residence orders made on or after 30 December 2005, irrespective of whether the application for the order was made before or after that date. Where local authorities are involved with carers seeking a residence order they may wish to inform them of these changes.

Step-Parent Parental Responsibility Orders

16 Step-parent parental responsibility orders will not be introduced until 30 December 2005. There are therefore no transitional arrangements. However, if local authorities are approached before 30 December by eligible individuals wishing to secure parental responsibility or considering adoption they may wish to provide information on the availability of such orders from 30 December.

AGENCIES

Establishing Panels

17 Most agencies will already have an adoption panel in place on 29 December 2005. By virtue of AAR 10.1 all members of the panel will cease to hold office on 30 December. The agency will therefore be required to establish a new panel in accordance with AAR 3 and 4 on 30 December. See Chapter One.

Medical Advisor

18 Agencies should have a medical advisor nominated on 29 December 2005 by virtue of AAR 1983: 6.4. If the agency wishes to retain this medical advisor, they need not do anything. On 30 December that nomination will be treated as if it was made under AAR 9 by virtue of paragraph 1 of Schedule 4 of the 2002 Act.

Policies and Procedures

19 Agencies are required by AAR 7 to put in place clear policies and procedures on 30 December 2005. It is recommended that these policies and procedures are finalised and shared as early as possible. Where agencies consult the adoption panel and medical advisor appointed under the AAR 1983 prior to 30 December this may be construed to meet the requirements of AAR 7.

Panel Functions

20 Specific transitional provisions have not been put in place for the exercise of panel functions. However agencies will wish to note that:

- Cases considered prior to 30 December 2005 will be subject to the requirements of the 1976 Act, the AAR 1983 and the 2003 Hague Convention Regulations.
- Unless a recommendation has been made and article 3 or 6 of the transitionals Order applies (see below), where the panel reconvenes to consider a case on or after 30 December, this will be under the 2002 Act and the information provided to them must therefore comply with the AAR and the FER where relevant.
- Where the panel meets to consider a case on or after 30 December 2005 this will be under the 2002 Act and the information provided to them must therefore comply with the AAR and the FER where relevant.

21 This means that where an agency refers reports and papers to its adoption panel prior to 30 December 2005 for consideration on or after 30 December the agency must ensure that the reports and papers meet the requirements of the AAR (and the FER if relevant). If these requirements are not met in such cases, the reports and papers should be withdrawn, updated and resubmitted.

Decisions

22 AAR 19, 27, and 33 and FER 16, 40 and 45 only apply to cases considered by the adoption panel on or after 30 December. Articles 3 and 6 of the transitionals Order make clear that, where a case has been considered by the adoption panel prior to 30 December 2005 and a recommendation has been made, the agency decision maker must make a decision and the agency must issue notifications as set out in the AAR 1983 and the 2003 Hague Convention Regulations. This applies to decisions about whether adoption is in the best interests of a child, the suitability of a prospective adopter to adopt a child, and whether a child should be placed for adoption with a particular prospective adopter.

Qualifying determinations – time limit for making representations or applying for a review by the independent review panel

23 Where the decision maker considers that the prospective adopter is not suitable to adopt a child (a qualifying determination) both AAR 1983: 11A.4 and AAR 27.4 require the agency to notify the prospective adopter of the reasons in writing and to invite him or her to submit any representations to the panel or apply to the Independent Review Panel administrator for review by an independent review panel. However, the time limit for this is increased from 28 calendar days under the AAR 1983 and the 2003 Hague Convention Regulations to 40 working days of the date that the notification is sent under the AAR.

24 Article 3(5) of the transitionals Order extends the time limit for making representations or applying for an independent review from 28 calendar days to 40 working days for any case where:

- The decision maker writes indicating that they are minded to make a decision that the prospective adopter is not suitable to adopt a child prior to 30 December 2005 but the 28 day limit would have expired on or after 30 December, or
- The decision maker writes indicating that they are minded to make a decision that the prospective adopter is not suitable to adopt a child on or after 30 December 2005 under the AAR 1983 or the 2003 Hague Convention Regulations by virtue of the fact that the case was considered by the adoption panel prior to 30 December.

Qualifying determinations – consideration of representations by the adoption panel or review by the independent review panel

25 Articles 3(4) and 6(4) of the transitionals Order ensure that cases considered by the adoption panel and the decision maker under the AAR 1983 or the Hague Convention Regulations 2003 will continue to be considered by either the adoption panel or the independent review panel under the 1976 Act until a decision is made by the adoption agency under the AAR 1983 or the Hague Convention Regulations 2003.

Placements by adoption agencies

26 Where the panel considered a proposed placement prior to 30 December 2005 any decision that the child should be placed for adoption with the prospective adopter will be made under the AAR 1983. In these cases the placement will go ahead using the AAR 1983 and there will be no requirement to obtain an authority to place by virtue of Article 3(6) of the transitionals Order.

27 Placements that have not been considered by panel prior to 30 December will be considered and made under the 2002 Act. This means that the local authority must secure authority to place the child for adoption prior to making a placement.

Placements made under the AAR 1983

28 Where a child is placed for adoption prior to 30 December 2005 or is placed using the AAR 1983 after 30 December, there will not be any requirement for local authorities to secure a retrospective authority to place (see article 3(6) and 3(7) of the transitionals Order).

Placements of Children Free for Adoption

29 Where a child is free for adoption by virtue of an order under Section 18 of the 1976 Act but a placement with a specific prospective adopter has not been considered by panel prior to 30 December 2005 (and a recommendation made) the AAR will apply to any placement. By virtue of article 4 of the transitionals Order a freeing order will allow the local authority to place the child for adoption under the 2002 Act.

30 Article 4 of the transitionals Order also provides that AAR 36 applies as if the adoption agency is authorised to place the child but has not yet placed the child for adoption, and the child is subject to a placement order. The child's case must be reviewed within three months of 30 December 2005.

31 Where a freeing order application is pending and the adoption panel has not made a recommendation in respect of a proposed placement with a prospective adopter prior to 30 December, the child may not be placed until either the freeing order is made or an alternative authority to place is secured.

Reviews and Monitoring – Suitability of adopters

32 No specific transitional provision has been put into place. However, AAR 29 allows an agency to review any approval made under the AAR 1983 in advance of the statutory requirement to review the approval within one year if the agency considers it necessary (eg it may wish to ensure that the requirements in relation to offences in the AAR are met due to the list of specified offences being more extensive as it takes account of the Sexual Offences Act 2003).

Reviews and Monitoring – Placements

33 Article 3(6) of the transitionals order makes clear that all placements made under the AAR 1983 will be treated as if they were made under the AAR. This means that from 30 December 2005 all placements (whether made under the AAR 1983 or the AAR) should be monitored and reviewed in accordance with AAR 36 and the agency should appoint an independent reviewing officer under AAR 37.

Adoption Support

34 ASR 24 provides that on 30 December 2005 existing cases are transferred to the new system. Any request for assessment, plan, review or adoption support service shall, from 30 December be treated as an assessment, plan, review or adoption support service under the ASR. See Chapter 9.

35 From 30 December responsibility for carrying out assessments of need will remain with the placing authority for three years after the making of an adoption order. This will apply to all cases. However, where any assessment is currently underway the local authority must complete this under the ASR and should provide such services as it deems necessary.

Preparation of Reports

36 Individuals who do not meet the requirements of ARR 3 may not prepare any of the reports set out in ARR 4 from 30 December 2005. See Chapter 1.

37 The agency should ensure that any reports being prepared for it by someone who will not meet the requirements of ARR 3 on 30 December are either completed in advance of 30 December or handed over to the agency incomplete by 29 December. Where a report is incomplete the agency should make arrangements for someone who does fall within the definition of ARR 3 to complete this work.

38 There may be cases where a social worker or social work student has not completed a report by 30 December, and does not meet the requirements of the ARR 3 for the reason that they are not appropriately supervised. In such cases, it would be preferable for the agency to ensure that the social worker or social work student is supervised in compliance with the regulations so that they may complete the report.

Access to Information

39 It has not been necessary to put in place specific transitional provisions in relation to access to information. There is a clear dividing line between those adoptions made prior to 30 December 2005 and those made on or after 30 December 2005. See Chapters 10 and 11.

Storage and Retention of Records

40 Article 13 of the transitionals Order provides that records relating to adoptions made prior to 30 December 2005 must be stored, preserved and treated as confidential in accordance with the requirements of the AAR 1983.

41 Records relating to adoptions made after 30 December 2005 must be stored, preserved and treated as confidential in accordance with the requirements of AAR 39, 40 and 41 and AIR 4, 5, 6 and 7.

Fees – intercountry adoption

42 No specific transitional arrangements have been put into place. However, any rights to payment that adoption agencies have accrued for the provision of adoption services that would have been legally payable under the 1976 Act may still be paid after 30 December 2005.

ADOPTION SUPPORT AGENCIES

Current independent adoption support providers

43 Where an adoption support provider is operational before 30 December 2005 and wishes to continue, it should submit an application to CSCI for registration as an Adoption Support Agency. The adoption support provider will be able to continue to operate on or after 30 December without operating outside of the law, subject to its application for registration being received by CSCI before 30 December. This situation will last until registration is granted or denied. During this period, providers will have to operate within the ASAR and meet the National Minimum Standards for ASAs.

Current VAAs

44 A VAA registered with the CSCI for its activity in relation to making arrangements for adoption and which provides adoption support services, will need to ensure that its registration is varied to include its adoption support services.

45 CSCI will contact all VAAs before 30 December 2005 asking them to inform CSCI of any adoption support services they provide. Where services are provided the VAA's registration will be varied and its adoption support services provision will be inspected at its next scheduled inspection. If the VAA does not provide adoption support services or it fails to complete and submit the form by 30 December, it will become a condition of its registration as a VAA that it does not provide adoption support services. This means that it will not be able to legally provide adoption support on or after 30 December.

46 Arrangements are being put into place to change the registration arrangements for those VAAs registered with CSCI under the Care Standards Act 2000 and the Secretary of State under the 1976 Act, which no longer wish to make arrangements for adoption, but wish to become an Adoption Support Agency. CSCI will be writing to all VAAs to enable them to apply for the transfer of their registration from a VAA to an ASA.

INDIVIDUAL CASES WITHIN THE SYSTEM

47 This section provides a checklist which sets out when and how ongoing adoption cases should be transferred into the new system. It also outlines the key actions the agency should take.

Children – Agency Cases

48 In all cases children should be informed of the change to the law and the counselling requirements of the AAR2005 and, where relevant, the FER should be met, subject to their age and understanding.

Checklist:

Stage reached (at 30 December 2005)	Handling & key points to note
Child being considered for adoption (ie the child's plan is for adoption following a statutory review).	• Transfer to new system. • Secure authority to place. • Ensure counselling requirements of AAR 13 and 14, and where relevant FER 36 are met.
Child's case referred to adoption panel but yet to be considered.	• Transfer to new system. • Secure authority to place. • Panel will consider any case on or after 30 December under AAR 18. • Reports and papers for the panel should comply with the requirements of AAR 17, otherwise these documents will need to be withdrawn, revised and re-submitted.

Stage reached (at 30 December 2005)	Handling & key points to note
Child's case considered by adoption panel and awaiting a decision.	• Continue under the 1976 Act until decision made. • Secure authority to place. • Subsequent steps in the process, such as matching and placement proposal, to be made under new system. • Ensure counselling requirements of AAR 13 and 14 and, where relevant, FER 36 are met.
Decision made that a child is to be placed for adoption but yet to be matched.	• Decision stands. • Secure authority to place (unless a freeing order is in place). • Subsequent steps in the process, such as matching and placement proposal, to be made under new system. • Ensure counselling requirements of AAR 13 and 14 and, where relevant, FER 36 are met.
Child provisionally matched with a prospective adopter but case yet to be considered by the adoption panel.	• Transfer to the new system. • Secure authority to place. • Panel will consider any case on or after 30 December under AAR 32. • Reports and papers for the panel should comply with the requirements of AAR 31. Any referred to the panel that do not will need to be withdrawn, revised and re-submitted.
Match considered by adoption panel and awaiting agency decision.	• Make decision under the AAR 1983. • No authority to place required. • Placement takes place under the AAR 1983. • Visits and reviews in accordance with AAR 36.
Decision maker decided child should be placed with prospective adopter but child yet to be placed.	• Decision stands. • No authority to place required. • Placement takes place under the AAR 1983. • Visits and reviews in accordance with AAR 36.
Child placed for adoption but no application made.	• Transfer to the new system. • No authority to place required. • Visits and reviews in accordance with AAR 36. • Ensure counselling requirements of AAR 13 and 14 and, where relevant, FER 36 are met.
Application for adoption made.	• Continue with old system until the application is disposed of. This to include preparing Schedule 2 report that meets the requirements of the 1976 Act.

Child's Parents

Checklist:

- The child's family should be informed of the change to the law and the implications (if any) for their case.

- Agencies must ensure that where the case has been transferred to the new system the counselling requirements of the AAR 14 and, where relevant, FER 37 are met.
- Agencies should be prepared to offer support to a child's parents who have previously relinquished their child and are distressed to be informed of the need to have their consent witnessed by a CAFCASS officer.

Prospective Adopters (Domestic)

Checklist:

Stage reached (at 30 December 2005)	Handling & key points to note
Expressed an interest in adoption.	• Transfer to the 2002 Act immediately. • Inform them of the up-coming changes to the system as early as possible.
Written application submitted but assessment process yet to start.	• Transfer to 2002 Act. Application handled under the AAR. • Ensure informed of the changes to the law.
Assessment process underway but papers yet to be put to adoption panel.	• Transfer to the 2002 Act. Comply with AAR 21 to 29. • Inform prospective adopters of changes to the law and ensure requirements of AAR 21 are met. • Review any police checks carried out under the AAR 1983 and ensure AAR 23 has been complied with. • Ensure preparation for adoption is offered in accordance with AAR 23 and that all the information required by AAR 25 is in place prior to putting the case to panel.
Assessment completed and case referred to panel but yet to be considered.	• Panel will consider any case on or after 30 December under AAR 26. • Reports and papers for the panel should comply with the requirements of AAR 25, otherwise these documents will need to be withdrawn, revised and re-submitted.

Stage reached (at 30 December 2005)	Handling & key points to note
Panel has considered the case but agency is yet to make a decision.	• Decision made and prospective adopters notified in accordance with AAR 1983 or the 2003 Hague Convention Regulations by virtue of Articles 3 and 6 of the transitionals Order. • Where minded not to approve, time for representations to the adoption panel/referral to the independent review panel extended to 40 working days by virtue of Articles 3(5) and 6(4) of the transitionals Order. • Where minded not to approve, reconsideration of the case, decision and notification then made in accordance with AAR 1983 or the 2003 Hague Convention Regulations and IRP Regulations. • Where approved as suitable to adopt this decision is treated as if it were made under the AAR and subsequent work (including reviews, matching and placement) undertaken under the AAR.
Agency decision maker has notified the prospective adopter that he is minded not to approve them.	• Where the deadline for representations would have expired on or after 30 December the time for representations to the adoption panel/referral to the independent review panel extended to 40 working days by virtue of Articles 3 and 6 of the transitionals Order. • Reconsideration of the case, decision and notification made in accordance with AAR 1983 or the 2003 Hague Convention Regulations and IRP Regulations. • Where approved as suitable to adopt this decision is treated as if it were made under AAR 19 and subsequent work (including reviews, matching and placement) undertaken under the AAR.
Decision maker had decided to approve the prospective adopters but is yet to notify them.	• Notification made in accordance with AAR 1983 or the 2003 Hague Convention Regulations. • Where approved as suitable to adopt this decision is treated as if it were made under AAR 19 and subsequent work (including reviews, matching and placement) undertaken under the AAR.
Decision maker has approved prospective adopters and notified them of this but are yet to be matched with a child.	• Decision is treated as if it were made under AAR 19 and subsequent work (including reviews, matching and placement) undertaken under the AAR.
Approved prospective adopters have been provisionally matched with a child but panel are yet to consider.	• Transfer immediately to new system. • Panel will consider any case on or after 30 December under AAR 32. • Reports and papers for the panel should comply with the requirements of AAR 31, otherwise these documents will need to be withdrawn, revised and re-submitted.

Stage reached (at 30 December 2005)	Handling & key points to note
Proposed placement has been considered by panel but decision is yet to be made.	• Decision made under AAR 1983. • Placement made under AAR 1983. • Reviews and visits in accordance with AAR 36.
Decision maker has decided child should be placed with prospective adopter but child yet to be placed.	• Decision stands. • Placement made under AAR 1983. • Reviews and visits in accordance with AAR 36.
Child placed for adoption.	• Placement reviewed under AAR 36. • Agency should make the prospective adopters aware of the change to the law and the implications for their case.
Adoption order application made.	• Continue under 1976 Act until application disposed of.

Prospective Adopters (Intercountry – Convention Cases)

Checklist

As for domestic adoption for all cases up to, and including, those who have been approved as suitable to adopt. Then:

Stage reached (at 30 December 2005)	Handling & key points to note
Decision maker has approved prospective adopters and notified them of this but papers are yet to be sent to DfES.	• Papers sent to DfES for processing as usual. • Certificate of eligibility issued in accordance with the FER. • Papers legalised and notarised as necessary prior to sending abroad. • If match received all requirements in FER must be complied with.
Papers have been sent to DfES.	• Papers processed as usual. • If not already issued, Certificate of eligibility issued in accordance with the FER. • Papers legalised and notarised as necessary prior to sending overseas. • If match received all requirements in FER must be complied with.
Papers have been processed and sent to the country being applied to.	• If match received the prospective adopter must comply with all the requirements in FER.
Match proposed by country being applied to but prospective adopters yet to travel to meet the child.	• Prospective adopter must ensure that the requirements of FER have been complied with.

Stage reached (at 30 December 2005)	Handling & key points to note
Prospective adopters have travelled to meet child.	• Prospective adopter must ensure that the requirements of FER have been complied with.
Prospective adopters have had child entrusted to them in State of origin.	• Must notify agency as per FER 19.3.c and comply with subsequent parts of the FER.
Prospective adopters have brought child into the UK but the 14 days are yet to expire and no notice has been given.	• When notice is given it is given under Section 44 of the 2002 Act and FER 5 applies, as modified by FER 25.
Prospective adopters have brought the child into the UK and given notice of their intention to adopt.	• Notice given under Section 22 of the 1976 Act treated as if given under Section 44 of the 2002 Act. • FER 5, as modified by FER 25, applies to such an extent as it has not already been applied by virtue of article 8 of the transitionals order.
Application for an adoption order has been made.	• Continue under 1976 Act until application is disposed of.

Prospective Adopters (Intercountry – Non-Convention cases)

Checklist

As for domestic adoption for all cases up to, and including, those who have been approved as suitable to adopt. Then:

Stage reached (at 30 December 2005)	Handling & key points to note
Decision maker has approved prospective adopters and notified them of this but papers are yet to be sent to DfES.	• Papers sent to DfES for processing as usual. • Certificate of eligibility issued. • Papers legalised and notarised as necessary prior to sending abroad.
Papers have been sent to DfES.	• Papers processed as usual. • If not already issued, Certificate of eligibility issued. • Papers legalised and notarised as necessary prior to sending abroad. • Conditions in FER 4 must be complied with.
Papers have been processed and sent to the country being applied to.	• Await decision from country being applied to. If match received the prospective adopter must comply with the conditions in FER 4.

Stage reached (at 30 December 2005)	Handling & key points to note
Match proposed by country being applied to but prospective adopters yet to travel to meet the child.	• Prospective adopter must ensure that the requirements of FER 4 have been complied with. The conditions in FER 4 (2)(a) will have been met prior to 30 December.
Prospective adopters have travelled to meet child but are yet to return to the UK with the child.	• Prospective adopter must ensure that the requirements of FER 4 have been complied with except for FER 4.2.b to d which do not apply by virtue of article 7(2) of the transitionals Order.
Prospective adopters have brought child into the UK but the 14 days are yet to expire and no notice of intention to adopt has been given.	• Prospective adopter must ensure that the requirements of FER 4 have been complied with except for FER 4.2.b to d and 4.3 which do not apply by virtue of article 7(3) of the transitionals order. • When notice is given it is given under Section 44 of the 2002 Act and FER 5 applies.
Prospective adopters have brought the child into the UK and given notice of their intention to adopt.	• Notice given under Section 22 of the 1976 Act treated as if given under Section 44 of the 2002 Act. • FER 5 applies to such an extent as it has not already been applied by virtue of article 8(2) and (3) of the transitionals order.
Application for an adoption order has been made.	• Continue under 1976 Act until application is disposed of.

Non-Agency Placements – Protected Child Status

49 Where notice of intention to adopt has been given under Section 22 of the 1976 Act prior to 30 December 2005, this will be treated as if notice was given under Section 44 of the 2002 Act by virtue of paragraph 1 of Schedule 4 of the 2002 Act. As the 2002 Act does not replicate the protected child provisions in the 1976 Act protected child status within the meaning of Section 32 of the 1976 Act will no longer apply and the local authority will no longer be obliged to protect the welfare of children under Section 33 of the 1976 Act.

50 However, other safeguards may be invoked by the local authority. Where the local authority conducts the investigation required under section 44(5) of the Act and becomes concerned for the welfare of the child the authority may apply for an emergency protection order under the 1989 Act. The local authority will also remain obliged to provide adoption services and carry out assessments of need for adoption support services in accordance with its duties in Sections 3 and 4 of the 2002 Act.

Intercountry Adoption

51 Where the child has been brought into the UK for the purposes of adoption (irrespective of the prospective adopter's relationship to the child) article 8 of the transitionals Order makes clear that from 30 December FER 5 will apply to the extent that it has not already been complied with as the result of the child being a protected child.

52 Where the local authority has not visited the child and prospective adopter prior to 30 December and more than one week has elapsed since the receipt of the notice of intention to adopt, 30 December 2005 shall be treated as the date of receipt of that notice for the purposes of FER 5.1(e) and (f).

53 Where the local authority has visited the child and prospective adopter prior to 30 December, the authority must carry out the reviews and visits imposed by FER 5.1(e) to (h) in so far as it has not already done so.

54 Where the review considering the matters referred to in FER 5.1(g) has not already taken place, 30 December 2005 shall be treated as the date of receipt of the notice of intention to adopt for the purposes of regulation 5.1(f).

Relatives – Domestic Arrangements

55 Where the child is living with a relative who falls within the definition in Section 105 of the Children Act 1989, and the child has not been brought into the UK for the purposes of adoption, the local authority will not be required to monitor the placement. It will, however, be expected to prepare a report for the Court in accordance with Section 44(5) and (6) of the 2002 Act and to use its powers in the 1989 Act if concerns for the child's welfare come to light.

Other Cases

56 Where the child is under 16 and the prospective adopter is not a relative within the definition of Section 105 of the 1989 Act, the child will be privately fostered by virtue of Section 66 of the 1989 Act and The Children (Private Arrangements for Fostering) Regulations 2005 (the Private Fostering Regulations) will apply.

57 Article 5 of the transitionals Order provides that:

- Where notice of intention to adopt has been given an individual will not be considered to be in breach of Regulation 5 of the Private Fostering Regulations.
- Where the notice of intention to adopt does not contain the information referred to in Schedule 1 to the Private Fostering Regulations the prospective adopter must provide this no later than 30 January 2006.
- Consent to the private fostering arrangements shall be treated as given until such time as the authority considers the information supplied by the prospective adopter and notifies the prospective adopter that consent to the arrangements is refused under section 68(4) of the Children Act 1989.
- Where the local authority has not already visited the child and met the requirements of Regulation 7.1 of the Private Fostering Regulations the authority must carry out this visit no later than 7 February 2006 and make the report required by Regulation 7.2.
- Where a visit has already taken place before 30 December 2005 the arrangement will be treated as if it began on 30 December 2005 for the purposes of identifying the intervals for subsequent visits required by Regulation 8.

58 It is recommended that, before 30 December 2005, local authorities write to prospective adopters who fall into this category to notify them of the change in their status and the requirement to provide information.

Index

Access to information
  Adopted Children Register
    connecting information   6.7–6.10
    entry system   6.4
    generally   6.1–6.3
    index   6.5–6.6
    person adopted after commencement   6.14–6.16
    person adopted before commencement   6.11–6.13
  Adoption Contact Register   6.17–6.22
  confidentiality   6.47–6.48
  disclosure of information
    generally   6.23–6.26, 6.43–6.45
    involving a child   6.38–6.40
    not involving a child   6.37
    person aged 18   6.41–6.42
    qualifying determinations   6.46
    system for   6.27–6.36
  privacy   6.49–6.52
Adopted Children Register
  connecting information   6.7–6.10
  entry system   6.4
  generally   6.1–6.3
  index   6.5–6.6
  person adopted after commencement   6.14–6.16
  person adopted before commencement   6.11–6.13
Adoption agencies. *See* Agencies
Adoption Contact Register   6.17–6.22
Adoption orders
  applicants for, eligible
    age of   4.10
    couples as   4.12–4.14
    domicile of   4.11
    father as sole   4.18–4.20, 4.75–4.84
    generally   4.9
    mother as sole   4.18–4.20
    partner as   4.15–4.16, 4.68–4.74
    probationary periods   4.25–4.31
    residence of   4.11

Adoption orders – *contd*
  applicants for, eligible – *contd*
    single married person as   4.17
    single people as   4.12–4.14
    step-parent as   4.15–4.16, 4.68–4.74
    suitability of   4.22–4.23
  babies   4.85–4.90
  conditions for making
    consent   4.42–4.44
    freeing   4.48–4.50
    placement   4.45–4.47
  consent   4.42–4.44
  contact arrangements and   4.40, 4.62–4.67
  generally   4.1–4.90
  notice and   4.35–4.36
  parental consent and   2.3–2.10
  parental responsibility and   4.3
  preliminaries to   4.21
  previous refusal of   4.37–4.38
  procedural steps   4.51–4.61
  reports   4.32–4.34
  requirements for obtaining   4.6–4.8
  restrictions on, contraventions of   4.39
  suitability for
    of applicant   4.22–4.23
    of child   4.24
Adoption panel
  function of   8.10–8.13
Adoption support services
  assessments   8.54–8.58
  financial support   8.59–8.63
  generally   8.51–8.52
  meaning of   8.53
  plans   8.54–8.58
  pre-provision procedure   8.64–8.66
  reviews   8.67–8.68
Advance consent   2.14–2.17
Age
  of applicant for adoption   4.10
  of child, welfare principle and   1.10
Agencies
  cases involving. *See* Agency cases

Agencies – *contd*
  decisions of
    generally   8.14
    review of   8.70–8.76
  duties
    proposed placement, regarding   8.24–8.30
    prospective adopter, regarding   8.17–8.23
    where considering adoption   8.5–8.9
    generally   8.1–8.76
  notification of parents by   8.14
  powers of   1.16–1.17
  regulations on   8.4–8.76
  requirements before placement   8.31–8.33
  reviews by   8.34–8.40

Agency cases
  removal of child
    consensual placements   3.113
    placement order cases   3.114–3.115
    return of child   3.116–3.118

Appeals
  effect of   7.165–7.178
  generally   7.146
  grounds   7.149
  notices   7.157–7.160
  permission for   7.150–7.156
  procedure following permission   7.161–7.164

Arrangements for adoption, prohibition upon making   5.3–5.7

Assessments
  adoption support services   8.54–8.58

Baby adoptions   4.85–4.90
Background, child's, welfare principle and   1.10

CAFCASS officer, appointment of   8.15–8.16
Care order
  pending application for
    consent to placement and   3.17
  placement order, effect of   3.39

Care proceedings
  placement order proceedings and   3.130–3.131

Case management   7.10–7.14

Child
  adopted
    status of   4.4–4.5
  age of, welfare principle and   1.10
  background of, welfare principle and   1.10
  cultural background of, welfare principle and   1.15
  disability of, welfare principle and   1.11
  'looked after'
    placement for adoption and   3.4
    review procedures for   3.58–3.68
  needs of, welfare principle and   1.6
  'protected'   3.111
  racial origin of, welfare principle and   1.15
  religion of, welfare principle and   1.15

Child – *contd*
  removal of
    agency cases   3.113–3.115
    non-agency cases   3.119–3.120
    return of, agency cases   3.116–3.118
  solicitor for   7.63–7.68
  special needs of, welfare principle and   1.11
  suitability for adoption   4.24
  surname following placement   3.107–3.110
  wishes of, welfare principle and   1.5

Child assessment order
  agency cases and   3.113
  placement order, effect of   3.41

Children and family reporter
  excluded applicants   7.84–7.85
  role of   7.71–7.72

Children's guardian
  appointment of   7.52–7.57
  duties
    exercise of   7.61–7.62
    generally   7.58–7.60
  excluded applicants   7.84–7.85
  powers   7.58–7.60
  solicitor for child   7.63–7.68

Confidentiality   6.47–6.48
Consensual route for placement   3.10–3.21

Consent, parental
  adoption order, to making of   4.42–4.44
  advance   2.14–2.17
  adoption and   2.3–2.10
  dispensing with
    generally   2.31
    grounds for   2.34–2.43
    paramountcy principle   2.32
    procedure for   2.44–2.46
    welfare checklist   2.33
  meaning of   2.11–2.13
  placement and   2.2, 3.10–3.15
  placement order and   3.31–3.35
  procedure for   2.22–2.30
  reporting officer's role in obtaining   2.28–2.30
  withdrawal of   2.18–2.21, 8.41

Contact order
  consent to placement, effect of   3.20–3.21
  effect of   3.20–3.21, 3.41
    placement order, effect of   3.41
  s 26, under   3.99–3.106
  placement procedure and   3.85–3.98
  post-adoption arrangements   4.40, 4.62–4.67

Costs   7.179–7.180

Couples
  as applicants for adoption   4.12–4.14

Court's duties after issue of application   7.29–7.30, 7.31, 7.32–7.35

Index

Cultural background, child's, welfare principle and	1.15
Delay, welfare principle and	1.4
Disability, child's, welfare principle and	1.11
Disclosure of information	
generally	6.23–6.26, 6.43–6.45
involving a child	6.38–6.40
not involving a child	6.37
person aged 18	6.41–6.42
qualifying determinations	6.46
system for	6.27–6.36
Dispensing with parental consent	
generally	2.31
grounds for	2.34–2.43
paramountcy principle	2.32
procedure for	2.44–2.46
welfare checklist	2.33
Domicile	
of applicant for adoption	4.11
Experts	7.127–7.145
Family, loss of membership of	1.7–1.9
Family Procedure (Adoption) Rules 2005	
appeals	
effect of	7.165–7.178
generally	7.146
grounds	7.149
notices	7.157–7.160
permission for	7.150–7.156
procedure following permission	7.161–7.164
case management	7.10–7.14
children and family reporter. *See* Children and family reporter	
children's guardian. *See* Children's guardian	
costs	7.179–7.180
court's duties after issue of application	7.29–7.30, 7.31, 7.32–7.35
experts	7.127–7.145
final hearing	7.42–7.51
first directions hearing	7.36–7.41
generally	7.1
litigation friend. *See* Litigation friend	
overriding objective	7.2–7.9
Part 5 procedure	7.26
Part 9 procedure	7.86–7.110
Part 10 procedure	7.111–7.126
parties	7.27–7.28
reporting officer, role of. *See* Reporting officer	
starting proceedings	7.15–7.25
Father	
as sole applicant for adoption	4.18–4.20
Father – *contd*	
unmarried	
with parental responsibility	4.75–4.77
without parental responsibility	4.78–4.84
Final hearing	7.42–7.51
Financial support	
adoption support services	8.59–8.63
First directions hearing	7.36–7.41
Foster parents, local authority	3.6
Freeing	
adoption order, condition of	4.48–4.50
orders, demise of	3.7–3.8
Grounds	
of appeal	7.149
for dispensing with parental consent	2.34–2.43
Harm, welfare principle and	1.12
Illegal placements	
arrangements, prohibitions on making	5.3–5.7
generally	5.1–5.22
payments, prohibitions on	5.13–5.16
reports, prohibitions on	5.8–5.12
Litigation friend	
role of	7.73–7.83
Local authority foster parents	3.6
'Looked after' child	
placement for adoption and	3.4
review procedures for	3.58–3.68
Mother	
as sole applicant for adoption	4.18–4.20
Needs, child's, welfare principle and	1.6
'No order' principle	1.38–1.40
Notices	
adoption orders and	4.35–4.36
in appeals	7.157–7.160
Options for court or agency, range of	1.18–1.19, 1.20
Paramountcy principle	
parental consent, dispensing with, and	2.32
Parent	
meaning of, for consent purposes	2.13
Parental consent. *See* Consent, parental	
Parental responsibility	
adoption order and	4.3
placement procedure and	3.81–3.84
unmarried fathers and	4.75–4.77, 4.78–4.84
Part 5 procedure	7.26
Part 9 procedure	7.86–7.110
Part 10 procedure	7.111–7.126
Parties	
adoption application	7.27–7.28

Partner
   as applicant for adoption   4.15–4.16, 4.68–4.74
Payments for adoption
   prohibitions on   5.13–5.16
Permanence, alternative options for   1.18–1.19
Permission for appeal
   generally   7.150–7.156
   procedure following   7.161–7.164
Placement for adoption
   as condition of adoption order   4.45–4.47
   consent and   3.10–3.15
   consequences of   3.81–3.84
   contact and   3.85–3.98
   contact order, application for, and   3.99–3.106
   definition of   3.3
   generally   3.1–3.131
   illegal   5.1–5.22
   'looked after' child and   3.4
   other orders, effect on
      care order, pending application for   3.17
      contact order, existing   3.20–3.21
      residence order   3.18
      special guardianship order   3.19
   parental consent and   2.2
   parental responsibility and   3.81–3.84
   routes for
      consensual   3.10–3.21
      placement order   3.22–3.57
Placement order
   agency cases   3.114–3.115
   circumstance, relevant   3.36–3.37
   conditions for making   3.27
   consent and   3.31–3.35
   definition of   3.26
   effective period of   3.28
   generally   3.22–3.57
   other orders, effect on
      care order   3.39
      child assessment order   3.41
      contact order   3.41
      s 8 order   3.40–3.41
      special guardianship order   3.43–3.44
      supervision order   3.41
   parties to application   3.45–3.48
   procedure   3.45–3.57
   proceedings for, care proceedings and   3.130–3.131
   review of   3.58–3.68
   revocation of   3.28, 3.69–3.75
   removal of child under   3.29, 3.111
   threshold criteria   3.30
   variation of   3.76–3.80
Powers, of court or agency, range of
   generally   1.16–1.17
   'no order' principle   1.38–1.40
   options, range of   1.20

Powers, of court or agency, range of – *contd*
   permanence, alternative options for   1.18–1.19
   residence orders   1.21–1.24
   special guardianship orders   1.25–1.29, 1.30–1.37
Privacy   6.49–6.52
Probationary periods
   adoption orders and   4.25–4.31
Procedure
   adoption order, application for   4.51–4.61
   adoption support services, prior to providing   8.64–8.66
   consent
      dispensing with   2.44–2.46
      giving   2.22–2.30
   Part 5   7.26
   Part 9   7.86–7.110
   Part 10   7.111–7.126
   permission to appeal, following   7.161–7.164
   placement order, application for   3.45–3.57
   recovery order, application for   3.125–3.129
Prohibitions
   arrangements, on making   5.3–5.7
   payments, on   5.13–5.16
   reports, on   5.8–5.12
'Protected child'   3.111
Racial origin, child's, welfare principle and   1.15
Recovery orders, following removal of child
   applicable cases   3.121
   'authorised persons'   3.123
   procedure for application   3.125–3.129
Relatives, relationship with, welfare principle and   1.13–1.14
Religion, child's, welfare principle and   1.15
Removal of child
   agency cases
      consensual placements   3.113
      placement order, under   3.29, 3.111
      return of child   3.116–3.118
   non-agency cases   3.119–3.120
   recovery orders following
      applicable cases   3.121
      'authorised persons'   3.123
      procedure for application   3.125–3.129
Reporting officer
   excluded applicants   7.84–7.85
   role of
      consent, obtaining   2.28–2.30
      generally   7.69–7.70
Reports
   adoption orders and   4.32–4.34
   prohibitions on making   5.8–5.12
Residence
   of applicant for adoption   4.11
Residence orders
   consent to placement, effect of   3.18

Index

Residence orders – *contd*		Surname of child, following placement	3.107–3.110
generally	1.21–1.24	Threshold criteria	
Return of child		placement order	3.30
agency cases	3.116–3.118	Variation	
Reviews		of placement order	3.76–3.80
adoption support services	8.67–8.68	Welfare	
agencies, determinations of	8.70–8.76	age and	1.10
Revocation		background and	1.10
of placement order	3.28, 3.69–3.75	checklist, on dispensing with parental consent	2.33
Single married person		child's needs and	1.6
as applicant for adoption	4.17	child's wishes and	1.5
Single people		cultural background and	1.15
as applicants for adoption	4.12–4.14	delay and	1.4
Solicitor for child	7.63–7.68	disability and	1.11
Special guardianship orders (SGOs)		generally	1.1–1.40
consent to placement, effect of	3.19	harm and	1.12
generally	1.25–1.29	membership of family, loss of and	1.7–1.9
placement order, effect of	3.43–3.44	paramountcy of	1.2
procedure for	1.30–1.37	racial origin and	1.15
Special needs, child's, welfare principle and	1.11	relatives, relationship with and	1.13–1.14
Step-parent		religion and	1.15
as applicant for adoption	4.15–4.16, 4.68–4.74	special needs and	1.11
Suitability for adoption process		Welsh family proceedings officer,	
of applicant	4.22–4.23, 8.43–8.50	appointment of	8.15–8.16
of child	4.24	Wishes, child's, welfare principle and	1.5
Supervision order		Withdrawal of parental consent	2.18–2.21
placement order, effect of	3.41		